Innovation & Intellectual Property
Collaborative Dynamics in Africa

EDITORS:
JEREMY DE BEER, CHRIS ARMSTRONG,
CHIDI OGUAMANAM AND TOBIAS SCHONWETTER

Published by UCT Press in association
with the IP Unit, Faculty of Law,
University of Cape Town (UCT) and
Deutsche Gesellschaft für Internationale Zusammenarbeit (GIZ).

UCT
PRESS

Innovation & Intellectual Property: Collaborative Dynamics in Africa

First published 2014 by UCT Press
an imprint of Juta and Company Ltd
First floor, Sunclare Building
21 Dreyer Street
Claremont, 7708
South Africa

www.uctpress.co.za

This book is published by UCT Press. This work was carried out with the aid of a grant from the International Development Research Centre, Ottawa, Canada, with financial support from the German Federal Ministry for Economic Cooperation and Development (BMZ), and in cooperation with Deutsche Gesellschaft für Internationale Zusammenarbeit (GIZ).

ISBN (Print) 978-1-91989-599-4
ISBN (ePub): 978-1-77582-143-4
ISBN (Web pdf) 978-1-77582-142-7

Project manager: Glenda Younge
Editor: Daphne Burger
Proofreader: Alfred LeMaitre
Indexer: Ethné Clarke
Cover designer: Farm Design

Typeset in 10.5 pt on 13 pt Minion Pro by: Integra
Printed and bound in the Republic of South Africa by Mega Digital (Pty)Ltd

This book has been independently peer-reviewed by academics who are experts in the field.

Contents

Preface ... v
Acknowledgements ... ix
About the Editors ... xiii
About the Contributors ... xiv
Acronyms and Abbreviations ... xvii

Chapter 1
Innovation, Intellectual Property and Development Narratives in Africa ... 1
Jeremy de Beer, Chidi Oguamanam and Tobias Schonwetter

Chapter 2
Frameworks for Analysing African Innovation: Entrepreneurship, the Informal Economy and Intellectual Property ... 32
Jeremy de Beer, Izabella Sowa and Kristen Holman

Chapter 3
Informal–Formal Sector Interactions in Automotive Engineering, Kampala ... 59
Dick Kawooya

Chapter 4
Geographical Indication (GI) Options for Ethiopian Coffee and Ghanaian Cocoa ... 77
Chidi Oguamanam and Teshager Dagne

Chapter 5
A Consideration of Communal Trademarks for Nigerian Leather and Textile Products ... 109
Adebambo Adewopo, Helen Chuma-Okoro and Adejoke Oyewunmi

Chapter 6
The Policy Context for a Commons-Based Approach to Traditional Knowledge in Kenya ... 132
Marisella Ouma

Chapter 7
Consideration of a Legal "Trust" Model for the Kukula Healers' TK Commons in South Africa ... 151
Gino Cocchiaro, Johan Lorenzen, Bernard Maister and Britta Rutert

Chapter 8
From *De Facto* Commons to Digital Commons?
The Case of Egypt's Independent Music Industry 171
Nagla Rizk

Chapter 9
Reflections on Open Scholarship Modalities and the
Copyright Environment in Kenya 203
Ben Sihanya

Chapter 10
African Patent Offices Not Fit for Purpose 234
Ikechi Mgbeoji

Chapter 11
The State of Biofuel Innovation in Mozambique 248
Fernando dos Santos and Simão Pelembe

Chapter 12
Reflections on the Lack of Biofuel Innovation in Egypt 267
Bassem Awad and Perihan Abou Zeid

Chapter 13
Effects of the South African IP Regime on Generating
Value from Publicly Funded Research: An Exploratory
Study of Two Universities 282
Caroline Ncube, Lucienne Abrahams and Titilayo Akinsanmi

Chapter 14
Towards University–Industry Innovation Linkages in Ethiopia 316
Wondwossen Belete

Chapter 15
Perspectives on Intellectual Property from Botswana's
Publicly Funded Researchers 335
Njoku Ola Ama

Chapter 16
Current Realities of Collaborative Intellectual
Property in Africa 373
Jeremy de Beer, Chris Armstrong, Chidi Oguamanam and Tobias Schonwetter

Index 395

Preface

This book is among the key outputs of the Open African Innovation Research and Training (Open A.I.R.) Project. Based on case study research in nine African countries, the book examines the recent history and current on-the-ground realities of innovation and intellectual property (IP) in African settings. In doing so, the book reveals complex collaborative dynamics across a range of different countries, sectors and socio-economic contexts, and generates recommendations for how innovation and IP can be married with social and economic development objectives in African settings. This book's sister report, *Knowledge and Innovation in Africa: Scenarios for the Future,* situates the current realities covered in this book within a much longer historical trajectory and multiple potential futures.

Conceived in 2009, established in 2010 and launched in 2011, Open A.I.R. is a pan-African and globally interconnected research and training network, which was established to:

- raise IP awareness in African settings and facilitate critical policy engagement;
- empower a networked, epistemic IP community in Africa;
- identify IP-related innovation bottlenecks and modes of open collaboration; and
- interrogate IP-related innovation metrics, capital and power structures.

Open A.I.R. is financially supported by Canada's International Development Research Centre (IDRC) and Germany's Federal Ministry for Economic Cooperation and Development (BMZ), and collaborates with numerous other organisations and individuals – all of whom are recognised in the Acknowledgements' pages of this book. In addition to the aforementioned case study and foresight research, the Open A.I.R. network engages in a wide range of training, capacity building, outreach and policy engagement activities – both on the African continent and in settings outside the continent where matters of African innovation and IP are engaged. These engagements target external stakeholders capable of changing policies and practices, including:

- innovators, creators and entrepreneurs – individuals and companies;
- business groups such as chambers of commerce and industry associations;
- national, regional and international law-makers and policy-makers;
- issue leaders, such as politicians, judges, professors and practitioners;
- scientific and cultural research and development funding bodies;

- university researchers, administrators and technology transfer officials;
- rights-holders and collective rights management organisations; and
- representatives of indigenous and local communities.

Open A.I.R. is motivated by a vision in which innovation and creativity in Africa are sustainable, properly valued, collaborative, widely accessible and result in benefits that are distributed throughout society. Based on this vision, the network's mission is to better understand how innovation and IP processes work in African settings, how knowledge and technology currently protected by IP can be mobilised, and how IP systems can be harnessed or adapted in a manner that fosters openness-oriented collaborative innovation resulting in just distribution of new knowledge and technology.

This book and the *Scenarios* volume are two parts of a much broader attempt, by Open A.I.R. and other initiatives, to facilitate, in the medium to long term, the emergence of new, pragmatic means of valuing and facilitating innovation and creativity in Africa. Contextually appropriate metrics sensitive to the monitoring of meaningful changes in behaviour around innovation and creativity could be instrumental for promoting African grassroots entrepreneurship, broad-based business development, and a vibrant private sector built on small and medium-sized enterprises (SMEs) with a sustained ability to innovate. And the opportunities for innovation-driven SMEs could also benefit from policy-maker adoption of appropriate metrics when designing the policy and regulatory frameworks necessary to ensure predictable innovation environments for stakeholders.

Open A.I.R.'s core funders, IDRC and BMZ, have provided a framework for Open A.I.R.'s objectives. Open A.I.R. fits within the IDRC's Science and Innovation programme, which supports research and policy engagement in relation to how science, technology and innovation (STI) can be engines of socio-economic development. Within this programme, the Information and Networks (I&N) initiative, which funds the Open A.I.R. Project, aims to better understand the linkages among innovation, creativity, networked collaborations (often enabled via information and communication technologies [ICTs]), and determinants of openness – including IP rights. The IDRC also supported the precursor network to Open A.I.R., the African Copyright and Access to Knowledge (ACA2K) Project, which ran from 2007 to 2011 and generated the nucleus of the expert network now driving Open A.I.R.

BMZ supports Open A.I.R. via Germany's Deutsche Gesellschaft für Internationale Zusammenarbeit (GIZ), under the GIZ commons@ip – Harnessing the Knowledge Commons for Open Innovation initiative. The commons@ip initiative focuses on how IP rights interact with open innovation, the knowledge commons, open licences and collaborative innovation. It is part of the BMZ-mandated Train for Trade programme, which aims at strengthening the private sector and its constituent bodies in the Southern African Development Community (SADC) region through training and capacity building in export promotion, quality control and promotion of open innovation – as well as through promotion of local and regional economic development and trade.

Open A.I.R.'s training and capacity building components include:

- building the network's capacity – through online platforms, network-wide workshops, research methodology support, scenario-building meetings and thematic seminars;
- awarding Open A.I.R. Fellowships to emerging IP scholars and potential leaders – from Tanzania, Kenya, Uganda, Ethiopia, Cameroon, Nigeria and Egypt;
- exchanging knowledge through Africa-wide and South–South knowledge networking at seminars, workshops and conferences;
- growing awareness among African creators, innovators, entrepreneurs and policy-makers of openness-oriented approaches to innovation and IP matters in Africa; and
- teaching at African tertiary educational institutions, including development of a replicable, open course curriculum on IP law and development.

Because of the immense geographic size of the African continent, and unique logistical challenges of African intra-continental travel, ICTs have been instrumental in empowering the research network's "community of practice". Open A.I.R. has an offline presence in 14 African countries and in multiple countries outside the continent. Online, the network includes hundreds of individuals and institutions throughout Africa and from all corners of the globe, linked via a suite of online networking and social-media tools. The Open A.I.R. community of practice advances a culture of multidirectional exchange among African innovative and creative communities and external actors – with a view to sustainably empowering local communities and SMEs. Network members promote cross-fertilisation of ideas via original thinking and partnerships with national and international institutions, scholars, funding agencies, civil society organisations and other willing partners. Those wishing to join the community can visit http://www.openair.org.za/join.

Acknowledgements

True to its emphasis on "collaborative dynamics", this book is the product of the collective energy of dozens of people and institutions in many countries, all of whom work within the Open African Innovation Research and Training (Open A.I.R.) network. Open A.I.R. currently has core network members and institutions in 14 African countries, spanning North Africa (Egypt, Tunisia), West Africa (Senegal, Ghana, Nigeria, Cameroon), East Africa (Ethiopia, Uganda, Kenya, Tanzania) and southern Africa (Malawi, Mozambique, Botswana and South Africa). Other network members and institutions are in Canada, the United States, the United Kingdom, Germany and France. These members are, in turn, linked – via online and offline interactions – to a broader Open A.I.R. network of hundreds of individuals and institutions, including people and entities in Brazil, India, Malaysia, Australia, Switzerland and the Netherlands. The network receives generous financial support from Canada's International Development Research Centre (IDRC) and Germany's Federal Ministry for Economic Cooperation and Development (BMZ).

Each of the editors and authors of this volume is part of, and collaboratively exchanges knowledge and expertise with, this large network, and we the editors, and each of the contributors, are profiled in "About the Editors" and "About the Contributors" sections of this book and on the Open A.I.R. website's Team page, http://www.openair.org.za/content/open-air-team. On this Team page, one can also find the names and contact details of Open A.I.R. Fellows and other network members and institutions. The network is also accessible via its social media platforms, featured at http://www.openair.org.za/join

Open A.I.R.'s administrative hub is the IP Unit in the University of Cape Town Faculty of Law, where Project Manager Nan Warner and Administrator Phyllis Webb are the key operational drivers. Warner and Webb receive management support from two of the editors of this book (and the co-Principal Investigators of the Open A.I.R. Project), UCT IP Unit Director Tobias Schonwetter and Jeremy de Beer of the University of Ottawa Faculty of Law. Also supporting project management are Julie Nadler-Visser of UCT's Research Contracts and IP Services (RCIPS) unit, members of the UCT Finance Department and Faculty of Law Finance Department, and another editor of this book: Chris Armstrong of the LINK Centre at the University of the Witwatersrand (Wits) in Johannesburg.

Network strategic guidance is provided by a Steering Committee composed of De Beer, Schonwetter, Warner, Chidi Oguamanam (another of this book's editors) of the University of Ottawa Faculty of Law, Nagla Rizk of The American University in Cairo (AUC), Sisule Musungu of IQsensato in Nairobi, Khaled Fourati of the IDRC office in Cairo, and Balthas Seibold of Germany's Deutsche Gesellschaft für Internationale Zusammenarbeit (GIZ) in Bonn. Further strategic support from the IDRC is, or has been, provided by Naser Faruqui, Simon Carter, Laurent Elder, Fernando Perini, Matthew Smith, Heloise Emdon and Phet Sayo; Karim Badran and Rose-Marie Ndiaye Pereira on financial matters; and Michelle Hibler and Nola Haddadian on publications. GIZ's involvement is focused on the capacity-building components of the network, which are carried out in collaboration with the GIZ's commons@ip – Harnessing the Knowledge Commons for Open Innovation initiative. At GIZ, in addition to support from the aforementioned Steering Committee member Balthas Seibold, who advises on matters of international knowledge cooperation and networking, support has also come from Petra Hagemann, Christine de Barros Said, Ursula van Look, Marina Neuendorff, Margrit Brockhaus and the Working Group of German Development Organisations on Promoting Innovation Systems. At UCT, as well as those already mentioned, key supporters and collaborators have been the Dean of Law, PJ Schwikkard, Lee-Ann Tong in the Faculty of Law, and, in the IP Unit, the Unit's founder Julian Kinderlerer, its Deputy Director Caroline Ncube and its Senior Research Fellow Bernard Maister. At the University of Ottawa, in addition to those already mentioned, support has been provided by the Dean of the Faculty of Law, Common Law Section, Nathalie Des Rosiers, and Former Dean Bruce Feldthusen.

For this book, key network participants were the team of JD candidates in the University of Ottawa Faculty of Law – Lukas Frey, Will Sapp, Phil Holdsworth, Maya Boorah, Kristen Holman and Saara Punjani – who provided long hours of diligent editorial assistance. In addition, because the research case studies presented in this book all required collection of data from human subjects – via interviews and/or focus group discussions and/or written surveys – this book would not have been possible without the cooperation of dozens of respondents across the countries of study. For reasons of confidentiality, most survey and interview respondents are not named in this book, but we are sincerely grateful for their contributions. Also contributing to the research outlined in this book was Donna Podems of OtherWISE in Cape Town, who advised on research methodologies and supported a methodology workshop for several of the authors featured in this volume, in addition to her support of Open A.I.R.'s monitoring and evaluation (M&E) framework. At this book's publisher, UCT Press, the key drivers have been Publisher Sandy Shepherd and Project Manager Glenda Younge. The cover design for this volume is by Elsabe Gelderblom of Farm Design in Cape Town, who does all of Open A.I.R.'s design work for its website, social media tools, PR materials,

Briefing Notes and the network's other substantial publication output, the Open A.I.R. *Scenarios* compendium – which is available in hard-copy, and on the Open A.I.R. website, as a separate published output and companion to this book.

Network headquarters at the UCT IP Unit serves as Open A.I.R.'s Southern Africa Hub, coordinated by Project Manager Warner. There are also four other Hubs: the North Africa Hub at the Access to Knowledge for Development Center (A2K4D) of the School of Business at The American University in Cairo (AUC), coordinated by Nagham El Houssamy under the direction of Nagla Rizk; the West Africa Hub at the Nigerian Institute of Advanced Legal Studies (NIALS) in Lagos, coordinated by Helen Chuma-Okoro under the direction of Adebambo Adewopo; the East Africa Hub at the Centre for IP and IT Law (CIPIT) of Strathmore University, Nairobi, coordinated by CIPIT Director Isaac Rutenberg; and the Canada Hub at the University of Ottawa Faculty of Law, coordinated by De Beer and Oguamanam. Contact can be made with these Hubs and Hub Coordinators via the aforementioned Open A.I.R. website Team page.

Also integral to the success of the network are its nine Fellows, each of whom has spent time at the UCT IP Unit in Cape Town. The Fellows have contributed to Open A.I.R.'s case study and foresight research, to outreach and training work, and to building the network. The nine Fellows are: Esther Ngom of the Ngo Nyemeck law firm in Yaoundé; Seble Baraki of the Justice and Legal System Research Institute (JLSRI) in Addis Ababa; Moses Mulumba of the Centre for Health, Human Rights and Development (CEHURD) in Kampala; Douglas Gichuki of CIPIT in Nairobi; Milton Lore of Bridgeworks Africa in Nairobi; Eliamani Laltaika of the Tanzania Intellectual Property Rights Network (TIP-Net) in Dar es Salaam; Alexandra Mogyoros, a student in the Faculty of Law at the University of Ottawa; West Africa Hub Coordinator Helen Chuma-Okoro of NIALS in Lagos; and North Africa Hub Coordinator Nagham El Houssamy of A2K4D in Cairo.

Other collaborating institutions are the Program on Information Justice and Intellectual Property (PIJIP) at the Washington College of Law at American University in Washington, DC; the Centre for Technology and Society (CTS) in Brazil; the Centre for Internet and Society (CIS) in India; and the Open Society Foundations, where Open A.I.R.'s key partner is Vera Franz. The Open A.I.R. network has also benefited from interaction with staff at the World Intellectual Property Organisation (WIPO) headquarters in Geneva. In London, Shirin Elahi of Scenarios Architecture is the driver of Open A.I.R. foresight research work, as featured in the aforementioned *Scenarios* compendium that provides an important forward-looking complement to the current picture offered by this volume. Jo Higgs of Go Trolley Films in Cape Town did post-production on the videos available on the Open A.I.R. YouTube channel – videos which show how the network came into being and how the research was conceptualised.

All the people and institutions mentioned here have in one way or another played a role, by collaborating within the Open A.I.R. network, in the conceptualisation, planning, data collection, data analysis, writing, editing, design and production processes that resulted in successful research and the completion of this book. It is hoped that this volume's free availability online, under a Creative Commons (CC) licence, will ensure that the book's collaborative dynamics do not end here at the moment of publication, and continue long into the future in the work of the still-growing Open A.I.R. community.

Jeremy de Beer, Chris Armstrong, Chidi Oguamanam, Tobias Schonwetter
September 2013

About the Editors

Prof. Jeremy de Beer is an Associate Professor in the Faculty of Law, University of Ottawa, and co-Principal Investigator of the Open African Innovation Research and Training (Open A.I.R.) Project. His edited books include *Access to Knowledge in Africa: The Role of Copyright* (UCT Press, 2010), and *Implementing the World Intellectual Property Organization's Development Agenda* (Wilfred Laurier University Press, 2009). jeremy.debeer@uottawa.ca

Dr Chris Armstrong is a Visiting Researcher at the LINK Centre, University of the Witwatersrand (Wits), Johannesburg, publishing and communications consultant for the Open African Innovation Research and Training (Open A.I.R.) Project, and former Research Manager of the African Copyright and Access to Knowledge (ACA2K) Project. He is an editor of *Access to Knowledge in Africa: The Role of Copyright* (UCT Press, 2010). c.g.armstrong@gmail.com

Dr Chidi Oguamanam is an Associate Professor in the Faculty of Law, University of Ottawa, a lawyer with Blackfriars LLP in Lagos, a co-investigator for the Open African Innovation Research and Training (Open A.I.R.) Project, and former Director of the Law and Technology Institute at Dalhousie University, Halifax, N.S., Canada. He is author of the books *Intellectual Property in Global Governance* (Routledge, 2012) and *International Law and Indigenous Knowledge* (University of Toronto Press, 2010). coguaman@uottawa.ca

Dr Tobias Schonwetter is Director of the IP Unit in the Faculty of Law, University of Cape Town (UCT), African Regional Coordinator for Creative Commons (CC), co-Principal Investigator for the Open African Innovation Research and Training (Open A.I.R.) Project, and former co-Principal Investigator for the African Copyright and Access to Knowledge (ACA2K) Project. He is an editor of *Access to Knowledge in Africa: The Role of Copyright* (UCT Press, 2010). tobiasschonwetter@gmail.com

About the Contributors

Dr Perihan Abou Zeid is a Senior Lecturer in the Faculty of Legal Studies and International Relations, Pharos University in Alexandria (PUA), a Post-doctoral Fellow in the Centre of Economic Law and Governance at Vrije University, Brussels, and a volunteer attorney for Public Interest Intellectual Property Advisors (PIIPA). perihan.abouzeid@pua.edu.eg

Lucienne Abrahams is Director of the LINK Centre, University of the Witwatersrand (Wits), Johannesburg, and a former board member of South Africa's National Advisory Council on Innovation (NACI) and National Research Foundation (NRF). luciennesa@gmail.com

Prof. Adebambo Adewopo is a Professor of Law at the Nigerian Institute of Advanced Legal Studies (NIALS), Abuja, a Principal Partner at L&A Legal Consultants, Lagos, and former Director-General of the Nigerian Copyright Commission (NCC). tonade@yahoo.com

Titi Akinsanmi is Policy and Government Relations Manager at Google, Johannesburg, an African Regional Representative on the At-Large Advisory Committee of the Internet Corporation for Assigned Names and Numbers (ICANN), and a former Research Associate at the LINK Centre, University of the Witwatersrand (Wits), Johannesburg. titi.akinsanmi@gmail.com

Prof. Njoku Ola Ama is an Associate Professor in the Department of Statistics, University of Botswana, Gaborone. amano@mopipi.ub.bw

Dr Bassem Awad is a Judge at the Appeal Court of Egypt, an Adjunct Professor in the Faculty of Law at the University of Western Ontario, London, Ont., Canada, and a Tutor at the Academy of the World Intellectual Property Organisation (WIPO). awad_bassem@hotmail.com

Wondwossen Belete is President of the Society for Technology Studies (STS), Addis Ababa, former Manager of International Creativity and Innovation Development Support Services (ICIDSS), and former Director of IP Protection and Technology Transfer at the Ethiopian Intellectual Property Office (EIPO). wondwossenbel@yahoo.com

Helen Chuma-Okoro is a Research Fellow at the Nigerian Institute of Advanced Legal Studies (NIALS), Lagos, a Research Fellow of the Open African Innovation Research and Training (Open A.I.R.) Project, and Coordinator of Open A.I.R.'s West Africa hub in Lagos. helenchuma@gmail.com

Gino Cocchiaro is a lawyer with Natural Justice: Lawyers for Communities and the Environment, Cape Town, and a former Legal Researcher at the International Development Law Organisation (IDLO), Rome. gino@naturaljustice.org

Dr Tesh Dagne is an Assistant Professor in the Faculty of Law, Thompson Rivers University, Kamloops, B.C., Canada. tdagne@tru.ca

Fernando dos Santos is Director-General of the African Regional Intellectual Property Organisation (ARIPO), Harare, a Tutor at the World Intellectual Property Organisation (WIPO) Worldwide Academy, Geneva, a former Lecturer in Law at Eduardo Mondlane University (UEM) and the Technical University of Mozambique, Maputo, and former Director-General of the Mozambican Industrial Property Institute (IPI). fsantos@aripo.org

Kristen Holman is a JD candidate in the Faculty of Law, University of Ottawa. kristen.holman@gmail.com

Dr Dick Kawooya is an Assistant Professor in the School of Library and Information Science, University of South Carolina, Columbia, SC, and former Lead Researcher of the African Copyright and Access to Knowledge (ACA2K) Project. He is an editor of *Access to Knowledge in Africa: The Role of Copyright*, (UCT Press, 2010). kawooya@sc.edu

Johan Lorenzen is an LLB candidate at the University of Cape Town (UCT) and a former consultant with Natural Justice: Lawyers for Communities and the Environment. yolorenz@gmail.com

Dr Bernard Maister is a Senior Research Fellow in the IP Unit, Faculty of Law, University of Cape Town (UCT), practised as an IP (patent) lawyer in the US, and is one of the authors of *Harnessing Intellectual Property Rights for Development Objectives* (Wolf Legal, 2011). maisterb@gmail.com

Dr Ikechi Mgbeoji is an Associate Professor at Osgoode Hall Law School, York University, Toronto, and a lawyer with Blackfriars LLP, Lagos. His authored books include *Global Biopiracy* (UBC Press, 2006). ikechimgbeoji@osgoode.yorku.ca

Dr Caroline Ncube is an Assistant Professor, and Deputy Director of the IP Unit, in the Faculty of Law, University of Cape Town (UCT), and lectures in the Master of IP programme of the World Intellectual Property Organisation (WIPO) and African Regional Intellectual Property Organisation (ARIPO) at Africa University, Mutare, Zimbabwe. caroline.ncube@uct.ac.za

Dr Marisella Ouma is Executive Director of the Kenya Copyright Board (KECOBO), Nairobi, an Advocate of the High Court of Kenya, has taught IP Law at the University of Nairobi, and lectures in the Master of IP programme of the World Intellectual Property Organisation (WIPO) and African Regional

Intellectual Property Organisation (ARIPO) at Africa University, Mutare, Zimbabwe. mwarsie@justice.com

Dr Adejoke Oyewunmi is a Senior Lecturer in the Faculty of Law, University of Lagos (Unilag), Akoka, and a former Adjunct Lecturer in the Master of IP programme of the World Intellectual Property Organisation (WIPO) and African Regional Intellectual Property Organisation (ARIPO) at Africa University, Mutare, Zimbabwe. aoyewunmi@unilag.edu.ng, adejoke21@yahoo.com

Simão Pelembe is a legal advisor at Petróleos de Mozambique (Petromoc), Maputo, a Master's candidate in Business Law at Instituto Superior de Ciências e Tecnologia de Moçambique (ISCTEM), and serves on the boards of Petromoc group companies Petrogás, Somotor, Petroauto, Ecomoz and Somyoung Motors. simao.pelembe@petromoc.co.mz

Dr Nagla Rizk is Professor of Economics at the School of Business, The American University in Cairo (AUC), founding Director of the Access to Knowledge for Development Center (A2K4D) at AUC, a Faculty Associate at Harvard University's Berkman Center for Internet and Society, an affiliated Fellow of Yale University's Information Society Project (ISP), and a founding member of the Access to Knowledge Global Academy. She is co-editor of, and contributor to, *Access to Knowledge in Egypt: New Research on Intellectual Property, Innovation and Development* (Bloomsbury Academic, 2010), and a co-author of *Arab Knowledge Report 2009*. naglarzk@aucegypt.edu

Britta Rutert is a PhD candidate in Anthropology at the Free University of Berlin and a Researcher for Natural Justice: Lawyers for Communities and the Environment in Bushbuckridge, South Africa. britta.rutert@gmail.com

Prof. Ben Sihanya teaches at the University of Nairobi Law School, is CEO of Innovative Lawyering and Sihanya Mentoring, Nairobi, and is former Dean of Law and Chair of the Department of Commercial Law at the University of Nairobi. His edited books include *Intellectual Property Rights in Kenya* (Konrad Adenauer Stiftung, 2009), and he is the author of *Intellectual Property and Innovation in Kenya and Africa* (Innovative Lawyering and Sihanya Mentoring, 2013) and *Presidency and Administrative Bureaucracy in Kenya* (forthcoming, 2013). sihanyamentoring@gmail.com, sihanya@innovativelawyering.com

Izabella Sowa is a JD candidate in the Faculty of Law, University of Ottawa. sowa.izabella@gmail.com

Acronyms and Abbreviations

A2K	access to knowledge
A2K4D	Access to Knowledge for Development Center (The American University in Cairo, Egypt)
AAU	Addis Ababa University
ABS	access and benefit-sharing
ACA2K	African Copyright and Access to Knowledge Project
ACP	African, Caribbean and Pacific Group of States
ACTS	African Centre for Technology Studies (Kenya)
ADPP	Ajuda de Desenvolvimento de Povo para Povo (Mozambique)
AERC	African Economic Research Consortium
AFTE	Association for the Freedom of Thought and Expression (Egypt)
AGOA	African Growth and Opportunity Act
AIM	Agência de Informação de Moçambique
AmCham	American Chamber of Commerce (Egypt)
ARC	Aquaculture Research Centre (Egypt)
ARIPO	African Regional Intellectual Property Organisation
ASSAf	Academy of Sciences of South Africa
ASTII	African Science, Technology and Innovation Indicators
ATO	alternative trading organisation
ATPC	African Trade Policy Centre
ATPS	African Technology Policy Studies Network
AU	African Union
AUC	The American University in Cairo
B-BBEE Act	Broad-Based Black Economic Empowerment Act 53 of 2003 (South Africa)
BCP	bio-cultural community protocol
BIH	Botswana Innovation Hub
BMZ	Federal Ministry for Economic Cooperation and Development (Germany)
BoI	Bank of Industry (Nigeria)
BOTEC	Botswana Technology Centre
BPR	business process re-engineering
CAA	Cocoa Abrabopa Association (Ghana)
CARICOM	Caribbean Community
CBD	Convention on Biological Diversity
CBN	Central Bank of Nigeria

CC	Creative Commons
CCIA	Computer and Communications Industry Association
CEDAT	College of Engineering, Design, Art and Technology (Makerere University, Uganda)
CEHURD	Centre for Health, Human Rights and Development (Uganda)
CEPIL	Centre for Public Interest Law (Ghana)
CIGI	Centre for International Governance Innovation
CIPC	Companies and Intellectual Property Commission (South Africa)
CIPIT	Centre for IP and IT Law (Strathmore University, Kenya)
CIPO	Canadian Intellectual Property Office
CIPR	Commission on Intellectual Property Rights (UK)
CMO	collective management organisation
COCOBOD	Ghana Cocoa Board
CPD	Centre for Policy Dialogue (Nigeria)
CRTT	Centre for Research in Transportation Technologies (Makerere University, Uganda)
CSIR	Council of Scientific and Industrial Research (India)
CTEA	Copyright Term Extension Act (US)
CVCP	Committee of Vice-Chancellors and Principals (UK)
DACST	Department of Arts, Culture, Science and Technology (South Africa)
DEST	Department of Education, Science and Training (Australia)
DFID	Department for International Development (UK)
DHET	Department of Higher Education and Training (South Africa)
DNS	domain name system
DRC	Democratic Republic of Congo
DRM	digital rights management
DRST	Department of Research, Science and Technology (Botswana)
DST	Department of Science and Technology (South Africa)
DTI	Department of Trade and Industry (South Africa)
EAEP	East African Educational Publishers (Kenya)
EC	European Commission
ECBP	Engineering Capacity Building Program (Ethiopia)
ECOWAS	Economic Community of West African States
ECX	Ethiopia Commodity Exchange
EEAA	Egyptian Environmental Affairs Agency
EIPO	Ethiopian Intellectual Property Office
EIPRL	Egyptian Intellectual Property Rights Law
EPA	Environmental Protection Authority (Ethiopia)
EPO	European Patent Office
EST	environmentally sound technology

EU	European Union
EUEI	EU Energy Initiative
Eurostat	Statistical Office of the European Communities
FAO	UN Food and Agriculture Organisation
FCN	Friendship, Commerce and Navigation (Kenya)
FDI	foreign direct investment
FDRE	Federal Democratic Republic of Ethiopia
FDSE	Free Day Secondary Education (Kenya)
FES	Friedrich Ebert Stiftung (Germany)
FLO	Fairtrade Labelling Organisations International
FOSS	free and open source software
FPE	Free Primary Education (Kenya)
FTA	free trade agreement
GDP	gross domestic product
GEM	Global Entrepreneurship Monitor
GERD	gross expenditure on research and development
GI	geographical indication
GIPC	Global Intellectual Property Center
GIZ	Deutsche Gesellschaft für Internationale Zusammenarbeit (Germany)
GM	genetically modified
GOAN	Ghana Organic Agriculture Network
GOK	Government of Kenya
GR	genetic resources
GTZ	German Technical Cooperation
HSRC	Human Sciences Research Council (South Africa)
ICANN	Internet Corporation for Assigned Names and Numbers
ICIDSS	International Creativity and Innovation Development Support Services (Ethiopia)
ICJ	International Commission of Jurists
ICLS	International Conference of Labour Statisticians
ICPSK	Institute of Chartered Public Secretaries of Kenya
ICT	information and communication technology
ICT4D	ICT for development
ICTSD	International Centre for Trade and Sustainable Development
IDC	Industrial Development Corporation (South Africa)
IDLO	International Development Law Organisation
IDRC	International Development Research Centre (Canada)
IDS	Institute of Development Studies (Kenya)
IE	informal economy

IFC	International Finance Corporation
IICA	Inter-American Institute for Cooperation on Agriculture
IIDMM	Institute of Infectious Disease and Molecular Medicine (South Africa)
IIED	International Institute for Environment and Development
IIPA	International Intellectual Property Alliance
IISD	International Institute for Sustainable Development
ILC	indigenous and local community
ILO	International Labour Organisation
INAO	Institut national des appellations d'origine (France)
IP	intellectual property
IPA	Industrial Property Act (Botswana)
IPC	International Patent Classification
IPI	Industrial Property Institute (Mozambique)
IPR-PFRD Act	Intellectual Property Rights from Publicly Financed Research and Development Act (South Africa)
IRB	Institutional Review Board (Botswana)
IRENA	International Renewable Energy Agency
ISAS	integrated seawater agriculture system
ISCTEM	Instituto Superior de Ciências e Tecnologia de Moçambique
ISI	Institute for Scientific Information
ISO	International Organisation for Standardisation
ISP	Information Society Project (Yale University, US)
ITC	International Trade Centre
JBEDC	Japan Bio-Energy Development Corporation
JITAP	Joint Integrated Technical Assistance Programme
JLSRI	Justice and Legal System Research Institute (Ethiopia)
K2C Biosphere	Kruger to Canyons Biosphere (South Africa)
KE	knowledge economy
KECOBO	Kenya Copyright Board
KENFAA	Kenya Nonfiction and Academic Authors' Association
KES	Kenyan Shilling
KHA	Kenya Historical Association
KICD	Kenya Institute of Curriculum Development
KIPI	Kenya Industrial Property Institute
KIPPRA	Kenya Institute for Public Policy Research and Analysis
KNAS	Kenya National Academy of Sciences
KOLA	Kenya Oral Literature Association
KTO	knowledge transfer office
LBC	Licensed Buying Company (Ghana)
LDC	least developed country

LE	Egyptian Pound
LINK Centre	Learning Information Networking Knowledge Centre (Wits University, South Africa)
LSK	Law Society of Kenya
MAN	Manufacturers Association of Nigeria
MANCAP	Mandatory Conformity Assessment Programme (Nigeria)
MCH	Maasai Cultural Heritage Organisation (Kenya)
MCST	Ministry of Communications, Science and Technology (Botswana)
MCT	Ministério da Ciência e Tecnologia (Mozambique)
MDCA	Malindi District Cultural Association (Kenya)
MDG	Millennium Development Goal
MEA	Multilateral Environmental Agreement
MIST	Ministry of Infrastructure, Science and Technology (Botswana)
MIT	Massachusetts Institute of Technology
MOA	Ministry of Agriculture (Ethiopia)
MOE	Ministry of Education (Ethiopia)
MOFA	Ministry of Food and Agriculture (Ghana)
MoFED	Ministry of Finance and Economic Development (Ethiopia)
MOST	Ministry of Science and Technology (Ethiopia)
MoU	memorandum of understanding
MRC	Medical Research Council (South Africa)
Natoil	Natural Oil Company (Egypt)
NACI	National Advisory Council on Innovation (South Africa)
NCC	Nigerian Copyright Commission
NDA	non-disclosure agreement
NEP	National Enquiry Point (Botswana)
NEPAD	New Partnership for Africa's Development
NESC	National Economic and Social Council (Kenya)
NESTI	National Experts on Science and Technology Indicators
NIALS	Nigerian Institute of Advanced Legal Studies
NRF	National Research Foundation (South Africa)
NGO	non-governmental organisation
NIALS	Nigerian Institute of Advanced Legal Studies
NIPMO	National Intellectual Property Management Office (South Africa)
NIS	national innovation system
NMIMS	Narsee Monjee Institute of Management Studies (India)
NPR	National Public Radio (US)
NPSB	National Policy and Strategy on Biofuels (Mozambique)
NRC	National Research Centre (Egypt)

NREA	New and Renewable Energy Authority (Egypt)
NWLR	Nigerian Weekly Law Report
OA	open access
OAPI	Organisation africaine de la propriété intellectuelle
OCEES	Oxford Centre for the Environment, Ethics and Society
OCFCU	Oromia Coffee Farmers Cooperative Union (Ethiopia)
ODEL	open, distance and electronic learning
ODI	Overseas Development Institute (UK)
OECD	Organisation for Economic Co-operation and Development
OER	open educational resource
Open A.I.R.	Open African Innovation Research and Training Project
ORD	Office of Research and Development (Botswana)
PBIP	place-based intellectual property
PCT	Patent Cooperation Treaty
Petromoc	Petróleos de Mozambique
PIIPA	Public Interest Intellectual Property Advisors (US)
PIJIP	Program on Information Justice and Intellectual Property (American University, US)
PPS	probability proportional to size
PRO	public research organisation
ProBEC	Programme for Basic Energy and Conservation in Southern Africa
R&D	research and development
RCIPS	Research Contracts and IP Services unit (UCT, South Africa)
RIPCO (B)	Rural Industrial Promotion Company (Botswana)
RMI	rights management information
SADC	Southern African Development Community
SARUA	Southern African Regional Universities Association
SCE	Society for Critical Exchange (Kenya)
SID	Society for International Development (Kenya)
SINER-GI	Strengthening International Research on Geographical Indications
SME	small and medium enterprise
SMIEIS	Small and Medium Industries Equity Investments Scheme (Nigeria)
SMME	small, micro and medium enterprise
SNA	social network analysis
SON	Standards Organisation of Nigeria
SPS	sanitary and phytosanitary measures
STCI	Science and Technology Capacity Index
STEP	Science Technology and Economic Policy (US)
STI	science, technology and innovation
STS	Society for Technology Studies (Ethiopia)

SVKM	Shri Vile Parle Kalamani Mandal (India)
TBT	technical barriers to trade
TCE	traditional cultural expression
TGE	Transitional Government of Ethiopia
THE	Times Higher Education (UK)
THRIP	Technology and Human Resources Programme (South Africa)
TIA	Technology Innovation Agency (South Africa)
TIP-Net	Tanzania Intellectual Property Rights Network
TISC	Technology and Innovation Support Center
TK	traditional knowledge
TKDL	Traditional Knowledge Digital Library (India)
TPMs	technological protection measures
TRIPS	Agreement on Trade-Related Aspects of Intellectual Property Rights
TTO	technology transfer office
TVET	Technical and Vocational Education and Training (Ethiopia)
UB	University of Botswana
UCC	Universal Copyright Convention
UCITA	Uniform Computer Information Transactions Act (US)
UCT	University of Cape Town (South Africa)
UEM	Eduardo Mondlane University (Mozambique)
UGT	Uganda Gatsby Trust
UK	United Kingdom
UM	utility model
UNCST	Uganda National Council for Science and Technology
UNCTAD	UN Commission on Trade and Development
UNDESA	UN Department of Economic and Social Affairs
UNDP	UN Development Programme
UNECA	UN Economic Commission for Africa
UNEP	UN Environment Programme
UNESCAP	UN Economic and Social Commission for Asia and the Pacific
UNESCO	UN Educational, Scientific and Cultural Organisation
UNFCCC	UN Framework Convention on Climate Change
UNICAMP	University of Campinas (Brazil)
UNIDO	UN Industrial Development Organisation
Unilag	University of Lagos
US	United States
USAID	US Agency for International Development
USPTO	US Patent and Trademark Office
WAK	Writers Association of Kenya
WATH	West Africa Trade Hub

WBCSD	World Business Council for Sustainable Development
WCT	WIPO Copyright Treaty
WEF	World Economic Forum
WEP	World Employment Programme
WHO	World Health Organisation
WIPO	World Intellectual Property Organisation
Wits	University of the Witwatersrand (South Africa)
WPIS	WIPO Patent Information Service
WPPT	WIPO Performances and Phonograms Treaty
WTO	World Trade Organisation
ZAR	South African Rand

Chapter 1

Innovation, Intellectual Property and Development Narratives in Africa

Jeremy de Beer, Chidi Oguamanam and Tobias Schonwetter

1. Context

Human development, including not just economic growth but also the capability for longer, healthier and more fulfilling lives, depends on innovation and creativity. While various economic, technological, social and other factors influence innovative and creative activity, intellectual property (IP) rights – copyrights, patents, trademarks, trade secrets and other appropriation mechanisms – play an increasingly important role. How IP rights help or hinder innovation and creativity in different contexts in Africa is the subject of this book.

The chapters that follow canvass aspects of the current reality of IP in nine different countries from the four main regions of the African continent. The chapters contain contextual analyses as well as on-the-ground case studies based on empirical, qualitative and quantitative research – and cut across diverse socio-economic contexts and legal systems, and a spectrum of formal, informal and traditional sectors. Examined as a whole, the evidence in this book helps build understanding of the ways in which the dual goals of protecting IP *and* preserving access to knowledge can be balanced. The book also provides indications of the roles that are being, and can be, played by collaborative and openness-oriented dynamics in relation to innovation, creativity and IP. A better understanding of the nuances and dynamics of IP is essential to creating policy frameworks and management practices that balance IP protection and access in such a way that African regions, nations and communities can harness IP as a tool to facilitate collaborative networking within diverse systems of innovation and creativity.

The proliferation and polarisation of opinion

Influential actors – multinational companies, developed-country governments, international organisations, academics, civil society groups – promote opposing views on how IP protection interacts with innovation and creativity. One view is that IP protection is inevitably and necessarily an incentive for innovation and creativity. The opposing view is that IP protection is not required to facilitate innovation and creativity and, rather, is an impediment to the free and open exchanges of technology, culture and knowledge that form the core of innovative and creative modalities. These polarised views persist because, in fact, little is really known about how IP environments do or could influence innovation and creativity as a means to development. A recent, wide-ranging review (Hassan *et al.*, 2010) of the growing but still "surprisingly scarce" literature on IP and developing countries uncovered little consensus and even less clear evidence on the key questions facing IP policy-makers (2010, p. xiv). It follows that policy-makers who seek to encourage creators and innovators tend to struggle to develop appropriate IP systems. Bottlenecks and systemic inefficiencies occur as law-makers and policy-makers make hazy efforts, based on insufficient information, to calibrate national IP environments in support of innovation and creativity.

Overzealous IP protection regimes may indeed raise the costs of future innovations and may, therefore, discourage potential innovators and creators who cannot afford high up-front investments. Also, over-protection of IP may result in innovators and creators being unable to organise collaborative relationships in strategically optimal ways. On the other hand, under-protection of outputs may indeed be an investment disincentive for a significant proportion of potential innovators and creators, and may therefore be a threat to development.

Despite the lack of consensus about the influence of IP on innovation and creativity for development, some new narratives seem to be emerging. For most of the 20th century, the orthodox assumption was that IP protection is good for development. The wisdom was that if some protection is good, more is even better. The origins and spread of such narratives are explained especially clearly in the literature on the history of the World Trade Organisation's (WTO's) Agreement on Trade-Related Aspects of Intellectual Property Rights (TRIPS) and in the leading work on the international political economy of IP more generally (e.g. Drahos and Braithwaite, 2002; May, 2010; May and Sell, 2005; Sell, 2003).

From the 1994 passage of TRIPS onwards, political and economic pressures to increase IP protection succeeded in raising both IP protection standards and awareness of IP in developing countries. But the protectionist pressures led to backlashes against IP systems that were seen as insensitive to local contexts. This was especially true where IP protection impacted other public policy priorities, especially on matters of health, education and cultural participation. The work of scholars such as Barbosa *et al.* (2007), Boyle (1997, 2003, 2004), Chon (2006), Okediji (1996, 2000) and others was influential in that context. Such scholarship contributed indirectly to reform initiatives undertaken by international organisations including the WTO, the World Health Organisation (WHO) and the World Intellectual Property Organisation (WIPO). A "development agenda", or indeed a suite of related agendas, emerged as a new paradigm focused on recalibrating international IP law and policy (De Beer, 2009; Deere, 2009; Gervais, 2007; May, 2007; Meléndez-Ortiz and Roffe, 2009; Netanel, 2008; Yu, 2009). Moreover, an *ad hoc* movement of civil society advocates and scholarly researchers came together under the framework of "A2K" (access to knowledge), a civil society coalescence which fundamentally reframed the terms of global IP debates (De Beer and Bannerman, 2013; Kapczynski, 2008; Kapczynski and Krikorian, 2010). An illustration (as this book was being finalised in mid-2013) of the continuing momentum of the A2K movement was the outcome of the WIPO Diplomatic Conference of June 2013 in Marrakesh, at which more than 50 countries signed the Marrakesh Treaty to Facilitate Access to Published Works for Persons Who Are Blind, Visually Impaired, or Otherwise Print Disabled (Marrakesh Treaty, 2013).

A number of important recent works demonstrate the integration of development principles and A2K perspectives into mainstream analyses of IP (e.g. Wong and Dutfield, 2011). Several scholars emphasise the complex, dynamic and multi-level nature not just of IP rules, but also of the broader governance of knowledge (e.g. Burlamaqui *et al.*, 2012; Chon, 2011; Oguamanam, 2011). The complexity of the scholarly endeavour has led to contrasting disciplinary perspectives and subtly different framings of IP issues. For example, some works characterise the basic problem as protecting "poor people's knowledge" (Finger and Schuler, 2004); others promote the recognition of "indigenous people's innovation" (Drahos and Frankel, 2012). A particularly important theme is the human impact of IP policy, i.e. the impact on individual fulfillment and well-being (Sunder, 2012).

Despite this rapidly growing global body of work, there is still little research examining systemic IP governance or knowledge governance in Africa. More than two decades ago, Juma and Ojwang (1989) urged African countries to examine their IP policies and "introduce laws that reflect the imperatives of national sovereignty" (1989, p. 3). Since then, there have been valuable in-depth examinations of particular issues, such as textiles and traditional knowledge (Boateng, 2011), or access to learning materials (Armstrong *et al.*, 2010; De Beer, 2013). In addition, some researchers have conducted regional analyses of A2K – in North Africa, for example (Shaver and Rizk, 2010) – and sub-Saharan African perspectives on IP and economic development have been put forward (e.g. Blackeney and Megistie, 2011), along with analyses of topics such as neo-colonialism and IP (e.g. Rahmatian, 2009) and African IP organisations (Kongolo, 2000). African-based researchers Pistorius, Harms and Visser have done strong work on the intersections among development and aspects of IP such as copyright (Pistorius, 2007) and international legal and political IP paradigms (Harms, 2012; Visser, 2007). But many gaps in our understanding of IP and development, especially development in African settings, remain.

Particular blind spots relate to the dynamic and contextual roles of IP in different kinds of African innovation and creation modalities, particularly collaborative and openness-oriented modalities. The researchers who contributed to this book responded to an open public call to investigate matters that would help answer the following question: *How can existing or potential IP systems be harnessed to appropriately value and facilitate innovation and creativity for open development in Africa?* This framing provoked a range of connected questions. Practically, how do African innovators or creators exploit, adapt to, or work around, IP environments? Conceptually, are exclusive IP rights compatible with collaborative, openness-oriented innovation and creativity in Africa, and with inclusive development more generally? What are the on-the-ground interplays between openness and protection in relation to IP in African innovative and creative settings? At a more systemic level, to what extent, and how, have policy-makers in Africa attempted to calibrate IP frameworks in such a way that they can maximise innovative and creative potential? Current research addressing these important questions, as presented in the available literature and translated into practice, remains scarce and often appears to reflect rhetorical polarisation more than objective investigation. This volume seeks to begin to fill that research gap, by presenting findings from studies which explored the role of IP in innovation and creativity within collaboration- and *openness*-based conceptions of development in the African context. In other words, the book is *not* about innovation systems or creative industries in general; it is about the roles that IP rights do, and could, play *within* such systems and industries, specifically *in* Africa, specifically in relation to collaborative, openness-oriented dynamics.

Emphasising Africa

Questions about IP law, policy and practice may appear to be most suitably addressed globally, not least because several multilateral instruments, such as TRIPS, strive to introduce uniform minimum standards of IP protection around the world. This book, however, takes the view that examination of the global setting is insufficient, because regional, national and sub-national characteristics and perspectives must be taken into account and examined. As the research presented in this book reveals, examination of IP environments at African regional, national and local settings has much to offer.

At the outset, it must be emphasised that Africa is an enormous and diverse continent, not a single country. Therefore this book's exploration of the role of

IP in systems of innovation and creativity in African settings seeks to avoid perpetuation of stereotypes of African homogeneity. This book also emerges from an awareness that, in the context of humanity's continual strivings for innovation and creativity, African nations and communities have typically been assigned least-performing status. Africa's contributions have tended to be positioned as confined to the ancient world or the prehistoric era, sometimes via dubiously benevolent attempts to acknowledge the continent's role as the starting place (the "cradle", no less) of humankind. Africa has also tended to be subjected to depictions as a "dark" continent, a disease and affliction hotspot dominated by poverty. Juxtaposing the concept of "modern" innovation with the word "African" has, for much of the past few centuries, been positioned (particularly in the "developed" world) as a contradiction in terms. African knowledge has typically been cast as "traditional", which, as Dutfield (2002, p. 22) points out, implies the opposite of innovative or creative. While there is some very recent evidence of less pejorative media narratives emerging in relation to African innovation (see *The Economist*, 2013), most countries on the continent are still seen as having a long way to go if they wish to become hotbeds of 21st-century innovation.

There are various interrelated, IP-connected reasons that might explain the power of narratives suggesting that creativity and innovation in most parts of Africa appear to fall short of innovative and creative activity in other regions, particularly developed-world regions. This book investigates two possible reasons in particular: first, that African creativity and innovation are not properly valued by prevalent IP systems and assumptions; and second, that African creativity and innovation are being constrained by sub-optimal IP-related policies and practices. Using a range of research methods, the chapters in this book investigate both possibilities: that prevalent IP modalities might be (1) *undervaluing* African innovation and creativity, and/or (2) *undermining* African innovation and creativity. It must be made clear in this introductory chapter, however, that in exploring the possibilities just mentioned, the research outlined in this book was premised on certain assumptions, chiefly that current IP modalities can and do contribute to facilitation of innovation and creativity in some African settings, but that at the same time, the facilitative róle of IP modalities in African settings can be improved.

Undervaluing African innovation and creativity?

It would appear that IP-related measurement tools for contributions to innovation do not sufficiently consider how innovation and creativity actually happen on the ground in African settings. It cannot be doubted that, amongst the rank of African and African diaspora intelligentsia, dating back millennia and certainly from pre-colonial times, there is no lack of epochal innovative and creative accomplishments in virtually all categories of human endeavour. And Africa remains a continent whose diverse natural and human resources are clearly integral to humanity's collective quest for innovative solutions to pressing problems. The issue is, therefore, not whether there is African innovation, but rather whether Africa's real and potential contributions to innovation are properly identified or valued by IP.

It seems likely that certain formal, or informal, or mixed formal–informal, modes of innovation and creativity in Africa cannot be fully or properly accounted for through the Western-oriented prism of patents, copyrights, trademarks and other formal IP outputs. Many measurements used in developed countries, and exported to developing countries, betray apparent misunderstandings of the nuances of IP law, policy and practice, e.g. through blind citation of statistics regarding "patenting by population" or "share of world patents" or "cross-border trade-marks" (e.g. Conference Board of Canada, 2010). Such measurements inevitably influence decision-makers, often through mainstream media coverage. For example, a 2010 media headline proclaimed "Southern Africa: Region Failing to Innovate, Says Study", and cited a study by the UN Educational, Scientific and Cultural Organisation (UNESCO) that concluded as follows: "Countries in southern Africa are producing so few scientific publications and patents that the region's social and economic progress is threatened" (Campbell, 2010, citing UNESCO, 2010). That Africa needs more patents is currently a key message being conveyed to African national policy-makers, who are, in turn, naturally tempted to seek to bolster their nations' statistical ranking via patent-centric policies, laws and regulations – even if the effects of such policy-making may well be counterproductive in the long term.

Simply citing numbers of patents issued is at best an incomplete attempt to measure innovation, and is at worst inappropriate, especially when in some cases these very patents could be clogging innovation systems with bottlenecks that impede collaboration. Some scholars in the developed world are now writing about such problems (Bessen and Meurer, 2008; Jaffe and Lerner, 2006), and influential bodies such as the Organisation for Economic Co-operation and Development (OECD) are beginning to recognise that sole reliance on such measurements of innovation is inadequate (OECD, 2010). Arguably, conventional IP metrics are especially improper for validation or empowerment of African innovators and creators at the "base of the pyramid", i.e. the most marginalised (yet often most resilient) segments of society.

But while the developed world seems to be advancing towards more sophisticated measurement and understanding of IP's actual roles in innovation and creativity, there is evidence – e.g. the UNESCO study referred to above – to suggest that African policy-makers continue to be offered relatively stale, globalist, protection- and harmonisation-centric IP narratives containing insufficient counterbalancing via references to nationally or locally contextualised IP realities and imperatives. This is despite decades-old pleas to look beyond patents for appropriate knowledge-governance frameworks:

> Patent protection *per se* is too narrow to account for most of the innovative activity going on in the region. A new regime of intellectual property protection should be introduced to cover traditional technologies, intermediate innovations, inventions and other products of innovative activity. It should take into account the national development needs, regional co-operation, and international competitiveness (Juma and Ojwang, 1989, p. 2).

Undermining African innovation and creativity?

The still-dominant paradigm of IP protection, globally and in Africa, promotes IP as a "power tool" to facilitate economic growth (Idris, 2003), i.e. growth through private sector monopolies that temporarily limit competition and thereby provide financial incentives to invest human and financial resources into innovative and creative endeavours. It seems clear that IP does, to some extent, have a positive role to play in incentivising innovation and creativity. But it also seems clear that too little consideration is given, in the dominant discourses of IP training, education and capacity building finding their way to Africa, to the potential socio-economic externalities of the existing system (De Beer and Oguamanam, 2010). Moreover, the focus of most existing research on IP and innovation is on *formal* sectors of the economy, with little effort made to date to understand IP's interactions with *informal* modes of innovation and creativity (informal modes which are particularly prevalent in developing-world settings).

If IP-related decisions are made based on narrow understandings of the true nature and value of IP in varying contexts, then human resources, venture capital and other factors influencing creativity and innovation might be misdirected in contexts (e.g. the African contexts that are the focus of this book) that do not conform to the tidy assumptions generated by narrow perspectives. There is a view, shared by the editors of this volume, that better understanding of the nuances of IP law, policy and practice in myriad settings (including, for the purposes of this book, African settings) can help policy-makers and practitioners more effectively harness the potential of what has come to be known as the "knowledge commons" (see Hess and Ostrom, 2006). According to the knowledge commons idea, knowledge is shared by groups of people and governed by dynamic mixes of formal and informal norms of ownership and control – by ownership and control systems that are sometimes closed, sometimes open, and often a combination of both.

Accordingly, the research studies detailed in this book sought to give proper due to dynamic fusings of formality and informality in relation to IP and innovation. In addition, the studies sought to examine whether greater attention should and could be paid to potential leveraging of existing IP systems, or refinement of existing IP systems, in ways suited to more participatory, collaborative, democratic and just models of innovation and creativity, i.e. leveraging or refinement of IP systems in ways suited to enablement of openness-oriented modalities for development, modalities that some have come to call "open development" – a notion covered in this chapter's next subsection, on openness.

The concept of openness

At present, it would seem that IP is, for the most part, not conceptualised in an openness-oriented way in Africa. Central to this book is the question of whether conceptualisations giving primacy to openness-based collaboration can help bridge the polarisation in IP discourse. This subsection explains how openness may be situated in respect of IP policy and practice, and the relationships between open IP models and openness more generally (as applied, for example, to notions of open development).

Open development

Open development is a relatively new concept that has only just begun to be investigated, let alone defined. Potential confusion around the concept stems from the elusiveness of agreement about what *openness* is. Whether a system can be considered open or not depends on a variety of factors including, significantly, the degree to which people are free, or even empowered, to universally access a system and to participate, collaborate and share within that system (Smith *et al.*, 2011). Early brainstorming around the idea of open development has centred around principles of collaboration, participation and inclusiveness in the political, legal, economic, social, cultural, technological and other institutions (broadly conceived) that shape people's lives.[1] Examples of open development applied in practice might include open government, open communications networks, open access to content, open-sourced research, open product development and commons-based peer production (Benkler, 2006; Wunsch-Vincent *et al.*, 2007). Similar principles can be found in discussions using the label "inclusive development", both generally (IDRC, 2011) and in the specific context of innovation (OECD, 2012).

---

1 One such brainstorming event was the IDRC Open Development Workshop in Ottawa, Canada (6–7 May 2010); more information about the workshop as well links to 21 paper abstracts are available at: www.idrc.ca/en/ev-140364-201-1-DO_TOPIC.html [accessed 12 April 2013].

Proponents of the value of open or inclusive development paradigms tend to gravitate towards calls for increasing democratic engagement, and they tend to emphasise the distributive implications of the benefits that accrue, from such modes of development, to the most marginalised segments of society. It can even be argued that openness breeds more openness, so that it is a game-changing force for unlocking innovation and creativity. That said, the potential downsides of openness should not be overlooked, including, in the realm of IP protection, the risk of misappropriation and, perhaps, challenges faced in seeking to find financial incentives for innovative and creative activity. The potential advantages and disadvantages make it necessary to consider appropriate degrees of openness that balance benefits with costs. Such balancing tends to be a constantly dynamic process, which further complicates a possible definition of openness in the context of developmental processes. Another challenge in arriving at a clear understanding of open development and related openness-focused concepts is the paradox that one person's freedom often requires another's constraint. Despite these conceptual and definitional challenges – and also to a great extent because of them – this book seeks to help build a better understanding of what the concept of open development might look like in one particular set of contexts: African contexts involving elements of IP, innovation and creativity.

Collaborative innovation and creativity

The term "innovation" has in recent years become a buzz word among government policy-makers, the private sector, civil society and academics. However, its meaning is not self-explanatory. The rich literature on innovation and its connections to entrepreneurship and formal and informal economic systems is canvassed in the De Beer *et al.* Chapter 2 of this book. In this introductory chapter, it will thus suffice to foreshadow the deeper analysis in Chapter 2 by providing an initial definition of innovation, making a rough distinction between the twin notions of innovation and creativity, and drawing some generalised connections among IP, innovation, creativity and openness.

A useful definition of innovation is contained in a handbook known as the *Oslo Manual*, a joint publication of the Organisation for Economic Co-operation and Development (OECD) and Eurostat (OECD and Eurostat, 2005). The *Manual*, now in its 3rd edition, provides guidelines for researchers and statisticians collecting and interpreting data regarding indicators of technological innovation in countries around the world. According to the *Manual*, an innovation can take the form of a new technological product (or service offering), a new production process, a new marketing method or a new organisational practice. Significantly improved products/services, processes, methods and practices also qualify as new, according to the *Oslo Manual*. But to be an innovation, the new product/service, process, method or practice must be implemented, not merely abstract. Implementation usually refers to market availability, with the market understood broadly so that public sector social innovations may be included.

In this chapter, and in this book as a whole, there is frequent reference made to "innovation and creativity" as twin ideas. This is because this volume seeks to be inclusive of a wide range of innovation and creative practices potentially relevant to IP modalities, and some branches of conventional IP privilege the notion of innovation while others privilege creativity. Reference in this book to innovation and creativity as twin notions should *not*, however, be mistaken as implying that the two are equivalent. As outlined above with reference to the *Oslo Manual*, for something to be called an "innovation" it typically requires implementation via market availability (with the market broadly defined). "Creativity", on the other hand, does not, in the understanding adopted by the editors of this book, necessarily imply implementation via market provision. In many cases, an instance of creativity may be but one link in the chain leading towards a market-available innovation; in other cases, an instance of creativity may remain as non-market-implemented, and thus not, strictly speaking, an innovation according to the *Oslo Manual* definition adopted by this volume.

In the context of IP law and policy, the term "innovation" is most often used during discussions of patents, while creativity is more typically mentioned alongside copyrights. This discourse results from the mistaken belief that patents are the most (or only) relevant IP right with respect to science and technology, while copyrights are the most (or only) important right in cultural industries. The emerging reality is that patents, trade secrets, copyrights, trademarks and other forms of IP protection are relevant across sectors, and that most industries are impacted by all of these issues (as explained in further detail below). Thus, among the reasons why this chapter typically mentions the concepts of innovation and creativity in conjunction with each other is our desire to move away, to the extent possible, from the tendency to bifurcate between patent-centric innovation analyses and copyright-centric creativity analyses.

Several important concepts emerge from the scholarly literature related to IP environments and collaboration- and openness-oriented innovation and creativity (or what we call, in this chapter, collaborative innovation and creativity). First, collaborative innovation and creativity need to be situated within the more general literature on innovation systems. One of the founders of the concept of innovation systems, Lundvall, has argued that research on formal aspects of innovation is evolving well, even in the developing world, including Africa (Lundvall *et al.*, 2009; see also Oyelaran-Oyeyinka and McCormick, 2007). However, to bridge innovation systems research and development studies, one of Lundvall's suggestions is to study the intersections among formal and informal dimensions of innovation (e.g. between patent statistics and social networks) (Lundvall *et al.*, 2009; Oyelaran-Oyeyinka and McCormick, 2007). The emerging conceptualisations of collaborative innovation and creativity seem to present opportunities for examination of formal–informal innovation intersections (Esalimba and New, 2009), and some of the chapters in this book (particularly Chapters 2 and 3) take up the challenge.

Current thinking about collaborative innovation and creativity can be unpacked into two relatively discrete components, which are very often conflated or misunderstood: *macro-level* IP public policies, and *micro-level* IP management practices. For example, when Chesbrough (2003) uses the term "open innovation", it refers to the strategic exploitation of IP rights by private firms in ways that are, in fact, sometimes open and sometimes closed. Such a conception seems to reflect only one part of the picture of innovation's role in development. The work of Chesbrough, and others such as Tapscott and Williams (2006) and Shirky (2008), has focused on the self-structuring behaviours of individuals and firms, albeit in the context of collective action. Communities built around initiatives like the Creative Commons, or the free and open source software (FOSS) movement, are likewise concerned mostly about organising actors within the respective communities. The work of researchers such as Lemos on the topic of "open business" also demonstrates how specific industries or parts of an industry can be developed using social rather than strict legal norms to govern expectations around content production, distribution and revenue-sharing (Lemos and Castro, 2008). In this subset of research, the adjective "open" as applied to innovation, creativity or business models is used in a variety of different and sometimes incompatible ways across disciplinary boundaries.

Moreover, even if a uniform understanding of the term *open* existed, it seems clear that while openness principles (however defined) work well in relation to IP in some sectors (such as software, content publishing, music distribution in some genres, health care, agriculture), they are more difficult to apply in other contexts (such as biotechnology research and development [R&D]) (see Adelman, 2005; Boadi and Bokanga, 2007; Boettinger and Burk, 2004; Clark *et al.*, 2000; Connett-Porceddu, 2004; Feldman, 2004; Halewood and Nnadozie, 2008; Hope, 2008; Kuchma, 2010; Nolan-Stevaux, 2007; Octaviani, 2008). Which sectors are most amenable to openness around IP, and why? There are very few studies that investigate multiple sectors simultaneously to determine which strategies might be viable on a larger scale or to draw other broad lessons (see Gastrow [2009] for one example of a multiple-sector study). This knowledge gap is a potential impediment to effective design and implementation of IP management policies and practices seeking to harness openness dynamics.

Another apparent gap in our understanding of the relationships between openness and IP is caused by the fact that, in both the scholarly and practical contexts, the potential public policy consequences of private orderings are usually discussed implicitly rather than explicitly. At the same time, research focused on high-level legal and policy issues – e.g. examination of whether building openness into IP policy will result in greater opportunity for developing countries to transform into equitable and sustainable knowledge societies – tends to fail to appreciate the practical implications of those public policies on private actors. That is, attention tends to be directed at either one or the other of these components of openness (private ordering or public policies) in relation to innovation and creativity, rarely making sufficient connections. It is hoped that this book's research findings and analysis offer some useful connections, or at least the beginnings of useful connections, between the actions of private and public sector actors in relation to IP, openness and collaboration.

2. The research

Analytical framework

The research framework for this book is pragmatic. Chapter authors approached their research on the basis of actual or likely practices of innovators and creators of valuable intangible assets. The researchers were at the same time asked to juxtapose these practices with the overarching legal, economic and policy systems governing people's behaviours, particularly behaviours in relation to IP, in the countries of study. While the point of departure for the research was the existing legal system of IP protection, a meaningful analysis of the ramifications of IP laws necessitated due consideration of disciplines other than law, such as political science, economics, business, engineering, philosophy and sociology. The multidisciplinary constitution of the network of researchers who contributed chapters to this book duly reflects this approach.

It also needs to be stressed that many of the research studies covered in this book sought to approach IP, innovation and creativity from the perspectives of relatively vulnerable and marginalised collectives of people. The data and analyses presented in this volume are grounded in the need, in the African settings researched, for more equal and just distribution of the benefits of socio-economic development.

Methods

As explained in the Preface, the Open African Innovation Research and Training Project (Open A.I.R.) (www.openair.org.za), of which this book is part, adopted a two-phase approach to researching the role of IP rights in relation to collaborative innovation and creativity with developmental intent: (1) the case studies, described in Chapters 3 to 15 in this book, seeking to reflect the *status quo* and develop some recommendations for the near future; and (2) scenario-building exercises seeking to understand what the intersection of IP, innovation, creativity and Africa's socio-economic development could look like two decades in the future. The second-phase findings, the scenarios, are documented in separate publications from this book, because the foresight work was geared towards strategic thinking and planning for the future. This book, meanwhile, offers the fruits of the first research phase, the case studies of the present.

The particular case studies in this book sought to lay the groundwork needed for new ways of identifying and valuing innovation and creativity in Africa. The case study method helps to humanise otherwise abstract information and yields understanding into complex systems of interacting variables. Case studies were thus chosen by the Open A.I.R. network as the necessary empirical tool for counteracting the formalistic tendencies of predominant IP measurements and analyses. The case study researchers adopted a range of methods. However, notwithstanding the Open A.I.R. network's interdisciplinary framework, IP is a decidedly legal construct, making legally focused desk research, including statutory analysis, an important part of most of the studies. Most of the researchers analysed a range of materials on the legal and policy contexts for their studies, including international treaties, national policies, statutes and regulations, and scholarly articles. The researchers also consulted a range of non-legal, non-policy sources, in order to generate coherent socio-cultural and economic contexts for their studies. While two of the chapters contain statistical analyses and quantitative data collected through surveys (Chapter 15 on Botswana's publicly funded researchers, and Chapter 8 on production and consumption of Egyptian independent music), most drew primarily on qualitative data from interviews, focus group discussions and qualitative written questionnaires. Such methods are not often used in legally oriented research (especially not regarding IP law), but are common in other areas of the social sciences. As will become clear to the reader, the qualitative data gathered were rich and facilitated author insights into a range of conceptual and practical elements, problems and solutions – insights which almost certainly could not have been generated via desk research alone.

Thematic research areas

The research featured in this book examined a diverse but interconnected range of phenomena in the following thematic areas related to IP: (1) informal appropriation, (2) trademarks and geographical indications, (3) traditional knowledge,

(4) copyrights, (5) patents and (6) publicly funded research. Collectively, these six interconnecting research foci, as brought together in this volume, offer insights into the extent to which IP systems are being, or could be, harnessed in African contexts to enable successful collaborative peer-production and distribution of knowledge-related goods and services.

Many previous and ongoing research projects have done, or are doing, valuable work by looking at particular topics within the framework of IP and development. For instance, there is much value in the work considering copyright's influence on access to learning materials, or strategies to increase access to patented knowledge, or the role of international organisations in local IP systems design. But analysing these issues in silos risks missing the bigger picture. Moreover, segregating topics such as patents, copyrights and trademarks into separate projects ignores the practical reality of how IP is managed on the ground. Any innovator, creator, entrepreneur or supporting policy-maker can attest to the fact that the key, overarching, real-world issue is how valuable intangible resources *of any sort* are protected, managed and mobilised. Whether the legal regime of patents or trademarks or copyrights is the particular tool being utilised in an effort to perform the desired management or mobilisation is of secondary importance to ultimate objectives. Many of the stakeholders affected by IP rights in any particular setting will often be unaware of the technical distinctions among branches of IP. A holistic approach was therefore necessary to achieve the objectives of the Open A.I.R. research programme that generated the content of this book.

Take just one of many possible practical examples: collaborative models of R&D in the biofuel sector. In some respects, this is clearly a patent-related issue. To the extent that patents may pose a problem for the development or deployment of innovative technologies, licensing strategies such as patent pools can be used to overcome such challenges. A wealth of scientific and technical information is contained in electronic patent databases, which are increasingly recognised for their potential value in facilitating North–South technology transfer and collaborative partnerships. Organisations that manage these databases, such as WIPO (via national IP offices), are right now implementing several large-scale online, networked projects to disseminate patent-related information throughout Africa as part of WIPO's development agenda. The information and communication technology (ICT) systems involved, however, are themselves layered with copyright protection. Moreover, the scientific and technical information contained in patent databases is at best incomplete and at worst useless without corresponding information contained in the scientific literature, the latter of which is protected by copyright and often technological protection measures (TPMs) too. To make matters more complex, the scientific research sector is built to a great extent upon public–private partnerships, with huge sums of both private and public funding supporting R&D, making issues of IP ownership fraught. How are IP rights to be managed to reduce bottlenecks and facilitate collaborative innovation in such circumstances? Despite the convenience of compartmentalisation, investigating IP issues in separate silos, through different programming areas or research projects, may miss important analytical insights and opportunities for influencing behavioural change. By combining the findings from case studies in different but related fields of IP, this book not only reflects research synergies and efficiencies, it also seeks to facilitate overarching insights into certain social, economic, political or other problems related to IP.

However, it must also be said that the book makes no claim to be comprehensive. No project of this nature could cover all relevant fields. Moreover, the case studies presented in the book were generated via responses that the Open A.I.R. network received from an open public call for research proposals. Thus the spread of topics and the countries covered was largely determined by the interests expressed by the researchers who initially came forward to propose studies and who successfully completed their studies. As a result, some topics that some readers may regard as central to understanding IP in relation to African innovation, creativity and development – e.g. access to medicines, plant breeders' rights, farmers' rights, video industries, biodiversity, utility models (UMs), industrial designs – receive only cursory mention, or no mention at all, in the chapters which follow. And while the editors of this volume were pleased to be able to include research from all four main regions of Africa – North, West, East and southern – there will undoubtedly be some readers not satisfied with the fact that only one North African country (Egypt) is featured, and that none of the research was conducted in a Francophone African country. Once again, on this matter of the geographical spread of the chapters of this book, the editors were restricted to consideration of the successful case studies which emerged via the open call.

Also, it is in the nature of the case study method that successful case studies tend to focus selectively on precise, somewhat narrow sub-issues within broader thematic areas, and often seek to chart new paths in a research landscape that already has some frequently examined features. So, within the patents theme, the researchers who contributed to this volume did *not* dwell upon the fairly well-covered issues of patents and access to medicines (see Abbott and Dukes, 2009; Adusei, 2012; 't Hoen, 2002) or patents and control of food (see Tansey and Rajotte, 2008). Instead, researchers concentrated on the emerging issue of patents and renewable energy, specifically biofuels – a source of energy promising to have significant impacts on both rural small-scale farmers and national economies in Africa, not to mention the global environment. Likewise, within the area of traditional knowledge (TK), researchers did *not* attempt to engage with the broad debates about international regimes for access and benefit-sharing (ABS) or similarly high-level topics. Researchers instead concentrated on one specific question – the viability of "TK commons" models in Africa – as one possible solution to TK-related IP challenges.

The following six subsections go into more detail about the thematic areas covered in the book and the author contributions to each theme.

Informal management of knowledge

One cannot understand African innovation without understanding the vibrant, entrepreneurial informal economy (IE) operating in African nations. But Africa's IE tends to be conceptually disconnected from the leading scholarly literature on innovation, entrepreneurship and IP. In this volume, a pair of chapters (Chapters 2 and 3) – which should ideally be read as companion pieces – seek to begin to bridge this gap, by (in Chapter 2) establishing an IP and innovation conceptual framework inclusive of the IE, and (in Chapter 3) reflexively engaging with that framework via evidence collected on the ground in the Ugandan capital city Kampala. In Chapter 2, De Beer, Sowa and Holman review concepts developed to understand and measure innovation, and then outline frameworks useful for drawing links, in Africa, between innovation and paradigms of entrepreneurship, the IE and IP. The authors conclude that the time is ripe for African policy-makers to seek holistic approaches to building innovation and, in turn, fostering socio-economic development.

In Chapter 3, Kawooya provides findings from his Ugandan case study of interactions between informal-sector Kampala automotive artisans and formally employed researchers at Makerere University's College of Engineering, Design, Art and Technology (CEDAT). The site of the interactions studied was CEDAT's formal–informal hybrid (or "semi-formal", as Kawooya calls it) entity, the Gatsby Garage automotive workshop. By probing the innovation practices at Gatsby Garage and at linked sites of informal activity, the research found that the informal artisans follow largely non-protectionist approaches to IP, both in their interactions with formal-sector partners and in their collaborations with counterparts in the informal sector.

Collaborative branding through trademarks and geographical indications

Throughout Africa, the agricultural sector remains central to economic and social development. New strategies are being developed to help brand African agricultural products with the unique product and production qualities they possess. Trademarks and related concepts such as certification marks and geographical indications (GIs) are important determinants of the likely success of such strategies. For many innovators, creators and entrepreneurs, especially those working as or with small- and medium-sized enterprises, their brand may well be their most valuable intangible asset in need of protection. In Africa, there are various examples of collectivities of citizens, firms or other organisations who are interested in collectively protecting brands. The latent commercial and non-commercial value in agricultural products and processes is often interconnected with the TK of indigenous and local communities (ILCs) (Dagne, 2010). But in the absence of a satisfactory protection mechanism for TK, communities must use other tools. In some circumstances, GIs might be used to associate products or processes with desirable qualities attributable to specific geographic locations. In other contexts, ordinary trademarks might be used to protect (or stop others from protecting) words and marks that might confuse consumers in the marketplace. Related to these legal strategies are systems of certification marks, which might shift market power in favour of producers of certified organic or fairly traded goods and services. Effectively, collaborative branding through certification marks or geographical indications presents a possible counter-narrative to the openness instincts that dominate the A2K movement's perspective on copyright and patent issues. Similar to patent pooling, these branding tools create systems that are open on the inside yet closed to outsiders. Studying the nuances of such arrangements holds great potential for contributing to better understanding of the role that IP plays in openness-based innovation and creativity settings.

In Chapter 4, Oguamanam and Dagne examine the Ethiopian coffee and Ghanaian cocoa industries in order to determine their potential to benefit from *sui generis* GIs as a model for practical adoption of IP for open development objectives. Through local field work, the authors investigate whether or not GIs could be successfully and sustainably used as instruments of place-based IP (PBIP). The authors submit that the implementation of GIs involves a range of tasks, including: the establishment of legal and institutional structures; maintaining the quality, reputation or characteristics of the products; enforcing and defending rights; and developing product awareness in international markets. These tasks involve significant costs and efforts that need to be measured and weighed against the expected benefits.

Chapter 5, authored by Adewopo, Chuma-Okoro and Oyewunmi, describes and interprets the findings of a case study into the potential application of communal trademark systems for certain Nigerian leather and textile products. The authors consider the national legal and regulatory environment, the levels of standardisation practised by small-scale leather and textile producers, and the views of producers regarding the viability of communal trademarking. The authors find interest, among the producers they survey, in communal trademarking, but at the same time they identify potential legal and practical challenges.

The potential of traditional knowledge (TK) commons arrangements

The question of how the TK of ILCs in Africa and elsewhere can and should be protected against misappropriation has been controversially discussed for decades. African countries currently protect TK in a wide variety of ways: some by way of *sui generis* systems, others via incorporation of TK into existing sets of IP laws. Interestingly, in the context of TK, many countries in Africa find themselves in the unaccustomed position of being net *exporters* of knowledge rather than, as is the case with most other types of IP, net *importers*. This situation results at times in high-level calls by African and other developing countries (at WIPO, for instance) for stronger protection of TK through IP laws – a position which contrasts with these countries' frequent demands for generally more flexible standards of IP protection. In other words, on TK matters there tends to be an inversion of typical North–South protectionist dynamics, with African and Southern nations to some extent taking up elements of the protectionist IP logic more usually associated with the stances of Northern governments and firms.

Within African ILCs, TK has typically been managed as a collectively held, shared and preserved resource. But recent decades have seen increased private sector proprietary, closed, commercial exploitation of TK, often in ways that do not benefit the communities that have created and preserved the knowledge. Chapters 6 and 7 look at one particular aspect of the current debate on exploitation of TK: the idea of a "TK commons". The current prospect that faces many ILCs is unregulated access to their knowledge, leaving it open to abuse or requiring negotiation of a separate ABS agreement for every non-commercial use. TK commons systems seek to provide another possible model, whereby TK can be promoted and circulated without having either to place it in the unrestricted public domain, where it is "free for all", or to deny all access to it entirely.

In Chapter 6, Ouma looks at the policy context for a possible TK commons in Kenya. Previous projects in Kenya, such as a digital archive documenting Maasai knowledge, have laid the groundwork for positive TK commons policy initiatives in Kenya, and the country has a National TK Policy (and draft law) seemingly capable of supporting commons approaches. But, the author concludes, collaboration between Kenyan government entities and ILCs is, at present, insufficient for full realisation of a TK commons. In Chapter 7, authors Cocchiaro, Lorenzen, Maister and Rutert outline their research findings from a legal, social and anthropological examination of the TK commons adopted by a grouping of traditional medicinal practitioners in the Bushbuckridge region of South Africa. Based on findings generated through embedded participatory research and legal analysis, the authors argue that one potential way for these traditional healers to improve management of the TK in their commons could be via establishment of a legal "trust" mechanism.

Copyrights and empowered creativity

The two copyright chapters in this book seek to break down assumptions that creators and users of cultural outputs hold homogeneous perspectives. In particular, both chapters reveal that not all creators need or want more or maximum copyright protection. This suggests a need for outside-the-box solutions, which Chapters 8 and 9 explore. In Chapter 8, Rizk presents findings from an extensive survey of creators and consumers of independent music in Egypt. The author seeks to determine, in the case of the output of the independent musicians, the potential applicability of alternative business models (see reference to the work of Lemos earlier in this chapter) which could enhance copyright compliance and still respect the wishes of both musicians and listeners. The research found a complex web of behaviours and perspectives (among both creators and consumers) in relation to the music and in relation to compliance, or lack thereof, with Egyptian copyright law. Key findings were that neither the musicians nor the consumers of their work are concerned by the lack of copyright compliance inherent in the widespread pirate copying and illegal commercial exploitation of independent music, as both the listeners and the creators regard paid-for live performances as the preferable means of commercial exploitation. While acknowledging the reticence among the musicians surveyed towards forms of commercialisation beyond payment for live performances, Rizk highlights the potential utility of an online Creative Commons-based "digital commons" arrangement for the music. Online combination of access to free and paid-for content and services (a kind of "freemium" model) could, the author argues, serve to simultaneously legalise, accommodate and refine the Egyptian grassroots music sector.

In Chapter 9, Sihanya reflects on the state of Kenyan scholarship in relation to the country's copyright environment. Sihanya researched attitudes and experiences among Kenyan scholarly publishing stakeholders in relation to emerging notions of "open scholarship" and alternative publishing with relaxed copyright restrictions. The author uncovered support for open scholarship among librarians and users, and a mixture of enthusiasm and reticence among scholarly authors. The primary interest of the scholarly authors Sihanya surveyed was wide dissemination of their ideas (an interest potentially well-served by open access [OA] and other alternative online publishing approaches). But, at the same time, the authors surveyed said they do not want to open themselves up to abuse of their economic rights, i.e. to jeopardise their ability to control commercial exploitation of their works. Sihanya concludes that Kenya's copyright environment, particularly in relation to enforcement of authors' economic rights, needs to be clarified and solidified in order for Kenyan authors to more fully embrace open scholarship and alternative publishing.

Patenting dynamics and African innovation policy priorities

Chapters 10, 11 and 12 investigate patenting and related matters relevant to African innovation objectives. Mgbeoji's Chapter 10, based on a survey of patent stakeholders in 44 African countries, focuses on the practical realities of patent examination in Africa. Mgbeoji found that most African patent offices are ill-equipped to discharge their two crucial functions: evaluation of the merits of an invention (to determine whether the criteria of patentability have been met); and collation and dissemination of patent information for the use of researchers, industry and other interested members of society. Mgbeoji argues that these weaknesses at African patent offices have the potential to hamper technology transfer and, in turn, retard domestic industrial development.

Chapters 11 and 12 look at specific issues connected to biofuel patenting, in Mozambique and Egypt, respectively. Both the developed and developing worlds face sustainable development crises for which energy matters are both cause and cure. In addition to wind, solar, geothermal, tidal and other sources, biofuels hold particular promise for the future, while at the same time triggering ethical, environmental and economic challenges. IP plays a little-studied role in this context. IP rights have the potential to induce investment in, and facilitate transfer of, innovative biofuel technologies, but at the same time can conceivably restrict R&D in the sector. Only very recently has attention begun to focus on this topic (see UNEP, n.d.). In Chapter 11, Dos Santos and Pelembe present their findings in Mozambique from a study of national biofuel policy-making and a biofuel patent landscaping exercise. The authors found strong Mozambican government policy commitment to development of small-scale biofuel enterprises and innovation, but, at the same time, a potentially countervailing dominance, by foreign firms, of biofuel technology patenting. Dos Santos and Pelembe argue that strong government support is necessary in support of locally driven biofuel technology research, innovation and development. Among other things, government needs to, according to the authors, facilitate affordable access to technology for small farming and producing enterprises. In Chapter 12, Awad and Abou Zeid outline their findings on Egypt's legal environment for biofuel patenting, and on the country's dearth of domestic biofuel innovation. The authors suggest policy and practical mechanisms that could help spark more Egyptian innovation in this area, with their recommendations including consideration of a clean energy "patent commons".

Ownership of outputs from publicly funded research

The patent chapters just outlined segue into the broader debate on the African continent – which forms the context for Chapters 13, 14 and 15 – about how IP policy can help or hinder the derivation of benefit from publicly funded research.

Scientific research resulting in innovation, and therefore benefiting development, can be complex, requiring large data sets, diverse analytical skills, and sophisticated, expensive equipment. By participating in international consortia, African publicly funded research institutions benefit from collaboration with global leaders in various fields, as such collaborations expose African researchers to best practices and give early access to research data and cutting-edge research equipment. But will African policy and legislative initiatives modelled on foreign instruments such as the US Bayh-Dole Act of 1980 (which permits certain recipients of federal research funds in the US to obtain IP protection for their inventions), be suitable for Africa, i.e. will public research in African nations, at its current levels, benefit from a Bayh-Dole-style commercialisation focus for the IP produced? One Bayh-Dole style law already exists on the continent, in South Africa, and there is a likelihood that other African nations will follow South Africa's example.

In an effort to provide some empirical evidence in support of deliberations by African policy-makers and law-makers giving consideration to introduction or revision of Bayh-Dole-style legislation in their respective countries, Chapters 13, 14 and 15 examine matters of IP protection for the results of publicly funded research in three African countries. In Chapter 13, Ncube, Abrahams and Akinsanmi analyse evidence from two South African universities, the University of Cape Town (UCT) and Johannesburg's University of the Witwatersrand (Wits), in relation to how these universities' innovation and knowledge dissemination activities are potentially influenced by the country's IP regulatory environment for publicly funded research. The authors investigated the ways in which UCT and Wits interact with South Africa's relatively new Intellectual Property Rights from Publicly Funded Research and Development (IPR-PFRD) Act of 2008. The research found problematic aspects with the IPR-PFRD Act's emphasis on knowledge protection and commercialisation, but at the same time evidence was found of initiatives and mechanisms, separate from the Act, by which the need for knowledge "socialisation" (generating non-commercial, societal benefits) and the practices of "open science" (wide sharing of data in order to maximise dissemination and collaboration) in relation to publicly funded research can still be fulfilled in South Africa.

In Chapter 14, Belete analyses findings from research into an apparent disconnect in Ethiopia between the state's innovation policy objectives (which emphasise transfer of protected IP between universities and industry) and the practical on-the-ground realities of scientific research in the country. The author found a dearth of innovative research at Ethiopia's universities, and scant linkage between universities and the private sector. In the author's opinion, the Ethiopian government should, instead of focusing on IP protection, explore alternative ways of funding and facilitating dissemination and sharing of innovative research, i.e. to support the open science objectives also identified in Ncube *et al.*'s Chapter 13. The open science theme also emerges in Chapter 15, in which Ama outlines and analyses the perceptions of IP in public policy and among publicly funded researchers in Botswana. Based on review of policy and legal instruments and statistical analysis of original survey data, Ama found that (as in the South African and Ethiopian cases covered in chapters 13 and 14), the Botswana government is putting strong emphasis on taking advantage of IP-related opportunities in the service of national science, technology and innovation (STI) goals. However, at the same time, Ama's survey of Botswana's public researchers found that the researchers had low levels of awareness of both national and institutional IP frameworks governing research outputs. In addition, Ama found that the public researchers surveyed had a strong, open science-oriented commitment to wide dissemination of their outputs, a commitment potentially at odds with the patenting orientation of some of the elements of the IP policies of the Botswana government and public research institutions.

3. Comparative analysis: conclusions on the current reality

Chapter 16 is a synthesis and comparative analysis, collaboratively authored by the four editors. The chapter draws out the common and contrasting findings generated by the studies outlined in Chapters 2 to 15. As well as comparing and contrasting specific research findings, the chapter draws some broad conceptual conclusions regarding three key themes that are consistently present in the case studies: (1) *collaborative innovation and creativity*; (2) *openness*; and (3) *IP*. This concluding chapter seeks to give a sense of the *status quo*, i.e. the current functioning, in African settings, of collaborative innovation and creativity in relation to openness and IP modalities. And then, based on that *status quo*, the chapter, and the book, concludes with three broad, evidence-based recommendations for consideration by African policy-makers. These recommendations are to patiently avoid importing and entrenching foreign IP approaches that may not suit local conditions; to broaden conceptions of relevant IP rights beyond merely formal mechanisms in order to create collaborative knowledge governance systems; and to focus on the future rather than the past or present when implementing IP policies.

Bibliography

Primary sources

Agreement on Trade-Related Aspects of Intellectual Property Rights (TRIPS) (1994).

Marrakesh Treaty to Facilitate Access to Published Works for Persons Who Are Blind, Visually Impaired, or Otherwise Print Disabled (Marrakesh Treaty) (2013).

Secondary sources

Abbott, F.M. and Dukes, G. (2009), *Global Pharmaceutical Policy: Ensuring Medicines for Tomorrow's World*, Edward Elgar, Cheltenham, UK.

Adelman, D. (2005), "A fallacy of the commons in biotech patent policy", *Berkeley Technology Law Journal*, Vol. 20, pp. 985–1030.

Adusei, P. (2012), *Patenting of Pharmaceuticals and Development in Sub-Saharan Africa: Laws, Institutions, Practices, and Politics*, Springer, New York.

Armstrong, C., De Beer, J., Kawooya, D., Prabhala, A. and Schonwetter, T. (Eds) (2010), *Access to Knowledge in Africa: The Role of Copyright*, UCT Press, Cape Town.

Barbosa, D.B., Chon, M. and Von Hase, A.M. (2007), "Slouching towards development in international intellectual property", *Michigan State Law Review*, Vol. 2007 No. 1, pp. 114–23.

Barratt, A. (2010), "Lessons from Bayh-Dole: reflections on the Intellectual Property Rights from Publicly Financed Research and Development Act (South Africa)", *Journal for Juridical Science*, Vol. 35, pp. 30–69.

Barton, J. (2007), *Intellectual Property and Access to Clean Energy Technologies in Developing Countries: An Analysis of Solar Photovoltaic, Biofuel and Wind Technologies*, International Centre for Trade and Sustainable Development (ICTSD) Programme on Trade and Environment, Issue Paper No. 2, Geneva.

Bello, J.H. and Holmer, A.F. (1991), "The Uruguay Round: where are we?" *International Law*, Vol. 25.

Benkler, Y. (2006), *The Wealth of Networks*, Yale University Press, New Haven, CT.

Bessen, J. (n.d.), *Open Source Software: Free Provision of Complex Public Goods*, available at: http://citeseerx.ist.psu.edu/viewdoc/download?doi=10.1.1.22.4994&rep=rep1&type=pdf; (accessed 22 March 2013).

Bessen, J. and Meurer, M. (2008), *Patent Failure: How Judges, Bureaucrats and Lawyers Put Innovators at Risk*, Princeton University Press, Princeton, NJ.

Bishop, P., Hines, A. and Collins, T. (2007), "The current state of scenario development: an overview of techniques", *Foresight*, Vol. 9 No. 1, pp. 5–25.

Blackeney, M. and Megistie, G. (2011), "Intellectual property and economic development in Africa", *Journal of World Intellectual Property*, Vol. 14 No. 238.

Boadi, R.Y. and Bokanga, M. (2007), "The African Agricultural Technology Foundation approach to IP management", in Krattiger, A., Mahoney, R.F. and Mill, L.N. (Eds), *Intellectual Property Management in Health and Agricultural Innovation: A Handbook of Best Practices,* Centre for the Management of Intellectual Property in Health Research and Development and Public Intellectual Property Resource for Agriculture.

Boateng, B. (2011), *The Copyright Thing Doesn't Work Here: Adinkra and Kente Cloth and Intellectual Property in Ghana*, University of Minnesota Press, Minneapolis.

Boettinger, S. and Burk, D.L. (2004), "Open source patenting", *Journal of International Biotechnology Law,* Vol. 1, pp. 221–31.

Boyle, J. (1997), "A Politics of intellectual property: environmentalism for the net?" *Duke Law Journal,* Vol. 47, pp. 87–116.

Boyle, J. (2003), "The second enclosure movement and the construction of the public domain", *Law and Contemporary Problems*, Vol. 66 No, 2, pp. 33–74.

Boyle, J. (2004), "A manifesto on WIPO and the future of intellectual property", *Duke Law and Technology Review*, Vol. 9 No. 2, pp. 139–65.

Burlamaqui, L., Castro, A.C. and Kattel, R. (Eds) (2012), *Knowledge Governance: Reasserting the Public Interest,* Anthem Press, London.

Campbell, C. (2010), "Southern Africa: region failing to innovate, says study," 13 August, available at: http://allafrica.com/stories/201008130924.html (accessed 12 April 2013).

Cannady, C. (2009), *Access to Climate Change Technology by Developing Countries,* International Centre for Trade and Sustainable Development (ICTSD) Issue Paper No. 25, Geneva.

Chesbrough, H. (2003), *Open Innovation: The New Imperative for Creating and Profiting From Technology*, Harvard Business School Press, Boston.

Chon, M. (2006). "Intellectual property and the development divide", *Cardozo Law Review*, Vol. 27, pp. 2821–912.

Chon, M. (2011), "Global intellectual property governance (under construction)", *Theoretical Inquiries in Law*, Vol. 12 No. 1, Art. 12.

Clark, J., Piccolo, J. and Stanton, B. (2000), *Patent Pools: A Solution to the Problem of Access in Biotechnology Patents?* US Patent and Trademark Office (USPTO), Alexandria, VA.

Commission on Intellectual Property Rights (CIPR) (2002), *Integrating Intellectual Property Rights and Development Policy* (2002), UK CIPR, London, available at: www.iprcommission.org/graphic/documents/final_report.htm (accessed 22 March 2013).

Computer and Communications Industry Association (CCIA) (2010), *Fair Use in the U.S. Economy: Economic Contribution of Industries Relying on Fair Use*, available at: www.ccianet.org/CCIA/files/ccLibraryFiles/Filename/000000000354/fair-use-study-final.pdf (accessed 12 April 2013).

Conference Board of Canada (2010), *How Canada Performs: Innovation*, available at: www.conferenceboard.ca/HCP/Details/Innovation.aspx (accessed 12 April 2013).

Connett-Porceddu, M. (2004), "Intellectual property and promoting R&D for the public interest in the Asian region: inclusionary and distributive innovation systems options", paper prepared for UNCTAD/ICTSD/HKU/IDRC Regional Dialogue on "Intellectual Property Rights (IPRs), Innovation and Sustainable Development", 8–10 November, Hong Kong.

Copenhagen Economics and the IPR Company (2009), *Are IPR a Barrier to the Transfer of Climate Change Technology?* available at: http://trade.ec.europa.eu/doclib/docs/2009/february/tradoc_142371.pdf (accessed 12 April 2013).

Dagne, T (2010), "Law and policy on intellectual property, traditional knowledge and development: legally protecting creativity and collective rights in traditional knowledge based agricultural products through geographical indicators", *The Estey Centre Journal of International Law and Trade Policy*, Vol. 11 No. 1, available at: http://papers.ssrn.com/sol3/papers.cfm?abstract_id=1600293 (accessed 12 April 2013).

De Beer, J. (Ed.) (2009), *Implementing the World Intellectual Property Organisation's Development Agenda* (2009), Wilfred Laurier University Press, Centre for International Governance Innovation (GIGI) and International Development Research Centre (IDRC), available at: www.idrc.ca/en/ev-139311-201-1-DO_TOPIC.html (accessed 12 April 2013).

De Beer, J. (2013), "Mapping the outcomes of multidisciplinary intellectual property research: lessons from the African copyright experience", in Scassa, T. Goudreau, M., Saginur, M. and Doagoo, C. (Eds), *Intellectual Property for the 21st Century: Multidisciplinary Perspectives on Intellectual Property Law*, Irwin Law, Toronto.

De Beer, J. and Bannerman, S. (2010), "Foresighting the future of WIPO's development agenda", *The WIPO Journal*, Vol. 1 No. 2.

De Beer, J. and Oguamanam, C. (2010), *Intellectual Property Training and Education: A Development Perspective*, International Centre for Trade and Sustainable Development (ICTSD) Issue Paper, Geneva.

De Beer, J. and Bannerman, S. (2013), "Access to knowledge as a new paradigm for research on ICTs and intellectual property rights", in Emdon, H., Elder, L., Petrazzini, B., and Fuchs, R. (Eds), *Connecting ICTs to Development: The IDRC Experience*, Anthem Press, London.

Deere, C. (2009), *The Implementation Game: The TRIPS Agreement and the Global Politics of Intellectual Property Reform in Developing Countries*, Oxford University Press, Oxford.

Diop, C.A. (1987), *Pre-Colonial Black Africa: A Comparative Study of the Political and Social Systems of Europe and Black Africa from Antiquity to the Formation of Modern States*, Lawrence Hill Books, New York.

Drahos, P. and Braithwaite, J. (2002), *Information Feudalism: Who Owns the Knowledge Economy?* Earthscan, London.

Drahos, P. and Frankel, S. (Eds) (2012), *Indigenous Peoples' Innovation: Intellectual Property Pathways to Development*, Australian National University E Press, Canberra.

Dutfield, G. (2002), *Protecting Traditional Knowledge and Folklore: A Review of Progress in Diplomacy and Policy Formation*, UNCTAD-ICTSD Issue Paper No. 1, available at: http://ictsd.org/i/publications/11775 (accessed 12 April 2013).

Esalimba, R. and New, W. (2009), "Spurring local innovation in Africa by improving access to information", *Intellectual Property Watch*, 19 October, available at: www.ip-watch.org/weblog/2009/10/19/spurring-local-innovation-in-africa-by-improving-access-to-information (accessed 12 April 2013).

European Patent Office (EPO) (2007), *Scenarios for the Future: How Might IP Regimes Evolve By 2025? What Global Legitimacy Might Such Regimes Have?* available at: http://documents.epo.org/projects/babylon/eponet.nsf/0/63A726D28B589B5BC12572DB00597683/$File/EPO_scenarios_bookmarked.pdf (accessed 12 April 2013).

Feldman, R. (2004), "The open source biotechnology movement: is it patent misuse?" *Minnesota Law Journal of Science and Technology*, Vol. 6 No. 1, pp. 117–67.

Finger, J.M. and Schuler, P. (Eds) (2004), *Poor People's Knowledge: Promoting Intellectual Property in Development Countries*, World Bank and Oxford University Press, Washington, DC.

Foresight for Development (n.d.), website, available at: http://foresightfordevelopment.org (accessed 12 April 2013).

Gastrow, M. (2009), *Open Innovation in South Africa: Case Studies in Nano-technology, Biotechnology, and Open Source Software Development*, available at: http://globelics2009dakar.merit.unu.edu/papers/1238513970_MG.pdf (accessed 12 April 2013).

Gervais, D.J. (Ed.) (2007), *Intellectual Property, Trade and Development: Strategies to Optimize Economic Development in a TRIPS-Plus Era*, Oxford University Press, Oxford.

Ghosh, R.A. (2006), *Study on the Economic Impact of Open Source Software on Innovations and the Competitiveness of the Information and Communication*

Technology (ICT) Sector in the EU, available at: http://ec.europa.eu/enterprise/sectors/ict/files/2006-11-20-flossimpact_en.pdf (accessed 12 April 2013).

Gollin, M., Hinze, G. and Wong, T. (2010), "Scenario planning on the future of IP", in Dutfield, G. and Wong, T. (Eds), *Intellectual Property and Human Development*, Cambridge University Press, Cambridge, UK.

Halbert, D.J. (2001), "Intellectual property in the Year 2025", *Journal of Futures Studies*, Vol. 6 No. 1, pp. 25–60.

Halewood, M. and Nnadozie, K. (2008), "Giving priority to the commons", in Rajotte, T. and Tansey, G. (Eds), *The Future Control of Food: A Guide to International Negotiations and Rules on Intellectual Property, Biodiversity and Food Security*, International Development Research Centre (IDRC), Ottawa.

Harms, L.T.C. (2012), "The politics of intellectual property laws", *Tydskrif vir die Suid-Afrikaanse Reg*, No. 3, pp. 461–68.

Hassan, E., Yaqub, O. and Diepeveen, S. (2010), *Intellectual Property and Developing Countries: A Review of the Literature*, Rand Europe, available at: www.rand.org/pubs/technical_reports/2010/RAND_TR804.pdf (accessed 12 April 2013).

Heller, M. and Eisenberg, R. (1998), "Can patents deter innovation? The anticommons in biomedical research", *Science*, Vol. 280 No. 5364, pp. 698–701.

Hess, C. and Ostrom, E. (Eds) (2006) *Understanding Knowledge as a Commons: From Theory to Practice*, MIT Press, Cambridge, MA.

Hope, J. (2008), *Biobazaar: The Open Source Revolution and Biotechnology*, Harvard University Press, Cambridge, MA.

Idris, K. (2003), *Intellectual Property: A Power Tool for Economic Growth*, 2nd ed., World Intellectual Property Organisation (WIPO), Geneva.

International Development Research Centre (IDRC) and UN Educational, Scientific and Cultural Organisation (UNESCO) (2003), *Future Directions for National Reviews of Science, Technology, and Innovation in Developing Countries*, Ottawa and Paris.

International Development Research Centre (IDRC) (2011), *Innovation for Inclusive Development: Program Prospectus for 2011–2016*, Ottawa.

Jaffe, A. and Lerner, J. (2006), *Innovation and Its Discontents: How Our Broken Patent System is Endangering Innovation and Progress, and What to Do About It*, Princeton University Press, Princeton, NJ.

Juma, C. and Ojwang, J.B. (Eds) (1989), *Innovation and Sovereignty: The Patent Debate in African Development*, African Centre for Technology Studies (ACTS), Nairobi.

Kapczynski, A. (2008), "The access to knowledge mobilization and the new politics of intellectual property", *Yale Law Journal*, Vol. 117, pp. 804–85.

Kapczynski, A. and Krikorian, G. (2010), *Access to Knowledge in the Age of Intellectual Property*, Zone Books, New York.

Kerr, W.A. (2006), "Enjoying a good port with a clear conscience: geographic indicators, rent seeking and development", *The Estey Centre Journal of International Law and Trade Policy*, Vol. 7 No. 1, pp. 1–14, available at: www.esteyjournal.com/j_pdfs/kerr7-1.pdf (accessed 22 March 2013).

Kongolo, T. (2000), "African intellectual property organizations: the necessity of adopting one uniform system for all Africa", *Journal of World Intellectual Property*, Vol. 3 No. 2, pp. 265–88.

Kuchma, I. (2010), *Report on the Implementation of Open Content Licenses in Developing and Transition Countries*, available at: http://mobile.eifl.org/cps/sections/services/eifl-oa/docs/report-on-implementation9384/downloadFile/file/Report_on_open_content_licenses_July.pdf?nocache=1278675629. 7 (accessed 12 April 2013).

Lang, T. (n.d.), "Building social capital with scenario work", unpublished DPhil thesis summary, Oxford University.

Lemos, R. (2007), *From Legal Commons to Social Commons: Brazil and the Cultural Industry in the 21st Century*, Working Paper No. 80, Centre for Brazilian Studies, University of Oxford, available at: www.law.nyu.edu/ecm_dlv2/groups/public/@nyu_law_website__centers__information_law_institute/documents/documents/ecm_pro_060831.pdf (accessed 12 April 2013).

Lemos, R. and Castro, O. (2008), *Tecnobrega: Pará Reinventing the Music Business*, International Development Research Centre (IDRC), available at: www.idrc.ca/en/ev-139014-201-1-DO_TOPIC.html (accessed 12 April 2013).

Lerner, A., Matupa, O., Mothlathledi, F.M, Stiles, G. and Brown, R. (2010), *SADC Biofuels State of Play Study*, Southern African Development Community (SADC), Programme for Basic Energy and Conservation in Southern Africa (ProBEC) and GTZ, available at: www.probec.net/fileuploads/fl11092010040316_SADC_BIOFUELS_STATE_OF_PLAY_STUDY.pdf (accessed 12 April 2013).

Lundvall, B.A., Vang, J., Joseph, K.J. and Chaminade, C. (2009), "Bridging innovation system research and development studies: challenges and research opportunities", paper submitted for the 7th Globelics Conference, Senegal, 6–8 October, available at: http://vbn.aau.dk/files/19664141/Bridging_Innovation_System_Research_and_Development_Studies.pdf (accessed 12 April 2013).

May, C. (2007), *The World Intellectual Property Organization: Resurgence and the Development Agenda*, Routledge, London.

May, C. (2010), *The Political Economy of Intellectual Property Rights*, 2nd ed., Routledge, New York.

May, C. and Sell, S.K. (2005), *Intellectual Property Rights: A Critical History*, Lynne Rienner, Boulder, CO.

Meléndez-Ortiz, R. and Roffe, P. (Eds) (2009), *Intellectual Property and Sustainable Development: Development Agendas in a Changing World*, Edward Elgar, Cheltenham, UK.

Netanel, N.W. (Ed.) (2008), *The Development Agenda: Global Intellectual Property and Developing Countries*, Oxford University Press, Oxford.

Musungu, S. (2006), *Intellectual Property Rights and Biotechnology in Developing Countries: Key Research and Knowledge Gaps*, International Development Research Centre (IDRC), available at: http://idl-bnc.idrc.ca/dspace/bitstream/10625/27486/1/65262.pdf (accessed 22 March 2013).

Nolan-Stevaux, K.M. (2007), "Open source biology: a means to address the access and research gaps?" *Santa Clara Computer and High Technology Law Journal*, Vol. 23 No. 2, pp. 271–316.

Octaviani, A. (2008), "Biotechnology in Brazil: promoting open innovation", in Shaver, L. (Ed.), *Access to Knowledge in Brazil: New Research on Intellectual Property, Innovation and Development*, Bloomsbury Academic, London.

Oguamanam, C. (2011), *Intellectual Property in Global Governance*, Routledge, New York.

Okediji, R.L. (1996), "The myth of development, the progress of rights: human rights to intellectual property and development", *Law and Policy*, Vol. 18 No. 3/4, pp. 315–54.

Okediji, R.L. (2000), "Toward an international fair use doctrine", *Columbia Journal of Transnational Law*, Vol. 39 No. 1, pp. XI–76.

Open African Innovation Research and Training Project (Open A.I.R., n.d.) website, available at: www.openair.org.za (accessed 12 April 2013).

Organisation for Economic Co-operation and Development (OECD) (2008), *Green Fuels for Development?Improving Policy Coherence in West Africa*, available at: www.oecd.org/dataoecd/3/31/41387549.pdf (accessed 12 April 2013).

Organisation for Economic Co-operation and Development (OECD) (2010), *Measuring Innovation – A New Perspective*, available at: www.oecd.org/document/25/0,3343,en_41462537_41454856_44979734_1_1_1_1,00.html (accessed 12 April 2013).

Organisation for Economic Co-operation and Development (OECD) (2012), *Innovation and Inclusive Development: Conference Discussion Report*, conference held 21 November, Cape Town.

Organisation for Economic Co-operation and Development (OECD) and Statistical Office of the European Communities (Eurostat) (2005), *Oslo Manual: Guidelines for Collecting and Interpreting Innovation Data*, 3rd ed., available at: http://epp.eurostat.ec.europa.eu/cache/ITY_PUBLIC/OSLO/EN/OSLO-EN.PDF (accessed 22 April 2013).

Oyelaran-Oyeyinka, B. and McCormick, D. (2007), *Industrial Clusters and Innovation Systems in Africa: Institutions, Markets and Policy*, UN University Press, Tokyo.

Pistorius, T. (2007) "The impact of intellectual property law and policy on sustainable development", *South African Yearbook of International Law*, Vol. 32, pp. 376–95.

Pouris, A. and Pouris, A. (2011), "Patents and Economic Development in South Africa: Managing IPRs", presentation to Accelerating IP and Innovation in South Africa Conference, 18–20 September, Cape Town.

PlusNews (2010),"South Africa: government is first to join major patent pool", 12 May, available at: www.plusnews.org/report.aspx?ReportID=89102 (accessed 12 April 2013).

Programme for Basic Energy and Conservation in Southern Africa (ProBEC) (n.d), website, available at: www.probec.org/displaysection.php?czacc=&zSelectedSectionID=sec1194694609 (accessed 12 April 2013).

Rahmatian, A. (2009), "Neo-colonial aspects of global intellectual property protection", *Journal of World Intellectual Property*, Vol. 12 No. 1, pp. 40–74.

Royal Society (n.d.) "Strategic priorities", available at: http://royalsociety.org/Strategic-Priorities/ (accessed 12 April 2013).

Schonwetter, T., Ncube, C. and Chetty, P. (2009), *ACA2K Country Report: South Africa*, African Copyright and Access to Knowledge Project (ACA2K), available at: www.aca2k.org/attachments/154_ACA2K%20South%20Africa%20CR.pdf (accessed 12 April 2013).

Sell, S.K. (2003), *Private Power, Public Law: The Globalization of Intellectual Property Rights*, Cambridge University Press, New York.

Shapiro, C. (2001),"Navigating the patent thicket: cross licences, patent pools, and standards setting", in Jaffe, A.B., Lerner, J. and Stern, S. (Eds), *Innovation Policy and the Economy, Vol. 1*, MIT Press, Cambridge, MA.

Shaver, L. and Rizk, N. (Eds) (2010), *Access to Knowledge in Egypt: New Research on Intellectual Property, Innovation and Development*, Bloomsbury, London.

Shirky, C. (2008), *Here Comes Everybody: The Power of Organizing without Organization*, Penguin Press, New York.

Smith, M.L., Elder, L. and Emdon, H. (2011), "Open development: a new theory for ICT4D", *Information Technologies and International Development*, Vol. 7 No. 1, Spring (Special Issue: Open Development), available at http://itidjournal.org/itid/article/view/692/290 (accessed 12 April 2013).

Sunder, M. (2012), *From Goods to a Good Life*, Yale University Press, New Haven, CT.

't Hoen, E. (2002), "TRIPS, pharmaceutical patents, and access to essential medicines: a long way from Seattle to Doha", *Chicago Journal of International Law*, Vol. 3 No. 1, pp. 27–46.

Tansey, G. and Rajotte, T. (Eds) (2008), *The Future Control of Food: A Guide to International Negotiations and Rules on Intellectual Property, Biodiversity and Food Security*, Earthscan, Oxford.

Tapscott, D. and Williams, A.D. (2006), *Wikinomics: How Mass Collaboration Changes Everything*, Atlantic Books, London.

The Economist (2013), "Africa rising: a hopeful continent", in "Special report: emerging Africa", 2 March, available at: www.economist.com/news/special-report/21572377-african-lives-have-already-greatly-improved-over-past-decade-says-oliver-august (accessed 12 April 2013).

UN Environment Programme (UNEP) (n.d.), "Launch of UNEP-EPO-ICTSD Joint Study on Patents and Environmentally Sound Technologies," available at: www.unep.ch/etb/initiatives/Patents_ESTs.php (accessed 12 April 2013).

UN Environment Programme (UNEP) (2009), *Toward Sustainable Production and Use of Resources: Assessing Biofuels*, available at: www.unep.fr/scp/rpanel/pdf/Assessing_Biofuels_Full_Report.pdf (accessed 12 April 2013).

UN Educational Scientific and Cultural Organisation (UNESCO) (2010), *World Science Report 2010*, available at: www.unesco.org/new/en/social-and-human-sciences/resources/reports/world-social-science-report (accessed 12 April 2013).

US Patent and Trademark Office (USPTO) (2000), *Patent Pools: A Solution to the Problem of Access in Biotechnology Patents?* available at: www.uspto.gov/web/offices/pac/dapp/opla/patentpool.pdf (accessed 12 April 2013).

Van der Heijden, K. (1996), *Scenarios: Art of Strategic Conversation*, John Wiley and Sons, New York.

Visser, C. (2007), "International intellectual property norm setting: democratising the World Intellectual Property Organisation?" *South African Yearbook of International Law*, Vol. 32, pp. 222–32.

World Intellectual Property Organisation (WIPO) (2003), *WIPO Guide on Surveying the Economic Contribution of the Copyright-based Industries*, available at: www.wipo.int/export/sites/www/ip-development/en/creative_industry/pdf/893.pdf (accessed 12 April 2013).

Wunsch-Vincent, S., Reynolds, T. and Wyckoff, A. (2007), "Implementing openness: an international institutional perspective", *First Monday*, Vol. 12 No. 6, available at: http://firstmonday.org/htbin/cgiwrap/bin/ojs/index.php/fm/rt/printerFriendly/1914/1796 (accessed 12 April 2013).

Wong, T. and Dutfield, G. (Eds) (2011), *Intellectual Property and Human Development: Current Trends and Future Scenarios*, Cambridge University Press, Cambridge, UK.

Yu, P.K. (2009), "A tale of two development agendas", *Ohio Northern University Law Review*, Vol. 34.

Chapter 2

Frameworks for Analysing African Innovation: Entrepreneurship, the Informal Economy and Intellectual Property

Jeremy de Beer, Izabella Sowa and Kristen Holman

Abstract

This chapter reviews conceptual frameworks to understand and measure innovation, and then outlines links between innovation and the concepts of entrepreneurship, the informal economy (IE) and intellectual property (IP). The review suggests that the time is ripe for African policy-makers to seek more holistic approaches to facilitating innovation and, in turn, to fostering socio-economic development in African nations.

1. Introduction

Innovation is a key driver of economic development, but the gap between socio-economic climates that foster innovation in developed and developing countries, particularly the developing nations of Africa, is large (Aubert, 2006; GTZ, 2010). This is a problem that must be addressed. Innovation is affected by many variables, one of which is intellectual property (IP). While IP plays an especially important role in formal-sector innovation, its role in the informal economy (IE) is just beginning to be explored (De Beer *et al.*, 2013). The existing literature on the role of intellectual property in innovation, entrepreneurship, the IE and economic development is largely disconnected, providing inadequate bases for understanding how IP does, or could, function in a manner beneficial to social and economic progress.

For example, those who study or make policy on innovation usually rely on a definition in a document called the *Oslo Manual*, published by the Organisation for Economic Co-operation and Development (OECD) and the Statistical Office of the European Communities (Eurostat). The *Oslo Manual* defines innovation as

> [...] the implementation of a new or significantly improved product (good or service), or process, a new marketing method, or a new organisational method in business practices, workplace organisation or external relations (OECD and Eurostat, 2005, p. 46).

Citing this *Manual*, and the theoretical concepts and study methods contained in it, is trite for innovation scholars and policy-makers. But too few IP experts, especially intellectual property lawyers, are familiar with this well-established framework. For many people working on IP, innovation is less an established field of study than a rhetorical buzz word. Similarly, entrepreneurship is a concept intuitively connected to IP, but too often IP law, policy and practice are insufficiently tied to various theoretical models of how and why entrepreneurship happens. The problems with such gaps in the discourses and understanding among different fields of research are exacerbated in the context of Africa's predominantly informal economic activities.

To avoid, or at least mitigate, the pitfalls inherent in multidisciplinary analyses of intellectual property and innovation, this chapter begins to establish conceptual common ground. Inevitably, for some readers, the chapter will be too simple; for others, it may be the opposite. To strike a balance, the modest goal of this chapter is to examine linkages among disparate strands of thinking in the literature on these topics, and to weave the strands together in an interdisciplinary way, relevant to emerging realities on the African continent.

2. Innovation

Our understanding of the links between technological innovation, economic growth and human development has evolved significantly over the past century. Despite more sophisticated understandings of development, based on human freedom (Sen, 1999) or capabilities (Nussbaum, 2011), economic growth is still a key metric to measure success. Thus, this section begins by discussing the role of technological innovation in classical, neoclassical and Keynesian economic theory. Next, it explores the interdisciplinary conceptions of innovation as presented by proponents of development economics and modernisation theory. Third, this section discusses the systems approach to innovation, which in the 1970s aimed to address the fragmented research on the topic that had emerged up to that point. The section concludes by examining current views on the innovation–development nexus.

Classical and neoclassical economics

Since the 18th century, when classical economic theory emerged as the first modern school of economic thought, various conceptions of innovation have shaped the economic discourse. Adam Smith (1776), a leading proponent of classical economics, argued that savings and capital accumulation are the key determinants of economic growth, and that competitive markets facilitate invention and innovation. This reasoning endured until the late 19th century, when neoclassical economics displaced classical economic theory.

Neoclassical economists assumed: that individuals have rational preferences among various outcomes to which values can be attributed; that individuals maximise utility; that firms maximise profits; and that people base their economic decisions on full information. Alfred Marshall, a key figure in the neoclassical school, acknowledged the link between innovation and local economic development (Marshall, 1920). He argued that firms involved in similar activities and clustered in the same place can be more efficient than isolated producers, because locational proximity allows third-party firms to benefit from new, non-excludable ideas generated by other firms. This early insight laid the groundwork for contemporary discourse around open, inclusive, networked or community-driven innovation, discussed later in this chapter.

Dynamic development of economic systems

In the 1930s and 1940s, Joseph Schumpeter countered the neoclassical view of orderly economic change and market equilibrium, arguing that adjustments in the economy are abrupt and uneven. He sought to explain how productive innovations arise sporadically within capitalist systems, displacing old equilibriums and creating radically new and more efficient socio-economic conditions. Schumpeter (1934, 1942) argued that such productive innovations can occur through the introduction of a new good or a new quality of a good; the introduction of a new method of production; the opening up of a new market; the conquest of a new source of supply; and/or the carrying out of a new mode of organisation of an industry.

Notwithstanding Schumpeter's novel ideas about the dynamic development of economic systems, neoclassical economic theories dominated the subsequent decades. Our understanding of innovation was thus impoverished, because the prevalent assumptions of rational optimisation – full information availability and an obsession with determinate solutions to fully specified models – left little room for analysis of technological change (AU-NEPAD, 2010).

Keynesian economics and growth theory

During the post-war period, economists viewed growth as the key requirement for development, and a number of growth theories emerged based on Keynesian economic principles. Notably, the Harrod-Domar Growth Model posited that increased investment is a prerequisite for economic growth, and that the state should encourage savings in order to accumulate investment and should support technological advances to increase productive capacity and efficiency (Domar, 1947; Harrod, 1939; Peet and Hartwick, 2009).

In the late 1950s, Robert Solow (1957) presented a revolutionary growth model that focused on the role of technological development to explain economic growth that could not be accounted for by capital accumulation or labour productivity. Solow argued that technological progress is not a product of economic forces, but rather an exogenous collection of knowledge that is continuously expanding. In subsequent decades, economists relied heavily on Solow's growth model when formulating their development policy recommendations (Peet and Hartwick, 2009).

Development economics

The post-war period also saw the establishment of the development economics school, which was premised on the idea that economic processes in developing countries are distinct from those in developed ones. While institutions, technology and entrepreneurship were assumed to be exogenous in the neoclassical economics school, development economists considered these factors to be endogenous. Albert Hirschman (1958) argued that developing countries lack entrepreneurship, or the perception of opportunities for investment. Accordingly, Hirschman envisioned a role for the state that involved developing confidence among entrepreneurs, enabling them to make investments in key sectors such as manufacturing.

Other development economists focused on the link between geography, technological innovation and economic growth. François Perroux (1955) viewed the innovative capacities of propulsive industries as growth stimuli for geographically proximate firms involved in technologically complementary industries. Geographer Allan Pred (1965) shared this idea; he posited that the clustering of firms in specific locations would lead to the development of innovative centres, which would in turn attract economic activity. He also argued that there is a positive correlation between the importance of an innovative centre and the speed of its economic growth (Peet and Hartwick, 2009; Pred, 1965).

Modernisation theory

In 1959, Seymour Martin Lipset set the stage for the emergence of modernisation theory, which presented a sociological alternative to purely economic theories of development. According to Lipset, industrialisation leads directly to positive social change, because it facilitates the emergence of democratic political institutions (Lipset, 1959). Bert Hoselitz also espoused a sociological approach to development, focusing on cultural change as a prerequisite for economic growth. Hoselitz argued that capitalist entrepreneurs, who of necessity set themselves apart from the mainstream, are the ones who generate new ideas. Hoselitz also believed that cities, to a greater extent than rural areas, are birthplaces of innovation, and he thus favoured political power being held by entrepreneurs in urban areas (Hoselitz, 1960; Peet and Harwick, 2009). Sociologist Talcott Parsons (1966) considered the most successful societies to be those that are able to adapt and differentiate for the purpose of using resources effectively and gaining a competitive advantage over other societies.

Another group of modernisation theorists presented a more psychological orientation. David McClelland (1961) argued that economic development can only take place in a society that accords importance to the achievement of innovation and entrepreneurship. Everett Hagen (1962) argued that society's values would shift towards favouring innovation and economic growth once traditional peoples searching for new identities engaged in processes characterised by creativity and the need to achieve.

Alongside the development of these diverse perspectives on modernisation, the 1960s saw a resurgence of interest in the notion of innovation, with one area of particular interest being the inexplicably rapid rise of Japanese productivity (Freeman, 1987). Economists became interested in identifying factors instrumental in pushing countries along the path of modernisation. Walt Whitman Rostow (1960) argued that all societies pass through five sequential categories of economic development: (1) traditional society; (2) preconditions for take-off; (3) take-off; (4) the drive to maturity; and (5) an age of high mass consumption. In Rostow's thinking, technological development is the stimulus that moves a society from one stage to the next. As such, the emergence of new production functions, which facilitate rapid growth in primary sectors, is a prerequisite for development even in mature, industrialised economies.

Everett Rogers (1962) also devised a five-step theory, about the diffusion of innovation, whereby an individual (1) becomes aware of an innovation; (2) becomes interested in the innovation and seeks information about it; (3) chooses to either adopt or reject the innovation; (4) (if the innovation is accepted) puts the innovation to use on a small scale; and (5) adopts the innovation for continued use in the future. According to Rogers, the successful spread of an innovation follows an S-shaped curve: after the first 15% of people in a society adopt an innovation there is relatively rapid adoption by the remaining members.

During the years that followed the publication of Rogers' work, others put forward geographic versions of diffusion theory, highlighting the spatial aspects of modernisation. Peter Gould (1964) argued that new ideas are diffused from one area to another through communication. An innovation will be adopted earliest in areas of close proximity to the innovation's place of origin, and adopted much later in areas farther away. Gould, of course, was writing in the 1960s, an era when communications were limited by less sophisticated technologies than are available today.

Evolutionary economic theory

By the end of the 1970s, researchers were taking a view that prevailing theories were providing an inadequate picture of innovation, because the theories were fragmented across multiple intellectual disciplines. Moreover, neoclassical economists' preoccupation with profit maximisation and market equilibrium was causing them to overlook the uncertainty of innovation and the wide variety of institutions that support innovation across different sectors (Nelson and Winter, 1977). Richard Nelson and Sydney Winter developed an evolutionary theory of business capabilities and behaviour that was modelled on biology. Drawing on Schumpeter's ideas about discontinuous economic change, Nelson and Winter (1982) concluded that firms facing key business decisions rely not only on past experience, but also on innovative alternatives to their past behaviour.

Later in the 1980s, Christopher Freeman broadened the emerging field of evolutionary economics by stressing the importance of national systems of innovation, which he defined as "the network of institutions in the public and private sectors whose activities and interactions initiate, import, modify and diffuse new technologies" (Freeman, 1987, p. 1). Bengt-Åke Lundvall (1992) supported this view, concluding that the two key factors acting on a system of innovation are its structure of production and its institutional set-up. Charles Edquist (1997) presented a more general definition of systems of innovation, which included consideration of the economic, social, political, organisational and institutional factors that affect development and diffusion of innovation.

As economists began to experiment with models and surveys to measure innovation, the OECD's Working Party of National Experts on Science and Technology Indicators (NESTI) identified the need for a coherent set of analytical tools. Hence, in 1992, the OECD published the first edition of the aforementioned *Oslo Manual*, subtitled *Proposed Guidelines for Collecting and Interpreting Technological Innovation Data*. This first edition focused on technological product and process innovation in manufacturing: an innovation is considered implemented if it has been introduced to the market (product innovation) or used within a production process (process innovation). This first *Oslo Manual* identified scientific, technological, organisational, financial and commercial activities as innovations (OECD and Eurostat, 1992).

In parallel, Paul Romer (1992) proposed a new growth theory, which characterised technological advancements as an endogenous product of economic activity, and knowledge as the driver of progress. Other scholars corroborated the importance of the knowledge–development nexus. Richard Nelson and Nathan Rosenberg (1993) concluded that the main sources of innovation are organisations that promote the creation and dissemination of knowledge, and Joseph Cortright (2001) viewed government policies focusing on innovation and the diffusion of knowledge as instrumental to economic growth. Notably, Cortright argued that economic strategies should value not only the knowledge generated through scientific research, but also the innovation of frontline workers (Cortright, 2001; Peet and Hartwick, 2009). When the OECD published the second edition of its *Oslo Manual* in 1997, it recognised the importance of both the knowledge transfer and systems approaches to innovation. The 1997 edition of the *Oslo Manual* also expanded the definition of innovation to cover a wider range of industries, including construction, utilities, manufacturing and marketed services (OECD and Eurostat, 1997).

The current state of innovation literature

Research on innovation and development split in several directions around the start of the 21st century, partly due to shifts in global economic and geopolitical power triggered by the emergence of the BRICS nations of Brazil, Russia, India, China and now, South Africa (Lawson and Purushothaman, 2003). Recent literature on innovation and progress has begun to reflect global heterogeneity. For example, scholars examining African development using the systems of innovation approach have focused on indigenous knowledge and capabilities, because these factors emphasise learning and capacity building (Muchie *et al.*, 2003). Interestingly, such approaches mirror one proposed 30 years earlier in a UN-commissioned study entitled *Sussex Manifesto: Science and Technology for Developing Countries during the Second Development Decade*, which stressed the need for developing countries to nurture indigenous scientific capabilities rather than relying on technologies transferred from developed countries (Ely and Bell, 2009).

The current, third edition of the *Oslo Manual*, published in 2005, includes an annex on innovation surveys in developing countries. According to the OECD, these surveys are intended to serve as guiding tools for public policy development and business strategy designs that seek to incorporate new ideas and knowledge. The current OECD view is that measurement exercises should focus on the innovation *process* rather than its outputs, and should emphasise how countries deal with *capabilities* and *efforts* as well as results. The OECD now sees efforts made by firms and organisations (innovation activities) and capabilities (stocks and flows) as equal to, or even more important than, the results (innovations), as elements requiring determination and analysis by researchers. Factors that hamper or facilitate innovation are key indicators for gauging a country's innovative profile in this context (OECD and Eurostat, 2005).

The recently established African Science, Technology and Innovation Indicators (ASTII) initiative is working to improve the measurement of science and technology indicators by Member States of the African Union (AU-NEPAD, 2010). ASTII published the *African Innovation Outlook* report (2010), which provides an overview of science, technology and innovation (STI) activities in 19 African countries.[1] Notably, the report asserts that

> [g]iven the appropriate institutional context, entrepreneurship at all scales (in micro, small, medium and large enterprises) has the potential to meet the huge demands of the continent and its population of over one billion. Legitimate, participative governance, strengthened through an innovation systems policy perspective, will also improve social cohesion by reducing uncertainties and enabling evolutionary change. In combination, these discrete components of policymaking and coordination offer the continent the opportunity to escape the vicious cycles of underdevelopment. (AU-NEPAD, 2010, p. 30)

Innovation scholars also postulate that risk-taking entrepreneurs are the driving force behind innovative activities (Gault and Zhang, 2010). The AU's work connects the institutional context for entrepreneurship, including governance, with social cohesion and other, broader development objectives.

While this vision of a well-governed, cohesive entrepreneurial society is one prospect for parts of Africa, it is not the only plausible scenario for the future. To help imagine alternative evolutions of African entrepreneurship, the next section of this chapter examines the literature on entrepreneurship and highlights its linkages to economic development theory.

1 The 19 countries are: Algeria, Angola, Burkina Faso, Cameroon, Egypt, Ethiopia, Gabon, Ghana, Kenya, Lesotho, Malawi, Mali, Mozambique, Nigeria, Senegal, South Africa, Tanzania, Uganda and Zambia.

3. Entrepreneurship

Entrepreneurship defined

Development scholars have tended to define entrepreneurship extremely broadly. In particular, recent literature has deemed any form of innovation that creates or improves a product, service or process as entrepreneurship. One of the most commonly referenced definitions in development literature defines entrepreneurship as

> [t]he manifest ability and willingness of individuals, on their own, in teams within and outside existing organizations, to perceive and create new economic opportunities (new products, new production methods, new organizational schemes and new product-market combinations) and to introduce their ideas in the market, in the face of uncertainty and other obstacles, by making decisions on location, form and the use of resources and institutions. (Wennekers and Thurik, 1999, pp. 46–7; Caree and Thurik, 2003, p. 441)

This definition of entrepreneurship hinges on two aspects that jointly create capacity for entrepreneurship: an environmental component and a behavioural component. Thus, this definition links to the argument, seen in the work of McClelland (1961), that in order to foster entrepreneurship it is necessary to examine factors that exist at both the system level and the individual level of any given economy. This definition is also compatible with descriptions of entrepreneurship as a "process" rather than a somewhat static phenomenon that an economy seeks to achieve (UNCTAD, 2005).

But the relationship between entrepreneurship (so defined) and development requires a more precise indication of what type of entrepreneurship is being measured. In the contemporary literature, a distinction has been made between "necessity entrepreneurship" and "opportunity entrepreneurship", coupled with an assertion that levels of opportunity entrepreneurship are a more significant indicator of a nation's entrepreneurial capacity than necessity entrepreneurship (Acs, 2006, p. 97).

Entrepreneurship in the developing world

The national economies of countries with low levels of per capita income tend to be characterised by large numbers of micro and small enterprises (Ayyagari *et al.*, 2005). Higher per capita income levels tend to correspond with industrialisation, economies of scale and larger, established organisations satisfying increasing demand while increasing their relative roles in the economy. Thus, both the existence of small entrepreneurial ventures and their eventual growth into large ventures have important places in the transformation sequence of an economy from developing status to developed status. Early-stage entrepreneurial development and the growth of existing entrepreneurial ventures are two different, but equally important, matters.

Once an economy has moved to the industrialised phase of capitalist development, it can be argued that a "qualitative change in the drivers of economic growth occurs" (UNCTAD, 2005, p. 4). This theory of development is premised on the idea of "long cycles" of economic development, a concept attributable to Joseph Schumpeter. Schumpeter deemed the first long cycle of innovation as being the diffusion of the steam engine and textile innovations in the 18th century, followed by railway and steel innovations, electrical power and then the chemical industry (Schumpeter, 1934). He asserted that once an economy graduates from a threshold level of industrial development, technology and the accumulation of human knowledge become the primary drivers of economic growth.

Entrepreneurship is arguably the common denominator behind both technological advances and knowledge accumulation. In Schumpeter's theory, it is the ability and initiative of entrepreneurs – drawing upon the discoveries of scientists and inventors – that create new opportunities for investment, growth and employment (Schumpeter, 1934, pp. 83–4). For this reason, Schumpeter believed that "new combinations" of factors of production would be a form of entrepreneurial discovery that would drive economic development. Schumpeter's theory posits that the process of "creative destruction" would allow the innovative entrepreneur to take market share from existing suppliers and increase overall demand for the products offered in that market (Schumpeter, 1942; UNCTAD, 2005, p. 4).

Scholars asserting the importance of the entrepreneurship context have emphasised the critical importance of the "imitating" entrepreneur as opposed to the "innovating" entrepreneur (Schmitz, 1989). Imitating entrepreneurs are individuals who manipulate existing activities and put new products or methods into practice, thereby creating knowledge through a process that development scholars such as James Schmitz have characterised as learning by implementing (Schmitz, 1989). Critics of Schumpeter's theory have pointed out that in order for learning/growth by imitation to ensue, there must be a trigger innovation of sufficient scale, and the social climate in which it is born must be "favourable" (Freeman, 1982). As major innovations become part of an economy's backdrop, further growth in that economy can and should be spurred by the activities of individuals seeking to imitate and subtly vary existing innovations.

Mowery and Rosenberg (1979) have argued that the diffusion process of innovation cannot be viewed as one of simple carbon-copy replication. Rather, the economic growth that is spurred involves a sequence of *further* innovations: sometimes large, but mostly small, subtle innovations based on the larger technical innovation. This process is typically cast as an outcome of firms striving to gain an edge over competitors in an industry. As new industries emerge they each set in motion process innovations linked particularly to exploitation of economies of scale (Rosenberg, 1976; Mowery and Rosenberg, 1979). This characterisation of economic growth appears relevant to markets in which there is an abundance of small firms (rather than a few key heavyweight actors), because small firms hold the capacity to imitate existing innovations. The "imitating entrepreneur" is an especially important figure throughout the developing world.

Fostering an entrepreneurial environment in a developing economy

There are two foundational models outlined in development literature that attempt to link entrepreneurship to development.

The Wennekers and Thurik Model

The Wennekers and Thurik Model divides analysis of innovative capacity growth through entrepreneurship into three categories: (1) individual level, (2) firm level and (3) macro level (Thurik and Wennekers, 2001). Each level operates according to its own set of "conditions" for entrepreneurship, which researchers believe are the factors driving innovative potential in the form of distinctive "cultures": certain conditions are thought to be required in order for a certain type of culture to be achieved at each level. Each level has an impact on the capacity for entrepreneurship in a given economy, with the impact emanating from the individual level and moving towards the macro level. According to the Wennekers and Thurik Model, entrepreneurial activity originates with a single person, the entrepreneur, and entrepreneurship is, for the most part, dependent on factors affecting the individual. Capacity thus originates at the individual level and is later realised at the firm/institutional level. Innovation is stimulated by an individual's attitudes, motives, skills and assessment of market risk.

Though this model posits that the individual entrepreneur does not undertake innovation in a timeless/space-less vacuum, the context in which the entrepreneur is acting is given less emphasis than the psychological factors that play on the entrepreneur's decision to innovate. At the same time, psychological factors are understood to be influenced to some extent by cultural and institutional factors, the business environment and macroeconomic conditions: personal entrepreneurial qualities that cause one to innovate are necessary but not sufficient to foster entrepreneurship.

The Wennekers and Thurik Model asserts that entrepreneurial activity expands the productive potential of a national economy by inducing both "higher productivity" and "an expansion of new niches and industries" (UNCTAD, 2005, p. 7). These results are produced by the individual layer transforming the processes used for providing certain products and services. When factors at the individual level foster entrepreneurial qualities in individuals, there is greater potential for increasing the productive potential at the firm level and, in turn, at the macro level. Individual entrepreneurs learn from the successes and failures of innovation attempts undertaken by themselves and others. These successes and failures form the basis of what is often referred to as "knowledge capital" – the "know how". Knowledge capital drives research and development (R&D) in its purest and cheapest form: knowledge makes its way from the individual level to the firm and macro levels, increasing the potential for economic growth.

The GEM Model

The Global Entrepreneurship Monitor (GEM) Model depicts entrepreneurship as something that is fuelled at the macro level, with movement to the micro level (Reynolds *et al.*, 2000). According to this model, capacity for entrepreneurship is fuelled by an economy's social/political context: the context generates the economic conditions that allow for entrepreneurship to occur, resulting in opportunities/capacity at the individual level. This model views entrepreneurship predominantly as firm creation, defining entrepreneurship more strictly than does the Wennekers and Thurik Model. More particularly, the GEM Model measures entrepreneurship on the basis of new firm creation, as opposed to the Wennekers and Thurik Model's broader focus on entrepreneurship as innovation in its purest form (i.e. innovation demonstrated by any form of improvement or imitation of existing products and processes).

The GEM Model also embodies a heavy focus on the role of existing firms. Existing firms are thought to generate new market opportunities for small and medium-sized firms, whether by technology spillover or by increasing domestic demand. The number of firms operating in the economy is thus regarded as an indicator of growth. In essence, the GEM Model conceptualises economic growth as firm growth and firm creation. Entrepreneurship in this context depends on the "emergence and presence of new market opportunities" – often the product of existing firms themselves – and the "capacity, motivation and skills of individuals to establish firms" (UNCTAD, 2005, p. 8). This is a narrower conceptualisation of entrepreneurship as it places less focus on opportunities for existing firms to increase returns through innovations in their production process.

Entrepreneurship and IP

Where, then, might IP dynamics affect a national economy's capacity to foster entrepreneurship? A prudent approach to answering this question would seem to require consideration of both the Wennekers and Thurik and GEM models of building entrepreneurship. In fact, the models provide two distinct avenues through which to examine the potential for bolstering economic development through IP.

IP and the Wennekers and Thurik Model

Given the focus on the individual entrepreneur that is proposed by the Wennekers and Thurik Model, it is essential to consider how changes to IP law and policy affect attitudes, motives and assessment of market risk in the economy. It is necessary to flesh out the ways in which IP can create attitudes of openness to innovation, increase incentives for the individual to pursue innovation, and shape conceptions of innovation in products and services as carrying minimal risk if pursued appropriately. According to this model, changing perceptions at the individual level will be the primary way to increase innovation at the firm level and, in turn, to foster high productivity in the broader economy. Crafters of IP laws and policies must thus take into account bottom-up approaches to increasing innovative capacity in target countries.

The most prominent scholar in this area is Harvard psychologist David McClelland, who has highlighted the importance of the "motivational aspect" of the entrepreneur. McClelland's studies have demonstrated that entrepreneurial behaviour is "driven by a need for personal achievement leading to a clear proclivity for becoming an entrepreneur" (McClelland, 1961, pp. 358–99; UNCTAD, 2005, p. 10). Critically, McClelland's work emphasises the fact that entrepreneurs with high motivation will almost always find ways to maximise economic achievement. This view implies that the levels of motivation of entrepreneurs are more critical than the economic conditions supporting their potential innovations. McClelland has identified 10 entrepreneurial competencies that must be strengthened in order to increase entrepreneurial potential at the individual level: (1) opportunity-seeking and initiative; (2) risk-taking; (3) demand for efficiency and quality; (4) persistence; (5) commitment to the work contract; (6) information-seeking; (7) goal-setting; (8) systematic planning and monitoring; (9) persuasion and networking; and (10) independence and self-confidence (McClelland, 1961).

IP and the GEM Model

The GEM Model, in contrast to the Wennekers and Thurik Model, lends support to the notion that innovative capacity is impacted predominantly at the macro level and must trickle downwards. Viewed via the GEM Model, IP laws and policies could themselves be cast as the driving forces behind increases in entrepreneurship and innovation. The GEM Model would thus seem to favour a domestic

IP structure that specifically encourages: (1) the growth of existing large firms, thus generating profit opportunities for small and medium-sized firms; and (2) the establishment of new firms. Based on the GEM Model's focus on more formalised concepts of R&D, increasing innovative capacity would require some form of incentive system to encourage the formal sector to spend more on R&D.

Entrepreneurship and Africa

The scholarly literature on African entrepreneurship provides several explanations of why entrepreneurship has not succeeded in lifting the continent's people from poverty. There is less analysis of how entrepreneurship needs to be – and has the potential to be – a key force for economic growth in African countries. The limited literature that does exist in relation to the importance of entrepreneurship in Africa tends to single out large youth populations, high levels of youth unemployment and rural–urban shifts as primary reasons why entrepreneurship needs to, and can, spur development in the context of Africa.

There are concerns that a large portion of Africa's youth population[2] has become marginalised and excluded from access to education, health care and salaried jobs. There is extensive literature on the increased marginalisation of African youth, including their inability to create sustainable livelihoods for themselves, and there is also evidence that this marginalisation phenomenon has affected not only impoverished youth but also youth across a broad spectrum of socioeconomic classes, including the well-educated (Chigunta, 2002, p. 11; Chigunta *et al.*, 2005, p. 5).

Africa has a larger youth-to-adult ratio than any other continent, and this ratio is growing. The ILO determined that 62% of Africa's total population was below the age of 25 (ILO, 2006). This "youth bulge"[3] is most evident in the sub-Saharan region of Africa, a region noted as having the highest population growth rate in the world (Guarcello *et al.*, 2008). The population of the sub-Saharan region has quadrupled since 1950 and continues to grow. Its youth-to-adult ratio was, in 2002, increasing at a projected rate of 18% (Chigunta, 2002, p. 4; Sommers, 2010, p. 321). To provide some perspective on this figure, a study by Population Action International reveals that there are 46 countries where at least 70% of the population is under 30, and all but seven of those countries are in sub-Saharan Africa (Leahy *et al.*, 2007, p. 23). Meanwhile, Africa also has the highest youth rural–urban mobility rate of any continent. It is estimated that more than 50% of

2 The category of "youth" in Africa is generally deemed to be those individuals in the range of 15 to 30 years of age. The UN definition is individuals aged 15 to 24.

3 The term "youth bulge" was originally coined by demographer Gary Fuller (Hendrixson, 2005, p. 2).

African youth reside in urban centres (Chigunta, 2002, p. 12). At the same time, formal job opportunities in the urban centres are limited. A recent study by the UN Office for West Africa revealed that by 2020, one half of the African population would be living in cities, with more than 50% of urban inhabitants being under the age of 19 (UNOWA, 2005, p.1).

Having a large youth population that is not in the workforce has been consistently pegged in development literature as a significant indicator of risk of general civil instability (Urdal, 2004, p. 16). This concern is reflected in the development community, including at the US Agency for International Development (USAID), which has noted that: "Urbanization concentrates precisely that demographic group most inclined to violence: unattached young males who have left their families behind and have come to the city seeking economic opportunities" (USAID, 2005, p. 7). Of particular concern is evidence that large numbers of unemployed youth in Africa have come to engage in unconventional means of sustaining their livelihoods (Chigunta *et al.*, 2005). Finding formal sector work can be particularly difficult for urban youth, as there are few jobs and many youth lack the qualifications that formal-sector work often requires. For instance, a Sierra Leone study found that only 9% of the working-age population in that country had formal-sector jobs, with opportunities falling significantly lower for youth than the average adult (Peeters *et al.*, 2009). Another study, in Angola's capital city, Luanda, determined that the average age of individuals working in the city's outdoor market areas was 21, and that both male and female youth averaged just over five years of education, with the women being exposed to fewer opportunities and lesser pay (De Barros, 2005, p. 212).

The size of the African workforce, estimated at 492 million in 2012, continues to grow at an annual rate of 2.8% per year (the highest in the world), representing roughly 13.8 million new entrants a year, a rate that is declining only marginally year over year (ILO, 2013).[4] That said, accurate unemployment statistics for the African continent are notoriously difficult to come by. Unemployment information for Africa has proven both difficult to gather and difficult to calculate, due to varying definitions of employment. As a result of these difficulties, the range of reported youth unemployment statistics is described as "phenomenal" (Sommers, 2010, p. 322).

Extensive research has been conducted on the supply-side factors affecting youth unemployment in Africa. This research has pointed to two dominant barriers: (1) a deficiency in skills, and (2) an underlying perception that the only worthwhile employment is "formal employment" rather than less formal employment (the category in which entrepreneurship generally lies) (Chigunta *et al.*, 2005). When it comes to engaging youth, Mike Grant and Jamie Schnurr have argued

4 Between 2000 and 2012, the rate dropped from 2.9% to 2.7% (ILO, 2013).

that demand-side factors are just as critical as supply-side factors. These scholars posit that economic development cannot be bolstered simply by directing youth through "stationary" paths to formal employment roles but rather by creating more "flexible systems" to propel youth into the workforce (Grant and Schnurr, 1999). Michael Todaro (1997) similarly asserts that too much emphasis should not be placed on the formal means of bolstering African economies through youth employment. Thus, it can be inferred that creating favourable conditions for youth entrepreneurship would be a component of any plan to bolster economic development.

In contexts where it is essential that youth create their own employment opportunities, a lack of financial and business resources will be detrimental. Individuals often lack the support that is required to turn innovative ideas into reality. Government budgets are too limited to directly support the large population of unemployed and increasingly marginalised youth in their countries. However, African governments can help alleviate this burden by engaging youth in entrepreneurship. In particular, educational institutions could introduce entrepreneurial education designed to expose youth to entrepreneurship at an early age, increasing the prospect of more successful entrepreneurial ventures in Africa (Chigunta *et al.*, 2005, p. 165). This concept suggests the time is ripe to better understand where government spending should be aimed if it is to target potentially entrepreneurial individuals and to support existing entrepreneurship in Africa.

As part of the OECD's ongoing work on innovation, it partnered with the UN Educational, Scientific and Cultural Organisation (UNESCO) in 2009 to host an international workshop entitled "Innovation for Development: Converting Knowledge to Value". Participants highlighted, *inter alia*, the important role of local entrepreneurs with respect to innovation and the need to focus on "the generation, transfer and application of local knowledge" (UNESCO, 2009, p. iii). In developing countries, the institutional framework for knowledge transfer at local levels consists primarily of informal institutions and organisations. For example, in sub-Saharan Africa, informal employment represents nearly three quarters of non-agricultural employment. It contributes, on average, 41% of national GDP in these countries, and over 50% in individual countries such as Ghana, Togo and Niger (ILO, 2002).

As early as 2000, it was estimated that in Africa, two in three urban residents obtain their livelihoods from the informal economic sector, a sector thought to be growing at an annual rate of 7%. At this time, it was estimated that more than 90% of jobs would be created through informal economies (Karl, 2007, pp. 53–4). A failure to recognise the vitality and necessity of informal markets constitutes a denial of fundamental economic realities. Confirming this projection was the aforementioned Sierra Leone study finding that a mere 9% of the working-age population had formal sector jobs (Peeters, *et al.*, 2009). Such figures highlight the need to recognise and fully harness the informal sector's roles in innovation. Accordingly, Section 4 of this chapter now turns to an examination of the linkages between innovation, entrepreneurship and the informal sector in Africa.

4. The informal economy (IE)

The "informal sector" concept

According to the International Labour Organisation (ILO), the "informal sector" comprises non-agricultural, private, unincorporated enterprises that produce their goods or services for sale or barter and are not registered under national legislation (ILO, 1993). While this definition provides some direction with respect to measuring the size of the informal sector in a given economy, it does not capture the various discipline-specific approaches that have been developed over the past 60 years to value informal sector activities.

In 1954, William Arthur Lewis first conceptualised the economy as constituting more than one sector. Lewis posited a dual economy model, whereby "[t]he capitalist sector is that part of the economy which uses reproducible capital, and pays capitalists for the use thereof [and the] subsistence sector is by difference all that part of the economy which is not using reproducible capital" (Lewis, 1954, p. 407). Lewis believed that the flow of labour is unidirectional, moving from the subsistence sector into the more formal, capitalist sector. Two decades later, economic anthropologist Keith Hart (1973) presented a different approach to the dual economy analysis. While studying the economy of urban Ghana in 1971, Hart noted that a thriving "informal sector" exists alongside the formal sector in urban economies. According to Hart, labour flows back and forth between these sectors in response to the availability of employment in each one at any given time.

The prevalent economic thinking in the 1960s was that employment levels would increase if an economy achieved success in generating capital and promoting exports. However, in 1967 the ILO proposed that development efforts should focus on increasing employment as a distinct policy objective. Accordingly, the ILO established the World Employment Programme (WEP) and organised "comprehensive employment missions" to analyse employment in developing countries (Bangasser, 2000, p. 5).

During the WEP's 1972 mission to Kenya, the ILO acknowledged the informal sector concept that Hart had coined a year earlier. However, the ILO presented a more nuanced perspective, asserting that informal activities "are not confined to employment on the periphery of the main towns, to particular occupations or even to economic activities. Rather, informal activities are the way of doing things" (ILO, 1972, pp. 5–6). Based on this view, the ILO (1972) identified seven elements that characterise the informal sector: (1) ease of entry; (2) reliance on indigenous resources; (3) family ownership of enterprises; (4) small scale of operation; (5) labour-intensive and adapted technology; (6) skills acquired outside the formal school system; and (7) unregulated and competitive markets.

The years that followed saw a gradual recognition of the need for an international statistical definition of the informal sector (Hussmanns, 2004). Consequently, in 1993, the 15th International Conference of Labour Statisticians (ICLS) adopted the following definition:

> The informal sector may be broadly characterised as consisting of units engaged in the production of goods or services with the primary objective of generating employment and incomes to the persons concerned. These units typically operate at a low level of organisation, with little or no division between labour and capital as factors of production and on a small scale. Labour relations – where they exist – are based mostly on casual employment, kinship or personal and social relations rather than contractual arrangements with formal guarantees. (ILO, 1993, p. 2)

In 2001, the Expert Group on Informal Sector Statistics (Delhi Group) assessed existing methods for measuring informal sector employment, and highlighted the need for a definition of informal employment (Hussmanns, 2004). In 2003, the 17th ICLS responded by officially defining informal employment as "the total number of informal jobs [...] whether carried out in formal sector enterprises, informal sector enterprises, or households, during a given reference period" (ILO, 2003, p. 2).

The ILO has described a continuum of economic relations that exists in the informal sector: "production, distribution, and employment relations tend to fall at some point on a continuum between 'formal' relations (i.e., regulated and protected) at one pole and 'informal' relations (i.e., unregulated and unprotected) at the other" (ILO, 2002, p. 12). (See Chapter 3 of this volume for Kawooya's case study of linkages between the formal and informal sectors in automotive engineering in the Ugandan capital city, Kampala.) Steve Daniels recently built on this idea in his analysis of Kenya's local economy by noting that informality exists along a spectrum (Daniels, 2010). According to Daniels, enterprises in the country's formal and informal sectors differ, to varying degrees, with respect to several factors: business size, start-up capital, labour, labour protection, skills, selling price, raw materials, infrastructure, quality, resources, market linkages, flexibility, efficiency, self-sufficiency and culture. For example, in terms of business size, an enterprise at the informal end of the formal–informal spectrum has fewer than five employees, while an enterprise at the formal end has more than 50 (Daniels,

2010). Meanwhile, firms with 6 to 50 employees are situated somewhere along the spectrum. Given the varying levels of regulation and legal protection for those providing goods and services across the spectrum of informality, striking the optimal balance between tight and loose regulation is likely to be critical to harnessing the potential of Africa's IE to facilitate innovation and development.

Paul Godfrey (2011) has reviewed how various disciplines – ranging from economics to sociology to management – define the IE. Godfrey found that the term receives varying treatment across the literature. Some development economists see limited potential for efficiency in the informal sector due to the small size of local enterprises and these enterprises' lack of protection of property rights (Godfrey, 2011). Hernando de Soto (2000), for example, positions informal work arrangements as a rational response by micro-entrepreneurs to onerous regulations governing the licensing and registration of businesses. Not all business and economics literature characterises informality in that light. Sparks and Barnett (2010), for example, argue that the informal sector is a source of vibrant entrepreneurship and job creation.

Outside the field of economics, additional favourable narratives have emerged regarding the IE. Political scientists Gaughan and Ferman assert that "[i]nformal activity takes place largely in personal and intimate domains [...] reflect[ing] the nature of the personal ties between the participants, defined by norms and institutions that are in essence non-economic" (Gaughan and Ferman, 1987, p. 16). Sociologists Portes and Sensenbrenner believe that "[a] solidary ethnic community represents, simultaneously, a market for culturally defined goods, a pool of reliable low wage labor, and a potential source for start-up capital" (Portes and Sensenbrenner, 1993, p. 1329).

A joint IDRC/OECD-published volume has also acknowledged that innovation among micro and small firms in the informal sector "can result in benefits not only to informal entrepreneurs, but also to the society as whole; the informal sector in fact produces economically viable and beneficial innovations that affect a large proportion of the population" (Kraemer-Mbula and Wamae, 2010, p. 66). The most recent literature on IP and indigenous peoples' innovation further highlights the widespread recognition that "traditional knowledge systems are indeed innovative, dynamic and directly relevant to practical needs; that collective and cumulative forms of innovation and creativity have value and worth in themselves" (Drahos and Frankel, 2012, p. xv).

Measuring innovation in the informal sector

Emerging from the somewhat discipline-specific approaches to defining the IE are various means of measuring informal employment and activities. Historically, the

ILO measured informal employment using the residual method, which assessed existing statistical data from population censuses, labour force surveys and/or household surveys, and compared countries according to international benchmarks (ILO, 1993). In recent years, the OECD has begun to give greater emphasis to country-specific innovation surveys than to international comparisons, because the former are seen as more effective tools for policy-making and business planning to facilitate the building, sharing and application of new knowledge (OECD and Eurostat, 2005).

However, Fred Gault (2010) has highlighted the fact that, in many developing countries, measuring innovation in the IE is not amenable to standard innovation surveys. Gault has proposed the use of case studies, based on structured interviews, as an alternative research approach. According to Gault, " [t]he results may highlight the need, for example, to treat agriculture as a knowledge-based industry in a global world, rather than a subsistence activity, or the need to protect indigenous knowledge so that its use can continue to benefit the community that has developed it over time" (Gault, 2010, p. 133).

5. A framework for development through IP

Parallel to the emergence of a heterogeneous literature on innovation, entrepreneurship and the IE, researchers have constructed an increasingly sophisticated definition of "development" as encompassing not simply economic growth, but more fundamentally, the promotion of human freedom. For example, Amartya Sen (1999) focuses on political, economic and social rights and opportunities that advance the capabilities of the individual. Martha Nussbaum (2000; 2011) argues for an approach whereby all people are afforded a minimum threshold of capabilities, including bodily health and integrity, as well as control over their environments. Thus, while economics is still heavily influential in theories of development, it no longer dominates policy discourse. The dialogue has become infused with international affairs, political science and law (including IP law).

There is now concerted reflection on how innovation can best contribute towards achievement of the UN Millennium Development Goals (MDGs) by 2015. Calestous Juma and Lee Yee-Cheong (2005) have highlighted the important role that innovation and innovation policy can play in this regard. Juma and Yee-Cheong stress that innovation has the potential to increase the ability of existing science, technology and innovation programmes to reduce poverty and expand human capabilities, particularly in the areas of public health, agriculture, energy use and information and communication technologies (ICTs). Development scholars have also begun to explore how innovation can contribute solutions to global challenges (Kraemer-Mbula and Wamae, 2010), and it is likely that theorists will continue along this trajectory as they broaden their understanding of the innovation–development nexus.

As suggested above, innovation and entrepreneurship encompass not only "pure" forms of innovation, but also imitation as innovation: small but significant improvements on processes and design. Given the limited resources available to most individuals working in the IE, imitation entrepreneurship is inevitably a prominent kind of entrepreneurial activity in the IE. In the context of scarce resources, the creativity to alter and adapt design processes and products is essential and abundant.

However, despite this wealth of creative innovation, those operating in the IE are, in most cases, not optimally incentivised. Among the stifling forces for innovation in the IE are, it would seem, IP dynamics. In the IE, IP dynamics potentially operate negatively in at least two fashions: (1) pure innovations receive little to no IP protection, allowing for duplication by large players in the formal economy; and (2) entrepreneurs do not attempt to expand the reach of their products, perhaps because they fear they are infringing on the rights of IP holders. Such limitations – fear of IP exploitation and fear of IP infringement – may be a disincentive for IE players to innovate and expand the reach of their innovations. Thus, mismatched IP policies and structures may be among the factors hindering the IE's potential to trigger a new phase of economic development in Africa driven by entrepreneurship and innovation. This is among the overarching uncertainties probed throughout the chapters of this book.

It is necessary when interrogating the functioning of the IE in Africa to interrogate, *inter alia*, the IP system's potential limitations at both macro and micro levels. Certain macro-level policy changes favouring improved knowledge dissemination in the IE are likely to be necessary to help address innovators' fears of potential IP expropriation. At the micro level, grassroots programmes will likely be required to quash fears of IP infringement by IE entrepreneurs and to engage entrepreneurship at the individual level in order to bolster the "motivational aspect" of IE entrepreneurship as posited by McClelland (1961). Such micro-level work will likely need to involve programmes that allow for shifts in the mindsets of the individuals that comprise the IE.

Entrepreneurs should be taught not only how to protect and exploit their own IP, formally or informally within the pragmatic parameters of the environments in which they operate. They should also be aware that imitation and improvement of existing products and processes are acceptable and, in fact, encouraged when done within certain parameters. Such a shift from the dominant rhetoric about the perils of IP piracy would seem to be an important component of an innovation policy. A shift in mindset at the individual level could potentially enhance existing incentives for those participating in the IE and, in turn, push the IE's innovative potential beyond its current threshold.

Bibliography

Acs, Z.J. (2006), "How is entrepreneurship good for economic growth?" *Innovations: Technology, Governance, Globalization,* Vol. 1 No. 1, pp. 97–107.

African Union-New Partnership for Africa's Development (AU-NEPAD) (2010), *African Innovation Outlook 2010,* AU-NEPAD, Pretoria, available at: www.nepad.org/system/files/June2011_NEPAD_AIO_2010_English.pdf (accessed 11 April 2013).

Anand, S. and Sen, A. (1996), *The Income Component of the Human Development Index,* UN Development Programme (UNDP), New York.

Aubert, J. (2006), "Innovation systems in emerging and developing economies", in Blankley, W., Scerri, M., Molotja, N. and Saloojee, I. (Eds), *Measuring Innovation in OECD and non-OECD Countries,* Human Sciences Research Council (HSRC), Cape Town.

Ayyagari, M., Beck, T. and Demirgüç-Kunt, A. (2005), *Small and Medium Enterprises across the Globe,* World Bank Review on Small Business Activities, Washington, DC.

Bangasser, P.E. (2000), *The ILO and the Informal Sector: An Institutional History,* International Labour Organisation (ILO), Geneva.

Caree, M.A. and Thurik, A.R. (2003), "The impact of entrepreneurship on economic growth", in Acs, Z.J. and Audretsch, D.B. (Eds), *Handbook of Entrepreneurship Research: An Interdisciplinary Survey and Introduction,* Kluwer Academic, Boston/Dordrecht.

Chigunta, F. (2002), "The socio-economic situation of youth in Africa: problems, prospects and options", paper presented at the Youth Employment Summit, 7–11 September, Alexandria, Egypt.

Chigunta, F., Schnurr, J., James-Wilson, D. and Torres, V. (2005), *Being "Real" about Youth Entrepreneurship in Eastern and Southern Africa: Implications for Adults, Institutions and Sector Structures,* International Labour Organisation (ILO), Geneva, available at: www.ilo.org/youthmakingithappen/PDF/WP72-2005.pdf (accessed 11 April 2013).

Cortright, J. (2001), *New Growth Theory, Technology and Learning: A Practitioner's Guide,* Impresa, Portland, OR.

Daniels, S. (2010), *Making Do: Innovation in Kenya's Informal Economy,* Analogue Digital, available at: www.analoguedigital.com/docs/makingdo-download-lores.pdf (accessed 11 April 2013).

De Barros, M.C. (2005), "Profiling youth involved in the informal markets of Luanda", in Muloongo, K., Kibasomba, R. and Kariri, J.N. (Eds), *The Many Faces of Human Security: Case Studies of Seven Countries in Southern Africa,* Institute for Security Studies (ISS), Pretoria.

De Beer, J., Fu, K. and Wunsch-Vincent, S. (2013), "The informal economy, innovation and intellectual property – concepts, metrics and policy considerations", WIPO Economic Research Working Paper No. 10, July, available at: www.wipo.int/export/sites/www/econ_stat/en/economics/pdf/wp10.pdf (accessed 30 July 2013).

De Soto, H. (2000), *The Mystery of Capital*, Basic Books, New York.

Domar, E. (1947), "Expansion and employment", *American Economic Review*, Vol. 37 No. 1, pp. 34–55.

Drahos, P. and Frankel, S. (Eds) (2012), *Indigenous Peoples' Innovation: Intellectual Property Pathways to Development*, Australian National University E Press, Canberra.

Edquist, C. (1997), *Systems of Innovation: Technologies, Institutions, and Organizations*, Pinter, London.

Ely, A. and Bell, M. (2009), *The Original "Sussex Manifesto": Its Past and Future Relevance*, STEPS Centre, Brighton, UK.

Freeman, C. (1982), "Innovation and long cycles of economic development", paper presented at the International Seminar on Innovation and Development at the Industrial Sector, University of Campinas (UNICAMP), Campinas, Brazil.

Freeman, C. (1987), *Technology Policy and Economics Performance: Lessons from Japan*, Pinter, London.

Gaughan, J.P. and Ferman, L.A. (1987), "Toward an understanding of the informal economy", *Annals of the American Academy of Political and Social Science*, Vol. 493, pp. 15–25.

Gault, F. (2010), *Innovation Strategies for a Global Economy: Development, Implementation, Measurement and Management*, International Development Research Centre (IDRC), Ottawa.

Gault, F. and Zhang, G. (2010), "Challenges and directions", in Kraemer-Mbula, E. and Wamae, W. (Eds), *Innovation and the Development Agenda*, Organisation for Economic Co-operation and Development (OECD) and International Development Research Centre (IDRC), Paris-Ottawa, pp. 13–27.

Godfrey, P.C. (2011), "Toward a theory of the informal economy", *Academy of Management Annals*, Vol. 5 No. 1, pp. 231–77.

Gould, P. (1964), "A note on research into the diffusion of development", *Journal of Modern African Studies*, Vol. 2 No.1, pp. 123–25.

Grant, M. and Schnurr, J. (1999), *A Conceptual and Analytical Research Framework for Youth Enterprise and Entrepreneurship Development: Social Innovation towards Sustainable Livelihoods for Youth*, International Development Research Council (IDRC): Sustainable Livelihoods for Youth Exploration, Ottawa.

GTZ: Deutsche Gesellschaft für Technische Zusammenarbeit GmbH (2010), "Strengthening innovation systems in the context of development cooperation", workshop documentation, 5–8 October, Dortmund, Germany.

Guarcello, L., Manacorda, M., Rosati, F., Fares, J., Lyon, S. and Valdivia, C. (2008), "School-to-work transitions: regional overview", in Garcia, M. and Fares, J. (Eds), *Youth in Africa's Labor Market*, World Bank, Washington, DC.

Hagen, E. (1962), *On the Theory of Social Change*, Dorsey Press, Homewood, IL.

Harrod, R. (1939), "An essay in dynamic theory", *Economic Journal*, Vol. 49 No. 193, pp. 14–33.

Hart, K. (1973), "Informal income opportunities and urban employment in Ghana", *Journal of Modern African Studies*, Vol. 11 No .1, pp. 61–89.

Hendrixson, A. (2005), "Angry young men, veiled young women: constructing a new population threat", Corner House Briefing 34, December, available at: www.thecornerhouse.org.uk/pdf/briefing/34veiled.pdf (accessed 13 April 2013).

Herrington, M., Kew, J. and Kew, P. (2009), *Tracking Entrepreneurship in Africa: A GEM Perspective*, Global Entrepreneurship Monitor (GEM), Cape Town.

Hirschman, A. (1958), *The Strategy of Economic Development*, Yale University Press, New Haven, CT.

Hoselitz, B. (1960), *Sociological Aspects of Economic Growth*, Free Press, Glencoe, IL.

Hussmanns, R. (2004), *Measuring the Informal Economy: From Employment in the Informal Sector to Informal Employment*, International Labour Organisation (ILO), Geneva.

International Labour Organisation (ILO) (1972), *Employment, Incomes and Equity: A Strategy for Increasing Productive Employment in Kenya*, Geneva.

International Labour Organisation (ILO) (1993), "Resolution concerning statistics of employment in the informal sector", adopted by the 15th International Conference of Labour Statisticians (ICLS), ILO, Geneva, January, available at: www.ilo.org/wcmsp5/groups/public/@dgreports/@stat/documents/normativeinstrument/wcms_087484.pdf (accessed 11 April 2013).

International Labour Organisation (ILO) (2002), *Women and Men in the Informal Economy: A Statistical Picture*, Geneva, available at: www.ilo.org/dyn/infoecon/docs/441/F596332090/women%20and%20men%20stat%20picture.pdf (accessed 11 April 2013).

International Labour Organisation (ILO) (2003), "Guidelines concerning a statistical definition of informal employment", adopted by the 17th International Conference of Labour Statisticians (ICLS), ILO, Geneva, November, available at: www.ilo.org/wcmsp5/groups/public/---dgreports/---stat/documents/normativeinstrument/wcms_087622.pdf (accessed 22 April 2013).

International Labour Organisation (ILO) (2006), *Regional Labour Market trends for Youth: Africa*, Geneva.

International Labour Organisation (ILO) (2013), *Global Employment Trends 2013: Recovering from a Second Jobs Dip*, Geneva.

Juma, C. and Yee-Cheong, L. (2005), *Innovation: Applying Knowledge in Development*, UN Millennium Project, Earthscan Publications, London.

Karl, K. (2000), "The informal sector", *The Courier*, Vol. 178 (Dec. 1999–Jan. 2000), pp. 53–4.

Kraemer-Mbula, E. and Wamae, W. (2010), "Adapting the innovation systems framework to Sub-Saharan Africa", in Kraemer-Mbula, E. and Wamae, W. (Eds), *Innovation and the Development Agenda*, Organisation for Economic Co-operation and Development (OECD), Paris.

Lawson, S. and Purushothaman, R. (2003), "Dreaming with BRICs: the path to 2050", *CEO Confidential*, Issue 2003/12, Goldman Sachs Group, New York, available at: www.goldmansachs.com/ceoconfidential/CEO-2003-12.pdf (accessed 11 April 2013).

Leahy, E., Engelman, R., GibbVogel, C., Haddock, S. and Preston, T. (2007), *The Shape of Things to Come – Why Age Structure Matters to a Safer, More Equitable World*, Population Action International, Washington, DC.

Lewis, W.A. (1954), "Economic development with unlimited supplies of labour" in Agarwala, A.N. and Singh, S.P. (Eds), *The Economics of Underdevelopment*, Oxford University Press, London.

Lipset, S.M. (1959), "Some social requisites of democracy: Economic development and political legitimacy", *American Political Science Review*, Vol. 53 No. 1, pp. 69–105.

Lundvall, B. (Ed.) (1992), *National Systems of Innovation: Towards a Theory of Innovation and Interactive Learning*, Pinter, London.

Marshall, A. (1920), *Principles of Economics*, Macmillan, London.

McClelland, D. (1961), *The Achieving Society*, D. Van Nostrand, Princeton, NJ.

Mowery, D. and Rosenberg, N.S. (1979), *Technology and the Pursuit of Economic Growth*, Cambridge University Press, Cambridge, UK.

Muchie, M., Gammeltoft, P. and Lundvall, B. (Eds) (2003), *Putting Africa First: The Making of African Innovation Systems*, Aalborg University Press, Aalborg, Denmark.

Nelson, R.R. (Ed.) (1993), *National Innovation Systems: A Comparative Analysis*, Oxford University Press, New York.

Nelson, R.R. and Rosenberg, N. (1993), "Technical innovation and national systems", in Nelson, R.R. (Ed.), *National Innovation Systems: A Comparative Analysis*, Oxford University Press, New York.

Nelson, R.R. and Winter, S.G. (1977), "In search of useful theory of innovation", *Research Policy*, Vol. 6, pp. 36–76.

Nelson, R.R. and Winter, S.G. (1982), *An Evolutionary Theory of Economic Change*, Harvard University Press, Cambridge, MA.

Nussbaum, M. (2000), *Women and Human Development: The Capabilities Approach*, Cambridge University Press, Cambridge, UK.

Nussbaum, M. (2011), *Creating Capabilities: The Human Development Approach*, The Belknap Press of Harvard University Press, Cambridge, MA.

Organisation for Economic Co-operation and Development (OECD) and Statistical Office of the European Communities (Eurostat) (1992), *Oslo Manual: Proposed Guidelines for Collecting and Interpreting Technological Innovation Data*, OECD, Paris.

Organisation for Economic Co-operation and Development (OECD) and Statistical Office of the European Communities (Eurostat) (1997), *Oslo Manual: Proposed Guidelines for Collecting and Interpreting Technological Innovation Data*, 2nd ed., OECD, Paris, available at: www.oecd.org/science/inno/2367580.pdf (accessed 11 April 2013).

Organisation for Economic Co-operation and Development (OECD) and Statistical Office of the European Communities (Eurostat) (2005), *Oslo Manual: Guidelines for Collecting and Interpreting Innovation Data*, 3rd ed., available at: http://epp.eurostat.ec.europa.eu/cache/ITY_PUBLIC/OSLO/EN/OSLO-EN.PDF (accessed 22 April 2013).

Parsons, T. (1966), *Societies: Evolutionary and Comparative Perspectives*, Prentice Hall, Englewood Cliffs, NJ.

Peet, R. and Hartwick, E. (2009), *Theories of Development: Contentions, Arguments, Alternatives*, 2nd ed., Guildford Press, New York.

Peeters, P., Cunningham, W., Acharya, G., and Van Adams, A. (2009), *Youth Employment in Sierra Leone: Sustainable Livelihood Opportunities in a Post-Conflict Setting*, World Bank, Washington, DC.

Perroux, F. (1955), "Note sur la notion de pole de croissance", *Économie Appliquée*, Vol. 8, pp. 307–20.

Portes, A. and Sensenbrenner, J. (1993), "Embeddedness and immigration: notes on the social determinants of economic action", *American Journal of Sociology*, Vol. 98 No. 6, pp. 1320–50.

Pred, A. (1965), "Industrialization, initial advantage, and American metropolitan growth", *Geographical Review*, Vol. 55 No. 2, pp. 158–85.

Reynolds, P.D., Hay, M., Bygrave, W.D., Camp, S.M. and Autio, E. (2000), *Global Entrepreneurship Monitor 2000 Executive Report*, available at: www.gemconsortium.org/docs/download/2408 (accessed 11 April 2013).

Rogers, E.M. (1962), *Diffusion of Innovations*, Free Press, New York.

Romer, P. (1992), "Two strategies for economic development: using ideas and producing ideas", in *Proceedings of the World Bank Annual Conference on Development Economics 1992*, World Bank, Washington, DC.

Rosenberg, N. (1976), *Perspectives on Technology*, Cambridge University Press, Cambridge, UK.

Rostow, W.W. (1960), *The Stages of Economic Growth: A Non-Communist Manifesto*, Cambridge University Press, Cambridge, UK.

Schmitz, J.A. (1989), "Imitation, entrepreneurship and long-run growth", *Journal of Political Economy*, Vol. 97 No. 3, pp. 721–39.

Schumpeter, J. (1934), *The Theory of Economic Development*, Harvard University Press, Cambridge, MA.

Schumpeter, J. (1942), *Capitalism, Socialism, and Democracy*, George Allen and Unwin, London.

Sen, A. (1999), *Development as Freedom*, Oxford University Press, Oxford.

Smith, A. (1776), *The Wealth of Nations*, Random House, New York.

Solow, R. (1957), "Technical change and the aggregate production function", *Review of Economics and Statistics*, Vol. 39 No. 3, pp. 312–20.

Sommers, M. (2010), "Urban youth in Africa", *Environment and Urbanization*, Vol. 22 No. 2, pp. 317–32.

Sparks, D.L. and Barnett, S.T. (2010), "The informal sector in Sub-Saharan Africa: out of the shadows to foster sustainable employment and equity?" *International Business and Economics Research Journal*, Vol. 9 No. 5, pp. 1–12.

Todaro, M.P. (1997), *Economic Development*, 6th ed., Longman, New York.

Thurik, R. and Wennekers, S. (2001), *A Note on Entrepreneurship, Small Business and Economic Growth*, Erasmus Research Institute of Management, Rotterdam, available at: http://repub.eur.nl/res/pub/125/erimrs20011101173530.pdf (accessed 11 April 2013).

UN Conference on Trade and Development (UNCTAD) (2005), *Entrepreneurship and Economic Development: The Empretec Showcase*, Geneva, available at: http://unctad.org/en/Docs/webiteteb20043_en.pdf (accessed 11 April 2013).

UN Educational, Scientific and Cultural Organisation (UNESCO) (2009), *Innovation for Development: Converting Knowledge to Value: Summary Report*, UNESCO Forum on Higher Education, Research and Knowledge, co-hosted by the Organisation for Economic Co-operation and Development (OECD) and UNESCO, 28–30 January, available at: http://unesdoc.unesco.org/images/0018/001832/183288e.pdf (accessed 11 April 2013).

UN Office for West Africa (UNOWA) (2005), *Youth Unemployment and Regional Insecurity in West Africa*, Dakar, Senegal.

Urdal, H. (2004), *The Devil in the Demographics: The Effect of Youth Bulges on Domestic Armed Conflict, 1950–2000,* World Bank Social Development Papers: Conflict Prevention and Reconstruction Paper No. 14, Washington, DC.

US Agency for International Development (USAID) (2005), *Youth and Conflict: A Toolkit for Intervention,* Washington, DC.

Wennekers, S. and Thurik, R. (1999), "Linking entrepreneurship and economic growth", *Small Business Economics,* Vol. 13 No. 1, pp. 27–56.

World Intellectual Property Organisation (WIPO) (2013), *Conceptual Study on Innovation, Intellectual Property and the Informal Economy*, prepared by WIPO Secretariat in collaboration with De Beer J. and Fu, K., available at: www.wipo.int/meetings/en/doc_details.jsp?doc_id=232525 (accessed 11 April 2013).

Chapter 3

Informal–Formal Sector Interactions in Automotive Engineering, Kampala

Dick Kawooya

Abstract

This chapter provides findings from a Ugandan case study that examined innovation transfers between informal-sector automotive artisans and formally employed researchers at Makerere University's College of Engineering, Design, Art and Technology (CEDAT). The primary site studied was CEDAT's Gatsby Garage, an automotive workshop where it was found that the informal-sector artisans were central to innovative processes but were at the same time driven more by sharing impulses than by concern for the intellectual property (IP) implications of their work. Based on these findings, it is argued that Ugandan policy-makers need to seek policy tools to support innovation transfers between informal and informal sectors, and that the tools need to cater for a wide range of innovation incentives.

1. Introduction

Very little research has focused on the dynamics of intellectual property (IP) rights in Africa's informal sector. No research has, to my knowledge, analysed the role or impact of IP rights in the exchange or transfer of innovation between the formal and informal sectors in Africa. Seeking to fill this research gap, the study outlined in this chapter examined the nature and scope of transfers and diffusion of innovative ideas in the Ugandan capital city, Kampala, between a Makerere University research centre and informal-sector artisans involved in automotive mechanics and engineering. The findings of the study are potentially important because there is reason to believe that indigenous technology research and innovations generated locally in Uganda (and more generally in Africa) are increasingly competing with research and innovations sourced from outside the continent, which are often inappropriate or ill-suited to local circumstances. At the same time, it would seem that the formal and informal sectors in Africa often do not collaborate or "talk" to each other, as evidenced by the large body of African research and innovations that remain underutilised and not communicated beyond the confines of African universities (Hassan, 2001; Lor and Britz, 2005; Ondari-Okemwa, 2007; Ondari-Okemwa, 2004).

Disparaging portrayals of the informal sector in Africa (see Hart, 1973; ILO, 1972) do not encourage researchers in formal institutions to pay much attention to what their informal counterparts do. Communication by formal researchers with informal sector actors tends to be limited to occasional interactions in instances of research data collection or sourcing of specific skills. I am of the understanding that national government policies facilitating collaboration between Africa's formal and informal sectors are rare and, in some places, totally absent. I therefore anticipate that the findings of this study can potentially provide lessons relevant to the crafting of policy initiatives aimed at fostering research and collaboration between the formal and informal sectors in African nations, specifically in relation to innovations grounded in (and appropriate to) Africa's realities.

2. Conceptual framework

Dualistic conceptions of formal and informal

In defining formal and informal sectors in the context of this study, I focused on the elements that characterise each sector. Informal-sector activities are sometimes defined as those outside or beyond government regulatory reach. They are broadly defined to include, but are not limited to, activities not liable to taxation. Formal institutions and sectors, meanwhile, are broadly defined as those within the reach of government regulation or even government agencies themselves.

Another potential means of distinguishing between the informal and formal sectors is to highlight how they differ from each other, e.g.:

- automated production (formal) v. intensive labour (informal);
- high barriers to entry (formal) v. low barriers to entry (informal);
- new materials (formal) v. scrap materials (informal);
- large-sized business (formal) v. small-sized business (informal);
- skills acquisition via institutions (formal) v. via a mentor (informal); and
- foreign "Western" approach (formal) v. adaptable to market and indigenous culture (informal) (Daniels, 2010; ILO, 1972; Palmer, 2004; Tabak, 2000).[1]

1 I thank David Gildiner for helping expand this list of elements typically used to define the informal sector.

These dualistic characterisations and framings of the formal versus informal sector may be helpful at the broad conceptual level, but the reality in many African contexts is that the line between the formal and informal sectors is blurred. A rigid binary cannot capture the highly complex nature of the interrelationships between the formal and informal sectors, and between these sectors and the broader economy, in many African contexts. Moreover, despite numerous informal sector studies conducted in Latin America, Africa and some advanced economies (Palmer, 2004; Portes, 1983; Portes and Sassen-Koob, 1987), there is actually little agreement on the nature and scope of the informal sector. Conceptualising the informal sector continues to be difficult due to the sector's fluidity and constant interaction with the formal sector. Indeed, the dualistic framing of formal versus informal has been discredited and discarded, to some extent, by many informal sector scholars (ILO, 2002, 2003; Palmer, 2004; Portes, 1983; Portes and Sassen-Koob, 1987). (See Chapter 2 of this volume for discussion, by De Beer *et al.*, of the concept of the informal economy [IE].)

In practical terms, the formal and informal sectors interact symbiotically. For example, a government department's use of an informal car repair shop for its fleet illustrates a form of interaction between the formal sector (government) and an informal-sector entity (repair shop). Another example is the practical training that informal-sector enterprises provide to students of formal research and training institutions. Both examples illustrate the potential for knowledge transfer between the two sectors. And formal sector entities – e.g. music recording studios – may periodically operate underground to avoid or limit their tax burden.

A formal–informal continuum

Based on the above analysis, it can be argued that it is more appropriate to conceptualise a *continuum* from formal to informal, where activities with varying degrees of informality are situated at different points along the continuum. This view is consistent with the conclusions of International Labour Organisation (ILO) studies on labour issues in the informal sector (ILO, 2002, 2003; Palmer, 2004). At the most formal end of the continuum are fully documented, regulated and taxed enterprises; at the most informal end of the continuum are entirely hidden, underground enterprises far removed from government oversight and often associated with illegal activities. But along the continuum between formal and informal, between the extreme ends, there is a mix of actors and enterprises whose characteristics are complex and often difficult to measure in terms of their degrees of formality or informality. For this study, I was interested in informal-sector enterprises somewhat near the middle of the continuum – i.e. likely to be well-organised internally and in the conduct of their business operations but still operating outside formal government oversight – but at the same time, enterprises which, while informal, have some contact with the formal (or at least more formal) sector.

Choosing a point on the continuum

I determined that, in the Ugandan context, studying interactions between a formal university research institution (positioned to serve as an engine of research and innovation) and informal sector actors would offer insights, particularly given my intention to investigate matters of IP. I anticipated that, in the Ugandan context, university researchers and innovators, including both faculty and students, would be interacting with informal-sectors through a wide range of mechanisms. My choice of research focus was informed by awareness of anecdotal evidence suggesting that in African contexts, a number of quite formalised institutions partially rely on the informal sector, e.g. to, *inter alia*, absorb their graduates (a process of informal-sector engagement often starting via internships for graduates). I was interested in the effect that fresh graduates coming to the informal sector (with somewhat formalised knowledge and know-how) might be having on the informal sector and, in turn, the effect the informal sector might be having on the formal institutions from which the graduates were emerging.

From the formal sector side, I was interested in understanding whether university IP-related research and innovation were being diffused into the informal sector – and whether (and if so, how) that IP-related innovation translated into commercially viable goods and/or services in the informal sector (a sector which, unlike a publicly funded university, operates on the basis of profit maximisation for survival). However, while the goal was to focus on IP-related innovations, I did not expect or assume ahead of the study that the innovations in question would be protected by IP laws or, for that matter, that the actors in the formal or informal contexts to be studied would even be aware of, or preoccupied with, IP as part of their innovation processes. Nonetheless, I did assume that there were a number of innovations that originated in Ugandan universities and that some of the resultant goods and/or services were finding their way into the informal sector (such as, to take but one possible example, software applications developed in university research laboratories). Thus, the overarching goal was to gain a nuanced understanding of the innovation dynamics moving in two directions: from formal to (the relatively) informal, and *vice versa*.

3. The research

The overarching question for this case study was: *To what extent do the formal and informal sectors in Uganda exchange ideas and innovations, and what is the role of IP, if any, in that exchange?* The study's primary objectives were therefore to understand:

- the kinds of innovations that formal and informal sector actors are involved in;
- the processes of transfer of innovation (and IP) between the two sectors;
- the role of IP rights and IP protection in either facilitating or hindering innovation in either sector; and
- the role of IP rights and IP protection in either facilitating or hindering the exchange of ideas and innovations between the two sectors.

The main setting I identified for the study was Gatsby Garage, run by Makerere University's College of Engineering, Design, Art and Technology (CEDAT) in the Ugandan capital city, Kampala. Gatsby Garage is a formal-sector entity that procures some of its inputs from informal-sector artisans. The study employed a qualitative methodology using elements of the social network analysis (SNA) method. The SNA method, which has been applied in a variety of disciplines, aims to construct a picture of the complex networks that form based on individual and organisational relationships, collaborations and sharing mechanisms. The SNA in this study focused on the personal network of a formal-sector innovator as the starting point, followed by identifying informal-sector nodes and relations, as well as the channels and mechanisms for the diffusion of innovation from formal to informal sector, or *vice versa* (Hanneman and Riddle, 2005; Hanneman *et al.*, 2005). Given that this study began in the formal sector (at Makerere University), innovators in that sector formed the core of the network. I then identified and approached the informal-sector component via the Gatsby Garage manager. (It was found during the research that the title "Garage manager" did not fully capture the wide range of activities, skill-sets, experience – and passion for his work – of this individual.)

In determining which actors or nodes to include in the network, I used the "egocentric networks" approach, where a central "node" is selected followed by identifying nodes around it (Hanneman and Riddle, 2005). This approach does not require determination and complete analysis of the network around the central node. Therefore, in both the formal and informal contexts studied by this research, the depth of the network was largely determined by the extent of the ties and the strength of the nodes that emerged. For the most part, I did not go beyond two layers of analysis, meaning that from the central actor (the formal-sector contact, the Garage manager) or "ego", I elected to go to two layers of nodes (Hanneman and Riddle, 2005; Hanneman *et al.*, 2005). I initially selected informal-sector contacts directly linked to the Garage manager, followed by contacts of those informal-sector actors, many of whom were not in direct contact with the Garage manager (see diagram in the Appendix). At each node or alter,

I conducted in-depth qualitative interviews that probed not only the connections or relationships that a given individual had, but also the kinds of innovative activities in which the individual engaged. I also inquired about the factors that influenced the individual's innovations, including the adoption and exchange of innovations by others.

The study focused on product engineering, reengineering and metal fabrication by informal artisans, with specific reference to automotive engineering and repair. The interconnectedness of informal-sector artisans in Uganda means that those whose primary work area is automotive engineering and repair will often shift to other related work as opportunities present themselves. It is also not unusual for them to outsource work to colleagues outside of automotive repair. Therefore, the unstructured nature of the relationships among informal-sector artisans required that a non-linear methodology like SNA be used to study the linkages and exchanges amongst them.

Gatsby Garage

Gatsby Garage is a project of Makerere University's CEDAT, with funds from the Uganda Gatsby Trust (UGT), a UK-funded non-governmental organisation (NGO). The Garage, a semi-formal entity, was seen as a suitable research site for this study because both faculty and students at CEDAT use it, especially those involved in automotive engineering research and design; students use the Garage as an internship facility and a place to translate their models into products; and the Garage actively employs graduates from CEDAT as well as informal-sector artisans. The aforementioned Garage manager, who has over 10 years of experience in the field, is a graduate of CEDAT (formerly Makerere's Faculty of Technology). The UGT is a member of the Gatsby Charitable Foundation in the UK, and its focus is on small enterprise development and innovation (see UGT, n.d.). UGT's organisational structure and leadership mix private technology-industry leaders with senior faculty at CEDAT, seeking to ensure responsiveness to industry needs as well as CEDAT's research priorities (see CEDAT, n.d.).

One of the network connections discovered in pursuing the Gatsby Garage manager's associations in the informal sector was a connection to an electronic vehicle project at CEDAT called the Kiira EV Project. The Kiira EV, developed by CEDAT's Centre for Research in Transportation Technologies (CRTT), is a prototype electric car designed and developed in Uganda by engineering students and faculty at CEDAT – probably the first of its kind in East and Central Africa (see CRTT, n.d.). Of interest in the context of this study was the fact that some of the informal artisans working for Gatsby Garage were involved in the actual fabrication and production of some parts for this prototype car, with the parts based on designs from the engineering team at CEDAT. Further, some informal-sector artisans not directly connected to CEDAT were also involved in the production of some parts of the car, via their connections to informal-sector artisans working directly with CEDAT. I thus decided to interview the Technical Head and Manager of the Kiira EV Project, in order to better understand the innovations associated with the project and its connections with the informal sector.

Data collection

A qualitative interview instrument was developed for the interviews at each node, as well as a consent form to secure informed respondent participation. I received permission to conduct the study from the Ugandan Government through the Uganda National Council for Science and Technology (UNCST). Data were collected using a mix of written memos and notes, as well as audio and video recordings. The field work began with informal discussions with researchers at CEDAT,[2] followed by 11 in-depth interviews with informal-sector artisans, CEDAT researchers and a government official (the official responsible for science, technology and innovation [STI] at the UNCST). All of the interviewees were male, largely due to the fact that both the formal and informal automotive research and fabrication settings investigated were virtually all-male environments.

Interviews with artisans were always secured and coordinated by the Gatsby Garage manager. His insistence on introducing me to the artisans to establish rapport was immensely important. Interactions with artisans generally took the form of an interview, followed by a site visit to witness the artisan's activities. The initial interviews were generally done inside the manager's car, away from the artisans' garages or fabrication facilities. The site visits that followed the initial interviews were carried out without the presence of the Garage manager.

4. Findings

The research data provided clear indications that the formal and informal actors studied were exchanging ideas and/or innovations, often via Gatsby Garage. At the same time, the role of IP protection issues was found to be minimal in the actions and thinking of the informal artisans. IP only became an issue on occasions when formal-sector entities raised IP matters in the course of sharing their innovations

2 I was introduced to CEDAT researchers by Prof. Robert Ikoja-Odongo, who availed me of his extensive contacts (deriving from his work on the informal sector), which proved invaluable in finding the appropriate contacts (including the Gatsby Garage manager) to start the SNA work.

with informal-sector entities, as was the case when CEDAT outsourced some of the work on the Kiira project to artisans (as is described later).

Innovative work in the formal and informal sectors

Much of the innovation in the sector studied stemmed from the undersupply of affordable spare automobile parts imported from Japan. Parts available through formal-sector outlets, such as from local representatives of Japanese automakers, are generally too expensive for owners of used cars. This shortage of affordable parts presents opportunities for artisans to find solutions to fixing broken parts or fabricating new ones. Most cars imported into Uganda operate on rough roads, making the breakdown of cars and car parts fairly common. This environment creates a significant demand for the services of informal-sector artisans skilled in automotive engineering and repair.

The research found a great deal of innovation among both the formal-sector and informal-sector actors studied. Formal-sector Makerere staff and researchers affiliated with the semi-formal Gatsby Garage were found to have developed products such as carriers to enable inspection under the vehicle, a movable stand for proper handling of car engines, and a computer-aided system for managing vehicle maintenance projects at Gatsby Garage. In terms of the informal sector, there was evidence that the artisans affiliated with Gatsby Garage were finding solutions to a wide range of problems. The artisans were involved in activities that ranged from maintenance of parts – e.g. fixing car radiators, aluminium welding and working with metal forgers – to interior design. It was found that the artisans' vast experience and expertise in these areas were allowing some of them to fabricate parts (via a mix of repairing old parts and creating new ones) not readily available on the Ugandan market.

Apprenticeship as a means of learning

Learning to innovate in the informal sector studied was found to be linked to apprenticeship, wherein senior artisans train new ones. There is a dynamic of generosity, a willingness to help a relative or friend. In the words of one artisan:

> If I don't help relatives by training them and giving them hands-on skills to produce stuff or repair work, they will likely become a burden in future, or social misfits, or probably engage in criminal activities due to poverty and lack of skills to find jobs. Besides, I was helped by a relative, so it's imperative that I do the same for young relatives and friends. (Participant 2, 2012)

Almost all participants interviewed for this study said they had acquired skills from friends or relatives through an apprenticeship. Some acquired their skills at semi-formal entities such as Gatsby Garage, where there is a degree of informality even in the way untrained men come to be identified as trainees. According to the manager:

> It's very informal the way we get them. I mean, you know somebody and they say: "I have a son, I have somebody, please help them out", and so they come. (Garage manager, 2012)

The study found that it is common that once a young trainee or apprentice has acquired basic skills, they either establish their own garages or work in a specialised area. In either case, the nature of problems presented to them on a regular basis demands that they are constantly thinking of innovative solutions. However, according to the manager, not all artisans are open to innovation, especially innovation seen as originating from academia:

> [T]here is a challenge of acceptance and adaptability. Sometimes people prefer doing things the way they are always done. They prefer to continue with the *status quo*, so introducing the new technology or machine, there is always resistance. There is that feeling that this thing [new idea or way of doing something] belongs to the "book people". They [artisans] tell us, "this isn't our thing, for us we want to work with our hands", so there is always criticism. (Garage manager, 2012)

Another reason why senior artisans train new artisans is that the latter are eager to learn and are a source of cheap labour. Once a new artisan masters a particular skill-set, the senior artisan assigns him to routine or more mundane activities. As such, young or inexperienced artisans will deal with problems that do not necessarily require new solutions, but at the same time have a degree of complexity. The senior artisan's involvement with the newer artisan is then limited to supervising and dealing with complicated tasks (particularly tasks that require new methods for dealing with new problems that have emerged, or tasks related to designing a new part).

Networks, linkages between formal and informal sectors

The social networks between the two sectors are nurtured by Gatsby Garage's commitment to informal enterprises, as well as what the Garage manager referred to as the "vast and deep talent and skills available in Uganda's informal sector" (Garage manager, 2012). The manager specifically noted that Gatsby Garage staff generally approach artisans after they have "identified a particular skill-set in someone" (Garage manager, 2012). Ideally, these are skills that they do not have in the formal sector. The same sentiments were expressed by the head of the Kiira EV Project, whose production depended largely on the experience of the artisans. While the research team at CEDAT produced the Kiira EV computer designs and models, the project depended on informal artisans for small steps in the process, such as costing of the car materials and fabricating some car parts. As one artisan indicated:

> [The Kiira EV staff] approached me to provide cost estimates for the car based on the models and I did, but they didn't come back to me, probably preferring another artisan. (Participant 6, 2012)

While the above process might appear to be a simple exercise of costing the car and sourcing the most affordable artisans for the Kiira EV Project, the fact is that the informal artisans know the market for new and used automobile parts better than the formal-sector researchers. According to Participant 6, the Kiira EV researchers were inclined to select the artisans who know the best and cheapest sources for parts for the EV model they have designed. The relationships between formal and informal actors are also based on a degree of mutual trust and respect. The formal-sector actors recognise limitations in certain areas that can only be met by the practical skill-sets found in the informal sector.

The creation of the formal–informal networks was found to be a rather informal process. For example, a Gatsby Garage client recommends a young, unemployed relative with no formal training, but with skills in vehicle maintenance. In turn, the young relative, once taken on by the Garage, refers some of his work at the Garage to places where he had formerly worked. Alternatively, the manager is informally introduced to a respected mechanic who is well known for certain areas of speciality. In other cases, artisans who had previously worked with Gatsby Garage recommend or introduce the manager to other highly skilled artisans. Put simply, the processes of formal–informal sector linkages and network creation are informal and organic. (However, I learned from Gatsby Garage and the Kiira EV Project that there are now efforts being made by researchers at Makerere to pro-actively and systematically identify informal-sector artisans and to co-opt them into formal research and innovation centres.)

The relationships with formal institutions are of particular importance to informal-sector artisans; a matter of personal pride as formal-sector actors come to them, rather than *vice versa*. As one participant put it, "I am proud of helping those with PhDs and more advanced training than I have [...] me without significant formal education" (Participant 5, 2012). However, this participant also acknowledged that he had learned some new skills from his formal-sector contacts, particularly soft skills such as customer care (particularly important when an informal sector artisan is dealing with formal-sector clients).

Gatsby Garage primarily outsources work to informal-sector mechanics when its employees do not have the requisite expertise or cannot do the work efficiently in-house. However, the Garage only works with the best informal-sector actors –

individuals with many years of experience in a particular field. Therefore, despite their lack of formal education or training, Gatsby's informal-sector partners feel valued by the researchers in the formal sector.

Another relationship vividly described by one participant is the relationship between artisans and technology students, especially graduating students. The majority of technology students turn to informal artisans when translating product models or designs developed in their programme into finished products. As such, informal-sector garages serve as production facilities for products whose models were developed at the university. While the students proudly present the finished products to supervisors back at the university, they cannot overlook the fact that the process involved shared efforts between themselves and informal-sector artisans. In fact, there is evidence to suggest that without the ingenuity of the artisans, many of the models would remain theoretical ideas on paper.

The dynamics of the interactions among CEDAT, Gatsby Garage and the informal-sector artisans would appear to be consistent with the theoretical proposition, outlined above, of the formal–informal continuum. Gatsby Garage has had an ongoing relationship with artisans and conducts "informal" non-contractual paid work with them. Gatsby Garage represents a case of a semi-formal sector entity because it is situated at the centre – or near the centre – of the continuum. On the other hand, CEDAT is a more formal entity, fairly removed from the informal sector. Thus, certain formal–informal hybrid entities (of which Gatsby Garage is an example) can actually move along the continuum towards informality and serve as conduits or bridges for highly formalised actors existing far from the centre of the continuum but needing to reach the informal sector.

The data demonstrate that, in the case studied, formal-sector researchers and innovators both require and seek out informal-sector actors more than *vice versa*. However, this does not necessarily mean that there is wide diffusion of informal-sector innovations into the formal sector. Instead, in the case studied, it may be that formal-sector researchers are primarily using informal-sector solutions on an *ad hoc* basis as problems arise, with limited learning among formal-sector innovators when they take work or problems to informal-sector artisans.

Networks, linkages within the informal sector

While the primary focus of this study was formal–informal exchanges and linkages, the study also revealed that there are strong connections among informal-sector actors. For example, one of the interview participants from the informal sector who is affiliated with Gatsby Garage has a relationship with the Central Engineering Workshop (an informal-sector entity) located in Kalerwe, a suburb of Kampala. While this entity focuses primarily on agro-processing machinery (e.g. grinding mortars), most of the raw materials for the machinery produced come from automotive garages. Moreover, other parts – such as metal sheets for agro-processing machinery – can be easily sourced from automotive garages with old car body parts. Central Engineering Workshop has slightly more advanced production machinery than some of the artisans interviewed for this study. For this reason, when necessary, artisans go to Central Engineering to use machines such as rollers (which roll flat metal sheets to desired angles). Conversely, staff from Central Engineering source specific expertise from car artisans to help with the fabrication and production of their agro-processing machines. Indeed, the artisan who connected me with Central Engineering often sources work from the Workshop when he has no clients. The Workshop therefore provides a secondary source of income and opportunity for this artisan.

The data thus suggest that informal–informal connections are even more organic than the formal–informal connections. This is likely because informal-sector actors are more likely to speak the same language and operate by the same rules. Moreover, many informal actors might specialise in a particular area but do not limit themselves to that area if opportunities present themselves elsewhere. Switching from one area of speciality to another can happen even during the course of a single working day.

Sharing of innovations

The research found, in the interactions between the formal- and informal-sector actors studied, that there was a great deal of freedom to share – innovations, solutions to problems, and even product designs and models – between the two sectors. While I had anticipated this situation, the extent and freedom with which both sides were sharing ideas was rather surprising, because it happened much more easily and frequently than I had anticipated. Given the complicated and competitive economic climate, I expected less sharing than was revealed in this study. It is therefore important to try to understand the rationales and motives for the sharing identified.

On the part of informal-sector artisans, it would seem that the ability to translate theoretical concepts into finished products, mostly through processes and activities that require a great deal of improvisation, is something the artisans are extremely proud of. They legitimately can (and do) portray themselves as solvers of problems that have eluded formally trained researchers in the academic setting. I even detected among the informal-sector artisans a sense of inevitability underlying the freedom with which they share their knowledge and new ideas, i.e. the artisans feel that individuals in academic settings are simply incapable of taking ideas beyond theory and applying them to existing or new problems. According to the artisans interviewed, new problems call for thinking about new solutions, which many "ivory tower" individuals are incapable of.

Also relevant to understanding the sharing impulse is consideration of the dynamics of the artisans' relationships with their clients, be they formal-sector partners or informal-sector colleagues. Artisans stated that once a client has paid for a service or product, the artisan feels obliged to explain what he did and how he did it, even if this involves disclosing new ideas, products or innovative ways of solving new problems. Almost all of the artisans interviewed expressed this view, even after repeated probing about the possibility of the formal-sector clients doing the job themselves in the future or taking artisans' innovations and commercialising them.

One artisan did say that he would be reluctant to freely and openly share his ideas, saying that if some of his innovative approaches became publicly known, client retention would be jeopardised. Another interviewee approached the matter of sharing innovation from a very practical perspective. He said that even if artisans did sometimes feel the urge to keep innovations to themselves, working in open spaces prevented artisans from being able to keep their ideas out of the public eye:

> It would be good to have ownership of a new idea, but we work in open places and spaces making it difficult and impractical to protect new ideas. Everybody can see what you're doing or working on every day. (Participant 7, 2012)

Also sometimes making it unrealistic for artisans to try to keep clients from seeing their innovations is a lack of trust. This is particularly true for clients from formal settings who may not have the same level of trust artisans have among themselves. One participant indicated that:

> [M]ost of our clients tend to stay around as we work on their cars. As such, they will get to know exactly what we do and whatever ideas and solutions we apply to whatever problems their cars present. Clients stay around and observe because they are not sure about [the] security of their cars. If we were a company, they wouldn't necessarily stay around. (Participant 7, 2012)

IP dynamics

Among the informal-sector artisans, the role of IP rights and IP protection was found to be of little or no concern in relation to their collaborations with the formal sector. With the exception of one artisan, the participants found the notion of owning ideas, innovations or inventions antithetical to the workings of the informal sector, where collaboration and sharing is the norm rather than the exception. This view was consistent regardless of whether sharing involved a vertical collaboration between formal and informal or a horizontal collaboration among informal-sector actors. Indeed, the notion of owning ideas was closely associated with preventing access and application of such ideas. This notion was understood to mean working in secrecy. One artisan asked:

> If my mentor had withheld his knowledge and new ideas from me, how on earth would I have acquired the knowledge I got from him? If I withhold the knowledge I have, how am I supposed to teach the next generation of artisans?

While young apprentices are often charged small "training fees", it is never the case that expectations go beyond that requirement. Usually, a small fee or even a family or friendship tie is sufficient for the senior artisan to freely pass on his knowledge without any expectation that it is protected "property". This mentality also enables experienced or senior artisans to share new ideas and ways of doing things when new problems or tasks arise. None of the informal-sector participants was aware of IP laws that could protect their innovations. Furthermore, they remained unconcerned about IP even after I provided a brief explanation. And apparently Gatsby Garage was not particularly concerned about IP protection in its relationship with informal-sector actors.

However, unlike Gatsby Garage and the Garage's informal-sector partners, the formal-sector actors studied were found to be increasingly aware of IP and wary of the possibility that their ideas could be "misappropriated". For instance, the Kiira EV Project within CEDAT signed formal memoranda of understanding (MoUs) with Gatsby Garage and the informal-sector artisans, and each MoU contained non-disclosure clauses. Also, at the time of the field work for this study, Kiira EV Project researchers were in the process of pursuing IP protections related to a number of innovations or inventions from the project. Notably, the Kiira EV manager did not feel that informal-sector artisans made a large enough contribution to warrant being part of the resultant IP, and thus whatever IP protection came out of the filings would go to the CEDAT researchers and Makerere University.

Notwithstanding the MoUs, the Kiira EV project manager was aware that informal-sector artisans came into contact with the project's IP in the form of designs that they could easily exploit. However, he was not concerned about informal-sector partners "stealing" or "commercialising" any of these ideas, because he felt that doing so would require heavy capital investment, which informal-sector artisans would be incapable of mobilising.

Policy-making

According to the official interviewed at the UNCST, the government of Uganda has neither studied, nor has experience with, the relationship between the formal and informal sectors. Instead, emphasis is placed on formal-to-formal sector linkages, such as university–industry linkages or collaborations and exchanges of innovation through formal "clusters" (UNCST official, 2012). The rationale is that these relations are easier to foster than formal-to-informal sector linkages and *vice versa*. The official stated: "Actually, we are working with Makerere University's Innovation System and Clusters Programme. They have clusters, and we are trying to study the relationships within those clusters" (UNCST official, 2012). The UNCST official said he hoped that, through such clusters, the university might bring informal actors on board. However, Makerere's Clusters Programme currently focuses on formal industry actors.[3] Arguably, these clusters present an easier means of dealing with IP issues than if the university were to collaborate extensively with informal-sector artisans.

5. Conclusions

This research found a striking absence of concern among the informal-sector actors studied about IP protection or IP rights in relation to their innovative collaborations with other informal actors or with formal-sector players. Meanwhile, the formal sector was found to be showing increasing interest in IP protection, but it was notable that the formal sector's formal–informal proxy entity, Gatsby Garage, appeared not to bring IP considerations into play during collaborations with the informal-sector artisans. These findings suggest there is a great deal of dynamism inherent in non-IP-based incentive modalities. Examination of how policy-makers might be able to optimise the incentive mechanisms at play in the settings studied in the course of this research was beyond the scope of the study, but there is clearly a need for substantial African-focused research in this area.

Government policies are needed in Uganda, and perhaps similarly in other African nations, to support formal–informal and informal–informal sector knowledge exchanges, so that innovations extend beyond project-specific or institution-specific initiatives. The incentive mechanisms included in such policy tools will need to be grounded in nuanced understanding of the complex mixes of motivations at play at different points along the formal–informal continuum.

3 Details about Makerere's Clusters Programme are available at: http://cedat.mak.ac.ug/ktp/cluster-programs.html.

Appendix 3.1: Visual representation of networks among study participants and entities

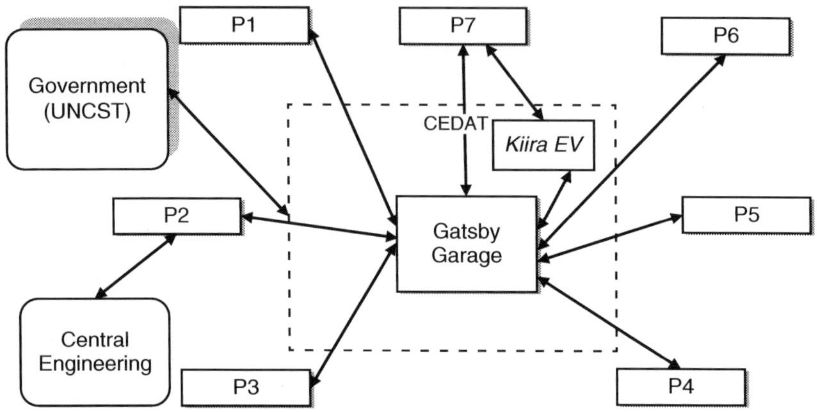

P =Participant
CEDAT = College of Engineering, Design, Art and Technology (Makerere University)

Bibliography

Centre for Research in Transportation Technologies (CRTT) (n.d.), Makerere University, Kampala, available at: http://cedat.mak.ac.ug/research/crtt.html (accessed 5 April 2013).

College of Engineering, Design, Art and Technology CEDAT (n.d.), Makerere University, Kampala, available at: http://cedat.mak.ac.ug (accessed 5 April 2013).

Daniels, S. (2010), *Making Do: Innovation in Kenya's Informal Economy*, available at: http://analoguedigital.com/makingdo/ (accessed 5 April 2013).

Freeman, L. C. (2004), *The Development of Social Network Analysis: A Study in the Sociology of Science*, Empirical Press, Vancouver.

Hanneman, R. A. and Riddle, M. (2005), *Introduction to Social Network Methods*, University of California, Riverside, available at: http://faculty.ucr.edu/~hanneman/ (accessed 5 April 2013).

Hanneman, R.A., Martinez, J. and Holguin, R. (2005), *Spatial Dynamics of Human Populations: Basic Models*, available at: http://faculty.ucr.edu/~hanneman/spatial/ (accessed 5 April 2013).

Hart, K. (1973), "Informal income opportunities and urban employment in Ghana", *The Journal of Modern African Studies*, Vol. 11 No. 1, pp. 61–89.

Hassan, M.H. (2001), "Can science save Africa?" *Science*, Vol. 292 No. 5522, pp. 1609–10.

Horn, P., Xaba, J. and Motala, S. (2002), *The Informal Sector in Sub-Saharan Africa*, Working Paper on the Informal Economy, Employment Sector – International Labour Organisation (ILO), Geneva.

International Labour Organisation (ILO) (1972), *Employment, Incomes and Equality: A Strategy for Increasing Productive Employment in Kenya*, Geneva.

International Labour Organisation (ILO) (2002), *Decent Work and the Informal Economy*, Report VI presented at the 90th session of the International Labor Conference, Geneva.

International Labour Organisation (ILO) (2003), "Guidelines concerning a statistical definition of informal employment", adopted by the 17th International Conference of Labour Statisticians (ICLS), ILO, Geneva, November, available at: www.ilo.org/wcmsp5/groups/public/---dgreports/---stat/documents/normativeinstrument/wcms_087622.pdf (accessed 22 April 2013).

Lor, P.J. and Britz, J. (2005), "Knowledge production from an African perspective: international information flows and intellectual property", *The International Information and Library Review*, Vol. 37 No. 2, pp. 61–76.

Ondari-Okemwa, E. (2004), "Impediments to promoting access to global knowledge in sub-Saharan Africa", *Library Management*, Vol. 25 No. 8/9, pp. 361–75.

Ondari-Okemwa, E. (2007), "Scholarly publishing in sub-Saharan Africa in the twenty-first century: challenges and opportunities", *First Monday*, Vol. 12 No. 10, available at: http://journals.uic.edu/ojs/index.php/fm/article/view/1966, (accessed 5 April 2013).

Palmer, R. (2004), *The Informal Economy in Sub-Saharan Africa: Unresolved Issues of Concept, Character and Measurement*, Occasional Paper No. 98, Centre of African Studies, University of Edinburgh.

Portes, A. (1983), "The informal sector: definition controversy, and relation to national development", *Review*, Vol. 7, pp. 151–74.

Portes, A. and Sassen-Koob, S. (1987), "Making it underground: comparative material on the informal sector in Western market economies", *The American Journal of Sociology*, Vol. 93 No. 1, pp. 30–61.

Rogers, E.M. (1983), *Diffusion of Innovations*, 3rd ed., Free Press, New York.

Tabak, F. (2000), "Informalization and the long term", in Tabak, F. and Crichlow, A.M. (Eds), *Informalization: Process and Structure*, Johns Hopkins University Press, Baltimore, MD, pp. 1–19.

Tijssen, R.J.W. (2007), "Africa's contribution to the worldwide research literature: new analytical perspectives, trends, and performance indicators", *Scientometrics*, Vol. 71 No. 2, pp. 303–27.

Uganda Gatsby Trust (UGT) (n.d.), available at: www.gatsbyuganda.com (accessed 5 April 2013).

World Bank (2006), *Kenya Inside Informality: Poverty, Jobs, Housing and Services in Nairobi's Slums*, Report No. 36347-KE, Washington, DC.

Chapter 4

Geographical Indication (GI) Options for Ethiopian Coffee and Ghanaian Cocoa

Chidi Oguamanam and Teshager Dagne

Abstract

This chapter outlines research into the Ethiopian coffee and Ghanaian cocoa industries that sought to determine the potential for the local communities and diverse stakeholders participating in the two industries to benefit from sui generis *geographical indications (GIs). The research was premised on the notion that GIs have the potential to serve as instruments for practical adaptation of intellectual property (IP) to open development. It was found that the degree to which GIs could be successfully and sustainably used as tools of place-based intellectual property (PBIP) – i.e. instruments of origin-designation – for Ethiopian coffee and Ghanaian cocoa would likely depend on the economic implications of the establishment of GI modalities. The implementation of GIs involves a range of tasks, including establishment of legal and institutional structures; maintaining the "quality, reputation or characteristics" of the products; enforcing and defending rights; and developing product awareness in international markets (TRIPS, 1994). These tasks involve significant cost and effort that would need to be measured and weighed against the expected benefits.*

1. Introduction

Geographical indications (GIs), a form of place-based intellectual property (PBIP)[1] protection, emphasise an agricultural product's particular qualities linked to an identified geographical area. Through the use of PBIP strategies, products originating from a certain geographical location are differentiated from other

1 We recognise the complex and overlapping applications that exist, both within and outside IP analysis, of the notions of place, origin and geographical delineation, and later in this chapter we briefly interrogate the distinction between place and origin.

products in markets (Higgins *et al.*, 2008), with the aim of opening up "alternative markets for higher-value products" (World Bank, 2008). GIs and other PBIP strategies potentially offer local, traditional agricultural producers a means to capitalise more effectively on any unique, authentic and positive images linked directly to the places of origin of their products.

For traditional European agricultural producers in civil law countries, *sui generis* (i.e. unique) systems of GIs have proved to be the most popular PBIP strategy. In the common law jurisdictions of the UK and former British colonies, GI protection is typically pursued via the conventional trademark system through the use of speciality trademarks such as collective trademarks, certification marks and, rarely, ordinary trademarks. A third type of PBIP strategy consists of non-trademarked certification schemes such as certain types of fair trade labelling, environmental certifications and organic labelling. Any of the three categories of PBIP differentiation – a *sui generis* GI protection, GI-based trademarks, non-trademark certifications – can be adapted, to varying degrees, to advance development objectives. Labelling and various certification schemes may or may not serve geographical or origin-identification objectives. As well, they may not have direct IP ramifications. However, IP, especially trademarks, is crucial for translation of such schemes into practical positive impact for those who deploy them. (See Chapter 5 in this volume for the Adewopo *et al.* case study of the potential sustainability of communal trademarks in selected Nigerian leather and textile sectors.)

The research outlined in this chapter examined the potential applicability of PBIP strategies to the production and marketing of Ethiopian coffee and Ghanaian cocoa. The next section (Section 2) outlines the conceptual framework for the research, and Section 3 outlines the research study itself. Section 4 examines the value chains in the Ethiopian coffee and Ghanaian cocoa sectors (as determined through the research) and the existing differentiation strategies in each sector. Section 5 interrogates the feasibility of GI use for the two sectors, and Section 6 provides conclusions.

2. Conceptual framework

It is often argued that we live in a global knowledge economy in which knowledge and intellectual capabilities play a significant role in value creation, productivity and economic growth (Florida and Kenney, 1993). In this knowledge economy, intangible IP-based valuations of products sometimes exceed the tangible physical value of products as the main source of income (Layton and Wiseman, 2008). The knowledge economy is also characterised by large multinational actors producing and selling the most lucrative IP-based products. Meanwhile, even in the knowledge economy context, the income of agricultural producers in developing countries continues to a great extent to depend on production and sale of products often categorised as raw or as having minimal value-add.

The World Bank found that the richest countries in the final three decades of the 20th century were those that exported mostly IP-based products (Boehlje *et al.*, 1999). Meanwhile, economists have estimated that from the beginning to the end of the 20th century, global trade in physical commodities shrank from approximately 70% of world trade to about 20%, mainly because commodities would earn much lower economic returns than IP-based manufactured goods (Boehlje *et al.*, 1999). The dominant actors in the 21st century agricultural market (i.e. multinational corporations) utilise IP as a mechanism of "valorising [i.e. adding value] to GRs [genetic resources]" at the final stage of the value chain (Prentice and Andersen, 2007). These IP-based products receive premium prices in international trade, while distinctive agricultural products from Africa, which are often at the initial stage of the global supply chain, with perceived lower levels of value-add, receive relatively low prices. Even in the face of clear evidence of the ever-shrinking physical value of low-value-add agricultural products, rural development strategies have continued to respond to the ascendance of high-yield, technology-based agriculture by seeking to boost low-tech agricultural production (Dedeurwaerdere *et al.*, 2007). Such rural economic development policies in many developing countries have proven to be ecologically unsustainable (McManis, 2003).

We contend in this chapter that one way producers of distinctive agricultural products can potentially improve their position in international trade is to use IP-based strategies. However, conventional IP rights tend to be amenable primarily to the needs of owners of technological and biotechnological knowledge and skills (Dutfield, 1999) – because IP rights operate in a market system where the norms of privatisation, enclosure and transferability guide resource allocation. Most traditional agricultural producers in African countries operate under informal frameworks of social organisation, supervised by local customary rules and ethics – systems which are conditioned to relatively open access to knowledge and skills (Hansen and Van Fleet, 2003). In these informal frameworks, community members freely share substantial amounts of information and resources. Introducing the Western model of IP rights into such open and traditional agriculture settings could potentially threaten existing practices of relatively free exchange and mutual communal support (Cottier and Panizzon, 2004), i.e. IP could become a barrier to the openness necessary for modes of development whereby individuals exploit resources left in a public domain. However, at the same time absolute rejection of IP protection – under the pretext of preserving the public domain – could undermine efforts to create a proprietary system for recognising traditional knowledge (TK) as a valuable asset of indigenous and local communities (ILCs) (Sunder, 2007). The conceptual question thus arises: to what extent can IP play a positive role in development in contexts where high levels of collaboration and openness are integral to knowledge production? The emerging concept of "open development" (Smith *et al.*, 2011) is helpful in tackling this question. Open development is a conception which holds that a key engine of contemporary socio-economic development is often a strong element of networked, relatively open collaboration among numerous stakeholders, often enabled to some extent by information and communication technologies (ICTs). At the core of the research study outlined in this chapter was our desire to determine the degree to which GIs could be a form of IP amenable to protection and preservation of certain rights to locally specific TK-based agricultural production while at the same time allowing for continuation of networked openness and collaboration (i.e. the "open development" dynamic).

GIs are forms of IP that seek to harness the value of the geographical origin of a product where the origin contributes to a "given quality, reputation or other characteristic of the good" (TRIPS, Art. 22.1). Worldwide, as mentioned above, the legal means for protecting GIs predominantly take one of two forms: protection through *sui generis* systems, or protection through conventional IP rights, typically a form of trademark. It can be argued, as we do, that GIs, particularly when protected via *sui generis* regimes, offer greater potential than other forms of IP protection (when deployed as part of a diversified set of strategies) to promote the economic competitiveness of TK-based agricultural products. *Sui generis* GI systems typically accommodate, at their core, distinctive attributes of localised TK. In contrast, the more typical and internationally standardised forms of IP – copyrights, patents, trademarks – tend to have poor credentials in relation to TK protection because the dominant notions of these IP rights delineate them as individual-focused private property rights.

Contrary to the individualistic orientation of conventional IP, TK is typically defined in terms of the collective and communal identity of its holders. For example, the agricultural systems of most ILCs regard the efforts of traditional breeding and selection of plant varieties as collective, rather than individual, exercises (Salazar *et al.*, 2007). As such, protecting TK typically involves the recognition of the collective rights of a community that holds and identifies with it (Taubman, 2006). GI systems, whether *sui generis* or trademark-based, have the advantage, in relation to TK, of according exclusive rights to an indefinite number of producers in a specific geographic area, represented by a name or sign which typically defines the producers' particular product (Cottier and Panizzon, 2004). GIs protect goodwill and reputation developed through the participation of a group of producers in an area, thus allowing for collective ownership of the proprietary value (WIPO, 2010a). In addition, GIs are not transferable from one owner to another, thus emphasising the relationships between human cultures and their lands and environments in collective societies (Prakash, 2000). This description applies to most GI-relevant agricultural products.

Collective entities – such as cooperative bodies made up of producers or members of a group or community – participate in the use and protection of GIs based on their adherence to traditional methods of production in a defined geographical area. Unlike other forms of IP where a specific owner acquires exclusive rights during the term of protection, with a GI, whosoever adheres to the sanctioned methods of production qualifies for GI protection. GI systems foster preservation of recognised traditional production methods linked to a territory, and can accommodate trans-generational territorial TK, an important factor given that TK often reflects the relationship between agricultural communities and their lands and territories that go far back into history (Rangnekar, 2004). GIs also afford protection in perpetuity, another feature that makes them potentially suitable instruments for protecting TK-based resources. Most forms of IP accord their owners a limited term of protection, based on the "contractarian or contract-based" rationale for IP which regulates the relationship between the creator and society (Oguamanam, 2009). GI rights, in contrast, potentially remain valid in perpetuity, i.e. as long as the rights-holders maintain the collective tradition (as represented by the GI) in a specified geographical area. With a GI, producers lose the right to use the GI only if their practices fall below the specified standards of production or fall outside the geographical area of production (Lorvellec, 1996). Thus a GI does not provide monopoly control over the knowledge represented by the indication; rather, it conditions access to the economic use of products based on adherence to TK-based production methods. In this sense, a GI promotes a dual dynamic of *open* access to knowledge and culture among a *closed* group of communities who comply with the communities' requirement for a culturally acceptable method of production in a restricted geographical boundary. Beyond their economic significance, GIs can also prevent cultural appropriation by ensuring that a product is associated with a defined geographical place where communities have established bonds between culture, ancestral lands, resources and the environment (Ray, 1998).

Most IP models tend to operate as barriers to openness by putting essential public goods into private hands, outside the reach of collective entities. The amenability of GIs to the traditions of collective production and collective decision-making allows ILCs to exercise power over their knowledge and resources, making GIs tools which are potentially relevant to the aforementioned concept of open development. GIs are functionally suited to facilitate collaborative knowledge production and advance open development outcomes, because they increase the competitiveness and overall empowerment of traditional agricultural communities. However, they do not have as broad recognition as other differentiation strategies typically adopted in developing countries.

3. The research

The overarching research question for this case study was: *how do stakeholders in the value chains of Ethiopian coffee and Ghanaian cocoa participate in international trade, and what roles do/could GIs and other types of PBIP have in empowering participants and facilitating open development?* From the central research question, sub-questions arose: (1) To what extent do/could GI and other PBIP strategies offer potential for local agricultural producers to collaboratively control their knowledge-based agricultural products in order to effectively participate in the global economy? (2) Which initiatives are under way to support GI and other PBIP initiatives in Ethiopia and Ghana? (3) How do different forms of GIs compare with existing initiatives? (4) Which legislative and regulatory approaches are needed to support GI models?

The study deployed two research methods, both qualitative. A desk-based analysis of primary and secondary sources was conducted, which focused on mapping the existing legal framework for PBIP in the two jurisdictions. The second method was an empirical value chain analysis of Ghanaian cocoa and Ethiopian coffee. A value chain is defined as the

> [...] full range of activities which are required to bring a product [...] from conception, through the different phases of production [...], delivery to final customers, and final disposal after use. (Hellin and Meijer, 2006)

Actors identified as being in the value chain of the two products included individual producers (farmers) and their producer groups (farmer associations, farmer cooperatives and cooperative unions); local collectors (buyers), wholesalers and exporters; importers, processors, roasters and retailers; sector-specific regulatory agencies in production and marketing; and farmer support groups and experts related to production and marketing. Due to time and logistics constraints, the research concentrated on the roles of producer groups in each value chain. The study covered, to a lesser extent, the roles and activities of regulatory bodies, support institutions, traders and other relevant actors, i.e. all the other categories of actors in the chain of activities and linkages to the products (as is customary in value chain analysis). This primary focus on producer groups was recognised as a potential research limitation. However, an advantage of this somewhat narrow focus was that it generated reasonably deep qualitative data. The tools employed for the value chain analysis were questionnaires, semi-structured interviews, informal focus group discussions and personal observations.

Three different questionnaires were prepared, one each for (1) individual producers and representatives of producer cooperatives and associations; (2) local buyers, exporters, processors and other intermediaries; and (3) qualified experts and other informants in the two sectors, such as members of fair trade, organic and other special interest-based product-certifying organisations. For the semi-structured interviews, guides were prepared based on the areas covered in the questionnaires. Stakeholders interviewed included representatives of: the Ethiopian Intellectual Property Office (EIPO), the Ethiopian Ministry of Agriculture (MOA), Ghana's Registrar General's Department, Ghana's Ministry of Trade, and the Ghana Standards Authority. The informal focus group discussions were conducted with key informants: producers, regulators and miscellaneous collections of stakeholders. Some of the focus group participants had already been interviewed through semi-structured interviews, while others only participated in the focus groups. In the focus group meetings, participants discussed the research themes in an open-ended manner and shared their experiences with one another.

In addition, we generated our own personal observations during site visits in Ethiopia, to a coffee processing and storage facility owned by a producer cooperative, and to the country's Coffee Quality Control and Inspection Centre. Moreover, we personally engaged in the administration of the research instruments in the two study countries, allowing for observation of the social and physical contexts associated with the information gathered. The next three sections of this chapter (Sections 4, 5 and 6) provide the research findings, analyse the findings, and draw conclusions.

4. The value chains

Ethiopian coffee

Ethiopia is believed to be the birthplace of arabica coffee, which has traditionally served as a social drink throughout the country. It has also attained a pre-eminent place in both the country's economy and its national identity. Coffee is Ethiopia's number one source of foreign exchange earnings (International Trade Centre, 2011). According to the Ethiopian Ministry of Agriculture (MOA), coffee accounts for more than 25% of the country's GNP, 40% of total export earnings and 25% of all employment opportunities across both rural and urban inhabitants (MOA, 2009). The country's coffee production system is customarily classified into four categories: forest coffee (8–10%), semi-forest coffee (23–35%), garden coffee (50–55%) and plantation coffee (5–6%) (MOA, 2009).

The key production actors were found to be small-scale coffee producers (farmers), coffee producer cooperatives, private investors and three state-run coffee producing enterprises. Small-scale coffee producers grow "shade-grown" coffee without chemical inputs, and hold the lion's share of overall coffee production (Stanculescu *et al.*, 2011). Ethiopian coffee producers often collect only about 10% of the profits from their coffee; the rest goes to coffee industry players: buyers, exporters, international importers, distributors and roasters (Oxfam, 2002).

Ethiopia has a multitude of coffee varieties with distinctive features linked to the culture and tradition of production in particular coffee-growing regions. It is believed that there are 6,000 Ethiopian coffee varieties with different flavors (Sereke-Berhan, 2010). The most popular coffee varieties grow in the regions of Sidama, Yirgacheffe and Harrar. For quality-grading purposes, the coffee varieties are classified based on three processing methods: sun-dried, washed and semi-washed. Each in this range of coffee varieties has a unique flavour, and the country's long and deep cultural appreciation of good-quality coffee has generated these varieties' strong reputations in the speciality coffee market.

Ethiopian coffee marketing is largely conducted through a centralised trading system at the Ethiopia Commodity Exchange (ECX). Established in 2008, the ECX aspires to create a marketplace that "serves all market actors, from farmers to traders to processors to exporters to consumers" (ECX, n.d.). The ECX conducts quality control at local markets and facilitates trade between local collectors, wholesalers, exporters and foreign importers through a competitive bidding system (on its trading floor in Addis Ababa, which conducts trading sessions according to different classes and types of coffee) (ECX, 2011b). All coffee produced by small-scale growers in the country is sold and purchased through the ECX. However, farmer cooperatives and large-scale growers do not use the ECX. Rather, they have direct linkages to the international market, and are able to bypass the ECX. At the time of our field visit to Ethiopia in mid-2012, the prices for coffee traded through the ECX ranged between US$2.01 and US$2.04 per pound, while coffee sold outside the ECX process (by cooperatives and large-scale growers through fair trade and other certification schemes) was receiving a US$0.20 certification premium and, usually, an improved base price (ECX, 2011a).

Producer cooperatives are coalitions of farmers who live or work within a given area. In mid-2012, there were roughly 265 primary coffee cooperatives in Ethiopia. Most of these cooperatives were integrated into nine Farmers Cooperative Unions in an attempt to directly access the international market through fair trade, environmental and organic certification/labelling. Coffee trading activities via these differentiation strategies constitute an alternative value chain intended to shorten supply chains in the commodity market. The goal of shortening the supply chain is to bring traditional agricultural producers into closer contact with consumers and, in the process, to cut out middlemen who take their own cut of profits. Given the existence of this alternative value chain via certifications, it is our view that the use of GI instruments could provide an additional differentiation strategy, enabling participants in this alternative value chain to gain even greater control of the market for their premium coffee varieties and other gourmet products.

Ghanaian cocoa

Ghana ranks second in world cocoa production, and Ghanaian cocoa is known worldwide for its high quality. Cocoa production accounts for nearly 8% of Ghana's gross domestic product (GDP), 25% of its agricultural GDP, 28% of its foreign exchange earnings and 5% of government revenue (ODI, 2007). Ghana's cocoa grows in thickly forested parts of six main regions: Ashanti, Brong Ahafo, Eastern, Volta, Central and Western. Ghanaian cocoa farmers predominantly harvest three varieties of cocoa: Tetequarshie, Amazonian and Hybrid. Tetequarshie and Amazonian have a gestation period of seven and five years, respectively. The Hybrid variety becomes ready for harvesting after between three and four years.

The Ghanaian government plays a significant role in cocoa production and marketing through the Ghana Cocoa Board (COCOBOD). In addition to performing various pre-harvest and post-harvest activities, the COCOBOD has a monopoly over both the export and marketing of Ghanaian cocoa. The COCOBOD retains 30% of the price it receives from the export of cocoa and is expected to spend a portion of this amount on farmer support activities such as pesticide control, providing agricultural inputs and research and development. The COCOBOD also controls the internal marketing of cocoa through a network of Licensed Buying Companies (LBCs), which purchase cocoa from farmers for delivery to the COCOBOD on a commission basis. A number of farmer groups and cooperatives are licensed as LBCs. These LBCs participate in certification schemes and distribute the benefits of the certification premium earned to their members. In 2012 there were 29 LBCs, of which about half a dozen were farmers' groups.

Differentiation strategies

Within the Ethiopian coffee and Ghanaian cocoa sectors, there is widespread use of strategies to differentiate products with a specific quality or characteristic on account of their geographical origin.

Fair trade certification

Fair trade certification schemes provide support to small-scale producers who could otherwise be marginalised by the global trading system. These schemes emerged in direct response to the poor income profile of small-scale producers. They serve as alternative trading channels that enable traditional farmers to reach "socially conscious consumers" through direct access to markets in industrialised countries (Barrientos, 2012). There are two main ways in which fair trade schemes are being implemented internationally: via alternative trading organisations (ATOs), and via Fairtrade Labelling Organizations International (FLO). ATOs are charity humanitarian organisations, mostly located in Europe and North America, that work to boost the incomes of small-scale producers in developing countries. These organisations include, for example, Oxfam, Fairtrade Federation, the Association for Promoting Fairtrade in Finland, Economic Development Imports and Fair World Designs.[2] Meanwhile FLO, established in 1997, grants Fairtrade certification (via the Fairtrade Foundation) and licenses the "FAIRTRADE™" mark to organisations that comply with standards of minimum social and economic requirements — with only "small producer organizations" being eligible for Fairtrade certification (Fairtrade, n.d.).

The Fairtrade scheme includes a set of requirements related to the production, trade and dealings in a product according to generic trading and product-specific standards. In general, the generic and product-specific standards focus on labour, social, economic, and environmental concerns. FLO-Cert, a company separate from FLO, certifies compliance with these fair trade standards and ensures that producers receive an improved price. With respect to Ethiopian coffee, FLO conducts Fairtrade certification for groups of smallholder producers organised as farmer cooperatives. In 2012, FLO was certifying 50 coffee-producing cooperatives organised under the umbrella of four major Farmers' Cooperative Unions: Oromia Coffee Farmers Cooperative Union, Yirgacheffe Coffee Farmers Cooperative Union, Sidama Coffee Farmers Cooperative Union and Kafa Forest Coffee Farmers Cooperative Union. Members of these cooperative societies were receiving two kinds of payments for their coffees: a Fairtrade minimum price and a premium for compliance with specified standards.

In Ghana, the Kuapa Kokoo Farmers Union is the main Fairtrade-certified cocoa-producing cooperative. The cocoa produced is sold in the UK and US markets via Divine Chocolate Inc., a chocolate manufacturing company based in the UK and partly owned by the Kuapa Kokoo Farmers Union in cooperation with

2 For a comprehensive list of ATOs and their websites, go to http://faircompanies.com/news/view/caalternative-trading-organization-ato/ (accessed 25 April 2013).

the Fairtrade Foundation in the UK (Divine Chocolate, n.d.). At the time of the research, the Cocoa Abrabopa Association (CAA), the largest association of cocoa farmers in Ghana, was in the process of seeking Fairtrade certification (Mustapha interview, 2012).

Environmental certification

Whereas fair trade certification deals with the social conditions of production, environmental certification is largely concerned with the ecological and sustainability conditions surrounding production. As with fair trade strategies, environmental certification is typically used as a tool to address inequalities in the global economy by offering opportunities for traditional agricultural producers to target niche markets. Environmental certification can generally be understood as certification

> [...] which conveys information about the environmental impact of *producing, processing, transporting, or using a food product* [...] in one or more of several dimensions: soil, water, and land-use practices; pest control practices. (Barham, 2002, italics in original)

Thus environmental certification involves the standardisation of principles and prescriptive criteria in terms of environment, health, safety and sustainability. Most often, independent third parties set the labelling standards. In Ethiopia, key environmental certification organisations include UTZ KAPEH, the Forest Stewardship Council, the Rainforest Alliance and a number of other organisations that have their own standards of certification (Volkmann, 2008). There are currently approximately 19 entities in Ethiopia involved in one way or another with environmental certification, including coffee-producing cooperatives, commercial actors and a public enterprise. In Ghana, the Rainforest Alliance and UTZ KAPEH are the dominant certifying organisations overseeing environmental standards for cocoa production (FAO, 2007). The Cocoa Abrabopa Association and a number of small-scale producer associations operate under various environmental certification schemes.[3]

3 For example, the Agro Eco-Louis Bolk Institute runs environmentally certified cocoa production projects in various regions of Ghana: Fine Flavor, the Nyinahin Sustainability Cocoa Production and Community Empowerment Project and the Ntobroso Rainforest Alliance Cocoa Farmers Union projects in the Ashanti region; the Mars Partnership for African Cocoa-Communities of Tomorrow; the Asankrangwa project in the Western and Central regions; and the Aponoapono Biakoye Organic Cocoa Farmers Association and Cocoa Organic Farmers Association projects in the Eastern region.

Organic certification

Organic certification schemes arose from consumer-driven organic movements across Europe and the US that opposed the perceived unsustainable character of agricultural biotechnology and also had reservations about the safety of genetically modified (GM) foods (Mansfield, 2004). Organic production schemes are those in which farmers' management of agriculture is based on natural methods of enhancing soil fertility – a conscious intermingling between human-based farming systems and natural systems. It can be argued that most informal farming in Africa is already *de facto* organic (Osei-Asare, 2007).

Unlike environmental certification, organic certification standards are usually institutionalised through national legislation. Under these systems, certification is generally overseen by governmental bodies. Producers cannot use the term "organic" without proper certification. Internationally, the International Federation of Organic Agriculture Movements has prompted multilateral efforts to harmonise standards for organic certification. In Ethiopia, the government enacted the Organic Agriculture System Proclamation of 2006 with two main objectives, namely, (1) to protect consumers of Ethiopian organic products against fraudulent acts such as use of misleading labels, and (2) to facilitate international recognition and acceptance of the Ethiopian organic products system in the international market. The MOA has the power to issue implementing directives and establish an "organic agricultural product council" to inspect and certify products bearing the label "organic" (Organic Agriculture System Proclamation of 2006). Despite our finding that there is a perceived absence of the strong MOA supervision envisaged by the Proclamation, there were, in mid-2012, an estimated 79 Ethiopian coffee cooperatives and 28 private coffee growers certified "organic" by foreign certifiers, often supported by capacity-building NGOs.

In Ghana, the Ghana Standards Board issues Codes of Practice for Organic Farming and oversees producers' compliance for certification, but there is no comprehensive legislation on organic certification akin to what is present in Ethiopia. A recent study revealed that farmers had little awareness of the Standards Board's Codes of Practice (Osei-Asare, 2007). Similar to the situation in Ethiopia, a number of NGOs in Ghana support capacity building for organic certification for farmer groups in collaboration with foreign certifiers. For example, some of the projects run by the Agro Eco-Louis Bolk Institute (see footnote 3) specialise in organic certification.

Assessing certification schemes

Most of the leaders of cooperative unions and farmers' associations interviewed for this research lauded the impact of existing certification schemes in terms of the financial and material support they offered in the form of premiums for small-scale producers.[4] However, even though the differentiation schemes have proved to be largely successful instruments for improving market access for agricultural producers in the international market, the lack of domestic certification capacity – and hence, reliance on foreign standards and certifying bodies – was cited by interviewees as raising a number of concerns.

One such concern cited is the fact that the system of certification in fair trade and eco-labelling incorporates expensive procedures of rigorous inspection and certification that some producers claim are too burdensome (G/Kidan interview, 2012). Interviewee Asinakech Thomas, Ethiopia's only female miller-exporter of Amaro Gayo Coffee, and who works closely with farming communities in the Amaro Gayo district, said she does not see the need for such an expensive process of organic certification through foreign-based certifiers (Thomas interview, 2012). Thomas argued that the farmers in her coffee-producing region already strive for the finest quality of coffee through traditional production methods that preserve the natural ecosystem and the human culture connected to that ecosystem. As noted earlier in this chapter, agricultural production in Africa is largely *de facto* organic. Given this context, the use of GIs could provide an opportunity to implement the standards of organic certification by incorporating requirements (such as preferences for environmentally sensitive methods of production, GM-free production, and maintenance of production conditions free of chemical pesticides and contaminants) in GI regulations as recognised methods of production. With effective implementation of GIs, small-scale farmers could be empowered to participate in international trade on their own terms.

A second concern arising from dependence on certification schemes relates to the fact that most of the schemes focus on a homogeneous set of certification practices that sometimes deviate from local realities (Mutersbaugh, 2002). Interviewee Tsegaye Anemo, General Manager of the Sidama Coffee Farmers Cooperative Union, stated that production standards in certification schemes do not take the unique circumstances and existing methods of production into account (Anemo interview, 2012). This opinion is commonly held among critics of certification schemes who often point out that the formalisation and standardisation of certification practices do not accommodate "varied and complex ecological, economic, and socio-cultural contexts" (Getz and Shreck, 2006). In contrast, GI protection is fundamentally premised on a desire to preserve local, national and regional distinctness in agricultural production (FAO, 2008).

A third concern expressed by interviewees was that the existing certification schemes prescribe different sets of standards and criteria that often overlap. Fair trade certification prescribes environmental standards that are also required in

4 Focus group discussion with Ato Tadesse Meskela (OCFCU) and Isa Mustapha (Executive, CAA).

organic certification and *vice versa*. However, producer groups that qualify for organic certification also have to undergo an independent certification process for fair trade and environmental certification. In addition to the cost producers incur in the form of application fees, the subjectivity and lack of uniformity in criteria-setting and conformity-assessment procedures across the schemes make attaining certification challenging. A number of respondents suggested the need for a harmonisation of standards in certification schemes in order to achieve more coherent and effective agricultural development.

5. Feasibility of GIs

Certification schemes appeal primarily to consumers willing to pay a higher price out of consideration for the socio-economic conditions of agricultural producers or out of consideration for the minimal environmental impact of the producers' methods of production. GIs, in contrast, make an appeal to consumers based on perceived quality, reputation or other distinctive characteristics of the product itself. GIs and certification schemes also significantly differ in the degree of control each offers to the communities who embrace them. GIs are unique types of IP, and as such they grant their owners all the attributes of property ownership, including: the power to control the resource; the right to determine what use is made of it and under what conditions; and, most importantly, the right to exclude others from use of it (Strahilevitz, 2006). GIs provide their owners with better leverage (than that afforded by certification schemes) to bargain for improved prices for their products through collective proprietary control.

Because of the fundamental distinction between the two, GIs and certification schemes tend to fall into distinct regimes. GIs mostly fall under IP legal regimes; fair trade labelling schemes and environmental or organic labelling schemes are generally voluntary initiatives and do not fall into a particular legal regime, even though they can be enhanced by trademarks. For example, some labelling organisations, such as Fairtrade, have registered their labels as trademarks in order to achieve a higher level of protection. In such cases, labelling schemes often overlap and are conflated with trademarks. Organic certification schemes are, in some ways, exceptions, to the extent that they are typically institutionalised through national legislation such that producers cannot use the term "organic" without certification by government or a government-mandated agency.

The price in the alternative value chain (through certification schemes) for Ethiopian coffee and Ghanaian cocoa largely reflects the conventional international price for the two products. According to the latest data available, certification schemes were connected to only 5% of Ghanaian cocoa and about 28% of

Ethiopian coffee (Fairtrade, n.d.; McCarthy, 2007). Therefore, the alternative value chains for Ethiopian coffee and Ghanaian cocoa were not found to be broad in scope. However, given consumers' increased interest in certification schemes – due to the work of advocacy networks – there is reason to believe that the bolstering of certification initiatives via GI initiatives could improve the market share for GI-protected goods.

Challenges of introducing GIs: structural

Introducing a functional system of GIs requires the establishment of institutional, legislative and organisational frameworks. As in many other developing countries, Ethiopia and Ghana do not have a developed system of GIs. At the time of writing, Ethiopia had draft legislation on GIs: the Proclamation for the Registration and Protection of Designation of Origin, and the Draft GIs Proclamation. These two pieces of draft legislation were under the auspices of the Ethiopian Environmental Protection Authority (EPA) and the EIPO, respectively. The EIPO had taken responsibility for integrating the legislation and preparing laws that would drive the application of GIs for a wide variety of agricultural products (Adelo interview, 2012). Meanwhile, Ghana was in the process of revising its Geographical Indications Act of 2003 to make it applicable to cocoa, pineapple, *kente*, *adinkra* and other export-based Ghanaian products.

In addition to a legal framework, GI protection requires institutional and administrative mechanisms for the identification and registration of eligible products. Also required are infrastructure and expertise to establish, monitor and control production methods to ensure that products are GI-compliant. Active coordination and cooperation between national, regional and local administrative authorities and producer groups are also necessary in order to adopt and administer compliance mechanisms for agricultural production (Rangnekar, 2007). Once GI protection is extended to the product, these mechanisms are necessary to ensure that the GI product does not become generic through unregulated production processes.

At least four government branches in Ethiopia claim to have a mandate relevant to the implementation of GIs: the MOA, the EIPO, the EPA and the Ministry of Trade. The MOA provides farmer support programmes that extend to the lowest administrative levels through its Agricultural Extension Directorate. A task force of nine people, composed of farmers, farmer association representatives and MOA employees, oversees the maintenance of quality in coffee production and processing (MOA interviewee, 2012). The MOA official interviewed for this research expressed concern that the cost of monitoring production, demarcating areas of production and ensuring quality in the event of GI protection could be challenging. However, given the potential for improved income, interviewees seemed optimistic that the benefits of GI protection would outweigh the costs.

Ethiopia's Coffee Quality Control and Marketing Proclamation of 2008 provides for a quality control system at the local production level. Pursuant to the objectives of the Proclamation, the MOA issued a Coffee Quality and Marketing Implementation Manual that details the methods of coffee production and precautions necessary for producing quality coffee beans (MOA, 2009). The Manual provides detailed guidelines on coffee production, beginning with the selection of beans and moving on to the planting of beans, care of seedlings and overall harvesting. The Proclamation also provides for the establishment of "coffee quality liquoring and inspection centres" to inspect and grade coffee supplied from production areas (Art. 2(20)). We found that a coffee quality liquoring and inspection centre established within the MOA was issuing certificates of grades based on representative samples of all coffee destined for the export market. Similarly, the ECX had quality inspection centres at primary markets in localities where the exchange was being performed between farmers and coffee supplier merchants. All producers who directly exported coffee from their own farm via alternative value chains, or those who exported via the ECX, were required to submit a representative sample of their product to the MOA's central coffee quality liquoring and inspection centre for grading before and after processing for export.

In Ghana, we found that the development of a legal framework for protection of GIs was part of a wider reform of the country's IP law (Ishaaque interview, 2012). According to interviewee Grace Ishaaque, then Principal State Attorney at the Registrar General's Department, Ghana's Ministry of Agriculture was to be entrusted with drafting detailed regulations and directives dealing with practical implementation once the Parliament of Ghana had approved amendments to the 2003 GIs law (Ishaaque interview, 2012). Ishaaque stated that the task of implementing GIs would be challenging, and emphasised the need for capacity building through training and experience-sharing with countries that have well-developed systems of GIs, particularly countries in the EU (Ishaaque interview, 2012). Similarly, interviewee Safoa Osei, a Senior Standards Officer at the GSA, noted that the GSA was currently maintaining quality at the farm level by the issuing of good agricultural practice guidelines (Osei interview, 2012). Osei stated that there was a need for a policy that would provide incentives based on quality of production and a form of regulation that would focus on training farmers, quality inspectors and others in the cocoa value chain (Osei interview, 2012).

Another economic consideration relevant to introducing GIs is the cost and burden for producer communities who seek to register GIs. GI legislation typically requires producers to perform specific tasks in order to tap into opportunities.

The successful implementation of GIs requires the presence of producer organisations and collectives with a structure that allows collaborative participation in registering, maintaining and protecting GI rights (INRA, 2008). In the cases of both Ethiopian coffee and Ghanaian cocoa, we saw above that a significant number of producer cooperatives and farmer associations operate in the alternative value chains through certification schemes. In Ethiopia, numerous cooperative societies – composed of 10 or more coffee farmers who produce in a defined geographical area – have been established. These societies have then formed larger cooperative unions. The Oromia Coffee Farmers Cooperative Union (OCFCU), for instance, is composed of 217 primary societies that have an annual combined production of more than 300,000 tonnes of five varieties of coffee. The coffee varieties are Sidama, Harar, Jimma, Nekemte, and Limmu (OCFCU, n.d.). According to interviewee Tadesse Meskela, OCFCU's General Director, the Union strives to guarantee traceability of coffee produced by its members – from harvesting to final market destination (Meskela interview, 2012). During our visit to the Union's coffee processing and storage facility in Addis Ababa, the Union demonstrated the traceability (through meticulous labelling) of the sources of different varieties of coffee arriving at its warehouses, down to the least of the coffee production areas. These traceability systems are intended to help farmers add value and find new market niches through systems of certification. The Sidama and Yirgacheffe Coffee Farmers Cooperative Unions have similar systems with primary coffee farmer societies operating within a functional system of quality control at grassroots level.

In Ghana, it was found that a number of cocoa farmers' associations, such as the Cocoa Abrabopa Association, were playing significant roles in ensuring the maintenance of quality through, for instance, improved farming techniques. The aforementioned state body, COCOBOD, through its Quality Control Division, was also found to be undertaking various activities to maintain quality.

The existence of the aforementioned structures would be of paramount significance in implementing the production-level quality control measures needed to form the basis of any GI system. In fact, we are of the view that the introduction of GI systems could, in the Ethiopian and Ghanaian cases, provide opportunities to empower and encourage greater levels of collective action among producers through their existing producer cooperatives and farmer associations. Existing networks of farming groups with shared commitments to both value-based production and the sanctity of place-based reputation could provide effective channels for enforcing the production standards central to GI protection. However, the existence of primary societies and cooperative unions does not necessarily eliminate the potentially prohibitive costs of implementing GIs. In the event of GI protection, additional activities related to protecting and maintaining GI rights by farmers would likely require a strengthening of organisational and managerial capacities of farmer associations and their cooperative unions, and would likely require collaboration with public agencies and development partners.

In registering the rights and ensuring the maintenance of standards of production, *sui generis* forms of GI protection typically incorporate both *ex officio* and *ex parte* protections. *Ex officio* protection is when public authorities take the initiative in relation to a product without being asked to, while *ex parte* protection is that which is provided at the request of an interested party, typically a producer grouping (Vassilakis, 2009). The GI systems of the EU, Switzerland, Croatia and Japan allow *ex officio* protection of GIs. The GI legislation of China, Algeria, Tunisia and Mauritius provides both *ex officio* and *ex parte* protections. Under the EU's GI system, states are expected to apply *ex officio* protection of GIs by establishing integrated control plans in sector-specific areas. The tasks that public authorities undertake in the EU are similar to those that producer organisations undertake in countries with less-developed systems of GIs, such as the inspection and monitoring of production. An *ex officio* feature in GI protection could benefit the largely small-scale Ethiopian coffee and Ghanaian cocoa producers because it could allow competent authorities to take the lead, either directly in registering and maintaining GI rights or indirectly in building the capacity of producer groups. As evidenced by the progressive partnership developments on GIs in India, Brazil and Indonesia, it is possible that Ethiopia's MOA and Ghana's COCOBOD could engage development partners, such as the UK Department for International Development (DFID), the UN Commission on Trade and Development (UNCTAD) and others, in supporting GI implementation.

In assessing the potential economic benefits and costs of GI implementation, some argue that requiring farmers to adhere to traditional methods of production as a condition for GI protection could have the effect of denying farmers the benefits of increased productivity via industrialised agriculture methods (Shepherd, 2006). In the course of this research, farmers, producer groups and individuals working with farmers were asked whether they agreed, disagreed or slightly ("somewhat") agreed with the hypothesis that producers' adherence to traditional methods of production would reduce productivity. Out of seven responses, four disagreed with the proposition while two chose "somewhat agree" and one agreed. In response to another suggestion, that sticking to traditional methods of production for GI-compliance could result in additional production costs, four disagreed, three agreed and one chose "somewhat agree". Most of the respondents who disagreed with the above assumptions argued that coffee and cocoa farmers do not use fertilisers anyway, and that farmers have not yet maximised the productivity potential of their products even within the traditional system of production (Meskela interview, 2012). Some respondents argued that adherence to traditional production methods provides cost savings via shunning of agricultural inputs such as chemical fertilisers and pesticides.[5] Some argued that the largely small-scale nature of production does not allow for the use of mechanised agriculture (Tessema interview, 2012) (meaning that the adoption of GIs could help to prevent the displacement of small-scale farmers by commercial producers who resort to large-scale agricultural production methods). In any event, we came to the conclusion that, in a successful implementation of GIs for Ethiopian coffee or Ghanaian cocoa, any decrease in yield due to the non-application of mechanised agriculture would likely be offset through improved prices for the products that would remain clearly differentiated from generic products in commodity markets.

Operational challenges

Getting consumers to know the quality, reputation or characteristic of a GI-protected product would be crucial to broad recognition of the product in the market. A significant number of respondents in the study recognised the need for strategies that broaden the market share for their products. One interviewee, a cocoa farmer from the Western region of Ghana, expressed the view that it would be worth the risk to invest in promotional activities in international markets, given the quality of his products (Quam interview, 2012). Meanwhile, all of the respondents in the Ethiopian coffee and Ghanaian cocoa sectors gave the response "agree" or "somehow agree" with the view that because some varieties of their products have existing market reputation, no significant expenses in advertisement and brand management would be expected. The leaders of farmers' associations and cooperative unions said they recognised that any GI strategy would present the opportunity to further engage in promotional activities.[6]

There is evidence that many distinctive agricultural products from African countries already have broad reputations in their respective markets.[7] But a problem for most producers of these products is that the premium prices that the products garner tend to benefit outside commercial entities, namely, intermediaries in the value chain of the products. In this context, it can be argued that,

5 Focus group discussion among coffee farmers, 15 June 2012, held at the office of the OCFCU.

6 Personal communications with leaders of the OCFCU, Sidama Coffee Farmers Cooperative Union, Yirgacheffe Coffee Farmers Cooperative Union and the CAA.

7 These products include, for example, Madagascar Bourbon, Ugandan Vanilla, Kenya's indigenous tea varieties such as Kericho tea, South Africa's indigenous tea product Rooibos, and the Chili de Mamou from the Republic of Guinea.

given the potential for GIs to balance the power relations between producers and intermediaries, marketing and brand management activities for the GI-protected products could be recoverable expenses.

Another potential challenge with a GI system is the cost of product quality improvement in response to changing consumer preferences (Lewin *et al.*, 2004). There is an argument that, for it to be viable to extend GI protection to distinctive agricultural products in developing countries, besides "tradition and authenticity" a target product must embody attributes that are "constantly subject to change and adaptation" in response to evolving consumer and market demands (Winter, 2003). In turn, it is argued that, because farmers and producers in developing countries are more familiar with subsistence production than with commercial production, small-scale producers may find it too difficult and expensive to engage in activities that respond to the latest consumer interests in the course of GI use (Larson, 2007). However, it is our view that the current global market environment is receptive to traditional agricultural products because of "a voracious appetite for exoticism and romanticism around cultural products from 'pristine' communities" (Oguamanam, 2009).

The earlier examination of the economic impacts of certification schemes demonstrated that marketing strategies based on local, territory-based and TK-based attributes of products have presented significant marketing opportunities in the global market for traditional agricultural food products. This increasing interest in traditional agricultural products – a feature of today's post-modern economy – largely dispels the concern that an absence of experience in adapting to changing consumer preferences would limit the effectiveness of GI protection. Consumer appetite for agricultural products from tradition-based agricultural producers can in fact be expected to rise even further in the future, given the growing consumer scepticism towards the health and safety aspects of many agro-biotechnology products. Thus, the association of most African products with local territory, culture and tradition has the potential to constitute an important feature of the marketing of any African products protected by GIs (Addor and Grazioli, 2002). Unlike corporate strategies that devise market-responsive methods of adding value to agricultural products, the commercial success of GI protection in the Ethiopian coffee and Ghanaian cocoa contexts could be expected to depend largely on defending and using the same traditional techniques that form the basis of "reputation, quality or other characteristics" of these products. This does not, however, mean that producers of these distinctive agricultural products would not need to formulate strategies to widen and control their market share.

During our interviews with producer cooperative members and farmers, one of the identified expectations of GIs was a need to control and protect Ethiopian coffee and Ghanaian cocoa brands from being undermined by counterfeit products of other countries. Many distinctive agricultural products from developing countries that have already acquired strong market presence and broad recognition have been subjected to different forms of counterfeiting and falsification in international markets. For example, the Tea Board of India reports that the district of Darjeeling produces only 10,000 tonnes of tea a year, while roughly 40,000 tonnes of tea is annually sold worldwide as "Darjeeling" (Kenny, 2004). The region of Antigua in Guatemala produces some 6 million pounds of genuine Antigua coffee per year (Grote, 2009), yet some 50 million pounds of coffee are sold annually under the "Antigua" designation around the world (EC, 2003). Ghana's *adinkra* and *kente* cloths are globally dispersed through sources traced to China (Boateng, 2011). GI implementation could provide the legal means to control and protect the Ethiopian coffee and Ghanaian cocoa brands (which can, like Ghanaian cloths, be subjected to counterfeiting and falsification), but producers would have to defend and enforce GIs in order to prevent any incidents of falsification of the origin of products and the counterfeiting of the product names. Such activities could require enormous resources for monitoring foreign producers, enforcing GI rights and engaging in proceedings in foreign courts or before quasi-judicial forums.

However, while absolute enforcement of GIs in foreign jurisdictions might be burdensome, the economic implications of protecting GIs could be minimised if there were increased protection for GIs at the international level via collaborative GI implementation. Increased international protection for GIs could be achieved by the World Trade Organisation (WTO) if it were to extend the WTO's highest level of GI protection – currently restricted to wines and spirits only – to other agricultural products. Under the minimum level of GI protection in the WTO TRIPS Agreement, GIs for agricultural products other than wines and spirits are protected against "the use of any means [...] that indicates or suggests that the good in question originates in a geographical area other than the true place of origin" (Art. 22.2(a)). However, such protection is qualified by the TRIPS provision that the use of GIs by other parties is prohibited only if the other parties use the indication either "in a manner that may mislead the public" or in a way which may "constitute an act of unfair competition" (Art. 22.2(a)–(b)). In terms of this TRIPS provision, the use of a designation for another product that is identical or similar to a GI-protected product may be possible under a number of scenarios, the validity of which can be determined only through legal contest. In terms of this provision, protection against unfair and misleading use of GIs means that aggrieved parties – holders of GI rights over a product – need to prove not only that the use of an indication is not correct, but also that such a use may mislead the public or may constitute unfair competition. Such a task would involve arduous and costly legal proceedings in cases where the indication was used outside jurisdiction.

The degree of GI protection for wines and spirits under Article 23 of TRIPS is such that only producers whose products actually originate from a geographical area are identified as having rights to use the indication. Competitors in international markets are prohibited from using the indication – even where they clearly indicate the true geographical origin of the good in question or use the GI sign or terms "accompanied by expressions such as 'kind', 'type', 'style,' 'imitation' or the like" (Art. 23). Under this enhanced level of GI protection for wines and spirits, therefore, producers are shielded from expensive legal proceedings that may be required (under the lower level of GI protection) to prove unfair competition and public deception in the use of an indication (Correa, 2002). Thus, higher WTO protection of *all* GIs at the international level would result in lower economic burdens for producers of Ethiopian coffee and Ghanaian cocoa were their products to be GI-protected.

In the absence of strong international protection for non-wine/spirit GIs, collaborative efforts, through state-led initiatives, would likely be needed to support small-scale agricultural producers. GIs are essentially agricultural instruments that historically have not been considered part of private property, unlike other regimes of IP such as trademarks (Aubard, 2010). The advantage of *sui generis* forms of protection is that GIs can be conceptualised as "publicly oriented" rights, rather than as the private business assets of individuals (FAO and SINER-GI, 2009). *Sui generis* systems of GIs allow state agencies to take an active role in enforcing GI rights in foreign jurisdictions, as evidenced by the actions of France's Institut national des appellations d'origine (INAO). The involvement of the state in GI protection is justified based on the public objectives of preventing consumer confusion, preserving cultural heritage and conserving agricultural systems for multiple benefits (Lukose, 2007).

The Ethiopian coffee trademark and licensing initiative

Before seeking to arrive at conclusions regarding the applicability of *sui generis* versus conventional trademark approaches to GI protection for Ghanaian cocoa and Ethiopian coffee, it is necessary to give consideration to the existing Ethiopian coffee trademark and licensing initiative, launched by the EIPO in 2004. The initiative involved the trademark registration of three of the country's coffee designations – Yirgacheffe, Sidama and Harrar – in major foreign markets. An in-depth analysis of the pros and cons of this initiative is beyond the scope of this study. However, a few observations can be made in order to understand whether the chosen strategy of trademark registration and licensing is an optimal strategy as compared to a GI system. One of the reasons why the EIPO embarked on trademark-based protection is that the *sui generis* option for GIs, as practised in

Europe and most notably in France, was not considered feasible, given the enormous efforts required to implement it (Adelo interview, 2012; Mengistie interview, 2012). This decision is understandable because of the need to build institutional infrastructures and expertise that ensure the establishment, monitoring and controlling of production and marketing of the GI product. However, as this research study has found, there is evidence to suggest that the establishment of the structures necessary for GI protection in Ethiopia would *not* need to start from nothing as far as coffee production in the alternative value chain is concerned. Some of the structures – and motivations from producers – with regard to GIs already exist in the Ethiopian coffee sector. If a *sui generis* system of GIs were found to be suitable – and perhaps more suitable than a trademark-based IP strategy – the tasks involved in introducing and implementing GIs do not appear to be out of reach.

6. Conclusions

There is demonstrable evidence of a networked collaborative tradition of knowledge generation among local communities and diverse stakeholders involved in the production of premium Ethiopian coffee and Ghanaian cocoa. These entities' suitability to adapt GIs as *sui generis* IP models for open development outcomes in the two countries is a very plausible potential of their traditional orientation and operational module. It is clear, however, that the practical implementation of GIs in the two countries could involve significant burdens, given that the system of GIs is relatively foreign to them. What is required is a strategic approach to using GIs in ways that alleviate, not increase, cost burdens for producer groups.

The research findings suggest that the burdens of implementing GIs are not insurmountable, for three reasons. First, the experience of differentiation through certification marks (for fair trade and organic certification) has meant that the preconditions for success of GI strategies already exist in the alternative value chains of each country. GI strategies for the two products could thus be based on the experience and strength of existing differentiation strategies, in cooperation with farmer cooperatives and associations. Second, cost implications could be contained by exploiting the flexibility offered by the choice between *sui generis* and trademark-based systems of GI protection. Third, the potential of GI implementation in harmony with the practice and institutional settings of cooperative unions and farmers' associations, as well as the involvement of the state in the process, are important considerations. Together these factors help mitigate the cost concerns usually presented in arguments against the adoption of GIs in developing countries. Developing countries such as Ethiopia and Ghana must weigh these considerations in determining whether to introduce GIs in their jurisdictions.

Trademark GIs v. sui generis *GIs*

The method by which GIs are protected – *sui generis* or trademark-based – determines how far they can be harnessed to enhance collaborative innovation and creativity in agricultural production. In this respect, it is necessary to draw attention to Ethiopia's initiative of registering trademarks over its coffee GI names in major international markets such as the US, Japan, Australia and European countries.

Two observations deserve attention in considering whether trademark-based registration of GIs or a *sui generis* method is suited to the goal of participatory agricultural development in the Ethiopian coffee and Ghanaian cocoa sectors. The first relates to the amenability of each instrument to certain policy contexts and objectives in agricultural development, such as ecological, cultural and biodiversity goals. The second relates to the degree of control that each instrument allows rights-holders in guaranteeing authenticity of the products and in preventing unauthorised and falsified use of the products by third parties.

First, unlike trademark protection, GI protection can be acquired in other countries only if there is strong protection at the local level in the country of origin. The very nature of a GI system is dependent on the link between a product and a geographical location that forms the basis of the product's distinctive attributes. The task of maintaining a territorial link between a product and its area of production should be considered an opportunity for African producers to establish collective rights over traditional resources in a defined geographical area without the need to designate individual rights-holders. Given the territorial nature of most agricultural practice in Africa, a geographical link as a condition for GI protection adds significant value to GIs as tools to contextualise policy objectives in the protection of biodiversity, the preservation of cultural identity and the prevention of biopiracy. Adoption of a *sui generis* GI system could make it possible for local cultural systems to govern, *inter alia*, an agricultural product's methods of production, allocation of different production roles, and classification of a specific knowledge of production and the procedures of its transfer and the modes of its utilisation. Thus, a *sui generis* method of GI protection could serve to formalise production methods developed and generated through local consensus. The basis of GI protection in a *sui generis* model could, *inter alia*, be crafted in such a way as to comply with the requirements ingrained in local protocols and traditional rules regarding the management and conservation of biodiversity in the particular territory from which the product originates. The requirement for the establishment of GI systems within the domestic legal framework could also serve to prevent or reduce the likelihood of internal fraud (within the country of origin) that could compromise the quality of a product and the validity of GI protection for the product in other jurisdictions. This would advance the authenticity of the product in order to claim continued protection of the GI in other jurisdictions.

Regarding the second observation, a *sui generis* form of GIs could potentially offer a greater degree of control to the IP-holders than trademark protection. In a trademark-based GI, third parties are only prohibited from using a GI in foreign markets either "in a manner that may mislead the public" or in a way that may "constitute an act of unfair competition" (TRIPS, Art. 22.2(a)–(b)).[8] In the trademark context, protection against unfair and misleading use of a GI means that the aggrieved party – i.e. coffee producers in the case of Ethiopian coffee – needs to prove not only that the use of an indication is not correct, but also that such a use may mislead the public or may constitute unfair competition. As previously noted, such a task involves arduous and costly legal proceedings in cases where the indication is used in another jurisdiction. For example, third-party retailers may sell Ethiopian coffee under their own brand, using such phrases as "Sidama-style coffee", so long as they clearly indicate that it is actually blended with coffee imported from a country or location distinct from the Sidama region of Ethiopia. In such a case, it could persuasively be argued that the use of the indication "Sidama" does not mislead the public and thus is not a trademark violation. However, with a *sui generis* form of GI protection, it is theoretically only producers whose products actually originate from the respective region who have exclusive rights to use the indication in any GI form, even with the addition of a descriptive word or phrase.

In trademark-based GI protection, proprietary value attaches to a geographical sign or term only if, through continuous use in relation to a product, the sign or term has become distinctive in the minds of consumers as an indicator of the source of the product (Farley, 2000). In their *sui generis* form, GIs convey proprietary rights in and of themselves, even before they are invested with a meaning that results from use in the market. The recognition of GIs on a proprietary basis allows producers to exercise a bundle of ownership rights irrespective of the existence of market reputation for the brands. The proprietary nature of rights in *sui generis* forms of GIs grants producers better leverage for dealing with intermediaries such as wholesalers, importers, distributors, manufacturers and retailers of their products. Producers can potentially stipulate conditions under which their products are supplied to the market (Marette *et al.*, 2007). These conditions can cover, *inter alia*, requirements for the product's distribution. As GI rights-holders, producers have exclusive rights to control the GI-relevant product, determine what use is made of it and under what conditions, and, most important, to

8 The two phrases, laid out under Article 22.2(a) and (b) of TRIPS, are reflective of countries' legal standards in the protection of trademarks.

exclude others from the use of an indication that reproduces, imitates or falsifies the indication in any form. Producers could, as a condition of trading over their products, prohibit downstream operators in the market, such as distributors, manufacturers and retailers, from blending the product with cheap coffee or cocoa supplies that do not originate from the area signified by the indication. In the long term, this would allow coffee and cocoa farmers to differentiate their distinctive products from commodity chains and to negotiate the price of their product independently.

Bibliography

Primary sources

Legal instruments

Ethiopia:

Coffee Quality Control and Marketing Proclamation, *Negarit Gazette*, No. 602/2008.

Ethiopia Commodity Exchange Establishment Proclamation, *Negarit Gazette*, No. 550/2007.

Ethiopian Organic Agriculture System Proclamation, *Negarit Gazette*, No. 488/2006.

Ghana:

Ghana Cocoa Board Law of 1984 (PNDC L. 81).

Geographical Indications Act 659 of 2003.

International:

Agreement on Trade-Related Aspects of Intellectual Property Rights (TRIPS) (1994).

Interview and focus group transcripts

Adelo, Berhanu (15 June 2012), personal communication.

Ahmed, Hussien (15 June 2012), personal communication.

Anemo, Tsegaye (15 June 2012), personal communication.

Focus group discussion A (7 June 2012): Isa Mustapha, Executive Chairman, Cocoa Abrabopa Association; Benjamin Gyan, Educational and Training Officer at the Cocoa Abrabopa Association; David Kpelle, Coordinator, African Cocoa Coalition.

Focus group discussion B (15 June 2012): coffee farmers, Office of Oromia Coffee Farmers Cooperative Union (OCFCU).

G/Kidan, Yilma (15 June 2012), personal communication.

Gyan, Benjamin (7 June 2012), personal communication.

Ishaaque, Grace (7 June 2012), Principal State Attorney, Registrar General, personal communication.

Mengistie, Getachew (15 June 2012), personal communication.

Meskela, Ato Tadesse (12 June 2012), Director-General, Oromia Coffee Farmers Cooperative Union (OCFCU), personal communication.

MOA interviewee (16 June 2012), Anonymous (Interview code 012), personal communication.

Mustapha, Isa (7 June, 2012), personal communication.

Osei, Safoa (7 June 2012), Senior Standards Officer, Standards Authority, personal communication.

Quam, Silvester (8 June 2012), Tebase, Western Region, personal communication.

Tessema, Meskerem (14 June 2012), Deputy Manager, Yirgacheffe Coffee Farmers Cooperative Union, personal communication.

Thomas, Asinakech (15 June 2012), personal communication.

Secondary sources

Addor, F. and Grazioli, A. (2002), "Geographical indications beyond wines and spirits", *Journal of World Intellectual Property,* Vol. 5 No. 6, pp. 865–97.

Aubard, A. (2010), *The Use of Geographical Indications to Promote Economic Development: Issues, Opportunities, Policy Options,* paper commissioned by the ACP-EU TradeCom Facility, Brussels.

Barham, E. (2002), "Towards a theory of values-based labelling", *Agriculture and Human Values*, Vol. 19, pp. 349–60.

Barrientos, S. (2012), *Ethical Sourcing in the Global Food System,* Routledge, New York.

Boateng, B. (2011), *The Copyright Thing Doesn't Work Here: Adinkra and Kente Cloth and Intellectual Property in Ghana*, University of Minnesota Press, Minneapolis.

Boehlje, M.D., Hofing, S.L. and Schroeder, R.C. (1999), *Value Chains in the Agricultural Industries*, Purdue University Staff Paper No. 99–10, West Lafayette, IN.

Burch, D. (2007), *Supermarkets and Agri-Food Supply Chains: Transformations in the Production and Consumption of Foods*, Edward Elgar, Cheltenham, UK.

Correa, C.M. (2002), *Protection of Geographical Indications in CARICOM Countries*, available at: www.crnm.org/index.php?option=com_docman&Itemid=82 (accessed 12 April 2013).

Cottier, T. and Panizzon, M. (2004), "Legal perspectives on traditional knowledge: the case for intellectual property protection", *Journal of International Economic Law*, Vol. 7 No. 2, pp. 371–99.

Dedeurwaerdere, T., Krishna, V. and Pascual, U. (2007), "An evolutionary institutional approach to the economics of bioprospecting", in Kontoleon, A. and Pascual, U. (Eds), *A Handbook of Biodiversity Economics*, Cambridge University Press, Cambridge, UK, pp. 417–45.

Divine Chocolate (n.d.), available at www.divinechocolate.com (accessed 8 April 2013).

Dutfield, G. (1999), *Sharing the Benefits of Biodiversity: Access Regimes and Intellectual Property Rights*, Science, Technology and Development Discussion Paper No. 6, *Oxford* Centre for the Environment, Ethics and Society (OCEES), Oxford.

Ethiopia Commodity Exchange (ECX) (n.d.), available at www.ecx.com.et (accessed 8 April 2013).

Ethiopia Commodity Exchange (ECX) (2011a), "Market at a glance", *Daily Market Bulletin*, Addis Ababa.

Ethiopia Commodity Exchange (ECX) (2011b), *The Operation of the Ethiopia Commodity Exchange and Roles of Stakeholders*, Addis Ababa.

European Commission (EC) (2003), *Intellectual Property: Why Do Geographical Indications Matter to Us?* Background Note 01/04, available at: http://trade.ec.europa.eu/doclib/docs/2003/october/tradoc_113900.pdf (accessed 12 April 2013).

Fairtrade (n.d.), available at: www.fairtrade.org.uk (accessed 8 April 2013).

Farley, C.H. (2000), "Conflicts between US law and international treaties concerning geographical indications", *Whittier Law Review*, Vol. 22, pp. 73–88.

Florida, R. and Kenney, M. (1993), "The new age of capitalism: innovation-mediated production", *Futures*, Vol. 25, pp. 637–51.

Food and Agriculture Organisation (FAO) (2007), *Agri-business Models and Export of Organic and Fairtrade Certified Products from Ghana*, proceedings of workshop held in Accra, 24–25 January.

Food and Agriculture Organisation (FAO) (2008), "Promotion of traditional regional agricultural products and food: a further step towards sustainable rural development", 26th FAO Regional Conference, Agenda Item 11, Rome.

Food and Agriculture Organisation (FAO) and SINER-GI (2009), *Linking People, Places and Products: A Guide for Promoting Quality Linked to Geographical Origin and Sustainable Geographical Indications*, Rome.

Food and Agriculture Organisation (FAO) (2010), *Creating Conditions for the Development of GIs: The Role of Public Policies*, available at: www.fao.org/docrep/012/i1057e/i1057e07.pdf (accessed 8 April 2013).

Gade, D. (2004), "Tradition, territory, and terroir in French viniculture: cassis, France, and appellation controlee", *Annals of the Association of American Geographers,* Vol. 94 No. 4, pp. 848–67.

Gangjee, D. (2007), "Quibbling siblings: conflicts between trademarks and GIs", *Chicago-Kent Law Review,* Vol. 82 No. 2, pp.1253–91.

Getz, C. and Shreck, A. (2006), "What organic and fair trade labels do not tell us: towards a place-based understanding of certification", *International Journal of Consumer Studies,* Vol. 30 No. 5, pp. 490–501.

Grote, U. (2009), "Environmental labeling, protected geographical indications, and the interests of developing countries", *The Estey Centre Journal of International Law and Trade Policy,* Vol. 10 No. 1, pp. 94–100.

Hansen, S.A. and Van Fleet, J.W. (2003), *A Handbook on Issues and Options for TK Holders in Protecting their Intellectual Property and Maintaining Biological Diversity,* American Association for the Advancement of Science, Washington, DC.

Hellin, J. and Meijer, M. (2006), *Guidelines for Value Chain Analysis,* available at: www.fao.org/fileadmin/templates/esa/LISFAME/Documents/Ecuador/value_chain_methodology_EN.pdf (accessed 14 April 2013).

Higgins, V., Dibdenb, J. and Cocklinc, C. (2008), "Building alternative agri-food networks: certification, embeddedness and agri-environmental governance", *Journal of Rural Studies,* Vol. 24 No. 1, pp. 15–27.

L'Institut national de la recherche agronomique (INRA) (2008), *Agriculture and Biodiversity: Benefiting from Synergies,* available at: http://inra.dam.front.en.pad.brainsonic.com/ressources/afile/234090-93eed-resource-expert-report-on-agriculture-and-biodiversity-summary.html (accessed 12 April 2013).

International Trade Centre (2011), *Ethiopia Coffee Quality Improvement Project,* Aid for Trade Global Review 2011: Case Story, Geneva.

Kenny, G. (2004), "Intellectual property rights of Darjeeling tea in the age of globalization and world trade", *Trade and Environment Database Journal,* available at: www1.american.edu/ted/darjeeling.htm (accessed 12 April 2013).

Kerr, W.A. (2006), "Enjoying a good port with a clear conscience: geographic indicators, rent seeking and development", *The Estey Centre Journal of International Law and Trade Policy,* Vol. 7, pp. 1–14.

Larson, J. (2007), *Relevance of Geographical Indications and Designations of Origin for the Sustainable Use of Genetic Resources,* Global Facilitation Unit for Underutilized Species, Rome.

Layton, R. and Wiseman, M. (2008), *Distinctive Values in African Exports: How Intellectual Property Can Raise Export Income and Alleviate Poverty,* Light Years IP, Philadelphia.

Lewin, B., Giovannucci, D. and Varangis, P. (2004), *Coffee Markets: New Paradigms in Global Supply and Demand,* World Bank, Washington, DC.

Lorvellec, L. (1996), "You've got to fight for your right to party: a response to professor Jim Chen," *Minnesota Journal of Global Trade*, Vol. 5, pp. 65–80.

Lukose, L.P. (2007), "Rationale and prospects of the protection of geographical indication: an inquiry", *Journal of Intellectual Property Rights,* Vol. 12 No. 2, pp. 212–23.

Mansfield, B. (2004), "Organic views of nature: the debate over organic certification for aquatic animals", *Sociologia Ruralis,* Vol. 44 No. 2, pp. 216–32.

Marette, S., Clemens, R. and Babcock, B.A. (2007), *The Recent International and Regulatory Decisions about Geographical Indications,* Matric Working Paper 07-MWP, Midwest Agribusiness Trade Research and Information Centre, Ames, IA.

McCarthy, S. (2007), "Ethiopia's coffee cooperatives: a case study", presentation to the World Bank Workshop on Rural Institutions, Washington, DC.

McManis, C.R. (2003), "Intellectual property, genetic resources and TK protection: thinking globally, acting locally", *Cardozo Journal of International and Comparative Law,* Vol. 11, pp. 547–83.

Ministry of Agriculture (MOA) (2009), *Sustainable Production and Supply of Fine Arabica Coffee to the World: Coffee Ethiopia's Gift to the World*, Addis Ababa.

Mutersbaugh, T. (2002), "The number is the beast: a political economy of organic-coffee certification and producer unionism", *Environment and Planning,* Vol. 34 No. 7, pp. 1165–84.

National Institute for Agricultural Research (2008), *Agriculture and Biodiversity: Benefiting from Synergies*, Paris.

O'Connor, B. (2004), *The Law of Geographical Indications*, Cameron May, London.

Oguamanam, C. (2009), "Beyond theories: intellectual property dynamics in the global knowledge economy", *Wake Forest Intellectual Property Law Journal,* Vol. 9 No. 2, pp. 104–54.

Oromia Coffee Farmers' Cooperative Union (OCFCU) (n.d.) "Oromia Coffee Farmers' Union (Members size, land possessed and expected production)", unpublished document, on file with authors.

Osei-Asare, Y.B. (2007), *Status of Organic Agriculture in Ghana: A Survey of Consumers, Producers, and Marketers,* UN Food and Agriculture Organisation (FAO), Ghana Organic Agriculture Network (GOAN), and Ministry of Food and Agriculture (MOFA), Accra, available at: www.ifoam.org/sites/default/files/page/files/status_of_organic_agriculture_in_ghana-_a_survey_of_consumers_producers_and_marketers_.pdf (accessed 8 April 2013).

Overseas Development Institute (ODI) (2007), *Production, Markets and the Future of Smallholders: The Role of Cocoa in Ghana*, ODI Workshop, Accra.

Oxfam (2002), *Crisis in the Birthplace of Coffee,* Oxfam International Research Paper, Oxford.

Prakash, S. (2000), *Indigenous Knowledge and Intellectual Property Rights*, World Bank IK Notes No. 19, available at: www.worldbank.org/afr/ik/iknt19.pdf (accessed 8 April 2013).

Prentice, R. and Andersen, V. (2007), "Creative tourism supply: creating culturally empathetic destinations", in Richards, G. and Wilson, J.C. (Eds), *Tourism, Creativity and Development*, Routledge, Oxford, UK.

Rangnekar, D. (2004), *Demanding Stronger Protection for Geographical Indication*, UN Discussion Paper Series 2004/11, Maastricht, Netherlands.

Rangnekar, D. (2007), *Trade and Environment: A Resource Book*, International Institute for Sustainable Development (IISD), Geneva.

Ray, C. (1998), "Culture, intellectual property and territorial rural development", *Sociologia Ruralis,* Vol. 38 No. 1, pp. 1–19.

Salazar, R., Louwaars, N.P. and Visser, B. (2007), "Protecting farmers' new varieties: new approaches to rights on collective innovations in plant genetic resources", *World Development,* Vol. 35 No. 9, pp. 1515–28.

Selleyfan, K. (2012), "Uganda: branding cotton, sesame and vanilla", *WIPO Magazine,* Issue 3/2012.

Sereke-Berhan, H. (2010), *Coffee, Culture, and Intellectual Property: Lessons for Africa from the Ethiopian Fine Coffee Initiative,* The Pardee Papers No. 11, Frederick S. Pardee Center for the Study of the Longer-Range Future, Boston.

Shepherd, B. (2006), *Costs and Benefits of Protecting Geographical Indications: Some Lessons from the French Wine Sector*, GEM Working Paper, Groupe d'economie mondiale (GEM), Sciences Po, Paris.

Smith, M.L., Elder, L. and Emdon, H. (2011), "Open development: a new theory for ICT4D", *Information Technologies and International Development*, Vol. 7 No. 1, Spring (Special Issue: Open Development), available at: http://itidjournal.org/itid/article/view/692/290 (accessed 25 April 2013).

Stanculescu, D., Scholer, M. and Kotecha, S. (2011), *Ethiopian Coffee Quality Improvement Project,* 2011 Aid for Trade Global Review: Case Story, International Trade Centre, Geneva, available at: www.intracen.org (accessed 25 April 2013).

Strahilevitz, L. J. (2006), "Information asymmetries and the rights to exclude", *Michigan Law Review*, Vol. 104 No. 8, pp. 1835–98.

Sunder, Madhavi (2007), "The invention of traditional knowledge", *Law and Contemporary Problems,* Vol. 70 No. 2, pp. 97–124.

Taubman, Anthony (2006), "Is there a right of collective personality?" *European Intellectual Property Review,* Vol. 28 No. 9, pp. 485–92.

UN Conference on Trade and Development (UNCTAD) (2009), *Review of the Technical Cooperation Activities of UNCTAD and their Financing,* TD/B/WP/222/Add.1, Geneva.

Vassilakis, G. (2009), "The *ex officio* protection", minutes of the Round Table on Geographical Indications, Brussels.

Volkmann, J. (2008), *Assessment of Certification Options for Wild Forest Coffee in Ethiopia,*CoCEProjectReportSubproject5.4,availableat:http://evolve-sustainable-development.de/index.php?option=com_content&task=view&id=5&Itemid=7 (accessed 14 April 2013).

Winter, M. (2003), "Embeddedness, the new food economy and defensive localism," *Journal of Rural Studies,* Vol. 19 No. 23, pp. 23–32.

World Bank (2008), *World Development Report 2008: Agriculture for Development,* Washington, DC.

World Intellectual Property Organisation (WIPO) (2010a), *Policies, Measures and Experiences Regarding Intellectual Property and Genetic Resources,* WIPO/GRTKF/IC/16/INF/13, ICIPGR, Geneva.

World Intellectual Property Organisation (WIPO) (2010b), *Project on Intellectual Property and Product Branding for Business Development in Developing Countries and Least-Developed Countries,* CDIP, Fifth Session, Geneva.

Chapter 5

A Consideration of Communal Trademarks for Nigerian Leather and Textile Products

Adebambo Adewopo, Helen Chuma-Okoro and Adejoke Oyewunmi

Abstract

This chapter describes and interprets the findings of a case study into the possible applicability of communal trademark systems for certain Nigerian leather and textile products. Consideration is given to the national legal and regulatory environment, to the level of standardisation currently practised by small-scale leather and textile producers, and to the views of producers regarding the viability of communal trademarking. The study found producer interest in communal trademarking, but also several potential undermining factors of a legal and practical nature.

1. Introduction

Small-scale enterprises constitute an integral part of the formal and informal sectors of the Nigerian economy (Osotimehin *et al.*, 2012). Such enterprises are also increasingly vulnerable to the adverse impacts of globalisation and trade liberalisation. They appear ill-equipped to compete favourably with other manufacturers in terms of the standards, quality and marketing strategies necessary to comply with regulatory policies and consumer demand on the local and global stage (UNESCAP, 2009, p. 34). The key challenges that have been identified for these small-scale enterprises are: meeting standards and quality requirements; marketing their products and building brands; identifying and exploiting the unique characteristics of their products; and protecting their brands in the global environment (UNIDO, 2010).

The status of Nigeria's textile and leather manufacturing sectors is strongly impacted by the general character of the Nigerian economy, which has been dominated by the oil sector since the late 1970s. A significant proportion of current exports is constituted by crude oil and associated products (CBN, 2012, p. 179;

ECOWAS, 2008; UNCTAD, 2008, p. 167). The supremacy of the oil sector has led to the neglect of other sectors, generating negative consequences for employment generation, self-reliance and sustainability (Azinge, 2011). The Nigerian government has recently recognised the need to diversify the economy by promoting growth in other sectors, including textiles and leather (Azinge, 2011; Briggs, 2007; Obasanjo, 2000).

There is evidence to suggest that Nigeria's textile and leather industries have strong existing and potential markets at both the local and international levels (see Mark, 2012). Indeed, the textile industry once ranked high as a major contributor to Nigeria's revenue generation and gross domestic product (GDP) (Njoku, 2004). It is widely held that agro-based products and textiles offer strong export potential if these sectors are given an enabling environment (ECOWAS, 2008; Quartey, 2006). Beyond the economic context, textiles hold special social and cultural value for West African countries. The art of handmade fabrics is part of a cultural endeavour and tradition that cuts across communities in Nigeria. Nigeria's leather sector exports processed hides and skins into a market dominated by Italy and China (Amakon, 2006). Nigeria has been identified as a potential leading contender in the export of leather (UNCTAD, 2009, p. 104), and various studies have indicated a vibrant local market and a market in neighbouring countries for Nigerian leather as a raw material for the manufacture of leather-based products and accessories including shoes, bags and furniture (UNIDO, 2002, 2003).

Nigeria's leather and textile sectors, however, face serious challenges from other players in international markets, from high international standards requirements and from technical barriers. Textiles and leather are products that attract high World Trade Organisation (WTO) and environmental standards requirements and strict technical regulations falling under the discipline of the WTO and Multilateral Environmental Agreements (MEAs) in respect of production processes, labelling, packaging and product standards as prescribed by individual countries (see Cordero *et al.*, 2008; UNCTAD, 2004). Amakon (2006) reports that Nigerian leather is often rejected in developed countries as raw material because of its low quality. These factors have severely constrained the capitalisation of market potential that exists locally and internationally.

One of the factors blamed for low quality is a lack of local grades and standards for branding (USAID, 2002). For small-scale enterprises, the challenges in the international market are even more daunting since these enterprises generally lack the individual wherewithal to meet product requirements (UNIDO, 2010). A recent statement credited to the Director of International Standards and SMEs at the Standards Organisation of Nigeria (SON), Robert Okiyie, noted that in Nigeria only 10 SMEs have the international quality certification mark from the International Organisation for Standardisation (ISO) (Ayankunle, 2011).

The local and regional West African market for textiles is also threatened by the proliferation and influx of cheap, low-quality imitations by foreign manufacturers, chiefly Chinese, of the designs of the local industries (see Abdullah, 2010).

At the same time, there is increasing evidence internationally that entrepreneurs from both developed and developing countries can find ways to overcome limitations of scale and survive the onslaught of globalisation and trade liberalisation. Among the methods being used by small-scale entrepreneurs to secure global market bases for their products is the use of the intellectual property (IP) tool of establishing legally enforceable communal trademarks: certification marks, collective marks and geographical indications (GIs) (UNESCAP, 2009). In India, for example, communal trademarks are instrumental in the branding of products of the small-scale producers of Darjeeling tea made in West Bengal, pashmina textiles made in Kashmir, and leather products, toys and wall decorations made in Andhra Pradesh (see UNIDO, 2010).

An example of communal use of trademarks in Africa is the Ethiopian initiative (see Chapter 4 of this volume) that saw the registration of three brands of Ethiopia's fine coffee produced by local farmers (Yirgacheffe, Sidama and Harrar). The utility of communal trademarks hinges on the fact that they provide a platform to achieve market growth and competitiveness through "partnership collaboration between the producers concerned, joint standardisation of product quality, monitoring of compliance with agreed production procedures and collective marketing" (UNIDO, 2010, p. 2).

The research study outlined in this chapter investigated the potential feasibility of communal trademark strategies in the leather and textile sectors of Nigeria. The study sought to investigate the potential of communal trademarks as strategic vehicles for branding and market access. The assumption underlying the study was that such collective strategies carry the potential to offer – in ways that might not be feasible through the use of individual trademarks – qualitative and quantitative synergies (based to some extent on collaboration and openness dynamics) that can help small entities distinguish their products and build a positive reputation in competitive environments. Section 2 of this chapter delineates the relevant concepts and the contours of the two sectors studied. Section 3 outlines the research, Section 4 provides the findings and Section 5 offers conclusions.

2. Definition of concepts, profiling of the sectors

Communal trademarks

Communal trademarks differ from the classical trademark paradigm. Classical trademarks conceive of the marks as owned and used by an individual entity to distinguish its product from others. In its most conventional context, a trademark has been defined as "a badge of origin" indicating the source or the trade origin of the item on which it is used (Kitchin *et al.,* 2005, p. 9). In most jurisdictions, a trademark can apply to goods and services alike. However, in Nigeria the Trade Marks Act does not protect services, though such protection has been imputed through a circuitous registration in class 16 and more recently with the Trade Mark Regulation allowing service mark registration. It thus remains debatable whether this action is valid (Trade Marks Act of 1965 [Cap. T13 LFN 2004]).[1]

It is frequently argued that one of the basic utilities of trademarks is to boost competitiveness (Landes and Posner, 1987, pp. 268–70), i.e. a mark with a positive reputation can enhance the competitiveness in the global economy of the goods on which it is affixed (UNESCAP, 2009; UNIDO, 2010). In the context of modern commerce, trademarks can indeed serve several valuable functions, not only in communicating the origin and quality of goods, but also in providing the incentive and security for investment in quality assurance and marketing (Landes and Posner, 1987; Leaffer, 1998). Communal trademarks potentially offer additional merits over traditional trademarks – additional merits germane to the marketing efforts of small entities. The potential underlying incentives for communalism in this context are the qualitative and quantitative synergies envisaged from collectiveness. Such potential synergies can be generated through the use of certification marks, collective marks or GIs. The World Intellectual Property Organisation (WIPO) defines a "collective mark" as "a sign capable of distinguishing the geographical origin, quality or common characteristics of goods or services of different enterprises that simultaneously use the collective mark under the control of its owner" (WIPO, 2004). As noted by Kitchin *et al.* (2005, p.120), the major purpose of a collective mark is to distinguish, for promotional purposes, the product produced by members of an associated group.

The first kind of communal trademark, a collective mark, is uniquely defined by its ownership structure. Collective marks are owned by an association (public or private), and intended for use exclusively by the individual members of the association. It is the responsibility of the organisation that registers the mark to ensure standard compliance by its members (Kitchin *et al.*, 2005, p. 69). A well-known example of a collective mark is the "CA" mark used by the Institute of Chartered Accountants.

The second type of communal trademark, the certification mark, is similar to a collective mark because it too is registered by a single entity and used by the collective. However, unlike with collective marks, the owner of a certification

1 See also *Hanover Star Milling Co. v Metcalf,* 240 US 403, 412 (1916); *Ferodo Ltd v Ibeto Ind. Ltd* (2004) 5 *Nigerian Weekly Law Report* (*NWLR*) Pt. 866 at 317–47.

mark may be a certifying authority rather than the association using the mark. "Woolmark" is an example of a certification mark. Use of the mark is open to anyone who complies with the necessary standards (WIPO, 2004, p. 69). This makes certification marks valuable to small entities that lack the wherewithal to develop their reputation independently. Certification marks are frequently used to guarantee compliance with specific standards. They also provide a platform to regulate standards in a sector where standards are demanded (Belson, 2002).

The third type of communal trademark, a GI, can be protected as either a collective mark or as a stand-alone IP right. A GI signifies a product possessing unique qualities, or reflecting the reputation attributable to its origin. The GI's value therefore lies in giving the product an association with its place of origin – a place of origin that holds particular qualitative advantages. Such advantages could include traditional skills, methods or modes of manufacturing, or unique elements determined by the particular characteristics of the geographical location (WIPO, 2004, p. 120).

Nigeria's leather and textile producing sectors

The textile sector in Nigeria is marked by a mix of large and small enterprises. The small enterprises primarily produce man-made textiles using traditional methods (Quartey, 2006). The small enterprises in this context could be more narrowly classified as micro or cottage enterprises, which are defined as employing fewer than 10 individuals (Abor and Quartey, 2010; EC, n.d., p. 14; IFC, 2012, p. 1; Kozak, 2007; Udechukwu, 2003). The Nigerian leather industry consists predominantly of small enterprises, with only a handful of large enterprises in this market (UNIDO, 2002). Nigeria's small-scale leather and textile production locations are generally formed in clusters around the country. While the nature and location of the leather and textile clusters differ, there are some systemic conditions and challenges common to both sectors, regarding mainly the legal and policy environment under which they operate. Beyond these lie distinct circumstances and attributes that may influence the feasibility of communal trademarks differently in the different locations.

Textile production is indigenous to the western part of Nigeria, which hosts the largest cluster of small-scale textile production in the country. This area is home to the Yoruba people, for whom textile production has historical, cultural and economic significance (Akinbogun and Ogunduyile, 2009; Maiwada *et al.*, 2012). The indigenous textile products of Nigeria are exported as raw material or sold and used locally to produce other items such as dresses, handbags and bedspreads for export. The textile industries in Nigeria are facing stiff competition from foreign markets (Ogunnaike, 2010, p. 32), and the survival in the global market of indigenous modes of textile production is under threat.

The Nigerian leather industry has two dimensions: leather tanneries and leather accessories. The tanneries are clustered in the northern regions of Nigeria, where livestock rearing is prevalent. Odularu (2008) notes that "Nigeria is internationally efficient in goat and sheep skin leather exports", with the red skin goat of unique quality highly coveted by foreign markets (USAID, 2002). Odularu further observed that exports in these products accounted for less than 1% of total exports in 2003. This suggests "that further development of the sector could result in [increased market access] for these products" (Odularu, p. 88). Makers of leather-based accessories and finished products are also located in the Northern region and in the cities of Lagos, Onitsha and Aba.

3. The research

The study aimed to investigate the feasibility of using communal trademarks to promote quality, competitiveness and market access of leather and textile products produced by small entities in Nigeria. The investigation focused on:

- analysis of the framework for the protection of communal trademarks;
- identification of specific challenges faced by the producers that could be addressed through use of communal trademarks; and
- identification of potential challenges to the use of communal trademarks.

The study consisted of desktop research combined with a field work component that used a survey questionnaire and interviews. Leather and textile producers were chosen for study because of the socio-economic relevance of these sectors in relation to employment generation and poverty alleviation. In the case of textiles, their economic importance is inherent in the fact that Nigeria hosts whole sectors devoted to textile production, which are unique to the country. Second, the unique African fabrics and materials have distinctive local and international appeal. Third, the manual, family-based and other operators in the sector who apply traditional knowledge (TK) in the production processes have to contend with stiff competition and strong standards in the international market. This creates barriers to market access that would seem to make intervention necessary. A 2006 technical report on textile certification under the African Growth and Opportunity Act (AGOA) noted that although AGOA's Category 9 scheme for qualifying folkloric textile products represented an attempt to encourage exports of small-scale, handmade folklore articles and ethnic printed fabrics, it often proved difficult to provide the historical and cultural documentation required to place a garment under Category 9 (WATH, 2006).

Interviews were conducted in person and via telephone. The interviewees were key personnel of stakeholder institutions in government and industry working on matters related to the textile and leather sectors. Questionnaires were then distributed to textile and leather enterprises using cluster sampling of small enterprises – mostly micro and cottage enterprises. The selection of the clusters for the study was narrowed by the existence of previous studies that provided basic background on the two sectors (UNIDO, 2002, 2003; USAID, 2002). Three cluster groups in three localities were surveyed via the questionnaires: leather shoemakers in Aba; local textile producers in Itoku-Abeokuta; and leather tanners in Kano.

In Aba, the shoe manufacturers are located in delineated zones hosting manufacturers specialising in respective leather-based accessories, mainly shoes, bags, boxes and belts. The shoemakers are located in four contiguous zones, and the study focused on three of these zones hosting over 100 shoe lines: Shoe Plaza with 41 lines, Bakassi Zone with 80 lines (with approximately 50% specialising in leather shoes) and Imo Avenue, which also specialises in leather shoes. Figure 5.1 shows the structure of the Aba shoe cluster in relation to two of the three zones studied (Bakassi Zone and Imo Avenue), in which stakeholders include: a national association, a state association (at Abia State level), the two zonal associations, product lines under each zone (coordinated by union structures), and then the individual shops.

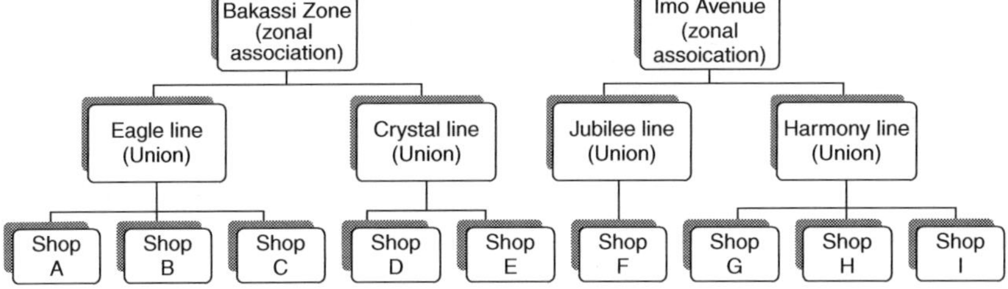

Figure 5.1: Typical structure of organisation in the Aba cluster (Bakassi and Imo Avenue zones)

Sources: As described to the authors by the interviewed executives of the zonal associations and unions of the Aba cluster; additional information from UNIDO (2003).

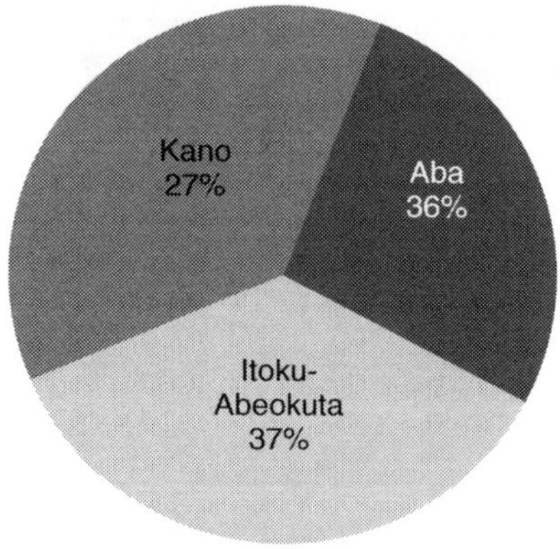

Figure 5.2: Percentage breakdown of the 120 responses across three clusters

Source: Authors' data analysis.

The three Aba zonal associations – Bakassi Zone, Imo Avenue and Shoe Plaza – were selected because they are adjoining groups forming a larger cluster; their leadership was cooperative and receptive to the investigation; and they all specialise in leather shoes.

A total of 170 questionnaires were distributed to individuals selected randomly in the three clusters studied: 60 questionnaires in Aba, 60 in Itoku-Abeokuta and 50 in Kano. The ultimate criterion for selecting the respondents was their position as line leaders and consequently leaders of the respective unions organised horizontally across each cluster at the lowest level (Figure 5.1). Of the 170 questionnaires distributed, 120 were completed and returned. Of the 120 completed questionnaires 36% came from Aba, 37% from Itoku-Abeokuta and 27% from Kano (see Figure 5.2).

The study's field-work findings were based on data drawn from the 120 questionnaires and from interviews with representatives of key stakeholders, including the Standards Organisation of Nigeria (SON), the Manufacturers Association of Nigeria (MAN), the Bank of Industry (BoI), the Nigerian Export Promotion Council, the Trademarks Registry, the country office of the UN Industrial Development Organisation (UNIDO Nigeria) and the US Agency for International Development (USAID).

4. Findings

Legal and regulatory framework

Trademarks are protected in Nigeria under the Trade Marks Act of 1965 (Cap.T13 LFN 2004). Of the three models of communal trademarks under consideration in this study, only certification marks are specifically covered in the Act, under Sections 43 and 67. The procedure for the registration of certification marks is contained in the First Schedule to the Act. Collective marks and GIs cannot be registered in Nigeria in terms of the Act. It can be argued, however, that Section 43 of the Act allows the registration of GIs as a kind of certification mark that distinguishes the product by origin.The Act's Section 43(1) discusses certification marks as follows:

> A mark adapted in relation to any goods to distinguish in the course of trade goods certified by any person in respect of region, material, method of manufacture, quality, accuracy or other characteristic, from goods not so certified, shall be registrable as a certification trade mark in Part A of the register in respect of those goods in the name, as proprietor thereof, of that person: provided that a mark shall not be so registrable in the name of a person who carries on a trade in goods of the kind certified. (Sect. 43(1))

This issue of GI registration has not been tested in court, and thus the lack of specific provisions for GIs constitutes a present limitation to the options available to producers and businesses contemplating use of communal trademarks in Nigeria.

Regarding international protection, Nigeria is a signatory to the WTO Agreement on Trade-Related Aspects of Intellectual Property Rights (TRIPS) and the Paris Convention for the Protection of Industrial Property (Paris Convention). Nigeria has not, however, ratified the Madrid Agreement Concerning the International Registration of Marks and the Protocol Relating to the Madrid Agreement Concerning the International Registration of Marks. Unlike the TRIPS Agreement, which can potentially be enforced in Nigeria, the Paris Convention remains unenforceable in Nigeria in the absence of domestication by the National Assembly. Nigeria ratified the Paris Convention in 1963 but is yet to domesticate it as required by Section 12 of the 1999 Constitution. Article 2 of TRIPS imposes an obligation on State Parties to apply the standards and obligations of the Paris Convention relating to trademarks. Thus, it can be said that the provisions of the Paris Convention regarding trademarks also apply *mutatis mutandis* to the TRIPS Agreement and so should be read together. Apart from GIs, no express provision is made for the protection of communal marks as such in TRIPS. However, this can be implied from the tone of Article 2 – which consequentially incorporates Article 7*bis* of the Paris Convention protecting collective marks – and Article 15(1). Article 15(1) of TRIPS defines the subject matter of protection broadly and accommodates collective marks to the extent that they are "signs or a combination of signs, capable of distinguishing the goods or services of one undertaking from those of other undertakings" (TRIPS, Art. 15(1); Pires de Carvalho, 2011, p. 293). However, with regard to certification marks, neither TRIPS nor the Paris

Convention appears to offer them any protection (Pires de Carvalho, 2011). Both TRIPS (Part II, Sect. 3) and the Paris Convention protect GIs as *sui generis* IP rights and appellations of origin distinct from trademarks. Article 1(2) of the Paris Convention includes "indications of source" and "appellations of origins" as protectable subjects. The treaties define GIs as indications which identify goods as originating in the territory of a Member, or a region or locality in that territory, where a given quality, reputation or other characteristic of the good is essentially attributable to its geographical origin. Indication of source means any expression or sign used to indicate that a product or service originates in a country, a region or a specific place, while an appellation of origin is the geographical name of a country, region or locality, which serves to designate a product originating therein, the quality and characteristics of which are due exclusively or essentially to the geographic environment, including natural and human factors. Thus, both geographical indications and appellations of origin require that there must be a link between the product and the place designated. However, while appellations of origin require that such link be attributable to the quality or characteristics derivable from the environment, geographical indications extend the basis for the link to reputation, i.e. public perceptions, impressions and expectations about a good and its geographical origin (Oyewunmi, 2012). (See Chapter 4 in this volume for discussion of GIs in relation to the Ethiopian coffee and Ghanaian cocoa sectors.)

With the exception of certification marks, Nigeria has a substandard national legal framework for the protection of communal trademarks. Failure to ratify the Madrid Protocol also undermines protection of a successful Nigerian trademark against international infringement outside the borders of Nigeria. The Madrid Protocol facilitates multiple registrations of trademarks in different countries by providing an international procedural mechanism whereby a single application filed and registered with a national or regional trademark office has effect in each of the countries designated by the applicant. Non-ratification of the Madrid Protocol therefore deprives Nigerian citizens of the benefits of a system intended to eliminate the inconvenience of having to file trademark applications in other countries where protection is desired. Meanwhile, in other countries, there is evidence of increasing recognition of communal trademarks as instruments for facilitation of trade and economic development from grassroots level upward. Since the 1990s, India, South Africa and the UK have all recognised the benefits of communal trademarks by amending their laws accordingly.

The success of a communal trademark would also depend to a great extent on assurance of quality. The Standards Organisation of Nigeria Act of 1970 regulates standards of locally produced textiles and leather, with the Standards Organisation of Nigeria (SON) administering the Act. SON's major responsibility is to prepare and enforce standards related to products in the formal and informal sectors, and its work is mainly targeted at protecting consumers from "locally manufactured sub-standard and/or unsafe products, which do not meet the minimum requirements of the relevant" standards, and by so doing, generating "confidence in Made-in-Nigeria products" (SON, n.d.). SON requirements for textile and leather products are, however, not standardised. On the contrary, standards are fixed on a case-by-case basis. It was also found in the course of the research that SON was not enforcing standards requirements on small-scale manufacturers of leather and textile products – apparently (according to the interviewed SON officials themselves) on the grounds that SON did not want to discourage enterprises that would be unable to satisfy such standards. At the same time, only 7% of the survey respondents were aware of the existence of government regulatory standards.

Existing cluster dynamics

Standard-setting initiatives were found to be lacking at the industry level in all three clusters surveyed. In a few cases, local unions and associations were attempting some measure of self-regulation by requiring the registration of individual products and mandating the use of specified materials in production. However, nearly a third of the respondents stated that they did not work within the specifications of any externally set standard requirement (see Figure 5.3).

Industry operatives at associations and unions did, however, express a willingness to implement standards requirements to enhance the businesses under their associations or any other competent body. In fact, where they exist, standards imposed by unions are strongly adhered to and enforced. This suggests that

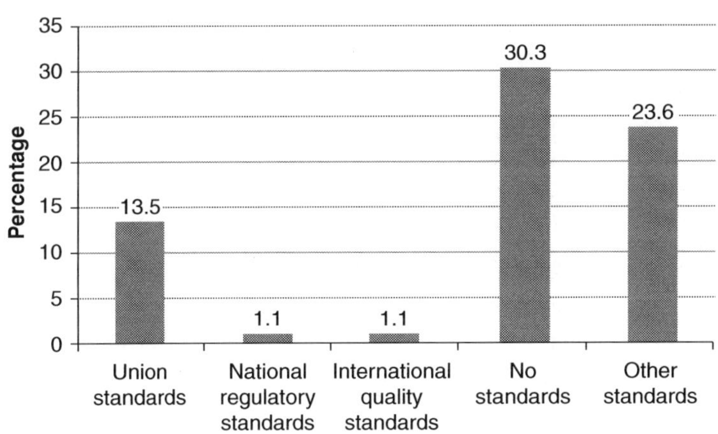

Figure 5.3: Respondent adherence to standards

Source: Authors' data analysis.

if standards were introduced at a higher level and in an appropriate manner, they would be respected. Without high-level standardisation, the goods in question cannot exhibit an assurance of quality, creating potential challenges to establishing and nurturing a successful certification or collective marks system. However, at the same time, implementation of standardisation could potentially create strong incentives for the use of certification marks by manufacturers, and could trigger government interest and support.

The success of a communal trademark system also requires the existence of an institution embodying ownership of the mark (UNIDO, 2010, p. 2). For the Aba cluster (see Figure 5.1), organisational infrastructure was found to exist, while the Itoku-Abeokuta and Kano clusters were found to have less (but still some) organisational structure. The Itoku-Abeokuta cluster, for instance, had an association of textile producers consisting mainly of the traders in the Itoku-Abeokuta market. The existing organisational bodies in all three clusters were providing administrative support, dispute settlement and disciplinary functions to their members – therefore signifying an existing system and a ready-made platform that could be harnessed to build a communal trademarks system at the market level. The Aba cluster was noteworthy here. It was found that in the Aba cluster, it was standard practice for there to be registration of labels and designs with the Aba unions (as protection from copying by other members of the union). The Aba unions were also providing support services and assistance in the form of finance and logistics to their members. The unions were formulating rules to protect the individual and collective interests of their members and were enforcing these rules.

One of the major potential challenges to adoption of a communal trademark by the Aba cluster was found to be the apparent lack of unity in the management structure. It was found that market leaders were prone to fragmentation and rivalry, due to competing interests. However, in the Itoku-Abeokuta cluster (unlike the Aba cluster), management fragmentation was not apparent. The traders' association in Itoku-Abeokuta was found to have a well-respected executive, headed by its Iya Oloja (executive head), which met regularly as a team. The Iya Oloja also held periodic meetings with the traders to discuss issues of common interest, to disseminate information, and to try to foster communal wellbeing in the market. The Itoku-Abeokuta cluster was therefore found to present an environment potentially more suited than the Aba cluster to successful implementation of communal trademarks. Unlike among the Aba respondents (where some misgivings were registered), the Itoku-Abeokuta respondents expressed confidence in their executive team to liaise with authorities to explore possible processes for establishing and using communal trademarks.

Existing knowledge of IP

It was clear from the data gathered that knowledge of trademarks was poor at all levels in the three clusters surveyed. But for a few ordinary (non-communal) trademarks officially registered in accordance with the Nigerian Trade Marks Act in the Kano leather tannery sector, and the printing of business names on packaging bags for textiles at Itoku-Abeokuta, there was a total absence of IP protection for the designs of the clusters surveyed. There were no instances found of registration of a communal trademark.[2] Design theft was found to be endemic in the clusters and a cause of concern for many. While entrepreneurs in Aba were seeking to protect their designs or labels by registering them with their local unions, this provided only limited protection – as it only extended to those operating within the jurisdiction of the unions. It was found that non-union members often copied such registered designs without incurring repercussions or liability from the registered owner.

Most of the respondents across the three clusters struggled to conceive of a suitable communal trademark. Meanwhile, only 12.2% had their businesses registered with the relevant government agencies. Despite the lack of existing knowledge of communal trademark modalities, the majority of respondents expressed willingness to participate in any collaborative trademarking strategy targeted towards standardising quality and price and improving market access. Roughly 80% of respondents favoured a model that would permit the use of common marks in addition to their personal packaging designs and labels.

Market challenges

It was found that the Kano leather tanners and Aba shoemakers produced for both local markets and markets in neighbouring countries. The Aba shoemakers sampled claimed to have clients both domestically and in neighbouring countries, with more than half of the leather products from Aba designated for export. But the Kano and Aba products were generally not performing well in these markets, in spite of the distinctiveness of some of the products, e.g. products made from red goat skin. The Itoku-Abeokuta textile enterprises surveyed said they had a diversified clientele, both within and beyond the African continent. Across the three clusters, 95.5% of respondents identified competition from foreign products –

2 At the same time, it must be noted that the study was not sufficiently in-depth as to be able to make a categorical conclusion that there is no single instance of registration of a communal trademark in Nigeria under the Trade Marks Act, with the greatest challenge in confirming this position being the lack of a proper and organised database for registered trademarks in Nigeria. This study was also not able to draw conclusions regarding the volume of use of unregistered trademarks.

particularly those from China – as being harmful to their business. They stated that, while local products were usually of higher quality than Chinese imports in terms of the materials used and the craftsmanship, Chinese-made products were cheaper and more aesthetically appealing in design and finishing, thus making them more attractive to customers. Most respondents felt that to remain competitive in this environment, local products would have to compete more favourably in terms of both price and design.

More than 75% of respondents indicated that they faced challenges in producing their goods to their desired specifications. The challenges identified in the Aba and Kano clusters included the high cost of quality raw materials, lack of expertise and equipment, lack of capital and lack of basic infrastructure. The problem of raw materials was particularly significant to the study. The field results indicated that local producers of leather and textiles used mostly (60%) high-cost international raw materials, and only 40% locally sourced materials. This revealed the potentially strategic position for Aba shoemakers of the leather tanning sector in Nigeria (e.g. in Kano) should it in the future be able to provide higher-quality materials to local manufacturers of leather products.

The research found that there were no dynamic marketing strategies in place in any of the three clusters. Manufacturers relied on marketing strategies with limited impact, such as simple displays of their products and offering customers business cards. The majority of respondents of the Aba cluster argued that one reason they did not want to advertise was because it would encourage further copying of their designs. As outlined above, even in cases where designs were registered with a union, protection was still lacking when an infringer was not a member of the union. It seemed clear that this area – design protection – was one in which the synergies provided by communal trademarks could be potentially useful.

Less than 50% of respondents shared their labels or designs with others. Nevertheless, many respondents expressed a willingness to be more open with their creative works if these were better protected. Respondents feared the absence of an efficacious framework that would protect their uniquely developed designs and labels from unfair competition. There was a strong impression that the absence of protection against infringement discourages serious investment in design and quality improvement. In the Itoku-Abeokuta textile cluster, members expressed strong interest in promoting their communal interests by association with high-quality, unique, handmade tie-and-dye products. They also expressed a willingness to share designs with fellow operators in their cluster – as the copying they opposed was the unacknowledged copying of their designs by clusters in other parts of the country and by international manufacturers.

Leather and shoe manufacturers in Aba reported that they distinguished their products from competitors mainly by using higher-quality materials and implementing unique designs. Unfortunately, the Aba respondents said, their consumers (middlemen traders) generally preferred foreign labels. As a result, the manufacturers said they often marked their products with false foreign labels, thus compounding the existing problem – because consumers then attributed whatever satisfaction they derived from the use of the product to a misleading origin.

5. Conclusions

Small-scale operators engaged in the production and manufacture of leather and textile goods in Nigeria hold great potential for improved economic performance, but they face myriad challenges. Key among these challenges is market access, both locally and internationally. Based on the findings of this research study, we are of the view that one of the tools with potential to ameliorate the market position of the three producer clusters studied is the use of communal trademarks (i.e. certification marks, collective marks and/or GIs).

The findings indicate that the use of communal trademarks could be feasible in the clusters investigated. One respondent aptly described the potential direct benefits of group identification as follows: "We will look out for each other's interests, and [at the same time] the competition will lead to high quality standards even within the group" (interviewee, 2012).With a communal trademark arrangement in place, areas of collaboration could include marketing and branding, enforcement of rights, and accessing credit facilities. For example, a properly conceptualised communal trademark with positive, far-reaching reputation could gain acceptance as security for loans to its adherents, thus opening up a new vista in Nigeria in the area of securitisation of intangibles. More generally, the successful implementation of a communal trademark could have many economic and social benefits, including increased income levels and livelihood opportunities for the large and growing percentage of the population made up of young Nigerians.

Of particular potential for implementation of a communal trademark among the three clusters studied was, in our view, the Itoku-Abeokuta textiles cluster. We saw above that this cluster had an orderly and respected management structure, and in this cluster there appeared to be clear incentives towards adoption of a communal trademark in order to, *inter alia,* distinguish the handmade original tie-and-dye brands from the imitation machine-made brands; to safeguard the indigenous art and TK of local people; to protect consumers from confusion and deception; and to ensure that the industry is protected against unfair competition.[3] The Itoku-Abeokuta cluster could deploy a GI or other kind of communal trademark to foster a collective identity and image and to promote Itoku-Abeokuta as the home of genuine handmade tie-and-dye. A communal trademark would also safeguard the integrity of their products – against counterfeiters who sell cheap, non-durable products – as original Itoku-Abeokuta tie-and-dye.

If a communal trademark model is pursued, it must be appropriate to the particular producer or manufacturer group. For the Itoku-Abeokuta textile cluster, a GI would seem to be the most appropriate kind of communal trademark, because of the cluster's deployment of traditional methods of production handed down through (mostly maternal) lineage specific to the locality. This strong localised TK element gives the Itoku-Abeokua products a unique quality that distinguishes them from textile products of different origins or produced by different methods. For this cluster, a GI could solidify the pedigree generated by the longstanding production in this locality – production which has led to positive reputation in both local and foreign markets. In contrast to the Itoku-Abeokuta cluster, the Aba cluster would seem well-suited to the existing legal framework of certification marks in Nigeria (the framework which does not at present appear to protect GI-based communal trademarks). Aba-made shoes lack a common geographical quality, but manufacturers possess individual quality standards and creativity that distinguish their designs – thus potentially making a non-GI certification mark more suitable to these manufacturers (i.e. based on a strong desire to standardise quality and distinguish their products via quality standards).

Crucially, there is a clear need for law reform in Nigeria to expand protection to all three main communal trademark models – certification marks, collective marks, and GIs – and to this end it is in Nigeria's interest to ratify the Madrid Treaty (so as to protect any Nigerian mark in regional and international markets). As one respondent stated,

> [...] when it comes to protection, we really do not have any body or institution looking out for our interests in those foreign lands and as such, anything can happen. The solution will be to register the products in the various international markets for easy identification and protection. (Interviewee, 2012)

This underscores the need for Nigeria to ratify the Madrid Treaty and amend its laws accordingly. As far as the law is concerned, the process of effecting the necessary amendments to the Nigerian Trade Marks Act to bolster protection of

3 These incentives suggest a public interest rationale for a communal trademark, thus satisfying the "public interest" condition specified as required for the registration of a certification mark under the Nigerian Trade Marks Act (First Schedule, Para. 5).

communal trademarks does not appear to raise extra costs or externalities. The law will likely be amended regardless of whether communal trademarks are contemplated. Short-term cost issues have the potential to present a challenge to producers, in the form of fees for registration procedures and professional services. However, there is reason to believe that these costs could be offset by long-term growth and development of the affected sectors. The introduction of a common trademarks system within the existing Economic Community of West African States (ECOWAS) trading bloc (of which Nigeria is a member) would also be helpful, by establishing a common West African system for IP protection of textile and leather products. Such an initiative, as seen in other regions, could offer valuable legal and institutional platforms for the establishment and West African enforcement of communal trademark models.

In addition, a detailed cost-benefit analysis (which was beyond the scope of this exploratory study) is required before any producer group embarks on the process of establishing a communal trademark.

A successful mark depends on public confidence and a positive reputation. SON is not at present enforcing standards in the market, and while this may in the short term seem to benefit the producers, in the long term it will be detrimental to the growth and development of the sectors. Collaborative efforts are needed between SON and cluster leaders to determine the best approach to establish and implement standards. If standards enforcement is implemented in a uniform, fair and transparent manner, cluster operators can be expected to bear the initial financial strain based on the promise of quality standardisation and market growth.

Beyond IP and standardisation matters, there is a need to address factors leading to the high cost of production. Policies are needed to minimise the manufacturing costs of local manufacturers, so that they can compete with imported products in terms of quality and price. For example, the leather tanneries in Kano need to be positioned for greater competitiveness, and promoting local production of cotton would help to lower textile input costs and generate additional employment.

In addition, the product producers and manufacturers need to become better informed, e.g. about existing financial support facilities and schemes, such as those provided by the Bank of Industry (BoI) and SON. SON provides Duty Drawback Schemes in collaboration with other government agencies (namely, the Nigerian Export Promotion Council, the Nigerian Customs Service and the Central Bank) through which importers may claim repayment of import duty paid for material used in the production of local goods that are exported. The scheme is established to provide relief for producers of various export goods (including leather and textile goods).There is a need for the relevant bodies to assist the manufacturers in benefiting from such schemes.

Bibliography

Primary sources

Legal instruments

International:

African Growth and Opportunity Act (AGOA) (2000).

Agreement on the Application of Sanitary and Phytosanitary Measures (SPS) 1867 UNTS 493 (1994).

Agreement on Technical Barriers to Trade (TBT), 1868 UNTS 120(1994).

Agreement on Trade-Related Aspects of Intellectual Property Rights (TRIPS) (1994).

Madrid Agreement Concerning the International Registration of Marks (1891, as amended on 28 September 1979).

Paris Convention for the Protection of Industrial Property (Paris Convention) (1883, as revised at Stockholm on 14 July 1967, and as amended on September 28, 1979).

Protocol Relating to the Madrid Agreement Concerning the International Registration of Marks (1989, and as amended on 12 November 2007).

Nigeria:

Standards Organisation of Nigeria Act of 1970 (Cap. S9 LFN 2004).

Trade Marks Act of 1965 (Cap. T13 LFN 2004).

Cases

Hanover Star Milling Co. v Metcalf, 240 US 403, 412 (1916); *Ferodo Ltd v Ibeto Ind. Ltd* (2004) 5 *Nigerian Weekly Law Report* (*NWLR*) Pt. 866 at 317–347.

Secondary sources

Abdullah, N. (2010), "Inside Ghana's collapsing textile industries", *Sunday Trust Magazine,* 20 June, available at: http://sundaytrust.com.ng/index.php/feature/3209-inside-ghanas-collapsing-textile-industry (accessed 10 April 2013).

Abor, J. and Quartey, P. (2010), "Issues in SME development in Ghana and South Africa", *International Research Journal of Finance and Economics,* No. 39, pp. 218–28.

Adeyemo J. and Bankole, S. (2003), "Standards, technical regulations, and product quality: institutional evidence from Nigeria", in *Standards and Global Trade: A Voice for Africa,* World Bank, Washington, DC.

Adjasi, C. K. and Kinful, E. (2008), "Trade policies and development in Africa: the Doha development agenda, the EU EPAs and ECOWAS", paper presented at "Future of Global Economy", the Eleventh Annual Conference on Global Economic Analysis, 12–14 June, Helsinki.

Akinbogun, T.L. and Ogunduyile, S.R. (2009), "Crafts engagement in the economic survival of South-Western Nigerian rural women", *Journal of Enterprising Communities: People and Places in the Global Economy,* Vol. 3 No. 2, pp. 217–34.

Aldaz-Carroll, E. (2006), *Regional Approaches to Better Standards Systems,* World Bank Policy Research Working Paper No. 3948, available at: http://ssrn.com/abstract=923255 (accessed 10 April 2013).

Amakon, U. (2006), *Export Constraints of the Kano Leather Industry: A Study of Industrial Clusters in Nigeria,* Department of Economics, Nnamdi Azikiwe University, Awka, Nigeria available at: www.csae.ox.ac.uk/conferences/2007-EDiA-LaWBiDC/papers/050-Amakom.pdf (accessed 10 April 2013).

Ayankunle, T. (2011), "Only 10 SMEs, 270 firms have ISO certification", *The Nation,* 1 December, available at: www.thenationonlineng.net/2011/index.php/author/Tunde/(accessed 10 April 2013).

Azinge, E. (Ed.) (2011), *A Book of Communiques: 2011 Roundtables of the Nigerian Institute of Advanced Legal Studies,* NIALS, Lagos.

Belson, J. (2002), *Certification Marks,* Sweet and Maxwell, London.

Briggs, I. N. (2007), *Nigeria: Mainstreaming Trade Policy into National Development Policies,* African Trade Policy Centre (ATPC) Work in Progress No. 52, UN Economic Commission for Africa (UNECA), Addis Ababa.

Central Bank of Nigeria (CBN) (2012), *2011 Annual Report,* available at: www.cenbank.org/Out/2012/publications/reports/rsd/arp-2011/Table%20of%20Contents%20and%20Summary.pdf (accessed 10 April 2013).

Chuma-Okoro, H. (2011), "The trade and environment nexus: issues for Nigeria as a developing economy", *NIALS Journal of Environmental Law,* No. 1, pp. 230–65.

Cordero, P., Sepulveda, S. and Rodriguez, A. (2008), *Trade and Environment Issues: Rural Development Technical Handbook No. 25,* Inter-American Institute for Cooperation on Agriculture (IICA), San Jose, Costa Rica.

Cornish, W.R. and Llewelyn, D. (2003), *Intellectual Property: Patents, Copyright, Trade Marks and Allied Rights,* 5th ed., Sweet and Maxwell, London.

Economic Community of West African States (ECOWAS) (2008), *ECOWAS Handbook on International Trade,* Lagos.

European Commission (EC) (n.d.), *The New SME Definition: User Guide and Model Declaration,* EC Enterprise and Industry Publication, available at: http://ec.europa.eu/enterprise/policies/sme/files/sme_definition/sme_user_guide_en.pdf (accessed 10 April 2013).

Ganguli, P. (2009), "Geographical indications ... its [sic] evolving contours", SVKM's NMIMS University Institute of Intellectual Property Studies, available at: http://iips.nmims.edu/files/2012/05/main_book.pdf (accessed 10 April 2013).

Graber, C.B. and Lai, J.C. (2011), *Indigenous Cultural Heritage and Fair Trade – Voluntary Certification Standards in the Light of WIPO and WTO Law and Policymaking*, Working Paper No. 1, University of Lucerne, Switzerland.

International Finance Corporation (IFC), (2012), *Interpretation Note on Small and Medium Enterprises and Environmental and Social Risk Management*, available at: www1.ifc.org/wps/wcm/connect/de7d92804a29ffe9ae04af8969adcc27/InterpretationNote_SME_2012.pdf?MOD=AJPERES (accessed 10 April 2013).

Janke, T. (2003), *Studies on Intellectual Property and Traditional Cultural Expressions*, Study No. 1, World Intellectual Property Organisation (WIPO), Geneva.

Khatun, F. (2009), *Environmental Related Trade Barriers and the WTO*, CPD Occasional Paper Series 77, Centre for Policy Dialogue (CPD), Dhaka.

Kitchin, D., Llewelyn, D., Mellor. J., Meade, R., Moody-Stuart, T., Keeling, D. and Jacob, R. (2005), *Kerly's Law of Trademarks and Trade Names*, 4th ed., Sweet and Maxwell, London.

Kowalski, S.P. (2009). "SMEs, open innovation and IP management: advancing global development", presentation to WIPO-Italy International Convention on Intellectual Property and Competitiveness of Micro, Small and Medium-Sized Enterprises (MSMEs), 10-11 December, Rome, available at: www.wipo.int/edocs/mdocs/sme/en/wipo_smes_rom_09/wipo_smes_rom_09_b_theme02_2.pdf (accessed 10 April 2013).

Kozak, M. (2007), *Micro, Small and Medium Enterprises: A Collection of Published Data*, International Finance Corporation (IFC), Washington, DC.

Landes, W. M. and Posner, R. A. (1987), "Trademark law: an economic perspective", *Journal of Law and Economics*, Vol. 30, pp. 265–309.

Leaffer, M.A. (1998), "The new world of international trademark law", *Marquette Intellectual Property Law Review*, Vol. 2 No.1, pp. 1–31.

Maiwada, S., Dutsenwai, S. and Waziri, M. (2012), "Cultural industries and wealth creation: the case of traditional textile industry in Nigeria", *American International Journal of Contemporary Research*, Vol. 2 No. 5, pp. 159–65.

Mark, M. (2012), "African fashion week: Lagos event set to become fixture of global style calendar", *The Guardian*, 12 March, available at: www.guardian.co.uk/world/2012/mar/12/africa-arise-fashion-week-lagos (accessed 10 April 2013).

Njoku, U.A.A. (2004), *Marketability of Made in Nigeria Textile Materials*, available at: http://stclements.edu/grad/gradnjok.pdf (accessed 10 April 2013).

Obasanjo, O. (2000), *Obasanjo's Economic Direction 1999–2003*, Office of the Honourable Minister of Economic Matters, Nigeria.

Odularu, G.O. (2008), *Nigeria-US Trade Relations in the Non-Oil Sector*, Dissertation. com, Florida.

Ogunnaike, O. (2010), "Nigerians' perception of locally made products: a study on textile fabrics consumers in Kaduna State", *Petroleum-gas University of Ploiesti Bulletin*, Vol. 62 No.1, pp. 30–6.

Olajide, D.M., Ajiboye, O.J. and Ajayi, B.J. (2009), "Áso-Oke production and use among the Yoruba of South Western Nigeria", *The Journal of Pan African Studies*, Vol. 3 No 3, p 55.

Olaoye, R.A. (2005), "Cloth talks: study of cloth among the Yoruba in Nigeria", *Africa Update Newsletter*, Vol. 12 No. 3, http://web.ccsu.edu/afstudy/upd12-3.html (accessed 10 April 2013).

Osotimehin, K.O., Jegede, C., Akinlabi, B.H. and Olajide, O.T. (2012), "An evaluation of the challenges and prospects of micro and small scale enterprises development in Nigeria", *American International Journal of Contemporary Research*, Vol. 2 No. 4, pp. 174–85.

Oyewunmi A.O. (2012), "Environmental sustainability, intellectual property and socio-economic development in Africa: what role for geographical indications?" *NIALS Journal of Environmental Law*, Vol. 2, pp. 32–66.

Pires de Carvalho, N. (2011), *The TRIPS Regime of Trademarks and Designs*, Kluwer Law International, Alphen aan den Rijn, Netherlands.

Quartey, P. (2006), "The textile and clothing industry in Ghana, 2006", in Jauch, H. and Traub-Merz, R. (Eds), *The Future of the Textile and Clothing Industry in Sub-Saharan Africa*, Friedrich Ebert Stiftung (FES), available at: http://library.fes.de/pdf-files/iez/03796/10ghana.pdf (accessed 10 April 2013).

Reynolds, B.J. (2007), *Branding for Success: Trademark Law, Product Certifications Important to Many Cooperatives*, available at: www.rurdev.usda.gov/rbs/pub/mar07/content.htm (accessed 10 April 2013).

Standards Organisation of Nigeria (SON) (n.d.), "About Us" and "MANCAP", available at: www.son.gov.ng (accessed 15 September 2013).

Udechukwu F.N. (2003), "Survey of small and medium scale industries and their potentials in Nigeria", in *Central Bank of Nigeria Seminar on Small and Medium Industries Equity Investments Scheme (SMIEIS)*, Central Bank of Nigeria (CBN) Training Center, Lagos, pp. 1–14.

UN Conference on Trade and Development (UNCTAD) (1997a), *Elements of the Positive Agenda on the SPS Agreement*, Geneva.

UN Conference on Trade and Development (UNCTAD) (1997b), *Opportunities for Vertical Diversification in the Food Processing Sector in Developing Countries*, available at: www.unctad.org/en/docs/c1em2d3.en.pdf (accessed 10 April 2013).

UN Conference on Trade and Development (UNCTAD) (2004), "Environmental requirements and market access for developing countries", Note by the

UNCTAD Secretariat, TD (XI) BP/1, available at: www.unctad.org/en/docs/tdxibpd1_en.pdf (accessed 10 April 2013).

UN Conference on Trade and Development (UNCTAD) (2008), *Handbook of Statistics*, Geneva.

UN Conference on Trade and Development (UNCTAD) (2009), *Investment Policy Review Nigeria*, available at: www.unctad.org/en/docs/diaepcb20081_en.pdf (accessed 10 April 2013).

UN Economic and Social Commission for Asia and the Pacific (UNESCAP) (2009), *Globalisation of Production and the Competitiveness of Small and Medium-Sized Enterprises in Asia and the Pacific: Trends and Prospects*, available at: www.unescap.org/tid/publication.tipub2540.pdf (accessed 10 April 2013).

UN Environment Programme (UNEP) (2005), *Environment and Trade: A UNEP Handbook*, 2nd ed., International Institute for Sustainable Development (IISD), Geneva.

UN Industrial Development Organisation (UNIDO) (2002), *Hides and Skins Improvement in Northern Nigeria,* Technical Report prepared for the Government of Nigeria, UNIDO SF/NIR/01/E01, Vienna.

UN Industrial Development Organisation (UNIDO) (2003), *Assistance to the Leather Industry Cluster in Aba,* UNIDO SF/NIR/01/D01, available at: www.unido.org/fileadmin/import/32799_BergRep1a.pdf (accessed 10 April 2013).

UN Industrial Development Organisation (UNIDO) (2010), *Adding Value to Traditional Product of Regional Origin: A Guide to Creating a Regional Consortium*, available at: www.unido.org/fileadmin/user_media/Publications/Pub_free/Adding_value_to_traditional_products_of_regional_origin.pdf (accessed 26 August 2012).

US Agency for International Development (USAID) (2002), *Subsector Assessment of the Nigerian Hides and Skins Industry,* available at: http://pdf.usaid.gov/pdf_docs/PNACY673.pdf (accessed 10 April 2013).

West Africa Trade Hub (WATH) (2006), *Export of Handloomed Textiles and Folkloric Articles: A Guide for Obtaining Category 9 Certification as Required by the African Growth and Opportunity Act (AGOA),* WATH Technical Report No. 12, January, available at: http://www.agoatoolkit.com/agoa/English/Export%20Guides/27-Guide%20for%20obtaining%209%20Category%20Certification.pdf (accessed 10 April 2013).

Wong, T. and Dutfield, G. (Eds) (2011), *Intellectual Property and Human Development: Current Trends and Future Scenarios,* Cambridge University Press, Cambridge, UK.

World Intellectual Property Organisation (WIPO) (2004), *WIPO Intellectual Property Handbook: Policy, Law and Use*, WIPO Publication No. 489(E), Geneva.

World Intellectual Property Organisation (WIPO) (2006), *Making a Mark: An Introduction to Trade Marks for Small and Medium Scale Enterprises,* Intellectual Property for Business Series No. 1, Geneva.

World Trade Organisation (WTO) (2005a), *Trade Policy Review: Nigeria Report by the Secretariat,* Document WT/TPR/S/147, Geneva.

World Trade Organisation (WTO) (2005b), *Trade Policy Review: Guinea Report by the Secretariat,* Document WT/PR/S/158, Geneva.

Chapter 6

The Policy Context for a Commons-Based Approach to Traditional Knowledge in Kenya

Marisella Ouma

Abstract

This chapter outlines research into the policy context for a commons approach to traditional knowledge (TK) in Kenya. The TK commons concept on which the research study was premised addresses protection, preservation, access, terms of use, licensing and benefit-sharing. The research examined the Constitution of Kenya, the National TK Policy, the Draft TK Bill, and intellectual property (IP) laws that provide a basis for a legal and policy framework for a TK commons in Kenya. The research sought to determine the degree to which existing law and policy in Kenya, along with reform proposals, have the potential to support a commons approach to TK management. The chapter assesses the degree to which such laws, policies and proposals might be able to protect the interests of indigenous and local communities (ILCs) in Kenya who hold TK, while at the same time promoting collaborative, networked "open development" objectives. The chapter argues that previous initiatives, such as a project to produce a digital archive documenting Maasai knowledge, have laid the groundwork for positive initiatives in support of a TK commons. However, a lack of collaboration between ILCs and Kenyan governmental organisations has left this potential unrealised. The chapter provides recommendations for, inter alia, *how to improve collaboration between government and ILCs.*

1. Introduction

Until recently, formal protection of intellectual property (IP) in African countries primarily addressed conventional IP – copyright, patents and trademarks. The emerging emphasis is on enforcement of IP according to minimum standards that have been set out in international instruments such as the World Trade Organisation (WTO) Agreement on Trade-Related Aspects of Intellectual

Property Rights (TRIPS). Against this backdrop, a fundamental question is whether existing IP policy frameworks facilitate open innovation and creativity in Africa. Of particular interest to this author, and the focus of this chapter, is the degree to which creativity and innovation in relation to a different form of IP, traditional knowledge (TK), is being catered for by IP policy instruments (Bergy, 2011).

There has tended to be a presumption that TK (including traditional cultural expressions [TCEs] and folklore, as well as traditional medicinal, ecological and other knowledge) is knowledge that is in the public domain and, thus, available to all. However, the reality is that indigenous and local communities (ILCs) who are the custodians of TK have systems of customs and taboos in place to ensure that certain TK is not made widely known, while at the same time is preserved and passed on from one generation to the next within the ILC. In the case of traditional medicine, for instance, specific families or persons, such as the *olaibon* among the Maasai in East Africa, hold knowledge and put it into practice. Such knowledge preservation systems can also be found in relation to genetic resources. In the case of music, specific composers within ILCs are often rewarded for their creativity by being recognised as custodians of the compositions. Certain forms of artwork and design often *belong* to certain members of ILCs. Many types of TK held by ILCs in Kenya, and in East Africa more generally, are thus kept within the custody of a selected few, to the exclusion of all others.

There is increasing interest in matters of law and policy in relation to TK, particularly TK in biological resources and in cultural goods. This heightened focus on TK policy is due to, among other things, evidence of increased commercialisation of TK in agricultural, pharmaceutical and cosmetic industries, as well as in creative industries such as visual art and design, performance and music. There have been numerous documented examples of third parties unscrupulously misappropriating TK, resulting in suspicion and mistrust between ILCs and third parties, posing obstacles to potentially beneficial partnerships.[1]

The need for appropriate policy instruments is twofold. On one hand, there is a need to limit practices whereby TK commercialisation takes place without the consent of the custodians or holders of the TK, and without benefits accruing to them (Tingoi, n.d.[a]). On the other hand, there is a need to ensure that the TK holders are able to exploit the knowledge to its full potential. TK is often not documented but passed on orally from generation to generation, and this can limit access to, or dissemination of, knowledge. In some cases, the TK can be lost forever.

1 For further reading, see Edmonds Institute and African Centre for Biosafety (2006) and Society for Critical Exchange (SCE) (2004).

Policy approaches are needed that can enhance ILCs' control over commercialisation and exploitation of their TK and restore ILCs' confidence in the communal spirit of TK-sharing. It is this author's view that legal policy instruments should seek to enhance communal approaches to TK protection and management, via enabling environments for documentation and value enhancement practices that can ensure the perpetuity and dynamism of ILCs' TK. One such approach would be to support formalisation of TK "commons" structures – structures whereby commonly held TK is shared and preserved within an ILC in a manner guided by an agreed instrument giving a measure of formality and enforceability to the ILC's TK commons.

Among the elements of the potential dynamism of TK that this author is concerned with is the potential for TK – when governed according to TK commons principles – to increasingly make information available to third parties for purposes not only of commercialisation and benefit-sharing, but also broader collaboration for socio-economic development – a collaborative developmental dynamic that has begun to be conceptualised in the development literature as "open development" (Smith *et al.*, 2011). The open development concept views networked, collaborative relationships – often enabled by information and communication technology (ICT) platforms – as integral to sustainable socio-economic development.

This chapter outlines the findings from a Kenyan research study into the degree to which Kenyan TK commons modalities are effectively catered for by existing international and Kenyan national legal and policy mechanisms. The study was premised on the assumption, grounded in the open development concept, that it is necessary to have a legal and policy environment for TK that can balance TK custodians' complex mix of social and economic needs (knowledge-sharing and preservation, knowledge protection, controlled knowledge exploitation and benefit-sharing) while at the same time fostering increased dynamism within the custodians' already-implicit TK commons – dynamism whereby TK-based creativity, innovation and open development can be optimised by the TK holders.

Among the contemporary commons-based approaches to TK are ICT-based efforts to digitally document TK in a manner that enhances preservation and equitable exploitation while at the same time encouraging follow-on innovation. In India, for instance, the Council of Scientific and Industrial Research (CSIR) has developed a digital database, the Traditional Knowledge Digital Library (TKDL), which captures information on India's existing TK. The information in the TKDL is used, among other things, by patent offices to verify applications based on Indian TK, especially in the area of pharmaceuticals.[2] This database model is currently under investigation by Kenyan government agencies.

2 For more information on India's TKDL, see Council of Scientific and Industrial Research (CSIR) (n.d.).

2. The research

The main research question the study sought to answer was: *How and to what extent does the Kenyan legal and policy environment cater to the creation and implementation of TK commons modalities conducive to open innovation and collaborative creativity?* The core research question raised the following sub-questions:

- What are the existing laws and policies in Kenya in relation to access to TK?
- Which laws and policies exist in Kenya to ensure perpetuity and third-party access to TK?
- How do relevant actors, such as the government, universities, research institutions and TK holders, contribute to TK commons modalities?
- What are the actual or potential roles of ICTs in TK commons modalities?

The study analysed:

- the existing legal and policy framework for the protection of TK in Kenya and how it potentially affects or contributes to TK commons structures among ILCs;
- the potential role of Kenyan policy actors in fostering an enabling environment for TK commons modalities in Kenya; and
- the potential role and impact of the digital environment in support of Kenyan TK commons practices.

Data were collected via library and online research, and via qualitative focus group discussions and interviews. The library and online research looked at national, regional and international papers, articles and stakeholder reports on TK protection and TK commons modalities. Also examined were provisions related to TK in the Constitution of Kenya, Kenyan Acts of Parliament, national policies and relevant international legal instruments in the context of IP protection of TK. Qualitative research consisted of practically oriented discussions with policy actors, to gauge understanding of the concept of a TK commons, with the policy actors drawn from ILCs, government, research institutions and universities. Focus groups and interviews were carried out between May and July 2011.

First, the research identified two communities to engage in the study, namely, the Maasai and Miji Kenda communities. The Maasai community was selected because it is the site of a project, supported by the World Intellectual Property Organisation (WIPO), on digitisation of the Maasai culture (which touches on the issue of documentation of TK). The Miji Kenda community was selected based on the work that has been done by the Malindi District Cultural Association (MDCA) to formalise the custody and continuity of the Miji Kenda TK. Of particular interest was to get a sense of the Miji Kenda community's views on the potential impact of ICTs on solidification of its TK commons. Next, the research team conducted focus group discussions with potential policy actors and elders within the two communities, primarily via the MDCA and the Maasai Cultural Heritage Organisation (MCH).

Interviews were then carried out with representatives of various institutions involved in policy creation and implementation at the national level, including the Office of the Attorney-General and the Department of Justice, the Kenya Copyright Board (KECOBO), the Department of Culture, the Kenya Industrial Property Institute (KIPI), the University of Nairobi and National Museums of Kenya. The focus groups and interviews were semi-structured to ensure flexibility and to allow for purposive identification of additional interviewees.

The next section (Section 3) outlines the research study's conceptual framing in relation to notions of TK and commons modalities. Section 4 outlines the study's findings regarding the Kenyan legal and policy environment. Section 5 provides and analyses the research findings from the qualitative focus group discussions and interviews. Section 6 draws conclusions based on the study findings. (See Chapter 7 in this volume for discussion of the dynamics of an existing TK commons that has been set up by traditional medicinal practitioners in the Bushbuckridge region of South Africa.)

3. Conceptual framework

The term "traditional knowledge" does not have a universally accepted definition. Some believe this is due to the diversity of traditions and culture at both the domestic and international levels (WIPO, 2001). Several attempts have been made to define TK (which, for the purposes of this study, included primarily TCEs and folklore).[3] TK is diverse, dynamic and varies from community to community. One study by Ostrom (1990) revealed that TK has a strong cultural and socio-economic impact on ILCs. The main challenge lies in the documentation and preservation of TK, and is well summed up in the words of a member of the Maasai community in Kenya: "When an elder dies, it's just

3 See, for instance, Article 7(II), Brazil's Provisional Measure No. 2.186-16, available at: www.wipo.int/wipolex/en/details.jsp?id=5897 (accessed 10 April 2013); Article 3(1), Portugal's Decree-Law No. 118/2002, available at: www.wipo.int/wipolex/en/details.jsp?id=5897 (accessed 10 April 2013); and Hansen and Van Fleet (2003).

like a light burning out, so we want to get that knowledge before this generation goes" (Tingoi, n.d.[b]). The challenge of documenting and preserving TK is exacerbated by the typically low literacy levels among the communities who are custodians of the knowledge.

The concept of a "commons" derives from the idea of community ownership of property (*res communes*), founded on the principle that certain resources and things, tangible and intangible, are owned and shared by a community as a network of people and guided by a predetermined set of rules and regulations that sets the boundaries and limitations of such use. There are different kinds of commons, including a material commons, a social commons (Nonini, 2007) and a knowledge commons. This study was based on the notation of a knowledge commons, organised around shared intellectual and cultural practices. Unlike material resources, these intellectual and cultural resources are often non-rival and non-subtractive because one person learning or using knowledge does not prevent another person from doing the same (Nonini, 2007). Further, a knowledge commons can be *generative*, in the sense that it can "scale up" as it develops (Nonini, 2007). According to Nonini:

> The more users, the better the commons functions, since the marginal cost of adding users is zero, and new users are not only the recipients of the gift of non-rival knowledge from others in the commons, but they also reciprocate by producing new knowledge for them refined on the basis of knowledge previously received. (2007, p. 71)

According to Abrell (2009), a commons involves the continual "movement and growth of knowledge that benefits not just the original community that provided the knowledge but other communities too" (2009, p. 16). Benkler (2006) explains that a commons refers to a particular institutional form of structuring rights to the access, use and control of resources:

> Commons are another core institutional component of freedom of action in free societies, but they are structured to enable action that is not based on exclusive control over resources necessary for action. (Benkler, 2006, p. 24, quoted in Abrell *et. al.*, 2009, p. 16)

TK accounts for an invaluable part of the lives of ILCs, and this study proceeded on the presumptions that:

- there is a need to preserve and protect TK;
- preservation and protection should not inhibit access;
- access should encourage open collaboration and collaborative creativity for open development; and
- access should take into account existing cultural norms and practices of ILCs.

4. Findings: the Kenyan legal and policy environment

At local, regional and international levels, two forms of legal protection of TK are prominent. There is *defensive* protection, intended to prevent others from asserting or acquiring IP rights over TK subject matter. Such protection may include making information available to patent and trademark examiners – so that formal IP rights are not granted for TK that is in the public domain (as far as patents are concerned) or that is a protectable element of identification of indigenous peoples and traditional communities (as far as trademarks are concerned).

One type of defensive TK protection is databases or other inventories of TK available to patent and trademark examiners (WIPO, 2003a, para. 12). One such model is the aforementioned TKDL in India (CSIR, n.d.). There is also *positive* protection of TK, which is intended to give TK holders the right to take action or seek remedies against certain forms of misuse of their TK. Positive protection of TK includes the use of existing IP systems, adaptations and *sui generis* elements of existing IP regimes, and wholly *sui generis* protection (WIPO, 2003b).

International and regional legal instruments

Kenya is a party to several international and African regional treaties, conventions and protocols that directly and indirectly protect various forms of IP rights, including patents, copyright and related rights, trademarks, industrial designs, utility models, geographical indications, trade secrets, plant breeders' rights and TK. This section examines some of the instruments that have a bearing on the protection of TK – and potentially on the formalisation of a TK commons – in Kenya.

Convention on Biological Diversity (CBD) (1992)

Article 1 of the CBD aptly captures the central role of the CBD in the protection of TK and genetic resources *vis-à-vis* a TK commons for development purposes. Article 8(j) of the CBD provides the legal framework that deals with the preservation and process of adding value to TK. Article 17 seeks to promote exchange of information, including indigenous knowledge and TK, from all publicly available sources relevant to the conservation and sustainable use of biological diversity, taking into account the special needs of developing countries. This provision has the potential to promote knowledge-sharing for research and development. The language of the CBD articles in relation to TK has the potential to facilitate the core elements of a TK commons: non-appropriation, recognition of existing cultural norms and regulations that govern TK, freedom of access and prior informed consent. The CBD also leaves room for flexibility, as it provides minimum standards, but not mandatory harmonisation.

Paris Convention for the Protection of Industrial Property (1883)

The Paris Convention was the first major treaty designed for the international protection of intellectual creations in the form of industrial property rights, including inventions (patents), trademarks and industrial designs. In the context of a potential TK commons, the Paris Convention's provisions on geographical indications, collective marks and certification marks all have the potential to play roles in identification of particular types of TK commons (Art. 7*bis*).

Patent Cooperation Treaty (PCT) (1970)

The PCT provides a system of simultaneous patent application filing for an invention in each of a large number of countries. The existing patent search databases maintained by the International Bureau of WIPO and other regional and national registration bodies could be helpful in the case of formalisation of a TK commons via establishment of an electronic TK database (see CSIR, n.d.).

International Treaty on Plant Genetic Resources for Food and Agriculture (International Seed Treaty) (2001)

This treaty recognises the contribution of ILCs in farming, conservation and development of plant varieties, and aims to ensure that any benefits derived from the use of genetic resources by third parties are shared with the communities from which they originate.

UN Declaration of the Rights of Indigenous Peoples (2007)

This declaration emphasises the rights of indigenous peoples in relation to the maintenance and strengthening of their own institutions, cultures and traditions, and their rights to pursue their development in keeping with their own needs and aspirations, including through documentation systems.

Swakopmund Protocol on the Protection of Traditional Knowledge and Expressions of Folklore (2010)

In the context of potential formalisation of a TK commons, the Swakopmund Protocol, developed by Member States of the African Regional Intellectual Property Organisation (ARIPO), reaffirms the fact that TK ought to be recognised, respected, preserved and protected from misuse, unlawful exploitation and misappropriation, while at the same time access is encouraged for the benefit of society. The Protocol limits the rights of access and exchange of TK to the TK's holders within the traditional context (Sect. 11). Article 8 of the Protocol allows TK holders to *generally* conclude licensing agreements for use of their TK, provided the agreements are in writing and approved by the competent national authority. In addition, the Protocol obliges contracting states to ensure that appropriate enforcement and dispute resolution mechanisms, sanctions and remedies are available where there is breach of provisions relating to the protection of TK (Sect. 23.1).

Kenyan national legal and policy framework

The Constitution of Kenya of 2010 provides a potentially strong framework for the creation of enabling policies to ensure that benefits of TK accrue to ILCs, and to promote access and preservation of TK for the sustainability of ILCs. The Constitution is the supreme law of the Republic of Kenya and binds all persons and all state organs (Art. 2(1)). The Constitution specifically defines property to include IP (Art. 260). In addition, the Constitution recognises culture as the foundation of the nation and as the cumulative civilisation of the Kenyan people and state (Art. 11(1)). The Constitution provides the Kenyan state with a duty to promote all forms of national cultural expression, to recognise the role of indigenous technologies in development and to promote the protection of IP rights (Art. 11(2)). In addition, the state has to support, promote and protect the IP rights of the people of Kenya (Art. 40(5)). The Constitution also provides for the sustainable management and use of natural resources, and for protection of biodiversity and genetic resources (Art. 69(1)). These provisions provide the potential framework for drafting laws that go beyond protecting and preserving and, for example, make provision for the creation of TK databases.

Kenya has no specific law on the protection of TK but there are several laws that touch on the subject matter as it relates to copyright, biodiversity, genetic resources, agriculture, forestry and wildlife. The main legal instruments for the protection of IP in Kenya are the following:

- Anti-Counterfeit Act 13 of 2008.
- Copyright Act of 2001 (Cap. 130).
- Industrial Property Act of 2001 (Cap. 507).
- National Museums and Heritage Act 6 of 2006.
- Seeds and Plant Varieties Act of 1991 (as revised in 2012) (Cap. 326).
- Trade Marks Act of 1994 (Cap. 506).

The Industrial Property Act contains some elements that could be built upon to create a database for defensive protection of TK. The Copyright Act, meanwhile, gives the Attorney-General the power to authorise and prescribe terms and conditions governing the commercial use of expressions of folklore (Sect. 49). With regard to the Trade Marks Act, the provisions relating to legal protection of collective marks and geographical indications are relevant to this study. One of the objectives of the National Museums and Heritage Act is the identification, protection, conservation and transmission of the cultural and natural heritage of Kenya – provisions relevant to creating a database of TK. (Also potentially relevant, if they come to fruition, will be the proposed geographical indications law and proposed TK and TCEs law.)

At the policy level, Kenya has a National Policy on Traditional Knowledge, Genetic Resources and Traditional Cultural Expressions (hereafter "National TK Policy"). This National TK Policy, finalised in 2009, provides for a national framework that recognises, preserves, protects and promotes the sustainable use of TK to enhance the mainstreaming of TK systems in pursuit of national development objectives. The Policy recognises that there is a need to ensure that TK is not only protected but is also accessible for innovative, developmental uses. The Policy envisages a system that contributes to open innovation and collaborative creativity, while at the same time ensuring that TK is preserved and well documented. In order to achieve the above core objectives, the following guiding principles are identified as forming an integral part of the Policy: respect; full disclosure; prior informed consent; confidentiality; good faith; compensation; equitable benefit-sharing; sustainable development; access; and international cooperation. Most of these guiding principles will be directly relevant to any attempts to establish defined TK commons arrangements in Kenya. This National TK Policy is, at the time of writing, being used as the basis for a draft law, the Draft Bill on Protection of Traditional Knowledge and Traditional Cultural Expressions (hereafter "Draft TK Bill"), which was published for comment in May 2013.[4]

Another policy that has potential bearing on the creation of TK commons arrangements is the 2009 National Policy on Culture and Heritage. Under this Policy, the government must:

- promote culture as the centrepiece and driving force behind human, social and economic development, and encourage cultural pluralism; and

4 KECOBO convened a national consultative forum on 8 May 2013 where the Draft TK Bill was presented and discussed by various stakeholders. The Draft Bill was then made available on the KECOBO website, to allow for further comment before submission to the Office of the Attorney-General.

- take appropriate measures for the protection, conservation and preservation of tangible and intangible national heritage situated within its boundaries.

These two policies, though silent on the notion of a TK commons, clearly articulate the important role government institutions are expected to play in the protection of Kenyan culture, heritage and folklore/TCEs. Article 4(1) of the Draft TK Bill provides for KECOBO to be the "National Competent Authority" for implementation of an eventual TK law, while Article 4(3) provides for the establishment of the National Cultural Agency.

5. Findings: stakeholder perspectives

TK among the Maasai and Miji Kenda communities encompasses traditional medicine and healing processes, rituals, traditional cultural expressions (beadwork, music and designs), preservation of food, nutrition and diet, agriculture and animal husbandry. Certain aspects of TK, such as the farming methods, preservation of food, nutrition, diet, animal husbandry, art and design, are shared freely within the community. Traditional medicine and healing are practised by specific persons within the community. In the case of music, there were specific composers and authors who were recognised and rewarded for their creativity. Knowledge is, thus, limited to a specific family or person. These communities have systems of customs and taboos that ensure the preservation of TK. This also helps in the preservation of genetic resources.

The respondents from three government agencies – KECOBO, National Museums of Kenya and KIPI – were of the considered opinion that TK deserves to be protected but that at the same time it is important to ensure the TK is documented and made accessible for appropriate uses.

Legal/policy framework and role of government

Some of the respondents were not aware of the notion of a TK commons. However, they raised concerns about the use of their knowledge by third parties to their detriment if that knowledge was made available without a proper legal or policy framework. There was, at the same time, a general understanding that the lack of documentation of TK left it open to misappropriation and exposed the communities to the risk of possibly losing the knowledge upon the death of its holders. This concern has been captured in the National TK Policy, among other challenges. The Miji Kenda community members articulated a desire to preserve and share their knowledge in an "open manner", with the exception of their sacred and secret TK (interviewees, 2011).

The interviews and focus group discussions exposed several challenges surrounding the preservation of TK within ILCs in Kenya, which in turn could have an impact on the creation of a TK commons. With the rapid modernisation within the communities, the younger generation is shunning traditional cultural practices and traditions. And because of low literacy levels, especially among those who hold the TK, the communities are finding it difficult to record their knowledge for future generations. For example, the *dhome,* a traditional Miji Kenda educational evening where elders pass on knowledge, is no longer held. As a result, there is a risk of the knowledge disappearing.

Interviewees and focus group participants from both the Miji Kenda and Maasai communities expressed deep concerns about the lack of proper legal and administrative structures to facilitate the preservation and perpetuation of their traditions and cultures in the face of modern socio-economic pressures. Their concerns present a potentially strong justification for the development of law and policy that can effectively facilitate protection and preservation of TK and, at the same time, sharing of the TK in a manner that can spur innovation, creativity and (open) development.

Apart from their concerns about the lack of a legal framework, the Miji Kenda perceive a tension between their own cultural conception of a TK commons and that expressed in government policies. There is a perception among the Miji Kenda that government policies are skewed in favour of other cultural communities, and that the National Museums of Kenya seem to institutionalise practices of favouritism. These tensions between the community and the government within the coastal region have a negative impact on the feasibility of the creation of a TK commons.

Other challenges to the creation of a TK commons cited by interviewees include financial constraints, especially in the creation of databases for the preservation of TK. The communities lack the facilities for documentation and rarely receive government support for such initiatives. They have to rely on community-based initiatives, which are usually underfunded. This is well illustrated by the experience of the Maasai community in the aforementioned process of digitising their culture. After the initial support received under the auspices of WIPO, they have not been able to secure any further funding, e.g. from the government of Kenya. Alarmingly, some interviewees were confused about the nature of TK and measures to protect it, due to the proliferation of research studies by different organisations. Some reports are inaccurate, and some researchers failed to disclose the purpose of their research to the communities in question. This undermines trust, and threatens the potential to develop inclusive policy proposals.

There is at present only limited collaboration between ILCs and government agencies such as KECOBO, National Museums of Kenya, KIPI and the Plant and

Health Inspectorate. The lack of collaboration creates impediments to the documentation and preservation of TK. There is also some unwillingness on the part of ILCs to share sacred or secret TK, especially as it relates to medicine and healing practices. Custodians are, understandably, not willing to share sacred knowledge with third parties, so this knowledge can only be conveyed through the traditional community systems. Some steps have been taken to try to address these challenges, including the digitisation of culture project among the Maasai community, and partnerships through community-based organisations, such as the MDCA, with government departments. Such initiatives potentially contribute to the formalisation of TK commons modalities within the communities.

The National TK Policy of 2009 takes cognisance of several challenges, such as: lack of recognition and lack of mainstreaming of TK systems in national policies and decision-making processes; lack of a TK database; inadequate capacity; and lack of TK linkage with IP, creativity and innovation. The main objective of the Policy is "to enhance and coordinate the application of traditional knowledge, innovations and practices in sustainable use of genetic resources and sustainable development in Kenya" (National TK Policy, 2009). This would include, among other things, the provision of the necessary legal and institutional framework for the documentation and application of TK, and fostering the use and dissemination of TK while ensuring that the ILCs benefit and enhance partnerships in the access and utilisation of TK innovations and practices (interviewees, 2011). Respondents from KECOBO, National Museums of Kenya and KIPI noted that the lack of implementation of this Policy to date has presented a challenge to the creation of TK commons structures. There is a need for a definite legal and administrative framework that will enable the achievement of the objectives of the Policy.

Use of information and communication technology (ICT)

With the advent of digital technology and the proliferation of the internet, works are reduced to digital format and can be reproduced, accessed and disseminated with relative ease across networks. An online licensing system could work well by affording a large degree of transparency. TK could be digitised and stored in an electronic database that has controlled or limited access. A good example is the TKDL in India. It provides information to specific patent offices and is also a tool for defensive protection of TK. The TKDL can also be used for research and development.

The Maasai interviewed for this study stated that there was a need to establish communication channels with relevant government departments and agencies, as well as research institutions and universities, to forge collaborative partnerships. Their TK is currently being preserved through the oral tradition, but there have been attempts by individuals within and from outside the community to document the traditions. They believe that the cultural digitisation project will eventually provide a platform for TK documentation as well as provide access. The project on digitisation of culture among the Kenyan Maasai community in Laikipia does indeed provide a potential starting point for documentation of traditional cultural practices, including TK and TCEs. The project was carried out under the auspices of WIPO through what is known as Digitising Traditional Culture in Kenya, under WIPO's Creative Heritage Project. There was no documentation of the Maasai TK prior to the WIPO project on digitisation of culture, and the full impact of the project is yet to be felt by the community.

KECOBO and KIPI, in consultation with WIPO, are planning to set up a digital library for TK. Although the Copyright Act requires the users of TK (specifically TCEs) to obtain authority to use the works (and to pay a fee), there is no database in place. The setting up of a digital library for TK would facilitate the establishment of this database. KECOBO and KIPI have proposed amendment of the Copyright Act to provide a substantive provision for the creation of the database, which would be maintained by KECOBO and be accessible by the public. The first step would be to engage the ILCs in the collection of the data. KECOBO and KIPI are currently studying the TKDL model in India to develop the necessary ICT tools, and a KIPI representative was sent to India to obtain first-hand exposure to the workings of the TKDL. Although KECOBO and KIPI view the TK digital library initiative as a form of defensive protection, they also see it as a means to facilitate access to TK for future innovations.

6. Conclusions

Most interviewees were not aware of the concept of a TK commons. However, after some probing and discussion, they were able to have insightful discussions on the policy considerations and challenges as well as the legal, economic, social and cultural dimensions of such a commons. The IP regime emphasises *defensive* protection of TK, as it is intended to prevent others from asserting or acquiring IP rights in TK. The proposed *sui generis* protection of TK by way of a commons offers *positive* protection, which affords flexibility for access and the creation of databases. It is important to have a clear understanding of the dynamics within a given community in order to engage the members in a productive discussion in relation to TK commons and openness-based approaches to development (open development).

The current legal regime, to a certain extent, provides a framework for the creation of a TK commons. However, the laws have limitations, as the framework only covers what is related to conventional IP. In some cases, the IP regime may limit the creation of commons modalities, as it provides exclusive rights to the exclusion of all others for a certain period of time. There is need for a legal framework that provides for the protection of TK as well as providing for access, i.e. a TK law aligned with the National TK Policy. (The aforementioned Draft TK Bill, published in May 2013 and under review at time of writing, will presumably lead to a law that addresses this need for a dedicated legal framework for TK.)

Communities face social and economic challenges that will affect the creation of a TK commons, increasing the need for government involvement. However, there is a clear gap between the policy-makers at the government level and the ILCs in Kenya. Collaboration between the policy-makers, users and TK custodians is required to facilitate discussions on policy issues.

The focus group and interview findings also clearly demonstrated a need for training and capacity building, including creating awareness among government, universities and research institutions, about the role of TK in (open) development. The creation of an electronic database of TK could further capacity building, and requires the support of government institutions such as KECOBO, National Museums of Kenya and KIPI – as well as the ILCs who are custodians of the TK.

Collaborative creativity and open innovation require access to TK. Technology is crucial for the creation of databases such as a TK digital library, which would provide access but remain within the control of the ILCs. This would also address the issue of preserving TK, which is at risk of being lost with diminishing intergenerational cultural knowledge transfer practices. Commons modalities involve the evolution of knowledge in service to both the original community and other communities. The creation of a TK commons in Kenya would encourage the sharing of information that could be utilised better for purposes of open development.

There is a need to provide for the implementation of the National TK Policy to ensure that it facilitates the creation of the TK commons modalities that can encourage innovation and collaborative creativity for development. The Draft TK Bill currently has provisions that provide for an institutional framework for TK management, with KECOBO (as the National Competent Authority in terms of the Draft Bill) expected not only to ensure the protection of TK but also to create a TK framework (which could potentially be favourable for establishment of a TK commons) through the creation of a database (which the Draft Bill describes as "a record of traditional owners and/or knowledge and traditional cultural expressions" (Draft TK Bill, 2013). Concerted and/or collaborative policy efforts on a TK commons should be pursued with the twin objectives of perpetuating TK and enhancing its value in a mutually beneficial manner for creativity and open development. The National TK Policy and Draft TK Bill take into account the preservation and protection of TK, and the facilitation of access and dissemination of TK, thus appearing to take into account the concerns raised by the custodians of TK (some of which have been documented in this study). The Policy, if properly implemented via, *inter alia*, an eventual TK law, provides for engagement with TK by policy actors both within government and in communities.

Bibliography

Primary sources

Statutes, regulations and draft bill

Kenya:
Anti-Counterfeit Act 13 of 2008.
Constitution of Kenya of 2010.
Copyright Act of 2001 (Cap. 130).
Copyright Regulations of 2005.
Draft Bill on Protection of Traditional Knowledge and Traditional Cultural Expressions (Draft TK Bill) (2013).
Industrial Property Act of 2001 (Cap. 507).
National Museums and Heritage Act 6 of 2006.
Seeds and Plant Varieties Act of 1991, as revised in 2012 (Cap. 326).
Trade Marks Act of 1994 (Cap. 506).

Other:
Decree-Law No. 118/2002, Government of Portugal, available at: www.wipo.int/wipolex/en/details.jsp?id=5897 (accessed 10 April 2013).
Provisional Measure No. 2.186-16, Government of Brazil, available at: www.wipo.int/wipolex/en/details.jsp?id=5897 (accessed 10 April 2013).

Regional and international instruments

Agreement on Trade-Related Aspects of Intellectual Property Rights (TRIPS) (1994).
Berne Convention for the Protection of Literary and Artistic Works (1970 Act).
Convention on Biological Diversity (CBD) (1992).
International Convention for the Protection of New Plant Varieties (1978).
International Treaty on Plant Genetic Resources for Food and Agriculture (2001).
International Convention on Economic and Social Rights (1966).
Paris Convention for the Protection of Industrial Property (1883).
Patent Cooperation Treaty (PCT) (1970).

Swakopmund Protocol on the Protection of Traditional Knowledge and expressions of Folklore (2010).
Universal Declaration of Human Rights (1948).
UN Declaration of the Rights of Indigenous Peoples (2007).

Kenyan Policies

National Policy on Traditional Knowledge, Genetic Resources and Traditional Cultural Expressions (National TK Policy) (2009).
National Policy on Culture and National Heritage (2009).

Secondary sources

Abrell, E. (2009), *Implementing a Traditional Knowledge Commons: Opportunities and Challenges*, Natural Justice, available at: http://naturaljustice.org/wp-content/uploads/pdf/Implementing_a_TKC-2009.pdf (accessed 10 April 2013).

Abrell E., Bavikatte, K.S., Cocchiaro, G., Jonas, H. and Rens, A. (2009), *Imagining a Traditional Knowledge Commons: Opportunities and Challenges*, Natural Justice and International Development Law Organisation (IDLO), available at: www.idlo.int/publications/Traditionalknowledge.pdf (accessed 10 April 2013).

Action Research Resources (n.d.), "Grounded theory", available at: www.scu.edu.au/schools/gcm/ar/arp/grounded.html (accessed 10 April 2013).

Benkler, Y. (2006), *The Wealth of Networks*, Yale University Press, New Haven, CT.

Bergy, B. (2011), "A multi-faceted approach to the support and conservation of folklore, traditional culture", paper delivered at the International Symposium on Protection and Legislation of Folk/Traditional Culture, 18–20 December, Beijing.

Council of Scientific and Industrial Research (CSIR) (n.d.), "Traditional Knowledge Digital Library", India, available at: www.tkdl.res.in/tkdl/langdefault/common/Home.asp?GL=Eng (accessed 10 April 2013).

Edmonds Institute and African Centre for Biosafety (2006), *Out of Africa: Mysteries of Access and Benefit Sharing*, available at: www.newscastmedia.com/4investors_africa.pdf (accessed 10 April 2013).

Folke, C. (2004), "Traditional knowledge in social-ecological systems", *Ecology and Society*, Vol. 9 No. 3, available at: www.ecologyandsociety.org/vol9/iss3/art7 (accessed 10 April 2013).

Hansen, S. and Van Fleet, J. (2003), *Traditional Knowledge and IP: A Handbook on Issues and Options for Traditional Knowledge Holders in Protecting their IP and Maintaining Biological Diversity*, available at: http://shr.aaas.org/tek/handbook/handbook.pdf (accessed 10 April 2013).

Hudson E. and Kenyon, A.T. (2006), *Copyright and Cultural Institutions: Guidelines for Digitisation*, available at: http://papers.ssrn.com/sol3/papers.cfm?abstract_id=881699 (accessed 10 April 2013).

Nonini, D.M. (2007), "Introduction: the global idea of 'the commons'", in Nonini, D.M. (Ed.), *The Global Idea of "the Commons"*, Berghahn Books, New York, pp. 1–25.

Oguamanam, C. (2006), *International Law and Indigenous Knowledge: IP Rights, Plant Biodiversity and Traditional Medicine*, University of Toronto Press, Toronto.

Ostrom, E. (1990), *Governing the Commons: The Evolution of Institutions for Collective Actions*, Cambridge University Press, Cambridge, UK.

Smith, M.L., Elder, L. and Emdon, H. (2011), "Open development: a new theory for ICT4D", *Information Technologies and International Development*, Vol. 7 No. 1, Spring (Special Issue: Open Development), available at http://itidjournal.org/itid/article/view/692/290 (accessed 10 April 2013).

Society for Critical Exchange (SCE) (2004), *Case Study: Hoodia Cactus*, Case Western Reserve University, available at: www.case.edu/affil/sce/authorship-spring2004/hoodia.html (accessed 10 April 2013).

Tingoi, J.O. (n.d.[a]), "Community documentation of cultural heritage: Laikipia Maasai community experience – Kenya", available at: www.wipo.int/edocs/mdocs/tk/en/wipo_tk_mct_11/wipo_tk_mct_11_ref_t_4_1.pdf (accessed 10 April 2013).

Tingoi, J.O. (n.d.[b]), "Creative Heritage Project: digitizing traditional culture in Kenya", available at: www.wipo.int/portal/en/wipo_untv_maasai.html (accessed 10 April 2013).

Tingoi, J.O. (n.d.[c]), "Digitizing traditional culture in Kenya", available at: www.wipo.int/portal/en/wipo_untv_maasai.html (accessed 10 April 2013).

Torsen, M. and Anderson, J. (2010), *IP and Safeguarding of Traditional Cultures: Legal Issues and Practical Options for Museums, Libraries and Archives*, World Intellectual Property Organisation (WIPO), Geneva.

Trochim, W.M.K. (2006), "Research methods knowledge base: qualitative measures", available at: www.socialresearchmethods.net/kb/qual.php (accessed 10 April 2013).

Wane, N.N. (2000), "Indigenous knowledge: lessons from elders – a Kenyan case study", in Dei, G.S., Hall, B.L. and Rosenberg, D.G. (Eds), *Indigenous Knowledges in Global Contexts: Multiple Readings of Our World*, University of Toronto Press, Toronto, pp. 54–69.

World Intellectual Property Organisation (WIPO) (2001), *Intellectual Property Needs and Expectations of Traditional Knowledge Holders: WIPO Report on Fact-Finding Missions on IP and Traditional Knowledge (1998–1999)*, Geneva.

World Intellectual Property Organisation (WIPO) (2003a), *Consolidated Analysis of the Legal Protection of Traditional Cultural Expressions/Expressions of Folklore*, Geneva.

World Intellectual Property Organisation (WIPO) (2003b), *Consolidated Survey of Intellectual Property Protection of Traditional Knowledge*, WIPO/GRTKF/IC/5/7, Geneva.

World Intellectual Property Organisation (WIPO) (2003c), *Overview of Activities And Outcomes of the Intergovernmental Committee on Intellectual Property and Genetic Resources, Traditional Knowledge and Folklore*, WIPO/GRTKF/IC/5/12, Geneva.

Yin, R.K. (2009), *Case Study Research: Design and Methods,* 4th ed., Sage, Thousand Oaks, CA.

Chapter 7

Consideration of a Legal "Trust" Model for the Kukula Healers' TK Commons in South Africa

Gino Cocchiaro, Johan Lorenzen, Bernard Maister and Britta Rutert

Abstract

In this chapter, the authors outline their research findings from examination of the evolution and current dynamics of the traditional knowledge (TK) commons of a large grouping of traditional healers – the Kukula Traditional Health Practitioners' Association – in the Bushbuckridge area of northeastern South Africa. The authors argue that one potential way forward for the healers towards securing improved protection, sharing and benefit from the intellectual property (IP) represented by their TK could be the setting up of a legal "trust" with the healers serving as the trust's beneficiaries. While such a trust would not solve all the problems related to IP protection, it would permit the healers to manage their commons more effectively and govern aspects of IP management such as "access and benefit-sharing" and "prior informed consent".

1. Introduction

The Kukula Traditional Health Practitioners' Association (the "Kukula Healers") is a group of traditional medicine practitioners who live in the Bushbuckridge area in northeastern South Africa. Spread across parts of two provinces (Mpumalanga and Limpopo), Bushbuckridge lies within the Kruger to Canyons (K2C) area, which the UN Educational, Scientific and Cultural Organisation (UNESCO) has registered as a Biosphere Reserve. The K2C Biosphere Region is managed by the K2C Management Committee comprising six individual stakeholders working in the tourism and political/government sectors in the region (K2C, n.d.). The K2C area contains an exceptionally wide array of animal and plant biodiversity. Moreover, there are various ethnic groups in the area, as reflected in members of the Kukula Healers' collective, who come from the Tsonga/Shangaan, Swazi,

Tswana, Bapedi (North Sotho) and Basotho (South Sotho) ethnic groupings. The K2C region is thus both socio-culturally multi-faceted and extremely biodiverse.

The K2C area is also one of the poorest regions of South Africa, with persistent rural poverty, high unemployment and high levels of HIV infection (Nyaka, 2013). Traditional healers provide primary health care services and counselling in the communities of Bushbuckridge. At the same time, the healers hold rich bio-cultural knowledge in relation to the landscape, the environment and the socio-cultural life of their communities. The healers are thus the custodians of a unique repository of physical, socio-cultural, medicinal and biological knowledge that finds expression in a bio-cultural way of being. This way of being is expressed in a variety of customary laws. To ensure the provision of health care service for their communities, the traditional healers require access to the surrounding landscapes so as to be able to collect medicinal plants. However, community access to medicinal plants is often restricted by access rights to the land (Du Plessis, 2012). Private and public nature and game reserves limit access to land that is far richer in biodiversity than the overgrazed and over-harvested communal areas controlled by local chiefs. The communal land is more easily accessible, but more difficult to control and maintain sustainably. For example, plant diversity in these areas is diminished due to grazing cattle and over-harvesting of trees and vegetation by local firewood collectors and *muti* (traditional medicine) hunters.[1] The *muti* hunters are organised collectors of medicinal plants who supply the large *muti* markets in the South African cities of Johannesburg and Durban.

With diminished access to land and, in turn, to medicinal plants, traditional healers' daily interactions with important biodiversity is minimised in the Bushbuckridge area, and these declining interactions could eventually lead to the loss of important traditional knowledge (TK). This situation poses a threat to the livelihoods of the area's traditional healers, and to their customary and culturally significant roles as custodians of TK. The potential loss of TK also threatens to further undermine traditional medicinal practitioners' already unstable position in communities increasingly exposed to modernising strands of South African society, to non-traditional health services, and to negative commentary from Western-oriented churches. The Bushbuckridge area's traditional healers have witnessed a steady decline in patient numbers, leading to reduced income and economic security (interviews with Kukula Healers, 2011–12).

The Bushbuckridge healers have in recent years given increasing consideration to means of protecting their already-diluting TK. As well as the aforementioned threats to the healers' TK, another threat is biopiracy: the unrewarded use of biological resources and TK. Biopiracy was largely a neglected issue until the

1 Spelled "muti" in isiZulu and "muthi" in isiXhosa, with both spellings found in the literature.

early 1990s and the drafting of the UN Convention on Biological Diversity (CBD) of 1992. The CBD, ratified in 1993, was the first binding international legal instrument to provide for the conservation, sustainable use and fair and equitable sharing of benefits arising from the use of biological resources and related knowledge. Prior to the CBD, natural resources and knowledge were treated as commonly held goods, to which broad rights of access for a wide variety of uses, including commercial uses, were taken for granted.

With the extension of the CBD through its Nagoya Protocol on Access and Benefit-Sharing (ABS) of 2010, community protocols, also known as bio-cultural community protocols (BCPs), have become a promising tool for indigenous and local communities (ILCs) to control their natural resources and TK. The Nagoya Protocol states that parties shall "take into consideration indigenous and local communities' customary law, community protocols and procedures" (Art. 12, Sect. 1), and support the development by ILCs of

> [c]ommunity protocols in relation to access to traditional knowledge associated with genetic resources and the fair and equitable sharing of benefits arising out of the utilization of such knowledge. (Art. 12, Sect. 3(a))

Responding to the threats to its TK, the Kukula Healers collaborated with the K2C Management Committee and the Natural Justice non-governmental organisation (NGO) in the development of a BCP aimed at strengthening their rights of access and protection (Kukula Healers, 2010).[2] BCPs are designed to assist communities in articulating the importance of self-governance and stewardship of their resources and associated TK; affirming their responsibilities to ensure the preservation of their communities' knowledge, lands and resources; and communicating their rights under customary, national and international law. According to Bavikatte (2011),

> [t]he value of community protocols lies in their ability to act as the glue that holds together the total mosaic of a community life that is fragmented under different laws and policies, with the understanding that the conservation of nature is a result of a holistic way of life. (Bavikatte, 2011, p. 23)

The Kukula Healers' BCP outlines their commitment to maintain the health of their communities – not only the physical, cultural and spiritual wellbeing of each community member, but also the protection of the biodiversity in their physical surroundings (Kukula Healers, 2010). The importance of the Kukula BCP lies in the fact that the communities it covers have, with some external support, now been

2 Natural Justice: Lawyers for Communities and the Environment is an international NGO comprised of lawyers working with ILCs on conservation, environmental sustainability and biodiversity. See Natural Justice (n.d.).

empowered to negotiate their rights (in the context of complex local, national and international policies) and to strengthen their capacity for self-governance. An important step in the development of the Kukula BCP was the traditional healers' agreement on the notion of a TK "commons", in which they would collectively pool their knowledge and share it with researchers or business partners. In 2011, in line with the provisions of the BCP, the Kukula Healers negotiated a non-disclosure agreement and agreed to share plant material with the South African cosmetics and bedding company Godding and Godding. In terms of the agreement, a transfer of plants with potential commercial value was completed between the healers and Godding and Godding in December 2011, with the support of members of the K2C Management Committee.

The purpose of this chapter is to give an account of the results of a research study, conducted in 2011–12, which examined the evolution and current functioning of the Kukula Healers' TK commons and sought to determine whether there were additional legal mechanisms for the healers to consider. We arrived at the conclusion that the setting up of a legal "trust" could potentially benefit the Kukula Healers. Section 2 of this chapter outlines the notion of the "commons" and provides an overview of the research study on which this chapter is based. Section 3 gives an account of the history, dynamics and current status of the Kukula Healers' TK commons. Section 4 outlines how a legal trust model could conceivably benefit the healers, and Section 5, the concluding section, summarises the potential efficacy of the trust model for the Kukula Healers.

2. Conceptual framework and methodology

The concept of a "commons"

The term "commons" refers to a resource shared by a group of people (Hess and Ostrom, 2007). In most cases, a commons is governed by the regulated right to access, use and control of resources (Ostrom, 1990). Benkler (2006) describes a commons as "a particular institutional form of structuring the right to access, use and control of resources". Abrell *et al.* (2009) refer to it as a resource that is controlled by a community through systematic rules that govern use of the resources. According to Hardin (1968), the commons model poses challenges for communities because "[f]reedom in a commons brings ruin to all" (Hardin, 1968, p. 1244), i.e. individual interests override community interests, resulting in the unsustainable use of resources. For example, common use of a pasture may lead to overgrazing. According to Hardin, publicly accessible resources tend to be misused and ultimately extinguished (Hardin, 1968).

We, however, support the argument that the TK commons model is not one that must of necessity result in "ruin for all" because, as Ostrom (1990) has argued, under certain conditions, conservation of TK and biodiversity is best ensured when decisions regarding communally managed resources are in the hands of the very communities who have historically been stewards of such knowledge and resources. These conditions are what Ostrom terms the eight "design principles" for effective common pool resource management, which are:

1. Define clear group boundaries.
2. Match rules governing use of common goods to local needs and conditions.
3. Ensure that those affected by the rules can participate in modifying the rules.
4. Make sure the rulemaking rights of community members are respected by outside authorities.
5. Develop a system, carried out by community members, for monitoring members' behaviour.
6. Use graduated sanctions for rule violators.
7. Provide accessible, low-cost means for dispute resolution.
8. Build responsibility for governing the common resource in nested tiers from the lowest level up to the entire interconnected system (Ostrom, 1990, p. 90). (See Chapter 6 in this volume for discussion of the potential for realisation of a TK commons in Kenya.)

The Kukula Healers' commons

The TK commons of the Kukula Healers is a commons created at the community level that aims to govern the healers' tangible and intangible resources, namely, traditional medicinal plants and TK, which, as described earlier, are both under threat due, on one hand, to biopiracy, and on the other hand, to shifting local social and economic dynamics. To address these challenges, the healers set up a commons to protect their resources and control access, through establishment of systematic rules to govern the use of the communally held resources. The rules allow healers to determine who is entitled to use the common resources (exclusion) and to what degree (subtractability). The Kukula Healers' knowledge commons is thus a common pool resource, whereby "a subtractable resource is managed under a property regime in which a legally defined user pool cannot be efficiently excluded from their resource domain" (Buck, 1998, p. 5). The TK commons of the Kukula Healers is based on a system of pooling and sharing elements of their bio-cultural knowledge and customary laws. It attempts to balance competing interests: disclosure versus secrecy, individual knowledge versus common knowledge. Formalised knowledge-sharing is relatively new to the healers, but it is at the same time grounded in their tradition. However, the Kukula Healers' knowledge commons does not at present carry the "legitimate" status that would be conferred if some form of property rights regime were to be adopted by the healers. Rather, the Kukula commons is a resource-based system, with knowledge constituting the resource of a specific group. We are of the view that using the legal model of a trust could – by generating a form of intellectual property (IP)-based property rights for the healers – serve to better govern the commons, while at the same time continuing to permit participants in the commons to use and share their resources on the basis of the existing rules of their established commons.

The research

To better understand the TK commons of the Kukula Healers, one of the authors of this chapter (Rutert, an anthropologist) conducted five months of participant observation, coupled with interviewing, in Bushbuckridge. Participant observation, a qualitative research method, requires the researcher to gather data through participation in the everyday lives of the people in the context being studied. For this study, Rutert lived in the home of the executive director of the Kukula Healers. The executive director supported the researcher's efforts by connecting her with other healers in the Association, so that she could conduct interviews and participate in their day-to-day activities. The participant observation process included: (1) involvement in traditional healers' everyday work, such as collecting plant material, consulting with patients and participating in ceremonies; and (2) participation in the Association's monthly meetings, at which current and future objectives and activities were discussed. In addition to participating in these activities, the researcher was able to conduct semi-structured interviews with 40 members of the Kukula Healers' Association. The interviews, conducted from December 2011 to May 2012, probed the healers on their knowledge commons, their knowledge protection and environmental protection, and their past and present socio-cultural, economic and political circumstances. The interviewees consisted of 12 male healers and 28 female healers. The interviewees were selected with the help of the executive director and with consideration of availability and accessibility. All interviewees were members of the Kukula Healers. Additional conversations with other healers, local authorities and residents of the area also contributed to the results.

3. Evolution of the Kukula TK commons

The Kukula Healers grouping started with 80 healers in 2009 and had grown to 300 members by the time of this research study in 2011–12. As mentioned above, the healers live in the Bushbuckridge municipality, an extensive area including parts of two South African provinces and bordering on the Kruger National Park. Because the members of the Kukula Association are spread across such a wide area, transportation between the villages is difficult and expensive, hindering regular gatherings of all 300 healers. Therefore, the Association formed a management sub-group, consisting of 26 healers, headed by an executive management committee of six healers (three female, three male) appointed in 2009. The executive management committee consists of the Association's CEO, three chairpersons, a treasurer and a secretary. This management committee meets on a regular basis to make important decisions and establish processes. It also convenes for joint meetings with the management sub-group to develop policies, such as the Kukula Healers' Code of Ethics (Kukula Healers, 2012).

In ILCs in South Africa, TK is intangible property held by actors embedded in a network of relationships. Traditional medicinal knowledge is typically regarded as belonging to the ancestors, and is transferred from generation to generation – either within family lines or in training schools – from a healer (*sangoma*) to an apprentice (*thwasa*). The ancestors are regarded as deceased members of an ongoing lineage. The healer evokes communication with the ancestors by using particular techniques, such as breathing, drumming or dancing. Communication with ancestors also occurs via (waking and sleeping) dreams, and through recital of particular prayers. This interplay between healers and ancestors connects the past with the present, the dead with the living. TK is thus a system of continuous connections and relations, or, according to Weiner (1985), an inalienable "object" that "acts as a vehicle for bringing past time into the present [...] To lose this claim to the past is to lose part of who one is in the present" (Weiner, 1985, p. 210).

According to the Kukula Healers, their traditional medicinal knowledge system originated from two ancestors, the brothers Nkomo le Lwandle and Dlamini. The healers recount that, hundreds of years ago, these two brothers split into separate, conflicting healing schools, in which slightly different forms of knowledge played significant roles. Each of these two healing traditions is characterised by, *inter alia*, specific knowledge of certain medicinal plants or healing performances. These schools, also called *imphande*, have a hierarchical structure, with the eldest healers serving as leaders (called *magobela*). The elders must be respected and obeyed by younger healers and former trainees, and respect is often expressed by kneeling down in front of the elder and offering gifts. The knowledge transferred in the *imphande* encompasses knowledge of medicinal plants and healing practices as well as ethical and moral norms of behaviour, referred to as customary laws. According to Abrell *et al.* (2009), "[c]ustomary laws are the principles, values, rules, codes of conduct, or established practices that guide the social practices of indigenous communities, including the use and management of natural resources" (Abrell *et al.*, 2009, p. 7). For the IIED (2009), customory laws "are locally recognized, orally held, adaptable and evolving", although they are often not recognised by state governments or courts, especially when they conflict with state laws (IIED, 2009, p. 5).

The Kukula Healers practise a holistic approach to knowledge-sharing that includes not only a transfer of knowledge but also a network of relationships ranging from past to present and interacting with both natural and cultural elements. Some knowledge may also be owned by one individual healer who, through the guidance of his or her ancestors, specialises in the treatment of particular diseases and ailments, using specific *muti* mixtures. Such specific healing capabilities typically lie in the family lineage, and are passed down from a grandfather or grandmother to a grandchild, skipping one generation. Accordingly, the transfer and collection of traditional medicinal knowledge in South Africa can be divided into three systems: (1) knowledge gained through training in a particular *imphande*; (2) knowledge gained through "private" ancestors in a family ancestral lineage; and (3) individually held knowledge gained through experience and the sharing of knowledge with other healers. All three systems are related to each other and simultaneously integrated in a complex set of relationships with ancestors, other healers, the environment and the plants with which the healers live and work. TK can thus be seen as a network of relationships among nature, the ancestors, the community and the individual.

The knowledge held by indigenous peoples has generally been acquired and refined over centuries.[3] Broadly, such knowledge may encompass topics such as those involving medicinal plants and animals and including such information as

> [...] where to find the medicinal [...] plant, animal or fungus [...] the cultural value; the specific collection practice; the exact part of the specimen that contains the active compound; the procedure for extracting the compound; and the different ways and timings to administer (or consume) the medicine (or food). (Bastida-Munoz and Patrick, 2006)

IP law, as it has developed in the context of industrialised nations, is incapable of dealing with TK. For example, one requirement of patentability requires that an invention be *novel*, whereas the knowledge that constitutes TK often will date back many generations. Copyright protection, with its requirements of "originality" and protection limited to that which is actually recorded, is not appropriate for the traditional songs and melodies of indigenous peoples, which often exist in

3 The nature of TK, who owns it, and what it involves, has been extensively covered in the literature. Some useful sources relating to TK and the difficulties encountered with current IP law protection include Bastida-Munoz and Patrick (2006), Correa (2004) and Drahos and Frenkel (2012).

oral form only. In the case of both patent and copyright protection, there has to be an identified inventor or author in whose name protection is sought. Clearly, in the case of multi-generational TK, identifying a single author or inventor is impossible. IP rights are usually granted to a single inventor or creator, or group of inventors or creators, and thereafter assigned to a single business entity such as a corporation.[4] As a consequence, secrecy is the primary means of knowledge protection.

According to the healers, knowledge cannot be shared with people outside the healers' community because knowledge is perceived as "sacred". If this knowledge were to leave the defined group, it would lose its power. Until recently, another factor mitigating against sharing the knowledge outside training schools was fear of persecution. In the pre-democratic era, before 1994, traditional healing practices were widely viewed as "witchcraft" and rendered illegal through the Witchcraft Suppression Act 3 of 1957. (See also the Mpumalanga Province draft Witchcraft Suppression Bill of 2007, and Niehaus [2005]).

During the research interviews with members of the Kukula Healers grouping, several claimed that they had been accused of witchcraft and some had been persecuted and received death threats, often within their own communities. This situation had, however, largely changed since the advent of democracy in 1994 and the development of government policy on traditional medicinal practices (i.e. the Biodiversity Act 10 of 2004, the Traditional Health Practitioners Act 35 of 2004 and the Indigenous Knowledge Systems Policy of 2004). The healers' reputation has improved in the democratic era, and they are able to perform their services in a less secretive and cautious way. The fact that healers can now provide their services more openly contributed to their decisions to set up the BCP and adopt a TK commons.

The system of sharing and transferring knowledge within the training schools and through ancestral communication could possibly already be regarded as a knowledge commons, or a knowledge commons pool, that is protected through customary law. Customary law is an intrinsic part of knowledge and, at the same time, an extrinsic regulatory system that protects the sensitive balance of all knowledge relations. It is a normative system that regulates moral and ethical behaviour in communities in general and in the healer community in particular. For the healers, customary law most often regulates sexual behaviour (e.g. no sexual intercourse while in training) and customs with regard to death and food.

4 It must, however, be noted that another key objection to granting patents as currently constituted in the context of TK is the issue of "prior art". Given the (usually) extensive prior knowledge of the subject matter (often a significant component of its power), TK is usually rejected by patent law as failing the "novelty" requirement.

All major aspects of the healers' practice are in danger of losing their purity, and hence power, when not guarded closely (Douglas, 1966). Customary law also regulates access and exposure to nature and the environment, and enforces the relational aspect of traditional healing. For example, customary law requires that the people seek permission from the ancestors to harvest plants and that they cover a plant's roots with soil after harvesting it.

The Kukula Healers' BCP was developed through a highly consultative process that allowed traditional health practitioners to define the essential elements of their practice and the core values that guide them. Notably, this process included detailing relevant customary laws and defining codes for knowledge-sharing with different parties, governance structures, ethics of conservation and commitments to holistic community wellbeing. The BCP was supplemented with direct references to relevant national and international law protecting this structure, and laid the foundation for the TK commons.

The TK commons of the Kukula Healers is based on a democratic group agreement that has evolved beyond their traditional methods of knowledge protection. The Kukula Healers agreed on a "TK commons pool" – a pool of knowledge that is shared among members of the Association, incorporating their conservation and "sustainable use" goals. Further, the members do not have to belong to the same healing tradition or *imphande*. The uniqueness of the TK commons pool lies in the very fact that the commons is based on a process of self-governance (although the contents of the TK commons pool might be similar to those of other area healers in terms of their medicinal knowledge). The TK commons, through its innovative combination of knowledge-sharing and protection, supports the Kukula Healers' ability to govern and further develop their knowledge while at the same time offering opportunities to form a coherent group identity.

The particularly multi-ethnic nature of the Bushbuckridge TK commons arises from the presence of different ethnic groups, predominantly the Shangaan and the Sotho peoples, in the region. The Bushbuckridge area is amongst the most ethnically heterogeneous areas of South Africa. Through diverse migration movements the area became a melting pot of different ethnic groups and consequently a region of many inter-ethnic traditions and customary laws, e.g. Shangaan men initiated under Sotho initiation rules (Niehaus, 2002). The different healing traditions continuously mingle and create a conglomerate of techniques and knowledge among the healers who have regular contact and tend to share their knowledge during ceremonial or informal meetings. This knowledge-sharing is largely based on the trust relationship between healers regardless of their ethnic affiliations or levels of experience. Notably, however, members of the group do not share all knowledge because of concerns that it could lead to the weakening of their individual healing specialisations.

When the TK commons system was established, Kukula members agreed that all knowledge that helps healers to improve their service to their communities and helps them to enter into negotiations with outside stakeholders can be shared according to strict rules. From their perspective, if knowledge is shared without limits, it loses its power. In their BCP, the Kukula Healers call for:

- increased access to conservation areas and reduction of over-harvesting of medicinal plants by others in communal areas;
- government recognition of their contribution to and benefits from the region's biodiversity;
- the establishment of a medicinal plants conservation and development area; and
- engagement with other local stakeholders to discuss the role of the traditional health practitioners in the communities (Kukula Healers, 2010).

The TK commons system adopted by the Kukula Healers currently permits them to pool and share their knowledge within their collective while, in general terms, keeping the knowledge secret from outsiders. One key question, however, remains: how is the knowledge to be best protected when the Kukula Healers engage with outside entities? Based on research evidence gathered on the functioning of the Kukula TK commons and BCP, one potentially beneficial legal model is that of a "trust".

4. Potential benefits of a legal "trust" for the Kukula Healers

As mentioned above, in 2011 the Kukula Healers entered into a non-disclosure agreement with a South African company, Godding and Godding, in terms of which the healers agreed to the transfer of certain types of knowledge to the company. This knowledge was to be used exclusively for lab testing in order to explore its efficacy and stability for cosmetics product development. The knowledge transfer was completed in a manner consistent with the customary laws of the Kukula Healers, including an acknowledgement that ownership of all knowledge they provided vests in their Association. Should the tests prove successful, a benefit-sharing arrangement will be required in order for Godding and Godding to commercialise any resulting products.

The agreement between the Kukula Healers and Godding and Godding is in line with, and reflects, international and national environmental legislation to protect TK. Specifically, Article 8(j) of the aforementioned CBD and the Nagoya Protocol grant ILCs, as custodians of TK, the right to consent to the use of their knowledge and to share in the benefits from its use. Parties are required to uphold the customary laws and community protocols of ILCs that regulate the use of their TK. In South Africa, protection of TK is governed by the Biodiversity Act 10 of 2004 and by the Bio-prospecting, Access and Benefit-Sharing Regulations of South Africa of 2008 which, *inter alia*, require ILCs to be identified and rewarded, and require signing of benefit-sharing agreements and securing of permits for bio-prospecting. However, these South African legal instruments fail to address certain questions, including: who provides consent for the use of TK that is communally held, how are the benefits to be communally shared, and what happens when communally held knowledge is privatised through the acquisition of IP rights by trading partners who ignore the original knowledge-holders? Thus far, the Kukula Healers have sought to address these matters through their BCP and their TK commons system. However, in order to give greater legal force to the TK commons, we propose that the Kukula Healers consider setting up a legal trust. The trust model is a legal mechanism with a long history in Western legal regimes, and in South Africa it is recognised and governed by the Trust Property Control Act 57 of 1988. This Act defines a trust as "the arrangement through which the ownership in property of one person" is placed under the control of another, the trustee, who then must administer such property "for the benefit of the person or class of persons designated in the trust instrument" (Trust Property Control Act 57 of 1988, Sect. 1).

The formation of a trust would not solve some of the problems created by trying to protect TK with existing IP law. Nevertheless, a trust would allow the Kukula Healers to manage their TK and any related products and facilitate the free sharing of TK at the local level, while at the same time ensuring (through imposing specific usage requirements) that any non-traditional uses of such knowledge comply with the norms and values of the community providing the knowledge – and ensuring that the community benefits from any commercial exploitation of its TK. The trust would also contribute to overcoming the problem of identifying the TK-holding community and the problem of deciding how to pay out benefits in a fair manner. With the passage of the CBD, mechanisms involving procedures such as "access and benefit-sharing" and "prior informed consent" have become integral to the management of TK. The structure of a trust would facilitate implementation of these mechanisms of TK management. For example, negotiating prior informed consent would be via the trustee whose fiduciary obligations would ensure that the best decision is made for the beneficiaries.

A single entity such as a trust would also more easily permit management of the TK as the trust's property (see below) since it provides a reliable mechanism for obtaining prior informed consent, the equitable sharing of benefits and enforcing the rights against infringement.

Setting up a trust would also have the benefit of requiring the Kukula Healers to precisely define and characterise their TK in order to determine the actual trust "property", a trust requirement discussed in more detail below. This would help in providing outsiders with information regarding the precise scope of TK controlled by the Kukula Healers. A further benefit of forming a trust, for the TK to be managed by it, would be that it permits the placing of conditions on the TK's use and exploitation consistent with the traditions of the healers. An arrangement of the sort described above, involving the non-disclosure agreement with the Godding and Godding cosmetics company, would, if a trust were in place, be entered into between the company and the trust rather than with the Kukula Healers. The conditions under which such an agreement would be reached – including how the knowledge is to be used, and who benefits should it be commercialised – would already be part of the conditions under which the trust functioned.

In the following subsections, the key elements of a trust are described.

Components of a legal trust

The "trust" as a legal entity is found in many legal systems. As discussed below, trust components are similar in different countries. As a result, it is a legal form that is familiar to, and readily accepted by, participants in international trade. South African law regarding the features of a trust follows the Hague Convention on the Law applicable to Trusts and their Recognition,[5] even though South Africa has not ratified or acceded to the Convention.[6]

The key components of a trust are: (1) the trustee, who is responsible for managing the actual definable property of the trust according to the terms of the trust, essentially one who is entrusted with the affairs of another; (2) the actual property comprising the trust; (3) the settlor (or "donor" or "creator") who creates the trust and establishes the conditions for its management (the "terms" of the trust); and (4) the beneficiaries to whom the benefits of the trust accrue and who may be considered the trust's ultimate purpose. The beneficiaries must be "definite", i.e. ascertainable at the time of creation of the trust or in the future. The "benefits and advantages" received by the beneficiaries, and the conditions under which these are made available, would be determined when the trust is created by its settlor. In cases of a "contingent entitlement", the beneficiaries might have to satisfy some requirement (e.g. attain a specific age) before being able to receive the benefit of

5 See the Hague Convention on the Law Applicable to Trusts and their Recognition (1985), and South Africa's Trust Property Control Act 57 of 1988, as amended by the Justice Laws Rationalisation Act 18 of 1996.

6 For a detailed discussion of this topic, see Cameron *et al.* (2002).

the trust. While the settlor has great freedom to determine the purpose of a trust, the trust must serve a lawful goal and cannot be used to achieve an invalid or illegal purpose.

The administrative and non-dispositive trust terms must relate to the purpose. While the wording of a written trust instrument is almost always the most important determinant of a trust's terms, the definition is not so limited. Oral statements, the situation of the beneficiaries, the purposes of the trust, the circumstances under which the trust is to be administered and, to the extent the settlor was otherwise silent, rules of construction, all may have a bearing on determining a trust's meaning.[7]

Trust "property"

A trust is created around designated "property" which must be definitely ascertainable at the time of trust creation. "Property" means anything that may be the subject of ownership, whether real or personal, legal or equitable, or any interest therein (US Uniform Trust Code, last reviewed or amended in 2005). In the South African Act, "trust property" means "movable or immovable property" that is managed by the trustee "in accordance with the provisions of a trust instrument" (Trust Property Control Act 57 of 1988, Sect. 1). "Knowledge" itself, of course, is not protected by statutory IP law – patents protect actual inventions (which incorporate the knowledge) – and, as noted above, only "secrecy" can protect this. Nevertheless, the actual products, or components, of such knowledge (such as an actual plant in its natural or processed state) or its active components (such as a plant's leaves, roots, etc.) could constitute the trust property and therefore be protected from outsiders. Other protectable property might include any medicinal preparations made from the plant or its products, provided these are manufactured in a reproducible manner, i.e. a consistent recipe. The land on which the plants grow, and its products (the plants), could be placed into a trust as well, managed by the trustee, with benefits accruing to the designated beneficiaries.

Determination of the nature of trust property and the specific ways in which it can be utilised or exploited are determined by the trust settlor. In the case of the Kukula Healers, there already exists *property* in the form of the products of TK (specific plants) made available to the Godding and Godding laboratories for testing with the goal of producing cosmetics. In order to clearly define the trust property, not only the exact plants but also the precise components of the plants should be defined (e.g. leaves, roots, stems). Various conditions, consistent with

7 See Restatement (Third) of Trusts Section 4 cmt. a (Tentative Draft No. 1, approved 1996); Restatement (Second) of Trusts Section 4 cmt. a (1959).

the healers' customary laws, could be included in the trust property description (e.g. time of harvesting, plant size). This of course presupposes that the Kukula Healers are able to claim ownership of the relevant plants and, ideally, the land on which they grow in order to maximise the benefits of the trust. For purposes of this report, we have assumed that such ownership, or at least control, of the land and the subject plants is within the power of the Healers' trust. Property can also include the land on which the plants grow provided the settlor (see below) is empowered to dispose of this land.

Important is the fact that the creation of a trust to manage the TK does not preclude the use of other legal mechanisms to protect the knowledge or, more specifically, any commercial products created. The trust would be able to avail itself of standard IP rights such as patents, trademarks, geographical indications and trade secrets, to mention a few examples.

The "settlor"

The trust settlor is the person or group of persons contributing property to the trust. In the case of the Kukula Healers, as noted above, the Association currently consists of 300 members with an overall management group of 26 people and an executive management committee of six individuals. The settlor could thus conceivably be the entire group of Kukula Healers, its executive committee, the K2C Management Committee, or specifically identified members of these groups such as the CEO of the Kukula Healers. However, it could be presumed that the Healers would want to follow their established practice, as per their Association, of using the management group to create and determine the conditions of the trust and the duties of the trustee(s). The Healers' Association has specific "Rules of Association" that determine how the association and executive are constituted and managed. Such rules would continue to exist independently of how a trust would be created and function, and are not the subject of this proposal.

"Terms"

The "terms" of a trust are a manifestation of the settlor's intent regarding a trust's provisions (US Uniform Trust Code). The provisions of the trust determine how the trust property, in this case the plants, may be used. Presumably the ultimate goal would be to commercialise the product for the benefit of the trust beneficiaries, by permitting a manufacturer to collect, process and sell to outsiders. The terms of the trust would determine, for example, how such a manufacturer would be chosen, whether products could be patented, how the beneficiaries would be remunerated etc. Conditions of particular significance to the Healers could be included as part of the trust instrument. For example, if the TK requires it, only members of the Association would be permitted to harvest the plants or the components required by the manufacturer.

Rules regarding the administration of the trust would be set out at the date of trust creation. Examples include such details as what constitutes a quorum of trustees for decision-making purposes, how often trustees should meet and whether any particular trustee has a deciding vote. The Healers' traditional decision-making rules could be incorporated into these. In addition, rules regarding how the product can be used or sold (e.g. only for cosmetic purposes and not as a poison) could be expressed in the terms of the trust but would additionally need to be outlined in any contract or licence with the manufacturer. The Kukula Healers would be able to add their customary norms for use of their TK as the terms of the trust.

The "trustee"

The term "trustee" means any person (including the founder of a trust) who acts as trustee by virtue of an authorisation under Section 6 of the Trust Property Control Act 57 of 1988. The essential duty of the trustee, who at all times is expected to act in good faith with reasonable care and with prudence, is to follow the terms and purpose of the trust and administer the trust solely in the interest of the beneficiaries. The duties of the trustee may be varied and include activities such as arranging to collect trust property, resolving any disputes concerning the trust or its administration and arranging contracts or licences with outside manufacturers and distributors. In South Africa, beneficiaries can also be trustees – provided, however, that the trustees include an unrelated individual qualified to act as a trustee, such as an accountant or lawyer.[8]

A major decision for the settlor would, in the case of a Kukula Healers' trust, be identification of a trustee or trustees. The trustee could be an outside entity – such as an independent lawyer or Natural Justice or the K2C Management Committee – or a group of individuals selected from among the members of the Kukula Healers. Essentially, the trustee can be a legal "person" with the legal capacity to administer the trust property. Ideally, this would be an individual, or group of individuals, respected by the Kukula Healers and having both the moral and legal authority to enforce the terms of the trust.

The "beneficiary"

The trust must have a designated beneficiary consisting of a legal "person" who is capable of holding legal title to property. Such a "person" may include partnerships

8 See *Land and Agricultural Bank of South Africa v Parker and others* 2005 (2) SA 77 (SCA).

or associations (incorporated or unincorporated), a requirement particularly relevant here given the existence of the Kukula Healers. In this regard, a class of persons could be named as the beneficiary of the trust, so long as the class is definitely ascertainable. The beneficiaries could be individual healers, children of the healers and/or the wider community. It is possible that the Kukula Healers Association's by-laws could define different groups in the Association, with only some constituting trust beneficiaries, e.g. all qualified traditional healers who are registered members of the Kukula Healers' Association, or those who have been members for more than five years. It must be noted that if the settlor's designation of beneficiaries was indefinite and made their identification difficult, the trust would fail as a legal entity.

5. Conclusions

Faced with uncompensated bio-prospecting, overharvesting of medicinal plants and continued marginalisation, the Kukula Healers have made efforts in recent years to protect their culture and identity, as well as to strengthen their livelihoods as traditional healers, through the development of their BCP and their TK commons. Their BCP and TK commons are attempts to preserve and utilise the values and norms intrinsic to the Kukula Healers' development and use, for several generations, of medicinal knowledge.

The Kukula Healers' pre-existing commons was one where sharing and transfer of knowledge were conducted through training schools and ancestral communication. The knowledge is often considered sacred and therefore has strict rules associated with its dissemination. A continuing challenge is the matter of how knowledge can flow through the TK commons system of the Kukula Healers in a manner ensuring its protection but not diluting the sanctity of the knowledge and values.

In their dealings with outsiders, the Kukula Healers have recently used their BCP and TK commons to engage with a local company. A non-disclosure agreement between the Kukula Healers and the company acknowledges the Healers' ownership of the knowledge and the necessity of a benefit-sharing agreement should the company's research result in a commercially viable product.

For the future, however, a trust model is a legal mechanism that could be useful to the Kukula Healers in order to more effectively manage their TK commons. It is important to recognise that the actual knowledge could not constitute the "property" for the purposes of a trust (as opposed to the property represented by the actual biological resource). The legal mechanism of a trust potentially offers a dynamic system, a system in which the products or manifestations of their knowledge could be protected and shared among the community of healers under certain clear terms, with benefits flowing back to the beneficiaries. Not only would it be useful to the commons but it is also a legal mechanism utilised by many national legal systems.

The options for protecting TK in established international or national IP law are limited, as this body of law was developed to suit innovation and development in countries that were already highly industrialised. As a consequence, TK-holders must consider other means of protecting their knowledge. As we demonstrate here, such protection may have to be indirect, utilising other well-established legal mechanisms such as the trust.

Bibliography

Primary Sources

Legal instruments

International:

Convention on Biological Diversity (CBD) (1992) 1760 UNTS 79, available at: www.cbd.int/doc/legal/cbd-en.pdf (accessed 30 April 2013).

Hague Convention on the Law Applicable to Trusts and on Their Recognition (1985).

Nagoya Protocol on Access to Genetic Resources and the Fair and Equitable Sharing of Benefits Arising from their Utilization to the Convention on Biological Diversity (Nagoya Protocol on Access and Benefit-Sharing) (2010), UN Doc UNEP/CBD/COP/10/27, 29 October, available at: www.cbd.int/abs/doc/protocol/nagoya-protocol-en.pdf (accessed 30 April 2013).

Uniform Trust Code, last reviewed or amended in 2005, United States.

South Africa:

Bio-prospecting, Access and Benefit-Sharing Regulations of 2008.

Kukula Healers (2010), Biocultural Protocol of the Traditional Health Practitioners of Bushbuckridge, available at: http://community-protocols.org/wp-content/uploads/documents/South_Africa-Bushbuckridge_Biocultural_Protocol.pdf (accessed 30 April 2013).

Mpumalanga Witchcraft Suppression Bill of 2007 [draft], suspended in 2008.

National Environmental Management: Biodiversity Act 10 of 2004.

Traditional Health Practitioners Act 35 of 2004.

Trust Property Control Act 57 of 1988, as amended by the Justice Laws Rationalisation Act 18 of 1996.

Witchcraft Suppression Act 3 of 1957.

Policies

Kukula Healers (2012), Code of Ethics.

Indigenous Knowledge Systems Policy of 2004.

Case

Land and Agricultural Bank of South Africa v Parker and others 2005 (2) SA 77 (SCA).

Secondary sources

Abrell, E., Bavikatte, K.S., Cocchiaro, G., Maister, B., Rens, A. and Von Braun, J. (2009), *Implementing a Traditional Knowledge Commons: Opportunities and Challenges*, available at: http://naturaljustice.org/wp-content/uploads/pdf/Implementing_a_TKC-2009.pdf (accessed 30 April 2013).

Ashforth, A. (2005), *Witchcraft, Violence, and Democracy in South Africa*, University of Chicago Press, Chicago.

Bastida-Munoz, M.C. and Patrick, G.A. (2006), "Traditional knowledge and intellectual property rights: beyond TRIPS agreements and intellectual property chapters of FTAs", *Michigan State Journal of International Law*, Vol. 14, pp. 259–89.

Bavikatte, K.S. (2011), "Stewarding the commons: rethinking property and the emergence of biocultural rights", in *Common Voices,* Issue 7, available at: www.fes.org.in/common-voices-7.pdf (accessed 30 March 2013).

Benkler, Y. (2006), *The Wealth of Networks: How Social Production Transforms Markets and Freedom*, Yale University Press, New Haven, CT.

Buck, S. J. (1998), *The Global Commons: An Introduction*, Island Press, Washington, DC.

Cameron, E., De Waal, M.J., Kahn, E., Solomon, P. and Wunsch, B. (2002), *Honoré: The South African Law of Trusts*, 5th ed., Juta, Cape Town.

Chhatre, A. and Agrawal, A. (2008), "Forest commons and local enforcement", *Proceedings of the National Academy of Sciences,* Vol. 105 No. 36, pp. 13286–91, available at: www.pnas.org/content/105/36/13286.full.pdf (accessed 30 April 2013).

Correa, C.M. (2004), *Update on International Developments Relating to the Intellectual Property Protection of Traditional Knowledge Including Traditional Medicine*, Trade-Related Agenda, Development and Equity (TRADE) Working Papers No. 18, South Centre, Geneva.

Douglas, M. (1966), *Purity and Danger: An Analysis of Concepts of Pollution and Taboo*, Routledge, London.

Drahos, P. and Frenkel, S. (Eds) (2012), *Indigenous People's Innovation: Intellectual Property Pathways to Development*, Australian National University E Press, Canberra.

Du Plessis, E. (2012), "Protection of traditional knowledge in South Africa: does the 'commons' provide a solution?" draft paper, Faculty of Law, University of Johannesburg.

Hardin, G. (1968), "The tragedy of the commons", *Science*, Vol. 162, pp. 1243–48.

Hess, C. and Ostrom, E. (Eds) (2007), *Understanding Knowledge as a Commons: From Theory to Practice*, MIT Press, Cambridge, MA.

International Institute for Environment and Development (IIED) (2009), "Key findings", in *Protecting Community Rights over Traditional Knowledge: Implications of Customary Laws and Practices. Key Findings and Recommendations 2005–2009*, available at: www.pubs.iied.org/14591IIED.pdf (accessed 30 April 2013).

Kruger to Canyons Biosphere Region (K2C) (n.d.), available at: www.kruger2canyons.org (accessed 30 April 2013).

Natural Justice (n.d.), available at: http://naturaljustice.org (accessed 30 April 2013).

Niehaus, I. (2002), "Ethnicities and the boundaries of belonging: reconfiguring Shangaan identity in the South African lowveld", *African Affairs*, Vol. 101 No. 405, pp. 557–83.

Niehaus, I. (2005), "Witches and zombies in the South African lowveld: discourse, accusation and subjective reality", *Journal of the Royal Anthropological Institute*, Vol. 11 No. 2, pp. 191–210.

Nyaka, F. (2013), "Concern over HIV-Aids numbers", *The New Age*, 14 March, available at www.journaids.org/images/uploads/0314_TNA_Concern_over_HIV_AIDS_numbers%282%29.pdf (accessed 19 March 2013).

Ostrom, E. (1990), *Governing the Commons: The Evolution of Institutions for Collective Action*, Cambridge University Press, Cambridge, UK.

Weiner, A.B. (1985), "Inalienable wealth", *American Ethnologist*, Vol. 12 No. 2, pp. 210–27.

Chapter 8

From *De Facto* Commons to Digital Commons? The Case of Egypt's Independent Music Industry

Nagla Rizk[1]

Abstract

This chapter provides the findings of a research study into the dynamics of Egypt's vibrant independent music industry, which previous research has identified as potentially having "commons" dynamics. Based on a survey of musicians and consumers, and interviews with key stakeholders, the research found a complex set of dynamics and attitudes at play in relation to distribution and consumption of the musicians' output. The research generated the conclusion that a Creative Commons-based "digital commons" business model using a "freemium" approach to payment may be worth exploring as a means to comply with copyright law in a manner that still caters to the existing priorities of musicians and consumers.

1. Background

The research case study outlined in this chapter explored the legal and sociocultural frameworks that reward creativity and enable knowledge-sharing in Egypt's independent music industry. Egypt is renowned for its entertainment industry and has been dubbed the "Hollywood of the East". Its long and extensive history has made Egypt a cultural powerhouse, dominating the film and music industries in the region and making it fertile ground for this research.

This research builds on the findings and recommendations of the author's previous work on Egypt's music industry, which concluded that "the live music scene in Egypt offers a special form of the commons [...] [dubbed the] *de facto*

---

1 The author is grateful for the work of the A2K4D research team, comprising Lina Attalah, Nagham El Houssamy, Mariam El Abd and Youssef El Shazli, and for the contribution to the field work by Marc Michael and Nagla Eid.

commons because it represents practices that have naturally emanated from the bottom up without any deliberate actions or conscious decision on the part of any organizing agency" (Rizk, 2010a, p. 128). I consequently recommended that "a more commons-based approach" to music be adopted through advertising or a subscription-based model "that incorporates social networking, virtual gift giving, and holding virtual parties. Such formats would be highly suitable to the Egyptian culture and practices of accessing music" (Rizk, 2010a, p. 128).

This case study comprised a collection of on-the-ground responses and evidence relating to music consumption patterns, and to the relevance and role of the current copyright regime in Egypt's independent music industry, from multiple perspectives: the musicians, consumers and other stakeholders, such as venue owners and lawyers. The work also examined the "open development" paradigm (see Smith *et al.*, 2011) by addressing the question of how to create a valid environment that would empower peer production and collaboration rather than marginalise selected stakeholders via intellectual property (IP) exclusion tools. (See Chapter 9 of this volume for discussion of the dynamics of copyright in relation to openness-oriented approaches to scholarly works.) Given the need for music-sharing among alternative Egyptian musicians, a valid IP environment in the country will be one with accepted and workable IP laws that eliminates the need for copyright infringement. Alternative musicians (as opposed to mainstream commercial musicians) were chosen as research participants because their field serves as a laboratory for studying the limitations of, as well as alternatives to, current IP regimes.

Music as a quasi-public good, and the access versus incentive tension

Music, like other knowledge goods, evokes the question of the extent to which it can be considered a public good or a private one. A public good is typically non-rivalrous (one person's use does not preclude another person's utility) and non-excludable (no member of the public can be denied access). Because adding an extra user has no effect on the cost of producing a public good, universal access is usually socially desirable because excluding people means sacrificing public welfare unnecessarily. For public goods, the marginal cost of production (what it costs to produce one extra unit of the good) is zero. Therefore, the provision of a public good is unsustainable as a market practice; no private entity has an incentive to produce it.

Music is conceptually non-rivalrous; one person's enjoyment of a song does not take away from another's. However, the non-rivalrous nature of music becomes complex when we consider different forms of music. The most common forms of music today are digital, as downloaded and stored in a computer or another digital device, packaged in a tape or CD, or delivered via live performances. Digital music is non-rivalrous and involves zero marginal cost of reproduction and distribution. On the other hand, packaged music makes music rivalrous, as the tape or CD is a private good by definition (Romer, 2002). Live performances by a particular musician also have an element of rivalry.[2] For concerts in closed halls with a limit on space, there are costs to expanding the size of the audience, and, for any concert, each additional person creates additional clean-up costs. In this way, a second cost adds to the marginal cost of expanding the audience size.

Given the rivalrous nature of some forms of music, it is clear that some forms can also be excludable, unlike a typical public good. Music can be technically excludable in the case of a record album that cannot be easily reproduced, or a digital file with technological protection measures (TPMs). Legal barriers in the form of IP rules that prohibit one musician from covering another musician's song, or that treat digital music-sharing as piracy, can also make music excludable. Physically, music can also be excludable in the case of a wall that blocks out members of the public who do not pay to see a live performance. Music can therefore be characterised as a *quasi*-public good, in the sense that it may be both non-rivalrous and possibly excludable at the same time. An additional user may not add to the marginal cost, yet excludability can be maintained by imposing a price (AmosWEB, 2013). It is possible to treat a *quasi*-public good as a purely private one by charging for access, but this is not economically efficient from the perspective of maximising social welfare. A trade-off emerges between maximising public welfare by expanding access and maximising private incentives by limiting access.

Egypt's music industry illustrates an access–incentive trade-off: music suppliers seek to maximise compensation through accruing monopoly rents via IP-based exclusion (incentive), whereas music consumers maximise their welfare by pursuing more access and sharing – using a variety of tools, including digital technologies (access). My previous research on Egypt's music industry found that in adapting to access–incentive tensions in the market and declining CD sales, the bulk of musicians' income comes from the live music scene, as opposed to copyrighted recordings. This live music scene, a type of social commons (coined "*de facto* commons" in my previous research), provides "a medium of bringing music creators and users together, without much need for the label, nor indeed copyright" (Rizk, 2010a, p. 127). According to Lemos (2007), social commons modalities

2 Live music performance may be non-rivalrous, since one person's enjoyment does not take away from another's, except if one is placed in a spot where he/she is blocked by the person in front. Free-riding can still occur when, for example, people listen to outdoor concerts from neighbouring surroundings (Lange, 2009). For open-air concerts, adding a user may not add to the marginal cost. In general, the possibility of non-rivalry and excludability qualifies the live performance as a quasi-public good.

thrive in situations where technology precedes the law, allowing independent creative industries based on free sharing and dissemination to appear. I referred to the live music scene in Egypt as a *de facto* commons because it represents practices that have naturally originated through a bottom-up approach, without any planned action or deliberate decision from any organising agency (Rizk, 2010a, p. 128). Such social commons models based on bottom-up approaches may be suited to developing countries where intellectual property regimes are not fully developed (Lemos, 2007). In a world of *de facto* commons, there is a convergence between the interests of musicians and users, without much need for copyright protection.

This *de facto* commons operates in parallel to the legal mainstream and serves both consumers and musicians. It also upholds the *quasi*-public nature of music goods (i.e. non-rival consumption but possibly excludable consumption), which renders traditional pricing mechanisms and typical IP maximalist motives in the music industry ineffectual in catering for economic efficiency. In relation to sustainable development, social commons or *de facto* models crystallise the meaning of knowledge as a form of public good that needs to be shared and disseminated (Rizk, 2010a, p. 101). Additionally, in a gift culture that "rejoices in sharing and gives little attention to individuality", the commons-based approach upholds the nature of music as a *quasi*-public good, whose value increases with the number of users (Rizk, 2010a, p. 126).

The legal context

Statutory protection of copyright in Egypt was introduced by the Copyright Law 354 of 1954, which was modified several times. In 2002 Egypt adopted a new law, the Egyptian Intellectual Property Rights Law 82 of 2002 (EIPRL, or "the Law"), which replaced the copyright statute and kept many of its provisions but expanded its scope by adding new ones, such as folklore protection. The Law generally protects all creative productions in the literary, scientific and musical domains, whatever their type or mode of expression. It provides protection for written works, oral works, paintings, sculpture, architecture, applied and plastic arts, theatre and musical pieces, photographs and cinematographic films, television and radio works, sketches, databases and computer software. Protection does not extend to mere ideas, procedures, systems, operational methods, concepts, discoveries and data. Protection does not cover information or ideas contained in a work; it only protects the original way in which information or ideas have been expressed. Protection for the author is automatic as soon as the original work is created in a fixed and tangible form of expression. While the Law requires publishers, printers and producers of works, sound recordings, performance recordings and broadcast programmes to "jointly deposit one or more copies, not exceeding 10, of their works", failure to deposit such copies "shall not affect the author's rights and related rights provided for under this Law" (Art. 184).

For musical recordings, Articles 160–165 of the Law grant copyright protection "for 50 years from the recording date if owned by a company and for 50 years after the death of the author if owned by an individual". Article 140.6 gives authors an exclusive right over musical works. Copyright violations are subject to fines ranging between LE 5,000[3] and LE 10,000 (approximately US$ 900 and US$ 1,800) per infringement and/or a minimum of one month imprisonment (Art. 181). Article 140(13) also protects derivative works and covers the "related rights" of performers such as musicians, actors, dancers, producers of phonograms (or sound recording such as CDs and cassettes) and broadcasting organisations. (See Appendix 8.1 for further review of the copyright provisions of the Law of 2002.) The Ministry of Culture is responsible for enforcing copyrights associated with music.

Alongside the Law's IP rights provisions, alternative licensing has sparked interest in Egypt. Creative Commons and other alternative licences are the product of individual negotiations for specific rights between the licensor (copyright owner) and the licensee, resulting in standardised licences for re-use cases with no commercial compensation sought by the copyright owner. Creative Commons licences enable creators to decide which rights they reserve and which rights they waive so that users and other creators can share, use and build upon the original work. Instead of falling under a typical copyright protection umbrella of "all rights reserved", alternative licences create an umbrella of "some rights reserved", creating "a balance between the reality of the Internet and the reality of copyright laws" (Creative Commons, 2012).

In June 2007, Egypt signed a memorandum of understanding with Creative Commons to adopt the alternative licence in accordance with Egyptian law. The licence was first translated into Arabic, and this "unported" licence (i.e. not associated with any specific jurisdiction) was carefully reviewed to ensure compatibility with the Egyptian law, including IP law and civil law. The revised Arabic Creative Commons licences were made available for discussion online in January 2010. In January 2013, as the research described in this chapter was being completed, Egypt was transferring the Egyptian licence to HTML to be posted online (Essalmawi, 2013).

IP law in practice

As evidenced by the abundance of illegally copied cassette tapes and CDs available on the market, Egyptian IP law as it applies to music is hardly respected or

3 LE stands for Egyptian pound.

enforced. There are no published local statistics on music piracy in Egypt; the only available figures are by the International Intellectual Property Alliance (IIPA), a coalition of associations representing US copyright-based industries. The IIPA reports that 75% of physical music (cassette and CD) distribution in Egypt consists of black market copies of a single original copy (IIPA, 2010). A popular form of illegal copying is the creation of "cocktails" – cassette and CD compilations of a variety of top hits sold on street kiosks downtown and elsewhere. These are part of an informal network of shops, street vendors and small-scale replication plants called "copy shops" that burn CDs on the spot (AmCham, 2005).

Mirroring the illegal music copying on Egyptian streets is an abundance of illegal access to music from the internet. Table 8.1 below offers an example of illegal download websites with the highest traffic in Egypt, which are among the top 75 websites most visited by Egyptians. These websites are easily accessible from home computers and PCs in internet cafés. The unlicensed software typically installed on computers in Egypt enables illegal downloading (AmCham, 2005). In 2008, the Egyptian music and record industry reported that illegal downloads represented 97% of all digital distribution of music in the country (IIPA, 2010, p. 177).

Table 8.1: Popular websites for illegal music downloads in Egypt

Alexa traffic rank *	Online music website
33	mazika2day.com
48	mawaly.com
60	melody4arab.com
75	Sm3na.com

* Rank among top websites visited in Egypt, as compiled from Alexa.com (January 2013). Alexa is an online provider of global web metrics that offers site analysis based on keyword, category or country.

Source: Alexa.com (2013)

The evidence on illegal copying, street "cocktails" and illegal downloading demonstrates that a great deal of music consumption in Egypt falls outside the scope of IP laws. Against this background, this case study explored how the consumption and production of independent music in Egypt, operate in the midst of restrictive copyright instruments and the mutual need of both consumers and producers for music sharing. This case study sought to bring the voices of central actors into the debate, namely, the consumers, musicians, producers and other stakeholders in the music industry. The study was the first to use field work to collect primary data on a large scale in Egypt on this topic, and it tapped into the perceptions behind music consumption habits and the thrust behind producing music outside the scope of the mainstream.

2. Research objectives and questions

How can independent music be nurtured and sustained within frameworks and models that reward creativity and enable knowledge-sharing, in a way that reflects the current practices of music consumption and production in Egypt? To answer this research question, field work was carried out to explore the prevailing perceptions of copyright and the practices of consumption and delivery of independent music. The research looked into the extent to which awareness of copyright and its breach intersects with trends in music delivery and consumption. It also looked at the gap in copyright awareness between physical and digital goods, whereby the notion of materiality directly correlates with the relevance of copyright. (This has its effect on the understanding of how products that are available online can be consumed and how the musicians behind them should be remunerated.) Accordingly, the study tapped into propositions on models that would legalise, accommodate and refine existing grassroots mechanisms for music production and sharing. The research also explored the possibility of creating a "*quasi*-commons" in which collaborators could be compensated for creativity and simultaneously satisfy the public interest in unhindered music-sharing. Specifically, the questions in the research included, but were not limited to:

- What are the prevalent trends of music consumption among users?
- What are the existing perceptions of copyright among users and producers?
- What types of reward are musicians seeking? Are they content with using their music as a channel for voicing opinion, or would they want to reap a monetary benefit as well, and, if so, how would that be possible?
- Which channels of remuneration do musicians prefer? Which ones do consumers prefer?
- How might it be possible to capitalise on the *quasi*-public, non-rival nature of music and yet create value that provides incentives to production?
- Which business models would be most suitable to empowering authors in the industry, bearing in mind socio-cultural factors?

The findings of this case study should prove valuable to policy-makers, as, in essence, the study addresses the core controversy inherent in any knowledge-embedded good: how can modern business models adapt to derive value from sharing and collaboration rather than resorting to maximalist IP tactics? If such models are to be developed, they will ultimately empower collaborators in the creative industry and encourage knowledge-sharing, thereby acting as a catalyst for invention, knowledge production and open development.

3. Methodology and design

The sample for this study consisted of a cross-section of 600 consumers of alternative music in Cairo and 38 individuals involved in the music industry (coming from creative, production, distribution and policy-making perspectives).[4] These included 24 independent musicians, five owners/managers of performance outlets, three owners/managers of digital platforms, two owners/managers from cultural centres, one policy-maker, one union lawyer, one producer and one copyright expert. (See Appendix 8.2 for a complete list of interviewees). A structured survey was deemed appropriate for the consumer group, whereas in-depth semi-structured interviews were utilised for the music industry sample. The survey allowed a larger number of consumers to be sampled in a cost-effective way, and the types of answers sought were straightforward enough to warrant beforehand-coding and very few open-ended questions. On the other hand, given that much less was known beforehand about the music industry and its operations – i.e. about the generation of musicians that constitutes the alternative music scene, their business models and the problems and successes they encounter – interviews were necessary so as to elicit more detailed information.

The consumer survey was carried out in Cairo – by a research team based at the Access to Knowledge for Development Center (A2K4D) at The American University in Cairo (AUC) – between March and April 2012. The survey followed a targeted stratified methodology. Appendix 8.3 provides the list of all institutions and venues targeted for the purposes of this study. These venues represent a cross-section of the most important institutional players on the Cairene alternative art scene. The researchers carried out the surveys at these alternative music outlets and performance and art spaces because the interested customer population was

4 The initial research plan included interviewing 60 individuals from the music industry, but, due to several constraints, that target was unattainable. One limitation in this study was the difficulty in contacting the originally desired number of musicians. This limitation should be taken into consideration in interpreting the numerical results of the musicians. This is, to some extent, compensated for by the anecdotes provided by musicians, which are reflected in the analysis.

more concentrated at those venues than among the general population, and in consideration of the high rates of non-response that were likely to occur had a random, door-to-door methodology been adopted. The sample was stratified according to gender only, given that for alternative music-consuming populations, older age groups might not be available. In absolute terms, a larger percentage of interviews was obtained from Sakiat al-Sawy (Al Sawy Cultural Wheel)[5] compared with other outlets, understandable given that venue's large capacity, diversity of audience and attendance rates. However, relative to their size, capacity and attendance rates, institutions were all fairly represented in the final sample of 600 respondents. (See Appendix 8.4 for more details on the consumer survey sample.)

For the semi-structured in-depth industry interviews, individuals involved in the alternative music and art industries were chosen according to criteria associated with their specific roles in the music industry. Musicians were chosen according to their visibility on the alternative music scene, as measured by their YouTube video click count or by their concert presence at the more frequented alternative venues. In this sense, the sample was also slightly stratified to include musicians whose music had "gone viral" and also those who were relatively well-known but had not broken through as yet. The policy-maker interviewed was selected according to his knowledge of the topic at hand.

4. Findings

Participants' knowledge of IP and perceptions of its relevance

The survey and interview results revealed a lack of relevance – from the perspective of consumers, musicians and other stakeholders – of copyright in relation to the Egyptian alternative music scene. This comes from their answers regarding three topics: (1) knowledge of the law; (2) obstacles hindering their creativity; and (3) incentives to comply with the law.

First, the lack of knowledge of the Egyptian copyright law by consumers and musicians pointed to the limited relevance of copyright in the independent music industry. While 71% of music consumers surveyed knew the general meaning of copyright and IP, only 26% of the total sample was familiar with the content of Egyptian copyright law. All of the musicians interviewed confessed they knew

5 Al Sawy Cultural Wheel was built on the site of a garbage dump under a flyover by the Nile. The centre transformed the role of the middleman in the music industry by "removing the concept of CVs", according to centre founder/director Mohamed Al Sawy (cited in Rizk, 2010a).

very little or nothing about copyright law in Egypt.[6] Additionally, the majority of musicians felt that the copyright regime was irrelevant to the art industry at large and to their own work. Only two out of 24 musicians thought copyright reform mattered, and stated it would only be effective if it shifted the balance of power away from production companies in favour of musicians. Hosam Loutfi, member of the Law Committee in the Supreme Council of Culture (and an IP lawyer), shed light on the lack of awareness of copyright in Egypt. He pointed out that independent musicians do not seek out the options available to them, and thus are not aware of how they could benefit from copyright (Loutfi, 2012). This perspective also explains the process by which copyright may have been rendered irrelevant in the minds of musicians.

Second, the musicians' perception of the lack of relevance of copyright could be deduced from their answers to questions on the obstacles hindering music and creativity in Egypt. None of the musicians cited the copyright regime as a main obstacle. Instead, they cited the role of production companies, media and government bureaucracy as the main obstacles. Furthermore, responses from other stakeholders also did not place importance on copyright. Dr. Ahmed El Maghraby, owner of Makan art outlet,[7] felt that, despite the existence of copyright in Egypt, the main obstacle facing musicians is the corrupt judicial process and court system, which hinder any protection that copyright could otherwise give to musicians (El Maghraby, 2012). Ahmed Mohamed, Partner and General Manager of Studio Vibe, mentioned the music syndicate laws as a major hindrance, since their requirements are too restrictive for young independent musicians. To illustrate this, Mohamed spoke of how requirements seek to compel musicians to be members of the syndicate in order to perform when, in fact, nowadays some young musicians have not reached the required membership age (Mohamed, 2012).

Third, copyright's lack of relevance is compounded by its absence as an incentive to musicians. Two main perspectives were voiced regarding copyright's apparent failure to incentivise. One view was that the legal coercion associated with enforcing copyright is a hindrance to musicians. Among the respondents voicing this view was Tarek Metwalli, founder of Who's Jammin?,[8] a digital platform composed of a worldwide private social network of musicians categorised by city and instrument. Metwalli spoke of copyright as a major obstacle in building a relationship between musicians and their consumer base. From his perspective,

6 Despite the musicans' little knowledge of the EIPRL, two musicians had heard of Creative Commons, and three felt that Creative Commons licensing would bring improvement to the Egyptian music landscape.

7 Makan is an art outlet in Cairo oriented towards cultural and heritage preservation/awareness.

8 A list of services provided by Who's Jammin? can be found at Who's Jammin? (n.d.).

copyrights promote a relationship of violent coercion, whereby the court system is involved and fines are imposed, rather than promoting a relationship of ethical consumption, whereby consumers want to do the right thing to support good art. Furthermore, Metwalli felt that copyright simply protected the rights of the industry and not that of the musicians (Metwalli, 2012). Another view was that the lack of enforcement of copyright laws deters musicians from pursuing a legal course of action in relation to copyright. When musicians were asked, "How would you feel about changes in copyright policies?" half of them said copyright did not matter because the law was a luxury irrelevant to most people's lives and it was impossible to get one's rights enforced in Egyptian courts. Makan art outlet owner El Maghraby also voiced this view, alluding to the corrupt judicial process and court system in Egypt (El Maghraby, 2012). Thus, in the perceived absence of incentives to comply with copyright, it becomes understandable why musicians see copyright as irrelevant.

Knowledge of the notion of a "digital commons"

In the next set of questions, consumers and musicians were asked about their perception of the notion of a "digital commons". The following is from the definition adopted for this research study:

> The digital commons comprises informational resources created and shared within voluntary communities of varying size and interests. These resources are typically held *de facto* as communal, rather than private or public (i.e. state) property. Management of the resource is characteristically oriented towards use within the community, rather than exchange in the market. As a result, separation between producers and consumers is minimal in the digital commons. (Stalder, 2010)

The sustainability of a digital commons model depends on its source of revenue. In the music context, revenue is commonly generated through advertising, sponsorships and subscription fees, which may include user payments in varying forms: direct payment in case of subscription, or a versioned user model with differential pricing possibly complementing advertising and/or sponsorships. Meetphool[9] is an existing digital platform based on sponsorship that seeks to develop a future model of user payment. Meetphool was established via a grant by the EU awarded in 2009 (Delegation of the EU to Egypt, 2011). Nada Thabet, Meetphool Concept and Technical Manager, explained that one element of the project is an effort to devise models for revenue generation in order to ensure sustainability (Thabet,

9 Meetphool is a platform that specialises in building a network for the performing arts, including music, with a regional focus seeking to bridge the Mediterranean and connect North African and European artists (Meetphool, 2012).

2012). Who's Jammin? founder Metwalli stated that his service's main source of revenue was studio bookings, and he hoped he would not have to resort to placing advertisements on the Who's Jammin? website. Metwalli added that Who's Jammin? will, however, eventually levy a subscription fee for non-musicians to get access to the music uploaded by member musicians on the digital platform (Metwalli, 2012).

Despite the existence of digital platform initiatives in Egypt, there was low familiarity with the notion of a digital commons among the surveyed sample. Initially, none of the consumers or musicians appeared to be familiar with the term. Once the concept was explained to them, just over one fifth of consumers and more than half of the musicians said they were familiar with the notion.

Half the musicians said they did not want to develop a digital commons model, partly because people do not buy music online and partly because they did not believe it could survive in Egypt. Of the total sample of music consumers, 96% said they downloaded music online, yet only 1% said they paid for it. The musicians dismissed alternative licensing and digital commons as irrelevant models for the improvement of the Egyptian independent music industry. Reasons included the lack of internet access and limited security for online payment, as well as the irrelevance of copyright as adequate legal protection. Meetphool interviewee Thabet also pointed to the problem of online payments in Egypt, stating that the country does not have a culture of online credit card use (Thabet, 2012).

Nevertheless, two musicians were in favour of developing a digital commons model to foster collaboration among musicians, citing the potential networking benefits of such a platform. As well, these two musicians expressed the view that a common digital platform could resolve the moral aspect of copyright. Citing YouTube as an example of a technology that helps address the issue of copyright, they felt that uploading a song to a digital platform obviates the need for recourse to a notary public or even to courts, i.e. they viewed uploading a video or a recording to YouTube as guaranteeing proof of authorship, with proof of date, without the hassle of the registration process. In addition, uploading music to YouTube was commended by musicians because, in their opinion, it blurred the distinction between promotion and protection.

Music consumption patterns

Most consumers surveyed were aware that street CDs were illegally copied, but the consumers did not seem to be deterred by this knowledge. Specifically, 97% of the consumers surveyed were aware that cheap street CDs were pirated and 91% believed it was illegal to buy them on the street. The EIPRL does not contain a specific clause for buying illegally copied CDs and thus it is not considered illegal to buy such copies.[10] More than three quarters of consumers surveyed believed that burning CDs was an illegal practice, but only 34% of all consumers were willing to pay more to purchase CDs that respected copyright.

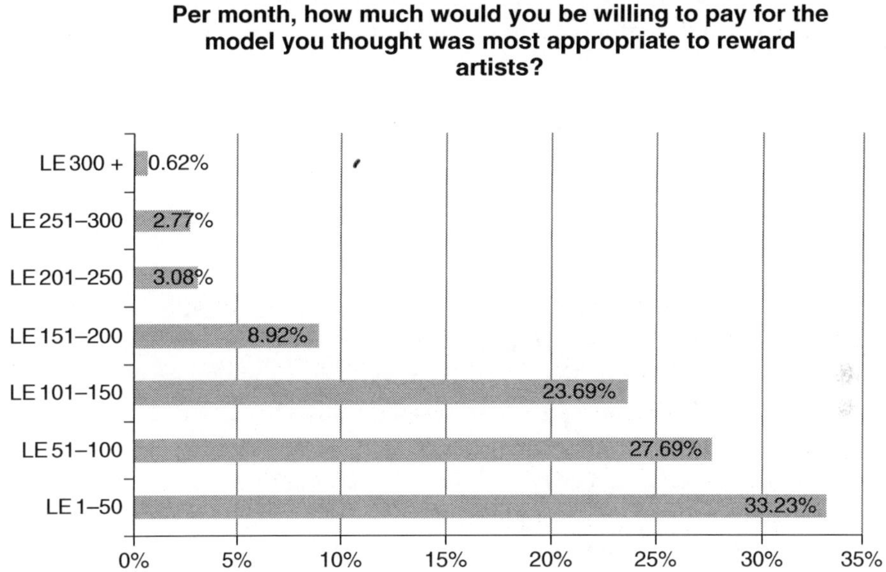

Figure 8.1: Amount respondent willing to pay per month to musicians

The survey asked consumers how much they would be willing to pay per month to reward musicians, regardless of the format of music delivery (Figure 8.1). While one third of the consumer sample was willing to pay between LE 1 and LE 50 (about US$ 0.17–0.18) per month to reward musicians, roughly one quarter of the sample was willing to pay between LE 51 and LE 100 (about US$ 8–16) per month, and slightly more than a quarter was ready to pay between LE 101 and LE 150 (about US$ 16–25). Together, this means that 85% of consumers were willing to pay some amount between LE 1 and LE 150 (US$ 0.17–25) per month, while only 15% were willing to pay more than that (LE 151–300 [US$ 25–50]).

Some questions were directed to the sub-group of consumers who use CDs or cassettes to listen to music (200 people, representing 33% of the sample). Of this sub-sample, 20% purchased illegally burned CDs and cassettes on the street at a cheaper rate, and 65% purchased them from stores with legal distribution

10 According to Article 181 of the EIPRL, it is illegal to sell burned/copied CDs. However, making a single copy of a CD for exclusive personal use is legal (Art. 171.2), provided that this copy shall not hamper the normal exploitation of the work nor cause undue prejudice to the legitimate interests of the copyright-holder.

rights. When asked about the reasons behind their consumption patterns, only 14% mentioned a respect for IP rights, as opposed to 86% who mentioned better quality as their primary reason.

In the sample of consumers, 33% (200 individuals) listened to CDs and cassettes that they purchased either in stores or on the streets. Consumers demonstrated a distinction in attitudes with respect to digital music. The prevailing view among the majority of consumers was that music available online is free and legally available for all. Consumption patterns reflected this view. Of the total sample of music consumers, 96% said they download music online, yet only 1% said they pay for it. Slightly more than 80% of respondents said they do not pay for the music they download due to the availability of free download sites. Another 14% held the view that websites and music available online are "free" (a misconception which reveals the lack of knowledge of online IP requirements and payment rules). The lack of knowledge of IP and payment rules suggests that there may be a widely held view that all virtual music products are implicitly free of charge by virtue of their online, unrestricted (in practical terms) accessibility.

Interviews with the independent musicians revealed a similar trend, whereby online digital music is perceived as "free". Streaming, in particular, was viewed by several musicians as a free-of-charge form of music. More than one musician noted, as obstacles for charging for digital downloads, the technical difficulties of tracking digital downloads and administering online payments in Egypt. Thus, while the concern for copyright and IP was found to be generally low among the sample of consumers and musicians, it was particularly low in respect of online digital music products. Music consumers and musicians both shared the view that virtual, online products are for free-of-charge use.

Remuneration, musicians' incentives and business models

The next set of questions explored the views of consumers and musicians regarding musicians' remuneration, incentives and business models. Out of the sample of consumers, 91% said they pay for music and 34% of the sample said they spend up to LE 50 (about US$ 8) on music per month (Figure 8.2). In comparison to spending money on CDs/cassettes or online music, consumers spend more money on concert-going. Almost 39% of consumers surveyed said they spend up to LE 100 (about US$ 16) on concerts per month (Figure 8.3).

On average, a respondent in the sample would spend LE 96 (about US$ 15) per month on concert-going, whereas the average respondent would spend a mere LE 14 (about US$ 2) per month on purchasing CDs/cassettes (and, in rare cases, online downloads), in other words approximately seven times less than on concert-going. And, as was mentioned above, although 96% of the sample reported downloading music online, only 1% of them reported paying for it, suggesting that the overwhelming majority of the "downloaders", 99%, download music free. Money spent on concerts, therefore, represents a disproportionately much larger

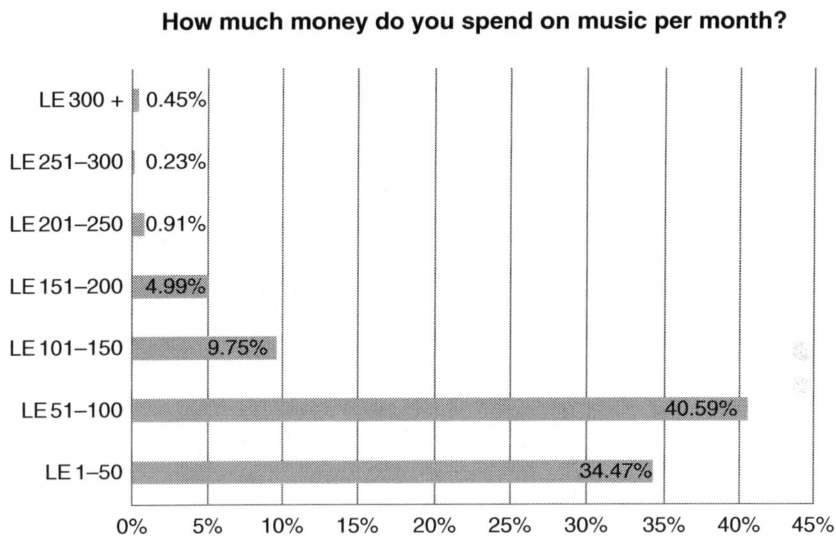

Figure 8.2: Money spent on music per month

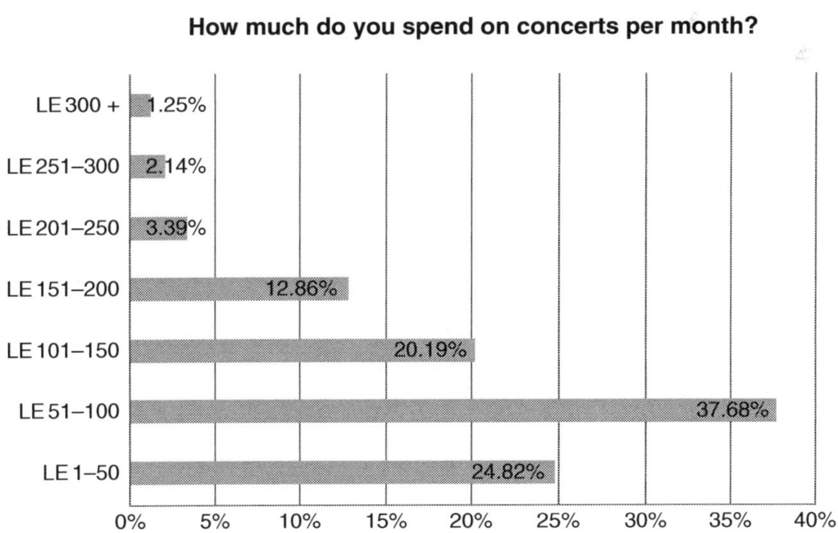

Figure 8.3: Money spent on concerts per month

sum than money spent on physical or online music goods. Confirming this trend, concerts and live performances were identified as the best medium of reward for musicians' work, with 59% of consumers sampled stating that they believe music creation is a real job that should be rewarded monetarily, and of that 59%, 76% saying that such work should be rewarded monetarily via paid attendance at concerts and performances (see Figures 8.4 and 8.5).

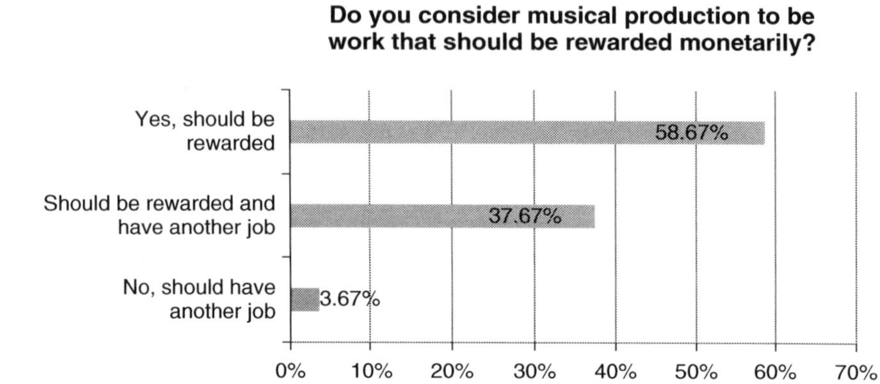

Figure 8.4: Monetary reward for production?

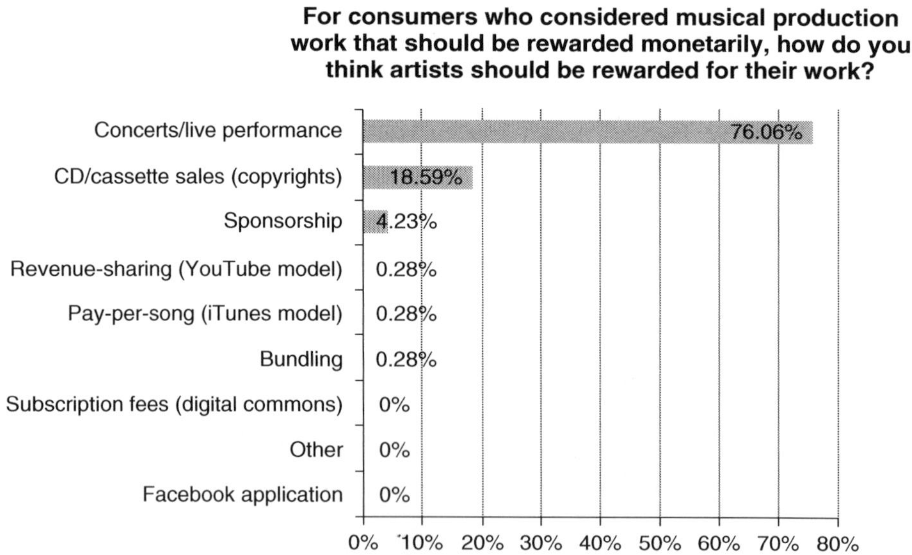

Figure 8.5: Method of monetary reward

Preference for the live scene as the main venue for music delivery was echoed by the musicians. One third of the musicians interviewed (8 out of 24) said they believe that, ideally, musicians should be remunerated for live performances, while half of them (12 out of 24) chose live performances as the first revenue source for themselves. Additionally, half the musicians (12 out of 24) said they get at least 50% of their music income from live performances, and 14 of them said they do not get any music income from copyright-protected recorded material. An exception is George Kazazian, a famous veteran star in the independent scene, who said copyrighted material represented a small amount of music income for him (Kazazian, 2012). For nearly half the musicians (10 out of 24), music is not their main source of income; they make most of their money from other occupations.

Other income for the musicians surveyed mostly comes from composing short jingles for advertisements, or from composing music for famous mainstream musicians. Rather than expecting to generate income from producing an album, a great majority of musicians who had recorded an album said they invested in its production with no hope of getting any direct return from it, demonstrating the fact that album production is viewed as a promotional exercise. Although 11 of the 24 musicians said they had produced one or more CDs, only one had actually signed with a label. Nine of the interviewed musicians agreed they would want to sign if offered the chance, but only if the conditions suited their tastes. They said they were concerned about "selling their souls" to production companies or labels.

For the majority of the alternative musicians surveyed, the importance of performances was said to be not merely an adaptation to the business realities of the contemporary independent music scene in Egypt, but also a lifestyle and ideological choice. This choice was reflected in the musicians' notable self-distancing from the notion of business models or the commercialisation of music practice. While 15 out of the sample of 24 musicians said they receive some income from music, the musicians were found to be uncomfortable when sharing their views about business models. They showed a lack of interest in making money, and were mostly interested in surviving by doing something they were passionate about. When asked, "What is your main incentive for producing music?" none of the independent musicians answered, "To make money". In fact, 16 of the respondents said they do not expect to make much money out of their music.

Many of the musicians surveyed voiced anti-commercialisation notions, perhaps as a reaction to the financially driven mainstream production universe. Almost half the musicians interviewed (10 of 24) highlighted that they would prefer to focus on their music as self-expression, rather than as a response to market demands. They said they did not want to commercialise themselves and preferred to continue creating their music to send their message. Three musicians emphasised the secondary importance of money and their willingness to struggle financially for their musical passion.[11]

In terms of the musicians' business model, more than half (13 of 24) the independent musicians interviewed said they had no business plan at all when they started, and that they still saw themselves as operating without a business plan. During the interviews, some musicians became annoyed or smiled at the mention of business terms, thus demonstrating their anti-commercial inclinations (as noted earlier). In the most extreme cases, the musicians argued against having business plans or considering financial success in order to progress in the field of art. The trend that emerged was that independent musicians accumulate and save money from multiple sources, mostly live performance or non-music-related work, to invest into the production of a recorded album, which is mostly seen as a tool of self-promotion, akin to a rite of passage rather than an important element of survival.

When asked whether they minded if their music is shared free, nine musicians answered that they did not, mostly because they said they see CDs as just a promotional tool and that the more people who listen, the better it is for them. This sentiment was present despite the fact that the musicians who said they do not mind their music being shared free tend to know that this sharing is illegal. Ten musicians agreed that art should be a public good, explaining that access to cultural production should be a human right.

However, despite the musicians' non-monetary and anti-commercial inclinations, some responses revealed propositions to make Egypt's independent music industry more economically viable. Fairuz Karawia, an independent musician, proposed an alternative remuneration model that would use mainstream IP for collaborative production of albums and collective licensing. This, according to Karawia, could be aided by consumers paying for material music goods such as CDs and cassettes. The proposed remuneration model was in line with Karawia's view that musicians should collaborate and devise business models to suit their own needs rather than complain about production companies (Karawia, 2012). Meanwhile, Emad Mubarak, the copyright lawyer interviewed, said he favoured

11 These statements echo those made by interviewees in my earlier research on Egypt's music industry. Moreover, in a National Public Radio (NPR) interview in 2008, independent Egyptian group Black Thema stated that it was not easy for the band to operate and they were working as musicians for almost no monetisation, because they refused to be part of the commercial music industry. The band said its music covered mundane Cairo life scenes so that it could provide "very real street-level views of Egypt", while focusing on raising the profile of a part of Egypt – Nubia – mostly ignored by popular music and musicians.

the notion of a sharing-based public licence coupled with ethical consumption, whereby consumers would pay symbolic prices for CDs and other artistic products subsidised by the state (Mubarak, 2012).

5. Conclusions

This study was an attempt to tap into the universe of independent music consumption and production in Egypt. Field questions focused on exploring the prevailing perceptions on matters of copyright, musician remuneration and consumption and delivery practices. The study found that the lack of awareness and the breach of copyright intersect with practices of music delivery and consumption. Moreover, there is a gap in copyright awareness with reference to physical goods versus virtual goods: respect for copyright is directly correlated with the physicality of the music product. This gap in copyright awareness is reflected in consumption and expenditure patterns by consumers and will need to be taken into consideration in proposing any model that would seek to legalise, accommodate and refine existing grassroots mechanisms for music production and sharing.

Through canvassing the prevalent trends in music consumption, it was found that Egyptian consumers do pay for music, albeit modestly. The majority of money spent on music goes towards attending concerts and barely any is spent on CDs or cassettes. Moreover, consumers who buy illegally copied street CDs and cassettes are not deterred by the counterfeit character of the goods. At the same time, online downloads are overwhelmingly done without any payment.

Consumers and musicians convey similar perceptions of copyright. While the majority of consumers (71%) surveyed knew of the general concept of copyright, only a minority were aware of the Egyptian law. All the musicians surveyed admitted to knowing very little about copyright, deeming it irrelevant to their practices. From the musicians' perspective, IP law is totally removed from people's lives and hence knowledge of it would not serve any end. Some musicians find the courts' approach to enforcing IP rights inadequate, thus rendering the IP regime even more irrelevant to them. Copyright law was not cited by any of the musicians as an obstacle to music production, and only a few of the non-musician stakeholders said that it was an obstacle. There thus appears to be a parallel and non-intersecting universe for independent Egyptian music alongside that of the mainstream universe of commercial production: a parallel independent music reality in which notions of copyright, cost and financial remuneration are of much less concern (than in the commercial dispensation) to both musicians and consumers.

An unexpected finding was the difference in perceptions (among both consumers and musicians) regarding physical versus virtual music. Most consumers surveyed said they felt that online music, unlike CDs or cassettes, was free from the legalities of economic rights (e.g. copyrights), given its immateriality. This view was shared by the independent musicians surveyed, for whom online platforms are primarily a vehicle not for monetary gain but rather exposure, promotion and sharing.

Despite its seeming potential, few respondents knew about the concept of a digital commons, and several musicians cast doubt on the feasibility of the concept for independent music in the Egyptian context. This lack of feasibility was, to a large extent, attributed by the musicians to the requirement that consumers would have to pay (directly or indirectly) for digital music in such a commons arrangement, a modality which musicians saw as running contrary to consumer expectation (as confirmed by the findings of this research) that online music is free of charge. Other potential structural impediments to a digital commons were, according to respondents, the lack of an e-commerce culture in Egypt and the overall low internet penetration.

In this author's analysis, however, the current reticence towards the idea of a digital commons for Egyptian independent music should not necessarily limit the possibility of promoting the concept. A digital commons platform could, in my view, resolve the moral element of copyright as it resonates with the spirit of EIPRL (which renders copyright protection for the artist automatically [see Appendix 8.1]). According to the EIPRL, moral rights are independent of economic rights and remain with the authors even after they transfer their economic rights (art. 143). The author of a work "cannot assign, waive, transfer or sell their moral rights", even if the owner of the economic rights is a different individual (Awad *et. al.*, 2010, p. 30). In addition, digital platforms could, for instance, allow for a "freemium" model (a mix of free and paid-for offerings) whereby free online music is bundled with forms of paid-for content and goods such as concert tickets (paid-for goods which clearly align with the musicians' ideologies towards their music and with the consumption patterns and economic preferences of consumers).

Egypt's independent musicians produce music for reasons other than monetary benefits. For most of the musicians surveyed, music is primarily a means of self-expression and voicing opinion. A few musicians surveyed did, however, note the importance of financial reward, albeit as a secondary motivation. Musicians could, in my analysis, reap an enhanced monetary benefit if they were to collaborate in the adoption of a business model that capitalised on the capacity of digital platforms to freely disseminate their artistic voice, promote their music and enable innovative means of remuneration.

Compensation for live performances was identified as the preferred channel of remuneration by both the musician and consumer sub-samples of the survey sample. Consumers spend as much as seven times more money on concert-going as they do on CDs/cassettes (and, extremely rarely, online music). A hybrid offering of live performances, CDs/cassettes and online music could represent a workable balance between public access and producers' returns. The sustainability of this balance would likely depend on factors such as the presence of spaces to host live performances, the adoption of alternative physical outputs of production (away from the expensive recording companies) for which consumers are willing to pay, and, finally, investment in more awareness about the promises and possibilities of a digital commons. One viable business model for Egypt's independent music scene could be based on a free digital commons licensed under an alternative licensing framework such as a Creative Commons.[12] Such a model could offer the option of direct purchase to support the idea of ethical consumption, and/or remuneration to musicians for their live performances (in alignment with the musicians' ideological stance of self-distancing from commercialised music practice).

Opening up an independent music digital commons is, in my analysis, realistic in Egypt, given the prevalent consumption patterns and the prevalent perceptions towards copyright and online payment modalities. Bundling free digital commons content with paid access to live performance (and optional contribution to the band and purchase of a physical CD or both) could be one way to capitalise on the nature of music as a *quasi*-public good (and also an "experience good" in a culture that thrives on social interaction). Business models that follow a *quasi*-commons approach to Egyptian independent music could offer an alternative, whereby collaborators could be compensated for creativity and could simultaneously satisfy the public interest in unhindered music-sharing. Such models could constitute one way of easing the tensions (between access and incentive) that have emerged with the expansion of free online music, while at the same time expanding user access and, through complementary means, generating musician remuneration.

Fine-tuning the appropriate business models as such would approach the "open development" paradigm. It would create a valid environment to empower music producers, promote collaboration and expand access, through an inclusive rather than exclusive IP paradigm. This would entail more sharing among musicians and, ideally, eliminate the need for copyright infringement.

12 There have been recent efforts (as mentioned above) to adapt Creative Commons licensing to the Egyptian context, as well as holding an event in December 2012 to promote the licence to artists in particular (Essalmawi, 2013).

Appendix 8.1: Review of Egyptian copyright provisions (in the EIPRL of 2002)[13]

1. Conditions of protection

Egypt's IP Law, the EIPRL of 2002, does not require any formalities for copyright protection. An author does not need to officially register, or apply, for copyright protection. Copyright protection exists as soon as an original work is created in a fixed and tangible form of expression.

In certain instances, however, keeping a private register of works *is* required by law. Article 187, for instance, provides as follows:

> Any establishment that puts in circulation works, recorded performances, sound recordings or broadcast programmes through sale, rent, loan or licensing, shall be required to:
>
> (1) Obtain a license from the competent minister against payment of a fee prescribed by the Regulations, not exceeding 1,000 pounds;
> (2) Maintain registers in which data and circulation year relating to each work, sound recording or broadcast programme are recorded [...].

Moreover, Article 149 of the Law, dealing with the right to transfer economic rights, requires any such transfer to be "certified in writing and contain an explicit and detailed indication of each right to be transferred with the extent and purpose of transfer and the duration and place of exploitation". Article 185 then goes on to require every competent ministry to establish a register in which any act of disposal relating to works, performances, sound recordings and broadcast programmes shall be recorded (Art. 185).

2. Core rights

Egypt is a civil law country and both moral rights and economic rights are protected. Economic rights allow authors to extract economic value from the utilisation of their works and moral rights allow authors to claim authorship and protect their integrity.

---

13 This Appendix was written by Bassem Awad, an IP specialist affiliated to A2K4D (where the author is Director) at The American University in Cairo (AUC). In addition to contributing this Appendix on Egyptian copyright provisions, Awad co-authored Chapter 12 of this book, on biofuel innovation and patenting in Egypt.

Moral rights include the right to make the work available to the public for the first time; the right to claim authorship; and the right to object to any distortion, mutilation or other modification of the author's work that might be prejudicial to his/her honour or reputation (Art. 143). These rights are independent of economic rights and remain with the author (and his/her successors) in perpetuity, even if he/she transfers his/her economic rights. Creators cannot assign, waive, transfer or sell their moral rights.

Economic rights cover any form of work exploitation. They provide the copyright-owner with an exclusive monopoly to do – and to authorise others to do – the following in relation to the copyright-owner's work: reproduce in various forms, adapt, translate, distribute, rent, lend, perform publicly, broadcast, communicate to the public and/or make available to the public (Art. 147).

In many countries, rights-holders in musical works have authorised so-called collective management organisations (CMOs) to license restaurants, retail outlets, broadcasting organisations and other users to perform/play/communicate their music. In Egypt, however, there is no CMO for copyright-holders. In countries with CMOs, the CMOs act on behalf of their members, negotiating rates and terms of use with users, issuing licences authorising uses and collecting and distributing royalties. The CMOs distribute the collected revenues, after the deduction of administration costs, to individual right-holders. There are typically various kinds of CMOs, depending on the category of works involved (e.g. music, dramatic works, multimedia productions).

3. Duration of protection

The Egyptian Law provides the standard term of copyright protection – 50 years – set out in international treaties. Copyrights are protected during the author, composer or lyricist's life and for 50 years after his/her death (Art. 160). The duration of protection of performer or producer "related rights" (also known as "neighbouring rights") is the same as that for the author/composer/lyricist rights: performers enjoy an exclusive right for the exploitation of their performances for a period of 50 years calculated from the date on which the performance/recording took place (Art. 166); and producers of sound recordings enjoy an exclusive economic right to exploit the recordings they produce for a period of 50 years calculated from the date on which the recording was made or made public, whichever comes first (Art. 167). Meanwhile, broadcasting organisations enjoy an exclusive right to exploit their programmes for a period of 20 years, calculated from the date on which the programme was first broadcast (Art. 168).

4. Administrative bodies

The following ministries and government authorities are responsible for enforcement of copyrights in Egypt:

Relevant government entity	Enforcement area
Ministry of Culture's Central Department for Audio-visual Censorship	Copyright and neighbouring rights for music, films and theatre performances; the Ministry of Culture does not enforce rights in literary works, databases and broadcasts
The Ministry of Information	Broadcasting rights
Ministry of Communications and Information Technology's Information Technology Industry Development Authority (ITIDA)	Software and databases
The Ministry of Trade	Counterfeits
The Cyber Investigation Unit of the Ministry of Interior Affairs	Internet copyright infringement

To promote stronger enforcement, Egypt in 1996 set up an IP unit within the police force, with the unit named the General Administration for the Prevention of Infringement of Intellectual Property Rights. In addition, teams of civil inspectors are authorised to remove infringing goods from the market, and an Economic Court was created in 2008 to handle several types of cases, including copyright disputes.

Appendix 8.2: List of interviewees

Digital platforms	Tarek Metwalli	Founder ,Who's Jammin?
	Nada Thabet	Concept and Technical Manager, Meetphool
	Mohamed El Ayat	Producer and founder of Underground Music Federation (UMF)
Outlets	Ahmed El Maghraby	Founder/Director, Makan
	Ammar Dajjani	Owner, Cairo Jazz Club
	Moataz Nasr El Din	Director, Darb 1718
	Ahmed Mohamed	Partner and General Manager, Studio Vibe
	William Wells	Director, Townhouse Gallery and Rawabet Gallery
Cultural institutes	Azza El Husseiny	Member of Organising Committee, El Fan Midan
	Mohamed Talaat	Project Coordinator, Jesuit Cultural Centre
Policy-maker	Hossam Loutfi	Member, Law Committee, Supreme Council of Culture (and IP lawyer)
Union	Emad Mubarak	Lawyer, Association for the Freedom of Thought and Expression (AFTE)
Stakeholder	Mohamed Khalifa	Producer, Bassem Youssef Show
IP rights officer	Hala Essalmawi	Principal Attorney and IP Rights Officer, Library of Alexandria

Continued

Appendix 8.2: List of interviewees *(continued)*

Independent musicians	Youssef Atwan	Like Jelly
	Georges Kazazian	Solo
	Nadia Chanab	Solo
	Mohamed Hassan	Solo rap/hip-hop
	Fairuz Karawia	Solo
	Moe (Mohamed El Arkani)	Percussion Show
	Hani Mustafa	HanyMust
	Hazem Shahin	Eskenderella
	Khaled Gabri	Ashara Gharby
	Ibrahim	Asphalt Band
	Gad	Asphalt Band
	Ahmed Mostafa	City Band
	Noor Ayman	Simplexity and Zabaleen Band
	Aya Metwalli	Solo and Mashrou3 Chorale
	Tarek El Borolossy	Digla
	Omar El Deeb	Simplexity
	Ousso (Mohamed Lotfy)	Eftekesat and Nagham Masry
	Ragui Akram	Karma Band
	Cherine Amr	Mascara Band
	Mado (Mohamed Adel Aal)	Taxi band
	Jimmy (Mohamed El Gohary)	Salalem
	Neobyrd	Solo DJ
	Aly B (Aly Bahgat)	Solo DJ
	Salam Yousry	Mashrou3 Chorale

Appendix 8.3: List of alternative art outlets in Cairo, as at May 2012

1) Cairo Opera House	El Borg Gezira, 11567, Cairo – Tel 0227390132
2) Darb 1718	Kast El Sham3 Street Al Fakhareen, Old Cairo, Cairo – Tel 0223610511
3) El Sawy (Culture Wheel)	End of 26th of July Street, Zamalek, Cairo- Tel 02 27368881, 2736 6178 – Email: info@culturewheel.com – Co-founder: Abdel Moneim El Sawy
4) Makan	1, Saad Zaghloul St, El Dawaween, Cairo – Tel 27920878, Dr Ahmad El Maghraby, Admin Secretary Dina Mohamed Said
5) Townhouse Gallery	Hussein El Me'amar Pasha St, off Mahmoud Basyouni St, Downtown Cairo – Tel 25768086 – Email: info@thetownhousegallery.com – Director: William Wells
6) Rawabet Theatre	3 Hussien El Me'amar St, ext. of Mahmoud Bassiouny St, from Talaat Harb – Tel 01275070727
7) El Gueinena Theatre / Beit El Harawi	Al Azhar Park, Salah Salem Street, Cairo – Tel 202 25103868 – 25107338 – Email info@alazharpark.com
8) After Eight	6, Kasr El Nil St, Downtown, Cairo – Tel 0103398000
9) Bikya	23, Dr Zaki Hassan St, off El Nasr Street, Nasr City, Cairo – Tel 224046688 – Email info@bikyabookcafe.com
10) Cairo Jazz Club	197, 26 of July Street, Sphinx Square, Agouza, Cairo – Tel 02 33459939 – Care of Mariam

Appendix 8.4: Consumer survey sample diagnostics

A problem encountered regarding the sample stratification was the gender balance. Although instructions were given to the research team in charge of the questionnaires, they were unable to respect a 50/50 gender balance due to the disproportionate number of men attending cultural events relative to women. The final gender distribution was 75/25 in favour of men, or 446 men and 154 women. Researchers reported, *ex post*, that the majority of women present at the venues were not particularly interested in music, and were simply there with their male partners/boyfriends or accompanying some friend/relative as a favour (encouraged by gender attendance policies which give preferential treatment [entry] to couples over young men).

In terms of age, the sample was, on average, younger than an average random sample of the population, as expected of alternative cultural outlets. Seventy per cent of the sample was aged 24 or younger, and 90% of respondents were 29 or younger. No respondents older than 44 were interviewed. Unsurprisingly, the majority of the respondents in the sample were students (62%). The fact that approximately 30% of the rest were employed by the private sector or in the liberal professions (e.g. lawyers, doctors, engineers) suggested a significantly more affluent segment of the population relative to the Egyptian average. This interpretation is further supported by the educational attainments of the sample: 83.5% of respondents had either already obtained or were in the process of obtaining a university degree. For only 10% of the sample was high school the highest educational attainment, and only 2.3% had obtained a technical licence.

To complete the picture, all but one respondent had access to the internet. For the greatest majority of internet users, the principal internet access point was at home (76.7%), while 15% accessed the internet primarily via mobile phone and 6% primarily at their workplaces. This high educational, class and connectivity profile was also mirrored in the linguistic abilities of the sample: only one third of respondents were Arabic-only speakers, whereas the majority (57%) spoke both Arabic and English, and 9% spoke Arabic and another language.

One of the more telling characteristics of the sample – considering its relative wealth, connectivity and high educational achievements – was its rate of bank account ownership. Only 34% of respondents reported having a bank account, a figure not disproportionately higher than the average population. Further, only half of the bank account holders in the sample reported using online banking features, and only a third felt safe using credit instruments for online purchases (i.e. 5% of the total sample). These characteristics severely restrict the ability of the vast majority in the sample to make online purchases of artistic products, including legal music downloads.

Bibliography

Primary sources

Legal instrument

Egyptian Intellectual Property Rights Law No. 82 of 2002 [in Arabic], available at: www.ecipit.org.eg/Arabic/pdf/IPR%20law%20no%2082%20year%202002%20 English.pdf (accessed 25 January 2013).

Interviews

Abdel Aal, M. Musician (2012), interview. Interviewed by A2K4D research team [personal interview], May 2012.

Akram, R. Musician (2012), interview. Interviewed by A2K4D research team [personal interview], May 2012.

Amr, C. Musician (2012), interview. Interviewed by A2K4D Research Team [personal interview], June 2012.

Atwan, Y. Musician (2012), interview. Interviewed by A2K4D research team [personal interview], April 2012.

Ayman, N. Musician (2012), interview. Interviewed by A2K4D research team [personal interview], June 2012.

Chanab, N. Musician (2012), interview. Interviewed by A2K4D research team [personal interview], April 2012.

Dajjani, A. Owner, Cairo Jazz Club (2012), interview. Interviewed by A2K4D research team [personal interview], April 2012.

El Arkani, M. Musician (2012), interview. Interviewed by A2K4D research team [personal interview], May 2012.

El Ayat, M. Producer and founder of Underground Music Federation (UMF) (2012), Interview. Interviewed by A2K4D research team [personal interview], April 2012.

El Borolossy, T. Musician (2012), interview. Interviewed by A2K4D research team [personal interview], May 2012.

El Deeb, O. Musician (2012), interview. Interviewed by A2K4D research team [personal interview], June 2012.

El Gohary, M. Musician (2012), interview. Interviewed by A2K4D research team [personal interview], June 2012.

El Husseiny, A. Member of Organising Committee, El Fan Midan (2012), interview. Interviewed by A2K4D Research Team [personal interview], June 2012.

El Maghraby, Dr. A. Founder and Director, Makan (2012), interview. Interviewed by A2K4D research team [personal interview], April 2012.

Essalmawi, H. Principal Attorney and the Intellectual Property Rights Officer at the Library of Alexandria (2013), interview (on the status of Creative Commons in Egypt). Interviewed by Nagla Rizk [telephone interview], 13 January 2013.

Gabri, K. Musician (2012), interview. Interviewed by A2K4D research team [personal interview], May 2012.

Hassan, M. Musician (2012), interview. Interviewed by A2K4D research team [personal interview], May 2012.

Ibrahim and Gad, Asphalt Band (2012), interview. Interviewed by A2K4D research team [personal interview], June 2012.

Karawia, F. Musician (2012), interview. Interviewed by A2K4D research team [personal interview], June 2012.

Kazazian, G. Musician (2012), interview. Interviewed by A2K4D research team [personal interview], May 2012.

Khalifa, M. Producer, Bassem Youssef Show (2012), interview. Interviewed by A2K4D research team [personal interview], May 2012.

Loutfi, H. Intellectual Property Lawyer (2012), interview. Interviewed by A2K4D research team [personal interview], June 2012.

Metwalli, A. Musician (2012), Interview. interviewed by A2K4D research team [personal interview], June 2012.

Metwalli, T. Founder, Who's Jammin? (2012), interview. Interviewed by A2K4D research team [personal interview], April 2012.

Mohamed, A. Partner and General Manager, Studio Vibe (2012), interview. Interviewed by A2K4D research team [personal interview], September 2012.

Mostafa, A. Musician (2012), interview. Interviewed by A2K4D research team [personal interview], June 2012.

Mubarak, E. Lawyer, Association for the Freedom of Thought and Expression (AFTE) (2012), interview. Interviewed by A2K4D research team [personal interview], May 2012.

Mustafa, H. Musician (2012), interview. Interviewed by A2K4D research team [personal interview], June 2012.

Nasr El Din, M. Director, Darb 1718 (2012), interview. Interviewed by A2K4D research team [personal interview], April 2012.

Neobyrd, Musician (2012), interview. Interviewed by A2K4D research team [personal interview], June 2012.

Shahin, H. Musician (2012), interview. Interviewed by A2K4D research team [personal interview], April 2012.

Talaat, M. Project Coordinator, Jesuit Cultural Centre (2012), interview. Interviewed by A2K4D research team [personal interview], April 2012.

Thabet, N. Concept and Technical Manager, Meetphool (2012), interview. Interviewed by A2K4D research team [personal interview], April 2012.

Wells, W. Director, Townhouse Gallery and Rawabet Gallery (2012), interview. Interviewed by A2K4D research team [personal interview], May 2012.

Secondary sources

Alexa.com (2013), "Top sites in Egypt," available at: www.alexa.com/topsites/countries/EG (accessed 27 April 2013).

American Chamber of Commerce in Egypt (AmCham) (2005), "Burn and loot," *Business Monthly*, July, available at: www.amcham.org.eg/resources_publications/publications/business_monthly/issue.asp?sec=5&im=7&iy=2005 (accessed 25 April 2013).

AmosWEB (2013), "Quasi public good," available at: www.amosweb.com/cgi-bin/awb_nav.pl?s=gls&c=dsp&k=quasi-public+good (accessed 15 April 2013).

Awad, B., El-Gheriani, M. Abou Zeid, P. (2010), "Egypt", in Armstrong, C., De Beer, J., Kawooya, D., Prabhala, A. and Schonwetter, T. (Eds.), *Access to Knowledge in Africa: The Role of Copyright*, UCT Press, Cape Town, pp. 22–56, available at: http://idl-bnc.idrc.ca/dspace/bitstream/10625/44667/1/131103.pdf (accessed 15 April 2013).

Creative Commons (2012), "About Creative Commons," available at: http://creativecommons.org/about (accessed 18 March 2013).

Delegation of the EU to Egypt (2011), "Launching of Meetphool.net!", available at: http://eeas.europa.eu/delegations/egypt/press_corner/all_news/news/2011/20110629_01_en.htm (accessed 25 April 2013).

International Intellectual Property Alliance (IIPA) (2010), *Egypt, Special 301 Report on Copyright Protection and Enforcement 2010*, available at: www.iipa.com/rbc/2010/2010SPEC301EGYPT.pdf (accessed 25 April 2013).

Lange, R. (2009), "Is digitized music becoming a quasi-public good?" International Communication Association Annual Meeting, 25 May, New York, available at: www.allacademic.com/meta/p13846_index.html (accessed 25 April 2013).

Lemos, R. (2007), "From Legal Commons to Social Commons: Brazil and the Cultural Industry in the 21st Century", Working Paper CBS 80-07, University of Oxford Centre for Brazilian Studies, available at: www.lac.ox.ac.uk/sites/sias/files/documents/R.%2520Lemos80.pdf (accessed 13 April 2013).

Macro-Fiscal Policy Unit (2012), *The Financial Monthly Bulletin*, available at: www.mof.gov.eg/MOFGallerySource/English/Reports/monthly/2012/November2012/full%20version.pdf (accessed 25 April 2013).

Meetphool (2012), available at: www.meetphool.net (accessed 18 March 2013).

Rizk, N. (2010a), "Notes from Egypt's alternative music scene: business models, commons and copyright", *The Journal of World Intellectual Property*, Vol. 13 No. 3, pp. 474–501.

Rizk, N. (2010b), "Stories from Egypt's music industry: *de facto* commons as alternatives to copyright", in Rizk, N. and Shaver, L. (Eds.), *Access to Knowledge in Egypt: New Research on Intellectual Property, Innovation and Development*, Bloomsbury, London, pp. 92–133.

Romer, P. (2002), "When should we use intellectual property rights?" *American Economic Review*, Vol. 92 No. 2, pp. 213–16.

Smith, M.L., Elder, L. and Emdon, H. (2011), "Open development: a new theory for ICT4D", *Information Technologies and International Development*, Vol. 7 No. 1, Spring (Special Issue: Open Development), available at http://itidjournal.org/itid/article/view/692/290 (accessed 25 April 2013).

Stalder, F. (2010), "Digital commons", in Hart, K., Laville, J.-L. and Cattani, A.D. (Eds), *The Human Economy: A World Citizen's Guide*, Polity Press, Cambridge, UK, pp. 313–24, available at http://felix.openflows.com/node/137 (accessed 25 April 2013).

Who's Jammin? (n.d.), http://www.whosjammin.com/services (accessed 25 April 2013).

Chapter 9

Reflections on Open Scholarship Modalities and the Copyright Environment in Kenya

Ben Sihanya[1]

Abstract

This chapter outlines findings from research into the attitudes of Kenyan scholarly publishing stakeholders towards open scholarship and alternative publishing. The findings indicate a mix of interest and reticence in relation to open access (OA) and other modes of alternative publishing. For instance, the authors surveyed recognise the potential of alternative publishing to enhance their scholarly profiles, but at the same time they fear potential dilution of the economic rights afforded to them by copyright law. The chapter concludes with suggestions on how Kenya's copyright environment could be made more amenable to open scholarship.

1. Introduction: open scholarship and copyright in Kenya

One of the most remarkable phenomena in the 21st century has been the emergence and development of the knowledge economy (KE), or "informationalism". The KE has been defined as one in which the generation and exploitation of knowledge plays a predominant part in the creation of wealth (Houghton, 2010). Castells (2004a) describes the concept of informationalism as a technological paradigm based on augmentation of human capacity for information processing and communication, made possible by revolutions in microelectronics, software and genetic engineering. Microelectronics, software, computation, telecommunications and digital communications are all components of one integrated system. This phenomenon of informationalism is characterised by a predominant position for knowledge in the creation of wealth and development, as precipitated

1 The author gratefully acknowledges the research assistance on this study provided by Timothy Wafula, James Mbugua, Enock Otieno and Martha Ndung'u, all of whom work for Innovative Lawyering and Sihanya Mentoring, Nairobi.

by the emergence of a new technological paradigm based on information and communication technology (ICT) (Benkler, 2006; Castells and Cardoso, 2005; Castells, 2004a). Rather than the mere opening up of new frontiers of knowledge, the KE is characterised by more effective use and exploitation of numerous types of knowledge in diverse types of economic activities.

Kenya, the case study country for this research project, is aspiring to become a knowledge-intensive economy. According to Kenya's current main policy blueprint, Vision 2030 (GOK, 2007), the country's development should be influenced by relevant educational provision and, in turn, by evidence-based policy-makers. Such education and decision-making require high-quality, creative and critical scholarly literature. The aforementioned new technological paradigm has changed the fundamentals of scholarly publishing globally and in Kenya. The new paradigm has resulted in a mix of offline print publishing and digital publishing via the internet and other related digital media.

Digital publishing outlets include e-journals, lists, blogs, websites, social networks and wikis. There have been radical changes in the traditional roles of authors, publishers, information managers and other key actors in the scholarly publishing arena. And a raging global debate has been sparked on the right to access knowledge freely as a "public good", and on the role of access to knowledge (A2K) (Benkler, 2006; Broumas, 2008). These arguments have often pitted the author and the user/consumer against each other. Proponents of "open access" (OA) by the public to scholarly works argue that free access to scholarly knowledge is essential to socio-economic development.

Also of relevance to the new publishing dynamics is the emerging concept of "open development": development powered by networked knowledge (see Smith *et al.*, 2011). Open development is centred around principles of collaboration, participation and inclusiveness in the networks and institutions, broadly conceived, that shape people's lives. Some of these principles have been recognised in the Constitution of Kenya of 2010 (Sihanya, 2013a, 2013b, forthcoming 2013).

Opposing the OA position are proponents of limited access, who argue that to sustain the generation of high-quality knowledge by the scholar, the scholar must be compensated by way of royalties and other forms of direct financial remuneration (Wasamba and Sihanya, 2012). "Open scholarship", via OA, has emerged as a concept that could change the business models in the education and information industries in Kenya and internationally. The traditional business model for publishing scholarly works primarily entailed the payment of royalties by the publisher to the author under a contract of transfer or assignment of copyright (for print publishing). Subscriber-based online access arrangements (for electronic publishing) then emerged (Wasamba and Sihanya, 2012). Today, three main alternative publishing models predominate: online subscription publishing, online OA publishing and online OA self-archiving (Houghton, 2010). Open scholarship and OA approaches alter the traditional relationships among the author, the publisher, the information manager or librarian and the knowledge consumer. OA approaches throw into confusion the main doctrine that has traditionally animated these relationships: copyright. There is now varied opinion as to whether copyright law promotes or undermines the momentum towards open scholarship.

The production of scholarly literature is at a sub-optimal level in Kenya. It seems likely that Kenya's dearth of scholarly publishing in some disciplines is due, to some extent, to limitations in author development and book authorship, and limitations in publishing and distribution (both off-line and online). It also seems likely, as this chapter argues, that the emerging open-scholarship publishing paradigm has yet to pick up momentum in Kenya partly because of the country's sub-optimal copyright environment.

Research problem

The emerging concepts of OA, open scholarship and alternative scholarly publishing pose challenges not just to authors, publishers, information managers and users, but also to policy-makers and related stakeholders. There are important questions regarding how authors and publishers are to benefit economically in an open scholarship context. And what role must copyright policy-makers and technocrats and administrators play? The design of copyright and related rights systems has traditionally been based on balancing two main theoretical perspectives: (1) that copyright protection acts as an incentive to promote innovation and creativity; and (2) that over-strong copyright protection will be an impediment to free and open exchange of educational and entertainment materials, culture and knowledge, thereby stifling creativity and development (Sihanya, 2013b). The concepts of OA, open scholarship and alternative scholarly publishing serve to intensify the tensions between these two perspectives.

I sought, through the research study outlined in this chapter, to take some initial steps towards understanding the dynamics at the intersection of open scholarship and copyright law, policy and practice in Kenya. The study sought to understand how the emergence of open scholarship may be affecting relationships among the stakeholders in the scholarly publishing process. The study also sought to probe the extent to which Kenya's copyright environment, in doctrinal and/or practical terms, might benefit from review so as to better facilitate open scholarship. (See Chapter 8 in this volume for another discussion of copyright dynamics, in this case in relation to the output of Egypt's independent musicians.)

2. Conceptual and practical framework

What are the conceptual, theoretical and pragmatic issues in relation to copyright and authorship in the context of Kenyan scholarship and publishing?

Conceptualising and contextualising copyright in Kenya

As stated above, the design of copyright and related rights systems has traditionally been based on two main competing theoretical perspectives: (1) the view that copyright protection acts as an incentive to promote knowledge development; and (2) the view that copyright protection can be an impediment to free and open exchange of knowledge (Cornish *et al.*, 2010). Neither of these views has been subjected to sufficient empirical research in Kenya. As a result, law- and policy-makers, as well as knowledge creators, will inevitably face problems if they seek to design and/or implement development-oriented approaches to copyright.

This study sought to partially fill the knowledge gap by examining the potential roles of copyright in relation to development-oriented open scholarship in Kenya. The main research methods used were desk research (literature review, document analysis, doctrinal analysis) and field research (surveying, interviewing and focus-grouping stakeholders), and emphasis of the data analysis was qualitative. The key doctrinal source was Kenya's Copyright Act No. 12 of 2001, which in Section 2 provides for copyright and related rights in primary works (such as literary, artistic and musical works), and in related, secondary, neighbouring or allied works (such as audio-visual works, sound recordings and broadcasts).

Who is an author?

The question of who is an author is contested in literary, legal and related scholarship (Bailey, 2000; Birnhack, 2008; Nehamas, 1986). This study focused on authorship in relation to literary works. Section 2 of Kenya's Copyright Act contains a broad definition of literary work, which includes:

- novels, stories and poetic works;
- plays, stage directions, film sceneries and broadcasting scripts;
- textbooks, treatises, histories, biographies, essays and articles;
- encyclopedias and dictionaries;
- letters, reports and memoranda;
- lectures, addresses and sermons;
- charts and tables;
- computer programs; and
- tables and compilations of data including tables and compilations of data stored and embodied in a computer or a medium used in conjunction with a computer, but does not include a written law or a judicial decision.

Further, this study focused on authors of scholarly literary works, i.e. scholarly works related to the arts, humanities, social sciences, law and the natural sciences (biological and physical sciences). Thus, authors of "popular literature" were not included. A scholarly work is typically defined as being a (critical) work that is peer-reviewed and publicly disseminated (Virginia Polytechnic Institute and State University, 2009). There are debates on disciplinary purity and interdisciplinarity: are there bright-line boundaries in the arts, humanities and social sciences (*cf.* Imbuga, 1993; Ogot and Ochieng, 1995; Ojwang, 1990; Okidi *et al.*, 2008; Okoth-Ogendo, 1990; Oloo, 2006; Outa, 2009; Oyugi *et al.*, 1988; Ruganda, 1992; Wanyande *et al.*, 2007)? Some have (problematically, in my view) placed law and legal studies under humanities and social sciences (Monahan and Walker, 2010).[2]

There has also been a long debate on what constitutes creative, critical, "committed" and "serious" literature on one hand, and popular literature on the other (Emenyonu *et al.*, 2006; Imbuga, 1991, 1993; Wanjala, 1982, 2007). The statutory definition of authorship has grown more problematic with the expansion of the subject matter of copyright. More particularly, problems have arisen in relation to technological developments, especially in entrepreneurial works and computer-generated works.

Establishing the identity of the author of a copyright work is important for at least four reasons. First, whether a work qualifies for protection at all depends on the status of the author. Section 23 of the Kenyan Copyright Act provides that copyright shall be conferred on every work eligible for copyright where the author, or any of the joint authors, is a citizen of, domiciled in or ordinarily resident in Kenya at the time the work is made, or is a corporate body incorporated under or in accordance with the laws of Kenya. Second, the identity of the author determines who becomes the first owner of the copyright. Section 31 of the Act provides that copyright conferred under Sections 23 and 24 of the Act vests initially in the author.

Third, for many works, the term of copyright is calculated by reference to the date of death of the author (Sect. 23(2) of the Act). For example, for literary, musical or artistic works other than photographs, the date of expiration of copyright in Kenyan law is 50 years after the end of the year in which the author dies. Fourth, in the case of many copyrighted works, the author has important moral rights. Section 32 of the Act provides for two types of moral rights accruing to the author: (1) the paternity right, which allows her/him to claim the authorship of the work; and (2) the right of integrity, which enables her/him to control the form of publication and to prevent her/him work from being distorted or mutilated.

2 For a review of the relationship, see Monahan and Walker (2010).

The foregoing is relevant to this study's focus on open scholarship. This is because, as shall be seen later in this chapter, scholarly authors' consideration of moral rights was found by this study to be generally more significant than their consideration of economic rights.

What is "scholarship"?

"Scholarship" has been conceptualised in various ways. Some have focused on the "product" of the scholarly, professional and creative work in conceptualising scholarship (Aseka, 1996; Diamond and Adam, 1993; Munene, 2012). Others have focused on the "process" of scholarship itself (Diamond, 2002; Glassick *et al.*, 1997). This study adopted a definition of scholarship as the creation, development and maintenance of the intellectual (architecture) of subjects and disciplines, in forms such as dictionaries, scholarly editions, catalogues and contributions to major research databases (Cohen and Atieno-Odhiambo, 1989, 2004; Halliday, 2001; Kipkorir, 2009).

In addition, the study adopted the perspective that a scholarly work is a creative work that is peer-reviewed and publicly disseminated (Virginia Polytechnic Institute and State University, 2009). Accordingly, there are at least three basic forms of scholarship: generation or discovery of new knowledge; development of new technologies, methods, materials or uses; and integration of knowledge leading to new understanding (Atieno-Odhiambo and Lonsdale, 2003).

This study also accepted the contention that scholarship involves communication. The term "scholarly communication" refers not merely to an output but also to an iterative process in which scholarship is communicated, used and developed within a community (Kling and McKim, 2000; *cf.* Imbuga, 1993; Ngugi wa Thiong'o, 1981; Njogu and Oluoch-Olunya, 2007; Ochieng, 2012; Ruganda, 1992). Scholarly publishing or communication fulfils at least three purposes: publicity, access, and trustworthiness (Kling and McKim, 1999). Björk (2007) outlines a life cycle of scholarship which involves conducting research and then communicating and applying the results across five stages: (1) fund research and research communication; (2) perform research and communicate the results; (3) publish scientific and scholarly works; (4) facilitate dissemination, retrieval and preservation; and (5) study publications and apply the knowledge.

Architecture for Kenyan scholarship

In Kenya, the architecture that directly supports, compromises or is neutral to scholarly endeavour includes universities, colleges, research institutes/centres, libraries, archives, publishers and scholarly consortia or communities.

Universities

There are two main types of universities in Kenya: public and private. There are 22 public universities established under the Universities Act of 2012. Private universities have registered exponential growth since about 2002, and with that there has been increased demand for copyrighted materials. University scholarship is mainly conducted by lecturers, professors, technical staff and postgraduate students. The largest university, the University of Nairobi, has about 5,400 staff and over 84,000 students (University of Nairobi, n.d.). It offers over 400 academic programmes in 26 faculties, schools and institutes (University of Nairobi, n.d.). Its budget for research and development (R&D) is estimated at KES500 million.[3]

Many universities now have a research and IP policy (Sihanya, 2013b). Polytechnics and other tertiary institutions are also engaged in research and development. Kenya has approximately six public scientific research institutions, which were established by the Science and Technology Act (Cap. 250), and one institute for the social sciences: the Kenya Institute for Public Policy Research and Analysis (KIPPRA). These research institutions have important collections in their libraries, most of which are still under copyright.

Libraries and archives

The Kenyan library system includes public libraries and institutional (both public and private) libraries. The Kenya National Library Service, established under the Kenya National Library Service Board Act (Cap. 225), manages public libraries. Another piece of legislation governing library services in Kenya is the McMillan Memorial Library Act (Cap. 217). Public, private, university and research institute libraries are increasingly playing an important, vital and unique role in scholarly research (Ouma and Sihanya, 2010).

Publishers

Publishers in Kenya are categorised into public, private and university (institutional) publishers. Private publishers include local and foreign publishers, and most of these focus on primary and secondary school publishing, because these areas provide the highest financial returns. These returns on investment have increased since 2003 when the Kenyan government strengthened the Free Primary Education (FPE) and Free Day Secondary Education (FDSE) systems. University publishers publish scholarly works targeted at university students, scholars and other information consumers seeking scholarly materials.

---

3 KES stands for the Kenyan Shilling, which at the time of writing in early 2013 stood at a value of approximately KES87 to US$1.

Scholarly consortia

Scholarly consortia in Kenya include the Kenya National Academy of Sciences (KNAS), the Kenya Nonfiction and Academic Authors' Association (KENFAA), the Kenya Oral Literature Association (KOLA), the African Economic Research Consortium (AERC), the Kenya Historical Association (KHA), the African Technology Policy Studies Network (ATPS) and the Writers Association of Kenya (WAK). They focus on publishing or disseminating the works of their members and other scholars.

Professional research and publishing

Professional membership organisations such as the Law Society of Kenya (LSK), the International Commission of Jurists, Kenya Section (ICJ-Kenya Section) and the Institute of Chartered Public Secretaries of Kenya (ICPSK) also occasionally publish reports on topical themes. The objective of such publishing is not to pursue a programmatic scholarly endeavour as such. But some, for instance the University of Nairobi's Institute of Development Studies (IDS) and Society for International Development (SID, a civil-society organisation), have tried to pursue scholarly themes.

Copyright communities

Copyright communities have been evolving in Kenya since the 1970s. These include collective management organisations (CMOs, which straddle the private and voluntary sectors), the Kenya Copyright Board (KECOBO) and the Copyright Tribunal (the "Competent Authority" cited in the Copyright Act). Related to these are the courts, which rule on copyright issues arising from scholarship and publishing, particularly the High Court, the Court of Appeal and the Supreme Court.

Digitisation and copyright

Digitisation facilitates acts of copying, first when developing a digital surrogate from a physical original, and second, when putting this surrogate on the internet, which multitudes of users can then access and copy onto their own computers (Dunning, 2004; Goldstein, 2005; Lessig, 2002, 2004). Digitisation enables materials to be used in different media, to be copied at the same quality as an original, to be manipulated and distorted, and to be distributed cheaply, easily and speedily (Benkler, 2006; Lessig, 2008; Mambi, 2010, p. 197). Digitisation enables, *inter alia*, libraries to have content accessible to the public via the internet (Boyle, 1997; Litman, 2006; Samuelson, 2000). Digitisation has generated numerous important issues in IP, including matters in relation to copyright, the domain name system (DNS), software patents and business method patents (Sihanya, 2012b, 2013b).

Digital information is protected under Kenya's Copyright Act of 2001, which incorporates the provisions of the World Trade Organisation (WTO) Agreement on Trade Related Aspects of Intellectual Property Rights of 1994 (TRIPS), and the World Intellectual Property Organisation's (WIPO's) "Internet Treaties" of 1996: the WIPO Copyright Treaty (WCT) and the WIPO Performances and Phonograms Treaty (WPPT). For any digital material to be protected under the Kenyan Copyright Act, it should fall within the definition of what is copyrightable subject matter. Section 22 of the Act lists what is copyrightable as literary work, musical work, artistic work, audio-visual work, sound recordings and broadcasts.

Open development

The emerging notion of open development refers to development systems in which people are free, or even empowered, to access networked development systems and to participate, collaborate and share within those systems. Aspects of open development include open government (Sihanya, 2006, 2007–8) (which is comparable to e-government and e-governance), open communications networks, open access to content and open-sourced research and product development as commons-based peer-production. In the context of OA and open scholarship, the challenge is balancing the competing interests of open development and the creative and innovation industries that benefit from appropriate incentives. (See Chapters 1 and 4 of this volume for more on the concept of open development.)

Open access (OA) and open scholarship

OA refers to works that are created with no expectation of direct monetary return, and which are made available at no cost to the reader on the public internet for purposes of education and research (Open Society Institute and the Soros Foundations Network, 2011). The Budapest Open Access Initiative stated that OA would permit users to read, download, copy, distribute, print, search or link to the full texts of works (Open Society Institute and the Soros Foundations Network, 2011).[4] Readers would also be able to trawl the works for indexing, pass them on as data to software, or use them for any other lawful purpose, without financial, legal or technical barriers other than those inseparable from gaining access to the internet itself. OA does not apply to materials for which the authors expect to generate direct revenue.

4 See other definitions at InTech (n.d.).

Jain (2012) outlines seven main characteristics of OA material:

1. It is free of charge.
2. It is free of (most or all) copyright and licensing restrictions.
3. The material is available online or on the internet.
4. The material is full text.
5. The material can be accessed by anyone and in any place subject to connectivity.
6. The material can be freely used by anyone who has access.
7. The materials can be in various formats, from texts and data to software, audio, video and multimedia, scholarly articles and their preprints. The concept of open scholarship has developed out of the concept of OA. It refers to OA practices as part of the scholarly publishing process.

As discussed above, new technologies and new means of research communication and dissemination are changing traditional publishing and enabling an increasing range of non-traditional forms of communication, such as via e-journals, lists, blogs and wikis (Bourne *et al.*, 2011). The development of OA and open scholarship principles has also resulted in the emergence of alternative scholarly publishing models. Under open scholarship, three main alternative publishing models have emerged: subscription publishing, OA publishing and OA self-archiving. Subscription or toll-access publishing refers primarily to academic journal publishing. It includes a publishing business model that imposes reader access charges and user restrictions (Murray, 2009, 2011; Murray and Moore, 2006). OA publishing refers primarily to journal publishing where access is free of charge to readers and the authors. The employing or funding organisations pay for publication. Use restrictions are minimal, as no access toll is imposed (EC, 2008; Houghton and Oppenheim, 2010). OA self-archiving refers to the situation where academic authors deposit their works in online OA repositories, making the works freely available to anyone with internet access.

3. The research

This study commenced in 2011 and was concluded in 2013. Its desk research consisted of: (1) reviewing and analysing literature on the key concepts under study; and (2) analysing existing legal instruments and policies in Kenya in relation to copyright. The field research consisted of surveys, interviews and focus group discussions, all guided by similar sets of questions. The focus of this field work was on gathering data from selected respondents on the emerging concepts of open scholarship and alternative publishing in Kenya in relation to the country's prevailing copyright environment. Respondents were drawn from the following groups of stakeholders:

- authors of scholarly works, including scholarly experts on copyright, literature, political science, history and sociology;
- publishers;
- information managers, including librarians, digital archivists, managers of digital repositories and conventional archivists;
- copyright administrators and regulators, including representatives of the Kenya Copyright Board (KECOBO), the State Law Office and collective management organisations (CMOs);
- information consumers, including general readers and representatives of consumer organisations and civil society organisations (CSOs) working on education, access to information and production of information; and
- research supporters and funders.

The research team encountered some challenges in carrying out the field research. Many of the respondents were unavailable for full face-to-face interviews, for various reasons. This forced the research team to leave survey questionnaires in the interviewees' offices and collect the completed questionnaires later. This had the potential to affect the quality of data received. In the end, it was decided that the most useful data came from four of the six stakeholder groups targeted (see Section 5 below).

4. Desk research findings

This section provides the findings from the literature review and analysis of legal instruments.

Development of copyright in Kenya and Africa

Sections 26–29 of the Kenya Copyright Act of 2001 define copyright as a set of exclusive rights granted to the author or creator of an original work. It is a bundle of moral and economic rights that subsist in the category of works outlined under Section 22 of the Kenya Copyright Act of 2001. Copyright includes the right to copy, distribute and adapt the work (Goldstein and Reese, 2010; Ouma and Sihanya, 2010; Sihanya, 2010).

Kenya's initial engagement with the copyright law was, as with many African countries, via its colonial experience under Britain. In Kenya, Uganda, Tanzania, Ghana, Nigeria, Zambia and South Africa, and in Anglophone Africa generally, copyright law began with the application of all or some of the UK Copyright Acts of 1842, 1911 and 1956. These statutes were applied together with the (English) common law of copyright. This was largely courtesy of the reception clauses of the respective countries (Seidman, 1969; Harvey, 1975). At transnational level, the Berne Convention on Literary and Artistic Works of 1886 and the Universal Copyright Convention (UCC) of 1952 were negotiated, signed and ratified on Kenya's behalf by British colonial authorities. After Kenya's independence in 1963, the treaties were applied through the doctrine of state succession (Sihanya, 2003, 2010). A number of Agreements on Friendship, Commerce and Navigation (FCN) also covered or laid a framework for copyright transactions and regulation.

The individual constitutions of most African countries tend not to deal with copyright matters directly. Significantly, however, Articles 11(2)(c), 40(5) and 69(1)(c) of the Kenyan Constitution of 2010 recognise IP generally by placing the duty of promoting the IP rights of the people of Kenya on the state. Specifically, Article 11(2) provides that the state shall promote all forms of national and cultural expressions (usually the domain of copyright and related laws), including folklore and traditional knowledge (TK). (See Chapter 6 of this volume for discussion of the policy framework for TK in Kenya.)

Copyright and scholarship in Kenya

The concept of open scholarship is not expressly provided for under the Kenyan Copyright Act of 2001. However, the Act has provisions which have the potential to promote authorship and scholarship, while at the same time seeking to balance or harmonise the interests of the various stakeholders in the copyright industry. The Act grants moral and economic rights to an author. Significantly for the concept of open scholarship, the Act of 2001 imposes several limitations on the author's rights in the interests of public access and usage. These limitations, in the Act, on the economic rights of an author are closely related to transnational standards for "fair practice" or "fair dealing", which will now be discussed.

Fair dealing

The Kenyan Copyright Act's provision for "fair dealing" is closely related to the notion of "fair practice" found under article 10 of the Berne Convention (Goldstein, 2001; Lewinski, 2008). The methodology and approach for fair dealing are not to be confused with the different, though in some respects similar in orientation, "fair use" doctrine in American copyright law (Goldstein, 2005; Goldstein and Reese, 2010). The fair dealing provision in Section 26(1)(a) of Kenya's Copyright Act of 2001 allows a person to deal with the copyrighted work of another for purposes of scientific research, private use, criticism or review and reporting. The conditions for such use are that it must constitute fair dealing and that the author must be acknowledged (Bainbridge, 2009; Cornish *et al.*, 2010; Goldstein and Reese, 2010; Ouma and Sihanya, 2010; Sihanya, 2010).

As McGreal (2004) notes, fair use in the US and fair dealing in the Commonwealth countries are the traditional exemptions to copyright allowed to the public, and specifically to educational institutions, for research and other uses such as parody or quoting (McGreal, 2004). There have been some notable Kenyan cases concerning application of the fair dealing provision in the Copyright Act: for example, the case of *Margaret Ogola & 3 Others v David Aduda and Another* (unreported). Margaret Ogola, a medical practitioner, wrote a novel entitled *The River and the Source.* It was, at one time, a literature set book for secondary school students in Kenya.[5] The defendant authored a students' guidebook to the novel and used, *inter alia*, the picture of a child from the cover of the original novel. Ogola and her publisher sued Aduda and his publisher for copyright infringement. In the proceedings for a temporary injunction and interlocutory orders, the defendants pleaded fair dealing on the grounds of criticism and review. The court declined to grant an interlocutory injunction, arguing that there were triable facts (Ouma and Sihanya, 2010).

School use

Section 26(1)(d) of the Copyright Act states that the author will not have a right to control the inclusion in a collection of literary or musical works of "not more than two short passages" from the work in question if the collection is designed for use in a Kenyan school or university and includes an acknowledgement of the title and authorship of the work. There are, however, challenges in operationalising such provisions (Ouma and Sihanya, 2010). It is not clear what constitutes "two short passages". Could any number of sentences, paragraphs or chapters qualify? What if the passages constitute the essential elements (the "pith and marrow") of the work – for instance, the refrain or chorus of a poem or song?

Several cases have emerged where learners were found to have infringed the rights of an author in using her work in a school. For example, in *Anne Nang'unda Kukali v Mary A Ogola & Another* ([2010] eKLR), Mary Ogola (first Respondent) had submitted a research proposal to the University of Nairobi (second Respondent) for the degree of Master of Arts in Project Planning and Management. The Applicant had allegedly presented similar material to Maseno University for the degree of Master of Education. The Applicant argued that at the time of the presentation, Ogola knew that the work was a copy of the Applicant's work, which Ogola obtained through a friend of the Applicant. The court, in granting an injunction, stated that

5 It is a set book once again from 2013.

the Applicant had shown that Ogola had used the Applicant's original work. Hence, should the Respondent's degree course be approved, the Applicant was likely to suffer substantial loss due to violation of her "intellectual rights". Problematically, there was no rigorous analysis in this case of originality and the different standards associated with plagiarism, on the one hand, and copyright infringement (which may be a civil wrong or criminal offence) on the other.

Instructional broadcasts

Section 26(1)(e) of the Copyright Act of states that the author will not have a right to control the broadcasting of a work if the broadcast is intended to be used for purposes of systematic instructional activities. This provision allows broadcasting of educational and scholarly materials where they are used for educational instruction. The clause may have the effect of supporting the Kenya Institute of Curriculum Development's (KICD's) broadcasts to schools. But what of virtual university systems, and open, distance and electronic learning (ODEL) in general? There is at present no clarity on these matters in Kenya.

Reading or recitation of an extract

Section 26(1)(g) of the Copyright Act requires that the author should not control the reading or recitation in public or in a broadcast by one person of any reasonable extract from a published literary work if accompanied by a sufficient acknowledgement of the author. Thus, a teacher, lecturer, student or pupil reading a publication to the class may not be infringing the copyright. But it must be relevant to the class and the extract must be "reasonable".

Compulsory licensing

Section 26(1)(h) of the Act gives the government power to compulsorily acquire a copyright or produce a copyrighted work where the reproduction is in the public interest and no revenue is derived from the reproduction.[6] It provides that the author does not have a right to control the reproduction of a work by or under the direction or control of the government. Moreover, the author may not control reproduction by such public libraries, non-commercial documentation centres and scientific institutions as may be prescribed in specified contexts. This provision is particularly relevant to where a work is important in an educational setting and the author is controlling or limiting reproduction to the detriment of the public.

6 *Cf.* Records Disposal Act (Cap. 14), Public Archives and Documentation Service Act (Cap. 19).

Assignments and licensing of scholarly works

Kenya's Copyright Act confers on the first owner of copyright certain exclusive economic rights over the exploitation of the work (Sect. 26 of the Act); unless there is evidence that the work should belong to the employer or commissioner (Sect. 31 of the Act). Only a few scholars have the financial ability, economic acumen or the willingness to undertake the process of scholarly publication and communication, i.e. printing and selling their own books and articles. Authors of books have traditionally found it advantageous in terms of the balance between the financial reward and the degree of risk involved to approach well-established publishers who then arrange for the printing, marketing and sale of the books or the story (*cf.* Chakava, 1996). The publisher is also better placed to monitor and take legal action against persons infringing the copyright.

Section 33 of the Kenya Copyright Act gives scholars other ways of exploiting their works, principally through assignment and licensing. Section 33(1) provides that copyright shall be transmissible by assignment, by licence, by testamentary disposition or by operation of law as movable property.

Copyright and open scholarship

The emergence of open scholarship and alternative publishing has upset the traditional relationship between the following stakeholders in the scholarship process: authors, peer reviewers or referees, research funders, publishers and libraries and archives as well as other repositories. The traditional interests and models of economic and non-economic rewards accruing to these parties have changed and thereby significantly altered the nature and character of transactions among them. Consequently, this has changed established views on the traditional doctrine of copyright, which shape the relationships among these parties.

Challenges to access to scholarly information

While it is true that there are immense advantages to be found via increasing access to knowledge in development, there are at least two counter-arguments and situations that negate free access to knowledge or information. First, there are arguments on the cost of information. The cost of published research in books and some journals and other media has been increasing, making it harder for individual readers, libraries and universities or colleges to access the information. Second, the copyright regime in place largely constrains free access to books and some journals.

In addition to the use of licences, numerous large commercial entities, especially publishers, have promoted legislation that creates limitations to the access and use of copyrighted materials. These include, for example, the US Digital

Millennium Copyright Act of 1998, the US Sonny Bono Copyright Term Extension Act (CTEA) of 1998 and the Uniform Computer Information Transactions Act (UCITA). There are also other laws in various jurisdictions that are traditional sources of quality research like the US, UK and Australia (Goldstein, 2001; Goldstein and Reese, 2010). The regime that may have similar effects in Kenya includes the Official Secrets Act (Cap. 187); Penal Code (Cap. 63); Public Officer Ethics Act of 2003; and the Anti-Corruption and Economic Crimes Act of 2003.

The Zwolle principles on scholarship and copyright management

The Zwolle group consists of academic authors, publishers and copyright experts. The group has developed seven "principles" aimed at "balancing stakeholder interests in scholarship-friendly copyright practices" (SURF Foundation, 2002). The principles are aimed at assisting stakeholders – including authors, publishers, librarians, universities and the public – to achieve maximum access to scholarship without compromising quality or academic freedom and without denying aspects of costs and rewards involved. The seven principles are, as quoted *in extenso* from the SURF Foundation's website (SURF Foundation, n.d.):

- First, achievement of this objective requires the optimal management of copyright in scholarly works to secure clear allocation of rights that balance the interests of all stakeholders.
- Second, optimal management may be achieved through thoughtful development and implementation of policies, contracts and other tools, as well as processes and educational programs, (collectively "Copyright Management") that articulate the allocation of rights and responsibilities with respect to scholarly works.
- Third, appropriate Copyright Management and the interests of various stakeholders will vary according to numerous factors, including the nature of the work; for example, computer programs, journal articles, databases and multimedia instructional works may require different treatment.
- Fourth, in the development of Copyright Management, the primary focus should be on the allocation to various stakeholders of specific rights.
- Fifth, Copyright Management should strive to respect the interests of all stakeholders involved in the use and management of scholarly works; those interests may at times diverge, but will in many cases coincide.
- Sixth, all stakeholders in the management of copyright in scholarly works have an interest in attaining the highest standards of quality, maximising current and future access and ensuring preservation; stakeholders should work together on an international basis to best achieve these common goals and to develop a mutually supportive community of interest.

- Seventh, all stakeholders should actively promote an understanding of the important implications of Copyright Management of scholarly works and encourage engagement with the development and implementation of Copyright Management tools to achieve the overarching objectives (SURF Foundation, n.d.).

The proposed amendments (in fact supersession) of the Kenyan Copyright Act currently being considered by the relevant policy-makers will thus need to secure balance in two contexts so as to help realise an appropriate digital copyright regime (Ouma and Sihanya, 2010; Sihanya, 2012a, 2012b, 2013; *cf.* Mwakisyala, 2000). There is need for balance between protection and access, and for balance between technological protection measures (TPMs), digital rights management (DRM) systems or rights management information (RMI), on the one hand, and market principles (or the price mechanism), social norms, copyright and related law, on the other (Sihanya, 2013b).

5. Field research findings

This report gives the findings based on the responses from four of the stakeholder groups surveyed: (1) authors of scholarly works, (2) publishers, (3) information managers and (4) information consumers. A separate questionnaire was prepared for each category surveyed. The questionnaires were designed to gather data on:

- motivation for publication of scholarly works by authors;
- rights in the scholarly work that the stakeholders, especially authors, consider most important;
- how the authors use scholarly works after publication;
- how the copyright policies of publishers affect authors;
- whether the stakeholders are familiar with the concepts of open scholarship and alternative publishing; and
- how open scholarship is affecting the relationships among authors and various stakeholders.

The field research generated several main findings, as detailed in the subsections which follow.

Motivation for authorship

The 20 authors surveyed were based at public and private universities. Most of these authors have published books, journal articles, articles in peer-reviewed magazines, book chapters, course materials and related scholarly materials. The questionnaire and focus group data found that the main motivation for most of the authors to publish scholarly works is attribution of the publication to their name. These authors thus consider moral rights to be of greater importance in scholarly publishing than economic rights. Economic rights – including royalties from publishers, fees from assignments and transfers of copyright – are considered by most authors to be secondary. The authors surveyed value recognition, via publication of their work, more than any aspect of monetary compensation that might result.

The primary motivating factors among authors for publishing scholarly works were found to be the following:

- attribution of the publication to the author's name (17 out of 20 authors cited this as a primary motivating factor);
- publishing in the spirit of promotion of scholarship and scholarly activities;
- promotion of knowledge;
- dissemination of information in their areas of expertise;
- a responsibility to the scholarly world and society; and
- advancement in the teaching profession, for example, in the hierarchy of lecturer, senior lecturer, associate professor and professor (4 out of 20 authors).

Secondary motivating factors for authors in publishing scholarly works were found to be as follows:

- royalties from publishers (17 out of 20 authors cited this as a secondary motivating factor); and
- fees from the transfer and assignment of copyright.

This position contrasted sharply with the position of some of the publishers surveyed, who consider the economic value of a scholarly publication to be more important.

Some of the authors stated that they have adopted the following strategies of authorship in the context of open scholarship:

- publishing on blogs;
- publishing on personal websites;
- keeping online journals; and
- providing their work to online OA libraries.

Some authors surveyed indicated that the movement towards open scholarship has yet to affect their relationship with other stakeholders like publishers and information managers. This is partly because the concept is still new in Kenya and has yet to be fully embraced. Some authors surveyed blame information managers for plagiarism and copyright infringement, especially where such information managers employ digital storage mechanisms. Information managers, on the other hand, stated that some authors and publishers have embraced the concept of open scholarship. Some information managers even stated that they have conducted open forums with authors on issues of free access to the author's works.

Use of scholarly works

The field research found that the authors surveyed seek a variety of uses for their scholarly works, including using such works as publications intended for other researchers; using the works as printed or electronic course materials for teaching; and using the works for general readership or scholarship. In using the scholarly works that they author in the above ways, the authors stated that they do so without asking for the permission of the publishers as to whether or not they have the right to re-use the articles in such a manner.

Some authors are of the opinion that most journals generally allow one to use the work published for teaching purposes. (These findings are consistent with recent developments in universities and colleges in Kenya, which have to cope with exponential growth in student populations without concomitant investment in the development or acquisition of the relevant literature.)

Copyright policies of publishers

It was found that not all authors pay attention to the copyright policies or practices of the publishers that publish their scholarly works. At the same time, it was found that, for some authors, the copyright policies or practices of publishers tend not to influence their decisions in selecting a publisher. There were a number of reasons given to the research team as to why some authors do not pay attention to the copyright policies or practices of publishers:

- Some of the authors surveyed lack adequate knowledge of the rights of the publisher and their own rights in relation to the published work.
- Some authors assume that the publisher has a duty to protect rights.
- Some authors are of the opinion that the agreements authors sign with publishers do not contain any clause on copyright. (Our research team experienced difficulties in ascertaining the veracity of this statement, because most publishers were uncooperative and thus we could not access the standard-form agreements of the publishers.)
- Some authors were of the opinion that it sometimes takes too long to deal with publishers and the authors therefore choose to fast-track the

publishing process by not raising too many questions concerning copyright and related issues.

- Some authors stated that their choice of a particular publisher is determined by the publisher's credibility in terms of reputation and publishing and distribution efficiency.

Thus, the key author interest expressed is in getting scholarly works published, and only secondarily in getting the necessary rewards in the form of royalties, grants or related payment (*cf.* Wasamba and Sihanya, 2012). The authors interviewed who said they do pay attention to the copyright policies or practices of publishers (12 out of 20 authors) stated that they do so because they know the agreement they sign with the publishers contains such policies and that such policies determine issues of royalty fee payments and certain distribution matters.

The concept of open scholarship

The field research also found that all the respondents are generally familiar with the concepts of open scholarship and alternative scholarly publishing. Some information managers at libraries based in institutions of learning shared examples with the research team of how they have developed programmes for accessing and sharing information. The information shared mainly concerns teaching materials and important course content. These materials are provided by lecturers, most of them the authors of the materials. Researchers using such libraries are thus able to access scholarly materials on the databases. Nine out of the 20 authors interviewed informed the research team that they have embraced online OA publishing of their articles in order for the articles to be accessed by more people.

However, some respondents were skeptical regarding the implications of open scholarship in the long run in Kenya. For example, some authors stated that they do not believe in concepts such as open scholarship, open access to information or open development. Some publishers shared this position. One respondent, a university professor, said nothing should be done "free". Some interviewees were of the opinion that the open scholarship concept is similar to killing authorship, and that creating free access might lead to misuse of scholarly works. Some authors stated that open scholarship is impractical in developing countries such as Kenya, since authors will have no rewards for their works. They stated that in developed countries open scholarship receives funding from donors, but this is not the case in developing countries.

Some respondents questioned why our research project was concentrating on the issue of online open scholarship whereas, in their view, there are other issues that remain unaddressed regarding copyright. They were of the opinion that the issue of authors benefiting from their works remains unresolved, and highlighted the issue of contracts between authors and publishers. One respondent (an author) was adamant in refusing to discuss open scholarship and instead dwelt on the copyright issues in traditional hard-copy publishing. Another author expressed his disappointment as his interview with a member of our research team came to a close. He said he had expected the interview to focus on the problems he is experiencing with his works in traditional hard-copy form.

However, while several authors surveyed have a sceptical view of the open scholarship concept, these authors nevertheless stated that some of their works have been made available on the internet and are available to the public on an OA basis. Other authors were strongly receptive to the idea of open scholarship, stating that it will promote scholarly activities. For example, one respondent, a university professor, stated:

> I do not care whether it is [an] open access journal or restricted journal. The biggest thing is whether the scholarly work is published. I do not believe that access to academic journals should be restricted. I give my scholarly works to my students freely. Ninety-nine per cent of my journals [articles] have been sent to open access journals (interviewee, 2012).

The field research found that information managers and information consumers were the categories of respondents most supportive of the open scholarship principle. Some librarians (i.e. information managers) stated that open scholarship has had a great impact in the information management business. They stated that they can now stock more materials and make them accessible to researchers and other information consumers. Some were of the opinion that online libraries have revolutionised access to information, and that very soon all libraries will go digital.

The information managers were of the view that other stakeholders, such as authors and publishers, will still benefit from digital libraries. For example, one suggested that DRM tools will control access to, and author and publisher benefit from, online publishing of content. In some DRM-controlled systems, only abstracts are free of charge and one pays for full access to works, either through paid subscriptions or one-off payments for each work accessed. Some information consumers stated that open scholarship has enhanced their consumption of academic materials, as it has become easier to access a wide range of scholarly materials from online databases. (Kenyan universities are increasingly subscribing to online databases.)

Some of the authors stated that in 10 years the idea of alternative scholarly publishing will no longer be "alternative" but rather traditional. To them, the idea of alternative publishing is taking over from the traditional publishing model. However, the authors still maintain that printed books will not disappear.

Copyright laws, policies and practices

Most of the authors interviewed were found to have limited information on Kenyan copyright laws. This was also found to be true of information managers and information consumers. Meanwhile, most publishers interviewed were reluctant to discuss copyright issues. Interviewees who had some knowledge of copyright law in Kenya were of the opinion that these laws cannot support and sustain open scholarship in Kenya. The main reasons advanced for this are the poor implementation mechanisms in Kenya to protect copyright, and the high level of ignorance regarding the laws, policies and practices.

Authors interviewed stated that the copyright laws cater for the interests of publishing stakeholders, and that publishers and information managers blatantly disregard copyright policies. The authors said weak implementation mechanisms subject them to exploitation. Information managers, on the other hand, were of the opinion that the current copyright law and policies cannot sustain open scholarship because they are too rigid and only encourage controlled and limited access to scholarly materials.

Most stakeholders identified implementation as the main copyright problem. They proposed that protection of the rights and interests of authors and other stakeholders will be more effective if there is greater education on, and sensitisation to, the realities of copyright laws, policies and practices in Kenya. Some proposed that more powers be given to copyright enforcement agencies, and some argued for stronger punishment for infringement.

6. Conclusions

The field research thus found a mixture of willingness and reticence among stakeholders in Kenyan scholarly publishing towards the idea of strongly embracing open scholarship and alternative publishing. The general view is that economic benefits might not be well protected under open scholarship. Thus, while alternative publishing as a concept is gaining in popularity in Kenya, the full exploitation of the model is held back by uncertainty regarding incentive or reward mechanisms, particularly economic rewards. Authors surveyed generally agree that open scholarship gives more voice and prominence to scholarly works, but that no (or limited) other benefits accrue (see also Wasamba and Sihanya, 2012).

Two broad recommendations emerge. First, the Copyright Act of 2001 and related laws should be reviewed, reformed and redesigned to clearly provide for and establish an explicit balance between an author's or scholar's rights, on the one hand, and the reader's or user's rights of access on the other hand. Reforms are needed to help ensure that copyright practices benefit authors and users under both the traditional *and* open, alternative scholarship and publishing models. The Copyright Act thus needs to be fundamentally reviewed (Ouma and Sihanya, 2010; Sihanya, 2009b, 2010). Some of the relevant proposals have been made to KECOBO and the State Law Office. These include clarifying owner's rights; and recognising limitations and exceptions to enhance access through Braille, audio or digital texts (Sihanya, 2013b). A national copyright policy should be developed to underpin the reform of the Act.

Second, there is a need to strengthen copyright administration and procedures. The operative regulations and administrative procedures should be reviewed to facilitate authors' and scholars' enjoyment of their rights (and compliance with their obligations) as well as users' enjoyment of their rights (and compliance with their obligations).

The following specific recommendations emerge, all with policy implications requiring appropriate intervention in order to promote copyright's progressive role in open scholarship and alternative publishing in Kenya:

1. Strengthen Kenya's architecture on copyright policy and administration regarding naming of authors, their recognition and their acknowledgement with regard to every work. There is a need to develop national and institutional policies on copyright, including on the character as well as on the limitations and exceptions on moral rights. These will guide the implementation and administration of the law, especially in the context of education, training, research and scholarship.
2. Ensure rewards for authors in Kenya for the use of their works in digital format, including through the internet, in ODEL and in open scholarship. The possible rewards include recognition, prizes, royalties, subsidies and related incentives.
3. Train authors and scholars in Kenya on the individual and social benefits of open scholarship.
4. Educate members of the public on copyright and related IP issues.
5. Create better mechanisms for the regulation of copyright and related issues. There is a need to strengthen the copyright licensing regime, as well as judicial and quasi-judicial mechanisms like the Copyright Tribunal (the "Competent Authority").
6. The penalty for infringing copyright laws should be revised and made more appropriate. The penalty is quite light and offenders will keep on infringing and paying whatever fine they are charged. In

addition, the Copyright Act and related laws should also be amended to facilitate incentives and systems that secure compliance. The possible incentives include financial and other rewards for those who comply with copyright, as well as "naming and shaming", or financial penalties, for those who do not comply.

7. Ensure financial and non-financial incentives to authors and scholars in order to increase the quality and volume of materials that can be made accessible via traditional and open scholarship in Kenya.

Bibliography

Primary sources

International instruments

Agreement on Trade-Related Aspects of Intellectual Property Rights (TRIPS) (1994).
Berne Convention on Literary and Artistic Works (1886).
Universal Copyright Convention (UCC) (1952).
WIPO Copyright Treaty (WCT) (1996).
WIPO Performances and Phonograms Treaty (WPPT) (1996).

Kenyan laws, regulations

Anti-Corruption and Economic Crimes Act of 2003.
Constitution of Kenya of 2010.
Copyright Act 12 of 2001.
Kenya National Library Service Board Act (Cap. 225).
McMillan Memorial Library Act (Cap. 217).
Official Secrets Act (Cap. 187).
Penal Code (Cap. 63).
Public Archives and Documentation Service Act (Cap. 19).
Public Officer Ethics Act of 2003.
Records Disposal Act (Cap. 14).
Science and Technology Act (Cap. 250).

Kenyan policies

Kenya Vision 2030: A Globally Competitive and Prosperous Kenya (2007), Ministry of Planning and National Development and the National Economic and Social Council (NESC), Government of Kenya, Nairobi (GOK, 2007).

Secondary sources

Amutabi, M. (2007), "Intellectuals and the democratization process in Kenya", in Murunga, G.R. and Nasong'o, S.W. (Eds), *Kenya: The Struggle for Democracy*, Codesria and Zed Books, Dakar and London.

Aseka, E.M. (1996), *Africa in the Twenty-First century*, Zapf Chancery, Limuru, Kenya.

Atieno-Odhiambo, E.S. and Lonsdale, J. (Eds) (2003), *Mau Mau and Nationhood: Arms, Authority and Narration,* James Currey, Oxford, East African Educational Publishers (EAEP), Nairobi, and Ohio University Press, Athens, OH.

Bailey, B.J. (2000), "What is an author?" *The Laryngoscope,* Vol. 110 No. 11, pp. 1787–88.

Bainbridge, D. (2009), *Intellectual Property,* 7th ed., Pearson Education, Harlow, UK.

Benkler, Y. (2006), *The Wealth of Networks: How Social Production Transforms Markets and Freedom,* Yale University Press, New Haven, CT.

Bently, L. and Sherman, B. (2002), *Intellectual Property Law,* Oxford University Press, New York.

Birnhack, M.D. (2008), *The Dead Sea Scrolls Case: Who Is An Author?* Tel Aviv University Law Faculty Papers, Working Paper 63, Tel Aviv.

Bix, B. (2009), *Jurisprudence: Theory and Context*, 5th ed., Sweet and Maxwell, London.

Björk, B.-C. (2007), "A model of scientific communication as a global distributed information system", *Information Research*, Vol. 12 No. 2, Paper 307, available at: http://informationr.net/ir/12-2/paper307.html (accessed 27 August 2012).

Bourne, P., Clark, T., Dale, R., De Waard, A., Herman, I., Hovy, E. and Shotton, D. (2011), *Force 11 White Paper: Improving the Future of Research Communications and e-Scholarship*", available at: http://force11.org/sites/default/files/attachments/Force11Manifesto20111028.pdf (accessed 5 April 2013).

Boyle, J. (1997), *Shamans, Software and Spleens: Law and the Construction of the Information Society,* Harvard University Press, Cambridge, MA.

Broumas, A. (2008), "Code, access to knowledge and the law: the governance of knowledge in the digital age", *University of Ottawa Law and Technology Journal,* Vol. 5 Nos. 1–2, pp. 221–59.

Castells, M. (2004a), "Informationalism, networks, and the network society: a theoretical blueprint", in Castells, M. (Ed.) *The Network Society: A Cross-cultural Perspective*, Edward Elgar, Northampton, MA.

Castells, M. (Ed.) (2004b), *The Network Society: A Cross-cultural Perspective*, Edward Elgar, Northampton, MA.

Castells, M. and Cardoso, G. (Eds) (2005), *The Network Society: From Knowledge to Policy,* Johns Hopkins Center for Transatlantic Relations, Washington, DC.

Chakava, H. (1996), *Publishing in Africa: One Man's Perspective,* Bellagio Publishing Network Research and Information Center, Boston.

Cohen, D.W. and Atieno-Odhiambo, E.S. (1989), *Siaya: The Historical Anthropology of an African Landscape*, James Currey, London.

Cohen, D.W. and Atieno-Odhiambo, E.S. (2004), *The Risks of Knowledge: Investigations into the Death of the Hon. Minister John Robert Ouko in Kenya, 1990,* University of Ohio Press and East African Educational Publishers (EAEP), Athens, OH, and Nairobi.

Cornish, W., Llewelyn, D. and Aplin, T. (2010), *Intellectual Property: Patents, Copyright, Trade Marks and Allied Rights*, 7th ed., Sweet and Maxwell, London.

Denscombe, M. (2011), *The Good Research Guide: For Small-scale Social Research Projects*, 4th ed., Open University Press and McGraw-Hill Education, Berkshire, UK.

Diamond, R.M. (2002), "Defining scholarship for the Twenty-First Century", *New Directions for Teaching and Learning*, Vol. 2002 No. 90, pp. 73–80.

Diamond, R.M. and Adam, B.E. (1993), *Recognizing Faculty Work: Reward Systems for the Year 2000,* New Directions in Higher Education, No. 81, Jossey-Bass, San Francisco.

Dunning, A. (2004), *Copyright and other rights issues in digitalisation,* available at: www.ahds.ac.uk/creating/information-papers/copyright-introduction/ (accessed 5 April 2013).

Emenyonu, P.T., Imbuga, F. D. and Gibbs, J. (2006), *New Directions in African Literature: A Review,* James Currey, Oxford.

European Commission (EC) (2008), *Open Access: Opportunities and Challenges,* UNESCO Handbook, available at: http://unesco.de/fileadmin/medien/Dokumente/Kommunikation/Handbook_Open_Access_English.pdf (accessed 5 April 2013).

Freeman, M.D.A. (2001), *Lloyd's Introduction to Jurisprudence*, 7th ed., Sweet and Maxwell, London.

Ghai, Y.P. (1987), "Law, development and African scholarship", *Modern Law Review,* Vol. 50 No. 6, pp. 750–76.

Ghai, Y.P. and McAuslan, J.P.W. (1970), *Public Law and Political Change in Kenya,* Oxford University Press, Nairobi.

Glassick, C.E., Huber, M.T. and Maeroff, G.I. (1997), *Scholarship Assessed: Evaluation of the Professoriate*, Jossey-Bass, San Francisco.

Goldstein, P. (1989), "Copyright law and policy", in Newberg, P. (Ed.), *New Directions in Telecommunications Policy: Vol. 2,* Duke University Press, Durham, NC.

Goldstein, P. (1997), "Copyright and its substitutes", *Wisconsin Law Review*, No. 5, pp. 865–72.

Goldstein, P. (2001), *International Copyright: Principles, Law and Practice,* Open University Press, New York.

Goldstein, P. (2003), *Copyright's Highway: From Gutenberg to the Celestial Jukebox,* revised edition, Stanford University Press, Stanford, CA.

Goldstein, P. (2005), "Copyright's commons", *Columbia Journal of Law and the Arts,* Vol. 29 No. 1, pp. 1–10.

Goldstein, P. and Reese, R.A. (2010), *Copyright, Patent, Trademark and Related State Doctrines: Cases and Materials on the Law of Intellectual Property,* revised 6th ed., Foundation Press, New York.

Halliday, L. (2001), "Scholarly communication, scholarly publication and the status of emerging formats", *Information Research,* Vol. 6 No. 4, July, available at: http://informationr.net/ir/6-4/paper111.html (accessed 15 April 2013).

Harris, J.W. (2005), *Legal Philosophies,* 2nd ed., Oxford University Press, New York.

Harvey, W.B. (1975), *Introduction to the Legal System in East Africa,* East African Literature Bureau, Nairobi.

Hoorn, E. (2005), *Towards Good Practices of Copyright in Open Access Journals: A Study Among Authors of Articles in Open Access Journals,* Pleiade Management and Consultancy, Amsterdam, available at: www.jisc.ac.uk/uploaded_documents/Towards%20Good%20Practices%20of%20Copyright%20in%20Open%20Access%20Journals%20-%20version%201.0new.pdf (accessed 15 April 2013).

Houghton, J. W. (2010), "Economic implications of alternative publishing models: self-archiving and repositories", *Centre for Strategic Economic Studies Quarterly Journal,* Vol. 19 Nos. 3–4, pp. 275–92.

Houghton, J.W. and Oppenheim, C. (2010), "The economic implications of alternative publishing models", *Prometheus,* Vol. 28 No. 1, pp. 41–54.

Hyden, G., Olowu, D. and Okoth-Ogendo, H.W.O. (1999), *African Perspectives on Governance,* Africa World Press, Trenton, NJ.

Imbuga, F.D. (1991), *Thematic Trends and Circumstance in John Ruganda's Drama,* East African Educational Publishers (EAEP), Nairobi.

Imbuga, F.D. (1993), *The Shrine of Tears,* Longman, Nairobi.

InTech (n.d.) "Open access resources", available at: www.intechopen.com/oa-resources.html (accessed 5 April 2013).

Jain, P. (2012), "Promoting open access to research in academic libraries", *Library Philosophy and Practice 2012,* available at: www.webpages.uidaho.edu/~mbolin/jain.pdf (accessed 5 April 2013).

Kipkorir, B. (2009), *Descent from Cherang'any Hills: Memoirs of a Reluctant Academic,* Macmillan, Nairobi.

Kling, R. and McKim, G. (1999), "Scholarly communication and the continuum of electronic publishing," *Journal of the American Society for Information Science,* Vol. 50 No. 10, pp. 890–906.

Kling, R. and McKim, G. (2000), "Not just a matter of time: field differences and the shaping of electronic media in supporting scientific communication", *Journal of the American Society for Information Science,* Vol. 51 No. 4, pp. 1306–20.

Lessig, L. (2002), *The Future of Ideas: The Fate of the Commons in a Connected World,* Vintage Books, New York.

Lessig, L. (2004), "The creative commons", *Montana Law Review,* Vol. 65 No. 1, pp. 1–13.

Lessig, L. (2008), *Remix: Making Art and Commerce Thrive in the Hybrid Economy,* Penguin Press, New York.

Lewinski, S.V. (2008), *International Copyright Law and Policy,* Open University Press, New York.

Liebetrau, P. and Mitchell, J. (2010), *Managing Digital Collections: A Collaborative Initiative on the South African Framework,* available at: http://digi.nrf.ac.za/publ/Managing%20Digital%20Collections.pdf (accessed 5 April 2013).

Litman, J. (2006), *Digital Copyright,* Prometheus Books, New York.

Macgoye, M.O. (1986), *Coming to Birth,* East African Educational Publishers (EAEP), Nairobi.

Mambi, A.J. (2010), *ICT Law Book: A Source Book for Information and Communication Technologies and Cyber Law in Tanzania and East African Community,* African Books Collective, Mkuki na Nyota Publishers, Dar es Salaam.

McDonald, I. (1996), "Digital publishing and copying: issues for authors and publishers", *Intellectual Property Law Bulletin, Vol. 9* No. 85.

McGreal, R. (2004), "Stealing the goose: copyright and learning", *International Review of Research in Open and Distance Learning,* Vol. 5 No. 3, available at: www.irrodl.org/index.php/irrodl/article/view/205/287 (accessed 15 April 2013).

Monahan, J. and Walker, L. (2010), *Social Science in Law: Cases and Materials,* 7th ed., Foundation Press and Thomson Reuters, New York.

Mouton, J. (1996), *Understanding Social Research,* revised ed., Van Schaik, Pretoria.

Mouton, J. (2001), *How to Succeed in Your Master's and Doctoral Studies: A South African Guide and Resource Book,* Van Schaik, Pretoria.

Mugenda, A.G. and Mugenda, O.M. (2012), *Research Methods Dictionary,* Applied Research and Training Services, Nairobi.

Munene, M. (2012), *Historical Reflections on Kenya: Intellectual Adventurism, Politics and International Relations,* University of Nairobi Press, Nairobi.

Murray, R. (2009), *Writing for Academic Journals,* Open University Press, New York.

Murray, R. (2011), *How to Write a Thesis,* Open University Press, New York.

Murray, R. and Moore, S. (2006), *The Handbook of Academic Writing,* Open University Press, New York.

Mwakisyala, J. (2000), "Tanzania Copyright Act is music to artists' ears", *East African,* 6–12 November.

National Library of South Africa (n.d.) "Digitisation", available at: http://www.nlsa.ac.za/index.php?option=com_content&view=article&id=98&Itemid=351 (accessed 5 April 2013).

Nehamas, A. (1986), "What an author is", *The Journal of Philosophy*, Vol. 83 No. 11, pp. 685–91.

Ngugi wa Thiong'o (1965), *The River Between*, Heinemann, Nairobi.

Ngugi wa Thiong'o (1981), *Decolonising the Mind: The Politics of Language in African Literature*, East Africa Educational Publishers (EAEP) and James Currey, Nairobi and London.

Njogu, K. and Oluoch-Olunya, G. (Eds) (2007), *Cultural Production and Social Change in Kenya: Building Bridges*, Twaweza Communications, Nairobi.

Ochieng, P. (2012), "Knowledge not the preserve of the academia", *Sunday Nation*, 3 September, available at: www.nation.co.ke/oped/Opinion/Knowledge+not+the+preserve+of+the+academia/-/440808/1492776/-/mwsdud/-/index.html (accessed 5 April 2013).

Ogot, B.A. and Ochieng, W.R. (1995), *Decolonization and Independence in Kenya, 1940–93*, James Currey, London.

Ojwang, J.B. (1990), *Constitutional Development in Kenya: Institutional Adaptation and Social Change*, African Centre for Technology Studies (ACTS) Press, Nairobi.

Okidi, C.O., Kameri-Mbote, P. and Akech, M. (2008), *Environmental Governance in Kenya: Implementing the Framework Law*, East African Educational Publishers (EAEP), Nairobi.

Okoth-Ogendo, H.W.O. (1985), *A Teaching Manual on the Law of Property in Kenya, Vol. 1–7*, University of Nairobi Law School, Nairobi.

Okoth-Ogendo, H.W.O. (1990), *Tenants of the Crown*, African Centre for Technology Studies (ACTS) Press, Nairobi.

Oloo, A. (2006), *Devolution and Democratic Governance: Options for Kenya*, discussion paper, Institute of Policy Analysis and Research, Nairobi.

Open Society Institute and the Soros Foundations Network (2011), "Read the Budapest Open Access Initiative", available at: www.soros.org/openaccess/read (accessed 5 April 2013).

Ouma, M. and Sihanya, B. (2010), "Kenya", in Armstrong, C., De Beer, J., Kawooya, D., Prabhala, A. and Schonwetter, T. (Eds), *Access to Knowledge in Africa: The Role of Copyright*, UCT Press, Cape Town.

Outa, G.O. (2009), *Performing Power: Ethnic Citizenship, Popular Theatre and the Contest of Nationhood in Modern Kenya*, Book Surge, Charleston, SC.

Oyugi, W.O., Atieno-Odhiambo, E.S., Chege, M. and Kitonga, A.K. (Eds) (1988), *Democratic Theory and Practice in Africa*, Heinemann, London.

Picciotto, S. (2002), "Copyright licensing: the case of higher education photocopying in the UK", *European Intellectual Property Review*, Vol. 24 No. 2, pp. 438–47.

Ruganda, J. (1992), *Telling the Truth Laughingly: The Politics of Francis Imbuga's Drama*, East African Educational Publishers, Nairobi.

Samuelson, P. (2000), "The digital dilemma: a perspective on intellectual property in the Information age", presentation to Telecommunications Policy Research Conference (with Randall Davis), available at: http://bthukuku.bilgi.edu.tr/documents/digital_dilemma.pdf (accessed 5 April 2013).

Seidman, R. (1969), "The reception of English law in colonial Anglophone Africa revisited", *East African Law Review,* Vol. 2 No. 1, pp. 47–85.

Sihanya, B. (2001), Opening Sources for Kenya's Development: The Discourse on Intellectual Property, Technology Transfer and Access to Software and Cyberspace in Kenya, unpublished Master's dissertation, Stanford Law School, Stanford, CA.

Sihanya, B. (2003), "Constructing copyright and literary creativity in Kenya: cultural politics and the political economy of transnational intellectual property", unpublished Doctoral dissertation, Stanford Law School, Stanford, CA.

Sihanya, B. (2006), *Legislative Reforms for Electronic Transactions in Kenya: Policy and Strategic Options,* report to Office of the President, Directorate of e-Government and UN Development Programme (UNDP), 8 February.

Sihanya, B. (2007–8), *Evaluation of the Automation of the Kenya Industrial Property Office: Impact, Challenges and Opportunities,* for World Intellectual Property Organisation (WIPO), Geneva, and Kenya Industrial Property Institute (KIPI), Nairobi.

Sihanya, B. (2008), "Intellectual property, quality assurance and ISO in Kenyan universities", *Law Society of Kenya Journal,* Vol. 4 No. 1, pp. 35–65.

Sihanya, B. (2009a), "Intellectual property and mentoring for innovation and industrialization in Kenya", *Law Society of Kenya Journal,* Vol. 5 No. 1, pp. 29–57.

Sihanya, B. (2009b), "Legislative reforms for increasing access to knowledge", paper presented at CEPIL-ACA2K National Stakeholders' Workshop on Copyright Exceptions and Limitations for Education and Research Environments, Centre for Public Interest Law (CEPIL) and African Copyright and Access to Knowledge (ACA2K) Project, Accra, 1 July.

Sihanya, B. (2010), "Copyright law in Kenya", *International Review of Intellectual Property and Competition Law,* Vol. 41 No. 8, pp. 926–47.

Sihanya, B. (2011), "The Presidency and Public Authority in Kenya's New Constitutional Order", Constitution Working Paper Series No. 2, Society for International Development (SID) Eastern and Central Africa and Regal Press, Nairobi.

Sihanya, B. (2012a), "Digital copyright in Kenya", *Law Society of Kenya Journal,* Vol. 8 No. 1, pp. 119–48.

Sihanya, B. (2012b), "Media law in Kenya in the era of digital broadcasting", *The Media Observer,* Journal of the Media Council of Kenya, Nairobi, July–October, pp. 12–14.

Sihanya, B. (2013a) "Public participation and public interest lawyering under the Kenyan Constitution: theory, process and reforms", *Law Society of Kenya Journal,* Vol. 9 No. 1, pp. 1-32.

Sihanya, B. (2013b), *Intellectual Property and Innovation in Kenya and Africa,* Innovative Lawyering and Sihanya Mentoring, Nairobi.

Sihanya, B. (forthcoming 2013), *Presidency and Administrative Bureaucracy in Kenya,* Innovative Lawyering and Sihanya Mentoring, Nairobi.

Smith, M.L., Elder, L. and Emdon, H. (2011), "Open Development: A New Theory for ICT4D", *Information Technologies and International Development,* Vol. 7, No. 1, Spring (Special Issue: Open Development), available at http://itidjournal.org/itid/article/view/692/290 (accessed 5 April 2013).

SURF Foundation (2002), "Copyright management for scholarship", available at: http://copyright.surf.nl/copyright/zwolle_principles.php (accessed 5 April 2013).

SURF Foundation (n.d.), available at: www.surf.nl/en (accessed 5 April 2013).

University of Nairobi (n.d.), available at: www.uonbi.ac.ke (accessed 5 April 2013).

Veitch, S., Christodoulidis, E. and Farmer, L. (2007), *Jurisprudence: Themes and Concepts,* Routledge-Cavendish, London.

Virginia Polytechnic Institute and State University (2009), "Faculty evaluation principles: scholarly activity definition", available at: www.cals.vt.edu/facultystaff/evaluation/documents/scholarlyactivity.pdf (accessed 5 April 2013).

Wanjala, C. (1982), *The Growth of a Literary Tradition in East Africa,* Institute of African Studies, University of Nairobi.

Wanjala, C. (2007), "Popular culture in East Africa", in Nyairo, J. and Nyairo, J. (Eds), *Urban Legends Colonial Myths: Popular Culture and Literature in East Africa,* Africa World Press, Trenton, NJ.

Wanyande P., Omosa M. and Ludeki C. (2007) *Governance and Transition Politics in Kenya,* University of Nairobi Press, Nairobi.

Wasamba, P. and Sihanya, B. (2012), "What do Kenyan artists get for their skill? Reforming compensation under copyright", *Journal of African Cultural Studies,* Vol. 24 No. 2, pp. 171–83.

Williams, A. (2000), "Intellectuals and governance", in Hyden, G., Olowu, D. and Okoth-Ogendo, H.W.O. (Eds), *African Perspectives on Governance,* Africa World Press, Trenton, NJ.

Yin, R.K. (2009), *Case Study Research: Design and Methods,* 4th ed., Sage, Thousand Oaks, CA.

Chapter 10

African Patent Offices Not Fit for Purpose

Ikechi Mgbeoji

Abstract

This chapter outlines the findings from research into the capacities of African patent offices. The research, which surveyed and interviewed patent stakeholders from 44 African countries, found that most of the national patent offices were ill-equipped to discharge their two main functions: examining patent applications and collating patent information so that it can be made publicly available for public and inventor follow-on use. It was found that there was a dearth of substantive examination, and record-keeping and public access to records were poor. The research generated the conclusion that the weaknesses of African patent offices have the potential to hamper technology transfer and domestic industrialisation on the continent, and that there is a compelling need to re-examine the operational capacities of these offices.

1. Research question and context

Patents are public documents, issued to inventors by individual states, certifying that the named inventor has been granted a limited monopoly to exclude other persons from working, selling or using an identified invention without the consent or permission of the inventor or her/his assignees or successors-in-title during the life span of the patent. The regime of patents is built on the theoretical assumption that, in exchange for a limited monopoly over a fixed period, an inventor discloses the knowledge embodied in an invention to the state in trust for the public. Key to this assumption is that society has a system in place in which experts in the respective fields to which the inventions pertain have the capacity to:

- Evaluate the merits of the claimed invention in terms of the well-established criteria for patentability, namely: novelty, ingenuity, industrial applicability and compatibility with accepted subject-matter classification (Mueller and Chisum, 2008).

- Collate patent applications and systematically organise the documents in such a manner that: they can be used as a reference body of knowledge both for the purposes of assessing whether subsequent patent applications have not been pre-empted by information in the public domain and to increase the general stock of knowledge in the public domain; and they can be made accessible to interested stakeholders for the purposes of spurring innovation.

The central question of the research study described in this chapter was whether patent systems in African states have the capacity to perform the two aforementioned functions. This question has its foundation in what is the *raison d'être* of the patent system: the system's need to facilitate exchange of valuable information between inventors and society. The bargain or contract between a patentee and society operates on the theoretical premise that, in exchange for a limited monopoly on use of an invention for 20 years, society has access to the ingenious information embodied in that invention. This research sought to find out whether this theory is supported by the reality of patent offices in Africa, i.e. do patent offices in the continent function as they should?

Roles of patent offices

A patent office functions as a gatekeeper: it keeps out dubious applications whilst accrediting meritorious ones. A central element of a patent office's gatekeeping process is ensuring that patents are not granted for inventions that have been anticipated by pre-existing knowledge (technically referred to as "prior art") (see Atal and Bar, 2010; Dolak and Goldman, 2001; Wainwright, 1999). Towards this end, it is reasonable to assume that a patent office must commit itself to a search process, i.e. the office must be geared towards granting patent rights commensurate with innovation and not clutter the public domain with dubious patent grants (Kesan and Banik, 2000; Lichtman *et al.*, 2000). As well as a commitment to granting only meritorious patents, a credible patent office must have the personnel, equipment and capacity to evaluate the substantive merits or lack thereof in each application for patent (Lerner, 2005). Substantial personnel and expertise are needed because the scope of the search must of necessity be global, and not restricted to a state's jurisdiction (Bagley, 2003). It is widely recognised that the patent offices of many states grant overly broad patents because they have insufficient knowledge of the relevant prior art, especially in high technology areas. Second, beyond the primary function of accrediting meritorious applications, a patent office must have the capacity to reliably and accessibly store the patent information for society to draw from to enrich the public domain and advance the wellbeing of society.

Implicit in the foregoing is the assumption that the institutions and mechanisms by which patent applications are examined for compliance and, at the same time, collated and disseminated for public use, are crucial institutions and mechanisms for a nation's developmental goals. Among the objectives potentially served (or undermined) by national patent offices are: development of science and technology; facilitation of transfer of technology; creation of a significant publicly available database of innovative information; and development of a local cadre of scientists and technologists. This brings us back to the central research question addressed by the study outlined in this chapter: do the patent offices of African states perform their necessary functions; i.e. are they "fit for purpose"? The next section (Section 2) outlines the research conducted. Section 3 outlines and analyses the findings from the study, and Section 4 offers some conclusions.

2. The research

The research question (as outlined above) was derived from the observation, made by many patent agents and scholars familiar with patent law regimes in Africa, that, across the continent, there tends to be a gap between national statutory provisions on patents and the actual practices in patent offices. My practical, personal experiences made this observation compelling. Some years ago, I was instructed by a US-based client to file an application in Nigeria for patent protection of an invention. In the course of submitting the application, mistakes were made: a few pages were omitted. However, the patent was nonetheless issued. When I subsequently applied for a correction of the mistakes arising from the missing pages of the description and claims, the official response from the Patent Office in the Nigerian capital city, Abuja, was that the original application could not be traced and that a brand-new application should be resubmitted. The resubmitted application was then approved, without reference to the earlier application.

The implications of this experience with the Abuja Patent Office were clear: the original application had not been examined for correctness and compliance with the statutory requirements for patentability; and the patent office seemed not to have a facility for storage and retrieval of documents. The gatekeeping role of the patent office was, thus, practically nonexistent. In effect, the Abuja Patent Office seemed clearly to be unfit for purpose, and was serving primarily as a clerical outpost more interested in collecting fees than in facilitating the disclosure of useful information to society (Lemley, 2001; Lemley and Sampat, 2012). Decisions to allow or reject patents seemed to be based not on the merits of the applications but on the basis of the ability to make payment of prescribed government fees. The seeming absence of capacity for storage and retrieval of vital patent documents in the Abuja Patent Office clearly undermined its ability to serve as a collator and disseminator of patent information for societal (including follow-on inventor) use. I came to wonder whether the situation in Abuja was reflective of a widespread state of affairs in the African continent. This research study emerged as an effort to test the situation across several African states.

The study was primarily conducted through a questionnaire administered (via email and phone) to key patent stakeholders in more than 40 countries, with the stakeholders including: experienced patent lawyers, administrators in patent offices, users of patent offices and selected inventors. Survey responses were received from 44 countries (see Appendix for listing of the countries and the number of respondents in each country). The study also generated data via site visits to patent offices and exploratory interviews with some of the stakeholders who responded to the survey. The research also required doctrinal analysis of legal texts in each country, to determine which countries' statutes provide for domestic examination of patent applications (this data is provided in the Appendix).

The research was tightly focused on understanding the degree to which national patent offices were delivering on their statutory mandates. The survey and interviews were thus limited to questions of whether the patent offices were conducting substantive examination of both domestic and international patent filings, and whether the offices were collating the patent information and making it accessible to the public. (A potential weakness of the research was that not all patent offices in African states were surveyed – largely as a result of the unwillingness or inability of stakeholders to respond to the questionnaires either by way of emails or phone calls. There were eight countries from which responses were not received: Botswana, Comoros, Democratic Republic of Congo (DRC), Djibouti, Mauritania, Niger, São Tomé and Principe, and Swaziland. However, responses were received from the vast majority of the countries of Africa (44 out of 55), as well as the two African regional bodies dealing with patents, the African Regional Intellectual Property Organisation (ARIPO) and the Organisation africaine de la propriété intellectuelle (OAPI). Many Anglophone African states are members of ARIPO, headquartered in the Zimbabwean capital, Harare, while many Francophone African states are organised under OAPI, based in Yaoundé, Cameroon. The research also sought evidence of influence from the international, Geneva-based patent examination regime aligned to the Patent Cooperation Treaty (PCT). The two key questions posed by the survey questionnaire and in interviews were as follows:

- Does your country's patent law provide for examination of patent applications?
- Does your country have patent examiners employed for the examination of patent applications?

Respondents were also asked to provide information about:

- whether their country was a member of an African regional IP organisation (i.e. ARIPO or OAPI) and whether membership in that organisation was helping to support the patent examination process in their country;
- whether their country was a member of the PCT, and if so, whether patent examinations conducted by the PCT in Geneva were final and binding on their country's national patent office; and
- the extent of public, online access to national patent filings.

3. The findings

The research findings revealed a patchwork of approaches to the issue of patent law administration in the African states from which responses were received. Most of the approaches were found to be based on colonial antecedents, while only a few reflected modest improvements on the *status quo* since the colonial era. In the vast majority of the states surveyed, most patent applications filed were drafted by foreign patent lawyers, examined at the PCT Office in Geneva, and mailed to African capital cities simply for filing. In only a few countries was there found to be some domestic infrastructure and capacity for examination of patents, via national patent offices or via the regional patent organisation ARIPO. The vast majority of states surveyed continued to rely on foreign examination for domestic registration of patents – in spite of statutory provisions, in the vast majority of the countries surveyed, for local inspection of patent applications (see Appendix).

The research also found a near-total lack of capacity to electronically store and disseminate patents filings for the use of follow-on innovators and other stakeholders. Thus, in the majority of the countries surveyed, regardless of whether the national patent office examined patent applications, the patent office was not equipped to readily disseminate patent filings to interested stakeholders, i.e. the technical and scientific information contained in patent applications was not publicly available. It was also found that membership in the aforementioned regional IP bodies ARIPO and OAPI was not substantially ameliorating the infrastructural deficiencies in the administration of patent law in most of the countries surveyed. It was also found that two of Africa's leading economies, South Africa and Nigeria, did not require local patent examination, and that most of the stakeholders surveyed, including many of the IP lawyers, were not concerned about the issue. The education and training of IP lawyers in Africa does not seem to be instilling a desire to rethink or change the *status quo* with regard to patent filing on the continent.

More encouraging was the discovery of a sense of professionalism, however frail, in some national patent offices. Kenya, for example, was found to have a professional cadre of patent examiners responsible for conducting examination in respect of national patent applications. However, the number of examiners is limited, and in most cases the Kenya Industrial Property Institute (KIPI) opts for the use of international search authorities when determining prior art. It was also found that both Morocco and Mauritius have examiners, but only two or three at any one time. Also potentially positive was the finding that many of the African states surveyed have, through membership of World Trade Organisation (WTO) and World Intellectual Property Organisation (WIPO), begun to update and modernise their patent laws.

It was found that the existence of regional groupings ARIPO (see Sayre, 2012) and OAPI had improved the patent examination situation only slightly. These bodies have teams (albeit skeletal) of patent examiners, and for ARIPO's 17 Member States, ARIPO headquarters in Harare is empowered, under the Harare Protocol, to receive and process patent and industrial design applications on Member States' behalf. Evidence was also found that ARIPO, unlike most of the national patent offices surveyed, conducts substantive patent examination (actively evaluating novelty, inventive step and industrial applicability), with the examinations done by ARIPO examiners drawn from Member States. However, it is well to bear in mind that ARIPO patents do not have region-wide effect, and a substantive complicating factor for the ARIPO examiners is that the 17 Member States of ARIPO do not have the same patent laws. (There are some general similarities, but also peculiarities, across the pieces of patent legislation in the Member States.) While studies have found that ARIPO examiners are well trained, this has to be placed in the context of the *mélange* of patent laws which the examiners have to see patent applications through (Thambisetty, 2009). As Sayre (2012) observes,

> [...] patent applications allowed by ARIPO may be declined by national patent offices if, for example, [they pertain] to subject matter excluded from patent eligibility by national law (e.g., in the realm of biological organisms). (2012)

Also important to note is that the vast majority of patent applications filed with ARIPO in Harare emanate from US and European pharmaceutical companies (see Drahos [2010] for the economic implications of this trend, which was not the focus of this research). Another notable reality in respect of ARIPO, observed by Sayre (2012), is that virtually all the applications filed at ARIPO are drafted by foreign patent agents, suggesting a near-total absence of African patent agents skilled in the drafting of patent claims and applications. In the words of Sayre,

> [...] many African nations have at least a couple or a few strong technological universities and research institutions that are generating new technologies targeted to local needs and challenges, though a dearth of skilled patent agents across Africa has hampered the patenting activity of those institutions. Via annual patent-drafting workshops across Africa, however, we are working to gradually [...] build that capacity, as more and more workshop graduates find opportunities to begin drafting and filing patent applications in their home countries. (2012)

In this author's view, it could well be that the dearth of patent agents in Africa is not so much a result of a shortage of training workshops but rather a function of the weak patent examination regimes in most of the continent – weak regimes which mitigate against active indigenous participation in patenting processes.

4. Conclusions

It seems clear from the research findings that the patent systems of many African states lack the safeguards and quality control mechanisms necessary to ensure that only inventions that meet the requisite threshold are conferred with patent protection. In addition, there is clearly a lack, in many African countries, of the infrastructure needed to ensure that the information contained in patent applications is collated and made electronically available to members of the public, researchers and technology-oriented industries. In general, the research findings suggest that a large number of African states are at present serving as dumping grounds for patents, with little examination of the merits of patent applications and little public access to the contents of the patent filings (contrary to the provisions and spirit of national patent laws).

Rigorous examination of patent applications requires governments to devote substantial resources to the objective. According to Lemley (2001), because the overwhelming majority of patents are never argued or licensed (i.e. asserted against a competitor), it is arguably financially efficient for a country to make detailed validity determinations in respect of *only* the few argued and licensed cases rather than in all patent examinations generally (many of which "will never be heard from again" [Lemley, 2001]). This raises the question: are African states perhaps being "rationally ignorant" of the objective validity of patents? That is, it may well be that it is too costly for African patent offices to discover all the necessary facts.

However, the phenomenon of poor record-keeping reveals that there is more than rational ignorance at play in African patent offices' lack of delivery on their statutory obligations, because poor record-keeping goes entirely against the disclosure objectives of patent frameworks (Ghosh and Kesan, 2004). Further, the argument for rational ignorance is undermined by the reality that a rational national patent regime would be concerned with assessing both the costs and benefits of the patent system on all actors, as opposed to just (in the case of non-examination of applications) the apparent fiscal and operational efficiencies sought by a patent office.

Where patent offices do not provide substantive examination of applications, they encourage foreign patent applicants to seek to overwhelm weak patent offices with dubious applications, in the (entirely reasonable) hope that dubious applications will slip through and be granted juridical validity. Such occurrences would be a deep disservice to the nation concerned. Some scholars have suggested that the patent system could be improved by structuring an incentivised payment system for patent examiners (Burke and Reitzig, 2007; Geller, 2003). A simplified example would be to use court rulings as a measure of performance, i.e. a patent examiner could be sanctioned if a patent application which he/she approved via examination (or had another role in the processing of) is later invalidated in court. However, certain practical issues reduce the usefulness of this kind of recommendation, e.g.:

- the rare occurrence of patent disputes and a strong tendency to settle out of court;
- long delays, in patent disputes, between patent issuance and final court judgments;
- other technical grounds for patent invalidations not connected to the performance of examiners; and
- complex sources of prior art in multicultural and multilingual African settings, making accurate examination or search extremely difficult.

A recommendation that cannot be argued against, however, is that there is a need for better training of legal counsel and judges in IP matters in Africa. A high-quality patent system is impossible to achieve with poor-quality lawyers and inexperienced judges; ineffective examination protocols assist to infiltrate the public domain with harmful and oppressive monopolies (Katznelson, 2010). Patent law requires a heterogeneous national administrative regime, with the patent office in the central but not solitary role (Farrell and Merges, 2004). However, there seems to be, in the countries surveyed, a palpable lack of appreciation for patent administration within a multi-institutional context. Multiple sectors of government need to take a deep and critical interest in the context and operations of a country's patent office.

As stated at the beginning of this chapter, patent offices are meant to engage in two key activities:

- consistently assessing initial applications and granting of patents only to those applications that meet the necessary criteria; and
- ensuring that the database of patents is reliable and accessible to the public.

The evidence from this research suggests that quality of delivery on both of these services is, at present, deplorable in many African states. Of particular concern is the potential impact of these faulty African national patent regimes in relation to transfer of emerging technologies. (See Chapters 11 and 12 of this volume on patenting matters in relation to clean energy technology in Mozambique and Egypt, respectively.) Economic arguments for patent protection are founded on the need to incentivise research and development (R&D), disclosure of technological knowledge and facilitation of technology transfer. Such arguments collapse in the context of societies lacking the capacities to capture and disseminate technological knowledge. Technology contributes to social welfare, and if there is no effective transfer of technological knowledge via the patent system, the *raison d'être* for the patent system evaporates.

At present, African patent offices seem to be operating on what Drahos calls a "trust me" mantra (Drahos, 2008). Such trust, to the extent that it exists, would clearly be misplaced in the case of many of the national contexts surveyed in this study. African national policy-makers need to pay much more attention to what is happening in their patent offices. Transnational companies, the biggest users of the patent system, are happy to have a world in which, at a moment of their choosing, they can obtain high-value patents at a low cost. To such firms, Africa is at present a highway, with no speed limits, on which applications are rushed to patent offices. Business actors encourage the speeding up of the work of patent offices, and reductions in the cost and quality of the application processes (Geller, 2003; Jensen *et al.*, 2005).

There is therefore a clear need to, *inter alia*, utilise the teeming number of African science graduates to fill some of the gaps in the examination modalities. There is also an urgent need to improve the information technology facilities at African patent offices. Much of the scientific information contained in African patent applications is at present not electronically available to stakeholders. The result is that market monopolies are being granted to foreign and domestic patent-holders in exchange for nothing in terms of transfer or dissemination of crucial innovative knowledge. Patent offices are supposed to facilitate interactions between manufacturers, inventors and broader society. The offices are sustained not just by inventors but also by society, and therefore they owe a duty to society. When patent offices give short shrift to examination of applications, and fail to collate and publicly disseminate the patent application information they possess, they have clearly taken sides with the inventor.

Appendix 10.1: Survey data

Countries surveyed, number of respondents (email, phone), and national statutory provision ("Yes/No") for domestic patent inspection

Country	Number of respondents via email	Number of respondents via phone	Existence of national statutory provision for local inspection of patent applications?
1. Algeria	3	1	Yes
2. Angola	2		Yes
3. Benin	5		Yes
4. Burkina Faso	2		No
5. Burundi	2		Yes
6. Cameroon	3		Yes
7. Cape Verde	3		No
8. Central African Republic	2		No
9. Chad	4	2	Yes
10. Côte d'Ivoire	4	1	Yes
11. Egypt	3	2	Yes
12. Equatorial Guinea	3		Yes
13. Eritrea	1		Yes
14. Ethiopia		1	Yes
15. Gabon	1		Yes
16. Gambia	4	1	Yes
17. Ghana	3	3	Yes
18. Guinea	2		No
19. Guinea-Bissau	1	1	No

20. Kenya	4		Yes
21. Lesotho	1		No
22. Liberia	3	2	Yes
23. Libya	5	2	Yes
24. Madagascar	4	2	Yes
25. Malawi	4		Yes
26. Mali	1		Yes
27. Mauritius	3	1	Yes
28. Morocco	4	1	Yes
29. Mozambique	3		Yes
30. Namibia	3		Yes
31. Nigeria	3		Yes
32. Republic of Congo	3		Yes
33. Rwanda	5		Yes
34. Senegal	3		Yes
35. Seychelles	3		Yes
36. Sierra Leone	3		Yes
37. South Africa	2		Yes
38. Sudan	3		No
39. Tanzania	3		Yes
40. Togo	2		Yes
41. Tunisia	3	1	Yes
42. Uganda	4		Yes
43. Zambia	6		Yes
44. Zimbabwe	6		Yes

No responses were received from eight countries: Botswana, Comoros, Democratic Republic of Congo (DRC), Djibouti, Mauritania, Niger, São Tomé and Principe and Swaziland.

Bibliography

Primary sources

Harare Protocol on Patents and Industrial Designs within the Framework of the African Regional Industrial Property Organisation (1982).

Patent Cooperation Treaty (1970).

Secondary sources

Arezzo, E. (2007), "Struggling around the 'natural' divide: the protection of tangible and intangible indigenous property", *Cardozo Arts and Entertainment Law Journal*, Vol. 25 No. 1, pp. 367–416.

Atal, V. and Bar, T. (2010), "Prior art: to search or not to search?" *International Journal of Industrial Organization*, Vol. 28 No. 5, pp. 507–21.

Bagley, M.A. (2003), "Patent first, ask questions later: morality and biotechnology in patent law", *William and Mary Law Review*, Vol. 45 No. 2, pp. 469–547.

Burke, P.F. and Reitzig, M.G. (2007), "Measuring patent assessment quality: analyzing the degree and kind of (in)consistency in patent offices' decision making", *Research Policy*, Vol. 36, pp. 1404–20.

Chander, A. and Sunder, M. (2004), "The romance of the public domain", *California Law Review*, Vol. 92 No. 1331, pp. 1346–7.

Christie, A.F. and Lim, A. (2005), "Reach-through patent claims in biotechnology: an analysis of the examination practices of the US, European and Japanese patent offices", *Intellectual Property Quarterly*, Vol. 3.

De Beer, J. (Ed.) (2009), *Implementing the World Intellectual Property Organisation's Development Agenda*, Wilfred Laurier University Press, Centre for International Governance Innovation (CIGI) and International Development Research Centre (IDRC), available at: www.idrc.ca/en/ev-139311-201-1-DO_TOPIC.html (accessed 15 March 2013).

Dolak, L.A. and Goldman, M.L. (2001), "Responding to prior art rejections – an analytical framework", *Journal of Patent and Trademark Office Society*, Vol. 83, pp. 5–20.

Drahos, P. (2008), "'Trust me': patent offices in developing countries", *American Journal of Law and Medicine*, Vol. 34, pp. 151–70.

Drahos, P. (2010), *The Global Governance of Knowledge: Patent Offices and Their Clients* Cambridge University Press, Cambridge, UK.

Drahos, P. (n.d.), *The Universality of Intellectual Property: Origins and Development*, Intellectual Property and Human Rights paper, available at: www.wipo.int/tk/en/hr/paneldiscussion/papers/pdf/drahos.pdf (accessed 15 March 2013).

Farrell, J. and Merges, R.P. (2004), "Incentives to challenge and defend patents: why litigation won't reliably fix Patent Office errors and why administrative patent review might help", *Berkeley Technology Law Journal*, Vol. 19, pp. 1–25.

Geller, P. (2003), "An international patent utopia?", *European Intellectual Property Review*, Vol. 25, pp. 515–32.

Ghosh, S. and Kesan, J.P. (2004), "What do patents purchase? In search of optimal ignorance in the patent office?", *Houston Law Review*, Vol. 40, pp. 1219–40.

Jensen, P.H., Palangkaraya, A. and Webster, E. (2005), *Patent Application Outcomes Across the Trilateral Patent Offices*, Melbourne Institute Working Paper No. 5/05, Melbourne.

Katznelson, R.D. (2010), "Bad Science in Search of 'Bad Patents'", *Federal Circuit Bar Journal*, Vol. 17, pp. 1–8.

Kesan, J.P. (2002), "Carrots and sticks to create a better patent system", *Berkeley Technology Law Journal*, Vol. 17 No. 2, pp. 763–97.

Kesan, J.P. and Banik, M. (2000), "Patents as incomplete contracts: aligning incentives for R&D investment with incentives to disclose prior art", *Washington University Journal of Law and Policy*, Vol. 2, pp. 23–38.

Lemley, M.A. (2001), "Rational ignorance at the patent office", *Northwestern University Law Review*, Vol. 95, pp. 4–20.

Lemley, M.A. and Sampat, B. (2012), "Examiner characteristics and patent office outcomes", *The Review of Economics and Statistics*, Vol. 94 No. 3, pp. 817–27.

Lerner, J. (2005), "150 years of Patent Office practice", *American Law and Economics Review*, Vol. 7, pp. 112–26.

Lichtman, D., Baker, S. and Kraus, K. (2000), *Strategic Disclosure in the Patent System*, University of Chicago Law and Economics, Olin Working Paper No. 107, Chicago.

Masur, J. (2010), "Costly screens and patent examination", *Journal of Legal Analysis*, Vol. 2, pp. 687–705.

May, C. (2008), "The World Intellectual Property Organization and the development agenda", *Global Society*, Vol.11 No. 22, pp. 97–130.

Mgbeoji, I. (2006), *Global Biopiracy: Patents, Plants and Indigenous Knowledge*, UBC Press, Vancouver.

Mgbeoji, I. and Allen, B. (2003), "Patent first and litigate later! The scramble for speculative and overly broad genetic patents: implications for access to health care and biomedical research", *Canadian Journal of Law and Technology,* Vol. 2 No. 2, pp. 83–98.

Miller, J. (2010), "Substance, procedure, and the divided patent power", *Administrative Law Review*, Vol. 63, pp. 25–40.

Morris, D. (1924), "The object and duties of the Patent Office", *Journal of the Patent Office*, pp. 104–23.

Mueller, J.M. and Chisum, D. (2008), "Enabling patent law's inherent anticipation doctrine", *Houston Law Review,* Vol. 45, pp. 1101–26.

Murray, K.N. (2008), "The cooperation of many minds: domestic patent reform in a heterogenous regime", *IDEA: The Intellectual Property Law Review*, Vol. 48, pp. 289–300.

Oguamanam, C. (2006a), "Intellectual property rights in plant genetic resources: farmers' rights and food security of indigenous and local communities", *Drake Journal of Agricultural Law,* Vol. 11, pp. 273–305.

Oguamanam, C. (2006b), *International Law and Indigenous Knowledge: Intellectual Property, Plant Biodiversity, and Traditional Medicine*, University of Toronto Press, Toronto.

Oguamanam, C. (2008), "Local knowledge as trapped knowledge: intellectual property, culture, power and politics", *The Journal of World Intellectual Property,* Vol. 11 No. 1, pp. 29–57.

Sayre, R.J. (2012), "Inside perspective on patenting at the African Regional Intellectual Property Office", inovia.com, available at: http://info.inovia.com/2012/01/inside-perspective-on-patenting-at-the-african-regional-intellectual-property-office/ (accessed 15 March 2013).

Thambisetty, S. (2009), *Legal Transplants in Patent Law: Why Utility is the New Industrial Applicability*, LSE Law, Society and Economy Working Papers 6/2008, reprinted in (2009) *Jurimetrics*, Vol. 49, pp. 155–5.

Wainwright, D.S. (1999), "Patenting around nuisance prior art", *Journal of Patent and Trademark Office Society*, Vol. 81, pp. 221–30.

Chapter 11

The State of Biofuel Innovation in Mozambique

Fernando dos Santos and Simão Pelembe

Abstract

This chapter provides findings and analysis from a study of the potential relevance of intellectual property (IP) dynamics (specifically patent dynamics) to small-scale, locally driven biofuel production in Mozambique. Through a policy and legal analysis, a patent landscaping exercise and stakeholder interviews, it was found that patenting is not at present the central barrier to successful small-scale biofuel exploitation in the country, but that patenting (and protection of utility models) is likely to become a more prominent issue in the coming years as Mozambique moves from first to second generation biofuel technologies. The chapter concludes that the government of Mozambique's vision of a flourishing sector of small-scale biofuel producers will require aggressive government support, in line with its National Policy and Strategy on Biofuels (NPSB) of 2009, for a range of measures in support of locally driven technology research, innovation and development. Among the issues the government will need to tackle, according to this chapter, is the matter of how to ensure affordable access to technology – whether patented or non-patented – for small farming and producing enterprises to use and adapt (with use of "petty patent" utility models potentially being appropriate in some cases).

1. Introduction

A number of local and foreign companies in Mozambique are producing, or setting up production facilities for, biofuels (ethanol and biodiesel) from agricultural products such as coconuts, jatropha and sugar cane.[1] The government of Mozambique is actively seeking to create the optimal policy framework for

---

1 For an in-depth account, from a non-IP-focused perspective, of Mozambique's biofuel strategies see Schut *et al.*, (2010).

biofuels production in the country. According to the government's National Policy and Strategy on Biofuels (NPSB) of 2009, one of the key policy aims is:

> To promote and explore agro-energy resources to guarantee energy security and sustainable socio-economic development in order to contribute to the reduction of the emissions of gas with greenhouse effect, which contributes to the global warming, through selection and adoption of appropriate production technologies and methods in agriculture and industry. (NPSB, 2009, translated from Portuguese by the authors)

The NPSB is based on several studies commissioned by the government, including a 2007 study that recommended pursuit of ethanol as a petrol additive and pursuit of biodiesel (Econergy, 2007). The Econergy study report, released in 2008, found that, for ethanol production, sorghum and sugar cane should be clear priorities, along with cassava (Econergy, 2008). For biodiesel, the best-suited crops among those already being cultivated were identified as coconut, sunflower, African palm, castor seed and jatropha. (The jatropha tree is a drought resistant and fast-growing plant that produces non-edible seeds high in oil that can be used for biofuel.) The 2008 Econergy report also concluded that implementation of a biofuel policy and strategy would have significant benefits for Mozambique, including:

- expansion of the agriculturally productive area in order to produce raw materials;
- reduction of fuel importation, then estimated as costing US$20 million per year;
- increased tax revenues;
- creation of 150,000 new jobs;
- increase of exports; and
- growth in the transportation sector (e.g. increase of traffic in ports) (Econergy, 2008).

However, notably absent from the narratives of the private sector, foreign governments and the government of Mozambique is mention of a possible intellectual property (IP) dimension (specifically a patent dimension) to the drive towards large-scale biofuels production for the country. For instance, the aforementioned assessment of biofuels in Mozambique, commissioned by the government and conducted by Econergy, which formed the basis for the adoption of the NPSB of 2009, does not contain a single reference to the role of IP in the development of the biofuels industry in Mozambique (Econergy, 2008).

We set out to discover whether the lack of focus on IP issues in Mozambique's biofuels strategy is perhaps a gap that needs filling. The study sought to understand the degree to which the biofuel technologies being deployed in (and/or being planned for) Mozambique are patent-restricted. Among the reasons for our desire to probe this question was the government of Mozambique's emphasis, articulated in the NPSB of 2009, on development of localised technologies and small-scale rural enterprises via biofuels production, an emphasis which would be undermined if small-scale actors are not able to gain access to the relevant technologies. (See Chapter 12 of this volume for research into patenting and technology transfer in Egypt's biofuel sector; and see Chapter 10 of this volume for discussion of deficiencies on the African continent in national patent examination and record-keeping.)

2. The research

The central research question for the study was: *To what extent is, or will, IP play a role in access, use and development of biofuel technologies in Mozambique?* This qualitative study, which we undertook between September 2011 and June 2012, consisted of:

- a review of the policy and legal framework relevant to biofuel exploitation, including the aforementioned NPSB of 2009;
- a patent "landscaping" exercise to determine the level of biofuel technology patenting in Mozambique; and
- visits in October 2011 to two provinces particularly active in the area of biofuels production from jatropha oil: Manica Province and Nampula Province.

The first research method, the policy and legal review, was made challenging by intensive activity towards development of the legal framework for biofuels exploitation during the time of the study, and continuing through to the time of finalisation of this report in April 2013. We were, however, fortunate in having access to a number of drafts of the policy instruments being developed. The second method, the patent landscaping exercise, looked at biofuel patents granted in Mozambique between 1999 to 2012, with the data collected from the Mozambican Industrial Property Institute (IPI) and from the African Regional Intellectual Property Organisation (ARIPO, of which Mozambique is a Member State). The data were gathered through direct contacts we have within the IPI and ARIPO.[2] The third method, the site visits to Manica and Nampula, focused on the

2 One of the authors of this study, Fernando dos Santos, served until the end of 2012 as Director-General of the IPI. In early 2013, he began a four-year term as Director-General of ARIPO.

production of jatropha oil and its transformation into biofuels. The objective of the visits was to allow direct observation of production sites and the technologies used therein. During both visits, the team conducted semi-structured interviews with stakeholders, based on a questionnaire consisting of 14 questions, seeking information on engagement with biofuel technology and IP matters related to the technology. Contact was also made with a team of three researchers from the state oil company, Petromoc, which had conducted site visits in 2010 to 39 biofuel projects across all 11 Mozambican provinces (Petromoc, 2010). We took into consideration the Petromoc team's report (see below).

3. Context: Existing studies of Mozambique's biofuel sector

Three existing studies were particularly valuable to our understanding of the biofuels context in Mozambique:

- a 2007 report by the UN Department of Economic and Social Affairs (UNDESA) entitled *Small-Scale Production and Use of Liquid Biofuels in Sub-Saharan Africa: Perspectives for Sustainable Development*;
- the aforementioned Econergy International Corporation report of 2008 entitled *Mozambique Biofuels Assessment – Final Report;* and
- the aforementioned Petromoc report of 2010, entitled *Relatórios de visitas aos projectos de biocombustíveis (Report of Visits to Biofuel Projects).*

UNDESA (2007)

This UNDESA study proposes a path for technology adoption for biofuels production in Africa. The study notes that local technologies have not yet been developed and access to foreign technologies may be restricted due to lack of technology information and the high costs. Therefore, the study proposes that governments should focus on the development of local technologies:

> In sub-Saharan Africa, there is a lack of locally available, locally produced biofuels technology, products, and equipment. Local developers may [...] not be aware of the available product offerings in the marketplace and how to obtain these, and foreign technology can be difficult to procure and expensive to purchase. Development of local technologies, products, and services matched to the needs of the marketplace will be important [to] the scale-up of small-scale biofuels throughout sub-Saharan Africa. (UNDESA, 2007, p. 31)

The study describes local technologies and projects related to local technologies for the production of biofuels and demonstrates their usefulness in local communities. It recommends that African governments:

> [a]dvance biofuels technology research, development, and demonstration in order to drive down costs for the technologies; enhance product and system performance, reliability, and efficiency; and expand the base of cost competitive end use applications. These activities should have a particular focus on local technology development and production. National/regional research centers that include small-scale biofuels technologies should also be encouraged. Up-to-date technology information and data exchanges should also be encouraged. (UNDESA, 2007, p. 35)

The approaches to building localised biofuel use and development which are recommended in the UNDESA report appear to be very similar to the approaches adopted by the government of Mozambique in its NPSB of 2009 (see below).

Econergy (2008)

This Econergy study was commissioned by the government of Mozambique and funded by the World Bank and the Italian Embassy in Maputo. The study assesses the baseline conditions in Mozambique; the different feedstocks for biofuels production; the market potential for biofuels; the competitiveness and feasibility of biofuel production; global biofuels production trends and technologies; and prospects for the implementation of projects in the biofuels sector in Mozambique that might align with the UN Framework Convention on Climate Change's (UNFCCC's) Clean Development Mechanism (established by Article 12 of the Kyoto Protocol).

The study reviews the available production technologies for biofuels, as well as technologies likely to emerge in the succeeding decade. The discussion of first generation biofuels production technologies clarifies that these technologies convert only a fraction of the feedstock (oils, sugars and starches) into fuel. The second generation technologies, meanwhile, represent an incremental improvement in feedstock utilisation efficiency by attempting to convert the remaining matter into fuel as well. These technologies are still in the very early stages of commercialisation in Europe and the US and therefore it is difficult to predict how soon they will be deployed in Mozambique. (Of note in this respect was a February 2012 report that Portuguese group Galp Energia is planning a EUR2 million project in Mozambique using second generation biofuel production from jatropha (Macauhub, 2012)).

The Econergy study does not indicate any particular method for how to develop or transfer biofuels production technologies, but suggests that Mozambique should follow the examples of Brazil and India in exploring partnerships with other countries possessing significant biofuel sectors, as well as exploring how biofuels production and exports might be a vehicle for increasing investment and improving technological knowledge and skills.

Petromoc (2010)

This fact-finding study by Petromoc, undertaken by three officers of the company's Office of Projects and Development, found 39 biofuel projects in Mozambique in 2010: 13 devoted to ethanol and 26 to biodiesel. The Petromoc team assessed, *inter alia*, the technologies used by the companies already producing biodiesel. Some companies did not indicate the type of technology in use, but, in general, those that disclosed such information applied first generation technology. The technology is mainly sourced from India, the Netherlands and South Africa.

4. Findings

Policy and legal framework

The NPSB, approved via Resolution No. 22/2009 of 24 March 2009, lists, *inter alia*, the following benefits Mozambique can achieve via biofuel production:

- gradual substitution of fossil fuels;
- exports via the existing free trade agreement (FTA) among Member States of the Southern African Development Community (SADC), of which Mozambique is a member and which has approximately 250 million inhabitants; and
- acceleration of research and development (R&D) activities to facilitate the adaptation and evolution of technology (NPSB, 2009).

The NPSB also calls for the promotion of participation by academic and research institutions and all components of the scientific community at national level in biofuels R&D. Further, the NPSB calls for development of technologies in local communities and support for small and medium enterprises (SMEs) in the biofuels sector. It is clear, then, that the government of Mozambique is setting great store in biofuels as a pathway to socio-economic development. There is also significant interest from the international private sector and from foreign governments (see NL Agency, 2011; 2012). Of note is Mozambique's biofuels support agreement with the EU and Brazil (ICTSD, 2010). Brazil, which has natural links to Mozambique via a shared Portuguese colonial heritage, is a world leader in biofuel production.

Since the approval of the NPSB, the government has enacted a number of legal instruments to implement the NPSB, including Decrees in 2011 providing for an Inter-Ministerial Committee on Biofuels and regulations for biofuel additives to commercialised fuel (Decrees No. 7/2011 and No. 58/2011). But we found that none of the legal instruments provides entirely concrete mechanisms to facilitate or enable the identification or development of appropriate technologies for production of biofuels in Mozambique. The NPSB itself, however, does aim to promote and explore agro-energy resources through selection and adoption of appropriate production technologies and methods in agriculture and industry. Indeed, one of the objectives of the NPSB is to promote research, by national teaching and research institutions, into technologies for production of biofuels, so that the technologies can be applied by local communities (NPSB, 2009).

The NPSB directs government to enact specific legislation on biofuels and to establish both a National Agenda for Research and Innovation in Biofuels and a National Programme on Biofuels Development. Among specific priorities of the proposed National Programme, some have a technological focus, such as the call for introduction of gel-fuel stoves and the call for R&D on new varieties of biofuel plants and biofuel technologies. In the National Agenda for Research and Innovation, research institutions are to be called upon to support development of the technical capacity necessary to the evolution of the National Programme, via use of conventional biofuel technologies, the emerging second generation technologies and any other technological advancements.

Meanwhile, the Inter-Ministerial Committee on Biofuels, decreed in July 2011 (Decree No. 7/2011), began operations in 2012, presided over by the Minister of Energy and including the Ministers of Agriculture, Science and Technology and Environment. The Committee has broad technological mandates:

- to promote research, development and innovation in the biofuels sector; and
- to coordinate the transfer and validation of technologies and establish demonstration units.

IP rights are recognised in Article 94 of the Mozambican Constitution of 2004, and in 2007, the government issued its Intellectual Property Strategy 2008–2018 (IP Strategy, 2007). In this Strategy, IP is positioned as an instrument for stimulating and protecting creativity and innovation to promote the country's economic, scientific, technological and cultural development. The IP Strategy does not make any specific reference to biofuel technologies. However, one of the Strategy's goals is the incorporation of IP strategy into all Mozambican sectors, both public and private, in a manner that benefits the development of the country. The IP Strategy also prioritises the promotion and safeguarding of technical solutions developed by local innovators. According to the Strategy, the development of simple, inexpensive technology can be incentivised by means of:

- innovation, by promoting the development of simple technology and safeguarding it by granting utility models (as provided for by Art. 95 in the IP Code of 2006);
- the adaptation of the technology to meet specific local needs; and
- recognising, safeguarding and rewarding inventors by granting utility models.

The IP Strategy also encourages the transfer of technologies, especially for use by SMEs. In terms of the legal framework, the industrial property system of Mozambique is based on the Industrial Property Code of 2006 (IP Code, 2006). The Code sets out the basic regulations regarding industrial property rights in Mozambique, including the definitions, durations of rights, registration procedures, administrative and judicial mechanisms for protection of rights, and anti-counterfeiting and border measures. To supplement domestic legislation, the government has ratified a series of regional and international instruments in the sphere of industrial property, including: TRIPS (1994), the Harare Protocol (1982), the Madrid Agreement (1891) and Protocol (1989), the Nice Agreement (1957), the Paris Convention (1883), and the Patent Cooperation Treaty (PCT) (1970) and Regulation (1993) (see Bibliography for the full names of these instruments). Patents and utility models are the main instruments for protection of technological innovations in the Mozambican IP Code of 2006. Patents are protected for 20 years (Art. 66) and utility models are protected for 15 years (Art. 95). The IP Code allows industrial property rights to be transferable *inter vivos* and *mortis causae* (Art. 17). Voluntary licences of rights are also available under the IP Code (Art. 84).

Legislative provisions for protection of utility models are potentially of particular importance in developing-world settings such as Mozambique, because, as the World Intellectual Property Organisation (WIPO) explains, "[t]he requirements for acquiring a utility model are less stringent than for patents", and "[u]tility models are cheaper to obtain and maintain" (WIPO, n.d.[b]). ARIPO also provides protection for utility models, which are sometimes called "petty patents" or "innovation patents" (WIPO, n.d.[b]).

The biofuel patent landscape

Our patent landscaping exercise revealed that there were 18 patents registered with Mozambique's IPI related to biofuels in Mozambique. All the patents had been filed by companies from foreign countries, i.e. Australia, Brazil, Germany, India, Italy, Japan, Mexico, South Africa, South Korea, Spain and the US. There was no patented, locally developed Mozambican biofuel technology, and only one patent originated from Africa (South Africa). (See Appendix for a listing of the 18 patents.) Fifteen of the biofuel patent applications had been filed via the PCT International Bureau in Geneva, one had been filed via ARIPO in Harare, and two had been filed directly with the IPI in Maputo. All but one of the patents had been granted between 2008 and 2011, with the other patent granted in 2000.

Key findings that emerge from this biofuel patent picture are: the surge in biofuel patenting activity from 2008 onwards; and the absence of locally developed patented biofuel technology. This picture raises the spectre of foreign control over biofuel technology implementation and development in Mozambique. However, we are cognisant of the fact that none of the simple (first generation) technologies cited in the aforementioned UNDESA study of 2007 are patented technologies. Thus it seems clear that first generation biofuel techniques are largely in the public domain in Mozambique, allowing for SME utilisation and adaptation. At the same time, it seems clear that many second generation technologies are likely to be under patent to a foreign firm at the time of their deployment in Mozambique.

The patent landscaping also found that patenting moves fast when companies sense a violation is imminent somewhere in the world. Data provided by the IPI showed that, as jatropha cultivation began to emerge in Mozambique for production of biofuels, a Japanese company, Sumitomo Chemical Company, filed two jatropha patents (related to controlling weeds in jatropha fields and controlling diseases to which jatropha is susceptible). These moves by the Japanese company show the efficiency and sensitivity of patent monitoring mechanisms by large developed-world firms (see Appendix for the formal details of these two patents).

Interview findings

Interviews were conducted with:

- a representative of Sun Biofuels Mozambique (in Manica Province);
- a representative of an ADPP community biofuel project (in Cabo Delgado Province); and
- a representative of Petromoc.[3]

Sun Biofuels Mozambique

Sun Biofuels Mozambique is a subsidiary of Sun Biofuels UK (Sun Biofuels Mozambique, n.d.). According to the interviewee, the company has developed

3 One of the authors of this chapter, Simão Pelembe, serves as a Legal Advisor to Petromoc.

2,300 hectares of jatropha plantations, which produced 560 tonnes of biodiesel in 2011. In July 2011, the media extensively reported the shipment of the first batch of biofuel produced by Sun Biofuels from the jatropha plant for use by the German airline Lufthansa (*Biofuels Digest*, 2011). According to the media reports, 30 tonnes of oil crushed from non-edible jatropha seeds were produced in Manica Province and sent to Germany. The remaining oil was used directly by the company in its vehicles. Sun Biofuels sourced the seeds from 11 varieties of plants from the Belgian company Quinvita. According to the interviewee, Sun Biofuels is now developing its own plant varieties. Its production of oil is based on a cold-pressing method of extraction technology, which is a non-patented first generation technology freely available in the public domain.

ADPP

ADPP stands for Ajuda de Desenvolvimento de Povo para Povo (People to People Development Aid), a Mozambican non-governmental organisation (NGO). The interview was conducted with a Danish teacher trainer (from DNS Denmark, an international teacher training college) who was coordinating an ADPP biofuel project in Bilibiza, Cabo Delgado Province.[4] Via that project, jatropha seeds produced by local small-scale farmers were being collected and oil extracted from the seeds for use in lamps (and in the production of soap). The technology used, a first generation public-domain (not under patent) cold-pressing method, had been acquired from similar projects in Arusha, Tanzania, via the DNS Denmark interviewee's direct observation of practices there.

Petromoc

This interviewee, in the Projects Division of Petromoc (the state-owned oil company), provided a general overview of the Petromoc projects under way in Mozambique in the area of biofuels. All the projects discussed were still in their initial phases. According to the interviewee, the biofuels industry will be sustainable in Mozambique only if clear national policies are designed that combine fiscal incentives, investments at start-up stage and regulations on the blending of fuel from fossil sources with biofuels. (The aforementioned Decree No. 58/2011 [of 11 November 2011] established that all commercialised fuel in Mozambique must contain at least 3% biofuels by 2015 and 10% by 2021.)

4 The interview was conducted in Nampula Province, but the key project discussed in the interview was in the adjacent Cabo Delgado Province.

5. Conclusions

The research found that, at present, much of the technology in biofuel production was non-patented first generation technology in the public domain. Thus it would appear that the patent regime was not, at the time of the study in 2011–12, hindering access to biofuel technology in use in Mozambique. However, the same may not apply to the more efficient second generation technology that is on the horizon, typically patented, and which is probably necessary to make Mozambique's biofuel industry a strong, sustainable one. Use of the more complex patented technology (by the local Mozambican biofuel producers and researchers envisioned by the NPSB of 2009) will likely require negotiation with the owners of the technology and payment of licensing fees.

The government of Mozambique is clearly going to have to play a strong role if its visions of 150,000 new jobs, localised biofuel technology innovation and vibrant local SME participation in the sector are to be realised. To that end, the Ministry of Science and Technology (Ministério da Ciência e Tecnologia [MCT]), has established a National Programme for the Promotion of Mozambican Innovators (see AIM, 2011; MCT, 2010). The inclusion of the Minister of Science and Technology in the newly established Inter-Ministerial Committee on Biofuels may pave the way for local research and innovation in the area of biofuels technology under the Promotion of Innovators Programme. (The programme had, at the time of the completion of this research study in 2012, already resulted in identification of more than 80 innovators and the filing of more than 40 patent applications. However, none of the innovations was related to biofuels.)

The standard technology transfer modalities will not be appropriate to achievement of the national objectives set out by the NPSB. The NPSB calls for selection and adoption of appropriate production technologies applicable to local communities, whereas the standard technology transfer model is one whereby the technology acquired tends to be for large-scale enterprises – in this case, large industrial biofuel processing plantations and plants. Such enterprises do not typically provide control to local small-scale actors, as such enterprises are incorporated into large bilateral investment projects requiring sophisticated licensing contracts and licensing and royalty payments.

Sophisticated, costly technology and machinery would likely hinder the vision put forward by the NPSB, which seeks SME access to technology. Already in the case of jatropha, we found (in our interviews) the view that small producers are generally not interested in processing jatropha into biofuel themselves. Small-scale jatropha producers seem, instead, more inclined to sell their harvests to large buyers who can transform the seeds into biofuels. Efforts thus need to be made, similar to the initiative we found under the auspices of ADPP, to encourage small-scale production and the use of liquid biofuels for localised energy needs (perhaps combined, as is the case with the ADPP project, with other uses such as for the production of soap), in order to ignite more SME interest in the planting and use of this particular crop. Accessing technology appropriate for processing of biofuels by small industrial units or local communities could potentially be achieved by:

- identification and use of simple (non-patented) public-domain technology already being used in other African countries or rural areas in Brazil and India;
- promotion of locally developed biofuels technology by empowering local innovators (e.g. the aforementioned National Programme for the Promotion of Mozambican Innovators); and
- provision of easy access to patent information on biofuels technology in order to foster local adaptations of the technologies to suit localised Mozambican needs.

Regarding the third of the three deliverables outlined above – access to patent information – we took note of the WIPO programme (as part of the WIPO development agenda) to support Technology and Innovation Support Centers (TISCs) in several developing countries, including Mozambique. TISCs aim to provide innovators in developing countries with access to locally based, high-quality technology innovation support, including up-to-date, easily accessible patent information. A TISC was established in Mozambique in September 2012, and two TISC focal points are now active (in the Ministry of Science and Technology and in the IPI).[5] Easy access to the patent information available in the TISC focal points has the potential to encourage localised use (and follow-on adaptation) of biofuels technologies of the kind identified by our patent landscaping exercise (and listed in the Appendix to this chapter). The TISC seems to have come at the right time for Mozambique, as it potentially constitutes a crucial bridge between local innovators and the fast-moving innovation systems of the developed world.

Also needed, in our analysis, is strong cooperation – with a clear division of roles – among Mozambique's research institutions, innovators, local industrial concerns and small-scale producers of feedstock – in order to potentially ignite the rise of localised small-scale processing and use of biofuels in Mozambique. The policy and legal instruments that emerge from the NPSB and the Inter-Ministerial Committee on Biofuels must thus provide concrete mechanisms to

5 In December 2011, WIPO reported that TISCs were active in 10 African countries (see WIPO, 2011b).

promote, facilitate and enable the identification of SME-appropriate, environmentally and economically sustainable technologies for the production of biofuels in Mozambique.

Also to be encouraged is informal technology transfer of the kind we found being practised by the ADPP NGO project, i.e. transfer of technology from Tanzanian small-scale farmer groupings to a Mozambican small-scale grouping. This is an example of African innovators transferring knowledge, on an open access basis, for the common good. Broad availability of locally developed technologies has the potential to boost and spread innovation in Africa. This successful free and open transfer of localised knowledge from rural communities in Tanzania to rural communities in Mozambique hints at the fact that focusing on development and sharing of local technologies could be a key path towards innovative, localised biofuels production in Mozambique (and elsewhere in Africa) that is sustainable in economic, environmental and social terms and, in turn, drives equitable socio-economic development.

It is urgent that the two key pillars of the NPSB of 2009 – the National Agenda for Research and Innovation in Biofuels and the National Programme on Biofuels Development – be implemented. To achieve the purpose for which they were created, it is fundamental that the two initiatives:

- prioritise processing of biofuels by small industrial units or local communities;
- promote identification and use of simple technology used in rural areas in other African countries, Brazil and India;
- encourage transfer of technologies, especially for use by SMEs, through appropriate incentives;
- encourage use of patent information and technological information services provided by TISC focal points to identify appropriate biofuels technology;
- promote synergies between research institutions, innovators, local industry and producers in order to identify non-protected technologies and provide for adaptation of such technologies to fit local needs;
- liaise with the National Programme for the Promotion of the Mozambican Innovator, developed by the Ministry of Science and Technology, in order to direct local innovation initiatives towards biofuels technologies; and
- promote the use of utility models, as recognised in the IP Code of 2006, by local innovators.

Appendix 11.1: Biofuel patents granted in Mozambique, 1999 to 2012

From the Patent Cooperation Treaty (PCT) International Bureau in Geneva:

- *Treatment of crude oils* – WO/2000/AU01390 (RMG Services, Australia);
- *Biodiesel fuel production from used vegetable oils for diesel engines, involves performing trans-esterification using triglyceride on used vegetable oils to form methyl ester compounds, and neutralising and purifying methyl ester compounds* – ES20050001805 (Fundacion Cidaut, Spain);
- *Biofuel composition and method for producing biofuel* – WO/2007/127059 (New Generation Bio Fuels Inc., US);
- *Algae Growth for Biofuels* –WO/2008/151373 (Nickolas Mitropoulos, Australia);
- *Integrated multistage supercritical technology to produce high quality vegetable oils and biofuels* – WO/2008/101200 (University of Syracuse, US);
- *Process to produce biodiesel and/or fuel oil* – WO/2008/BR00128 (Ouro Fino Participações e Empr, Brazil);
- *Production method of biofuel from pumpkin* – KR/2008/0045255 (Lee Jang Hoon and others, South Korea);
- *Procedure for the production of biofuel from organic wastes* – WO2009/101647 (Università degli Studi di Milano, Italy);
- *A biofuel composition, process of preparation and a method for fuelling thereof* – WO/2009/004652 (Big Tec Private Ltd., India);
- *Efficient operation of a biomass fermentation plant, comprises fermenting a fermentation substrate in a biogas plant and subsequently energetically utilizing the obtained biogases in a combined heat and power unit* – DE200910024536 (LTS Leipziger Technologie Serv, Germany);
- *Method for producing biofuel using marine algae-derived galactan* – WO/2010/131844 (Korea Institute of Industrial Technology, South Korea);
- *A biofuel composition, process of preparation and a method for fuelling thereof* – WO/2010/0412661 (Big Tec Private Limited, India);
- *Synthetic fuels and chemicals production with in-situ CO_2 capture*, WO/2011/031752 (Fanxing and Zeng Liang, US); and
- *Process and apparatus for extracting biodiesel from algae* – US/2008/0999794 (Echevarria Parres Antonio Jose de Jesus de San Juna, Mexico).

From ARIPO in Harare:

- *Biofuel production* – AP/P/2010/005413 (University of the Witwatersrand, Johannesburg, South Africa).

From applications made directly to the IPI in Maputo:

- *Method for controlling diseases of jatropha* – P175/2010 (Sumitomo Chemical Company, Limited, Japan); and
- *Method for controlling weeds in jatropha-inhabiting place*, P161/2009, P162/2009, P163/2009 (Sumitomo Chemical Company, Limited, Japan);

Bibliography

Primary sources

Legal Instruments

Mozambique:

Constitution of the Republic of Mozambique of 2004.

Decree No. 1/97 of 28 January 1997, defining the Regulations for Distribution and Marketing of Petroleum Products and Their Pricing, in National Territory – *Decreto No. 1/97 de 28 de Janeiro de 1997, define o regime a que ficam sujeitas as actividades de distribuição e comercialização de produtos petrolíferos e a fixação dos seus preços, em território nacional, in BR nº 004, I Série, 2º Supl. de 28 de Janeiro de 1997.*

Decree No. 04/2006 of 12 April 2006 establishing the Industrial Property Code (IP Code, 2006), available at: www.wipo.int/wipolex/en/text.jsp?file_id=128888 (accessed 13 April 2013).

Decree No. 63/26 of 26 December 2006, for Legal Provisions Pertaining to Importation, Distribution and Marketing of Petroleum Products, Including their Pricing – *Decreto No. 63/2006 de 26 de Dezembro de 2006, adequa as disposições legais relativas às actividades de importação, distribuição e comercialização de produtos petrolíferos, incluindo a fixação dos seus preços, in BR nº 051, I Série, 8º Supl. de 26 de Dezembro de 2006.*

Decree No. 7/2011 of 26 July 2011 establishing an Inter-Ministerial Committee on Biofuels – *Decreto Presidencial No. 7/2011 de 26 de Julho de 2011, cria a Comissão Interministerial de biocombustíveis, in BR, I série No. 29, 20 de 26 de Julho 2011.*

Decree No. 58/2011 of 11 November 2011 approving Regulation of Biofuels and their Mixtures with Fossil Fuels – *Decreto No. 58/2011 de 11 de Novembro de*

2011, aprova o Regulamento de Biocombustíveis e suas Misturas com combustíveis fósseis, in BR nº 045, I Série, 2º Supl. de 11 de Novembro de 2011.

International:

Agreement on Trade-Related Aspects of Intellectual Property Rights (TRIPS) (1994).

Harare Protocol (1982), Concerning the Regional Registration of Patents, Utility Models and Industrial Designs.

Kyoto Protocol (1997) to the United Nations Framework Convention on Climate Change.

Madrid Agreement (1891) and Protocol (1989) on the International Registration of Marks.

Nice Agreement (1957), Concerning the International Classification of Goods and Services for the Purposes of the Registration of Marks.

Paris Convention (1883), Concerning the Protection of Industrial Property.

Patent Cooperation Treaty (PCT) (1970) and Regulations (1993).

Policies

Intellectual Property Strategy 2008-2018 (2007) (IP Strategy, 2007), available at: www.wipo.int/wipolex/en/text.jsp?file_id=202232 (accessed 13 April 2013).

Resolution No. 22/2009 of 24 March 2009, approving the National Policy and Strategy for Biofuels (NPSB), Resolution No. 22 of 2009 (NPSB, 2009) – *Resolução No. 22/2009 de 24 de Março de 2009, aprova a Política e a Estratégia Nacional dos Biocombustíveis, in BR, I série No. 20, 20 de Maio 2009.*

Secondary sources

Agência de Informação de Moçambique (AIM) (2011), "Governo reconhece papel do inovador na produção" ("Government recognises the role of innovative production"), 26 May, available at: http://noticias.sapo.mz/aim/artigo/111326052011142005.html (accessed 13 April 2013).

Biofuels Digest (2011), "Sun Biofuels commences shipment of jatropha oil from Mozambique", 26 July, available at: www.biofuelsdigest.com/bdigest/2011/07/26/sun-biofuels-commences-shipment-of-jatropha-oil-from-mozambique (accessed 13 April 2013).

Denscombe, M. (2010), *The Good Research Guide: For Small-scale Social Research Projects*, Open University Press, Berkshire, UK.

Econergy (2007), "Biocombustíveis em Moçambique: custos e competitividade" ("Biofuels in Mozambique: costs and competitiveness"), Econergy International

Corporation presentation to Workshop on Potential for Development of Biofuels in Mozambique, Maputo.

Econergy (2008), *Mozambique Biofuels Assessment – Final Report*, Econergy International Corporation, available at: www.globalbioenergy.org/fileadmin/user_upload/gbep/docs/BIOENERGY_INFO/0805_WB_Italy_-_Mozambique_biofuels_assessment.pdf (accessed 13 April 2013).

European Energy Initiative (EUEI) (2012), *Biomass Energy Strategy Mozambique*, availableat:www.euei-pdf.org/sites/default/files/files/field_pblctn_file/EUEI%20 PDF_Mozambique_BEST_Fact%20file_Feb2013.pdf (accessed 13 April 2013).

Hart, D., Bauen, A., Chase, A. and Howes, J. (2003), *Liquid Biofuels and Hydrogen from Renewable Resources in the UK to 2050: A Technical Analysis*, available at: www.lowcvp.org.uk/assets/reports/liquid_biofuels_and_hydrogen_to_2050_-_e4tech_dft_-_december_2003.pdf (accessed 13 April 2013).

Inter-American Institute for Cooperation on Agriculture (IICA) (2010), *Biocombustíveis em FOCO (Biofuels in focus)*, Vol. 2 No. 14, available at: www.anbio.org.br/pdf/bio_foco_14.pdf (accessed 13 April 2013).

International Centre for Trade and Sustainable Development (ICTSD) (2010), "EU, Brazil, Mozambique to cooperate on biofuels production", *Bridges Trade BioRes*, Vol. 10 No. 14, 23 July.

Krattiger, A. (2007), *Executive Guide to Intellectual Property Management in Health and Agricultural Innovation: A Handbook of Best Practices*, available at: www.infodev.org/en/Document.647.pdf (accessed 13 April 2013).

Leite, R. and Leal, M. (2007), "O biocombustível no Brasil" ("Biofuels in Brazil"), *Novos Estudos*, No. 78, pp. 15–21, Centro Brasileiro de Análise e Planejamento, São Paulo.

Lerner, A. (2007), *Mozambique and the Biofuels Revolution: A Study on Mozambican Possibilities for a Pro-poor and Certified Sustainable Biofuels Growth*, School of Economics and Management, Lund University, Sweden.

Macauhub (2012), "Portugal's Galp Energia announces investments in biofuels in Brazil and Mozambique", available at: www.macauhub.com.mo/en/2012/03/07/portugal's-galp-energia-announces-investments-in-biofuels-in-brazil-and-mozambique (accessed 13 April 2013).

Ministry of Science and Technology (MCT) (2010), "Ministério da Ciência e Tecnologia realiza primeira gala do inovador moçambicano" ("Ministry of Science and Technology holds first Mozambican innovation gala"), available at: www.mct.gov.mz/portal/page?_pageid=617,2266889&_dad=portal&_schema=PORTAL (accessed 13 April 2013).

Nhantumbo, I. and Salomão, A. (2010), *Biofuels, Land Access and Rural Livelihoods in Mozambique*, International Institute for Environment and Development

(IIED), available at: http://dev.natureandpoverty.net/uploads/media/12563iied.pdf (accessed 13 April 2013).

NL Agency (2011), *Towards Sustainability Certification of Jatropha Biofuels in Mozambique*, Ministry of Foreign Affairs, Netherlands, available at: www.agentschapnl.nl/en/node/103474 (accessed 13 April 2013).

NL Agency (2012), *Factsheet: Mozambique – Market Opportunities for Bioenergy*, Ministry of Foreign Affairs, Netherlands, available at: www.agentschapnl.nl/sites/default/files/Factsheet%20Mozambique%20-%20Market%20opportunities%20for%20bioenergy.pdf (accessed 13 April 2013).

Oliveira, F.C.C., Suarez, P.A.Z. and Dos Santos, W.L.P. (2008), "Biodiesel: possibilidades e desafios" ("Biodiesel: possibilities and challenges"), *Quimica Nova na Escola*, No. 28, São Paulo, Brazil.

Organisation for Economic Co-operation and Development (OECD) (2008), *Green Fuels for Development? Improving Policy Coherence in West Africa*, available at: www.oecd.org/dataoecd/3/31/4187549.pdf (accessed 13 April 2013).

Perez Pugatch, M. (2011a), "When policy meets evidence: what's next in the discussion on intellectual property, technology transfer and the environment?" in *Global Challenges Report*, World Intellectual Property Organisation (WIPO), Geneva.

Perez Pugatch, M. (2011b), "The role of intellectual property rights in the transfer of environmentally sound technologies", in *Global Challenges Report*, World Intellectual Property Organisation (WIPO), Geneva.

Petromoc (2010), *Relatório de Visitas aos Projectos de Biocombustíveis (Report of Visits to Biofuel Projects)*, Maputo.

Programme for Basic Energy and Conservation in Southern Africa (ProBEC) (n.d.), available at: www.probec.org/displaysection.php?czacc=&zSelectedSectionID=sec1194694609 (accessed 13 April 2013).

Schut, M., Bos, S., Machuama, L. and Slingerland, M. (2010), *Working Towards Sustainability: Learning Experiences for Sustainable Biofuel Strategies in Mozambique*, Ministry of Foreign Affairs and Wageningen University, Netherlands, available at: www.open.ac.uk/technology/mozambique/sites/www.open.ac.uk.technology.mozambique/files/pics/d128235.pdf (accessed 13 April 2013).

Sitoe, A. (2008), *Relatório da Avaliação de Jatropha – Manica (Jatropha Assessment Report – Manica)*, Policy Brief, for Directorate-General for International Cooperation and Wageningen University, Netherlands, available at: www.wageningenur.nl/upload_mm/4/0/0/ed7208aa-2e2f-45fd-954c-6729bdd26908_MSccoursefieldreportjatrophamanica2008.pdf (accessed 13 April 2013).

Sun Biofuels Mozambique (n.d.), available at: www.sunbiofuelsmz.com/joomla (accessed 13 April 2013).

UN Department of Economic and Social Affairs (UNDESA) (2007), *Small-Scale Production and Use of Liquid Biofuels in Sub-Saharan Africa: Perspectives for Sustainable Development*, available at: www.energyandsecurity.com/images/csd15_bp2.pdf (accessed 13 April 2013).

UN Environment Programme (UNEP) (2009), *Towards Sustainable Production and Use of Resources: Assessing Biofuels,* UNEP International Panel for Sustainable Resource Management, available at: www.unep.org/pdf/biofuels/Assessing_Biofuels_Full_Report.pdf (accessed 13 April 2013).

World Business Council for Sustainable Development (WBCSD) (2007), *Biofuels Issue Brief*, available at: www.wbcsd.org/Pages/EDocument/EDocumentDetails.aspx?ID=106&NoSearchContextKey=true (accessed 13 April 2013).

World Intellectual Property Organisation (WIPO) (2011a), "How the private and the public sectors use intellectual property to enhance agricultural productivity", *Proceedings of a Seminar at WIPO,* 14 June, available at: www.wipo.int/freepublications/en/global_challenges/1027/wipo_pub_1027.pdf (accessed 13 April 2013).

World Intellectual Property Organisation (WIPO) (2011b), *Technology and Innovation Support Centers (TISC): Progress and Needs Assessment Questionnaire: December 2011 – Survey Summary Report*, available at: www.wipo.int/export/sites/www/tisc/en/doc/tisc_2011_survey_report.pdf (accessed 13 April 2013).

World Intellectual Property Organisation (WIPO) (n.d.[a]), "Technology and Innovation Support Centers (TISCs)", available at: http://www.wipo.int/tisc/en/ (accessed 13 April 2013).

World Intellectual Property Organisation (WIPO) (n.d.[b]), "Protecting innovations by utility models", available at: www.wipo.int/sme/en/ip_business/utility_models/utility_models.htm (accessed 13 April 2013).

Yin, R.K. (2009), *Case Study Research: Design and Methods*, 4th ed., Sage, Thousand Oaks, CA.

Chapter 12

Reflections on the Lack of Biofuel Innovation in Egypt

Bassem Awad and Perihan Abou Zeid

Abstract

This chapter outlines findings from research into Egypt's legal environment for biofuel patenting and the present state of biofuel innovation in the country. Based on evidence of only one domestically generated biofuel patent in Egypt at the time of the completion of the research in 2012, the chapter suggests policy and practical mechanisms which could help spark more innovation in this sector. The mechanisms suggested include online clean energy patent databases, a clean energy patent fast-tracking mechanism, and a green "patent commons".

1. Introduction

The energy sector in Egypt faces a number of challenges. The price of liquid petroleum has increased significantly in recent years, putting the country's oil reserves in decline and resulting in deterioration of the financial performance of the country's energy companies. An adequate and reliable supply of energy must thus be secured to support a growing population and to sustain economic growth. At the same time, as part of its commitments under the Kyoto Protocol and the UN Framework Convention on Climate Change (UNFCCC), Egypt must reduce greenhouse gas emissions and incorporate clean energy technology into its development plans.[1]

The government of Egypt has decided to diversify its energy supplies through the development of new and renewable energy sources. The country's national

1 Egypt is also a Member State of the International Renewable Energy Agency (IRENA), which promotes the adoption of clean energy technologies (IRENA, n.d.).

Renewable Energy Strategy was revised in 2007 (and the revisions made official in early 2008) to prioritise the use of natural resources in a more sustainable manner through the production of clean and renewable energy. Biofuels produced from rice straw, sugar cane, jatropha, jojoba or algae have been proposed as alternative fuel sources to solve some of the challenges facing the Egyptian energy sector.

Following the UNFCCC Bali meeting in 2007, the issue of the relationship between intellectual property (IP) mechanisms and clean energy technology innovation was brought to the fore. Laws and regulations governing patents have come to be viewed as possible barriers to the development of clean energy technology and its commercialisation. In 2009, at the UN Climate Change Conference in Copenhagen, countries such as Brazil, China and India proposed to adopt measures on flexibilities and exceptions for IP rights to ensure greater access to clean technology. They argued that new "green" technologies should be subject to an expanded use of existing flexibilities in the implementation of IP rights, including the measure of "compulsory licensing". Such a licensing system has been used in the health area where, for example, a particular lifesaving drug is prohibitively expensive, and the Group of 77 developing nations (G77), led *de facto* by China, has argued for analogous application of this logic to patents for technology related to climate change mitigation and adaptation (Kogan, 2010).

While patents and other forms of orthodox IP are not in themselves accurate indicators for innovation in African countries – for reasons discussed in chapters 1 and 16 of this volume – our research study, as outlined in this chapter, sought to investigate the degree to which Egypt's patent system is conducive to biofuel innovation, and to see whether there are any legal and practical steps needed to enhance the country's innovation potential in this important area. The research consisted of a legal analysis of Egyptian patent law (provided in Section 2 below) and an examination of the current realities of, and stakeholder perceptions of, biofuel patenting (Sections 3 and 4). Section 5 provides our reflections on possible ways forward. (See Chapter 11 of this volume for discussion of innovation and patenting matters in relation to biofuels in Mozambique.)

2. Egypt's patent system

IP protection for innovative research and development in the area of renewable energy can take one of three forms: trade secrets, patents or *sui generis* plant variety protection. Trade secrets have immediate effect, exist for an indefinite period – provided confidentiality is maintained – and have no registration costs. However, it can be risky and expensive to the holder to seek to keep the trade secret information confidential. The Egyptian Intellectual Property Rights Law (EIPRL) 82 of 2002, which consists of four Books, replaced all previous legislation related to IP rights in Egypt in order to ensure the country's compliance with the World Trade Organisation (WTO) Agreement on Trade-Related Aspects of Intellectual Property Rights (TRIPS). The executive regulation for the EIPRL's Book One (related to patents) and Book Four (related to plant varieties) was issued by Prime Ministerial Decree 1366 of 2003. This Decree addresses procedural issues not specified in the EIPRL itself.

The EIPRL grants patents to all types of inventions in all fields of technology, as long as these inventions meet certain basic criteria. An invention must show some new characteristic not known prior to the application date or priority date (absolute novelty). The invention must also be non-obvious to a person skilled in the particular field of the invention (inventive step). (The EIPRL does not, however, provide a definition for the requirements of an "inventive step".) Finally, an invention must be capable of being applied in industry in its broadest sense (industrial applicability). According to Article 1 of the EIPRL:

> A patent shall be granted, in accordance with the provisions of this Law, to any industrially applicable invention, which is new, involves an inventive step, whether connected with new industrial products, new industrial processes, or a new application of known industrial processes. (Art. 1.1)

At the same time, Article 2 of the EIPRL, modelled on Article 27.2 of TRIPS, excludes the following from patentability:

> 1 – Inventions whose exploitation is likely to be contrary to public order or morality or prejudicial to the environment, human, animal or plant life and health.
>
> 4 – Plants and animals, regardless of their rarity or peculiarity, and essentially biological processes for the production of plants or animals, other than microorganisms, non-biological and microbiological process for the production of plants. (Art. 2)

Egyptian patent law has therefore availed itself of Article 27 of TRIPS, which allows TRIPS Member States to prohibit patentability of inventions in order to protect public order or morality, including avoiding serious prejudice to the environment. We are of the view that the EIPRL made Egyptian IP law "greener" by excluding from patentability inventions that may cause prejudice to the environment as well as providing specific treatment for plant varieties. However, the Law does not provide a clear standard as to how to assess serious prejudice to the environment (Derclaye, 2010).

The EIPRL's Article 2 explicitly excludes plants from patent protection. The Law also establishes a *sui generis* system for plant varieties: Article 189 of the EIPRL states that plant varieties, whether derived inside or outside Egypt, shall be protected regardless of whether they were developed through biological or non-biological means. This provision is notable, because advanced plant breeding could lead to the development of new plant varieties with improved traits suitable for the production of biofuels, and such new varieties, while not eligible for patent protection, could be protected via *sui generis* methods (Al-Saghir, 2004). According to Article 194 of the EIPRL, any third party wishing to produce, propagate, circulate, sell, market, import or export the propagating material of a new plant variety has to obtain written consent from the breeder.

Article 195 of the EIPRL provides an exemption allowing free access to plant material in order to breed new varieties without having to obtain permission from the first breeder. This kind of "breeder exemption" is one of the cornerstones of plant variety rights systems. The same Article 195 also allows free activities related to experiments and scientific research purposes, as well as selected non-commercial uses and activities related to teaching and training. Article 10 of the EIPRL contains a list of exceptions to exclusive patent rights for the purposes of research or experimental use of an invention. Researchers often build upon existing inventions, and this exception could thus be relevant in the clean energy context where adaptation of technology to local needs and environments is particularly vital.

Formal requirements under Egyptian patent law do not concern the nature of the invention, but rather the manner in which the invention is submitted to the Egyptian Patent Office. According to Article 16 of the EIPRL, the filing of a patent application is followed by the processing of the application through a search of prior art, substantive examination of patentability, and deciding whether a patent is granted or refused. Identifying an invention requires a summary of all the particular features of the invention, such as a description, claim(s), drawing(s) and an abstract. Other formal requirements are evidence of ownership and the payment of fees to the Patent Office. The description filed with the Patent Office must disclose the invention in a clear and complete manner so that the invention could be carried out by a person skilled in the art (EIPRL, Art. 13.1).

Article 13 of the EIPRL includes specific provisions regarding the disclosure of the invention that are potentially relevant to biofuel innovation and other clean energy technology innovations. Article 13 adopts the highest possible level of disclosure, as it requires the patent applicant to disclose in the best possible way how the invention is executable at the time when the patent application is filed (Awad, 2007). Moreover, Article 13 states that, where the invention involves biological, plant or animal matter, traditional medicinal, agricultural, industrial or handicraft knowledge, or cultural or environmental heritage, the applicant should have acquired the source of such product, knowledge or heritage by legitimate means. The patent applicant must, according to Article 3(3) of the Executive Regulation of the EIPRL, submit to the Patent Office the documents indicating that he/she legally obtained such genetic resources or information according to the provisions of "the applicable legislations in Egypt", which require disclosure of the origin of genetic resources and prior informed consent of the use of traditional knowledge (TK) in patent applications. There are a number of developing countries that have adopted this kind of disclosure requirement as a formal condition for the granting and validation of patent rights. Failure to comply results in a rejection of the patent application (or invalidity of the patent if it was granted prior to the invalidation).[2]

According to the interpretation of Phillips *et al.* (2011), the reference in Article 3(3) of the Executive Regulation of the EIPRL to "the applicable legislations in Egypt" refers not only to national laws but also to the international conventions to which Egypt is a party, including the Convention on Biological Diversity (CBD) (1992). Phillips *et al.* explain that the EIPRL and its Regulation are drafted in light of the CBD, which recognises the sovereign rights of states over their natural resources and that the authority to determine access to genetic resources rests with the national governments (Art.15(1) and 15(4)–(5)). The EIPRL requirement for disclosure of origin aims to improve the transparency of use of genetic resources and TK so as to facilitate access to these resources and sharing of the benefits derived from their commercialisation. Meanwhile, the disclosure of the technical details of inventions aims to expand the public stock of technical knowledge and create competition among innovators and researchers.

3. Biofuels patenting in Egypt

In December 2011 we distributed a formal survey to academics, economists, scientists and technologists in industry to obtain concrete data for mapping the status of biofuels in Egypt. The results of the surveys were analysed to map the current clean energy landscape in the country. This first phase was followed by an examination of the Egyptian Patent Office database to find registered patents of clean energy technology in Egypt.

2 See, for example, Brazil's Provisional Measure No. 2.186-16, of 2001, Article 31; the Member States of the Andean Community (Bolivia, Colombia, Ecuador, Peru and Venezuela), Decision 391 of 1996, Articles 16, 26, 35 and second complementary provision and Decision 486 of 2000, Articles 3 and 75; Costa Rica's Law No. 7.788 of 1998, Article 81; and India's The Patents Act of 1970 (as amended by The Patents [Amendment] Act of 2002, Sect. 10, 25 and 64).

The data and information gathered indicate that research in Egypt includes different types of clean energy, ranging from solar and wind energy to biofuels (obtained from different sources such as jatropha and jojoba plantations, agricultural waste, cooking oil and recently also algae). Notably, solar and wind energy receive substantial government funding for research, specifically from the state's New and Renewable Energy Authority (NREA, 2011).

In general, we found the gathering of data and information on biofuels in Egypt to be a difficult task due to the scarcity of information, the lack of governing rules, the overlap between related public entities and the lack of coordination among different stakeholders. This in itself was a significant finding of this research, as information availability is central to the logic of patent systems as systems which balance the interests of patent-holders with the interests of stakeholders needing access to the patent information for purposes of experimentation and follow-on innovation (see Chapter 10 of this volume, which examines failure, by patent offices in much of Africa, to ensure sufficient public access to patent filings).

Statistics from the Egyptian Patent Office show that the process from the filing date of an application to the approval of a patent takes on average three years and 10 months. Our analysis of the Egyptian Patent Office procedures shows the need to establish an advanced database to make it easier to search for accepted applications and other relevant patent information. Patent information consists of the text of granted patents and published patent applications, including the abstract, specifications, drawings and claims. The information becomes accessible through its publication and the availability of the patent documents at the Patent Office. At the moment, however, it can be very difficult to obtain reliable information about the geographical coverage and status of patents in Egypt. There is also a noted delay in issuing the *Patent Gazette*. The accessibility of information needs to be improved, especially since the Egyptian Patent Office is now, as of 1 April 2013, one of the international searching and preliminary examining authorities under the Patent Cooperation Treaty (PCT) and is currently accepting patent applications from all over the world.

4. Stakeholder activities and perceptions

The final stage in the research consisted of field interviews with stakeholders and policy-makers from three categories: (1) scientists and academics, (2) public sector representatives and (3) private sector project managers. In general, it was found from the interviews that, while most stakeholders acknowledge the importance of biofuels in Egypt, scientific exploration and production remain limited in this area.

Scientists and academics

There is no specific research institute or department within a university faculty in Egypt that specialises in renewable energy or biofuels technology. Biofuel investigations are usually temporary projects. For example, at some engineering faculties and/or departments, such as those at Cairo University and the Arab Academy for Science and Technology and Maritime Transport, there is an interest in the development of biofuel refineries and in undertaking research to evaluate the quantity of energy that can be derived from different types of biofuels. In faculties of agriculture, the departments are mainly focused on studying plants, agricultural waste or algae and biofuel production methods (e.g. the Department of Animal and Fish Production, Faculty of Agriculture, Alexandria University). In environmental institutes, while research is focused on biofuel production in general, there is a focus on the environmental impact of biofuels.

The only important domestically generated biofuels patent we were able to find evidence of was obtained in 2009 by Bahaa Shawky, a professor at the Genetic Engineering and Biotechnology Research Division at the National Research Centre (NRC). The invention involves a pre-treatment method for facilitating the enzyme decomposition of different agricultural waste, e.g. rice straw. Facilitating enzyme decomposition helps generate sugar, which is then fermented to obtain bioethanol.[3] The patent was granted in 2009 but has not yet been commercialised at any level by industry, due in part to lack of government support. According to Shawky, this invention should ideally be considered for adoption as a national project, because it could help reuse, for energy production, the 40 million tonnes of agricultural waste produced annually in Egypt.

At the Faculty of Agriculture of Alexandria University, it was found that some researchers are trying to increase the amount of oil that can be extracted from algae, which can then be converted into biofuels (see Demirbas and Demirbas, 2010). Another important biofuels project was established by the Aquaculture Research Centre (ARC) in the Arab Academy for Science, Technology and Maritime Transport. The ARC managed to create algae powder on a small scale, using dehydration techniques. More importantly, the ARC successfully extracted biofuels from used cooking oil. After applying chemical conversion techniques, the ARC obtained biodiesel from the used cooking oil in a cost-effective manner with minimal environmental impact. For this purpose, the ARC signed agreements with hotels and restaurants to obtain used cooking

3 Patent No. 24507/2009, granted by the Egyptian Patent Office, for "a method and multipurpose apparatus for lignocelluloses materials pre-treatment to enhance subsequent enzymatic hydrolysis for producing fermentable sugars and ethanol".

oil instead of their disposing of it. The ARC team did not pursue the patent route due to the formalities and time required for patent review process at the Egyptian Patent Office.

Public-sector bodies

We were surprised to discover that Egypt's New and Renewable Energy Authority (NREA) does not have any departments that specialise in biofuels, and in fact is not conducting research pertaining to biofuels (NREA, 2012). The Authority's projects and research are mainly concerned with solar and wind energy production, with research on biofuels apparently a lower priority area.

The Egyptian Environmental Affairs Agency (EEAA), meanwhile, is undertaking several projects. One project relates to growing the jatropha plant (a commonly known source of biofuels) using treated waste water. The EEAA planted jatropha, using treated waste water, in the Suez and Luxor regions on land otherwise unsuitable for food agriculture, and the aim is to produce high-energy yields with low inputs of water, fertilisers and pesticides and on the smallest possible land area (Ministry of State for Environmental Affairs, 2012). One of the jatropha plantations was found to be very successful in comparison to its counterparts in other countries (JBEDC, 2008). However, the EEAA officials interviewed stated that Egyptian jatropha is not being used for biofuel production beyond the research setting, due to a lack of funding.

Private sector

Private-sector interviewees were found to be enthusiastic about biofuels, and they acknowledged the importance of biofuels to the country's future. At the same time, they stated that biofuel production has yet to become a commercial reality in Egypt. Energy Allied International, an international development firm, initiated investment in the biofuels sector in Egypt in 2005 and established a sub-company called New Nile Company. New Nile's vision was to adopt an integrated seawater agriculture system (ISAS) which utilises seawater for biofuel and food production (New Nile Company, 2012). New Nile also wanted to do some work in Egypt with a new variety of jatropha that it was developing in conjunction with an Indian company and that was thought to be suitable for the climate, agriculture and irrigation conditions in Egypt. However, after obtaining the necessary approvals, New Nile encountered a number of administrative hurdles which led it to abandon the project.

The private firm Egyptian Natural Oil Co. (Natoil), established in 1996, grows jojoba and sells its seeds and rooted seedlings for further planting (Natoil, 2012).

But while the company acknowledged the importance of jojoba as a source of biofuels, its existing focus is on cosmetic and medical applications, and it has even obtained two patents, from Egypt's Patent Office, the US Patent and Trademark Office (USPTO) and the European Patent Office, for the medicinal applications of jojoba (see El Mogy, 2010).

5. The way forward

Our research found little in the way of biofuels innovation in Egypt. This prompted us to cast our minds towards the future and to try to identify steps that could be taken to potentially boost innovation.

Fast-tracking

We found persuasive the ideas of Derclaye (2010), who has suggested that patent systems as tools for technological development and economic growth can benefit from "green" inventions receiving, among other things, fast-tracked examination, reduced application fees and exemption from deferred examination. Of particular interest is the idea of fast-tracking. The adoption of a fast-track administrative procedure in Egypt could help to encourage innovation in clean energy technology, including biofuels. A faster administrative process would allow clean energy innovations to receive patent protection more quickly and therefore to reach the market earlier. Ideally, faster procedures could encourage Egyptian innovators to invest local resources in developing new technologies and to provide those technologies to the marketplace.

Internationally, several major patent offices have instituted a fast-track mechanism for clean technology innovation. The UK Intellectual Property Office has introduced an initiative to give priority to patent applications directed to technology having environmental benefits. Instead of the typical average of two to three years for an application to get through the UK Intellectual Property Office, a patent application for a clean technology can be granted in just nine months. According to the Office, "[t]here is no specific environmental standard to meet in order to benefit from the Green Channel" (UK Intellectual Property Office, 2009): the applicant simply needs to provide as much justification as is necessary to explain why the invention is environmentally friendly.

The USPTO introduced a system in 2009 to process clean technology patent applications more quickly (USPTO, 2012). The Australian and South Korean patent offices have also launched similar schemes (IP Australia, 2012; Korean

Intellectual Property Office, 2009). South Korea currently provides the fastest examination period in the world for green technology: examinations can be completed in less than one month. In 2011, the Canadian Intellectual Property Office (CIPO) amended its patent rules to expedite the examination of patent applications related to green technologies (CIPO, 2011).

Early evidence suggests that, so far, only a small percentage of eligible patent applicants in the area of green technology make use of the opportunities for accelerated examination under the aforementioned programmes (Dechezleprêtre, 2013). However, in certain circumstances fast-tracking could still help increase the number of green technology patents in Egypt, e.g. if third-party investment is urgently needed, or in order to secure commercial partnerships.

Patent database

Based on the difficulty we faced in accessing reliable patent information for this research, we are of the view that the Egyptian Patent Office should move forward quickly on its plan for an advanced patent database, as a means to ensure wide public dissemination of patent-related information, including clean energy technology information.

Of relevance is the work of the World Intellectual Property Organisation (WIPO) on patent databases. The WIPO Patent Information Service (WPIS) facilitates access to technical information within patent documents (WIPO, 2012), and WIPO has even set up a special patent database related to biofuels, the IPC Green Inventory, which was developed by the International Patent Classification (IPC) committee of experts in order to facilitate searches for patent information relating to environmentally sound technologies (ESTs) as listed by the UNFCCC. The inventory attempts to collect ESTs in one place to facilitate the search for this type of technology innovation (WIPO, 2012), and allows users to search and display all international patent applications available through PATENTSCOPE (a WIPO database that aggregates PCT patent data from developed and developing countries).

A "patent commons"

Another possible approach would be an "open source" approach whereby there is free sharing of knowledge – within a "patent commons" – so as to maximise the collaborative elements of innovation. The Eco-Patent Commons is an interesting initiative of this sort. In January 2008, a number of large multinational companies, including IBM, Nokia, Sony and Pitney Bowes, in cooperation with the World Business Council for Sustainable Development (WBCSD), established the Eco-Patent Commons initiative to create a collection of patents that concern inventions that directly or indirectly protect the environment (Hall and Helmers, 2011). The patents are pledged by companies and other IP rights-holders and are made available to anyone free of charge. This patent commons is a resource for connecting those who have had success with a particular challenge to those who are facing similar challenges (WBCSD, 2011). Since the launch of the Eco-Patent Commons, 121 eco-friendly patents have been contributed by 13 companies worldwide (WBCSD, 2011). The patent commons model could be deployed in Egypt in order to pool Egyptian clean energy technology contributions and provide an institutional design that allows easy access to patented clean energy technologies.

Accordingly, a biofuels innovation pool that contains different licences from Egyptian patent-holders or breeders of new plant varieties could stimulate use of innovation for equitable reward. Those members of the private sector interested in investing in biofuels innovation could pay a reasonable fee for using these protected technologies. (See Chapters 6 and 7 in this volume for discussion of commons modalities in relation to traditional knowledge [TK].)

Research incentives

One of the main obstacles facing researchers and scientists in Egypt is a lack of funds. And several interviewees criticised the lack of government help in marketing their innovations, making it more difficult to recoup research expenses. Providing incentives in the form of research grants and awards could help promote innovation.

Stakeholder structures

There is neither a policy nor a holistic strategy for the development of biofuels in Egypt. A researcher, scientist or an investor in the field of biofuels does not have access to a governmental body that can provide guidance, funds or approvals in the context of biofuels. Thus Egypt is in need of a workable biofuels strategy and a body that is responsible for governing biofuels research with the objective of developing this important field of technology for national interests. The activities of this body could include:

- setting out a national holistic biofuels strategy that includes, but is not limited to, deciding the optimum level of biofuel generation that Egypt can implement along with providing the necessary infrastructure;
- gathering research data and literature regarding biofuels and compiling a list of research projects undertaken by research institutions in Egypt to facilitate effective research and cooperation among scientists;

- building effective public–private partnerships and collaborative research projects, which could be an effective way for the public sector, generally limited in resources, to achieve public policy objectives through working with the private sector; and
- administering biofuel-related activities and providing the necessary approvals in coordination with different government entities.

In addition, it is important to establish a national platform among researchers and the industry to establish priorities for short- and long-term timeframes for biofuels. Such a platform could act as a lobby to push Parliament towards adopting laws which, among other things, stipulate percentages of biofuels that need to be blended into gasoline, and establish implementation provisions.

Also, during the research interviews with the private sector, we noted that companies are not aware of each other's activities, and interviewees expressed the need for private-sector collaboration (and, in turn, investment) in order to take the biofuels industry forward strongly. The Egyptian government could play a role through creation of new tax and investment incentives for biofuels investors. Accordingly, small and medium-sized entrepreneurs and farmers should consider establishment of a consortium to help secure investments.

Bibliography

Primary sources

Legal instruments

Agreement on Trade-Related Aspects of Intellectual Property Rights (TRIPS) (1994).

Convention on Biological Diversity (CBD) (1992).

Egyptian Intellectual Property Rights Law (EIPRL) 82 of 2002.

Executive Regulation of Book One (patents) and Book Four (plant varieties) of the EIPRL issued by Prime Ministerial Decree 1366 of 2003.

Egyptian government documents

Ministry of State for Environmental Affairs (2012), "The national programme for safe use of treated sewage water for afforestation: planting jatropha in Egypt", available at: www.eeaa.gov.eg/english/main/env_forests_jatropha.asp (accessed 11 April 2013).

New and Renewable Energy Authority (NREA) (2011), *Annual Report 2010/2011*, available at: www.nrea.gov.eg/annual%20report/Annual_Report_English_2010-2011.pdf (accessed 11 April 2013).

New and Renewable Energy Authority (NREA) (2012), "Renewable energy", available at: www.nrea.gov.eg/english1.html (accessed 11 April 2013).

Renewable Energy Strategy of 2008, summary available at: www.nrea.gov.eg/english1.html (accessed 11 April 2013).

Secondary sources

Abbot, C. and Booton, D. (2009), "Using patent law's teaching function to introduce an environmental ethic into the process of technological innovation", *Georgetown International Environmental Law Review*, Vol. 21 No. 2, pp. 219–55.

Al-Saghir, H. (2004), "Protection of new plant varieties", presentation to WIPO National Training Workshop on Intellectual Property for Diplomats, World Intellectual Property Organization (WIPO) and Institute for Diplomatic Studies, 13–16 December, Cairo.

Awad, B. (2007), *Le brevet instrument d'incitation à l'innovation technologique en Égypte?* ANRT, Lille.

Canadian Intellectual Property Office (CIPO) (2011), *Expedited Examination of Patent Applications Related to Green Technology*, available at: www.ic.gc.ca/eic/site/cipointernet-internetopic.nsf/eng/wr02462.html (accessed 11 April 2013).

Dechezleprêtre, A. (2013), *Fast-tracking Green Patent Applications – An Empirical Analysis*, International Centre for Trade and Sustainable Development (ICTSD) ICTSD Global Platform on Climate Change, Trade and Sustainable Energy Series Issue Paper No. 37, available at: http://ictsd.org/downloads/2013/02/fast-tracking-green-patent-applications-an-empirical-analysis.pdf (accessed 11 April 2013).

Demirbas, A. and Demirbas, M.F. (2010), *Algae Energy: Algae as a New Source of Biodiesel*, Springer, New York.

Derclaye, E. (2010), "Not only innovation but also collaboration, funding, goodwill and commitment: which role for patent laws in post-Copenhagen climate change action?" *John Marshall Review of Intellectual Property Law*, Vol. 9 No. 3, pp. 657–73.

El Mogy, N. (2010), *Jojoba Shrubs: A New Hope for Desert Development*, available at: www.natoileg.com/english.htm (accessed 11 April 2013).

Hall, B.H. and Helmers, C. (2011), *Innovation and Diffusion of Clean/Green Technology: Can Patent Commons Help?*, available at: http://elsa.berkeley.edu/~bhhall/papers/HallHelmers13_patent_commons_JEEMfinal.pdf (accessed 11 April 2013).

International Renewable Energy Agency (IRENA) (n.d.), "About IRENA", available at: www.irena.org/Menu/index.aspx?PriMenuID=13&mnu=Pri (accessed 11 April 2013).

IP Australia (2012), "Fast tracking patents for green technology", available at: www.ipaustralia.gov.au/get-the-right-ip/patents/patent-application-process/expedited-and-modified-examination-for-standard-patents/green-patents (accessed 11 April 2013).

Japan Bio-Energy Development Corporation (JBEDC) (2008), *Project Report: Egyptian Biofuel Industry Development*, available at: www.jbedc.com/en/projects-2.html (accessed 11 April 2013).

Kogan, L.A. (2010), *Climate Change: Technology Transfer or Compulsory License?*, Institute for Trade, Standards, and Sustainable Development (ITSSD), available at: http://itssd.org/LKogan%20-%20Climate%20Change%20-%20Technology%20Transfer%20or%20Compulsory%20License%20-%20ANSI%20Luncheon%201-15-10.doc (accessed 11 April 2013).

Korean Intellectual Property Office (2009), "Thanks to super speed examination, green technology acquires patent in a month", available at: www.kipo.go.kr/kpo/user.tdf?seq=1305&c=1003&a=user.english.board.BoardApp&board_id=kiponews&catmenu=ek20200 (accessed 11 April 2013).

Maskus, K. E. and Okediji, R. L. (2010), *Intellectual Property Rights and International Technology Transfer to Address Climate Change: Risks, Opportunities and Policy Options*, International Centre for Trade and Sustainable Development (ICTSD) Intellectual Property and Sustainable Development Series Issue Paper No. 32, available at: http://ictsd.org/i/publications/97782/?view=document (accessed 11 April 2013).

Natural Oil Co. (Natoil) (2012), "Company business activity", available at: www.natoileg.com/english.htm (accessed 11 April 2013).

New Nile Company (2012), "Understanding ISAS", available at: www.newnileco.com/en/understanding-isas.html (accessed 11 April 2013).

Nuffield Council on Bioethics (2011), *Biofuels: Ethical Issues*, available at: www.nuffieldbioethics.org/sites/default/files/Biofuels_ethical_issues_FULL%20REPORT_0.pdf (accessed 11 April 2013).

Phillips, J., Sibanda, M., El Saghir, H., Garcia, E.R., Orlyuk, O.P. and Gabriel, C. (2011), *Study on Patents and the Public Domain*, study for World Intellectual Property Organisation (WIPO) Committee on Development and Intellectual Property, CDIP/4/3 REV./STUDY/INF/2, available at: www.wipo.int/edocs/mdocs/mdocs/en/cdip_4/cdip_4_3_rev_study_inf_2.pdf (accessed 11 April 2013).

UK Intellectual Property Office (2009), "Green Channel for patent applications", available at: www.ipo.gov.uk/pro-types/pro-patent/p-law/p-pn/p-pn-green.htm (accessed 11 April 2013).

US Patent and Trademark Office (USPTO) (2012), "Green petition report summary" 26 April, available at: www.uspto.gov/patents/init_events/green_report_summary 20120426.pdf (accessed 11 April 2013).

World Business Council for Sustainable Development (WBCSD) (2011), *The Eco-patent Commons: A Leadership Opportunity for Global Business to Protect the Planet*, available at: www.wbcsd.org/Pages/EDocument/EDocumentDetails.aspx?ID=13650&NoSearchContextKey=true (accessed 11 April 2013).

World Intellectual Property Organisation (WIPO) (2012), "IPC Green Inventory", available at: www.wipo.int/classifications/ipc/en/est (accessed 11 April 2013).

Chapter 13

Effects of the South African IP Regime on Generating Value from Publicly Funded Research: An Exploratory Study of Two Universities

Caroline Ncube, Lucienne Abrahams and Titilayo Akinsanmi

Abstract

This study analyses evidence from two South African universities of how innovation activity and research dissemination are being influenced by a new intellectual property (IP) commercialisation law for publicly funded research outputs. The study sought to understand the ways in which the Intellectual Property Rights from Publicly Financed Research and Development (IPR-PFRD) Act of 2008 and its Regulations influence the generation of value from research. The study was positioned within a theoretical frame which holds that maximalist approaches to IP protection tend to be sub-optimal for certain long-term socio-economic objectives inherent in research funding. The research found evidence of adaptation by both of the universities studied (UCT and Wits University) to the requirements of the Act, and evidence that the Act can have a positive influence on South Africa's innovation nexus provided that the Act's patenting orientation continues to be complemented by openness-oriented research dissemination and collaboration practices, including open access (OA) scholarly publishing.

1. Introduction and research design

The research outlined in this chapter investigated the potential impact of South Africa's Intellectual Property Rights from Publicly Financed Research and Development (IPR-PFRD) Act 51 of 2008 and its 2009 Regulations on the commercialisation of research and on research dissemination, including scholarly publishing. The study focused on practices at two leading public universities: the University of Cape Town (UCT) and Johannesburg's University of the Witwatersrand (Wits University).

The IPR-PFRD Act of 2008 and its Regulations of 2009 (which became effective in 2010) seek to promote the protection and commercialisation of intellectual property (IP) generated through South African public funding. The Act applies to IP emanating from publicly financed research and development (R&D), which is defined in Section 1 as "research and development undertaken using any funds allocated by a funding agency but excludes funds allocated for scholarships and bursaries". In particular, it applies to South Africa's higher education institutions, to its 10 listed research councils, and to any other institutions that shall be identified by the Minister of Science and Technology in the future (Sect. 1 and 3(2), and Sched. 1, of the Act). The Act and Regulations have been critiqued (Barratt, 2010; Chetty, 2009/2010; Gray, 2010) from a number of perspectives, including charges that they:

- may be counter-productive to achieving the objectives of promoting commercialisation;
- may have too broad an approach to conceptualisation of commercialisation, i.e. include knowledge that should be socialised rather than commercialised;
- approach IP protection in ways that may present potential obstacles to scholarly publication; and
- have provisions that may be unnecessarily onerous for universities and academics.

The critiques made to date have been primarily theoretical. The research presented in this chapter sought an evidence-based understanding of the effects of the Act and Regulations on research, innovation and scholarly publishing.

A mixture of research methods was employed: a legal doctrinal analysis and review of annual reports on UCT and Wits research were supplemented by interviews with leading academics who have created patentable inventions and also publish extensively, and senior administrators responsible for research productivity at the two universities. The study focused on research in health sciences and engineering sciences, two research fields which are among the "top 21" scholarly publishing fields in South Africa (Abrahams and Akinsanmi, 2011; Mouton *et al.*, 2008). The research did not aim to be a comparative case study between UCT and Wits, but rather to separately explore the experiences of UCT and Wits in order to find out what could be learned from each case.

Particular inter-relationships are believed to exist between innovation, closed or open IP systems, and socio-economic development, with these inter-relationships seen as sometimes being mutually supportive while at other times being in conflict (Bünemann, 2010; Gray, 2009/2010; Hargreaves, 2011). These inter-relationships, and the extent to which they exist, need to be better understood if research productivity and value are to be maximised.

Accordingly, this study included the following elements in its examination of the two selected fields of research (health sciences and engineering sciences) at UCT and Wits:

- identification of major research producers;
- investigation and cataloguing of research, innovation practices and scholarly publishing; and
- investigation of the potential effects of the Act and Regulations on the work of research administrators, IP creators and research collaborations.

The overarching research question was: *How does South Africa's 2008 IP commercialisation law potentially impact research, innovation and scholarly publishing in key fields at universities?* Three sub-questions were designed to answer the main question:

- Prior to the Act, how did universities approach IP generated by their scientific research output?
- What are the potential effects of the Act and Regulations on universities' IP protection and commercialisation of innovation?
- To what extent are universities' publicly funded research results being communicated through scholarly publishing channels, i.e. paid access and/or open access (OA) publication approaches, and to what extent are these approaches being impacted by the Act and Regulations?

UCT and Wits were selected for study based on their high levels of research performance and contribution to South Africa's national system of innovation. They are among South Africa's leading research-producing universities and have been identified as two of the major research universities in the southern African region (Mouton *et al.*, 2008). Thus, they were selected as *critical*, not *typical*, research settings in South Africa, as per Patton's (2002) research methodological distinction, i.e. the relatively narrow focus on UCT and Wits meant that there would be only limited general applicability of the research findings to other South African universities.

First, an analysis was conducted of relevant South African policy, and the IPR-PFRD Act and Regulations, in order to establish the legal requirements for publicly funded research institutions. Second, UCT's and Wits's annual research reports for 2010 and 2011 were analysed. Third, semi-structured interviews probed the experiences and perceptions of patent-holding academics and research managers who administer IP commercialisation at each university. Purposive sampling (Denscombe, 2010) was used to identify participants who could provide in-depth knowledge and experiential insights into the Act and Regulations and their practical implications. The criteria used to identify suitable researcher-inventor interviewees included strong research and publishing records and evidence of patent holdings. Identification of interviewees was done in consultation with relevant academic management at UCT and Wits, and with reference to the universities' research and innovation reports. The data were collected through document analysis and through interviews with nine key informants at UCT and Wits University: five researcher-inventors and four research-IP managers. The four research-IP manager interviewees were drawn from the UCT Research Contracts and IP Services office (RCIPS) and from Wits Commercial Enterprise (Pty) Ltd. (Wits Enterprise). The data were analysed thematically in order to determine the common and distinctive perceptions, at each university, of the extent of the impact of the Act on generating benefit from publicly funded research.

2. Conceptual framework

The study was grounded in several conceptual assumptions, as outlined in the subsections which follow.

IP protection

IP is created when new knowledge or creative work enjoys protection under common law or acquires a proprietary right pursuant to legal frameworks governing patents, copyrights, trademarks and trade secrets. Commercialisation of IP occurs when the value of new knowledge or creative work is realised in the marketplace through an IP vehicle that results in financial return (Geuna and Nesta, 2006). In a recent review of the IP environment in the UK, Hargreaves (2011) states that the UK IP framework has a tendency to act as a significant drag against innovation and economic growth. The Hargreaves Report finds this to be true not just within the creative works domain but increasingly and extensively with respect to business and academic innovation. South Africa, as a former British colony and a member of the Commonwealth, has an IP framework that, in many respects, reflects that of the UK. It follows, then, that some of the problems identified by Hargreaves with the existing UK IP framework may also characterise the South African context.

Central to this study's focus on connections between IP protection, commercialisation and research publishing is the contention that IP protection has the potential to limit access to knowledge (A2K), via explicit and/or implicit barriers, and that such limits on A2K undermine the balancing mechanisms inherent in the notion of IP protection. IP protection is not supposed to stifle A2K. In extreme instances, the protection of research findings via IP can constitute knowledge *hoarding.* Such hoarding has been found to lead to the "under-utilisation of research findings" (NACI, 2003). Access is necessary to allow others to build on prior knowledge, and IP should ideally improve conditions for sustained creativity and innovation. This research was premised on a view that knowledge will tend to have greater socio-economic impact where it is shared and utilised.

The aforementioned Hargreaves Report (2011) argues for increased flexibility in the publishing of publicly funded research. Hargreaves addresses the potential conflict between, on the one hand, facilitation by digital communication technologies of "the routine copying of text, images and data" (2011, p. 3) and, on the other hand, closed-off online sources operating within a framework of laws that constitute a regulatory barrier to the creation of new knowledge and business development. Hargreaves proposes the development of a "digital copyright exchange" (2011, p. 3) designed to increase consumer confidence in the use of copyrighted material for both private and public benefit. The Report advises that "there should be a change in rules to enable scientific and other researchers to use modern text and data mining techniques, which copyright prohibits" (2011, p. 4).

Commercialisation

Commercialisation of research output is typically premised on the acquisition of IP protection. In order to realise the value contained in the IP, the entity seeking to commercialise it must have an established proprietary right over the knowledge via an IP right. Such a process of commercialisation requires a robust approach to IP protection. It is important to note, however, that securing patent protection is not a guarantee that commercialisation will succeed.

Knowledge socialisation

Knowledge socialisation, or "socialisation of knowledge" as it is referred to in the relevant literature, involves the adoption or uptake of norms, customs and ideologies through which social, cultural and economic continuity are sustained (Halloran, 2011; Nonaka, 1991; Plaskoff, 2011). The concept applies to non-commercial integration of knowledge in society. The socialisation of knowledge is underpinned by one major imperative – that knowledge is shared. Sharing allows the knowledge to develop, as it is adopted and adapted by various sections of society. In the context of academic research and publishing, the ability of researchers to disseminate knowledge into the public domain significantly determines the extent to which such knowledge becomes socialised. Advances in technology have opened up myriad ways for knowledge to be rapidly socialised. Some consequences may be negative, i.e. in the internet age, untried, untested and sometimes unfounded knowledge can become social knowledge and prematurely become "truth". However, the positive consequences of rapid knowledge socialisation are substantial, with readily and rapidly accessible knowledge contributing to reductions in socio-economic inequality (De Assumpção, 2005).

Scholarly publishing

The trend towards the use of OA publishing, whereby works are made freely available online with minimal copyright restrictions, continues to grow in strength in relation to both learning materials and scholarly works. Proponents for and against OA publishing both agree that research findings should optimally benefit society. Some OA proponents argue that, where research publishing continues to be organised within the traditional closed access framework, only very slow increases will occur in the pool of quality researchers (Abrahams *et al.*, 2008).

At the same time, however, it must be borne in mind that the push towards OA can be daunting in developing countries, because the online platforms through which OA thrives are undermined in contexts where there are low levels of broadband internet access at higher education institutions. Online scholarly publishing is generally low in institutions located in developing countries and universities (Chan and Costa, 2005). Many scholars are restricted to publishing in Institute for Scientific Information (ISI) journals. Others publish in unrecognised platforms or fail to publish due to various restrictions, incapacities or resource limitations. Reductions in university library budgets, together with the increased cost of journals, foster demand for free access and alternative approaches to scholarly publishing and knowledge dissemination. OA publishing is a relatively inexpensive and inclusionary way of addressing this need but, at the same time, existing access barriers to publication are replicated in the digital world. Transitioning to OA publishing also generates issues of quality assurance, to ensure that research quality, credibility and ownership are not undermined.

Valuable, development-focused research is produced in Africa on an ongoing basis. While increasingly accessible online, dissemination of such research output is still considered low in the international context. In a report for Australia's Department of Education, Science and Training (DEST), Houghton *et al.*, (2006) recommend that greater levels of access to publicly funded research may be promoted by

> [...] [e]nsuring that the Research Quality Framework supports and encourages the development of new, more open scholarly communication mechanisms, rather than encouraging a retreat by researchers to conventional publication forms and media, and a reliance by evaluators upon traditional publication metrics (e.g., by ensuring dissemination and impact are an integral part of evaluation). (Houghton *et al.*, 2006, p. XIII)

Open science, open knowledge, open research

Interrogating the value of OA for research productivity, visibility, accessibility and knowledge in South Africa needs to be approached from a multi-disciplinary perspective. This entails moving beyond consideration of copyright and IP laws and traditional boundaries of scholarly publishing into consideration of the potential, offered by OA publishing, of what is sometimes referred to as "open science", "open knowledge" or "open research". The openness orientation implied by these terms entails the prioritisation of wide dissemination and sharing of the outputs of scientific research. This approach requires institution-wide commitment and change at universities. It requires the creation and/or strengthening of a research value chain that incorporates all levels of the academic hierarchy engaged in researching, writing and publishing. Abrahams *et al.* (2008) propose a framework "based on open knowledge approaches to knowledge production, publishing and dissemination in response to identified constraints and challenges to a productive academic research and publishing sector" (2008, p. 9).

This research endeavour thus combined consideration of ideas around IP commercialisation with consideration of the dynamics of knowledge socialisation and of the many transitions that are possible for managing IP and disseminating knowledge.

3. Findings Part 1: the Act and Regulations

Evolution of the South African approach, 1996 to 2012

The Act and Regulations have their roots (see Figure 13.1) in the government's 1996 White Paper on Science and Technology, which flagged the need for an IP regime that encourages innovation (DACST, 1996, Chap. 6). This orientation was reiterated in the Department of Science and Technology's (DST's) 2002 National Research and Development (R&D) Strategy, which lamented the absence of a formal policy framework for IP protection of publicly financed research and expressly mentioned the US Bayh–Dole Act as a model to emulate (DST, 2002, pp. 22, 67). The R&D Strategy was partially implemented by the creation of the Intellectual Property Rights from Publicly Financed Research Framework in 2006, which formed the blueprint for the eventual IPR-PFRD Act of 2008. The Framework preceded the publication by the Department of Science and Technology (DST) of a Ten-Year Innovation Plan in 2008 that identified financing and IP management as major challenges to successful IP commercialisation. Accordingly, the Ten-Year Plan provided for creation of the Technology Innovation Agency (TIA) to provide funding, and creation of the National IP Management Office (NIPMO) "to enhance protection of IPRs" (DST, 2008, pp. 22–23). Ultimately, the essential elements of the IP Framework articulated via the foregoing developments were enacted as the Act in 2008, supplemented by the Regulations of 2009 (effective in 2010).

Meanwhile, since the mid-2000s, the Academy of Sciences of South Africa (ASSAf) has sought to promote OA publishing. By 2011, ASSAf had adapted the Brazilian Scielo OA publishing platform to create Scielo South Africa, encouraging South Africa's top scholarly journals to locate there. In 2012, Scielo South Africa was endorsed by international publishing firm Thomson Reuters's Web of Science scientific citation platform, meaning that authors publishing in a journal hosted by Scielo South Africa are recognised to have published in a Web of Science indexed journal. At the National Scholarly Editors' Forum convened by ASSAf in July 2012, the Department of Higher Education and Training (DHET) indicated that it was considering requiring all accredited South African journals to publish either on the Scielo South Africa platform or on another internationally recognised platform such as Web of Science. Also in 2012, DHET's Green Paper for Post-School Education and Training in South Africa, released in February of that year, prioritised open educational resources (OERs), i.e. learning objects made freely available online with minimal copyright or usage restrictions.

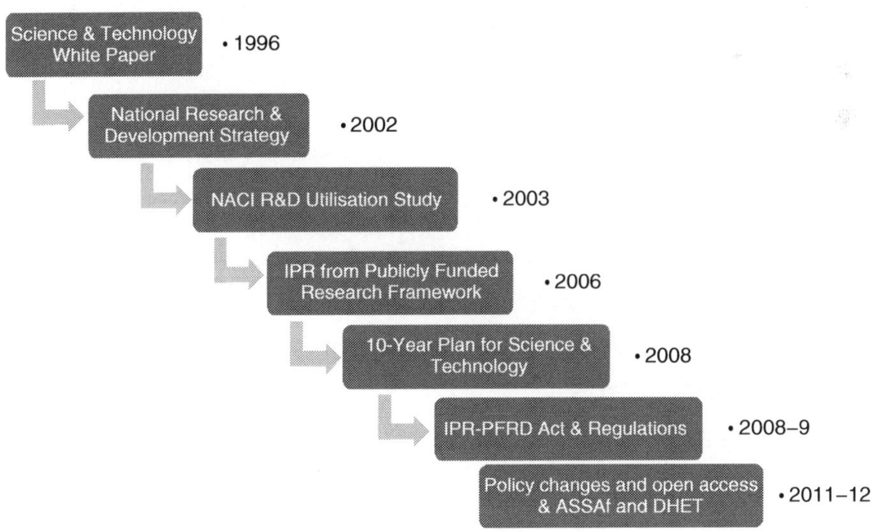

Figure 13.1: Evolution of the South African approach: timeline

Source: Authors' data collection.

Rationale

At the time of the IPR-PFRD Act's formulation, it was argued that the Act was essential to encourage publicly funded research institutions to be innovative and productive in the knowledge economy (DST, 2006, pp. 5–7). The lack of a national IP protection and commercialisation framework, it was argued, prejudiced South Africa because publicly funded research was being underutilised (NACI, 2003) and IP was being "lost to foreign jurisdictions" or "sitting on shelves" and failing to contribute to national socio-economic development (Sibanda, 2011). South Africa's poor patent profile was cited as an indicator of "a major weakness in South Africa's ability to become a full player in the global knowledge economy" and "[i]ncreasing patenting activity" and "building capacity in entrepreneurship and technology transfer within publicly funded institutions" were identified as remedial solutions (DST, 2006, p. 15). The legislation therefore provides for protection and commercialisation of IP from publicly funded research and places restrictions on offshore IP transactions to limit the loss of IP to foreign jurisdictions. There were also perceptions that a lack of clear incentive and benefit-sharing formulae were resulting in an environment with little or no motivation for researchers to innovate and commercialise inventions. The legislation, therefore, provides for benefit-sharing to incentivise researchers, an approach seemingly inspired by the approach adopted in the US via the provisions of the 1980 Bayh-Dole Act (see Chapters 14 and 15 of this volume for examples of attempted Bayh-Dole-type orientations in Ethiopia and Botswana, respectively).

Primary intent of the IPR-PFRD Act

The Act of 2008 defines "commercialisation" as

> [...] the process by which any intellectual property emanating from publicly financed research and development is or may be adapted or used for any purpose that may provide any benefit to society or commercial use on reasonable terms, and "commercialise" shall have a corresponding meaning. (Sect. 1 of the Act)

This definition is expounded by Section 1 of the Regulations, which defines "benefits" as:

> [...] contribution to the socio-economic needs of the Republic and includes capacity development, technology transfer, job creation, enterprise development, social upliftment and products, or processes or services that embody or use the intellectual property. (Sect. 1 of the Regulations)

These definitions result in a problematic conflation of IP commercialisation with socialisation of knowledge. The underlying theoretical perspective that informs the Act does not recognise the differing trajectories between research which is commercialised via IP protection and research which is socialised via sharing.

While the legislation requires attempted acquisition and commercialisation of IP generated from publicly funded research, the Act excludes from its provisions "copyrighted works such as a thes[e]s, dissertation[s], article[s], handbook[s] or any other publication which, in the ordinary course of business, is associated with conventional academic work" (Sect. 1 of the Act). Trademarks and designs are included in the provisions of the Act, and institutions may choose to use trade secrets as a form of protection. The legislation's emphasis on patenting as a means of economic development fails to recognise that patents do not always lead to commercialisation and economic growth (Webster and Jensen, 2011, p. 447). The legislation could, for instance, prod institutions to build large patent portfolios with little prospect for commercialisation, i.e. portfolios of weak patents barely meeting the statutory patentability requirements. Such a phenomenon is possible in South Africa because South Africa does not examine patent applications (see Chapter 10, this volume, for discussion on lack of patent application examination processes in Africa). The DST acknowledges that "patenting for the sake of patenting is not adequate", but argues that a focus on patenting is a prerequisite for successful commercialisation in alignment with South Africa's technological growth strategy (Sibanda, 2007, p. 31).

Meanwhile, despite the exclusion of copyrighted scholarly publications from its provisions, the Act's focus on patenting could still have a negative effect on written academic output. Rapid publication of research findings relating to potentially patentable inventions could potentially have to be curtailed in order to prevent the compromise of novelty requirements for patentability. If publications were to be routinely delayed (for the lengthy periods of time required to formalise a patent application), this would have a chilling effect on written scholarly outputs, making South African scholars less competitive on the global stage of academic exchange and less able to participate in the aforementioned open science and open knowledge paradigms.

Key provisions

Several provisions in the Act and Regulations have the potential to be counterproductive. Section 1 of the Act defines IP as:

> [A]ny creation of the mind that is capable of being protected by law from use by any other person, whether *in terms of South African law or foreign intellectual property law,* and includes any rights in such creation, but excludes copyrighted works [...] (Sect. 1 of the Act, emphasis added)

The inclusion of foreign IP law means that South African institutions are required to obtain statutory protection in foreign jurisdictions, even if the R&D in question is ineligible for IP protection in South Africa (Tong, 2010, pp. 409–10). This extension is understandable given that the underlying objective of the legislation is to increase South African local and international patenting. However, the extension raises two concerns. First, South African institutions will now have to ensure they possess adequate knowledge of foreign IP law, so that the required international protection is obtained. Second, acquisition of international IP protection is lengthy and costly, placing a heavy burden on institutions. The legislation seeks to answer these concerns by providing for partial or full funding for the "development of appropriately skilled personnel" in institutions through NIPMO (Sect. 6(4)*(b)*(iii)), and by establishing a national IP fund to finance institutions' acquisition and maintenance of local and foreign statutory IP protection (Sect. 13(2)*(a)*).

Institutional infrastructure

NIPMO, which oversees the Act (Sect. 8–9) and the IP fund, is mandated to financially support, manage and protect onshore and offshore IP efforts of publicly funded research institutions (Sect. 13). The Act provides for institutions to separately or collaboratively create technology transfer offices (TTOs) with the support of NIPMO. TTOs are to be "responsible for undertaking the obligations of the institution" (Sect. 6(1) and 6(3)) in respect of management of the identification, protection, development and commercialisation of IP, and to provide mandatory biannual disclosures to NIPMO (Sect. 5 and 7).

IP ownership and statutory protection

The Act provides for institutions, rather than researchers, to own IP derived from publicly financed research (Sect. 4(1)). However, where the full (as opposed to partial) cost of the research is privately funded, the IP does not fall within the ambit of the Act, i.e. the IP does not rest with the institution, but rather with the private funder (Sect. 15(4) of the Act).

The Act defines private entities or organisations as "a private sector company, a public entity, an international research organisation, an educational institution or an international funding or donor organisation" (sect. 15(5)). (This inclusion of "public entity" in the definition of a "private entity" is odd and, in the absence of a detailed explanatory memorandum accompanying the Act, is difficult to explain.)

The precise meaning of "full cost" has to be made clear within the policy prescripts of the institution, with full cost funding generally meaning that the funder pays the full cost of the research (including overheads) and, subject to agreement with the institution, owns any resulting patents. For partially privately funded research, the private funder takes precedence and must be offered the option to acquire ownership and statutory protection for the IP. The Act does not provide for, or stipulate, any level or threshold that must be passed by a partial funder in order to earn entitlement to be offered ownership of the IP. The Act merely provides that "where a private entity or organisation had provided some funding" it should be offered ownership of the IP ahead of the IP creator (Sect. 4(4)*(b)* of the Act). Therefore, such an offer must be made to any partial funder regardless of the extent of the funding granted by that funder.

When institutions choose to forfeit ownership and statutory protection of IP from a research undertaking, they must notify NIPMO and provide reasons (Sect. 4(2)). Section 2 of the Regulations provides factors that must be considered by institutions in making such a choice. These include South Africa's socio-economic needs, the costs and advantages of possible IP protection, the potential for commercialisation, and whether the IP should be placed in the public domain. Should the balance of factors lie with retaining ownership and obtaining IP protection but the institution chooses to do neither, NIPMO may, upon referral from the institution (Sect. 2(4) of the Regulations), acquire ownership of the IP and seek statutory protection. NIPMO can do so if it is of the view that the state would be prejudiced if statutory protection were not obtained (Sect. 4(3) of the Act).

When the balance of factors does not lie with securing IP ownership and protection – i.e. neither the institution nor NIPMO wishes to acquire IP ownership and protection – the institution must give the researcher(s) who created the IP the option to assert ownership and obtain IP protection (Sect. 4(4)*(b)* of the Act and Sect. 4(10)–(11) of the Regulations).

IP transactions

The Act also regulates IP transactions, which are defined as:

> [A]ny agreement in respect of intellectual property emanating from publicly financed research and development, and includes licensing, assignment and any arrangement in which the intellectual property rights governed by this Act are transferred to a third party. (Sect. 1 of the Act)

The Act preserves the right of institutions to determine the type and terms of IP transactions they enter into, provided preference is afforded to non-exclusive licensing, to broad-based black economic empowerment entities (as per South Africa's B-BBEE Act 53 of 2003), to small businesses and to parties who intend to use the IP for the benefit of South Africa's economy (Sect. 11(1)*(a)*–*(c)*). Section

11(1) of the Regulations provides for the terms of non-exclusive licences to be determined "on an arms-length basis". NIPMO's approval must be obtained in cases where the "consideration payable by a licensee to a recipient is not determined on an arms-length basis", or where royalty-free licences are granted, or where offshore exclusive licences are granted and/or where assignments of IP are made locally and offshore (Sect. 11(2) of the Regulations).

Conditions that apply to all licences

Section 11(1)*(e)* of the Act states that each IP transaction must provide the state with an irrevocable and royalty-free licence authorising the state to use or have the IP used throughout the world for South Africa's health, security and emergency needs. Section 11(2) of the Act provides that each IP transaction must contain a condition that "should a party fail to commercialise the intellectual property to the benefit of [South Africa], the State is entitled to exercise" walk-in rights provided for in Section 14 (see "state 'walk-in' rights" sub-section below). Section 11(3)*(a)* of the Act provides that where the relevant IP is assigned to a small business, the assignment agreement must contain a condition that if the business is liquidated, the IP will revert to the institution.

Conditions that apply only to exclusive licences

Section 11(1)*(d)* of the Act requires that "exclusive licence holders must undertake, where feasible, to manufacture, process and otherwise commercialise" the invention in South Africa, failing which NIPMO has the power to request that the exclusive licence be converted into a non-exclusive licence.

Conditions that apply to offshore transactions

Section 12 of the Act requires institutions to notify NIPMO and to obtain its approval before concluding offshore exclusive IP transactions (exclusive licences and assignment), i.e. licences and assignments granted outside South Africa. Such approval will only be given pursuant to a number of considerations, including the requirement that NIPMO is satisfied that there is insufficient capacity within South Africa to commercialise the IP.

State "walk-in" rights

Sections 14(2) and 14(3) of the Act and Section 14(1) of the Regulations require NIPMO to conduct annual reviews of non-commercialised IP in consultation with publicly funded research institutions. Should an institution fail to commercialise the IP after review and consultation, NIPMO may require the institution to grant a licence to a third party (Sect. 14(4) of the Act). The institution will be afforded an opportunity to challenge the exercise of the state's walk-in rights prior to NIPMO's final determination (Sect. 14(2) of the Regulations). Overall, the exercise of walk-in rights by the state must be reasonable and balanced in relation to other competing rights and must terminate once the specific health, security or emergency need has been met (Sect. 14(7) of the Regulations).

Benefit-sharing

Creators of IP from publicly funded research (or the creators' heirs) are entitled, under Section 10, to at least 20% of the first ZAR 1 million in revenues generated by the IP. They are also entitled to at least 30% of the net revenues in excess of the first ZAR 1 million earned. Revenues are to be shared equally among creators unless another benefit-sharing formula has been agreed to previously (Sect. 10(3)). Creators are entitled to timely access to monetary and non-monetary incentives (Sect. 19(1)). Section 9(3) of the Regulations also requires institutions to develop policies for sharing non-monetary benefits with IP creators for approval by NIPMO.

4. Findings Part 2: UCT and Wits University

The two studies, of research and IP management realities at UCT and Wits University, respectively, took different directions. These differences resulted to some extent from differences in data availability and to some extent from differences between the matters identified in each setting, during the course of the research, as being worthy of investigation and analysis.

UCT

Research and innovation indicators

UCT's IP Policy was amended in 2011 to implement the provisions of the Act (UCT, 2011b). The Policy addresses the role and duties of UCT's TTO, the roles and duties of UCT's Intellectual Property Advisory Committee, the ownership of IP, IP commercialisation and dispute resolution. UCT's *Innovation at UCT 2011* report outlines the institution's IP and commercialisation efforts, which are summarised in Table 13.1.

Table 13.1: Research indicators for UCT (ZAR = South African Rand, m = million)

Research contracts signed 1,056 (2010) 882 (2009)	Research contract value ZAR550 m (2010) ZAR543.9 m (2009)	Total research income ZAR760.5 m (2010) ZAR768 m (2009)
Foreign research funding ZAR382.5 m (2010) ZAR334.7 m (2009)	Local (South African) research funding ZAR167.7 m (2010) ZAR209.2 m (2009)	Publications* 1,188.22 (2010) 1,086.15 (2009)
Invention disclosures 31 (2010) 25 (2009)	Patent applications filed 57 (2010) 46 (2009)	Patents granted 36 (2010) 47 (2009)
Licence agreements 8 (2010) 6 (2009)	Materials transfer agreements (outbound) 29 (2010) 21 (2009)	Spin-out companies 0 (2010) 1 (2009)
Licence income ZAR3.5 m (2010) ZAR136,494 (2009)	Profit from UCT-incubated companies ZAR400,000 (2010) ZAR693,630 (2009)	Total income from IP ZAR3.9 m (2010) ZAR830,699 (2009)

Source: UCT (2011), p. 3.

* These publication counts have decimal points as a result of DHET's method of calculation, which translates publications into units and half units and shares them between institutions where a publication is co-authored.

Researchers in the Department of Chemical Engineering, the Department of Molecular and Cell Biology and the Institute of Infectious Disease and Molecular Medicine (IIDMM) are among UCT's top inventors, as evidenced by their very high publishing outputs (UCT, 2010, pp. 7–8). Recent research in these departments has been focused on minerals, the creation of human and animal vaccine candidates, preventive HIV vaccines, anti-malarial drug discovery and the development of a device that enables *in situ* evaluation of ferro-metallic catalysts (UCT, 2010, pp. 17–27, 65).

Administration perspectives

UCT's TTO function is performed by its RCIPS office, which in the last few years has focused its efforts on implementing the IPR-PFRD Act and Regulations. RCIPS has conducted a campus-wide education and awareness campaign, and runs seminars aimed at creating awareness about the Act and demonstrating UCT's compliance arrangements. According to an RCIPS staff member interviewed, there are minimal negative impacts on IP commercialisation under the Act, but implementation has presented practical challenges. For instance, researchers interested in socialising their ideas at conferences or through publication may face constraints or delays because of the prioritisation of patent filing. The interviewee said that, with proper planning, however, a patent application could be filed prior to conference presentations or publication. RCIPS strives to assist UCT's academics and researchers to "fit IP protection seamlessly into the publication or thesis submission process" (RCIPS interviewee, 2012).

However, in the RCIPS interviewee's opinion, it was not necessarily ideal for commercialisation of research to be mandated by legislation. While it was appreciated that the intent of the legislation was to more concretely motivate a reflective approach to commercialisation by publicly funded institutions, some research lends itself more readily to commercialisation, and thus implementation of the Act has to be reasonable and bear such distinctions in mind. The RCIPS interviewee also said that other elements of South African IP protection could be amended to become more conducive to commercialisation. For example, the fact that South African patents are not substantively examined leads to "commercial uncertainty, as the claims have not been tested by examination and can only be contested in court – which is an expensive process" (RCIPS interviewee, 2012). Funders are understandably hesitant to invest when faced with this state of unpredictability over the future of a patented invention.

Another concern voiced by the RCIPS interviewee related to the lack of funding for development of early-stage IP:

> This [early-stage funding] is scarce and significantly impedes actual transfer of technology. There is a need for development to mature the IP within a university to fashion it into a commercialisable form [...] I think that there is a need for a parallel stream of people working on development, rather than research, to focus on translating research findings into tangible outputs that can be of relevance in the marketplace. (RCIPS interviewee, 2012)

A UCT researcher-inventor interviewee stated that full funding by industry of South African university research (necessary for the funder to acquire full rights to the IP in terms of the Act of 2008) is "uncompetitive and expensive" (UCT researcher-inventor interviewee, 2012). As a reflection of this sentiment, the interviewee pointed to a small but significant loss of industry-contracted research at UCT. The interviewee stated that barriers also arise from the need to seek NIPMO permissions for certain IP transactions, as per the Act. This requirement lengthens research contract negotiations and their implementation, making the process more expensive and less attractive to industry.

Also having a potentially chilling effect on research funding, said a UCT interviewee, is uncertainty about the exercise of state walk-in rights in terms of the Act. Funders are unsure of how the government will exercise these rights and may be unwilling to invest in a project that may be subject to the exercise of such rights. An additional burden cited by a UCT interviewee is the fact that the university has had to increase its screening work, because more researchers are informing RCIPS of their inventions so that they can be scrutinised for patentability. Researchers now disclose everything, including borderline inventions. Before the Act, only clearly patentable inventions were disclosed (UCT researcher-inventor interviewee, 2012).

At the same time, it was argued by one UCT interviewee that the Act does not constrain socialisation of research, if one defines socialisation as compatible with both *financial* and *non-financial* returns from publicly funded research. This interviewee argued that the requirement that researchers screen their work for protectable IP prior to public disclosure may result in more reflective practices among scholars, due to the awareness raised and the duties imposed by the legislation. This interviewee went on to say that UCT research had habitually been socialised and identified with significant "societal benefit" prior to the introduction of the legislation, and the Act will not have an impact on this emphasis on socialisation. At UCT, the interviewee argued, societal benefit is a core objective and not "something that one will measure by monitoring protectable IP rights" (UCT researcher-inventor interviewee, 2012).

Indeed, evidence was found of significant knowledge socialisation by UCT researchers, through both traditional and emerging scholarly publishing and distribution channels. UCT has an online research portal through which its staff and postgraduate students can manage their research. UCT also disseminates publications and other research outputs through an open-licensed website called UCT OpenContent (http://opencontent.uct.ac.za), where Creative Commons (CC)-licensed learning materials are published. UCT motivates scholarly publishing by providing career progression and research funding incentives to academics who publish regularly. UCT uses open source software and CC licences to ensure wide promotion and dissemination of the knowledge it generates (UCT, 2011b). Many UCT researchers enter competitions and receive awards for their work, affording them opportunities for wider engagement beyond publishing. UCT also supports events and competitions that disseminate knowledge, and it seeks to report specifically on the societal contributions of its research and innovation. In 2011, UCT signed the 2002 Berlin Declaration on Open Access, affirming its commitment to distribution of UCT research output on an OA basis.

Another UCT researcher-inventor interviewee argued that the Act may hinder the socialisation of knowledge – because of the need, mentioned above, to consider obtaining IP protection before engaging in research dissemination. However, even this interviewee stated that in many instances, the cost of the publication delay would likely be outweighed by the benefits of commercialisation.

The RCIPS interviewee stated that there might be difficulties in situations where IP is jointly created or shared, resulting in a situation where one of the parties (i.e. UCT) is required to comply with the Act while others may not be required to do so. This would be the case where the other parties are not publicly funded and thus not obliged to comply with the Act. The interviewee expressed hope that NIPMO would issue guidelines addressing this concern. Thus far, UCT has negotiated such situations by obtaining the necessary approvals from collaborating partners. However, obtaining these approvals invariably delays the conclusion of an agreement. Meanwhile, some philanthropic donors do not use a full-cost pricing model (which would entitle them to the IP rights) and instead seek alternative approaches to IP protection, such as direct IP transfers to them, which are subject to NIPMO approval.

RCIPS often works with researchers and inventors to prepare patent applications. It was stated that NIPMO compliance is onerous for RCIPS, but that UCT's administrative practices (e.g. the use of databases) and the provision of funding by NIPMO to finance capacity enhancement are mitigating the burden. The RCIPS interviewee said that capacity development funding is critical because universities have to be

> [...] suitably capacitated to cope with the implementation of the IPR Act – both in terms of human resources [and] skills transfer to the research community, and [in terms of] funding both to support early commercialisation as well as to pay for patent application and maintenance. (RCIPS interviewee, 2012)

Researcher-inventor perspectives

The UCT researcher-inventor interviewees generally reported that they favour the notion of open research, i.e. they favour extensive dissemination and publication of their research findings, and participation in international research consortia. They also stated that it is critical that resources are not wasted, that research is properly directed, and that appropriate benefits accrue from their research. The interviewees reported that they employ both full-cost and partial-cost funding models. Sometimes the full-cost model of funding entails limitations on related publications and strict regulation of confidentiality through the use of non-disclosure agreements (NDAs). In contrast, the partial-cost model is one in which the funder does not cover all costs and therefore does not own the IP (but must, in terms of the Act, be offered the opportunity to acquire the IP). As noted above, this is in all cases where partial funding, regardless of extent, has been provided. Frequently, such funders only seek royalty-free use of the final product or process for five years, with the result that UCT researchers working on such projects have no restrictions related to publishing, conference presentations or other modes of socialisation of the knowledge they produce.

One researcher-inventor interviewee expressed concern that the full-cost model may starve some companies, who are unable or unwilling to provide full-cost funding of research inputs. The Act may also block UCT relationships with other universities because of the restrictions imposed by NDAs (interviewee, 2012). It was also stated by a researcher-inventor interviewee that, when a project has multiple funders, there may be difficulties in gaining consensus on matters of IP ownership.

The UCT researcher-inventor interviewees stated that academic publishing is their main mode of knowledge dissemination, and that the Act does not necessarily inhibit this kind of knowledge socialisation because delays occasioned by the need to maintain secrecy prior to the filing of a patent application can be minimised by proper planning. For instance, a provisional patent specification can be filed on short notice in a case where a researcher needs to make a presentation at an international conference that could potentially undermine the novelty of an invention if presented in advance of a patent application. There was consensus among UCT researcher-inventor interviewees that implementation of the Act must seek to minimise any negative impact on scholarly publishing. One researcher-inventor interviewee stated that "publishing, collaboration and the free exchange of info between the people in the world engaged in our area of research is the only way forward" (UCT researcher-inventor interviewee, 2012).

At the same time, UCT researcher-inventor respondents expressed the belief that if, for instance, students had to delay publishing their theses because of the requirements of the Act, it would in most cases be an acceptable trade-off relative to the potential benefit that could accrue from a related patent and from the student's participation in patentable innovation. One researcher-inventor interviewee recounted how a student had become co-author of a patent derived from joint research conducted jointly by the interviewee and the student. The licensing of the patent had resulted in significant benefits for the student.

Wits University

Research and innovation indicators

Wits engages in multiple international research collaborations and has plans to establish six global research institutes (Wits University, 2010). In 2010, Wits had research funding in excess of ZAR 426,691 million, of which ZAR 102,591 million constituted public funding from the National Research Foundation (NRF), the Medical Research Council (MRC) and other government departments and science councils, while ZAR 75,751 million came from external sources, including the private sector and philanthropic donations. The rest came from miscellaneous sources. The largest volume of research output in 2010, including graduate work, was in the Faculty of Humanities (433 research units), followed by the Faculty of Science (418 units) and the Faculty of Health Sciences (366 units). Most patentable inventions stemmed from faculty members in Science, in Health Sciences, and in the Faculty of Engineering and the Built Environment.

Patent filing

Working from its 2003 IP Policy, Wits has effectively complied with the Act, transferring IP from inventors to the university, in the process securing "a cupboard full of patents [while] the challenge is to take the stuff out of the cupboard, get it out to the market and have an impact on society" (Wits Enterprise, 2012). Historically, according to Wits Enterprise, the university has handled patenting more as an academic exercise, spending on patenting but not on transferring patents into outcomes. In the future, patenting decisions would need to be based on all available information, in order to patent only where it will create value. The Act also requires universities to drive IP for societal benefit, which, arguably, includes economic benefit. Of these two approaches, patenting comes with the biggest formal overhead and expense (Wits Enterprise, 2012). One of the key challenges for the TTO remarked on by Wits Enterprise is to find ways to assist researchers in becoming proficient in IP management. The institutional perspective is that there is an onus on academic researchers to work for the public good, and the Act guarantees that the inventor will share in the financial and non-financial benefits, even though the university owns the IP (Wits Enterprise, 2012). Wits's IP Policy has historically permitted funding for Wits Enterprise to facilitate technology transfer and patenting; however the university needs to research the market and network with industry to operate in the broader ecosystem. University management does not yet have all necessary systems in place (Wits Enterprise, 2012).

The Wits portfolio of patenting doubled every year between 2003 and 2011 (Wits Enterprise, 2012), following the introduction of the Wits IP Policy in 2003 (Wits University, 2003). Prior to this Policy, which requires academics to disclose research that can be patent-protected, only a few small pockets of patent activity existed at Wits, in industrial diamond technology, gene-silencing technology for hepatitis B, and in bone generation. Today, the university's patent portfolio covers a relatively wide range of activity, including inventions in Health Sciences,

Engineering and the Built Environment, and Science. In the Faculty of Health Sciences, the Department of Pharmacy and Pharmacology in the School of Therapeutic Sciences had, by 2010, filed 25 patents in a single patent class in South Africa. The research involved drug delivery technologies to enhance the efficacy of drugs, with the focus on improved drug delivery of existing molecules (at low cost) as compared to the development of new molecules (with extended time to develop/market and high cost) (Wits University, 2010, pp. 103–5). The inventors were the most highly published in the field of pharmacy in South Africa, and were publishing approximately 15 journal articles annually.

Between 2010 and 2012, Wits established a dedicated Technology Transfer Unit to perform TTO functions within its IP management unit, Wits Enterprise. Wits Enterprise is a stand-alone company, established by the university in 2002, and offers a wide range of IP management research contracts and short courses.

The cost of patent filing at Wits is covered by a mix of public funding and funding from the university (for the legal fees, via Wits Enterprise). Prior to the Act, Wits made only limited financial commitments to technology transfer from the university, because it apparently did not see value in protecting inventions if there was no intention to exploit them commercially. In 2011, Wits introduced funding of IP protection for the first time, and increased its budget for this activity in 2012 (Wits Enterprise, 2012). Wits records patents through the RIMS (InfoEd) patent database, which includes a technology transfer module and a database for patent filings. The InfoEd system prompts the inventor or system administrator to either file a patent or take another specific action. NIPMO has access to the system data (Wits Enterprise, 2012).

Research-IP manager perspective

Wits research-IP managers explained that many industry funders have had to re-evaluate their approach since the introduction of the IPR-PFRD Act, because most industrial support had not, before the Act, been on a full-cost basis. Before the Act, industry-funded research projects generally had additional university or government funding, and IP from this research belonged to Wits, according to its IP Policy. The university would then negotiate the industry funder's rights to the IP, e.g. rights to post-commercialisation reward. South African petrochemical parastatal Sasol is an example of a company that has restructured its approach since the promulgation of the Act. The company has, since the Act, developed a policy for university research funding that allows it to retain ownership of IP from research of high commercial value in return for paying full cost to the university (Wits Enterprise, 2012).

The view was expressed that most South African businesses do not fully understand IP. Since much IP comes from offshore, businesses know how to commercialise it but not how to manage it. Full-costing for industry research funding is seen as an essential way forward wherever possible, otherwise Wits owns the IP even where it may lack the capacity or the finance to develop such. Initially, there was a fear that the full-cost model would be a problem; as it turned out, key industry players were not fazed, but wanted to understand the risks and liabilities more explicitly (Wits Enterprise, 2012).

Wits Enterprise expresses the view that there have been limited developments at Wits regarding collaboration between the university, industry and government, i.e. "triple helix" collaborations. Examples cited of early-stage triple helix formation were the Technology and Human Resources Programme (THRIP) programme of the NRF and the Department of Trade and Industry (DTI), and the De Beers Element Six programme of funding for industrial diamond research. These, however, were funding approaches rather than cases of commercialisation of research output. It was apparently too early to gauge the degree to which the triple helix approach on the input side was resulting in triple helix in operation on the output side (Wits Enterprise, 2012).

Though Wits research-IP managers interviewed stated that converting IP to commercial products and services is becoming more active at Wits, traditional forms of academic achievement are still pre-eminent among the majority of Wits academics and, in the short period since the Act has taken effect, there has been very little impact on broader research practice at Wits. The majority of academics were in fact unlikely to be aware of the Act, though there were plans to raise awareness. Scientists in Engineering Science were said to be knowledgeable, while greater awareness of the Act was needed in Health Sciences (Wits Enterprise, 2012).

Meanwhile, in the realm of dissemination and publication, Wits in November 2012 signed the aforementioned Berlin Declaration on Open Access (which UCT signed a year earlier, in 2011). However, the interviews with Wits research-IP managers and a Wits researcher-inventor revealed that there is a degree of uncertainty at Wits regarding what should or should not be disclosed through OA publishing, and thus there is a need for greater clarity on the Wits approach to OA. The technology transfer process regulated by the Act does not prevent OA publishing. Because a regulator's permission is required in the case of publication of potentially patentable information, this hurdle to publishing ensures that motivation to publish includes inventors' consideration of their actions in terms of the best way to make the knowledge useful. This involves thinking through the issues, rather than simple regulatory compliance.

Since inventions can only be protected prior to publication, the university advises academics to attach draft conference papers or scholarly articles to their patent applications. Academics can then publish the paper or article once the provisional patent is filed and a priority date is given (Wits Enterprise, 2012).

The view was expressed that the requirements of the legislation have fostered a conversation about commercialisation and innovation at Wits – a conversation that would not have been possible prior to the Act of 2008 (Wits Enterprise, 2012). Wits is now beginning to build the commercialisation component of its innovation system, with Wits Enterprise emphasising that the IP protection strategy of the university must be linked to an ability to deploy IP in the market. Spending money on patenting commercially unviable inventions is pointless, because the roughly ZAR1 million required to file a single full international patent family application is a large financial commitment for an organisation with a research budget of under ZAR500 million. It is possible that the rate of patenting will decline as understanding of the commercial prospects of academic research grows (Wits Enterprise, 2012).

In working to build the resource base for commercialisation, both the research-IP managers and the researcher-inventor interviewed said they felt that there is a need for appropriately skilled technology transfer professionals. Such professionals are scarce, however, with some estimates suggesting there may be as few as 20 such experts in the country (Wits researcher-inventor interviewee, 2012). Because NIPMO, the TIA, the universities and the legal profession all need such expertise, this personnel shortage presents a major system constraint. It is therefore necessary to identify and train professionals to fill the gap in this field. Furthermore, effective access to information tools and databases that allow analysis of the industry and market (to support potential partnerships) is also needed (Wits researcher-inventor interviewee, 2012).

To commercialise technology, a university can either license its IP to existing parties or create a company to use the IP. Wits currently licenses IP generated at the university to firms that have the capacity for, and interest in, commercialising it. This is because much of the patentable IP produced by researchers at the university is very early-stage and requires a fair amount of development before it is market-ready. It would be very risky for the university to establish start-up companies, as this would require venture capital, entrepreneurial management and possible incubation centres or specialised laboratories. These necessary elements are not within the natural scope of university competency. Wits attempted the alternative avenue for commercialising IP by establishing two start-up firms. Both, however, were in the process of being closed in 2012 because they had proved to be too risky (Wits Enterprise, 2012).

Where highly specialised clinical trials are required, neither Wits nor local companies have access to the large financial investments necessary. In fact, access to venture capital in South Africa, on the whole, is limited by the country's relatively undeveloped venture capital sector. Local venture capital has historically failed to engage with very-early-stage high-tech start-ups. While institutions such as South Africa's Industrial Development Corporation (IDC) could potentially have some interest, the applicable university-based research is typically too early-stage to meet the criteria for IDC development financing (Wits researcher-inventor interviewee, 2012).

An important challenge and priority is funding of TTO functions at Wits Enterprise. More funding is needed from the university and NIPMO. For example, in one of the most advanced cases (as mentioned above) of invention and patenting at Wits, academics and research students in the School of Therapeutic Sciences are working on enhanced drug delivery technologies, potentially making an important contribution to knowledge. Now, argues Wits Enterprise, "[t]he university needs to assist in getting the most impact out of that science" (Wits Enterprise, 2012). This case suggests strong opportunity in the future for entrepreneurial science at Wits, facilitated by Wits Enterprise.

Researcher-inventor perspective

The researcher-inventor interviewed, working in the commercially oriented space, explained that the research team prioritises publishing academically. However, since inventions can only be protected prior to publication, the researcher-inventor pointed to a potential conflict between academic publishing and the exploitation of their knowledge through commercial channels. Some research team members would prefer to delegate the commercialisation aspect of their patents to Wits Enterprise, but are limited by the difficulties involved in commercialising early-stage research (Wits researcher-inventor interviewee, 2012). It was stated that global patenting is an important issue for certain research fields. By way of example, South Africa has no local pharmaceutical development industry so inventors can effectively only transmit their research for commercialisation in global R&D markets. Thus, with respect to the invention and patenting phase, local inventors in the pharmacy sector may benefit from global linkages and global clout. The Wits pharmaceutical research team had filed a provisional patent application locally first and then filed an international Patent Cooperation Treaty (PCT) application. However, the degree of protection that a local patent gives, in a context where no local R&D industry exists, is an important question that needs to be addressed (Wits researcher-inventor interviewee, 2012), as this could amount to an inefficient utilisation of scarce funds.

The investment of public funds in research is understood to place an obligation on researcher-inventors to ensure returns are realised in the local economy, while at the same time facilitating a competitive innovation sector. One of the most effective means of moving the research and commercialisation agenda forward in South Africa is seen to be through the global patenting market. At Wits, an advanced drug delivery platform is being developed for a disease that affects everyone globally, making the securing of patents in the US, EU and Japan (the major pharmaceutical markets) essential. In this context, Wits inventors are engaged in a global value creation process, while aiming to generate a revenue stream back to South Africa. South African scientists can have a global agenda, participating in global R&D markets in order to enhance competitiveness. It can be argued that a local patent has limited value if it pertains to a global disease where R&D occurs abroad (e.g. ulcerative colitis, cancer), while a local patent for HIV drug delivery has significant value. Both approaches can deliver positive macro-economic effects. Publication occurs after receiving the priority date in the case of a provisional patent application in South Africa (Wits researcher-inventor interviewee, 2012).

It was noted that knowledge gained through pharmaceutical R&D contributes to knowledge socialisation through the scholarly publishing and citation process. Inventors within the field of pharmaceutical research at Wits publish between 15 and 20 papers a year in high-impact international journals. The researcher-inventors publish in both paid-access (per article or via subscription) journals and via OA modes. OA scholarly publishing has been observed to increase citations, as more academics have access to the articles. Global researchers have approached the pharmaceutical research team for access to their findings, and OA simplifies the process for academics who cannot afford access to paid-access publications, while data related to patent filings that have commercial potential is not shared (Wits researcher-inventor interviewee, 2012).

It was argued that researchers who want visibility "to make ourselves known" value OA, as it has many benefits. OA publishing is observed to help validate the research, as international researchers find it valuable and cite it. For example, Wits research papers on advanced drug delivery platforms are extensively cited and high visibility has led to many expressions of interest in collaboration from researchers in, for example, Egypt, Argentina and Mauritius. Additionally, citations are among the criteria used for promotion, e.g. through reporting H-Index values. High citation rates suggest the article has created attention, something that is wanted in the innovation space. The objective is to create attention for the inventors, the institution and the country. Given the importance of OA in facilitating basic research, the view was expressed that the focus of the Act should not be solely on commercialisation (Wits researcher-inventor interviewee, 2012).

The Wits researcher-inventor interviewee's perspective includes the view that, in particular research fields, the officials scrutinising the patents should be experts. It was noted that the patent examination process in South Africa is not as stringent as it could be and that greater capacity is required at the patent office. However, researchers filing for patent protection are usually the local experts, and thus cannot also be active in a patent examination office. This raises questions regarding the exact nature of expertise needed at the point of patent scrutiny and where such expertise might come from. NIPMO and the Companies and Intellectual Property Commission (CIPC, formerly CIPRO) may need to engage in global and local collaborations for effective patent scrutiny. In this regard too, however, there is a risk of bias that would need to be managed (Wits researcher-inventor interviewee, 2012).

Ambiguities in the Act and Regulations

Since 2008, when the Act became law, the process of setting up the complementary Regulations, as well as the Act's implementing infrastructure, has remained gradual, and at the time of this study had yet to be completed. There is a sense of ambiguity and uncertainty regarding the Act's practical application, warranting the feeling that the Act needs redrafting (Wits Enterprise, 2012). While amendments to many of the ambiguous aspects of the Act were proposed by universities and other advocates prior to enactment, the amendments were not adopted. Furthermore, certain sections in the Regulations are inconsistent with the provisions of the Act. However, thus far, despite being "left with the chaos", as one respondent put it, Wits appears to have taken a goodwill approach to meeting the objectives of the Act through pragmatic adaptations and general commitment to make the Act work. In order to clarify areas of uncertainty in the Act and Regulations, the regulator has published guidelines. Practice notes, similar to those deployed on tax matters by the South African Revenue Service, have been proposed as another tool for NIPMO to use, but it is not yet known whether this approach will be introduced (Wits Enterprise, 2012).

A primary issue appears to be the matter of what falls within the scope of the Act, because the Act does not define R&D, referring only to IP emanating from publicly financed research. Regulatory guidelines are in the process of development, and South African universities have had some input into the guidelines, on a confidential basis. It is unclear whether the draft guidelines will be published for comment. (The regulator NIPMO is also focusing on getting its systems operational to guide the TTOs, but is under-resourced (Wits Enterprise, 2012).)

5. Conclusions

The evidence outlined in the previous two sections of this chapter – the legislative and regulatory analysis in Section 3 and the UCT and Wits case study findings in Section 4 – suggest that the research landscape for the two universities studied (and potentially for other South African research universities and public research entities) is experiencing a period of transition. The transition would seem to be from a more purely research orientation to more mixed research and innovation orientation.

The IPR-PFRD Act of 2008 is a primarily a patent act, not an omnibus piece of legislation for publicly funded innovation. The Act is therefore part of an innovation puzzle, in which the roles and contributions of various actors (DHET, the DST, ASSAf, universities and industry) are shifting from the historically more linear contributions to research towards a form of research-innovation interconnectedness or entanglement, to use the terminology of Hanauske *et al.*, (2007). The DST's initiative, via the Act, to promote and regulate the patenting of publicly funded research seems clearly to be prompting behaviour. At the same time, global trends in publishing are raising philosophical and ecosystem questions in South Africa about how to maximise the value of academic publication output – as evidenced by the aforementioned change of approach at ASSAf (with the support of the DST and DHET), and the adoption by Wits of the Berlin Declaration. Both the patenting and scholarly publishing environments in South Africa are thus in a state of flux.

While the evidence gathered by this research project suggests that there may have been an initial chilling effect on scholarly publishing following introduction of the Act in 2008, as well as a rearranging of industry finance for university research and increased emphasis on university-level IP policy and practice, it would appear that significant amounts of successful adaptation have occurred. The provisions of the Act and Regulations require, and appear to have prompted, investments in increased IP management capacity at state level and at the two universities studied. Further system-building and legal-regulatory mechanisms are likely still required, in order for the DST, TIA, NIPMO, universities and industry to create, and adapt to, the new rules of the game. There is also evidence that the scholarly publishing landscape is beginning to shift, based on new thinking about academic journal accreditation, OA publishing and financial incentives for scholarly publishing. The whole system of knowledge production is in motion. At the same time, the human and financial infrastructure to support patenting of university-based R&D is slowly unfurling. This system change has the potential to reset the "publish or perish" approach to a mixed "patent, publish, commercialise" and "publish and socialise" approach.

In conclusion, we now consider two particularly important themes that have emerged from this research:

Building the new ecosystem

The following are levers for building the new ecosystem for publicly funded research:

- from government: policy, legislation, regulations, supporting institutions (NIPMO, TIA) and funding frameworks;
- from universities and other publicly funded research entities: IP policy, externally funded work policy, TTOs and legal offices; and
- from industry: research funding approaches.

These levers are all necessary, and must be interlinked, in order for the knowledge capacity and base of publicly funded research entities to be aggregated and extended. For instance, legislation and regulations alone can only have limited impact on the challenge posed by the fact that South African university research tends to be underutilised at this stage in the country's knowledge production evolution, because most potentially commercialisable research is early-stage. In addition to the fact that the Act and Regulations only deal with a tiny slice of the research and innovation pipeline, we saw above that even on the matters specifically addressed by these legal instruments, the instruments are vague on important points, including the distinction between economic and social value and modes of support for key activities in the value chain of transformation of IP into both economic and social value.

Only an interlinked ecosystem, with the levers of government, public research entities and industry combining effectively, can improve utilisation of early-stage research and help bring it to later stages in a manner that can deliver on both commercial and social objectives. The components of South Africa's new ecosystem for publicly funded research are still at an early stage of development, with supporting institutions at state level and at public research entities (NIPMO, TIA, TTOs) still in their formative stages. The role of NIPMO is protection- and support-related; the role of the TIA is support-related; and the synergistic linkages between these two bodies, TTOs and public research entities are still in an early stage of evolution.

There is also the matter of how to give both patenting and scholarly publishing the attention they require for their combined future development. Attention to one without attention to the other limits the potential of the IP landscape as a whole. The Act's focus on patenting, and lack of emphasis on scholarly publishing, may be perceived as a weakness. This is because the production, commercialisation, dissemination and socialisation of knowledge are all related endeavours.

As such, some argue that legislation must treat them as related processes, on the grounds that if the legal-regulatory system does not address all elements of knowledge production in the IP ecosystem, systemic weaknesses will result, with every element of the ecosystem undermined. It can thus be argued that the IPR-PFRD Act should also have included proactive provisions on scholarly publishing. Such an argument is not persuasive, however, because scholarly publishing cannot and should not be driven by legislative requirements, so as to maintain the sanctity of university autonomy and the academic freedom of researchers and scholars. This research study has shown that there are non-legislative mechanisms which can, and are being, harnessed to build a scholarly publishing environment conducive to the new ecosystem.

Knowledge socialisation

The Act conceptualises commercialisation broadly, and potentially applies a commercialisation imperative to knowledge that should, in our view, be prioritised for socialisation. This over-broad conception of commercialisation requires forethought by universities and inventors at universities, so that knowledge production is not collapsed into a requirement that all knowledge be subject to patent applications by default.

Socialising knowledge is important because it forms the foundation of knowledge-building for future generations of researchers, inventors and universities. Whether published using paid-access journals or OA platforms, scholarly research is a specific form of knowledge socialisation. In the interests of socialising knowledge, UCT and Wits have both confirmed their institutions' commitment to OA by becoming signatories to the Berlin Declaration.

The Act, and the actors interviewed at UCT and Wits for this research, envision achievement of broad societal and economic impact through publicly funded research. Differences emerge, however, with respect to the means through which to foster such impact, with arguments ranging from calls to protect IP to calls for it to be made openly available. It is important to distinguish between two main kinds of potential impact: commercial and social. A university is, above all, a social institution of knowledge generation, with a broad societal role, not merely a narrow economic, commercial, instrumentalist one. We have seen that the emerging South African innovation landscape addresses patenting, licensing, commercialisation and scholarly publishing (in either paid-access or OA format), but narratives aligned with notions of open science, open research, open knowledge and "open development" (see Chapter 1 of this volume) are not prominent in the South African innovation and IP discourse, and they ought to be.

Finally, it is necessary to return to the research question for this study, as provided in the opening section of this chapter: *How does South Africa's 2008 IP commercialisation law potentially impact research, innovation and scholarly publishing in key fields at universities?* The research has found that the Act appears to have the potential to steer university research, innovation and scholarly publishing in new directions. However, it seems clear that if South African universities approach the Act simply from a compliance perspective, the R&D objectives of the Act could be lost. A compliance-based approach could lead to indiscriminate patenting, without consideration to real potential commercial and social benefits and costs. Such an approach would not achieve the developmental intentions of the Act, as it would not sufficiently engage universities and their inventors in the task of considering how best to transfer knowledge generated by public funds to industry and to society. A compliance-based approach would represent a lack of the philosophical questioning and iteration necessary for constructing a 21st-century knowledge and innovation ecosystem in South Africa.

Bibliography

Primary sources

Legislation, regulations

International:

Bayh-Dole Act, or Patent and Trademark Law Amendments Act (Pub. L. 96-517, December 12, 1980) (Bayh-Dole Act of 1980).

South Africa:

Broad-Based Black Economic Empowerment (B-BBEE) Act 53 of 2003.

Copyright Act 98 of 1978.

Designs Act 195 of 1993.

Intellectual Property Rights from Publicly Financed Research and Development (IPR-PFRD) Act 51 of 2008.

Intellectual Property Rights from Publicly Financed Research and Development Regulations, 2009, GN R675, in *Government Gazette* 33433 of [i.e. effective on] 2 August 2010.

Patents Act 57 of 1978.

Plant Breeders' Rights Act 15 of 1976.

Proclamation 34, *Government Gazette* 33422 of 30 July 2010.

Trademarks Act 194 of 1993.

Policies

Green Paper for Post-School Education and Training (2012), Department of Higher Education and Training (DHET), Pretoria (DHET, 2012).

Intellectual Property Rights from Publicly Financed Research Framework (2006), Department of Science and Technology (DST), Pretoria (DST, 2006).

National Research and Development Strategy (2002), Department of Science and Technology (DST), Pretoria (DST, 2002).

Ten-Year Plan for Science and Technology (2008). Department of Science and Technology (DST), Pretoria (DST, 2008).

White Paper on Science and Technology (1996), Department of Arts, Culture, Science and Technology (DACST), Pretoria (DACST, 1996).

UCT

University of Cape Town (UCT) (2008), "Comments on IPR from Publicly Financed Research and Development Bill".

University of Cape Town (UCT) (2010), *Innovation at UCT 2010.*

University of Cape Town (UCT) (2011a), *Innovation at UCT 2011.*

University of Cape Town (UCT) (2011b) Intellectual Property Policy, available at: www.uct.ac.za/downloads/uct.ac.za/about/policies/intellect_property.pdf (accessed 25 April 2013).

Wits University

Wits Commercial Enterprise (Pty) Ltd. (Wits Enterprise) (2012), data from interviews and unpublished documents obtained by the authors from Wits Enterprise, Johannesburg.

Wits University (2003), Intellectual Property Policy.

Wits University (2010), *2010 Research Report.*

Secondary sources

Abrahams, L. and Akinsanmi, T. (2011), "Revitalisation of higher education in Southern Africa: key themes and issues for the attention of policy-makers and university leadership", unpublished paper, LINK Centre, University of the Witwatersrand, Johannesburg.

Abrahams, L., Burke, M., Gray, E. and Rens, A. (2008), *Opening Access to Knowledge in Southern African Universities*, SARUA Study Series, Southern African Regional Universities Association (SARUA), Johannesburg.

Armstrong, C., De Beer, J., Kawooya, D., Prabhala, A. and Schonwetter, T. (Eds) (2010), *Access to Knowledge in Africa: The Role of Copyright*, UCT Press, Cape Town.

Barratt, A. (2010), "Lessons from Bayh-Dole: reflections on the Intellectual Property Rights from Publicly Financed Research and Development Act (South Africa)", *Journal for Juridical Science*, Vol. 35, pp. 30–69.

Bünemann, H. (2010), "Open access: the future for research?" *Mind Design*, Vol. 3 No. 28, pp. 1–3, available at: www.dcdr.dk/uk/menu/update/webzine/articles/open-access--the-future-for-research (accessed 25 April 2013).

Chan, L. and Costa, S. (2005), "Participation in the global knowledge commons: challenges and opportunities for research dissemination in developing countries", *New Library World*, Vol. 106 No 3/4, pp. 141–63.

Chetty, P. (2009/2010), "Review of IPR Act and Regulations: Intellectual Property Rights from Publicly Financed Research and Development Act, Act 51 of 2008, Republic of South Africa", *African Journal of Information and Communication*, No. 10, pp. 78–83.

Creswell, J. and Bean, J. (1981), "Research output, socialisation, and the Biglan Model", *Research in Higher Education*, Vol. 15 No. 1, pp. 69–91, available at: www.sciencedirect.com/science/article/pii/S0048733306000655 (accessed 25 April 2013).

De Assumpção, D.A. (2005), "Socializing knowledge and reducing regional inequalities: strategies for Brazil", in Willard, T., Andjelkovic, M., Vosloo, S., Mungai, W., Salas, M., Lall, A., Garai, A., De Assumpção, D.A. and Sobeih, A. (Eds), *A Developing Connection: Bridging the Policy Gap between the Information Society and Sustainable Development*, International Institute for Sustainable Development (IISD), available at: www.iisd.org/pdf/2005/networks_dev_connection_brazil.pdf (accessed 25 April 2013).

Denscombe, M. (2010), *The Good Research Guide*, 4th ed., Open University Press, Maidenhead, Berkshire, UK.

Geuna, A. and Nesta, L. (2006), "University patenting and its effects on academic research: the emerging European evidence", *Research Policy*, Vol. 35 No. 6, pp. 790–807.

Gray, E. (2009), *National Environmental Scan of South African Scholarly Publishing*, availableat:www.cet.uct.ac.za/files/file/OS%20PositionPaper2%20_%20%20Final%20typeset.pdf (accessed 25 April 2013).

Gray, E. (2009/2010), "Access to Africa's knowledge: publishing development research and measuring value", *African Journal of Information and Communication*, No. 10, pp. 4–19.

Halloran, P. (2011), "An infrastructure for process improvement, organisational learning and knowledge management", in Koohang, A., Harman, K. and Britz,

J. (Eds), *Knowledge Management: Theoretical Foundations*, Informing Science Press, Santa Rosa, CA.

Hanauske, M., Bernius, S. and Dugall, B. (2007), *Quantum Game Theory and Open Access Publishing*, available at: http://mpra.ub.uni-muenchen.de/15986/1/MPRA_paper_15986.pdf (accessed 25 April 2013).

Hargreaves, I. (2011), *Digital Opportunity: A Review of Intellectual Property and Growth*, independent report commissioned by the Prime Minister of the United Kingdom, available at: www.ipo.gov.uk/ipreview-finalreport.pdf (accessed 25 April 2013).

Houghton, J., Steele, C. and Sheehan, P. (2006), *Research Communication Costs in Australia: Emerging Opportunities and Benefits,* Australian Department of Education, Science and Training, Canberra, available at: http://dspace.anu.edu.au/handle/1885/44485 (accessed 25 April 2013).

Kahn, M. (2011), "A bibliometric analysis of South Africa's scientific outputs – some trends and implications", *South African Journal of Science*, Vol. 107 No. 1/2, pp. 1–6.

Kaplan, D. (2005), "South Africa's National Research and Development Strategy: a review" *Science Technology and Society,* Vol. 9 No. 2, pp. 273–94.

McQuail, D. (2005), *McQuail's Mass Communication Theory,* 5th ed., Sage, London.

Mouton, J., Boshoff, N., De Waal, L., Esau, S., Imbayarwo, B., Ritter, M. and Van Niekerk, D. (2008), "The state of public science in the SADC region", in Kotecha, P. (Ed.), *Towards a Common Future: Higher Education in the SADC region: Research Findings from Four SARUA Studies*, SARUA Study Series, Southern African Regional Universities Association (SARUA, Johannesburg.

National Advisory Council on Innovation (NACI) (2003), *Utilisation of Research Findings: Extent, Dynamics and Strategies,* discussion document, NACI, Pretoria.

National Intellectual Property Management Office (NIPMO) (2012), "The launch of Guideline 1 of 2012", available at: www.nipmo.org.za/node/1267 (accessed 25 April 2013).

Nonaka, I. (1991), "The knowledge-creating company", *Harvard Business Review,* Vol. 69 November/December, pp. 96–104.

Open Society Initiative (2003), Berlin Declaration on Open Access to Scientific Knowledge, available at: http://oa.mpg.de/lang/en-uk/berlin-prozess/berliner-erklarung/ (accessed 25 April 2013).

Patton, M. (2002), *Qualitative Research and Evaluation Methods,* 3rd ed., Sage Publications, Saint Paul, MN.

Plaskoff, J. (2011), "Intersubjectivity and community-building: learning to learn organizationally", in Easterby-Smith, M. and Lyles, M. (Eds), *Handbook of Organisational Learning and Knowledge Management*, 2nd ed., Wiley, Chichester.

Pouris, A. (2009), "How does South African academia rate internationally?" *Innovate,* No. 29, pp. 30–2.

Pouris, A. and Pouris, A. (2011), "Patents and economic development in South Africa: managing IPRs", presentation to Accelerating IP and Innovation in South Africa Conference, 18–20 September, Cape Town.

Sibanda, M. (2007), *The State of Patenting in South Africa: Special Report 2007,* The Innovation Fund, Pretoria, available at: www.rcips.uct.ac.za/usr/rcips/news/stateofpatenting_SA.pdf (accessed 25 April 2013).

Sibanda, M. (2011), "Ownership and commercialisation of publicly-funded research and innovation – goals and challenges in developing countries", presentation to Accelerating IP and Innovation in South Africa Conference, 18–20 September, Cape Town.

So, A., Sampat, B., Rai, A., Cook-Deegan, R., Reichman, J., Weissman, R., and Kapczynski, A., (2008), "Is Bayh-Dole good for developing countries? Lessons from the US experience", *PLoSBiol,* Vol. 6 No. 10, pp. 2078–84.

Southern African Regional Universities Association (SARUA) (2007), *Science and Technology: A Baseline Study on Science and Technology and Higher Education in the SADC Region,* SARUA, Johannesburg.

Times Higher Education (THE) (2012), *World University Rankings,* available at: www.timeshighereducation.co.uk/world-university-rankings/ (accessed 25 April 2013).

Tong, L. (2010), "Ownership of IP derived from publicly-funded research: the state steps in", *Journal of Intellectual Property Law and Practice,* Vol. 5 No. 6, pp. 409–11.

Webster, E. and Jensen, P.H. (2011), "Do patents matter for commercialisation?" *Journal of Law and Economics,* Vol. 54 No, 2, pp. 431–53.

Wellings, P. (2008), *Intellectual Property and Research Benefits,* Lancaster University, Lancaster, UK.

World Intellectual Property Organisation (WIPO) (2007), *Technology Transfer, Intellectual Property and Effective University-Industry Partnerships: The Experience of China, India, Japan, Philippines, the Republic of Korea, Singapore and Thailand,* available at: www.wipo.int/freepublications/en/intproperty/928/wipo_pub_928.pdf (accessed 25 April 2013).

Youngleson, J. (2011), "Ownership and commercialisation of publicly-financed research and innovation: implementation goals and challenges in developing countries", presentation to Accelerating IP and Innovation in South Africa Conference, 18 September, Cape Town.

Chapter 14

Towards University–Industry Innovation Linkages in Ethiopia

Wondwossen Belete

Abstract

This chapter analyses findings from research into the apparent disconnect in Ethiopia between the state's innovation policy and the practical realities of scientific research in the country. The research found that the Ethiopian government's emphasis – in its Science, Technology and Innovation (STI) Policy of 2012 – is on IP protection, and patenting of outputs from publicly funded research. Meanwhile, it was found, there is a dearth of innovative research at Ethiopia's universities, and scant linkage between universities and the private sector. The chapter argues that the Ethiopian government should look beyond the current focus on IP protection and patenting and seek the optimum balance among a variety of models of university–industry knowledge transfer.

1. Introduction

Ethiopia is the second most populous country in sub-Saharan Africa, with a population of 84 million. Agriculture accounts for 41% of gross domestic product (GDP) and 85% of employment, and is also the main source of foreign exchange and raw materials for domestic industry. Although the country is one of the poorest in the world, its economy has demonstrated signs of improvement in recent years. At the time of writing, Ethiopia had experienced double-digit GDP growth for nine consecutive years, making it one of the fastest-growing economies in Africa.

Despite promising signs of economic improvement, poverty eradication still remains a priority for the Ethiopian government. The country's low level of technological development is a major constraint on this national development objective. Promoting technological progress is therefore seen as essential to achieving broad-based, accelerated and sustained economic growth. The government in 2012 approved a Science, Technology and Innovation (STI) Policy based on a national innovation system (NIS) approach. The NIS approach is premised on the assumption that the flow of technology and information among people, enterprises and institutions is key to the innovative process. The Policy emphasises the need for strengthening the interaction among universities and industrial enterprises to enhance the innovative capacity of industry. Other government policies and programmes also view the wealth of knowledge generated through academic research as a source of industrial innovation and national competitiveness (FDRE, 2010a, 2010b, 2012; MOST, 2010).

In turn, intellectual property (IP) rights have been identified as important tools to facilitate the transfer of university-generated knowledge to industry. Various studies have recommended policies that permit universities and government research institutes to retain IP rights (EIPO, 2007; Mengistie, 2006; MOST, 2009). The studies do not mention specific foreign policies to be used as models, but a critical examination of the studies reveals that priority is being placed on the adoption of IP policies from developed countries in relation to the promotion of university–industry interaction (EIPO, 2007; MOST, 2009). These studies have had a significant influence on the IP strategy of the STI Policy – an important point, given that the recommended strategy provides for the development and implementation of institutional IP systems that could, if implemented, lead to increased privatisation of the knowledge outputs from publicly funded research (FDRE, 2012).

There are a number of challenges associated with cross-national emulation of STI policies between developed-world and developing-world contexts. STI policies need to cater to a country's socio-economic context, the research environment in its universities and research institutes, the capacity of a country's domestic firms to absorb external knowledge, and the availability in the country of resources for research and innovation. Hence the appropriate policies needed to enhance the benefits of STI are highly context-specific. In order to build an innovation system that works in the Ethiopian context, it is necessary to base STI policy development on research evidence reflecting the current situation of science and technology.

This study aimed to produce evidence on the potential impact of IP dynamics on university–industry interaction – a matter of heated debate in Ethiopian STI policy-making. The study sought to answer the question: *How does IP protection of academic research output potentially influence the performance of innovation in Ethiopian industry?*

The study reviewed the policies and laws in place in Ethiopia to promote a university–industry alliance, and examined the views of stakeholder groups regarding the different channels of knowledge transfer between universities and industry and the policy environment affecting that knowledge transfer. Establishing a system that stimulates effective university–industry interaction requires a clear understanding by academic researchers, industry managers and policy-makers of the relative merits of the different models of knowledge transfer, and this study sought to generate findings that can contribute to this process of understanding.

The next section of this chapter (Section 2) outlines the study's methodology. The third section reviews the relevant literature in order to establish the context of the study. Section 4 analyses the relationships between IP rights, publicly funded research and industrial innovation in Ethiopia on the basis of information gathered during the research. The fifth and final section provides conclusions and policy recommendations. (See Chapters 13 and 15 of this volume for more research, in South Africa and Botswana, respectively, into matters at the intersection of IP and publicly funded research.)

2. Research methods

This study used two main data collection methods: document analysis and questionnaires. The documents analysed included government policies, laws, plans, programmes and study reports. Also analysed were research strategies of universities and study papers produced during recent university reforms in Ethiopia – in order to gather information on research performance and management at the institutional level. In addition, previous research in this area was reviewed to identify questions that needed to be answered and to explore different viewpoints on the application of IP protection in relation to publicly funded research.

Questionnaires were used to collect information from groups categorised into (1) universities, (2) industrial enterprises and (3) government agencies. The universities included in the study were selected according to the following factors: number of academic staff, size of public research funding, research performance and previous experience in collaborations with industry. Researchers in universities who directly participate in publicly funded research, or who are involved in the process of design and implementation of research projects, were selected for the study. Industrial enterprises were chosen based on their levels of innovative activities and prior collaboration with universities. The respondents from enterprises were selected on the basis of their roles in research management and protection of enterprise IP. The government agencies included in the study were those with active roles in the development of STI policy. In these agencies, government officials with technical knowledge of IP rights administration were targeted as respondents.

Because the nature of the information gathered from each group had some level of variation, three separate questionnaires were developed. The questionnaires were delivered as attachments to e-mail messages. The questionnaires included background information about the study and posed questions intended to collect information on the impact of academic patenting on industrial innovation. Each question gave respondents a range of options to select from. In cases where answers did not fit into the given options, respondents were allowed to provide their own comments. The questionnaires also contained a section that allowed respondents to add their individual thoughts on IP and the dissemination of university research results.

Some of the university researchers targeted as respondents did not respond to the questionnaire. This limited the study's ability to incorporate the views of people with in-depth information on the subject. In addition, since the study focused on a recent policy issue that has not yet been extensively or systematically researched in the context of least developed countries (LDCs), it was difficult to find materials written from the perspective of such countries. Although innovation policies are context-specific, LDCs share commonalities associated with their low level of technological development.

3. IP rights and university research

IP and dissemination

Over the past three decades, IP protection of publicly funded university research has been the subject of intense policy debate in both developed and developing countries. Some people consider the dissemination of university research via patent licensing as a model that facilitates economic and social returns from university research. Others have highlighted the potential for this model to generate unintended and deleterious consequences for innovation systems (Boettiger and Bennet, 2006; Montobbio, 2009; Sampat, 2006).

The UK Commission on Intellectual Property Rights (CIPR) found that the underlying argument for patenting university inventions and exclusive licensing of technologies is to increase the rate of commercial application of knowledge by encouraging private sector investment (CIPR, 2002, p. 123). University inventions are often in the very early stages of development, and therefore require substantial development before commercial application. It is thus argued that unless companies are able to negotiate exclusive access to the IP from university research, the companies will not have the incentive to invest the resources necessary for developing marketable products. The argument for university ownership of IP rights, therefore, "pertains not to *ex ante* incentives for invention, but to incentives *ex post* for downstream users to invest in commercialization of federally funded inventions" (Thursby and Thursby, 2007, p. 4).

The opposing argument is that the interests of technology transfer and commercial application will be best served by the widest possible dissemination of knowledge in the public domain. According to this perspective, increased focus on IP protection of academic inventions is a threat to the objectives of universities (Davis *et al.*, 2011). Academic researchers have traditionally been committed to "open science", which involves peer evaluation, a shared culture of scientists that emphasises the importance of motivational factors other than economic ones, and the widespread dissemination of research findings (David, 2003; Dosi *et al.*, 2006; Liebeskind, 2001; Lundvall, 2008; Sampat, 2006). It is argued that the open science approach helps to avoid excessive duplication of research efforts, to promote information-sharing and to allow the development of a strong public knowledge base from which subsequent researchers can draw (Fabrizio, 2006).

Bayh-Dole and its international emulation

The 1980 Bayh-Dole Act in the United States permitted university patenting. Proponents of the Act argued that there was a significant informational divide between the world of academia and the world of industry, making it difficult to implement university inventions in practice (Colyvas *et al.*, 2002). Bayh-Dole aimed to promote the commercialisation of university research results that were seen as going to waste (Fabrizio, 2006). The Act responded to a belief by policy-makers that stronger protection for the results of publicly funded research and development would accelerate the commercialisation of these results and the realisation of economic benefits for US taxpayers (Mowery *et al.*, 2001). Furthermore, allowing universities to share in the proceeds from faculty inventions would create incentives for the universities to advertise these inventions to industry. Bayh-Dole "provided blanket permission for performers of federally funded research to file for patents on the results of such research and to grant licences for these patents, including exclusive licenses, to other parties" (Mowery and Sampat, 2005, p. 228).

Recent policy initiatives in a number of industrial economies have revealed that there is considerable interest in emulating the Bayh-Dole Act. Many European countries changed their innovation policies to accord with the American example, entrusting universities with IP management and providing support to intermediary units that help to facilitate the university–industry technology transfer process (Poglajen, 2012). Similarly, Bayh-Dole provided a model of reform for Japanese policy-makers (Walsh *et al.*, 2008). Several developing countries have also adopted legislation modelled on Bayh-Dole, while others are considering the introduction of such policies (Foley and Lardner, 2011; Graff, 2007; Koyama, 2010; Vartak and Saurastri, 2009).

Despite this apparent popularity of cross-national policy emulation in the case of the Bayh-Dole Act, there is a strong argument that policy copying without due consideration of country-specific situations is not desirable. Verspagen (2006) argues that the justifications given for the adoption of Bayh-Dole in the US may not be applicable in the European context. Crespi *et al.* (2006) used their data from a large-scale survey of European countries to argue against Bayh-Dole-like legislation in Europe. According to their argument, there is no indication of market failure, in the dissemination of university research in Europe, to justify legislative intervention. Mowery and Sampat (2005) argue that the emulation of Bayh-Dole in other industrial economies is based on a misreading of the empirical evidence of the effects of the Act, and a misreading of the importance of the facilitating role of IP rights in the transfer and commercialisation of university inventions. There is also a lack of firm evidence on the effect that Bayh-Dole has had on the quantity and quality of university research output and its level of commercialisation (CIPR, 2002).

Various authors have criticised the emulation of Bayh-Dole in developing countries. Anthony *et al.* (2008) are doubtful that the benefits of legislation modelled on Bayh-Dole can outweigh the costs in developing countries. Sampat (2009) examined the theory and evidence supporting the main goals of the draft Indian Bill for the Protection and Utilisation of Publicly Funded Intellectual Property. Like Bayh-Dole, India's proposed Bill was to apply to all research resulting from government grants. Sampat noted the difficulties inherent in cross-national policy emulation, and advised that India and other developing countries considering Bayh-Dole-like legislation should not precisely follow the American model. These insights are also applicable in Ethiopia.

4. IP, university research and industrial innovation in Ethiopia

Government policies

Seeking to foster the development of domestic technological capabilities, various government policies in Ethiopia emphasise the need for stronger interaction between universities and industry. These policies are intended to strengthen graduate training and university research, to establish mechanisms to facilitate collaboration and information flow, and to create industry demand for knowledge generated by universities.

Ethiopia issued its first national Science and Technology Policy in 1993 (TGE, 1993). This Policy contained directives intended to establish and/or strengthen science and technology institutes and research and development (R&D) centres. The Policy also addressed the need for dissemination and application of research results, and encouraged the private sector to invest capital, participate in the promotion and development of scientific and technological activities, and promote mutual support between research and production (TGE, 1993). However, the Policy followed a linear approach to innovation that limited its ability to create a strong alliance between universities and industry. The linear approach postulates that innovation starts with basic research, then adds applied research and development and ends with production and diffusion.

Hence in 2012 the government adopted a new STI Policy. This new Policy envisages the establishment of a national innovation system that strengthens the links between different innovation actors. The Policy contains strategies for creating strong connections between universities, research institutes and industry in the learning and adaptation of foreign technologies (FDRE, 2012).

The government's Education and Training Policy of 1994 emphasises the creation of an appropriate nexus between university research and industrial innovation. The Policy sets out the research-oriented role that higher education should play, in order to enable students to become problem-solving professional leaders who address broader societal needs in their fields of study. The approach gives priority to research with practical societal impact that fosters cooperation among stakeholders (TGE, 1994). The Higher Education Proclamation of 2009 serves to consolidate the Education and Training Policy. One of the objectives of the Proclamation is to promote and enhance university research by focusing on knowledge and technology transfers consistent with the country's priority needs (FDRE, 2009).

Industrial development and capacity-building policies also stress the importance of universities as sources of new ideas with industrial application. These policies consider the interface between universities and their socio-economic environment as one of the key factors for development. While giving recognition to the role of universities as breeding grounds for professional leaders and researchers, these policies emphasise that tertiary institutions should be engaged in activities aimed at generating knowledge that can be applied in industry. Universities are required to have a role in problem-solving activities that address the specific needs of industry and contribute to innovation through technology transfer (FDRE, 2002a, 2002b).

However, it is this author's view that there is no evidence to suggest that the focus of these policies – on universities as instruments for knowledge-based economic development and change – has yet brought the envisaged change in industrial innovation and economic growth in Ethiopia. Examination of the factors constraining the contribution of universities to technological capacity building and national competitiveness is a broad research subject that goes beyond the scope of this study. However, the following subsection outlines capacity-related constraints that seem to explain the scant collaborative links between universities and industry in Ethiopia.

University research and innovation performance of firms

Over the past 15 years there has been a significant expansion of higher education in Ethiopia, facilitating improved access to tertiary education for many young people. The number of universities increased from just two in 2000 to 32 in 2011. Undergraduate enrolment increased from 149,694 students in 2005 to 319,217 students in 2009. Postgraduate enrolment increased from 3,884 students to 10,125 students over the same period (MOE, 2005, 2010, 2011). University research has not, however, shown parallel growth. Only a handful of universities, chiefly Addis Ababa University (AAU), Haramaya University and Mekelle University, are engaged in notable research activities. Furthermore, it was found that there is a disconnect between the research focus of the universities and the needs of the economy. A situation analysis of research activity at AAU found that none of the units at the university had set research priorities based on national development objectives (Lemma *et al.,* 2008). A shortage of qualified researchers, lack of adequate research funding and weak research infrastructure have also been identified as factors limiting the involvement of universities in development-oriented research programmes (Belete, 2010; Lemma *et al.,* 2008).

The strength of university–industry links depends not only on the amount and orientation of university research activities, but also on the ability of industrial firms to identify, assimilate and apply knowledge generated in universities. The absorptive capacity of recipient firms is a major factor in potential transfer of university knowledge and effective university–industry interaction. Viewed from this perspective, most Ethiopian industrial enterprises have weak absorptive capacity for externally generated knowledge. They face problems related to their lack of information on available technological options, financial constraints and skill gaps (i.e. differences between the skill requirements of the enterprise and those possessed by graduates) (Belete, 2010). The resulting lack of required technical skills negatively influences the technological capabilities of enterprises. Most of the technical staff working in firms are trained by the Technical and Vocational Education and Training (TVET) institutes of Ethiopia. However, in my experience, many TVET graduates do not meet the expectations of industrial enterprises. TVET has traditionally concentrated on institution-based training, which favours theoretical instruction. Until recently, TVET training was input-oriented and followed curricular requirements instead of workplace and labour market requirements. Moreover, training and continuous upgrading for the existing workforce was only partially in place. A meaningful structure for steady adaptation to workforce demands and life-long learning was missing (MOE, 2005).

The structure of the industrial sector is another factor contributing to the innovative performance of industrial enterprises and their connections with universities. Ethiopia's manufacturing sector is dominated by small and medium enterprises (SMEs), which are often owned by individuals or families. These SMEs tend to be risk averse. Enterprises willing to invest in new management systems or new production processes are relatively scarce. It is rare to find separate units within these enterprises focusing on innovation; rather, innovative activities are carried out informally along with day-to-day manufacturing operations (Belete, 2010; UNCTAD, 2002).

The government has launched several initiatives aimed at improving the linkage between universities and industry in Ethiopia. Starting as early as 1986, these initiatives focused on encouraging industrially relevant university research and improving the capacity of industry to absorb and utilise university-generated knowledge (Gebreyesus, 1998; Kitaw, 2008; Wasmuth and Nebelung, 2006). The most recent of these initiatives is the Engineering Capacity Building Program (ECBP). In 2011–12, the ECBP established Institutes of Technology at different universities. The Institutes are engaged, *inter alia*, in an interdisciplinary approach to applied technology research and technology transfer, in an effort to impact the development of Ethiopia's regional and national economies. Also among the core tasks of the Institutes are the establishment of sustainable partnerships for development and mutual support between industry, the business community and national and international institutions (Edhardt and Scholz, 2009).

The national IP system and institutional IP management

IP protection is a relatively new concept in Ethiopia. The country's first patent law was adopted in 1995, and regulations implementing it were introduced in 1997. The national IP system began to take shape only after the establishment of the Ethiopian Intellectual Property Office (EIPO) in 2003. The EIPO operates as an autonomous government agency with responsibility for the administration of IP rights. It is also mandated to conduct studies in various IP fields and to recommend policies and legislation (FDRE, 2003).

Despite the demanding tasks entrusted to the EIPO, it suffers from a shortage of professionals with sufficient knowledge and skills to carry out its mandate.[1] The examination of patent applications is performed by personnel who lack the requisite training and experience. Moreover, there is a general lack of appreciation of how specific IP policies affect creativity.

Under Ethiopia's 1995 patent law, employers are the default owners of any patents on inventions created by employees in the course of employment. This provision may be interpreted as entitling universities to retain the IP rights on research conducted by academic staff using institutional resources. However, inventions that are not related to an employee's employment or service contract and were created without the use of the employer's resources, data, materials or equipment, belong to the employee (TGE, 1995). The Higher Education Proclamation of 2009 recognises individual IP rights and confidentiality agreements when university-generated knowledge is used for public benefit (FDRE, 2009). However, the Proclamation does not contain any explicit provisions for institutional ownership of patents on inventions generated by university research. Such a provision was included in the Research Policy at AAU, which was submitted for discussion to the academic community in 2011.The University's Research Policy requires all potentially patentable inventions conceived by academic staff in the course of their employment, and in sponsored projects, to be disclosed on a regular basis to the Office of the Vice President (AAU, 2011). This gives the University the right to patent inventions developed as a result of public funds or other public financing being channelled through the University. At the same time this AAU Research Policy creates the potential for delays in the publication of research results until a patent application is filed. The Research Policy of Adama University, like that of AAU, requires academic researchers to disclose all inventions resulting from their research activities in the course of their employment, so that the University may claim patent ownership. The University consequently gains the right to grant exclusive licences to industry (Adama University, 2010).

As a consequence of policy emphasis on strengthening university–industry interaction, technology transfer units were established within the organisational framework of some of the country's institutes of higher education, including the aforementioned universities in 2011–12. The technology transfer units are tasked with encouraging links between the institutes and the economy. Within this scope, the technology transfer units are responsible for the management of IP (Edhardt and Scholz, 2009). However, it is my view that the units are not

1 The author served as the EIPO's Director of Intellectual Property Policy and Planning in 2004–06, Director of Trademarks in 2007–10, and Director of Intellectual Property Protection and Technology Transfer in 2010–11.

sufficiently resourced to staff offices with adequately trained IP-knowledgeable professionals who can determine how and when to use IP as a tool for technology transfer.

Perspectives of policy-makers, industry managers and academic researchers

Effective interaction between knowledge-generating universities and industry is dependent on the capacity of IP policy-makers to appreciate the various factors affecting the relationships between research, innovation and economic development. However, this study found, via the questionnaires completed by government officials, that Ethiopia lacks sufficient IP expertise in the government agencies responsible for science, technology, industry and trade. Most policy-makers, understandably, have a limited understanding of the complex and multifaceted role of IP in national innovation systems. Those government officials with IP knowledge tend to have technical knowledge of IP rights administration and only a limited understanding of the role of IP as a tool of regulatory and economic policy.

The government respondents surveyed for this study cited an absence of noticeable transfer of knowledge between university research and industry. They indicated that universities are not engaged in large-scale research activities and argued that the small amount of university research lacks relevance to industrial innovation. Further, respondents pointed to the inadequacy of public funds allocated for university research. The absence of research infrastructure and a shortage of qualified researchers were also identified as factors limiting the amount of research conducted in universities.

The government officials responsible for STI policy cited a lack of clarity on IP ownership of university research as a factor limiting university–industry collaboration. They argued that IP policies allowing university ownership of publicly funded research outputs are essential for strengthening collaborative ties between universities and industry. A critical look at the questionnaire data found that government respondents viewed the alignment of national IP laws (as well as national and institutional IP policies) with international standards as necessary to build national competitiveness. Their views seem clearly to be influenced by the proclaimed positive impact, in developed countries, of IP on national innovation systems. Furthermore, the government respondents implicitly favoured the replication of IP policies of developed countries as important in strengthening university–industry linkages in Ethiopia.

At the same time, information obtained from government respondents demonstrated that universities in Ethiopia are not significant players in terms of ownership of IP rights. Most of the local applications received by the EIPO are from SMEs. These SMEs are mainly requesting utility model certificates for their incremental inventions (which may not fulfil the criteria of patentability). Government respondents considered the low utilisation of IP by universities as an outcome of the low level of awareness about IP among the academic community.

Respondents from industry shared the views of government officials regarding the scale and orientation of university research. All industry respondents considered universities to be relatively unimportant information sources for Ethiopian industry's innovative activities. New products and processes introduced over the last few years by their enterprises have, the respondents said, been mainly developed internally, while others have been acquired from local technology centres or foreign research institutes. The inadequate supply of industrially applicable university knowledge and the weak alliance between university and industry actors were both noted as factors limiting the transfer of innovation to industrial enterprises.

Most industry respondents' knowledge of IP systems was limited to the technical requirements for IP protection. While the views expressed by industry respondents varied according to their level of understanding of the subject matter, some opinions were found to be shared among respondents. First, they agree on the need to view the issue of IP, in the context of current STI policy efforts in Ethiopia, as a tool for potentially facilitating the development of domestic technological capability – with industrial enterprises used as loci of innovation. Second, they agree on the need to eliminate barriers constraining industrial enterprises in their efforts to access university knowledge. Third, respondents said they believe that there is a need to devise mechanisms that will stimulate university researchers to engage in industrially applicable research. Finally, industry respondents cited the need for balance between measures stimulating industry-oriented university research and measures ensuring improved access to university knowledge by industry.

Similar to the other two stakeholder groups surveyed, the academic researcher respondents demonstrated a low level of awareness and understanding of IP. The limited IP expertise that can be found at universities is apparently concentrated in the schools of law, which offer semester-long courses in IP. I found the lack of IP awareness surprising, given that the respondents who participated in this study are directly involved in research or research management at their respective universities. (It was therefore presumed that they would have an interest in IP in the university context and a greater level of understanding of the topic.) The researchers' primary concern is apparently funding. The respondents stated that inadequate funds hinder their ability to carry out meaningful research that will be considered worthy of industrial application. Also cited as problems were: inadequate research facilities; a shortage of qualified research staff; a lack of information resources; a lack of institutional incentive mechanisms; and a lack of clear research strategy. Researcher respondents were also critical of the heavy teaching loads and administrative burdens faced by most university professors, limiting their involvement in research.

The university researcher respondents indicated that the direct commercialisation of research outputs is not an incentive that drives research. Furthermore, they indicated that IP considerations play a negligible role in the transfer of university research output to industry. However, respondents were of the view that as long as mandatory requirements on patenting research are not imposed on researchers, IP can be used as but one in an array of mechanisms for the transfer of university-generated knowledge to industry. Conferences, workshops, journal articles and personnel mobility – more than IP rights – were all identified as the prevailing mechanisms for the dissemination of university research results.

The researcher respondents indicated that the potential mutual benefits that can accrue from universities working closely with industry include networking and researcher access to industry partners, access to industry laboratories and equipment, and financial benefits from consulting activities. Respondents did not place importance on the generation of income through IP protection for university research. According to the responses, the focus should be on improving knowledge transfer between universities and industry, and the patenting and licensing of university knowledge should be viewed as an option for income generation only so long as it does not constrain the academic objectives of open science. They consider IP as but one mechanism for commercialisation of university research, not as a default option.

5. Conclusions and recommendations

Ethiopia's national STI Policy of 2012 envisions building of capabilities to enable rapid learning, adaptation and utilisation of effective foreign technologies. The realisation of this vision depends on the existence of institutional structures that support the process of technological learning and innovation. Publicly funded university research, which forms an important element of such structures, can play a central role in the process of technological catch-up called for by the Policy of 2012, especially catch-up through adaptation of foreign technologies to suit local conditions. Promoting innovation in industrial enterprises requires wide dissemination of technology research outputs generated by universities.

Universities in Ethiopia were found by this study to be playing only a limited role as research centres for the adaptation of foreign technologies and as sources of knowledge for problems affecting industry. They have weak research capacities, both in terms of infrastructure and qualified manpower. Furthermore, the research activity in these institutions (what little there is of it) was found to be not aligned with the needs of industry, and thus it has little relevance to the economy. University institutional IP policies that prioritise patenting of academic inventions have the potential to further limit the degree and rate of academic knowledge transfer, thus slowing the rate of innovation.

The capacity of firms to absorb externally generated knowledge is an equally important issue for facilitating university knowledge transfer. Ethiopian firms are significantly limited in their capacity to seek out and make effective use of externally generated knowledge, due to a lack of investment in building internal research and innovation capacity. Companies depend heavily on minor in-house innovative activities aimed at adapting technologies to specific local circumstances. Moreover, most firms in Ethiopia operate on a small scale and face resource constraints, limiting their capacity to acquire university knowledge through mechanisms that may require some financial investment.

In this context, university–industry interactions that require less financial commitment by enterprises will contribute more effectively to the enhancement of technological capacities at the company level. For this reason, making university research available in the public domain could be a more effective way – more effective than the use of IP rights – of improving access to research knowledge by industry. Moreover, the Ethiopian government's current emphasis, on IP protection for the transfer and commercialisation of publicly funded university research outputs, may have undesired consequences for the innovation process. Patenting of publicly funded university research should be considered the best option only when there is empirical evidence to suggest that other models of knowledge transfer would fail to ensure effective utilisation of the research outputs.

This study's review of Ethiopian government policies clearly found that the underlying IP focus is on building the technological capability of local enterprises, by facilitating their access to improved technologies emerging from university research. The views expressed by the different stakeholders surveyed also emphasised the importance of strengthening the interaction between universities and industry through the flow of university knowledge. But there was a clear view among many of the researcher and industry respondents that the desired strong university–industry nexus is more likely to be achieved through encouraging knowledge transfer via open science methods – such as publications, conference presentations and informal contacts – than via formal technology transfer methods based on IP rights. Therefore, Ethiopia's government actors and policy community need to look beyond the current IP focus and seek the optimum balance between different models of university–industry knowledge transfer (with IP-related models as but one part of the mix).

For a developing country like Ethiopia, technological catch-up requires emphasis on the use of information in the public domain, not emphasis on privatisation of knowledge. The primary focus, therefore, should be on enhancing the research capacities of universities to improve the supply of research outputs with potential applications in industry. Rather than, or at least in addition to, relying on the privatisation of university research through IP, the research environment in universities can be improved by upgrading the skill levels of the researchers, increasing the research budgets, implementing a salary structure that incentivises research, and giving better recognition to the intellectual contributions of academic researchers. Such measures would, in this author's opinion, enhance universities' research performance and ensure wider dissemination of university knowledge for the improvement of social and economic returns from academic research.

Bibliography

Primary sources

Statutes, proclamations, regulations

Ethiopian Intellectual Property Office Establishment Proclamation of 2003, Proc. No. 320/2003, Federal Democratic Republic of Ethiopia, Addis Ababa (FDRE, 2003).

Higher Education Proclamation of 2009, Proc. No. 650/2009, Federal Democratic Republic of Ethiopia, Addis Ababa (FDRE, 2009).

Proclamation Concerning Inventions, Minor Inventions and Industrial Designs (1995), Proc. No. 123/1995. Transitional Government of Ethiopia, Addis Ababa (TGE, 1995).

Policies, strategies

Adama University (2010), Strategic Plans, Ethical Codes, Legal Rules and Guidelines for Adama University Research and Postgraduate Studies, Version 1.1, Office of VP for Research and Postgraduate Studies, Adama.

Addis Ababa University (AAU) (2011), Research Policy, presented for discussion by academic officers, available at: www.aau.edu.et/index.php/component/k2/item/2042-aau-academic-officers-discuss-gtp-polices (accessed 15 April 2012).

Capacity Building Strategy and Programmes (2002), Federal Democratic Republic of Ethiopia, Addis Ababa, (Amharic document) (FDRE, 2002a).

Education and Training Policy (1994), Transitional Government of Ethiopia, Addis Ababa (TGE, 1994).

Education Sector Development Programme III: Programme Action Plan (2005), Ministry of Education, Addis Ababa (MOE, 2005).

Education Sector Development Programme IV: Programme Action Plan (2010), Ministry of Education, Addis Ababa (MOE, 2010).

Green Paper on Science, Technology and Innovation Policy: Building Competitiveness through Innovation, Ministry of Science and Technology, Addis Ababa (MOST, 2010).

Growth and Transformation Plan (2010/11–2014/15): Vol. I: Main Text, Ministry of Finance and Economic Development, Addis Ababa (MoFED, 2010).

Industrial Development Strategy (2002), Federal Democratic Republic of Ethiopia, Addis Ababa (Amharic document), (FDRE, 2002b).

Intellectual Property Rights in National Innovation Systems: Background Paper prepared for the Science, Technology and Innovation (STI) Policy of Ethiopia, Ministry of Science and Technology, Addis Ababa (MOST, 2009).

Science and Technology Policy (1993), Transitional Government of Ethiopia, Addis Ababa (TGE, 1993).

Science, Technology and Innovation (STI) Policy of Ethiopia (2012), Federal Democratic Republic of Ethiopia, Addis Ababa (FDRE, 2012).

Secondary sources

Anthony, S., Sampat, B.N., Rai, A.K., Cook-Deegan, R. and Reichman, J.H. (2008), "Is Bayh-Dole Good for Developing Countries? Lessons from the US Experience", *PLoS Biol*, Vol. 6 No. 10, e262.doi:10.1371/journal.pbio.0060262, available at: www.plosbiology.org (accessed 15 April 2012).

Belete, W. (2010), "Current experiences and innovation support needs of industry and business: the case of Ethiopia", paper presented at WIPO Regional Conference on Technology and Innovation Support, Addis Ababa.

Boettiger, S. and Bennet, A. (2006), "The Bayh-Dole Act: implications for developing countries", *IDEA*, Vol. 46 No. 2, pp. 261–81.

Colyvas, J., Crow, M., Gelijns, A., Mazzoleni, R., Nelson, R., Rosenberg, N. and Sampat, B. (2002), "How do university inventions get into practice?" *Management Science*, Vol. 48, pp. 61–72.

Commission on Intellectual Property Rights (CIPR) (2002), *Integrating Intellectual Property Rights and Development Policy: Report of the Commission on Intellectual Property Rights*, London.

Crespi, G., Geuna, A. and Verspagen, B. (2006), *University IPRs and Knowledge Transfer: Is the IPR ownership model more efficient?* Mimeo SPRU, University of Sussex and Ecis, Eindhoven University of Technology, Brighton, UK, and Eindhoven, Netherlands.

David, P.A. (2003), "Can 'open science' be protected from the evolving regime of IPR protections?" *Journal of Institutional and Theoretical Economics,* Vol. 160 No. 1, pp. 9–34.

Davis, L., Larsen, M.T. and Lotz, P. (2011), "Scientists' perspectives concerning the effects of university patenting on the conduct of academic research in the Life Sciences", *The Journal of Technology Transfer*, Vol. 36 No. 1, pp.14–37.

Dosi, G., Llerena, P. and Labini, M.S. (2006), "The relationships between science, technologies and their industrial exploitation", *Research Policy*, Vol. 35 No. 10, pp. 1450–64.

Edhardt, U. and Scholz, G. (2009), *Framework and Change Management Concept for Setting up Institutes of Technology in Ethiopia,* Engineering Capacity Building Program, Addis Ababa, available at: www.ecbp.biz/fileadmin/editors/university/articles_for_download/Institutes%20of%20Technology%20Framework.pdf (accessed 20 April 2013).

Ethiopian Intellectual Property Office (EIPO) (2007), *Institutional and Policy Constraints to the Effective Use of the Intellectual Property System in Ethiopia: Assessment Report,* Addis Ababa.

Fabrizio, K. (2006), "The use of university research in firm innovation", in Chesbrough, H., Vanhaverbeke, W. and West, J. (Eds), *Open Innovation: Researching a New Paradigm,* Oxford University Press, Oxford, pp. 134–60.

Foley, M.L. and Lardner, L. (2011), "China Bayh-Dole Act: a framework fundamental to achieving the economic potential of China's National Patent Development Strategy (2011–2020)" , *China Quarterly Newsletter, Eye on China*, Spring 2011 edition of *Legal News*, available at: www.foley.com/intelligence/detail.aspx?int (accessed 20 April 2013).

Gebreyesus, Tarekegn (1998), "Past university–industry cooperation", paper presented at a workshop on University–Industry Cooperation, Addis Ababa.

Graff, G.D. (2007) "Echoes of Bayh-Dole? A survey of IP and technology transfer policies in emerging and developing economies", in Krattiger, A. (Ed.), *IP Handbook of Best Practices*, Chapter 3.3, available at www.iphandbook.org/handbook/ch03/p03/ (accessed 20 April 2013).

Kitaw, D. (2008), "Higher education – industry resource integration center – towards solving existing industrial problems", in Etzkowitz, H. and Roest, M. (Eds), *Transforming University-Industry-Government Relations in Ethiopia*: Proceedings of the Ethiopia Triple Helix Conference, Addis Ababa, pp. 86–101.

Koyama, M.M. (2010), "The privatisation of publicly funded research in South Africa: lessons from the US Bayh-Dole Experience", ACB Briefing Paper No.14, available at: www.acbio.org.za (accessed 20 April 2013).

Lemma, B., Yigeremu, M., Tefera, M., Alemu, G. and Mersha, G. (2008), *Business Process Re-Engineering (BPR): Situation Analysis on Research in Addis Ababa University*, Report Submitted to Vice President for Graduate Studies and Research, Addis Ababa University.

Liebeskind, J. (2001), "Risky business: universities and intellectual property", *Academe*, Vol. 87 No. 5, pp. 49–53.

Lundvall, B.-A. (2008), "Toward developmental university systems", paper presented at IKE-Workshop on Institutions, Innovation and Development, Aalborg University, Denmark.

Mengistie, G. (2006), *Intellectual Property Assessment in Ethiopia*, Ethiopian Intellectual Property Office (EIPO), Addis Ababa.

Ministry of Education (MOE) (2011), "List of public universities in Ethiopia", available at: www.moe.gov.et (accessed 20 April 2013).

Montobbio, F. (2009), "Intellectual property rights and knowledge transfer from public research to industry in the US and Europe: which lessons for innovation systems in developing countries", in *The Economics of Intellectual Property: Suggestions for Further Research in Developing Countries and Countries with Economies in Transition*, World Intellectual Property Organisation (WIPO), Geneva, pp. 180–209.

Mowery, D., Nelson, R.R., Sampat, B.N. and Ziedonis, A.A. (2001), "The growth of patenting and licensing by US universities: an assessment of the effects of the Bayh-Dole Act of 1980", *Research Policy*, Vol. 30, pp. 99–119.

Mowery, D.C. and Sampat. B.N. (2005), "Universities in national innovation systems", in Fagerberg, J., Mowery, D.C. and Nelson, R.R. (Eds), *Oxford Handbook of Innovation*, Oxford University Press, Oxford.

Poglajen, M. (2012), *University-Industry Knowledge and Technology Transfer: Isomorphism of University Technology Transfer Organizational Units*, Working Paper, University of Ljubljana, Slovenia.

Sampat, B.N. (2006), "Patenting and US academic research in the 20th Century: the world before and after Bayh-Dole", *Research Policy*, Vol. 35, pp. 772–89.

Sampat, B.N. (2009), *The Bayh-Dole Model in Developing Countries: Reflections on the Indian Bill on Publicly Funded Intellectual Property*, UN Conference on Trade and Development (UNCTAD)-International Centre for Trade and Sustainable Development (ICTSD) Project on IPRs and Sustainable Development, Policy Brief No. 5, Geneva.

Thursby, J. and Thursby, M. (2007), "Knowledge creation and diffusion of public science with intellectual property rights", Working Paper, Georgia Tech, available at: www.en.cams.bwl.uni-muenchen.de/files/thursby_ipchap.pdf (accessed 20 April 2013).

UN Conference on Trade and Development (UNCTAD) (2002), *Investment and Innovation Policy Review: Ethiopia*, UNCTAD/ITE/IPC/ Misc. 4, Geneva.

Vartak, R. and Saurastri, M. (2009), "The Indian version of the Bayh-Dole Act", *Intellectual Asset Management*, March/April, available at: www.iam-magazine.com (accessed 20 April 2013).

Verspagen, B. (2006), "University research, intellectual property rights and European innovation systems", *Journal of Economic Surveys*, Vol. 20 No. 4, pp. 607–32.

Walsh, J.P., Baba, Y., Goto, A. and Yasaki, Y. (2008), "Promoting university–industry linkages in Japan: faculty responses to a changing policy environment", *Prometheus*, Vol. 26 No. 1, pp. 39–54.

Wasmuth, N. and Nebelung, M. (2006), "Bridging universities and industry in Ethiopia", paper presented at the Conference on Launching a Program to Transforming [sic] University-Industry-Government Relations in Ethiopia, Engineering Capacity Building Program (ECBP), Addis Ababa.

Chapter 15

Perspectives on Intellectual Property from Botswana's Publicly Funded Researchers

Njoku Ola Ama

Abstract

This chapter outlines the findings from a case study of perceptions of intellectual property (IP) issues among researchers conducting publicly funded research in Botswana. The country's emergent legal and policy framework on IP and on science, technology and innovation (STI) shows that Botswana is actively seeking to position itself to take advantage of IP commercialisation opportunities. However, the data from this study's survey of publicly funded researchers reveal low levels of awareness among the researchers of both national and institutional IP frameworks governing the outputs of their research – and, at the same time, an apparent desire among the researchers for there to be a combined emphasis on commercialisation of knowledge while adhering to the principles of "open science". The study also found strong evidence of researcher desire for improved research climates at their institutions, in order to foster the high-quality research necessary to feed into open science dissemination and sharing, as well as commercialisation synergies with the country's parastatal and industrial entities.

1. Research problem

Owners of intellectual property (IP) will normally make works or inventions available to the public in exchange for exclusive rights granted for a limited time. Exclusive rights enable the IP owner to generate economic returns from protected works or inventions. Formal IP rights may take the form of a patent, industrial design, copyright or trademark. In many countries belonging to the Organisation for Economic Co-operation and Development (OECD), universities and public research organisations (PROs) that receive significant public research funding have become increasingly alerted to the value of IP. This is, to some extent, a result of a view taken by governments that placing the outputs of publicly funded research in the public domain is not sufficient to generate adequate social and economic benefits from research (Salter and Martin, 2001).

IP regulatory environments influence both the type of research that is publicly funded and the value that accrues from such research. IP is, therefore, part of a nation's public policy relating to the promotion of technological innovation in a knowledge-based economy. According to Huang (2006), a prevalent view of the value of a strong IP system, as typified by the US Patent and Trademark Office (USPTO), is that IP protection "contributes to a strong global economy, encourages investment in innovation and fosters entrepreneurial spirit" (Huang, 2006, p.12).

The question this research study sought to answer was: *How do Botswana's IP laws, and the policies of institutions doing publicly funded research, potentially impact on dissemination, utilisation and commercialisation of research output?* The question was premised on the assumption that benefits accruing to a country from publicly funded research can be influenced by the nation's IP regime, and the hypothesis that policies encouraging openness in the dissemination of research outputs may encourage more active participation in research and innovation.

Context

University research has historically formed the foundation for many of the most significant technological and industrial advancements (Holly, 2010). However many ideas and discoveries arising from university research are never fully developed. Social prosperity and economic growth are stimulated when academic discoveries are adopted and transformed by entrepreneurs and established corporations, but many great ideas springing from publicly funded research do not make the step from the laboratory to the marketplace. Several explanations have been offered for this problem, including: a lack of funding to scale and commercialise ideas; a lack of the business expertise required to understand the steps towards commercialisation; a scarcity of the human capital required to build start-up companies when needed; and inadequate mentoring and educational support for new entrepreneurs (Holly, 2010).

It has been persuasively argued that the innovation performance of a country largely depends on how its universities, PROs and parastatal and industrial enterprises relate to each other in the creation and use of knowledge, i.e. that the level and type of interaction between these major actors in a national innovation system determines the rate and direction of technological progress (OECD, 1997). The smooth operation of a national innovation system depends on, among other factors, wide dissemination of knowledge generated by universities and PROs in a way that maximises its developmental impact. The ability of parastals and industry to access knowledge from universities and PROs is thus crucial. The quality of public research infrastructure, and the infrastructure's links to industry, are among the most important national assets for supporting innovation.

But the relationship between IP and access to research results and innovation performance is, at the same time, contentious. One position posits that IP ownership by public institutions, and exclusive licensing of technologies by these institutions to the private sector, will increase the rate of commercial application of knowledge (GIPC, n.d.). This view is typified by the provisions of the US Bayh-Dole Act of 1980. The opposing view argues that the interests of technology transfer are best served by the widest possible dissemination of knowledge, through what has come to be known as "open science" (Sampat, 2002). The impact of IP on the growth, diffusion and use of scientific knowledge is thus a central issue for economists, law-makers, policy-makers, technology scholars, sociologists and decision-makers in public and private institutions (Campbell *et al.*, 2002; David, 2001; Heller and Eisenberg, 1998; Straus *et al.*, 2004; Walsh *et al.*, 2002). Heller and Eisenberg (1998) have argued that IP rights can have an "anti-commons" effect, deterring investment and stifling innovation rather than spurring it. Heller and Eisenberg, along with others, view IP systems as a potential impediment to the free flow of scientific knowledge and the ability of researchers to build cumulatively on each other's discoveries, particularly in the field of biomedical research (Heller and Eisenberg, 1998; David, 2004; Huang, 2006; Murray and Stern, 2007). This approach aligns with Weitzman's (1974) work on a "new economics" of scientific research, which itself built on Merton's (1942) "science first" position, which advocated for norms of full disclosure for knowledge dissemination. Dasgupta and David (1994) agree with Merton, arguing that full-disclosure systems reward scientific endeavour, through community recognition of those with the greatest knowledge contribution over a sustained period of time. Career incentives such as tenure also encourage open disclosure through, *inter alia*, publications (which help ensure that research outputs remain as public goods, readily accessible for application).

The US Bayh-Dole Act enabled universities to own and manage the IP arising from federally sponsored research, with royalty revenues shared between universities and inventors. From an economic development perspective, it has been argued by some that Bayh-Dole was a boon to local economies and to society at large, as new technologies were introduced to market (Holly, 2010). However, Sampat (2002) argues that Bayh-Dole was promulgated based on minimal evidence that the *status quo ante* resulted in low rates of commercialisation of university inventions. The Act neglected the economic importance of the public aspects of university research and ignored the possibility of potential negative effects of increased patenting and licensing on online-based science and other emergent channels of technology and knowledge transfer (Sampat, 2002). Mazzoleni and Nelson (2007, as cited in Sampat, 2009), argue that one of the main ways in which publicly funded research contributes to domestic innovation and productivity is by making knowledge and technology readily accessible to the public. The underlying logic of this view is that the outputs of academic research disseminated via open science contribute not only to industry, but also to future academic research (Salter and Martin, 2001). Put another way, the argument is that greater attention needs to be paid to the *socialisation* of knowledge for the benefit of society – as opposed to a narrower focus on generating primarily *commercial* value from knowledge.

In recent years, maximising the societal benefits of publicly funded research has become a subject of debate in some African countries, particularly those which have introduced, or are planning to introduce, legislation in this area. South Africa (see Chapter 13 in this volume) passed a law in 2008 dealing with IP from publicly funded research (IPR-PFRD Act of 2008). Other African countries are currently contemplating similar legislation. In Ethiopia (see Chapter 14 in this volume), the STI Policy of 2012 has identified building capacity to manage IP, at both national and institutional levels, as one of its strategies. However, there is a view that African countries, in developing policy and legislation related to IP from public research, must be careful not to blindly mimic the approach of the American Bayh-Dole Act – an Act adopted in national and global contexts different from the ones faced by African countries at present (Youngleson, 2012).

2. The research

The study reported in this chapter sought to probe the potential impact of Botswana's IP legal and policy environment on dissemination, utilisation and commercialisation of knowledge generated through publicly funded research. The study was exploratory in nature. Through examination of Botswana's legal and policy frameworks relevant to IP from public research, and a survey of researchers' perceptions of the IP situation at their institutions, the study sought to discover how Botswana's IP environment was interacting with publicly funded research. The primary contribution of this study is its focus not on abstract principles or secondary literature, but on empirical data regarding the understandings and beliefs of Botswana's researchers.

The core of the study was a structured survey questionnaire administered to researchers across three publicly funded research settings: (1) universities;

(2) PROs and government/NGO entities; and (3) parastatal/industry/consultancy institutions. To decide on the sample size for the survey of researchers, the Creative Research Systems (2010) *Sample Size Calculator* was used to determine an appropriate sample size to provide 95% confidence, and a 5% margin of error, so that responses from the sample would reflect those of the target population. For a population of 2,000 (the approximate size of the target community of Botswana's public researchers), the statistically desirable sample size was calculated at 323. However, because of budget constraints, the sample size for this study could only be 194 respondents (60% of the optimal sample size). The population was organised into the three aforementioned strata: universities, PROs and parastatal/industry institutions. The statistically determined sample size was allocated to each stratum using probability proportional to size (PPS) measures, which provided a more representative sample of the population than simple random sampling would have. A purposive sampling method was used to identify the individual researchers to be surveyed. This method enabled identification of researchers with the desired characteristics (e.g. those with a record of innovation, those belonging to particular disciplines central to innovative research, those whose research was publicly funded). Another method of non-random sampling – the snowball technique, relying on referrals from initial subjects to additional subjects – was also employed.

The questionnaire administered to each of the respondent researchers was completed in writing either (1) by research assistants during structured interviews adhering to the questionnaire or (2) by the respondents themselves. The questionnaire sought information from the researchers on:

- the nature and type of research they were involved in;
- their general knowledge and utilisation of IP;
- the IP-related activities of their institutions; and
- their views on the potential impact of IP on the publicly funded research environment.

The questionnaire was reviewed and ratified by the University of Botswana's Institutional Review Board (IRB) and then approved by the Ministry of Trade and Industry's Ethical Committee. In addition, permission to conduct the study was obtained from the heads of the institutions where the respondents were based. The trained research assistants informed respondents about the purpose of the study before the questionnaire was administered. Of the 194 respondents targeted, 187 questionnaires were completed and returned, providing a response rate of 96.4%. The questionnaire data were supplemented by key informant interviews with select policy-makers (Members of Parliament, ministry staff, councillors, village development committee members) and heads of institutions, directors of research and development, heads of IP units and some members of the judiciary.

Before describing and analysing the findings from the study (in Sections 4 to 6), it is first necessary (in the next section) to provide an understanding of the IP and science, technology and innovation (STI) legal and policy environment in Botswana.

3. Botswana IP and STI environment

IP rights are essentially territorial: they generally operate within borders. A number of international instruments attempt to establish uniform standards and overcome the difficulties that arise from this territorial nature of IP rights. To that end, Botswana is a contracting member of a number of international instruments.

Global instruments:

- Agreement on Trade-Related Aspects of Intellectual Property Rights (TRIPS);
- Berne Convention for the Protection of Literary and Artistic Works;
- Convention Establishing the World Intellectual Property Organisation (WIPO);
- Hague Agreement Concerning the International Deposit of Industrial Designs;
- Paris Convention for the Protection of Industrial Property;
- Patent Cooperation Treaty (PCT);
- Protocol Relating to the Madrid Agreement Concerning the International Registration of Marks;
- WIPO Copyright Treaty (WCT); and
- WIPO Performances and Phonograms Treaty (WPPT).

African instruments:

- Banjul Protocol on Marks within the Framework of ARIPO;
- Harare Protocol on Patents and Industrial Designs within the Framework ARIPO;
- Lusaka Agreement on the Creation of the African Regional Intellectual Property Organisation (ARIPO); and
- Swakopmund Protocol on the Protection of Traditional Knowledge and Expressions of Folklore within the Framework of ARIPO.

Botswana has signed treaties that fall into two general categories: those which aim to achieve harmonisation through the provision of minimum standards of protection (such as the Paris Convention and TRIPS) and those which aim to achieve international registration to obviate the need for an applicant to file applications in every country where protection is sought (such as the ARIPO Harare Protocol and the Madrid Protocol). International treaties have influenced Botswana's statutory IP protection framework. For example, Botswana's Industrial Property Act (IPA), which governs patents and trademarks, provides internationally recognised standards of protection for both foreign and domestic IP.

IP law in Botswana is regulated by a combination of common law and statute. Although applicable IP law is mainly statutory, there are many aspects of it – such as actions for unlawful competition – which are governed by the common law. For instance, under the common law, an Aquilian action *(actio legis Aquiliae)* can be instituted for the recovery of compensation for patrimonial loss caused by the unlawful conduct of another through acts such as breach of confidence, passing off and injurious falsehood. Botswana has grappled with the challenges of enacting laws that reflect the country's hybrid Roman-Dutch and common law legal heritage. In modernising its laws to keep pace with current developments to attract and retain foreign investors, Botswana has also incorporated many of the principles from international treaties into its domestic IP laws. Some of these domestic laws are:

- Copyright and Neighbouring Rights Act 8 of 2000;
- Industrial Property Act 14 of 1996 (replaced in 2010);
- Industrial Property Regulations, Statutory Instrument 78 of 1997; and
- Industrial Property Act 8 of 2010.

Prior to 1996, protection of industrial property rights (patents, trademarks and industrial designs) in Botswana was primarily via extension of protections granted in the UK and South Africa.[1] Botswana enacted the IPA, its first comprehensive legislation on the matter, in 1996. The IPA was restructured in the new IPA of 2010, and amendments came into force on 31 August 2012, by virtue of Statutory Instrument 69 of 2012. Unlike its previous incarnation, the 2010 IPA incorporates separate registers for traditional knowledge (TK) and geographical indications (GIs). Broadly, the IPA deals with the protection of patents, trademarks, utility models and industrial designs. The IPA also aims to encourage the diversification of industry, to expand the manufacturing base, to encourage small, micro- and medium-sized enterprises (SMMEs) and to improve overall economic growth. The 2010 IPA is conspicuously silent about IP emanating from publicly funded research and development, including its dissemination, utilisation, management and commercialisation. A new Act or amendments would be required to

1 For further discussion of this background, see Department of Research, Science and Technology (DRST) (2006, pp. 7–8).

streamline the issues of management of IP arising from publicly funded research in the context of Botswana's economic development.

IP and the University of Botswana (UB)

The IPA does, however, establish an IP framework for Botswana's higher education institutions and industry, which is indirectly relevant to publicly funded research. In response to the IPA, the University of Botswana (UB) has developed an IP policy designed to support publicly funded research (UB, 2004). The policy indicates that the University will own all original IP generated by its academic community. This includes official documents, experimental databases, computer programmes and software. Possible exceptions include: copyright held by staff and students, IP arising from work conducted outside of the University, work done by students (unless the University has paid for the work) and where there is a written agreement to the contrary between the inventor and the University (UB, 2004).

Subsection 10(4) of the 2010 IPA states that, in the absence of any agreement, IP of an employee belongs to the employer. The IPA recognises that when the owner of the IP is protected by a patent, he/she can license the IP to a business. The business then pays the owner a share of profits from the use of the licences. UB's IP policy recommends that the split of any profits from IP shall be 50% for the inventor and 50% for the University (after the University recovers costs) (UB, 2004). The UB Office of Research and Development (ORD) manages IP at the university. There are several units within ORD, including a knowledge transfer office responsible for the training of staff on commercialisation, ethics and how to source research funds internationally. ORD also has a project office for the management of research funds. In addition, the UB Research Commercialisation Unit works with the UB research community in the following areas:

- creating awareness and training on research commercialisation and its potential contributions to the University's mandate;
- fostering a culture of innovation for the UB research community as part and parcel of the broad research agenda of the University;
- availing relevant information and materials to researchers on technology transfer and the commercialisation process at UB in order to support the commercialisation of research at UB;
- assisting in identifying and protecting the IP generated by UB researchers through a variety of approaches, including patenting, copyrights and trademarks;
- performing due diligence studies and market studies to ascertain the commercialisation potential and potential markets for UB inventions and innovations;

- promoting and marketing opportunities for technology transfer to potential industry partners;
- negotiating licences with industry partners and other stakeholders for inventions which arise from UB research; and
- creating strong relationships between the UB research community and business, government, NGOs and other relevant stakeholders which can facilitate the translation of knowledge into products, policies and services (UB, 2008).

Ministerial powers and parastatal institutions

The Department of the Registrar of Companies, Business Names, Patents, Trademarks, Utility Models, and Industrial Designs, which operates within the Ministry of Trade and Industry, is responsible for implementing the IPA. The Department houses a National Enquiry Point (NEP) for IP matters. This NEP is a Joint Integrated Technical Assistance Programme (JITAP) project supported by the World Trade Organisation (WTO), the UN Conference on Trade and Development (UNCTAD) and the International Trade Centre (ITC). JITAP initiatives aim to help African member countries benefit from multilateral trade. The NEP is open to government officials, business representatives, university professors and students. Interested parties can obtain trade-related information resources with a specific emphasis on the WTO TRIPS Agreement (Government of Botswana, n.d.).

Botswana's Minister of Trade and Industry is empowered by the IPA to exploit a patented invention under compulsory licence (without authorisation of the owner) in the interests of nutrition, national security or health, or for the development of a vital sector of the national economy. Further, where the court determines that exploitation of a patent by the owner or licensee is anti-competitive, the Minister may infringe upon the owner's/licensee's patent rights in order to alleviate the anti-competitive situation (IPA of 2010; Benett and Chilume, 2007).

Other ministries also play a role in fields related to IP, in particular science and technology. In 1979, the Ministry of Infrastructure, Science and Technology (MIST) implemented, as a parastatal, the Botswana Technology Centre (BOTEC). BOTEC is part of a deliberate federal effort in Botswana to integrate traditional knowledge (TK) within international structures of IP. It aims to bridge publicly funded research institutions – such as UB, the Botswana Export Development and Investment Authority and the Botswana Innovation Hub (BIH) – with TK. BOTEC is viewed by international organisations such as WIPO as a successful model for other developing African countries to follow. BOTEC also played a critical role in developing the TK aspects of the new IPA of 2010. Today, BOTEC's mandate is tied to Botswana's Vision 2016 programme.

MIST also created the Rural Industrial Promotion Company Botswana (RIPCO (B)) and the BIH as parastatal organisations. Headquartered in Gaborone, RIPCO (est. 1974) is a research and development organisation that follows Botswana's broader objectives of improving the living standards of its citizens by developing and disseminating agriculture-related technology. The BIH (est. 2012), announced in a keynote address by the Vice President of Botswana in November 2012, was established to accelerate the country's Vision 2016 goals. Its aim is to promote "research, technology and innovation based entrepreneurship" through the interaction between academics, entrepreneurs and government (the so-called "triple helix" of research and development) (Government of Botswana, 2012). The BIH is a product of the Revised National Policy on Research, Science, Technology and Innovation (MIST, 2011). It was also developed in response to the World Economic Forum's (WEF's) *Global Competitiveness Report* (*2011–2012*), which highlighted Botswana's need to attract foreign direct investment (FDI). General statistical data also highlight Botswana's need for improvement in this area (WEF, 2012).

According to the Science and Technology Capacity Index (STCI), Botswana is a scientifically developing country. The STCI measures the ability to absorb and retain specialised knowledge and research, to meet needs and to develop efficient products and processes. Botswana also falls within the category of countries that are below the international mean for most components of science and technology indices. The gross expenditure on research and development (GERD) in Botswana is low, at 0.52% of GDP (World Bank, 2012), when compared to the recommended Southern African Development Community (SADC) and African Union (AU) investment targets of at least 1% of GDP. However, Botswana has a high proportion of PhD and MSc employees (at least 48% of research and development staff – higher than South Africa's 34%) (CSIR, 2005). The government of Botswana aims to invest at least 2% of GDP to develop scientific and technological research, consistent with SADC targets (MIST, 2011). Botswana's Vision 2016 objective for its science and technology environment aims to foster: (a) an educated, informed nation; (b) a prosperous, productive and innovative nation; and (c) a compassionate, just and caring nation. MIST's parastatal organisations and Botswana's leading research organisations have modelled their IP objectives around Botswana's Vision 2016 (Government of Botswana, 1997).

IP expertise and activity in Botswana

The total number of patents registered in Botswana is unknown, as there are inconsistencies in Botswana's patent registration system, and the list of registered patents is not available in electronic format. The Registrar of Companies estimates that between 15 and 30 patents are registered annually, and the majority of the patents are registered by foreign entities. Botswana has few legal firms with qualified IP professionals (e.g. attorneys, agents and licensing professionals) who are in a position to assist during the patent life cycle, i.e. the application process, the negotiation of a licence over patented technology and the settlement of disputes over IP rights. The only readily available IP case found in Botswana was *Botswana Football Association and Another v. Kgamane* [1998 BLR 153 (CA)]. This suggests minimal legal activity in Botswana related to IP.

However, since the 1970s, Botswana has taken progressive steps to improve its general IP framework. Furthermore, the country has attempted to develop the necessary institutional infrastructure to encourage and support its objectives. Botswana's Vision 2016 objectives and the broad integration between MIST, its parastatals and academic institutions such as UB are certainly steps in the right direction. Botswana is clearly cognisant that it needs to continue to improve its publicly funded research environment in order to stimulate research and to attract, support and retain academic talent. The data collected and analysed in the sections that follow provide some insights into researchers' perspectives on the existing public research environment.

4. Research findings Part 1: awareness, knowledge, institutional frameworks

Respondent demographics

Of the 187 researchers who participated in the study, 61.5% were married, 28.3% were single (never married) and 7% were divorced. The highest educational qualification of respondents was as follows: 58.3% PhD, 34.8% Master's degree, 5.9% Bachelor's degree. The age of the respondents varied as follows: 35.8% were between 40 and 49; 17.1% between 30 and 39; 16% between 50 and 59, and 22% did not state their age. Of the respondents, 67.4% were male and 32.6% female (see Figure 15.1).

Awareness of use of IP to protect research output

The study found that 84.5% of the researchers were aware that the intellectual output of their research activities (their IP) could be protected from being used, sold and copied by other individuals or organisations without their permission. Meanwhile, 11.8% were unaware of this fact, and 3.7% did not indicate. Researchers were aware of various methods of protecting IP: copyright (89.2%), trademark (77.8%), patent (75.9%), industrial designs (56.3%), geographical indications (50.6%) and trade secrets (49.4%) (Figure 15.2).

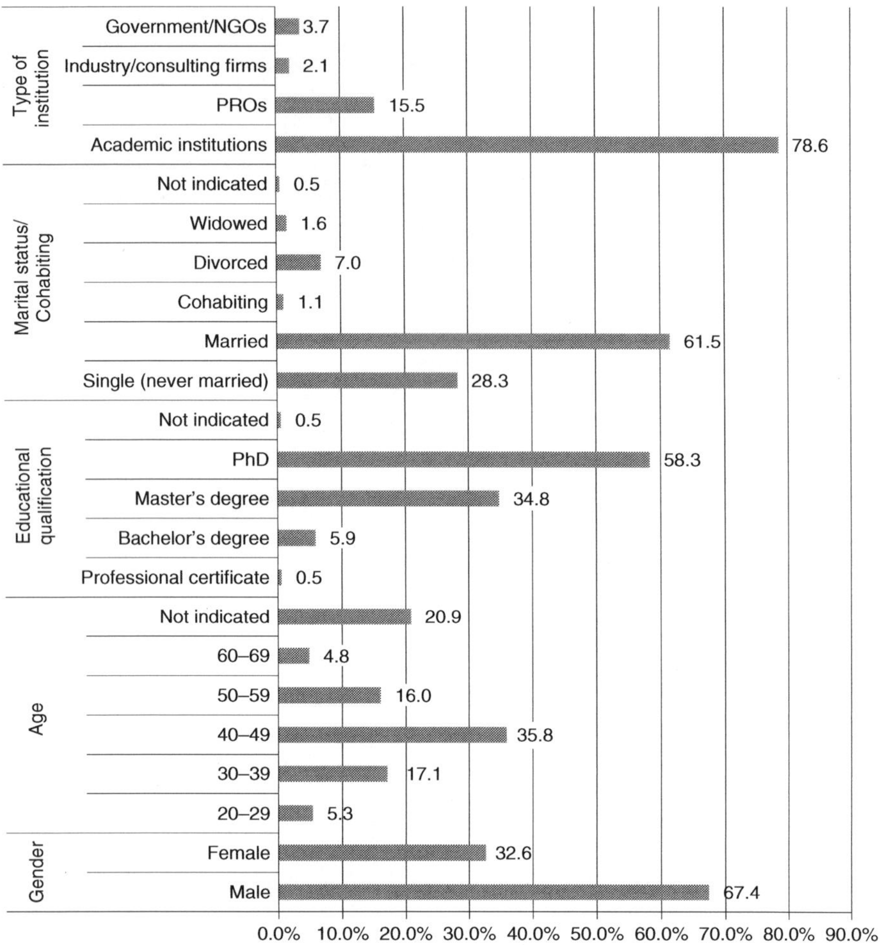

Figure 15.1: Demographic characteristics of respondents

When asked whether they knew how to use the various mechanisms to protect their IP, 81.5% of the researchers said they had knowledge of the use of copyrights, 65.5% said they knew how to use patents, 66.4% trademarks, 48.7% industrial designs, 42% geographical indications and 47.9% trade secrets (Figure 15.3).

On whether they had used IP protection methods, 62% stated they had used copyrights, 28% patents, 30% trademarks, 28% geographical indications, 24% trade secrets and 16% industrial designs (Figure 15.4).

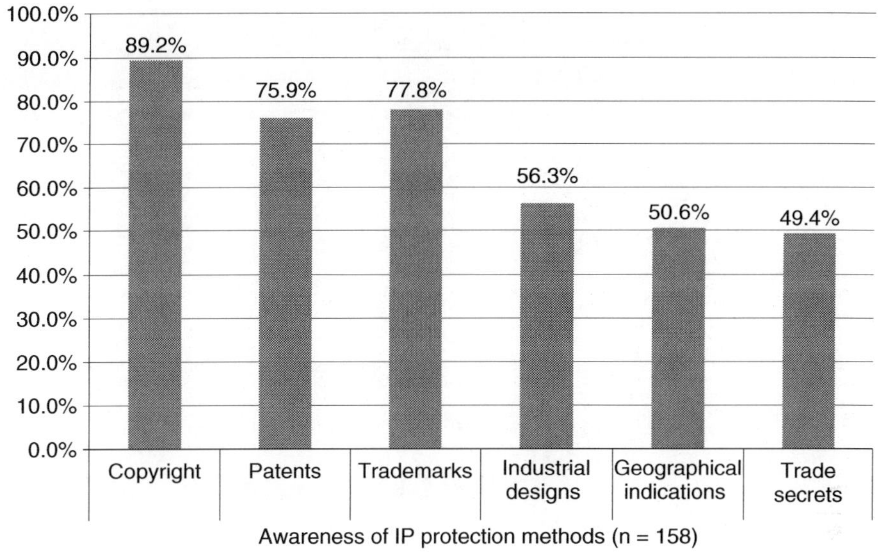

Figure 15.2: Awareness of IP as mechanism to protect research output

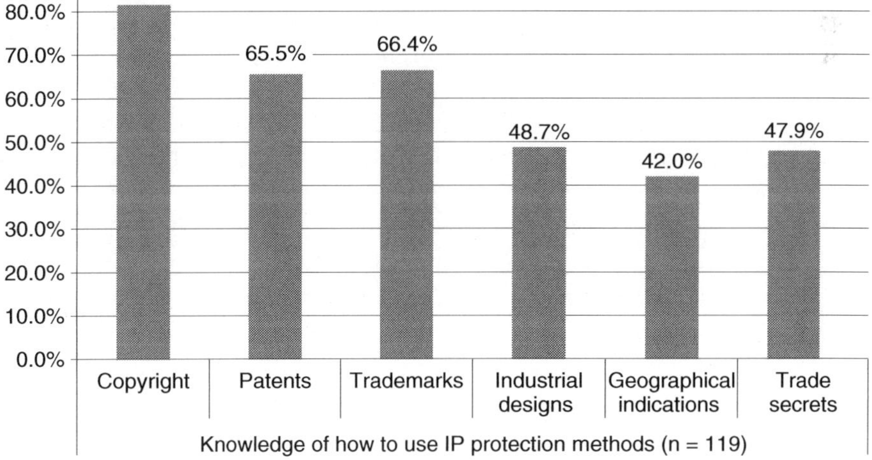

Figure 15.3: Knowledge of how to use IP

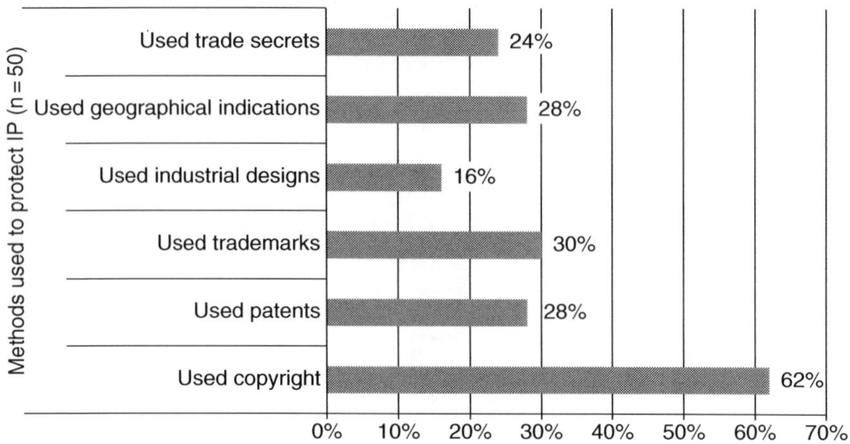

Figure 15.4: Use of IP

Framework for IP at institutions

The respondents were asked to indicate their knowledge of the existence or nonexistence of a policy and regulatory framework governing IP in their institutions on a three-point scale (1 = yes, 2 = no and 3 = don't know) and to answer five questions on the content and nature of the framework. The researchers' responses (see Table 15.1) showed a lack of knowledge of the prevailing IP conditions in their various institutions. While 54.2% of the researchers indicated that their institutions had IP policies, the majority of the researchers did not know whether the policy was environmentally friendly (53.2%), how ownership of the IP was managed (53.8%), or whether the policy encouraged openness in sharing information from publicly funded research (53.6%). In addition, 51% did not know whether the policy articulated the management of the IP.

The researchers were asked how the IP policies of their institutions impacted: (1) their knowledge dissemination; (2) their knowledge utilisation; and (3) their commercialisation of research output. The results elicited by these questions are shown in Tables 15.2 to 15.4. On knowledge dissemination (Table 15.2), between 52% and 58% did not know whether their institution's IP policy had provision to track the research projects that were publicly funded (57.7%); provision to review IP and associated commercial activities and outcomes (57%); or provision to clarify staff responsibilities in relation to IP (e.g. prevention of premature public disclosure of research results prior to obtaining IP [54.1%]). However, 42.3% of the researchers knew that the IP policies of their institutions provided guidance

Table 15.1: Knowledge of institutional IP policies

Institutional IP policies	Yes		No		Don't know	
	Number	%	Number	%	Number	%
Does your institution have an IP policy?	98	54.2	20	11.0	63	34.8
Is the policy environmentally friendly?	57	36.0	17	10.8	84	53.2
Does the policy encourage innovation?	60	38.5	22	14.1	74	47.4
Does the policy spell out the management of IP?	62	39.4	15	9.6	80	51.0
Does the policy clarify ownership of IP?	60	38.5	12	7.7	84	53.8
Does the policy encourage openness in sharing information from publicly funded research?	56	36.6	15	9.8	82	53.6

in relation to potential conflicts of interest concerning ownership, management, protection and exploitation of IP, and 41.7% knew of provisions recognising the IP rights and needs of stakeholders involved in research.

On how institutional IP policies impact knowledge utilisation, 56.3% of researchers understood that their institution's policy encouraged openness in sharing information from research, while 48.3% knew that it required researchers using public funds to publish outputs through open sources, conferences, workshops or through patenting. The majority of the researchers did not know whether knowledge transfer offices (KTOs) in Botswana were financially supported by several funding sources, including public authorities (64.1%); whether government policy in Botswana requires organisations receiving public funds to comply with any national interest policy (51.4%); whether Botswana national policy granted the public free and unrestricted access to cultural works supported by public funds and publicly funded collections and activities (57.1%), or free and unrestricted access to government-collected data (57%), or free and unrestricted access to output of publicly funded research (54%) (see Table 15.3).

The research (Table 15.4) found that the majority of respondents did not know that their institution's IP policy encouraged commercialisation of research output. For instance, 69.2% did not know whether Botswana's IPA assigned PROs

Table 15.2: Impact of institutional IP policy on dissemination

Impact of institutional IP policy on your knowledge dissemination	Yes		No		Don't know	
	Number	%	Number	%	Number	%
Provides for a review process to identify IP that can be protected and exploited	55	34.6	16	10.1	88	55.3
Guides researchers in assessing the existing IP that may affect their freedom to operate in their field of research	63	40.6	10	6.5	82	52.9
Recognises the rights and needs of all stakeholders involved in the research	65	41.7	10	6.4	81	51.9
Provides guidance in relation to potential conflicts of interest concerning ownership, management, protection and exploitation of IP	66	42.3	9	5.8	81	51.9
Clarifies staff responsibilities in relation to IP, including the prevention of premature public disclosure of research results prior to obtaining IP	65	41.4	7	4.5	85	54.1
Reviews IP and associated commercial activities and outcomes	47	30.1	19	12.2	90	57.7
Has provisions to track the research projects that are publicly funded	47	32.2	18	12.3	81	55.5

ownership of results and first right to inventions. A further 13.7% stated explicitly (and falsely) that the Act did not make such a provision. In addition, 64.2% of researchers did not know whether their institutional IP policies made provisions for conducting surveys to see how many publicly funded research endeavours produced patents and commercial outcomes such as spin-off companies; whether the policies defined the way in which benefits from the development and exploitation of IP would be allowed (60.8%); or whether the institution would claim

Table 15.3: Impact of institutional IP policy on knowledge utilisation

Impact of institutional IP policy on your cumulative knowledge utilisation	Yes		No		Don't know	
	Number	%	Number	%	Number	%
Grants the public free and unrestricted access to outputs of publicly funded research	58	38.7	11	7.3	81	54.0
Grants the public free and unrestricted access to government-collected data	52	34.9	12	8.1	85	57.0
Grants the public free and unrestricted access to cultural works supported by public funds and publicly funded collections and archives	52	35.4	11	7.5	84	57.1
Encourages openness in sharing information from research	80	56.3	6	4.2	56	39.5
Requires organisations receiving public funding to comply with a national interest policy	69	46.6	3	2.0	76	51.4
Requires researchers using public funding to publish research outputs through open sources, conferences, workshops or through patents	71	48.3	5	3.4	71	48.3
Knowledge transfer offices (KTOs) are financially supported by several funding sources, including public authorities	43	29.7	9	6.2	93	64.1

any ownership or associated rights to IP from publicly funded research, including research conducted by postgraduate students (60%). Only 38% of the researchers indicated that their institution's IP policies supported discoveries that may have commercial value.

Table 15.4: Impact of institutional IP policy on commercialisation

Impact of institutional IP policy on your commercialisation of research output	Yes		No		Don't know	
	Number	%	Number	%	Number	%
Supports researchers in recognising discoveries that may have commercial value	57	37.5	18	11.8	77	50.7
Outlines whether institution will claim any ownership or associated rights to IP from publicly funded research (including research conducted by postgraduate students)	47	31.5	12	8.1	90	60.4
Defines the way in which benefits from the development and exploitation of the IP will be allocated	43	29.1	15	10.1	90	60.8
Makes provisions for conducting surveys to see how much of the publicly funded research produces patents and commercial outcomes such as spin-off companies	33	22.3	20	13.5	95	64.2
Provides legal frameworks for IP that spell out clearly the ownership of IP	46	30.9	16	10.7	87	58.4
Encourages and strengthens links between the research base and industry	44	30.1	20	13.7	82	56.2
Assigns to institution ownership of results and first right to inventions	25	17.1	20	13.7	101	69.2

Between 17% and 37.5% of the researchers showed an understanding of the potential impact of their institution's existing institutional policy on improving the commercialisation of their research outputs (Table 15.4), while less than 50% showed an understanding that their institution's IP policy could impact on their knowledge utilisation (Table 15.3) and knowledge dissemination (Table 15.2).

Knowledge and perceptions of Botswana IP law and policy

Institutional IP policies in Botswana operate in relation to national laws and policies. The findings clearly illustrated that the researchers, although aware that national laws and policies relevant to IP did exist, knew very little about the content of those laws and policies and their potential impact on management of their IP derived from publicly funded research. The researchers were asked about their knowledge and perceptions of key elements in Botswana's IP law and policy environment (Table 15.5).

Thirteen per cent of the researchers knew that Botswana's IP law and policy framework provides for tax incentives to innovators for IP generated from their inventions and processes but 80% did not know this and 78.4% did not know that the framework provides for KTOs to be financially supported by several funding sources, including public authorities. Similarly, 74% had no knowledge that the framework assigns PROs ownership of research results and the first right to inventions. Thirty-seven per cent did know that the framework encourages pursuit of protection of innovative ideas and processes, and 34% knew that it promotes sharing of knowledge and collaboration.

5. Research findings Part 2: research activities, patenting, licensing, partnerships

Types of research conducted

The types of research most frequently conducted by respondents were: applied research (i.e. research undertaken to solve practical problems rather than acquire knowledge for knowledge's sake) (57.8%); literature/desk review (47.6%); basic research (i.e. experimental and theoretical work undertaken to acquire new knowledge without looking for long-term benefits other than advancement of knowledge) (44.9%); consultancies for industry (28.6%); evaluation research (27.6%); and epidemiological research (9.2%) (Figure 15.5).

When looking at the different types of research conducted by institutions, the results showed that about half of the research in academic institutions (53%) was applied research. This compares with an overwhelming majority of research in

Table 15.5: Knowledge of IP law and policy

Key elements of IP law and policy	Yes		No		Don't know	
	Number	%	Number	%	Number	%
It leverages the IP system to better mobilise knowledge within a global economy	41	26.6	10	6.5	103	66.9
It encourages sharing of knowledge and collaboration	51	33.6	16	10.5	85	55.9
It encourages pursuit of protection of innovative ideas and processes	57	36.8	9	5.8	89	57.4
It encourages trans-disciplinary understanding about the history of innovation	40	25.8	12	7.7	103	66.5
It facilitates the flow of information to solve problems through networks of collaborators	42	27.5	10	6.5	101	66.0
It facilitates knowledge networks and markets through university, industry and government	46	29.9	12	7.8	96	62.3
It emphasises managing IP in ways that facilitate innovation within the existing legislative framework	43	28.7	10	6.7	97	64.7
It encourages institutions to develop IP policies within the national framework	48	31.6	12	7.9	92	60.5
It ensures incentives are in place to encourage patenting of inventions in the country as well as strategic patenting of inventions from elsewhere	35	22.6	20	12.9	100	64.5
It spells out the sharing of proceeds from commercialisation of IP rights	29	19.0	14	9.2	110	71.9

Key elements of IP law and policy	Yes		No		Don't know	
	Number	%	Number	%	Number	%
It assigns to publicly funded research institutions ownership of research results and first right to inventions	25	16.3	14	9.2	114	74.5
It provides for knowledge transfer offices (KTOs) to be financially supported by several funding sources, including public authorities	23	15.0	10	6.5	120	78.4
It defines appropriate tax incentives to innovators for IP generated from their inventions and processes	20	13.2	10	6.6	121	80.1
It facilitates the exploitation of indigenous technologies and the evaluation, acquisition and adaptation of foreign technologies for increased competitiveness	33	22.1	14	9.4	102	68.5
It creates avenues to educate and sensitise all Batswana in matters of IP	29	19.2	19	12.6	103	68.2
It incorporates aspects of IP law in the school curricula at the various levels of education	15	9.9	28	18.4	109	71.7
It stimulates innovation nationwide by setting up an advisory network in the use, production, protection, and commercialisation of inventions and artistic works	28	18.3	19	12.4	106	69.3
It ensures that research in universities and public research organisations (PROs) is adequately transferred to the commercial sector	21	13.9	22	14.6	108	71.5

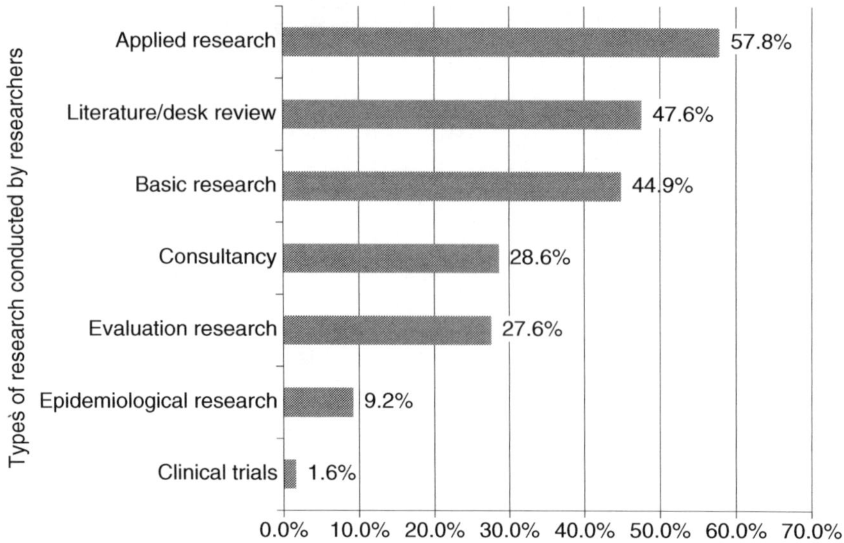

Figure 15.5: Types of research

PROs (86%), which was applied research (Table 15.6). In industry and consulting firms, most research (75%) was basic research. Government and NGO research was most likely to be applied (43%) or basic (29%).

Levels of research activity

Respondents were asked about their involvement in past and present research. The finding was that, while 94.1% of respondents had conducted research in the past, only 79.5% were at present actively engaged in research. In terms of perception of their institutions' involvement in research, 43.8% of respondents assessed the level as "medium" while 32.4% rated it "high" and 22.7% rated it "low" (Figure 15.6). The study results suggest that the level of involvement in research was significantly dependent on the type of institution. The majority of the researchers from academic institutions (48.3%) and research institutions (69%) rated their institution's level of involvement in research as medium, while 75% of researchers from industry rated it as high.

The magnitude of respondents' annual research activity was also assessed. Figure 15.7 aggregates the respondents' average annual research output over a five-year period (2006–10) across 13 kinds of outputs. The 187 respondents surveyed were found to have produced an annual average of 165 journal articles,

Table 15.6: Research emphasis of institutions

Type of research conducted	Type of institution				Total
	Academic institutions	PROs	Industry/ consulting firms	Government/ NGOs	
Basic research	44%	50%	75%	29%	45%
Applied research	53%	86%	50%	43%	58%
Literature/desk review	47%	57%	75%	14%	48%
Consultancy	26%	43%	50%	14%	29%
Clinical trials	1%	4%	0%	14%	2%
Epidemiological research	10%	7%	0%	14%	9%
Evaluation research	27%	32%	25%	29%	28%
Total	79%	15%	2%	4%	100%

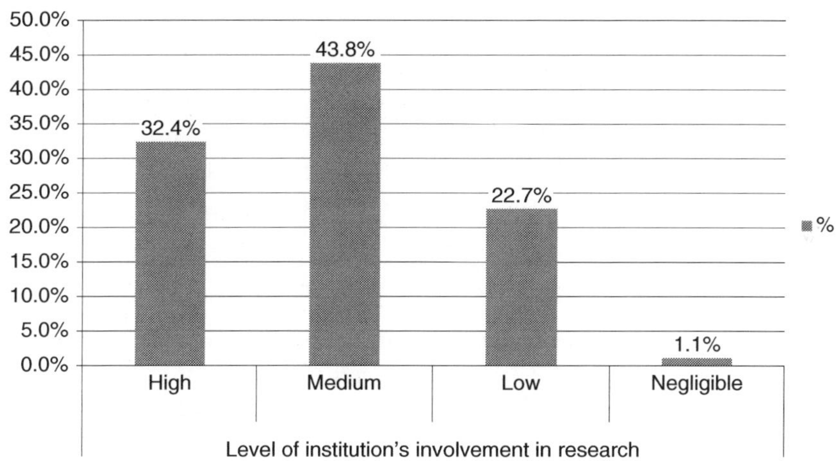

Figure 15.6: Perception of institution's research involvement

156 conference/seminar presentations, 70 published conference papers, 34 book chapters, 12 monographs and 2 books. On average only one patent was registered each year among the 187 respondents. This value is low considering the amount of applied research being conducted, and reflects the fact that most of the applied research does not yield patentable outputs.

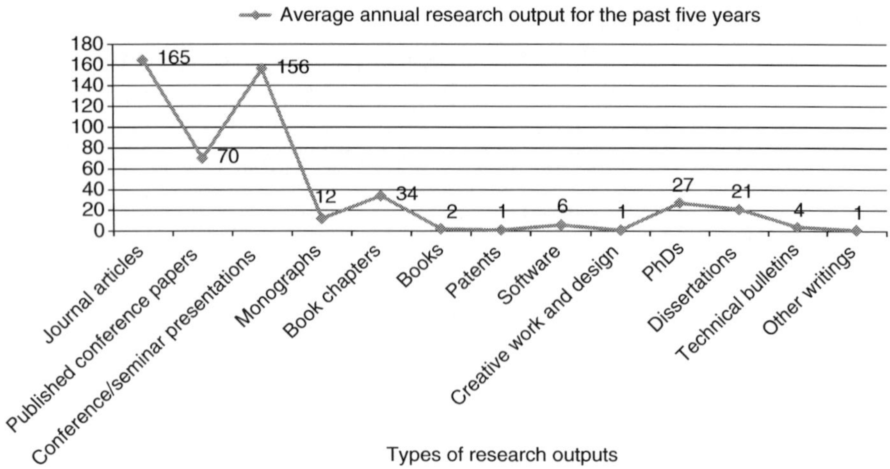

Figure 15.7: Respondents' average yearly research output

Use of IP procedures

The study found that only 28% of respondents (53 researchers) had (or were at institutions that had) attempted to use IP procedures. The methods are shown in Figure 15.8. The most common legal arrangement pertaining to IP, tried/used by 74% of respondents, was a research agreement or contract, while 20% had tried/used exclusive licences and 16% had tried/used joint ventures. Establishment of spin-off companies, or use of non-exclusive licenses, was found to be uncommon.

IP and research factors and commercialisation

Table 15.7 (on page 360) shows how respondents rated the importance of various IP and research factors in the commercialisation of research output on a four-point scale (1 = high; 2 = medium; 3 = low; and 4 = not important). The results show that the most highly rated factors enabling commercialisation of research outputs were: quality of the research base (81%); innovation (64.4%); availability of companies willing to implement research results (61%); openness in sharing information from research (59%); the strength of links between industry and research (56.6%); and maintenance of science and technology skills (56.6%). The number of patents (53.7%), timely protection of discovery (48.7%) and supportive IP policies that encourage sharing of benefits from research (46.8%) were considered the three least important factors.

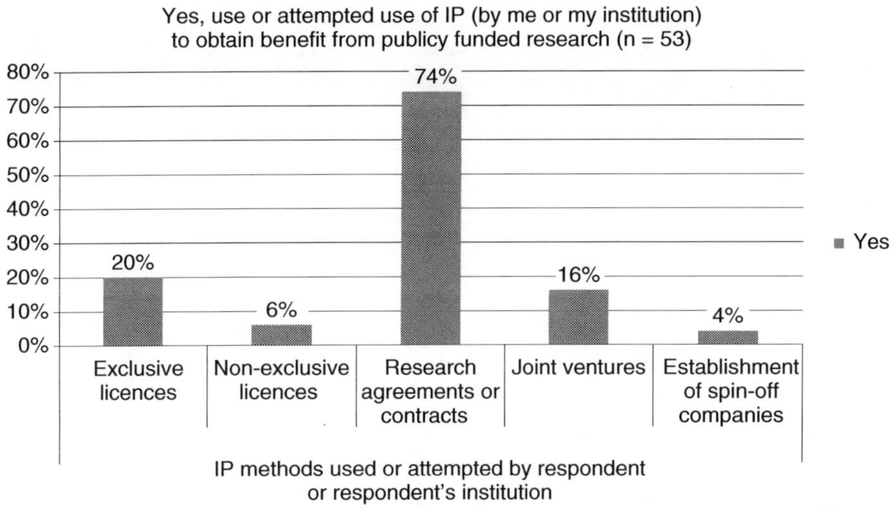

Figure 15.8: IP methods used or attempted by respondent or respondent's institution

IP and value from publicly funded research

Also surveyed were respondents' perceptions of the practices necessary in the IP and research environments in order to generate value from publicly funded research. Respondents assessed the practices on a four-point scale (1=high; 2=medium; 3=low; 4=not important). The results, in Table 15.8 (on page 361), indicate that the most highly rated practices were: creating the right academic environment (77.5%); innovation (66.5%); openness in sharing information from research (58.6%); increasing funds allocated to research (55.7%); and increasing capital to commercialise research and technology innovation (45.8%). Protection of invention and processes (51.6%), development of effective commercialisation support structures (50%), existence of an appropriate legal and regulatory environment for IP (45.9%) and IP policies in universities and institutions (46%) were less important.

Benefits to the economy and society

Respondents were asked to indicate their perceptions of benefits to the economy and society derived from publicly funded research. The responses in Figure 15.9 (on page 362) are the most highly rated benefits. Among the 186 respondents who answered this question, the majority identified the increase in stock of useful knowledge available for firms and other users (76%) as the most important benefit. Other benefits cited as important were: production of skilled graduates

Table 15.7: Importance of IP and other research factors to commercialisation

Perceived importance of IP and other research factors to commercialisation	Degree of importance							
	High		Medium		Low		Not at all important	
	Number	%	Number	%	Number	%	Number	%
Quality of the research base	145	81.0	32	17.9	1	0.6	1	0.6
Availability of companies willing and able to take up the results of research	108	61.0	51	28.8	15	8.5	3	1.7
Maintenance of science and technology skills	98	56.6	61	35.3	11	6.4	3	1.7
Strength of links between research base and industry	98	56.6	60	34.7	15	8.7	0	0.0
Availability of venture capital	69	41.8	68	41.2	25	15.2	3	1.8
Quality of management skills	69	43.7	64	40.5	22	13.9	3	1.9
Appropriateness of legal and regulatory environment	79	46.7	69	40.8	18	10.7	3	1.8
Competitiveness of business environment	80	46.8	66	38.6	19	11.1	6	3.5
Publication rate	78	47.6	66	40.2	19	11.6	1	0.6
Success in achieving external research grants	82	51.6	67	42.1	9	5.7	1	0.6
Innovation (ideas, processes)	103	64.4	54	33.8	3	1.9	0	0.0
Openness in sharing information from research	95	59.0	56	34.8	9	5.6	1	0.6
Number of patents	34	22.8	80	53.7	27	18.1	8	5.4
Legal framework for IP that clearly spells out the ownership of IP	69	44.2	68	43.6	17	10.9	2	1.3
Supportive IP policies that encourage sharing of benefits from research	68	43.6	73	46.8	12	7.7	3	1.9
Timely disclosure of discoveries	62	39.2	72	45.6	21	13.3	3	1.9
Timely protection of discoveries	60	38.5	76	48.7	13	8.3	7	4.5
Recognition of the researcher	4	57.1	3	42.9	0	0.0	0	0.0

Table 15.8: IP and research practices necessary for value

Perceptions of IP and research practices necessary to generate value from publicly funded research	Degree of importance							
	High		Medium		Low		Not important	
	Number	%	Number	%	Number	%	Number	%
Creating the right academic environment	141	77.5	35	19.2	6	3.3	0	0.0
Developing effective commercialisation support structures	51	31.1	82	50.0	26	15.9	5	3.0
Developing and expanding relationships with existing companies/industries	70	41.7	61	36.3	31	18.5	6	3.6
Facilitating and increasing the number of new spin-off companies derived from university research activities	50	29.9	74	44.3	37	22.2	6	3.6
Strengthening the corporate base	34	22.1	69	44.8	42	27.3	9	5.8
Increasing the amount of finance available for the commercialisation of research and technological innovation	77	45.8	65	38.7	20	11.9	6	3.6
Increasing the amount of funding allocated to research	93	55.7	58	34.7	16	9.6	0	0.0
Innovation	109	66.5	44	26.8	10	6.1	1	0.6
Openness in sharing information from research	99	58.6	58	34.3	11	6.5	1	0.6
Institutions' reward systems to innovators	69	42.6	68	42.0	21	13.0	4	2.5
Financial and taxation reward systems	38	23.9	66	41.5	40	25.2	15	9.4
An appropriate legal and regulatory environment for IP	57	36.3	72	45.9	25	15.9	3	1.9
Protection of inventions and processes	56	36.1	80	51.6	17	11.0	2	1.3
IP policies in universities and institutions	68	41.7	75	46.0	17	10.4	3	1.8

Figure 15.9: Benefits to economy and society from publicly funded research

and researchers (66%); enhancement of capacity for scientific and technology problem-solving (58%); provision of social knowledge (54%); improved quality of life (43%); development of networks and stimulation of social interactions (44%); influencing the decision-making apparatus of private and public enterprises (40%); and improving living standards (37%).

Institutional roles

Research institutions in Botswana are expected to play a key role in ensuring that IP policies encourage researchers to harness benefits from publicly funded research. These roles include, but are not limited to: providing an enabling environment for research; helping researchers patent the most promising concepts and license the work to firms that commercialise them into new products and services; and ensuring that important ideas generated from publicly funded research enter the marketplace. Government policy expects research institutions to provide funding to scale and commercialise ideas, business expertise to commercialise, human capital to build start-up companies, and mentoring and educational support for new entrepreneurs.

Table 15.9 shows respondents' views regarding the role institutions should play in generating benefits from publicly funded research. An overwhelming majority of the respondents (92%) stated that their institutions should notify

Table 15.9: Roles of institutions

Principal roles of your institution in harnessing benefits from publicly funded research	Type of institution				Total
	Academic institutions	PROs	Industry/ consulting firms	Government/ NGOs	
Notification of funding bodies of any identified valuable inventions created using public funds	95%	84%	67%	83%	92%
Taking ultimate responsibility for commercialising inventions by adopting a time limit for applying for a patent	74%	40%	67%	50%	67%
Establishment of an IP management infrastructure	91%	68%	67%	83%	87%
Allocating a certain proportion of granted funds towards exploitation of IP rights	83%	84%	67%	50%	81%
Ensuring the inclusion of knowledge transfer or commercialisation as an express component of mission statement	69%	72%	100%	67%	86%

funding bodies of any identified, valuable inventions created using public funds. The establishment of an IP management infrastructure was also considered important (87%). Respondents were also strongly concerned (86%) about ensuring the inclusion of knowledge transfer or commercialisation as an express component of their institutions' mission statements. Notifying funding bodies of valuable inventions created using public funds was a top priority of researchers in academic institutions and PROs (95% and 84%, respectively). Conversely, respondents from industry felt that the top priority of their institutions should be the inclusion of knowledge transfer or commercialisation as an express component of the institution's mission statement (100%).

Institutional IP environments

Respondents were asked to indicate if there were government IP policies that potentially inhibited their institution's innovation and generation of value from publicly funded research. It was found that 66% felt there were no policies that were having an inhibiting effect, while 34% took the opposite position. Several respondents pointed to non-IP obstacles, including the attitude of institutional policy-makers towards researchers and the fact that, in some institutions, non-researchers seem to benefit more from research outputs than do researchers.

The study also asked respondents how institutional IP policies could be improved so as to enhance the value gained from publicly funded research. As Figure 15.10 shows, 29% of respondents were unsure of what should be done, while 20% were content with the *status quo*. Others felt that IP policies should be disseminated to researchers through academic bodies (8%); that protective legislation for researchers' IP rights should be introduced (5%); that there should be IP policies developed at institutions that lacked them (5%); and that additional incentives – e.g. increased research funding, reduction in time allocated to teaching, and hiring of additional staff to assist in marking of class tests and tutorials – should be introduced to boost the activity of researchers (5%).

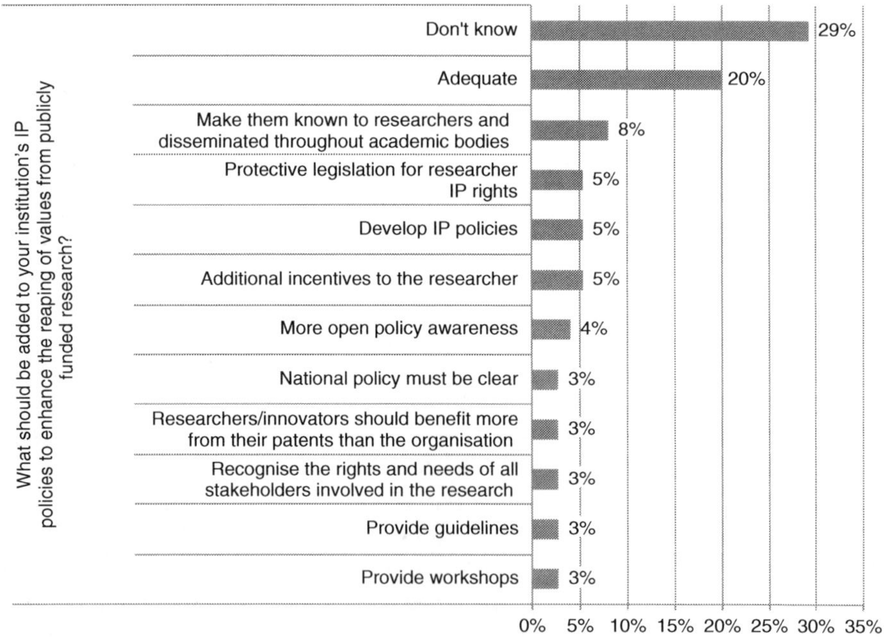

Figure 15.10: Institutional IP policies

Institutional funding for research

Respondents were asked to rate the level of funding for research at their institutions from four sources: government, NGO, international and institutional. As Table 15.10 shows, 66% of the respondents rated government research funding support to their institutions as low, while 9% said it was high. A majority of respondents (63%) rated funding support from NGOs as low. International funding support for research was rated by 40% as medium, while 25% said it was high. Institutional funding for research was assessed to be low by 46%, medium by 40% and high by 14%.

Table 15.10: Funding levels from different sources

Rating of research funding from	High		Medium		Low	
	Number	%	Number	%	Number	%
Government (n = 161 respondents)	15	9.3	40	24.8	106	65.8
Institution (n = 160 respondents)	23	14.4	64	40.0	73	45.6
International bodies (n = 159 respondents)	40	25.2	64	40.3	55	34.6
NGOs (n = 152 respondents)	16	10.5	40	26.3	96	63.2

6. Conclusions

The study found a lack of knowledge of the prevailing legal and policy frameworks governing IP at the institutional and national levels in Botswana. Although 54.2% of the researchers indicated that their institutions had IP policies, the majority of the researchers were unaware of the content of such policies. This lack of knowledge of the legal and regulatory framework is likely to hinder IP development and may be contributing to the low usage of IP rights. Maister *et al.* (2011) made similar observations about the lack of awareness of IP frameworks at research institutes and universities in Burundi and Rwanda, respectively.

The lack of knowledge about commercialisation of research output from publicly funded research indicates that most researchers have failed to engage with their institutional IP policies. Botswana has a very low level of patenting (MCST, 2005). The lack of knowledge about commercialisation may also point to the poor quality of research institutions' IP policies. Creating awareness of IP and its utility in generating value from research outputs is a key area that requires urgent intervention among researchers. The quality of the research base, innovation and the availability of companies willing and able to incorporate research were identified by researchers as major incentives for commercialising IP.

The key priorities identified by the researchers related to an improved scholarly setting. Researchers want: the right academic environment (77.5%); innovation (66.5%); openness in sharing information from research (58.6%); and an increase in the amount of funds allocated to research (55.7%). These findings correspond with the findings of other studies (Altschuld and Zheng, 1995; Jordan *et al.*, 2003; Ransley and Rogers, 1994; Ulwadia, 1990). It is thus important that an academic environment is created which includes: a reduced teaching load; availability and accessibility of research resources, including publications; and an IP environment that balances commercialisation efforts with encouragement of open sharing of research data and findings. University and PRO roles in research are measured in terms of attracting more students, retaining good scientists, and enhancing access to additional research and development funding opportunities. The extent to which they are able to accomplish this role depends on their ability to create the enabling and conducive environment cited as necessary by the majority of respondents to this study. Universities and PROs need to have guaranteed levels of research funding and strong links with funding agencies. Universities and PROs should take an active role in IP management by, *inter alia*, establishing clear and realistic objectives, ensuring adequate resources and setting up dedicated, professional technology transfer offices (TTOs). Creating awareness of existing IP policies at institutions should be prioritised.

At the same time, the study found that researchers believe that value from publicly funded research can be improved by openness in sharing information from research (58.6%). Access to research data was seen by the respondents as likely to increase the returns from public investment and reinforce open scientific inquiry. This is in line with the OECD view that openness encourages diversification of study and intellectual opinion by researchers, promoting the exploration of topics that had not been envisioned (OECD, 2007). According to the OECD, research policies, practices, support systems and cultural values all affect the nature of new discoveries, the rate at which they are made and the degree to which they are made accessible and used. Sharing and open access to publicly funded research data help not only to maximise research potential, but also to provide greater returns from public investment in research. Open publication or display of knowledge should be seen as an essential aspect of publicly funded science. Publications expand opportunities for access to the knowledge and skills of the scientific community, as created and supported by public investment in research (Dasgupta and David, 1994; Salter and Martin, 2001).

Bibliography

Primary sources

Botswana

Botswana Football Association and Another v. Kgamane [1998 BLR 153 (CA)].

Department of Research, Science and Technology (DRST) (2006), *Botswana Patents, Utility Models and Industrial Designs Manual*, Gaborone.

Government of Botswana (n.d.), "Intellectual property", available at: www.gov.bw/en/Business/Sub-audiences/Small--Medium-Businesses/Intellectual-Property/ (accessed 7 April 2013).

Government of Botswana (1997), Vision 2016: A Long Term Vision for Botswana.

Government of Botswana (2012), Keynote Address by His Honour, the Vice President of the Republic of Botswana Dr Ponatshego H. K. Kedikilwe, PH, MP at the Official Launch of the Botswana Innovation Hub, 11 December, available at: www.gov.bw/en/News/THE-OFFICIAL-LAUNCH-OF-THE--INNOVATION-HUB/ (accessed 7 April 2013).

Industrial Property Act 14 of 1996 (IPA of 1996).

Industrial Property Act 8 of 2010 [C.I.F. 2012] (IPA of 2010).

Ministry of Communications, Science and Technology (MCST) (2005), *Botswana National Research, Science and Technology Plan: Final Report*, MCST, Gaborone.

Revised National Policy on Research, Science, Technology and Innovation (2011), Ministry of Infrastructure, Science and Technology (MIST), approved by Parliament in 2012 (MIST, 2011).

University of Botswana (UB) (2004), University of Botswana Policy on Intellectual Property, RD 04/04K, RD04/04J, Office of Research and Development, University of Botswana, Gaborone.

University of Botswana (UB) (2008), *Research Commercialisation at the University of Botswana*, Office of Research and Development (ORD), Gaborone, available at: www.ub.bw/ord/ord_detail.cfm?pid=977 (accessed 7 April 2013).

University of Botswana (UB) (2010), *UB Annual Research Report 2010*, Gaborone, available at: www.ub.bw/ord/documents/UB%20Research%20Report%202010.pdf (accessed 7 April 2013).

Africa

African Regional Intellectual Property Organisation (ARIPO) (n.d.), "ARIPO patent registrations, ARIPO design registrations, ARIPO trademark registrations", ARIPO, Harare, available at: www.hahn.co.za/patent-serrvices-aripo.htm (accessed 7 April 2013).

African Regional Intellectual Property Organisation (ARIPO) (2012), "Legal framework, the ARIPO Protocols", ARIPO, Harare, available at: www.aripo.org/index.php/legal-framework (accessed 7 April 2013).

Banjul Protocol on Marks within the Framework of ARIPO.

Green Paper on Science, Technology and Innovation Policy: Building Competitiveness through Innovation, Ministry of Science and Technology (MOST), Federal Democratic Republic of Ethiopia, Addis Ababa. (MOST, 2010).

Harare Protocol on Patents and Industrial Designs within the Framework ARIPO.

Intellectual Property Rights from Publicly Financed Research and Development (IPR-PFRD) of 2008, Republic of South Africa (IPR-PFRD of 2008).

Lusaka Agreement on the Creation of the African Regional Intellectual Property Organisation (ARIPO).

Swakopmund Protocol on the Protection of Traditional Knowledge and Expressions of Folklore within the Framework of ARIPO.

International

Agreement on Trade-Related Aspects of Intellectual Property Rights (TRIPS) (1994).

Berne Convention for the Protection of Literary and Artistic Works.

Convention Establishing the World Intellectual Property Organisation (WIPO).

Hague Agreement Concerning the International Deposit of Industrial Designs.

Paris Convention for the Protection of Industrial Property.

Patent Cooperation Treaty (PCT).

Protocol Relating to the Madrid Agreement Concerning the International Registration of Marks.

WIPO Copyright Treaty (WCT).

WIPO Performances and Phonograms Treaty (WPPT).

Secondary sources

Altschuld, J.W. and Zheng, H.Y. (1995), "Assessing the effectiveness of research organisations: an examination of multiple approaches", *Evaluation Review*, Vol. 19 No. 2, pp. 197–216.

Bennett, B. and Chilume, Y. (2007), *Making the Most of Natural Advantages: Intellectual Property and Natural Products in Botswana*, Botswana Council of Non-governmental Organisations and Botswana Trade and Poverty Programme, Gaborone.

Campbell, E.G., Clarridge, B.R., Gokhale, M., Birenbaum, L. Hilgartner, S., Holtzman, N.A. and Blumenthal, D. (2002), "Data withholding in academic genetics: evidence from a national survey", *Journal of the American Medical Association*, Vol. 287 No. 4, pp. 473–79.

Council for Scientific and Industrial Research (CSIR) (2005), *Botswana National Research: Science and Technology Plan: Inventory and Assessment Report*, CSIR, Stellenbosch, South Africa.

Creative Research Systems (2010), *Sample Size Calculator*, available at: www.surveysystem.com/sscalc.htm (accessed 7 April 2013).

David, P. (2001), *From Keeping "Nature's Secrets" to the Institutionalization of "Open Science"*, Stanford Working Paper No. 01-006, Stanford University, Stanford, CA.

David, P.A. (2004), "Can 'open science' be protected from the evolving systems of IPR protections?" *Journal of Institutional and Theoretical Economics*, Vol. 160 No. 1, pp. 9–34.

Dasgupta, P. and David, P. (1994), "Towards a new economics of science", *Research Policy*, Vol. 23 No. 5, pp. 487–521.

Foray, D. and Lissoni, F. (2010), "University research and public-private interaction", in Hall B.H., and Rosenberg, N. (Eds), *Handbook of Economics of Innovation*, Elsevier, Amsterdam, pp. 276–308.

Gersbach, H., Sorger, G. and Amon, C. (2009), *Hierarchical Growth: Basic and Applied Research Economics*, Working Paper Series 09/118 CER-ETH, Center of Economic Research – Swiss Federal Institute of Technology, Zurich.

Global Intellectual Property Center (GIPC) (n.d.), *Open Licensing for Publicly Funded Research: Building Block or Barrier to Scientific Progress?*, GIPC White Paper Series, Washington, DC.

Heller, M.A. and Eisenberg, R.S. (1998), "Can patents deter innovation? The anti-commons in biomedical research", *Science*, Vol. 280 No. 5364, pp. 698–701.

Holly, K.Z. (2010), *IMPACT: Innovation Model Program for Accelerating the Commercialization of Technology: A Proposal for Realizing the Economic Potential of University Research*, White Paper, University of Southern California.

Huang, K.G. (2006), *Innovation in the Life Sciences: the Impact of Intellectual Property Rights on Scientific Knowledge Diffusion, Accumulation and Utilization*, PhD thesis, Massachusetts Institute of Technology (MIT), Cambridge, MA.

Jordan, G.B., Streit, L.D. and Binkley, J.S. (2003), "Assessing and improving the effectiveness of national research laboratories", *IEEE Transactions on Engineering Management*, Vol. 50 No. 2, pp. 228–35.

Kurosaki, T. (2003), "Specialization and diversification in agricultural transformation: the case of West Punjab, 1903–92", *American Journal of Agricultural Economics*, Vol. 85 No. 2, pp. 372–86.

Latif, A.A., Keith, M., Okediji, R., Reichman, J. and Roffe, P. (2011), *Overcoming the Impasse of Intellectual Property and Climate Change at the UNFCCC: A Way*

Forward, Policy Brief No. 11, International Centre for Trade and Sustainable Development (ICTSD), Geneva.

Maister, B., De Jonge, B. and Napier, G. (2011), *Harnessing Intellectual Property Rights for Development Objectives: The Double Role of IPRs in the Context of Facilitating MDGs Nos. 1 and 6*, Wolf Legal Publishers, Nijmegen, Netherlands.

Martin, B.R. and Tang, P. (2006), *The Benefits of Publicly Funded Research*, SPRU Working Paper Series No. 161, University of Sussex, Brighton, UK.

Martin, B., Salter, A., Hicks, D., Pavitt, K., Senker, J., Sharp, M. and Von Tunzelmann, N. (1996), *The Relationship Between Publicly Funded Basic Research and Economic Performance*, Science Policy Research Unit, University of Sussex, Brighton, UK.

Mazzoleni, R. and Nelson, R. (2007), "Public research institutions and economic catch-up", *Research Policy*, Vol. 36 No. 10, pp. 1512–28.

Merton, R.K. (1942), "Science and technology in a democratic order", *Journal of Legal and Political Sociology*, Vol. 1, pp. 115–26.

Murray, F. and Stern, S. (2007), "Do formal intellectual property rights hinder the free flow of scientific knowledge? An empirical test of the anti-commons hypothesis", *Journal of Economic Behavior & Organization* , Vol. 63, pp. 648–87.

Organisation for Economic Co-operation and Development (OECD) (2007), *OECD Principles and Guidelines for Access to Research Data from Public Funding*, Paris, available at: www.oecd.org/science/sci-tech/38500813.pdf (accessed 7 April 2013).

Pingali, P. (1997), "From subsistence to commercial production system: the transformation of Asian agriculture", *American Journal of Agricultural Economics*, Vol. 79 No. 2, pp. 628–34.

Pingali, L.P. and Rosegrant, M.W. (1995), "Agricultural commercialization and diversification: process and polices", *Food Policy*, Vol. 20 No. 3, pp. 171–85.

Ransley, D. and Rogers, J. (1994), "A consensus on best research and development practices", *Research Technology Management*, Vol. 37 No. 2, pp. 19–26.

Salter A.J., and Martin, B.R. (2001), "The economic benefits of publicly funded basic research: a critical review", *Research Policy*, Vol. 30 No. 3, pp. 509–32.

Salter, A.J., D'Este, P., Martin, B.R., Geuna, A., Scott, A., Pavitt, K., Patel, P. and Nightingale, P. (2000), *Talent Not Technology: Publicly Funded Research and Innovation in the UK*, Committee of Vice-Chancellors and Principals (CVCP), London.

Sampat, B.N. (2002), "Private parts: patents and academic research in the Twentieth Century", paper prepared at the Research Symposium of the "Next Generation" of Leaders in Science and Technology Policy, Washington, DC.

Sampat, B.N. (2009), "Academic patents and access to medicines in developing countries", *American Journal of Public Health*, Vol. 99 No. 1, pp. 9–17.

Scott, A., Steyn, G., Brusoni, S. and Steinmuler, E. (2002), *The Economic Returns of Basic Research and the Benefits of University-Industry Relationships: A Literature Review and Update of Findings*, Science and Technology Policy Research Unit, University of Sussex, Brighton, UK.

Snijders, T. (1992), "Estimation on the basis of snowball samples: how to weight?" *Bulletin de Méthodologie Sociologique*, Vol. 36, pp. 59–70.

Straus, J., Holzapfel, H. and Lindenmeir, M. (2004), *Genetic Inventions and Patent Law: An Empirical Survey of Selected German R&D Institutions,* VMD Verl, Munich.

Timmer, C.P. (1997), "Farmers and markets: the political economy of new paradigms", *American Journal of Agricultural Economics,* Vol. 79 No. 2, pp. 621–67.

Ulwadia, F.E. (1990), "Creativity and innovation in organisations", *Technology Forecasting and Social Change*, Vol. 38 No. 1, pp. 65–80.

UN Development Programme (UNDP) (2013), "Explanatory note on 2013 HDR composite indices: Botswana: HDI values and rank changes in the 2013 Human Development Report" in *Human Development Report 2013: The Rise of the South: Human Progress in a Diverse World*, available at: http://hdrstats.undp.org/images/explanations/BWA.pdf (accessed 16 August 2013).

Von Braun, J. (1995), "Agricultural commercialization: impacts on income and nutrition and implications for policy", *Food Policy,* Vol. 20 No. 3 pp. 87–202.

Wagner J.W. (2007), "Multiversity or university? Pursuing competing goods simultaneously", *Academic Exchange,* Vol. 9 No. 4, available at: www.emory.edu/ACAD_EXCHANGE/2007/febmar/wagneressay.html (accessed 7 April 2013).

Walsh, J.P., Arora, A. and Cohen, W.M. (2002), "Effects of research tool patents and licensing on biomedical innovation", in Board of Science Technology and Economic Policy (STEP) (Ed.), *Patents in the Knowledge-Based Economy*, The National Academies Press, Washington, DC.

Weitzman, M. (1974), "Free access vs. private ownership as alternative systems for managing common property", *Journal of Economic Theory,* Vol. 8 No. 2, pp. 225–34.

World Bank (2012), *World Bank Development Indicators Data: Research and Development Expenditure (% of GDP)* available at: http://data.worldbank.org/indicator/GB.XPD.RSDV.GD.ZS (accessed 7 April 2013).

World Economic Forum (WEF) (2012), *The Global Competitiveness Report 2011–2012,* available at: www3.weforum.org/docs/WEF_GCR_Report_2011-12.pdf (accessed 7 April 2013).

World Health Organisation (WHO) (2012), "Regulatory frameworks on intellectual property," available at: www.aho.afro.who.int/profiles_information/index.php/Botswana:Regulatory_frameworks_on_intellectual_property (accessed 7 April 2013).

World Intellectual Property Organisation (WIPO) (2012), "WIPO Assemblies agree roadmaps for new international instruments", PR/2012/723, available at: www.wipo.int/pressroom/en/articles/2012/article_0022.html (accessed 7 April 2013).

Youngleson, J.S. (2012), "Nightmares or opportunities? The IPR-PFRD Act – its implementation status, impact on contract research, patenting and other considerations", presentation to the Licensing Executives Society of South Africa AGM, Department of Science and Technology, Pretoria, available at: www.licensing.co.za/pdf/NIPMO-Presentation-LES-SA-AGM-2012.pdf (accessed 7 April 2013).

Chapter 16

Current Realities of Collaborative Intellectual Property in Africa

Jeremy de Beer, Chris Armstrong, Chidi Oguamanam and Tobias Schonwetter

1. Introduction

Drawing conclusions across numerous studies featuring qualitative and quantitative data collected from myriad settings on the African continent is no simple task. It is also a task that needs to be approached with caution lest it fall into the trap of totalising "African" experience (when, in fact, this book is to a great extent about the diversity of realities present across a continent of 55 nation-states and innumerable sub-national realities).

Apart from Chapter 2's overview of conceptual frameworks potentially applicable in any or all of Africa's national and local settings, Mgbeoji's study (Chapter 10) of patent offices in 44 countries, and Oguamanam and Dagne's Chapter 4 looking at settings in both Ethiopia and Ghana, each of the studies in this book looks at realities in a single country. And, in the chapters on Kampala's informal-sector auto mechanics (Chapter 3) and on the Kukula traditional healers of Bushbuckridge in South Africa (Chapter 7), the study settings are sub-nationally localised. Further diversification arises from the fact that the research findings in this book emerge from several different modes of innovation and creativity; from a variety of approaches to intellectual property (IP); and from several different orientations towards socio-economic development. The purpose of this concluding chapter is to identify compelling results, commonalities and contrasts across the studies, and to arrive at some overarching conclusions and recommendations.

The researchers who responded to our open call for case study proposals – which generated the evidence for the contributions to this book – were asked to address this question: *How can existing or potential IP systems be harnessed to appropriately value and facilitate innovation and creativity for open development in Africa?* What emerged were multiple, often overlapping interpretations of the question, and a range of relevant considerations in answering it. The research shed new light on the diverse nature of innovation and creativity in African settings, and on the different IP policies and practices related to innovation and creativity on the continent.

When linked with broader development objectives and models, the findings offer insights into the nature of IP-related dynamics in relation to innovation and creativity in Africa, and guidance towards IP policy and management possibilities. The next section of this chapter (Section 2) looks at the modalities of innovation and creativity uncovered through the case studies. Section 3 examines collaborative IP approaches across the studies. Section 4 looks at the visions of socio-economic development explicitly or implicitly present in the contexts studied. Section 5 summarises findings in relation to the book's three central themes: collaborative innovation and creativity, openness and IP. Section 6 concludes the book with recommendations to African policy-makers.

2. African innovation and creativity

The research outlined in this book reveals the need for restraint in drawing generalised impressions of the modes of innovation and creativity on the African continent. The diversity of settings studied refutes the temptation to use, as Muchie (2004) puts it, "the African nation as a unit of analysis" (2004, p. 318). The studies also challenge us to reflect on the appropriateness of (developed-world-centric) conceptualisations of "the idea of innovation in the African context" (Muchie, 2004, p. 318), i.e. to reflect upon the appropriateness of orthodox constructs of innovation, and innovative societies, in the context of African realities.

There are inherent and profound divergences among African countries' socio-cultural compositions and among their environments. At the same time, however, it cannot be denied that there is evidence of similarities at play across the African innovation landscapes. Such similarities point to systemic, albeit inchoate or open-ended, insights on innovation and creativity as the continent responds to the transformational pressures of market liberalisation and global IP norms. The results of the case studies make it apparent that, in Africa, innovation and creativity are not endeavours that inevitably take place in the context of market economic surveillance. Deliberate reification of commercial or organisational strategies for business and entrepreneurial advancement may be aspirational constructs, but they are not necessarily the mainstream of African orientation towards innovation. Indeed, at present the African context seems predisposed towards innovations and creations of *necessity* (as pointed out in the conceptual survey in Chapter 2).

Because of their pragmatic tenor, innovations and creativity in African settings tend not to be consciously oriented towards so-called frontier or high technologies. As Belete's Chapter 14 reveals in relation to the Ethiopian context, where there is a paucity of institutional infrastructure for research and development (R&D) and of industrial absorptive capacity for knowledge conversion, high-level science and technology innovation (STI) will not flourish. Coupled with evidence of poor funding for Ethiopian universities and their sub-optimal level of R&D personnel, the findings in Ethiopia almost certainly resonate with many other national settings on the continent (including Botswana, as examined in Ama's Chapter 15). However, within the variegated and less formalised platforms examined, particularly in Kawooya's Ugandan study in Chapter 3, the capacity for informal innovation and inversion of frontier technologies to meet local needs in unpredictable circumstances is clearly a prominent feature of the innovation-creation experience.

Outside conventional straight-jacketing, innovations and creations in African settings often consist of endeavours that create value, and add value to societies, through *pragmatic* means. Innovations occur in multiple contexts, including through historic and extant transformations, re-orientations, and renegotiations of indigenous knowledge systems. The sites of innovation and creativity are diverse, from, *inter alia*, traditional medicines (Cocchiaro *et al.*'s Chapter 7) to agricultural products (Oguamanam and Dagne's Chapter 4) to clothing (Adewopo *et al.*'s Chapter 5) to automobile parts (Kawooya's Chapter 3) to biofuels (Dos Santos and Pelembe's Chapter 11, Awad and Abou Zeid's Chapter 12).

Innovations also happen in the shadow of the continent's transition and response in relation to global IP trends and pressures. The pressures are being negotiated at national levels – e.g. Chapters 13, 14 and 15 on emergent regimes around publicly funded research in South Africa, Ethiopia and Botswana, respectively – but under weak and fledgling national and regional institutional constraints, especially those dealing with IP. The constraints are stark in Mgbeoji's Chapter 10, which provides an unflattering portrayal of African national patent offices and which is resonant with the context-specific constraints apparent in several other case studies in this volume.

The innovation-creation dynamics reflected in most of the case studies unavoidably generate doubt over the veracity, in African contexts, of the "firm" or the "organisation", as positioned by orthodox innovation inquiry (Shane *et al.*, 1995), as the default unit for knowledge transfer. In the African settings examined, the configurations of cultural strands, nodes and clusters interact at formal and informal scales to generate knowledge outside orthodox organisational paradigms. The singularities are present in every form of production, from Egyptian independent musicians, Nigerian textile makers, Ethiopian coffee growers and Ghanaian cocoa producers, to Ugandan auto mechanics, Kenyan scholarly authors, Botswana's publicly funded researchers, South African traditional healers and Mozambican jatropha growers.

Under the rubrics unveiled in the case studies, there are no clear individual-to-firm or firm-to-individual binary demarcations of the direction of knowledge of the kind recognised within orthodox innovation frameworks. Rather, knowledge transmission is mediated by myriad factors, including necessities generated by present dynamics, inter-generational obligations, and cultural sensitivities to experiences and knowledge from the (deep and/or recent) past. For instance, the studies found evidence of knowledge transmission being animated by individual pride within given trades, particularly those with sector-specific apprenticeship traditions (e.g., automobile repair, leather-crafting, textile design, feedstock agriculture, coffee production, traditional healing).

Tabulations of the quantity of science and engineering publications, yearly patent totals and other forms of R&D statistics reified by orthodox audits of innovation (see Bogliacino, *et al.*, 2012; Shane *et al.*, 1995) are but extremely blunt instruments for anyone seeking to distil the essence(s) of the innovations and creations present in the African settings analysed in this book. Given the predilection of the aforementioned R&D benchmarks for detection of (so-called) frontier technologies, it should not come as a great surprise that the oftentimes incremental, informal, traditional and/or accidental innovations and creations featured in this book (and discussed conceptually in De Beer *et al.*'s Chapter 2) do not readily submit to such benchmarks. For instance, Ouma's Chapter 6 and Cocchiaro *et al.*'s Chapter 7 draw attention to the contemporary salience of innovative knowledge systems arising from resourcefulness transmitted across the millennia via, *inter alia*, stewardship of plant genetic resources and other forms of traditional knowledge.

Current interest shown by some governments in Africa in calibrating university–industry liaisons through patenting and commercialisation of publicly funded research outputs (examined in Chapters 13–15) symbolises a response to the globalising world's innovation measurement imperative. Such attempted calibrations reflect exploration of the expansion of formal institutional channels for knowledge transformation in which the firm and other forms of local organisational structures would be conduits for knowledge transfer. The expansion of such formal institutional collaborations for innovation would likely result in increased relevance of orthodox benchmarking of innovation. But such changes might come at the expense of more context-appropriate approaches that better reflect realities in African settings. Quite unlike the orthodox, firm-centric organisational structure featured in conventional innovation discourse, actors in the African settings probed in this book are situated within heterogeneous socio-cultural ecosystems characterised by ongoing hybridisations among the "modern" and the "traditional"; the "developed" and the "developing"; the "Western" and the "African".

The case studies in this volume display pluralities of social units, associational frameworks and contexts for innovative and creative endeavour (King, 2001). Africa's diversity of social constructs cannot readily be compacted into a simplistic binary between so-called individualistic and collectivist societies. However, it is true that many of Africa's innovation contexts (including several of the contexts examined in this book) do not affirm the privileging of individualist cultures over so-called collectivist ones in innovation narratives (Shane, 1992; Taylor and Wilson, 2012). It is difficult to separate the presumptions in innovation studies about collectivist societies from the systematic under-reporting of the innovative credentials of contemporary African settings – with African contexts often uncritically pigeonholed into a collectivist framework posited as antithetical to aggressive innovation. The research findings presented in this volume suggest that the individual, the family, the community and various other social units and contingent entrepreneurial clusters, are all implicated in knowledge generation, innovation and creativity in the settings studied. This characteristic of African ingenuity should not be undermined or underestimated.

Based on the evidence presented in this book, it seems clear that, in contemporary African settings, innovative-creative modalities gravitate towards optimised hybrids: non-absolutist, adaptable mixes of openness and protection, of sharing and preserving, of informal and formal, of new and old, of open source and IP-protected. Such hybrids, arrived at via selective pragmatism, have the potential to accentuate the diversity of African innovation-creation practices and allow individuals, communities, regions and nations on the continent, and diasporic Africans, to more optimally participate in global IP structures – provided deployment of IP modalities is but one in the range of tools utilised in quests for acceleration of socio-economic development. IP law-making and policy-making in service to optimised hybrids are and will be complex, particularly given the fluidity of these hybrids. We now turn to examination of the various IP modes uncovered by the contributors to this book.

3. Collaborative intellectual property

The studies in this volume scrutinise several African IP frameworks and systems that govern knowledge. They do this by investigating six thematic areas covering a range of IP-related issues: informal protections; trademarks and geographical indications (GIs); traditional knowledge (TK); copyrights; patents and public policy; and ownership of publicly funded research outputs. Some of the case studies probe the relationship between IP and innovation in a selected setting without emphasising distinctions among specific kinds of IP (e.g. the Ugandan study in Chapter 3), but most focus on a specific area of IP and its impacts on certain sectors, communities and/or policy processes in a selected national or sub-national setting.

Across the studies, we can see examples of what seem to be potential middle-ground models of IP policies and practices, based on underlying principles of *inclusion* and *collaboration*. This middle ground emerges when one is willing to accept that absolute openness is not required to facilitate knowledge-sharing; and, at the same time, nor does IP protection inevitably preclude access to everyone but the individual proprietor. Situated in this middle ground are various forms of IP that can be used as tools to facilitate collaboration within or across communities of many kinds. As the Kawooya study shows, automotive mechanics and university researchers can and do share trade secrets among themselves, often pursuant to informal agreements enforced by social rather than legal norms. The studies by Oguamanam and Dagne and by Adewopo *et al.* found that groups of agricultural or industrial producers and retailers invoke place-based protections. Meanwhile, as evidenced by the Ouma study and the Cocchiaro *et al.* research, indigenous peoples manage cultural heritage or medicinal knowledge through a mix of customary laws and cultural norms, and/or through more formal mechanisms such a bio-cultural community protocol (BCP). Rizk found that musicians choose to confront the realities of copyright unenforceability through alternative business models, and Sihanya looked at how scholars and publishers can use copyright creatively to openly license learning materials. The studies by Dos Santos and Pelembe and Awad and Abou Zeid found evidence to suggest that the patent system could play a role in the sharing of technological knowledge between rights-holders and communities of potential users or collaborators, thus furthering particular industrial policy objectives, in respect of clean energy technologies. The Ncube *et al.*, Belete and Ama research findings suggest that appropriate IP management policies and practices can contribute to the ability of publicly funded researchers to put "open science" models into practice, i.e. to engage in wide online sharing of research data in order to spur collaborations and dissemination.

In none of these cases observed would IP owners be likely to see advantage in exercising the power to fully exclude others from the protected knowledge. Doing so would be counter-productive to underlying social, cultural and economic objectives present in the settings in which the knowledge is being deployed. Even in the context of indigenous and local communities (ILCs), sharing among select groups of stewards or practitioners is necessary to preserve and utilise TK. What we observe, then, are *degrees* of openness, where boundaries between communities and outsiders can become more or less porous, depending on the context. We have decided to call this phenomenon of selective inclusion "collaborative intellectual property".

The De Beer *et al.* Chapter 2 and the Kawooya Chapter 3 look at previously understudied modes of appropriation in the informal economy (IE). What the authors of these chapters describe in relation to the IE, theoretically in Chapter 2 and empirically in Chapter 3, would in high-income countries be commonly understood as trade secrecy. Trade secrets, confidential information and sharing or non-disclosure agreements are all well-accepted forms of IP management and play important roles in innovation systems. Yet, because secrecy does not produce a quantifiable output (e.g. a patent), its use and value in Africa's informal sectors are too often ignored. Experts such as Juma (see Juma and Ojwang, 1989) have argued that design patents or utility models (UMs) are appropriate modes of protection for the IE, because they are generally easier to obtain (and, consequently, offer weaker protection) than ordinary patents. Similarly, Dos Santos and Pelembe's Chapter 11 suggests that UMs may need prioritisation in Mozambique as a means to spur biofuel innovation. But, at the same time, as seen in Kawooya's Chapter 3, the Kampala informal-sector actors surveyed through interviews and other in-depth qualitative research techniques made no mention of any desire for such protection. Perhaps they are unaware of the benefits, or perhaps UMs are only of limited value in highly informal settings, because UMs, though less administratively cumbersome than patents, still depend on formal administrative and legal mechanisms to obtain and enforce. There is undoubtedly a need for further research on the issue of UMs in African settings.

The Oguamanam and Dagne and Adewopo *et al.* studies, outlined in Chapters 4 and 5, respectively, look at trademark certification schemes and origin-designated or place-based branding of GIs as underdeveloped forms of IP protection in the African context. Chapter 4 examines how GIs could benefit the Ethiopian coffee and Ghanaian cocoa industries. Chapter 5 considers how different kinds of communal trademarks or communal branding strategies (collective marks, certification marks and GIs) could improve the market position of leather and textile producer clusters in Nigeria. In both cases, however, prudent legal or policy reforms would be required. In Ethiopia and Ghana, as Oguamanam and Dagne emphasise, policy-makers need to seek a balance between protection, preservation, openness and collaboration. Based on the Nigerian case studied, the authors Adewopo, Chuma-Okoro and Oyewunmi note that the current national legal framework for the protection of at least two of the three forms of communal trademarks is inadequate.

Ouma's Chapter 6 and Cocchiaro *et al.*'s Chapter 7 both look at *commons*-based approaches to TK, in Kenya and in the Bushbuckridge area of South Africa, respectively. Kenya currently has no specific law on the protection of TK, but a draft TK law was published in mid-2013 (as this book was being finalised) and there are several Kenyan laws that touch on TK as it relates to copyright, biodiversity, genetic resources, agriculture, forestry and wildlife. In addition, Kenya's National TK Policy, which underpins the 2013 draft TK law, seeks to recognise, preserve, protect and promote the sustainable use of TK for national development purposes. Ouma concludes that reliance on existing Kenyan copyright law and industrial property law (which at present represent a conventional IP regime) would not be sufficient to ensure realisation of an effective commons modality in Kenya; rather, it is the National TK Policy (and draft law), coupled with emerging state interest in creating a Kenyan TK digital library, that show the most promise for the establishment of a TK commons that combines the objectives of protection, access and controlled exploitation.

Chapter 7's authors, Cocchiaro, Lorenzen, Maister and Rutert, share Ouma's scepticism expressed in Chapter 6 regarding the suitability of conventional IP laws for dealing appropriately with TK (in this case, the TK of the Kukula traditional medicinal practitioners). Problematic issues identified in Chapter 7 include the requirement of novelty in patent law (which contradicts the fact that knowledge constituting TK often dates back many generations) and the protection requirements, in copyright law, of originality and manifestation in material form (when, for instance, traditional songs and melodies of indigenous peoples often exist only in oral form). Both copyright laws and patent laws also require a single inventor-creator or a clearly distinguishable group of co-inventors or co-creators. In the case of multi-generational TK, identifying a sole inventor-creator or even a discrete group of inventors-creators is often impossible. Recognising these difficulties, the authors of Chapter 7 suggest that the group which was the focus of the authors' research, the Kukula Healers' collective, could benefit from the creation of a legal trust as a platform to, at the very least, more effectively manage its TK. Such an approach, according to the authors, could facilitate sharing of TK at the local level while ensuring that any non-traditional uses of such knowledge comply with the norms and values of, and provide benefits to, the community. Setting up a legal trust could also encourage the healer community to better document its TK, in order to determine the actual trust "property", which in turn could provide potential external partners with information regarding the precise scope of the TK.

The first of the two copyright-focused chapters, Chapter 8, provides an investigation of Egypt's vibrant independent music industry and the complex dynamics of distribution and consumption in that sector. The author, Rizk, observes a significant disconnect between the law on the books (which affords copyright protection to musical works) and consumption and distribution practices on the ground (which routinely violate copyright). Physical CDs and cassettes are copied and sold irrespective of the legal restrictions imposed by copyright law. As far as online material is concerned, the majority of consumers and independent musicians surveyed said that they regard such material as inherently free-of-charge. The surveyed musicians said they generally find the notion of copyright protection for their material irrelevant to their practices, in addition to being inadequately enforced. Rizk concludes that Egypt's independent musicians produce music primarily for self-expression and voicing opinion, and only expect remuneration for live performance. However, musicians could, in Rizk's analysis, reap an enhanced monetary benefit (and restore a measure of legitimacy to the Egyptian copyright regime) if they bundled free access to content in their "digital commons" with paid access to live performances (perhaps combined with optional contributions to the band and purchase of a physical CD), thus adopting a "freemium" approach to organisation and exploitation of their commons.

The other copyright-oriented chapter, Sihanya's Chapter 9, identifies a stumbling block for open scholarship and alternative publishing in Kenya in the existence of uncertainty among stakeholders regarding reward mechanisms, particularly economic rewards (even though, at the same time, the scholarly authors interviewed generally said they consider *moral* rights to their works to be of greater importance than *economic* rights). In order to overcome the uncertainties in terms of authors' control over economic rights, Sihanya recommends a revision of the Kenyan Copyright Act of 2001 with the aim of more clearly providing a balance between authors' economic rights and users' access rights – by, for instance, (a) clarifying owner's rights and more clearly recognising limitations and exceptions (e.g. exceptions for access through Braille), and (b) strengthening copyright administration.

Mgbeoji's Chapter 10, Dos Santos and Pelembe's Chapter 11, and Awad and Abou Zeid's Chapter 12 all address issues related to patent protection. Based on survey and interview responses from stakeholders in 44 African countries and at African regional IP bodies ARIPO and OAPI, Mgbeoji finds that African states are serving as "dumping grounds" for patents, with little or no examination or public access. Mgbeoji argues that national patent offices in Africa are thus insufficiently facilitating the legal bargain between inventors and society that is at the heart of patent law: i.e. the exchange whereby disclosure of inventions results in time-limited monopolies. According to Mgbeoji, this bargain requires a system in which experts evaluate the patentability of an invention, and patent offices collate and systematically disseminate patent documents in a publicly accessible manner. Mgbeoji argues that the wider significance of his findings is that dysfunctional national patent regimes not only contradict the spirit of national laws but may also disincentivise R&D and hamper the dissemination of technological knowledge, in turn undermining social welfare and development.

Dos Santos and Pelembe investigate the extent to which IP plays, or could play, a role in access to, use of, and development of biofuel technologies in Mozambique. The authors' focus is on patenting under the country's Industrial Property Code of 2006, combined with an analysis of two relevant policies: the National Policy and Strategy on Biofuels (NPSB) of 2009 and the Intellectual Property Strategy 2008–2018. The NPSB directs the Mozambican government to enact specific legislation on biofuels, and to establish both a National Agenda for Research and Innovation in Biofuels and a National Programme on Biofuels Development. The IP Strategy aims to stimulate creativity and innovation to promote economic, scientific, technological and cultural development. Both policies emphasise the need to support technological solutions developed by local innovators, and the NPSB emphasises the need for small-scale rural farming enterprises to be empowered via the country's biofuel exploitation. However, a patent landscaping exercise conducted by Dos Santos and Pelembe revealed that all 18 biofuel-related patents thus far registered in Mozambique have been filed by foreign companies, with only one patent originating from Africa (South Africa). The authors also found that *first generation* biofuel production technology in use in Mozambique appears to be mostly in the public domain, with a surge in biofuel patenting since 2008 resulting in the more efficient *second generation* technologies typically being patented. The authors conclude that, while patents do not hinder access to the first generation biofuel technologies, future use of second generation technology will likely require negotiation with the owners of the technology and payment of licensing fees, thus undermining participation by small enterprises. As mentioned earlier in this chapter, Dos Santos and Pelembe also call for greater Mozambican government attention to UMs as a potential form of IP protection for innovations that may not meet the criteria for full patenting. At the same time, the authors of this Mozambique study present an interesting example they discovered of informal, open access technology transfer (of a biofuel cold-pressing method) between Tanzanian rural small-scale farmer groupings and a similar Mozambican grouping. This informal mode of technology transfer (which resonates with the kind of knowledge-sharing found by the Kawooya research outlined in Chapter 3) could, in the view of the authors, be one of the paths towards innovative, localised, small-scale biofuels production in Mozambique and, more generally, environmentally sustainable socio-economic development.

The Awad and Abou Zeid study of Egyptian biofuel technology development was, to some extent, prompted by the growing view at international level (in evidence, for example, in talks related to the UN Framework Convention on Climate

Change [UNFCCC]) that laws and regulations governing patents can be barriers to sustainable development of clean energy technologies. Awad and Abou Zeid examine whether Egypt's patent system is conducive to biofuel innovation, and their legal observations include the finding that there is a *sui generis* protection regime in Egypt for plant varieties, and that a so-called "breeder exemption" exists, in the context of plant variety rights, in order to allow permission-free access to plant material so as to facilitate breeding of new varieties. Furthermore, Egyptian patent law requires, according to the authors, "the highest possible level" of disclosure in exchange for granting a patent. At the same time, the authors found that there is very little in the way of *actual* biofuel innovation in Egypt – with only one identified domestically generated biofuel patent to date (which has not been commercialised). Awad and Abou Zeid propose several mechanisms that, if adopted in Egypt, could increase clean energy innovation, including a clean energy patent fast-tracking system; an advanced patent database for wider dissemination of clean energy technology information; and a clean energy "patent commons" model that would facilitate the collaborative elements of innovation and allow easier access to patented clean energy technologies.

Ncube *et al.*'s Chapter 13, Belete's Chapter 14 and Ama's Chapter 15 address the issue of ownership of publicly funded research outputs. Ncube, Abrahams and Akinsanmi investigate the potential impact of South Africa's Intellectual Property Rights from Publicly Financed Research and Development (IPR-PFRD) Act on collaborative research, innovation and scholarly publishing at two of the country's top universities, the University of Cape Town (UCT) and Johannesburg's University of the Witwatersrand (Wits). The authors submit that the Act seems to have resulted in some change in behaviour, as the two universities studied are adapting to the realities of patenting and commercialisation under the new legislation. The authors caution against South African public research institutions approaching the Act's requirements from merely a compliance perspective. They recommend, instead, an ongoing process of considering the Act's full range of objectives and requirements, so as to avoid indiscriminate patenting without due consideration of social and broad economic benefits. The authors also highlight the need for state support of the open access (OA) publishing movement already apparent at both UCT and Wits and among other public research stakeholders, in order to ensure a counter-balancing of the Act's knowledge commercialisation emphasis by vibrant knowledge "socialisation" and open science activities.

Belete's Chapter 14 notes the Ethiopian government's emphasis on strengthening university–industry interactions, and the assumed important role of IP rights protection and commercialisation in facilitating knowledge transfer from universities to industry. Acknowledging global debates about IP protection for publicly funded research, Belete cautions against uncritical cross-national law and policy emulation, especially from high-income to low-income countries, because country-specific situations must be considered. In Ethiopia's case, for instance, universities currently have weak research capacities, which are often not aligned with industry needs. Meanwhile, private sector firms often have limited capacity to seek and utilise externally generated knowledge, due to financial constraints. In Belete's analysis, instead of emphasis on privatising knowledge by way of IP rights, the push should be towards the methods of knowledge transfer associated with the aforementioned concept of open science. IP-related models can still play a role in encouraging innovative research, Belete suggests, but other measures are even more important, such as increasing research budgets and creating salary systems that incentivise research activity and better recognise research contributions. Belete concludes that such strategies have the potential– more readily than IP commercialisation – to increase knowledge transfer from universities to the private sector.

Ama's Chapter 15 looks at IP matters in relation to publicly funded research in Botswana, examining the country's relevant policies and laws and presenting original survey data on public researchers' perceptions of IP matters. Key findings from the author's investigation include a general lack of awareness among researchers of the specifics of national and institutional IP law and policy frameworks. At the same time, Ama also found that Botswana's researchers do see value in the notion of commercialisation efforts facilitated by IP protection. However, resonant with Belete's analysis of the Ethiopian setting, Ama found that most of the Botswana researchers surveyed believe that value from publicly funded research is best served by approaches whereby research outputs are widely shared and openness and collaboration are prioritised, i.e. approaches founded on the notion of open science.

Thus the IP approaches identified as suitable by the research outlined in this book – i.e. approaches identified as being compatible with innovation and creativity in the African settings studied – tended to be characterised by a strong degree of openness and a balance between protection and collaboration objectives.

4. Visions of socio-economic development

As well as improving understanding (as outlined in the previous section) of the real and potential links between collaborative modes of IP management and innovation and creativity, the research outlined in this book has shed light on the roles that collaborative IP, innovation and creativity are being expected, or could be expected, to play in service to broader socio-economic development visions. For it is clear that, as demonstrated to some extent by De Beer *et al.* in Chapter 2, issues of innovation and creativity, and the potential of IP modalities as spurs to innovation and creativity, derive their importance primarily from being seen as having the capacity to stimulate socio-economic development. And it is thus necessary to take stock of the developmental visions present in the various African settings examined by the research in this book. A range of developmental visions was uncovered: high-level state policy visions (e.g. in Egypt, Ethiopia, Botswana, Mozambique and South Africa); mid-level visions (e.g. among small-scale, community-based associations and collectivities in Nigeria, Ghana, Ethiopia, Mozambique and South Africa); and grassroots, *ad hoc* visions of loose collectivities (e.g. among Egyptian independent musicians and Ugandan informal-sector auto mechanics.)

High-level, state visions

In the examinations of policies on IP from publicly funded research in South Africa, Ethiopia and Botswana (Chapters 13 to 15), we see the national governments in these three countries to some extent borrowing approaches from afar, in particular from the IP commercialisation orientation of the US Bayh-Dole Act. It remains to be seen whether such an orientation, fashioned more than three decades ago in the world's strongest economy, will be helpful in contemporary or future African contexts. The evidence provided in this book suggests that the IP commercialisation orientation for public research outputs will have a relatively benign impact in South Africa; potentially damaging consequences in the context of Ethiopia (with its moribund university–industry linkages); and highly uncertain results in Botswana (where the policy-making is very recent and awareness among public researchers very low).

The biofuel innovation context (covered in Chapters 11 and 12) is another area in which contributors to this book uncovered evidence of apparently strong, high-level, state developmental visions (in Mozambique and Egypt, respectively). Policy-makers in both these nations seem clearly to see domestic clean energy innovation as central to the national drive for sustainable socio-economic development (notwithstanding the extreme flux at national government level in Egypt as this book was being finalised in mid-2013). However, at the same time, in both the Mozambique and Egypt studies the research found evidence of highly uncertain feasibility in the visions of clean energy technology innovation as national development drivers, with potentially thorny IP matters, specifically patenting matters, seemingly receiving inadequate attention in both countries. In Mozambique, the Inter-Ministerial Committee on Biofuels, guided by the National Policy and Strategy on Biofuels (NPSB) of 2009, became operational only in 2012, and thus it is ultimately too soon to tell whether the state's developmental vision will align with the actual innovation and IP realities in the biofuels sector. The presence on this Inter-Ministerial Committee of three government Ministers (of Agriculture; of Science and Technology; and of Environment) suggests a high degree of state commitment to developmental goals via biofuels, but at the same time it is notable that there is no mention of IP in the NPSB of 2009. Meanwhile, in Egypt the feasibility of a developmental vision in relation to bioenergy innovation is called into question by the finding, by case study researchers Awad and Abou Zeid, that there appeared to be only one locally generated Egyptian bioenergy patent, and that the patent was not yet commercialised.

It must be borne in mind, however, that it is future possibilities, not current realities, that matter most when examining development pathways. The poor patent position of a country such as Mozambique may or may not place it at a competitive disadvantage. Important players with natural affinities to Mozambique through shared colonial history (and thus cultural, social, linguistic and economic linkage) – e.g. companies like Brazil's Petrobras – may see fit to make substantial local investments in Mozambican biofuel capacity. Also uncertain, because of the advent of new technologies to generate energy, in particular fracking to extract natural gas, is whether biofuels will remain a policy priority.

Mid-level, associational visions

In contrast to the bureaucrat-led state developmental visions described in several case studies were the seemingly more grounded developmental visions, found in other studies, of sector- and/or community-based associations. Whether it is the Ethiopian coffee and Ghanaian cocoa grower-producer collectives (Chapter 4), the leather and textile unions and associations in Nigeria (Chapter 5), the small-scale jatropha oil-pressing collective in Mozambique (Chapter 11) or the traditional medicinal practitioners in South Africa (Chapter 7), there is evidence in the behaviour of these groups of adoption of developmental visions which prioritise sustainable and realistic engagement with prevailing innovation (and to some extent IP) realities. And there is evidence to suggest that these associational collectivities have the dynamism to translate their development visions into workable innovations and IP engagements based on gradations of openness, collaboration and protection that they determine to be appropriate to local conditions. Put another way, these groupings appear to have the potential to harness the potential vitality – to the extent that it exists in their respective settings – of collaborative, openness-oriented (i.e. "open development"-oriented – see Section 5 below) approaches to the intersection of IP management, innovation and creativity, in service to livelihood development and socio-economic upliftment for association members.

Grassroots, ad hoc *visions*

Also uncovered by the research were instances of grassroots, *ad hoc* (and more implicit than explicit) developmental visions held by relatively unorganised actors with minimal associational support. The Ugandan auto mechanics (Chapter 3) and Egyptian independent musicians (Chapter 8) seem not to be engaged in the formation of overtly collective structures, but at the same time they seem to display strong, entrenched visions of how to achieve livelihood success. Chapter 2's conceptual survey helps us to see that the IE and informal economic and subsistence structures are emergent topics of interest in innovation research. The evidence in Chapters 3 and 8 of powerful-yet-informal developmental visions provides support for the view that the dynamics of informality in African settings require closer scrutiny and have many insights to offer to researchers.

Kawooya in Chapter 3 proposes the conceptual tool of the "continuum" between formality and informality, and it will be valuable to examine, in the years to come, where the Ugandan informal-sector mechanics and Egyptian independent musicians – and myriad other collectives of relatively informal actors in African settings – find themselves (or place themselves) on the continuum in their efforts to realise personal, familial or community developmental goals. In Chapter 8, Rizk provides thoughts on how a mix of digital commons and freemium approaches might allow Egypt's independent musicians to adopt greater adherence to formalised copyright realities while at the same time remaining true to the vision and practices organically developed in their loosely defined creative sector. Meanwhile, via the Ugandan study, Kawooya shows us that the Gatsby Garage is to some extent a formal–informal (or "semi-formal", in Kawooya's words) hybrid: a setting where both formalised actors (employed by Makerere University) and informal actors (contracted or paid on an occasional basis) collaborate and share ideas, innovations and trade secrets as IP. Such findings make it easy to imagine that formal–informal (semi-formal) hybrid encounters with innovation, creativity and IP will, in the years and decades to come, become increasingly prevalent engines of socio-economic development in African settings.

We have also seen stakeholders in the case studies, – e.g. the scholarly authors in Kenya, and (to a lesser extent) the public researchers in Ethiopia and Botswana – who, while they have formalised employment at institutions (e.g. universities) that are presumably governed in line with national developmental goals, seem to lack a strong connection to visions of socio-economic development. In the case of the researchers in Ethiopia and Botswana, there seems to be little linkage between high-level government socio-economic visions (in relation to innovation and IP) and the felt needs of researchers.

5. Current intersections: collaborative innovation and creativity, openness and IP

It is now necessary to draw out some of the key findings from across the chapters of this book in relation to the main themes proposed by the Open A.I.R. Project that supported the research: the themes of collaborative innovation and creativity, openness and IP.

Collaborative innovation and creativity

In almost every one of the cases outlined in this book, there are vibrant collaborative models at play in relation to innovation and livelihood development. The collaborations range from the extremely informal (e.g. the apprenticeship and referral networks among the Ugandan auto mechanics in Chapter 3); to the considerably more formal (the BCP instrument of the Kukula Healers in South Africa, Ghanaian cocoa's Licensed Buying Companies, and Ethiopian coffee's Farmers Cooperative Unions); to the somewhere in between (the Gatsby Garage in Uganda, the sometimes fractious union or association structures for Nigerian leather and textile producers, the oil-from-jatropha initiative in Mozambique). A crucial engine in these collaborative innovation-creation endeavours seems clearly to be openness.

Openness

In some of the studies featured in this book, we see what appears to be a strong emphasis on openness (with an almost complete absence of restrictions or closures) in relation to certain innovative, collaborative outputs. For instance, the Ugandan mechanics interviewed for Chapter 3 do not, as is the nature of the very open paradigm in which they innovate and develop their livelihoods, seek proprietary control over access to their innovative ideas and solutions. But in other chapters, we see that collaboration does not mean absolute openness. The Kukula Healers are committed to openness among the participants in their TK commons, but their BCP controls access to their commons (by both participants and non-members). Likewise, the leather and textile makers in Nigeria seek to share within their unions and associations, but at the same time they seek to prevent their designs from being used by non-union/association members. And while the Kenyan scholarly authors discussed in Chapter 9 are enthusiastic about the potential of OA publishing, they also want protection of their economic rights as creators. In these three cases, the *knowledge commons* present seems to be analogous to the traditional agricultural commons (in which there is sharing of the common land but not everyone [i.e. not someone who does not reside in the vicinity of the commons] has access to the common land).

As discussed in some detail in Chapter 1 and mentioned in other chapters (see Oguamanam and Dagne's Chapter 4, Ouma's Chapter 6, Rizk's Chapter 8, Sihanya's Chapter 9), the concept of "open development" is relatively new and still at an early stage of conceptual evolution. To the extent that the studies outlined in this volume suggest that collaboration is a primary engine of innovation and development in many African settings, then the conceptual emphasis of open development's proponents – the emphasis on networked collaboration – seems to fit. But it must also be borne in mind that the framers of the open development framework acknowledge that absolute openness will often not be beneficial or possible in developmental settings; there will usually need to be some parameters and restrictions (see Smith *et al.*, 2011). The findings generated by the studies in this book support the contention that open development cannot be conceived as a binary proposition, either open or closed. Nor would a metaphor of a spectrum, from more open to more closed, necessarily be apt: socio-economic development, especially when conceived as open development, is a far more complex process than that.

IP

Long before it became fashionable to extol the virtues of collaborative, open approaches to IP, these were factor endowments inherent in the African innovation and creation experience. These endowments are now assets (or can become assets) that African policy-makers and practitioners can bring to national, regional, continental and global IP policy and practical discourses. To do so, however – as the crosscutting nature of this volume's collection of case studies shows – African innovation policy-makers and actors will need to move away from dominant preconceptions of IP as involving mainly patent, copyright and trademark protections. Informal and flexible protections such as trade secrets seem much better suited to the informal sector, as the Kawooya study in this volume demonstrates. And Ouma, in her study, notes how orthodox IP institutions are inappropriate to protect TK, while Cocchiaro and his co-authors show how legal mechanisms outside of IP, such as trusts, may prove useful. A further indication that the conventional forms of IP are increasingly unsuited for more organic forms of innovation and knowledge generation emerges from the fact that several of the case studies in this book (e.g. the studies by Oguamanam and Dagne, Cocchiaro *et al.* and Awad and Abou Zeid) discuss or report on existing systems of *sui generis* protection for certain forms of IP (e.g. GIs, TK, plant varieties). The lack of salience, in many African settings, of conventional IP, drives home the fact (discussed in Chapter 1) that using patent numbers (commonly used as an indicator of innovation, thus positioning Africa as a continent that produces little or no innovation) is too crude an instrument to adequately measure innovation in Africa. Another factor mitigating against the salience of conventional IP in many African settings (in addition to the attractiveness of non-conventional approaches to IP), is the presence in many African countries of weak institutional infrastructure and a lack of context-sensitive policy orientation on IP (De Beer and Oguamanam, 2010).

Formal IP protection cannot exist in the absence of strong institutions, including not just IP offices that register, disclose and educate, but also a culture of respect and enforcement of IP rights. Several case studies in this book provide evidence that while IP laws are in place, their impact is minimal (or at least reduced) due to shortcomings in the administrative infrastructure needed to implement and enforce these laws. In many of the case study settings, the policy context is almost invisible, clearly divorced from the (often informal) economic and social structures central to innovation dynamics. Egypt's independent musicians and consumers of independent music are revealed, in Chapter 8, to behave (in their production and consumption, respectively) according to organically evolved motivations that take no account of mainstream music business models or copyright law. Chapter 10's findings reveal that many African national patent offices serve as a mere "clerical outpost" (to use author Mgbeoji's expression), with little regard for the statutory obligations at the basis of their existence. And there is a conundrum: attempts to boost IP infrastructure and enforcement can easily be viewed, particularly by marginalised communities who already perceive themselves to be on the wrong side of the prevailing IP exploitation equation, as introducing new tools of exclusion. Such perceptions would tend to decrease, rather than increase, respect for conventional IP modalities.

However, there is evidence, in some of the chapters of this book, of settings where improved institutional performance in relation to IP and related matters can be of potential benefit. In these settings, generally weak institutions impede effective policy implementation and compound the uncertainty already inherent in innovation environments. Kenya's scholarly authors would apparently, according to the research findings in Chapter 9, be more willing to embrace alternative publishing models if they had more faith in state protection of their economic rights under copyright. And Mgbeoji calls, in Chapter 10, for improved performance by African national patent offices, in their roles as examiners and disseminators of patent filing data, as a spur to localised innovation. Meanwhile, in Chapter 5 it is apparent that improved performance by a body not formally mandated as an institution of IP administration, the Standards Organisation of Nigeria (SON), would be of benefit to leather and textile innovation. We saw that the innovators studied in Nigeria have an inherently unpredictable relationship with SON, which has the power to regulate and standardise the quality of goods produced by small traders but does not at present adequately perform these functions. These findings connect to the crucial matter of how best to grow the small and medium enterprise (SME) sector on the continent – a sector made up of enterprises which, while suited to working within informal frameworks, can also benefit from a certain degree of regulatory predictability and formality in relation to the goods and services on which their business models are based.

Meanwhile, where there are state efforts to create more predictable and enabling IP policy environments for innovation, such as in South Africa, Ethiopia and Botswana, there is evidence of reliance on foreign models that are not necessarily well suited to local contexts. And hasty adaptations of such models – intended to superficially improve their suitability to African contexts – will likely make matters worse. While the American Bayh-Dole Act has been criticised for causing problems by giving publicly funded research institutions *the right to* patent outputs, we saw in Ncube *et al.*'s Chapter 13 that South Africa's IPR-PFRD Act of 2008 goes further by *requiring*, as a default, institutions to protect IP and to seek patent protection in any case where patentability seems possible. The Ncube *et al.* findings suggest that South African public research bodies will be able to construct workaround solutions to mitigate the potentially adverse impacts of the IPR-PFRD. But there are risks inherent in seeking to work around faulty policy – risks that are less likely to be present when policy-makers are truly attentive to emerging evidence and truly consultative with all relevant stakeholders.

6. Recommendations to African policy-makers

The final task of this chapter, and of this book, is to make some recommendations to African policy-makers: recommendations based on the evidence presented in the preceding chapters. IP policy-making in many African contexts is in a state of infancy. In many countries, IP is only now emerging onto the policy radar, and we hope that this book will enhance visibility of key issues. Growing interest in IP as a policy lever for innovation and creativity in Africa presents both profound opportunity and tremendous risk. Not only are emergent IP policies in Africa often driven by foreign interests and top-down assessments, but early African adopters of IP policy frameworks are in some cases leapfrogging developed-world models, and often not in a useful way.

Regardless of how little or how much the stakeholders who were surveyed, interviewed and observed in the studies done for this book are interacting with IP systems, policy frameworks (and the laws, regulations and institutions which seek to concretise the policy frameworks) have contextual importance in almost all of the settings studied. And, in most of the studies, the IP policy frameworks, no matter how faintly acknowledged, intersect with issues crucial to African nations' socio-economic development, including, but not limited to, science, energy, education, food, culture and communications. Given the range of important areas that IP policies and practices impact upon, and the often poor alignment (revealed by several studies in this book) between existing IP systems and present innovation realities, three key recommendations to African policy-makers emerge from, and provide a suitable conclusion to, this book.

Avoid mistakes

The first recommendation to African policy-makers is to avoid policy mistakes. Having no IP policy may be better than entrenching the wrong IP policy. This does not mean that policy-makers can ignore IP, but that they should be cautious and seek to make evidence-based rather than political decisions wherever possible. We have witnessed, in most of the case studies presented in this book, that actors innovate and create shared value through collaboration between interconnected communities (broadly defined). Collectivities in African settings continue to do what they have done – and done well – for millennia. Certainly, IP policies properly tailored to local contexts can enhance the benefits of innovation and creativity. But poorly designed policies can exacerbate problems, requiring risky and inefficient workarounds for innovation practitioners. Because, in many countries, IP policies are not yet locked in for the long term, the opportunity remains to leapfrog past many developed countries that are struggling with the adverse consequences of ill-conceived IP measures. But policy leapfrogging need not be a rapid endeavour. Learning from others' experiences, and then crafting context-appropriate responses, requires the willingness to collect evidence and consult broadly. Patience will provide African policy-makers an advantage.

Broaden IP conceptions

The second recommendation to policy-makers is to broaden conceptions of relevant and valuable IP practices. The studies presented in this book suggest that patent systems (even were the institutional capacity to exist, and in most cases it does not) are irrelevant to many of the modes of innovation and creativity happening in Africa. Copyright seems also to be ineffective in many African settings, because of its lack of enforceability.

We do not suggest putting an end to the building of capacity to conduct patent examinations and disseminate patent disclosures, or an end to the raising of copyright awareness in order to enhance copyright enforcement and compliance. These are potentially useful exercises. We believe it is better, however, to focus resources on mechanisms that are more relevant to localised, marginalised innovator communities. In many contexts, informal modes of IP protection, such as trade secrecy, coupled with limited knowledge-sharing within a defined group, seem better suited than formal IP mechanisms. Branding, whether through reputation alone or protected by geographic, communal or certification marks, may be another useful form of IP in many instances. Utility models and industrial designs deserve more careful analysis and consideration. And in the context of indigenous communities, it may be necessary to think more creatively about the kinds of mechanisms that have the potential to reinforce local customs and facilitate benefit-sharing, rather than building ways (as many emerging TK laws seem to be implicitly doing) to allow communities and/or governments to perpetually monopolise access to collectively generated knowledge. The crucial point is that IP can certainly be a practical tool for collaboration, but not if it is perceived narrowly or pursued dogmatically.

Look forward

The third, and perhaps most important, recommendation we can draw from the studies in this book is that African policy-makers need to look forward, not backwards. Through on-the-ground qualitative and quantitative data gathering, the researchers who have contributed to this volume have demonstrated the rapidly evolving dynamics of IP, innovation, creativity and development in African settings. This evidence provides a sense of the current realities in a wide variety of contexts. But simply observing the past and present cannot adequately prepare policy-makers and stakeholders for the future. Many African states appear to be at a crossroads in their paths towards negotiating their places in an increasingly globalised IP order. A narrative of Africa as "emerging Africa" (*The Economist*, 2013) has gained currency in recent years via African countries' relatively strong GDP growth in the wake of the 2008–09 global financial crisis (at a time when many "developed" states are experiencing stagnated GDP). This more positive view of the continent's prospects is potentially a welcome boost for African nations seeking to attract investment and partners. But this narrative whereby Africa is *emergent* also brings with it the danger of intensified pressure on African states to fine-tune national and regional laws and reorient knowledge production traditions into a globalised paradigm predicated on the market economy (in which orthodox approaches to IP rights have typically been positioned as sacrosanct). The findings in this book suggest that, going forward, African policy-makers, as with the innovators and creators whom the policy-makers are supposed to serve, must seek to harness IP rights on their own terms.

Bibliography

Bogliacino, F., Perani, G., Pianta, M. and Supino, S. (2012), "Innovation and development: evidence from innovation surveys", *Latin American Business Review*, Vol. 13, pp. 219–61.

De Beer, J. and Oguamanam, C. (2010), "Intellectual Property Training and Education: A Development Perspective", ICTSD Programme on IPRs and Sustainable Development, Issue Paper No. 31, International Centre for Trade and Sustainable Development, Geneva, pp. 1–58.

Juma, C. and Ojwang, J.B. (Eds) (1989), *Innovation and Sovereignty: The Patent Debate in African Development*, African Centre for Technology Studies (ACTS), Nairobi.

King, K. (2001), "Africa's informal economies: thirty years on", *SAIS Review of International Affairs*, Vol. 21, pp. 97–108.

Muchie, M. (2004), "Resisting the deficit model of development in Africa: re-thinking through making of an African national innovation system", *Social Epistemology*, Vol. 18, pp. 315–32.

Open African Innovation Research and Training Project (Open A.I.R., n.d.), available at: www.openair.org.za (accessed 12 April 2013).

Seriki, H.T., Hoegl, M. and Parboteeah, K.P. (2010), "Innovative performance in African technological projects – a multi-level study", *Journal of World Business*, Vol. 45, pp. 295–303.

Shane, S. (1992), "Why do some societies invent more than others?" *Journal of Business Venturing*, Vol. 7, pp. 29–46.

Shane, S., Venkataraman, S. and MacMillan, I. (1995), "Cultural differences in innovation championing strategies", *Journal of Management*, Vol. 21, pp. 931–52.

Smith, M.L., Elder, L. and Emdon, H. (2011), "Open development: a new theory for ICT4D", *Information Technologies and International Development*, Vol. 7 No. 1, Spring (Special Issue: Open Development), available at http://itidjournal.org/itid/article/view/692/290 (accessed 12 April 2013).

Taylor, M.Z. and Wilson, S. (2012), "Does culture still matter? The effects of individualism on national innovation rates", *Journal of Business Venturing*, Vol. 27, pp. 234–37.

The Economist (2013), "Africa rising: a hopeful continent", in "Special report: emerging Africa", 2 March, available at: www.economist.com/news/special-report/21572377-african-lives-have-already-greatly-improved-over-past-decade-says-oliver-august (accessed 12 April 2013).

Index

Please note: Page numbers in *italics* refer to figures, tables and appendices.

A

Academy of Sciences of South Africa (ASSAf) 289, 308
access and benefit-sharing (ABS) 15–16, 18, 151
  Nagoya Protocol 153, 161–162
  Regulations, South Africa 162
access to knowledge (A2K) 3, 17, 204, 285–286
Access to Knowledge for Development Center (A2K4D) 178
Adama University Research Policy, Ethiopia 325
Addis Ababa University (AAU) 323
  Research Policy 325
Africa 4–5, 61
  agricultural production 89
  diversity of social constructs 377
  net exporters of knowledge 18
  recommendations to policy-makers 391–393
  unemployment statistics 46
African Economic Research Consortium (AERC) 210
African Growth and Opportunity Act (AGOA) 114
African innovation and creativity
  undermining 5, 7–8
  undervaluing 5–7
African innovation policy priorities 20
African national patent regimes 242
African Regional Intellectual Property Organisation (ARIPO) 139–140, 237, 238, 239, 250–251, 256, 262, 381
African Science, Technology and Innovation Indicators (ASTII) 39
  African Innovation Outlook report 39
African Technology Policy Studies Network (ATPS) 210
African Union (AU) 344
African workforce 46
agricultural biotechnology 88
agricultural industries 133
agricultural producers 79
agricultural products 375
agricultural waste 272, 273
  rice straw 273
Agro Eco-Louis Bolk Institute 88
Ajuda de Desenvolvimento de Povo para Pova (ADPP), People to People Development Aid, Mozambique 257
  community biofuel project 256, 257, 258–259
  NGO project 260
algae 272, 273
alternative art scene, Cairene 178–179
alternative markets for higher-value products 78
alternative music and art industries 179
alternative music-consuming populations 179
alternative publishing models
  online subscription 204–205, 212
  online OA self-archiving 205, 212
alternative trading organisations (ATOs) 86
alternative value chain 90–91
American University in Cairo, The (AUC) 178
Anne Nang'unda Kukali v Mary A Ogola & Another, Kenya, 215–216
anti-commons effect 337
Anti-Counterfeit Act, Kenya 140
Antigue coffee, Guatemala 97
apprenticeship
  as means of learning 66–67
  sector-specific 376
Aquaculture Research Centre (ARC), Egypt 273
Arab Academy for Science, Technology and Maritime Transport 373
Arabic Creative Commons licences 175
architecture for Kenyan scholarship
  copyright communities 210
  libraries and archives 209
  professional research and publishing 210
  publishers 209
  scholarly consortia 210
  universities 209
Argentina 306
artisans 67
  and technology students 69
Association for Promoting Fairtrade in Finland 86
Australian patent office (IP Australia) 275–276
authorship 206–208
  motivation for 219–221
  and open scholarship 220–221
automobile parts 375

B

Bali meeting, UNFCCC 268
Banjul Protocol on Marks within the Framework of ARIPO 340
Bank of Industry (BoI), Nigeria, 116, 125

Bayh-Dole Act, US 21, 288, 290, 337–338, 391
international emulation 320–321
B-BBEE Act, South Africa 293
Berlin Declaration on Open Access 298, 303, 308, 310
Berne Convention for the Protection of Literary and Artistic Works 214, 340
bio-cultural community protocols (BCPs) 153, 378, 388
Biodiversity Act, South Africa 159, 162
biofuels 15, 375
agricultural products 248
ethanol and biodiesel 248–249
exploitation 250
innovations 270, 383, 385
legislation 254
patent landscape, Mozambique 255–256
policy and strategy, Mozambique 249
production methods 273
technology in production 258, 382
technology patenting 20
biopiracy 152–153
bio-prospecting 162
biotechnology 11
Botswana 385
benefits of public research to economy and society 359, *362*
framework for IP at institutions 348–353
importance of IP factors to commercialisation *360*
industrial property rights 341
institutional funding for research 365, *365*
institutional IP environments 364
institutional IP policies *364*
institutional IP policy on commercialisation *352*, 352–353
institutional IP policy on dissemination *350*
institutional IP policy on knowledge utilisation *351*
institutional roles 362–363, *363*
IPA and PRO ownership of results 350
IP and research practices necessary for value *361*
IP and STI environment 340–342
IP and University of Botswana (UB) 342–343
IP expertise and activity 344–345
IP law and policy 338, 353, *354–355*
IP management infrastructure 363
IP methods used *359*
IP for protection of research output 345–346, *347*
knowledge of how to use IP *347*
knowledge of institutional IP policies *349*, 353
levels of research activity 356–357
ministerial powers and parastatal institutions 343–344
Ministry of Trade and Industry 339, 343
publicly funded researchers 22, 335, 359, 384, 387
public policy 22
Registrar of Companies 344–345
research factors and commercialisation 358
"triple helix" of research and development 344
types of research 353, 356
university and PRO roles 366
use of IP procedures *348*, 358
Botswana domestic laws and regulations
Copyright and Neighbouring Rights Act 341
Industrial Property Act (IPA) 341
Industrial Property Regulations, Statutory Instrument 341
Botswana Export Development and Investment Authority 343
Botswana Football Association and Another v. Kgamane 345
Botswana Innovation Hub (BIH) 343, 344
Botswana Technology Centre (BOTEC) 343
Braille, audio or digital texts 225
branding 110
communal strategies 379
BRICS nations (Brazil, Russia, India, China, South Africa) 38
Budapest Open Access Initiative 211
Bushbuckridge, Kruger to Canyons (K2C) area, South Africa 151–168, 380
multi-ethnic nature of TK commons 160
municipality 157
registered as Biosphere Reserve 151
traditional medicinal practitioners 18, 386

C

Canadian Intellectual Property Office (CIPO) 276
capitalist entrepreneurs 36
Centre for Research in Transportation Technologies (CRTT), Makerere University, Uganda 64–65
certification
assessing schemes 88–90
critics of schemes 89
overseen by governmental bodies 88
marks 16–17, 78, 111, 112–113, 120, 123, 124
registration of marks 117
trademarks schemes 379
China 97, 110, 111, 122
clean energy technology 378, 383
Egypt 242, 267
fast-track administrative procedure 275–276
innovations 270, 385
and IP mechanisms 268
Mozambique 242
Climate Change Conference, UN, Copenhagen 268
clothing 375
Codes of Practice for Organic Farming, Ghana 88
collaborative, openness-oriented dynamics 4
collaborative branding, trademarks and geographical indications (GIs) 16–17

collaborative innovation and creativity 9–12, 22, 135, 388
collaborative intellectual property 377–384
collaborative partnerships 144–145
collective entities 81
collective management organisations (CMOs) 210
collective marks 111, 123, 124
  "CA" mark 112
collective rights of a community 80
College of Engineering, Design, Art and Technology (CEDAT), Makerere University 16, 63, 387
  IP dynamics 71–72
  Kiira EV Project 64–65, 67, 72
  Makerere Clusters Programme 73
  MoUs (memoranda of understanding) 72
  networks among study participants and entities *74*
  research centre and informal-sector artisans 59–60
  see also Gatsby Garage automotive workshop
commercialisation 320, 335
  in global R&D markets 305
  of IP 285, 286, 304
  of research output 348
Commission on Intellectual Property Rights (CIPR), UK 319–320
common law
  of copyright 214
  jurisdictions of UK and former British colonies 78
commons 137
  concept 154–155
  knowledge 137
  material 137
  social 137
  traditional agricultural 388–389
communalism 112
communal trademarks 109, 111–113, 120, 123, 379
  Ethiopian initiative 111
  feasibility 114
  models 124
  Nigeria 116–119
communication 37
communities
  closed group of 81
  traditional agricultural 82
Companies and Intellectual Property Commission (CIPC) (formerly CIPRO), South Africa 307
confidential information 379
construction, innovation in 38
consultancies for industry 353
consumer preferences 96
Convention on Biological Diversity (CBD) 138–139, 153, 271
cooking oil 272, 273–274
copyright 1, 3, 10, 132, 138, 346, 378
  American law 214–215
  development in Kenya and Africa 213–214
  economic rights 208
  and empowered creativity 19
  infringement 221
  laws, policies, practices 224
  moral rights 207, 208
  paternity right 207
  policy-makers 205
  protection 175, 205, 389
  in research 14
  right of integrity 207
  term in Kenyan law 207
  violations 175
  see also open scholarship and copyright, Kenya
Copyright Act, Kenya 140, 141
Copyright Tribunal, Kenya 210
cosmetic industries, and traditional knowledge (TK) 133
counterfeiting and falsification 97, 124
Creative Commons 11, 175
Creative Research Systems, *Sample Size Calculator* 339
creativity 1–2, 10, 133, 374, 375
cultural heritage 378
customary laws 157–158, 159

D

De Beers Element Six programme 303
demand-side factors 47
Department for International Development (DFID), UK 94
Department of Chemical Engineering, UCT 296
Department of Education, Science and Training (DEST), Australia 287
Department of Higher Education and Training (DHET), South Africa 289, 308
  Green Paper for Post-School Education and Training 289
Department of Molecular and Cell Biology, UCT 296
Department of Science and Technology (DST), South Africa 288, 308
Department of Trade and Industry (DTI), South Africa 303
design theft 121
diffusion
  geographic versions of theory 37
  process of innovation 41–42
digital commons business model 171, 387
  advertising and/or sponsorships 181
  knowledge of 181
  Meetphool digital platform181–182
  online digital music and streaming 184
digital copyright exchange 286
digital communications 203
digital rights management (DRM) 219, 223
digitisation and copyright, Kenya 210–211
discontinuous economic change 37

Divine Chocolate Inc, UK 86
domain name system (DNS) 210
Draft Bill on Protection of Traditional Knowledge and Traditional Cultural Expressions (Draft TK Bill), Kenya 141–142
dual economy model 48

E

Econergy International Corporation 249, 252–253
ecological and sustainability conditions, of production 87
Economic Community of West African States (ECOWAS) 125
economic development 36
  drive to maturity 36
Economic Development Imports 86
economic growth 33
economic strategies 38
economic systems
  classic and neoclassical 33–34
  development 33, 35
  dynamic development 34
  formal and informal 9
Eco-Patent Commons 276–277
ecosystem, building the new 309–310
"egocentric networks" approach 63
  selection of central node 63–64
Education and Training Policy, Ethiopia 322
Egypt 306, 385
  Al Sawy Cultural Wheel 179
  willingness to pay musicians *183*
  biofuel patenting 20, 271–272, 275–278
  biofuel technology development 382
  copyright law 174–175, 381
  Economic Court *194*
  "Hollywood of the East" 171
  illegally copied CDs and cassettes 183–184
  independent music industry 19, 171–172, 376, 380–381, 387
  IP law in practice 175–177
  alternative art outlets, Cairo *197*
  Patent Gazette 272
  patent law 270
  Patent Office 270–271, 272, 275, 276
  patent system 267–272
  private sector 274–275
  public sector 274
  research incentives 277
  stakeholders 272–275, 277–278
  see also music industry
Egyptian alternative music scene 390
  judicial process and court system 180, 181
  knowledge of copyright law 179–180
  relevance of copyright 180
Egyptian copyright provisions 268–271
  administrative bodies *194*
  conditions of protection *192*
  duration of protection *193*
  economic rights *192–193*
  Executive Regulation 270–271
  moral rights *192–193*
Egyptian Environmental Affairs Agency (EEAA) 274
Egyptian Intellectual Property Rights Law (EIPRL) 174–175, 182–183, 268–269
  Executive Regulation 271
  moral rights 190
electronic patent databases 14
electronic publishing 204
engineering, software and genetic 203
Engineering Capacity Building Program (ECBP), Ethiopia 324
enterprises, parastatal and industrial 336
entrepreneurial education 47
entrepreneurial environment in a developing economy 42–45
entrepreneurs
  "imitating" 41, 42
  "innovating" 41
  risk-taking 39
entrepreneurship 9, 32
  and Africa 45–48
  defined 40
  in developing world 40–42
  imitation 52
  and IP 43–44
environmental certifications 78, 87
  and labelling 84
Environmental Protection Authority (EPA), Ethiopia 91
environmental standards 110
environmentally sound technologies (ESTs) 276
ethanol 249
Ethiopia 21–22, 99, 316, 373, 375, 384, 385
  agriculture and GDP 316
  coffee industry 17, 77, 78, 84–85, 90–91, 376, 379, 386
  Coffee Quality Control and Inspection Centre 83
  Coffee Quality Control and Marketing Proclamation 92
  coffee trademark and licensing initiative 98–99
  Draft GIs Proclamation 91
  empirical value chain 82
  Farmers Cooperative Unions 84, 388
  foreign exchange earnings 83
  Forest Stewardship Council 87
  government policies 321–323
  institutional IP management 324–326
  IP rights and university research 319–321
  Ministry of Trade 91
  national IP system 324–326
  Office of the Vice-President 325
  Organic Agriculture System Proclamation 88

policy-makers, industry managers, academic researchers 326–328
poverty eradication 316–317
public researchers 387
Rainforest Alliance 87
university research and innovation by firms 323–324, 329
UTZ KAPEH 87
Ethiopia Commodity Exchange (ECX) 84
quality inspection centres 92
Ethiopian Intellectual Property Office (EIPO) 83, 91, 324–325, 327
trademark-based protection 98–99
Europe 99
European Patent Office 275
Eurostat (Statistical Office of the European Communities) 9, 32
evolutionary economic theory 37–38
Expert Group on Informal Sector Statistics (Delhi Group) 49

F
fair trade 84
certification 86–87, 89–90
labelling 78
Fairtrade Federation 86, 90
Fairtrade Foundation, UK 87
Fairtrade Labelling Organizations International (FLO) 86
FAIRTRADE™ mark 86
Fair World Designs 86
financial support facilities and schemes 125
FLO-Cert 86
Kafa Forest Coffee Farmers Cooperative Union 86
Oromia Coffee Farmers Cooperative Union 86
Sidama Coffee Farmers Cooperative Union 86, 89, 93
Yirgacheffe Coffee Farmers Cooperative Union 86, 93
folklore 133, 136, 214
foreign certifiers 88
foreign direct investment (FDI) 344
foreign markets 113
formal and informal sectors
dualistic conceptions 60–61
innovative work 66
networks, linkages between 67–69
sharing of innovations 70–71
formal–informal continuum 61–62, 387
choosing a point on 62
knowledge transfer 61
formal–informal exchanges and linkages 69–70
formal–informal innovation intersections 11
France 99
free and open source software (FOSS) movement 11
Free Day Secondary Education (FDSE), Kenya 209
Free Primary Education (FPE), Kenya 209
Friendship, Commerce and Navigation (FCN) Agreements 214

G
Galp Energia 252
Gatsby Garage automotive workshop, Uganda 16, 387, 388
IP protection issues 65–66
research 62–69
General Administration for the Prevention of Infringement of Intellectual Property Rights, Egypt 194
genetically modified (GM) foods 88
genetic resources (GRs) 79
geographical indications (GIs) 13, 16, 17, 77–78, 80–82, 89, 111, 113, 118, 123, 124, 138, 341, 346, 378
compliance and additional production costs 94
feasibility 90–91
legislation 92–93
operational challenges 95
origin-designated (or place-based) branding 379
potential economic benefits and costs 94
protection for wines and spirits 98
structural challenges 91–95
Ghana 48, 373
adinkra and *kente* cloths 97
certification schemes 85
Cocoa Abrabopa Association 87, 93
cocoa industry 17, 77, 78, 90–91, 376, 379, 386
empirical value chain analysis 82
Geographical Indications Act 91
good agricultural practice guidelines 92
government role in production and marketing 85
Kuapa Kokoo Farmers Union 86–87
Licensed Buying Companies (LBCs) 85, 388
Ministry of Agriculture 92
Ministry of Trade 83
Rainforest Alliance 87
Registrar General's Department 83
Standards Authority 83
Standards Board Codes of Practice for Organic Farming 88
UTZ KAPEH 87
Ghana Cocoa Board (COCOBOD) 85, 94
Quality Control Division 93
global diseases 306
Global Entrepreneurship Monitor (GEM) Model 43
and IP 44–45
globalisation 109, 111
global patenting market 306
greenhouse gas emissions 267
green inventions 275
green technologies 268, 276

gross domestic product (GDP)
Botswana 344
Ethiopia 316
Nigeria 110
gross expenditure on research and development (GERD) 344
Group of 77 developing nations (G77) 268

H
Hagen, Everett 36
Hague Agreement Concerning the International Deposit of Industrial Designs 340
Hague Convention on the Law applicable to Trusts and their Recognition 163
Haramaya University, Ethiopia 323
Harare Protocol on Patents and Industrial Designs within the Framework of ARIPO 255, 340–341
Hargreaves Report, UK 285–286
Harrod-Domar Growth Model 35
healing schools (*imphande*) 157
leaders (*magobela*) 157
Higher Education Proclamation, Ethiopia 322, 325
Hirschman, Albert 35
HIV infection 152
local patent for drug delivery 306
Hoselitz, Bert 36
human development 33

I
IBM 276–277
implementation, meaning of 10
inclusive development 8–9
India 118
Council of Scientific and Industrial Research (CSIR) 134
Darjeeling tea 111
Protection and Utilisation of Publicly Funded Intellectual Property 321
leather products, toys, wall decorations 111
pashmina textiles 111
indigenous and local communities (ILCs) 18, 80, 81, 144, 145, 146, 378–379
control over commercialisation and exploitation 134
control over natural resources and TK 153
Kenya 132, 133, 136–137
Kukula Healers, South Africa 161–162
and TK 17, 80
indigenous art 123
indigenous knowledge and capabilities 38
Indigenous Knowledge Systems Policy, South Africa 159
indigenous people's innovation 3
indigenous scientific capabilities 38
indigenous textile products, Nigeria 113
industrial absorptive capacity for knowledge conversion 375
industrial designs 138, 346
Industrial Development Corporation (IDC), South Africa 305
industrialisation 36
Industrial Property Act (IPA), Botswana 341
Industrial Property Act, Kenya 140, 141
Industrial Property Code, Mozambique 255, 382
Industrial Property Institute (IPI), Mozambique 250–251, 256
industrial property rights 255
informal appropriation, research on 13
informal economy (IE) 16, 32, 47–48, 52, 61, 379
"informal sector" concept 48–50
informal protections 378
international statistical definition 49
Kampala auto mechanics 373
networks, linkages in 69–70
information and communication technology (ICT) 204
efforts to digitally document TK 134, 136
systems 14, 51, 80
use of in Kenya 144–45
"informationalism" 203
innovation 1–2, 10, 33, 67, 133, 283, 288, 304, 339, 374, 375
conceptual frameworks 32
current state of literature 38–39
development and diffusion 37
and entrepreneurship 36, 52
five-step theory (Rogers) 36
in industrial enterprises 328
knowledge transfer approach 38
measurement in the informal sector 50–51
systems approach 33, 38
innovation–development nexus 33
innovation for development 47
innovative knowledge systems 376
Institute of Chartered Public Secretaries of Kenya (ICPSK) 210
Institute of Infectious Disease and Molecular Medicine (IIDMM), UCT 296
Institut national des appellations d'origine (INAO), France 98
instructional broadcasts 216
intangible resources 14
integrated seawater agriculture system (ISAS), Egypt 274
intellectual property (IP) 32, 77, 111, 248, 249, 268, 335, 373
Code, Mozambique 255
commercialisation 384
conventional rights 79
and dissemination 319–320
education and training of lawyers in Africa 238
fear of exploitation and infringement 52
framework for development 51–52
law and traditional healing 158–159

law, policy and practice 7, 10, 384
macro-level public policies 11
management, innovation, creativity 386
micro-level management practices 11
open or closed systems 283
policy instruments 133, 309
protection 319, 327, 346
rights 1–8, 22, 138, 317
rights in Africa's informal sector 59
South African public funding 283
training of legal counsel and judges 241
valorising (adding value to) GRs (genetic resources) 79
Western model of rights 79
Intellectual Property Rights from Publicly Financed Research and Development (IPR-PFRD) Act, South Africa 282–285, 288, 290, 302, 308, 310, 338, 383, 389–391
benefit-sharing 295
conditions that apply only to exclusive licences 294
conditions that apply to all licences 294
conditions that apply to offshore transactions 294
evolution of South African approach *289*
Framework, 288
institutional infrastructure 292
IP ownership and statutory protection 292–293
IP transactions 293–294
key provisions 291–292
primary intent of Act 290–291
Regulations 282–285
state "walk-in" rights 294–295
inter-ethnic traditions and customary laws 160
Inter-Ministerial Committee on Biofuels, Mozambique 254
regulations for biofuel additives to commercialised fuel 254
International Commission of Jurists (ICJ), Kenya Section 210
International Conference of Labour Statisticians (ICLS) 49
International Development Research Centre (IDRC), Canada 50
International Federation of Organic Agriculture Movements 88
International Institute for Environment and Development (IIED) 158
International Intellectual Property Alliance (IIPA) 176
International Labour Organisation (ILO) 45, 48–49, 51, 61
international markets
competition and standards 114
promotional activities in 95
International Patent Classification (IPC)
committee of experts 276
Green Inventory 276
International Organisation for Standardisation (ISO) 110
International Trade Centre (ITC) 343
International Treaty on Plant Genetic Resources for Food and Agriculture (International Seed Treaty) 139
inventions 304, 381
evaluation of merits 20
protection and processes 359
inventors 303
investment 35
Italian Embassy, Maputo 252
Italy 110

J

Japan
policy-makers 320
productivity 36
Joint Integrated Technical Assistance Programme (JITAP) 343
jojoba 274–275
medicinal applications 275
plantations 272

K

Kenya 380
alternative publishing 381
Anti-Corruption and Economic Crimes Act 218
civil society organisations 213
collaboration between government and indigenous and local communities (ILCs) 132
collective management organisations (CMOs) 213
conceptualising and contextualising copyright 206–208
Constitution 132, 140, 204, 214
Copyright Act 206, 211, 213, 214–217, 219, 224–226, 381
copyright law 380
Department of Culture 136
Department of Justice 136
Digitising Traditional Culture Initiative 145
Draft TK Bill 132, 146–147
fair dealing 214–215
funding 143
industrial property law 380
international and regional legal instruments 138–140
IP laws 132
IP rights 214
legal instruments for protection of IP 140–141
legal/policy framework and role of government 142–144

local economy 49
McMillan Memorial Library Act 209
National Cultural Agency 142
national and legal policy framework 140–142
National Museums of Kenya 136, 143–144
National TK Policy 18, 132, 142, 144, 146–147, 380
Office of the Attorney-General 136
Official Secrets Act 218
Penal Code 218
Public Officer Ethics Act 218
scholarly authors 376, 387, 388
Science and Technology Act 209
stakeholder perspectives 142–145
State Law Office 213, 225
TK commons 380
TK digital library 380
University of Nairobi 136
Vision 2030, policy blueprint 204
see also open scholarship and copyright, Kenya
Kenya Copyright Board (KECOBO) 136, 143–144, 145, 146, 210, 213, 225
National Competent Authority for traditional knowledge (TK) 142
Kenya Historical Association (KHA) 210
Kenya Industrial Property Institute (KIPI) 136, 142, 143–144, 145, 239
Kenya Institute for Public Policy Research and Analysis (KIPPRA) 209
Kenya Institute of Curriculum Development (KICD) broadcasts 216
Kenya National Academy of Sciences (KNAS) 210
Kenya National Library Service Board Act 209
Kenya Nonfiction and Academic Authors' Association (KENFAA) 210
Kenya Oral Literature Association (KOLA) 210
Keynesian economics and growth theory 33, 34–35
knowledge
African 5
capital 43
commercial application 337
commons 7, 388
dissemination 320, 348
economy 78–79
hoarding 285–186
informal management of 16
"know how" 43
poor people's 3
pre-existing ("prior art") 235
socialisation 21, 310–311, 338
technological 242
utilisation 348
knowledge-based economic development and change 322–323
knowledge–development nexus 38
knowledge economy (KE) 203
knowledge-governance frameworks 7
knowledge-sharing 178
knowledge transfer 375–376
knowledge transfer offices (KTOs), Botswana 349, 353
Kruger to Canyons (K2C) Biosphere Region, South Africa 151
ethnic groupings 151–152
K2C Management Committee 151, 153, 154, 165, 166
Kukula Healers 151–154, 373, 380, 388
Association 156–157, 167
bio-cultural protocol (BCP) 153–154, 160, 161
Code of Ethics 157
collective 380
commons 155–156
cosmetics 164
evolution of TK commons 156–161
Godding and Godding laboratories 164
holistic approach to knowledge-sharing 158
IP-based property rights 156
Nagoya Protocol 161–162
non-disclosure agreement with Godding and Godding 161–162
Traditional Health Practitioners' Association 151
trust as legal model 161–163, 166
Kyoto Protocol 252, 267

L

labelling 93
labour, flow of 48
Latin America 61
Law Society of Kenya (LSK) 210
least developed countries (LDCs) 319
legal profession and universities 304
legal trust components 163–164
licensing
alternative, in Egypt 175
and assignments of scholarly works 217
compulsory 216
learning materials 378
of rights, voluntary 255
and registration of businesses 50
Lipset, Seymour Martin 35–36
Luanda, Angola study 46
Lusaka Agreement on the Creation of ARIPO 340

M

Maasai, Kenya 142
community 135–136, 143, 144
knowledge 18, 132, 133
project on digitisation of culture 145
Maasai Cultural Heritage (MCH) Organisation, Kenya 136
Madrid Agreement Concerning the International Registration of Marks 117, 255, 340

Protocol 117, 118, 255, 341
Treaty 124–125
Malindi District Cultural Association (MDCA), Kenya 136, 144
Manufacturers Association of Nigeria (MAN) 116
manufacturing 35, 38
Margaret Ogola & 3 Others v David Aduda and Another, Kenya 215
marginalisation of African youth 45
marketed services, innovation in 38
Marshall, Alfred 34
mass consumption, age of high 36
Mauritius 306
McClelland, David 36
media coverage 6
medicinal knowledge 378
medicinal plants 152, 157
and animals 158
Mekelle University, Ethiopia 323
memoranda of understanding (MoUs) 72
microelectronics 203
micro-entrepreneurs 50
micro or cottage enterprises 113
Miji Kenda community, Kenya 135–136, 142, 143
Millennium Development Goals (MDGs) 51
Ministry of Agriculture (MOA), Ethiopia 83, 88, 91, 94
Agricultural Extension Directorate 91
Coffee Quality and Marketing Implementation Manual 92
Ministry of Infrastructure, Science and Technology (MIST), Botswana 343, 344, 345
modernisation theory 33, 35–37
Mozambique 379, 382, 385
applications to the Industrial Property Institute (IPI), Maputo 262
biofuels agreement with EU and Brazil 253
biofuel production 248–250
biofuel technology patenting 250, 256
Constitution 254
Inter-Ministerial Committee on Biofuels 259–260, 385–386
IP Code 255
IP Strategy 254–255
national biofuel policy-making and patenting 20
oil-from-jatropha initiative 388
patents granted 261
policy and legal framework 253–255
studies of biofuel sector 251–253
Multilateral Environmental Agreements (MEAs) 110
musicians
anti-commercialisation 187–188
business model 188
ethical consumption 189
non-monetary inclinations 188
remuneration model 188–189
sharing-based public licence 189
music industry 133
access versus incentive tension 172–174
commons-based approach 172, 190
consumers of alternative music, Cairo 178
consumption patterns 182–184
copyright and sharing 177–178
digital 172–173
"freemium" model 19, 171, 381, 387
illegal music copying, Egypt 176–177
independent music digital commons 191
jingles for advertisements 187
legal barriers and IP rules 173
live music scene, Cairo 173–174, 187, 190–191
monetary reward *186*
money spent on concerts *185*
money spent on music *185*
physical versus virtual 189–190
piracy in Egypt 176
as *quasi*-public good 172–174
remuneration, incentives, business models 184–189
websites for illegal music downloads, Egypt *176*
muti (traditional medicine) hunters, South Africa 152

N

National Agenda for Research and Innovation in Biofuels, Mozambique 254, 260
National Enquiry Point (NEP), Botswana 343
National Experts on Science and Technology Indicators (NESTI), OECD 37
national innovation system (NIS) approach 317
National IP Management Office (NIPMO), South Africa 288–289, 292, 294–295, 297–298, 302, 304, 307, 308, 309
National Museums and Heritage Act, Kenya 140, 141
National Museums of Kenya 142, 143
National Policy and Strategy on Biofuels (NPSB), Mozambique 248, 249, 250, 253, 258, 259, 382, 385–386
National Policy on Traditional Knowledge, Genetic Resources and Traditional Cultural Expressions (National TK Policy), Kenya 141
National Programme for the Promotion of Mozambican Innovators 258
National Programme on Biofuels Development, Mozambique 254, 260
National Research and Development (R&D) Strategy, South Africa 288
National Research Centre (NRC), Egypt 273
National Scholarly Editors' Forum, South Africa 289
Natural Justice non-governmental organisation (NGO) 153

neoclassical school 34
market equilibrium 34
orderly economic change 34
Natural Oil Company (Natoil), Egypt 274–275
New and Renewable Energy Authority (NREA), Egypt 274
New Nile Company, Egypt 274
Nigeria 379
Aba leather shoemakers *115*, 115–116, 120, 121–123
Central Bank 125
economy 109–111
existing cluster dynamics 119–120
existing knowledge of IP 121
export of leather 110
Itoku-Abeokuta textile producers 115, 120, 121–124
Kano leather tanneries 114, 115, 120, 121–122
leather and textile products 17, 78, 109–111, 113–114, 388
leather and textile unions and associations 386
legal and regulatory framework 116–119
market challenges 121–123
oil sector 109–110
Patent Office, Abuja 236–237
revenue generation 110
small-scale operators 123
textile makers 376
Trade Marks Act 112, 116–117, 121, 124–125
Yoruba people 113
Nigerian Customs Service 125
Nigerian Export Promotion Council 116, 125
Nokia 276–277
non-disclosure agreements (NDAs) 299–300
non-GI certification marks 124
non-trademarked certification schemes 78
North Africa 3
North–South protectionist dynamics 18

O
online Creative Commons-based "digital commons" 19
open, distance and electronic learning (ODEL) 216
open access (OA) 204, 211–212
to knowledge and culture 81
online publishing approach 19
publishing 289, 303, 383, 388
scholarly publishing 282, 287, 306
Open African Innovation Research and Training Project (Open A.I.R.) 12–15, 388
network's interdisciplinary framework 13
research programme 14
open development 8–9, 80, 134, 191, 204, 211, 386
open educational resources (OERs) 289
open innovation 135
open knowledge 288
openness 22, 388–389
open research 288
open scholarship 222–223, 381
challenges to accessing scholarly information 217–218
and alternative publishing, Kenya 225–226
and copyright, Kenya 19, 203–205, 211–212
open science approach 21, 288, 320, 335, 337
open source approach 276
Oromia Coffee Farmers Cooperative Union (OCFCU), Ethiopia 93
organic certification 84, 88, 90
schemes 90
through foreign-based certifiers 89
organic labelling 78
Organisation africaine de la propriété intellectuelle (OAPI) 237, 238, 239, 381
Organisation for Economic Co-operation and Development (OECD) 6, 9, 32, 38, 51, 335, 366
Working Party of NESTI 37–38
work on innovation 47
Oslo Manual: Proposed Guidelines for Collecting and Interpreting Technological Innovation Data (OECD and Eurostat) 9–10, 32–33, 37–39
ownership
and control systems 7
of IP rights 327
of outputs from publicly funded research 20–22, 378
Oxfam 86

P
Paris Convention for the Protection of Industrial Property 117–118, 139, 255, 340
Parsons, Talcott 36
patentability 234
patent commons 276–277
Patent Cooperation Treaty (PCT) 139, 237–238, 255, 272, 305, 340
International Bureau, Geneva 256, 261
Office, Geneva 238
patent data 276
patenting
and commercialisation 383
dynamics 20
university 320
patent offices in Africa 234
roles of 235–236
survey data *243–244*
patents 1, 10, 132, 138, 234, 248, 249, 346, 378
access to information 259
applications 236, 238
business method 210
database 276
design 379
"dumping grounds" 381
exclusive rights 270
incentivised payment for examiners 241
regimes in Africa 236–238

protection 381, 389
and renewable energy 15
in research 14
software 210
statistics 11
systems in African states 240–241
performance industry 133
Perroux, François 35
Petrobras, Brazil 386
Petromoc, Mozambique 251, 253, 257
"petty patent" utility models (UMs) 248
pharmaceutical industries 133, 134, 306
pharmaceutical research 306
Pitney Bowes 276–277
place-based intellectual property (PBIP) 17, 378
strategies 77, 78
plagiarism 221
Plant and Health Inspectorate, Kenya 143–144
plants 273
African palm 249
breeder exemption 270, 383
breeders' rights 138
castor seed 249
coconut 248, 249
genetic resources 376
jatropha 248, 249, 250, 251, 252, 256, 272, 274, 376, 386
sugar cane 248, 249
sui generis protection for varieties, Egypt 383
sunflower 249
variety rights systems 270
see also jojoba
Population Action International 45–46
preconditions for take-off 36
Pred, Allan 35
principles of inclusion and collaboration 378
prior informed consent 151
private-sector investment 319–320
probability proportional to size (PPS) measures 339
Proclamation for the Registration and Protection of Designation of Origin, Ethiopia 91
product
innovation 38
quality improvement 96
production cost 125
professionalism in patent offices 239
property ownership, attributes of 90
proprietary value 101
protection of IP 285–286
public good 172, 204
publicly funded research 14, 318, 320, 338, 351, 359, 375, 376, 384, 385
ownership of outputs 383
public–private partnerships 14–15
public research organisations (PROs), Botswana 335, 336–337, 339, 353, 363
publishers' copyright policies 221–222
publishing
digital 204
offline print 204
scholarly 204

Q

qualitative data 13, 373
quantitative data 13, 373
quasi-public good 173

R

reading or recitation of an extract 216
remuneration, direct financial 204
Renewable Energy Strategy, Egypt 268
research
analytical framework 12
applied 353
development-focused 287
emphasis on institutions *357*
epidemiological 353
evaluation 353
investment of public funds 306
literature/desk review 353
methods 12–13
multi-disciplinary network of researchers 12
perception of institution's involvement *357*
publicly funded entities 309
publishing 285
respondents' average yearly output, Botswana *358*
thematic areas 13–16
types *356*
under-utilisation of findings 286
research and development (R&D) 15, 20, 43, 45, 209, 242, 253, 254, 283, 305, 322, 375, 382
university-based 308
Revised National Policy on Research, Science, Technology and Innovation, Botswana 344
rights-holders 100
rights management information (RMI) 219
Rogers, Everett 36
Rostow, Walt Whitman 36
royalties 204
Rural Industrial Promotion Company (Botswana) (RIPCO (B)) 344
rural poverty 152

S

scholarly communication 208
scholarly publishing 203, 205, 287
literary works 207
scholarly works, use of 221
scholarship 208
see also architecture for Kenyan scholarship
school use and copyright 215–216
Scielo OA publishing platform, Brazil 289
Scielo South Africa 289
science and engineering publications 376
Science and Technology Capacity Index (STCI) 344

Science and Technology Policy, Ethiopia 322
"science first" position 337
science, technology and innovation (STI)
African Science, Technology and Innovation Indicators (ASTII) 39
Botswana 335, 344
national goals 22
Policy, Ethiopia 316–318, 322, 328, 338, 375
at Uganda National Council for Science and Technology (UNCST) 65
scientific information in African patent applications 242
scientific research, new economics of 337
scientists and academics 272–274
Schumpeter, Joseph 34, 41
Seeds and Plant Varieties Act, Kenya 140
sharing or non-disclosure agreements 379
Sierra Leone, study 48
small, micro- and medium enterprises (SMMEs) 341
small and medium enterprises (SMEs) 253, 255, 324, 327, 391
access to technology 258
utilisation and adaptation 256
small-scale enterprises 109
small-scale entrepreneurs 111
Smith, Adam 34
social and cultural value of textiles 110
social (*de facto*) commons 171–174
socialisation of knowledge 286–287, 299
socially conscious consumers 86
social network analysis (SNA) 63, 64
social networks 11
Society for International Development (SID), Kenya 210
socio-economic development 32, 134, 204, 283, 373, 382, 384–385, 387
grassroots, *ad hoc* visions 387
high-level, state visions 385–386
mid-level, associational visions 386
sociological approach to development 36
solar and wind energy 272
Solow, Robert 35
growth model 35
Sony 276–277
sorghum 249
South Africa 118, 385
traditional healers 376
traditional medical practitioners 386
South African Revenue Service 307
Southern African Development Community (SADC) 344
South Korean patent office (Korean Intellectual Property Office) 275–276
standardisation 109
Standards Organisation of Nigeria (SON) 110–111, 116, 118–119, 390–391
Director of International Standards and SMEs 110
Duty Drawback Schemes 125
respondent adherence to standards *119*
Statistical Office of the European Communities, *see* Eurostat
sub-Saharan Africa
informal employment 47
perspectives 3
"youth bulge" 45
youth-to-adult ratio 45
sui generis
ex parte form of GI protection 94
ex officio form of GI protection 94
geographical indications (GIs) 77–78, 80
protection of GIs, TK, plant varieties 389–390
regimes 80
systems 18
Sumitomo Chemical Company 256
Sun Biofuels Mozambique 256–257
Quinvita 257
Lufthansa 257
supply-side factors 47
Sussex Manifesto: Science and Technology for Developing Countries during the Second Development Decade 38
Swakopmund Protocol on the Protection of Traditional Knowledge and Expressions of Folklore within the Framework of ARIPO 139–140, 340

T

take-off preconditions 36
Tanzanian small-scale farmers 382
Tea Board of India 97
Technical and Vocational Education and Training (TVET), Ethiopia 323–324
technological development 35, 36
technological innovation 33
technological knowledge 242
technological protection measures (TPMs) 14, 173, 219
Technology and Human Resources Programme (THRIP), South Africa 303
Technology and Innovation Support Centres (TISCs), WIPO 259
Technology Innovation Agency (TIA), South Africa, 288, 304, 308, 309
technology research outputs 328
technology transfer offices (TTOs) 292, 296, 302, 307, 366
funding functions at Wits Enterprise 305
informal mode 382
and legal offices 309
telecommunications 203
Ten-Year Innovation Plan, South Africa 288
Thomson Reuters Web of Science 289
trade
global 79

liberalisation 109, 111
secrets 1, 10, 138, 346, 379, 389
trademark-based GI protection 101
trademark GIs versus *sui generis* GIs 100–102
ecological, cultural, biodiversity goals 100
trademarks 1, 10, 80, 132, 138, 346, 378
collective 78
conventional 78
ordinary 78
protection 389
registration and licensing 98
in research 13
speciality 78
see also communal trademarks
Trade Marks Act, Kenya 140, 141
Trademarks Registry, Nigeria 116
Trade-Related Aspects of Intellectual Property Rights (TRIPS) Agreement, WTO 2, 4, 117–118, 132–133, 255, 269, 340
traditional cultural expressions (TCEs) 133, 136, 145
traditional ecological knowledge 133
traditional healers, Bushbuckridge, South Africa 151–152
Traditional Health Practitioners Act, South Africa 159
traditional knowledge (TK) 80, 123, 136, 138, 214, 341, 376, 378
and biodiversity 155
biological resources and cultural goods 133
commercialisation 133
commons 16, 18, 134, 151
commons-based approach 380
commons pool 160
digital library initiative as defensive protection 145
exploitation of 18
legal trust mechanism 18
multi-generational 159, 380
patent applications 271
potential of commons arrangements 18–19
in production processes 114
in research 15
sui generis protection 145
TK-based agricultural products 80
TK-related IP challenges 16
trans-generational territorial 81
Traditional Knowledge Digital Library (TKDL), India 134, 144
traditional medicinal knowledge 133, 375
ancestors Nkomo le Lwandle and Dlamini 157
from healer (*sangoma*) to apprenctice (*thwasa*) 157
transfer and collection systems 158
traditional society 36
trust
administration rules 166
beneficiary 166–167
property 164–165
settlor 165
terms 165–166
trustee 166
Trust Property Control Act, South Africa 162–164, 166

U
Uganda 59, 375
auto mechanics 387
Central Engineering Workshop, Kampala 70
Kampala 59
policy-making 72–73
see also Gatsby Garage automotive workshop
Uganda Gatsby Trust (UGT) 64
Uganda National Council for Science and Technology (UNCST) 65, 72–73
UK 78, 94, 118, 319–320
Copyright Acts, colonial era 213–214
Intellectual Property Office 275
IP framework 285
UN
Commission on Trade and Development (UNCTAD) 94, 343
Declaration of the Rights of Indigenous Peoples 139
Department of Economic and Social Affairs (UNDESA) 251–252, 256
Educational, Scientific and Cultural Organisation (UNESCO) 6, 47, 151
Framework Convention on Climate Change (UNFCCC) 252, 267, 276, 382–383
Industrial Development Organisation (UNIDO) 116
Office for West Africa 46
unemployment 152
unfair competition 101
Universal Copyright Convention (UCC) 214
universities 338
university-generated knowledge 317
university–industry knowledge transfer, Ethiopia 316, 329, 376, 383
university–industry linkages 385
University of Botswana (UB) 339, 342, 345
Institutional Review Board (IRB) 339
Office of Research and Development (ORD) 342
research community 342–343
University of Cape Town (UCT) 21, 282–285, 383
commercialisation and dispute resolution 295
Creative Commons (CC)-licensed learning materials 298
Intellectual Property Advisory Committee 295
ownership of IP 295
research and innovation indicators 295–296, *296*
Research Contracts and IP Services office (RCIPS) 285, 296–297, 298, 299
researcher-inventor perspectives 299–300
UCT OpenContent website 298

University of Nairobi Institute of Development Studies (IDS) 210
University of the Witwatersrand (Wits University), South Africa 21, 282–285, 383
funding 302
IP protection strategy 304
patent filing 301–302
pharmaceutical research team 305
research and innovation indicators 300–301
researcher-inventor perspective 305–307
research-IP manager perspective 302–305
Technology Transfer Unit 302
Wits Enterprise (Wits Commercial Enterprise (Pty) Ltd) 285, 302–304, 305, 307
US
Agency for International Development (USAID) 116
Digital Millennium Copyright Act 217–218
Patent and Trademark Office (USPTO) 275–276, 336
Sonny Bono Copyright Term Extension Act (CTEA) 218
Uniform Computer Information Transactions Act (UCITA) 218
utilities, innovation in 38
utility models (UMs) 138, 248, 379

V

value chains 82
differentiation strategies 85–88
Ethiopian coffee 83–85
Ghanaian cocoa 85
intermediaries in products 95–96
visual art and design 133

W

Web of Science journal index 289
Wennekers and Thurik Model 42–43, 44
West African countries 110
White Paper on Science and Technology, South Africa 288
witchcraft 159
Witchcraft Suppression Act, South Africa 159
work policy, externally funded 309
World Bank 79, 252
World Business Council for Sustainable Development (WBCSD) 276–277
World Economic Forum (WEF) 344
Global Competitiveness Report 344
World Employment Programme (WEP), ILO 48–49
mission to Kenya 48–49
World Intellectual Property Organisation (WIPO) 3, 14, 18, 112, 143, 239, 255, 259
development agenda 3, 14, 259
Convention Establishing WIPO 340
Creative Heritage Project 145
digitisation of culture 145
digitisation of Maasai culture 135–136, 145
Diplomatic Conference, Marrakesh 3
Internet Treaties 211
Marrakesh Treaty to Facilitate Access to Published Works for Persons Who Are Blind, Visually Impaired, or Otherwise Print Disabled 3
patent databases 276
PATENTSCOPE database 276
Technology and Innovation Support Centres (TISCs) 259
WIPO Copyright Treaty (WCT) 211, 340
WIPO Patent Information Service (WPIS) 276
WIPO Performances and Phonograms Treaty (WPPT) 211, 340
World Trade Organisation (WTO) 2–3, 97, 110, 239, 269, 343
Trade-Related Aspects of Intellectual Property Rights (TRIPS) Agreement 2, 97, 117, 132–133, 211

Y

youth unemployment in Africa 46–47
deficiency in skills 46

Z

Zwolle principles, on scholarship and copyright management 218